Disruptive Technology and Digital Transformation for Business and Government

Kamaljeet Sandhu
University of New England, Australia

IGI Global
PUBLISHER of TIMELY KNOWLEDGE

A volume in the Advances in Business Strategy and Competitive Advantage (ABSCA) Book Series

Published in the United States of America by
IGI Global
Business Science Reference (an imprint of IGI Global)
701 E. Chocolate Avenue
Hershey PA, USA 17033
Tel: 717-533-8845
Fax: 717-533-8661
E-mail: cust@igi-global.com
Web site: http://www.igi-global.com

Library of Congress Cataloging-in-Publication Data

Names: Sandhu, Kamaljeet, 1970- editor.
Title: Disruptive technology and digital transformation for business and government / Kamaljeet Sandhu, editor.
Description: Hershey, PA : Business Science Reference, [2021] | Includes bibliographical references and index. | Summary: "This book offers a look at the key areas of digitalisation and global challenges, especially as shown during COVID-19 pandemic period presenting new and unique challenges that requires new knowledge for understanding the complex issues (technical --e.g. technology related and people related)"-- Provided by publisher.
Identifiers: LCCN 2021004482 (print) | LCCN 2021004483 (ebook) | ISBN 9781799885832 (hardcover) | ISBN 9781799885849 (paperback) | ISBN 9781799885856 (ebook)
Subjects: LCSH: Business enterprises--Technological innovations. | Technological innovations--Management. | Public administration--Technological innovations. | Internet in public administration.
Classification: LCC HD45 .D53 2021 (print) | LCC HD45 (ebook) | DDC 658/.05--dc23
LC record available at https://lccn.loc.gov/2021004482
LC ebook record available at https://lccn.loc.gov/2021004483

This book is published in the IGI Global book series Advances in Business Strategy and Competitive Advantage (ABSCA) (ISSN: 2327-3429; eISSN: 2327-3437)

British Cataloguing in Publication Data
A Cataloguing in Publication record for this book is available from the British Library.

Advances in Business Strategy and Competitive Advantage (ABSCA) Book Series

Patricia Ordóñez de Pablos
Universidad de Oviedo, Spain

ISSN:2327-3429
EISSN:2327-3437

Mission

Business entities are constantly seeking new ways through which to gain advantage over their competitors and strengthen their position within the business environment. With competition at an all-time high due to technological advancements allowing for competition on a global scale, firms continue to seek new ways through which to improve and strengthen their business processes, procedures, and profitability.

The **Advances in Business Strategy and Competitive Advantage (ABSCA) Book Series** is a timely series responding to the high demand for state-of-the-art research on how business strategies are created, implemented and re-designed to meet the demands of globalized competitive markets. With a focus on local and global challenges, business opportunities and the needs of society, the **ABSCA** encourages scientific discourse on doing business and managing information technologies for the creation of sustainable competitive advantage.

Coverage

- Resource-Based Competition
- Strategy Performance Management
- Differentiation Strategy
- Value Chain
- Value Creation
- Co-operative Strategies
- Strategic Alliances
- Economies of Scale
- Core Competencies
- Adaptive Enterprise

IGI Global is currently accepting manuscripts for publication within this series. To submit a proposal for a volume in this series, please contact our Acquisition Editors at Acquisitions@igi-global.com or visit: http://www.igi-global.com/publish/.

The Advances in Business Strategy and Competitive Advantage (ABSCA) Book Series (ISSN 2327-3429) is published by IGI Global, 701 E. Chocolate Avenue, Hershey, PA 17033-1240, USA, www.igi-global.com. This series is composed of titles available for purchase individually; each title is edited to be contextually exclusive from any other title within the series. For pricing and ordering information please visit http://www.igi-global.com/book-series/advances-business-strategy-competitive-advantage/73672. Postmaster: Send all address changes to above address.

Titles in this Series

For a list of additional titles in this series, please visit:
http://www.igi-global.com/book-series/advances-business-strategy-competitive-advantage/73672

Competitive Drivers for Improving Future Business Performance
Carlos Martins (Lusíada University of Porto, Portugal) and Paula Rodrigues (Lusíada University of Porto, Portugal)
Business Science Reference • © 2021 • 267pp • H/C (ISBN: 9781799818434) • US $225.00

Entrepreneurial Innovation for Securing Long-Term Growth in a Short-Term Economy
Jorge Gamez-Gutierrez (Universidad de la Costa, Colombia) and Jose Manuel Saiz-Alvarez (Universidad Católica de Santiago de Guayaquil, Ecuador & Universidad Autónoma de Manizales, Colombia & CEIEF-Universidad de Santiago de Chile, Chile)
Business Science Reference • © 2021 • 256pp • H/C (ISBN: 9781799835684) • US $215.00

Global Perspectives on Military Entrepreneurship and Innovation
Sanya Ojo (Nigerian Defence Academy, Nigeria)
Business Science Reference • © 2021 • 357pp • H/C (ISBN: 9781799866558) • US $195.00

Handbook of Research on Sustaining SMEs and Entrepreneurial Innovation in the Post-COVID-19 Era
Neeta Baporikar (Namibia University of Science and Technology, Namibia & University of Pune, India)
Business Science Reference • © 2021 • 676pp • H/C (ISBN: 9781799866329) • US $325.00

Revolutionizing Institutional Theory Through Stakeholder Capitalism
Neslihan Aydogan-Duda (UC Berkeley Extension, USA)
Business Science Reference • © 2021 • 300pp • H/C (ISBN: 9781799844921) • US $235.00

Creating Social Value Through Social Entrepreneurship
Mine Afacan Fındıklı (Beykent University, Turkey) and Duygu Acar Erdur (Beykent University, Turkey)
Business Science Reference • © 2021 • 369pp • H/C (ISBN: 9781799847274) • US $195.00

Handbook of Research on International Business and Models for Global Purpose-Driven Companies
Rafael Ignacio Perez-Uribe (EAN University, Colombia) Carlos Largacha-Martinez (Fundación Universitaria del Área Andina, Colombia) and David Ocampo-Guzman (EAN University, Colombia)
Business Science Reference • © 2021 • 589pp • H/C (ISBN: 9781799849094) • US $345.00

Cases on Internationalization Challenges for SMEs
António Carrizo Moreira (University of Aveiro, Portugal)
Business Science Reference • © 2021 • 333pp • H/C (ISBN: 9781799843870) • US $185.00

IGI Global
PUBLISHER of TIMELY KNOWLEDGE

701 East Chocolate Avenue, Hershey, PA 17033, USA
Tel: 717-533-8845 x100 • Fax: 717-533-8661
E-Mail: cust@igi-global.com • www.igi-global.com

I dedicate this book to the memory of my mother and father.

Editorial Advisory Board

Ramkrishna Ghosh, *Haldia Institute of Technology, India*

Ayse Gunsel, *Kocaeli University, Turkey*

Farid Huseynov, *Gebze Technical University, Turkey*

Ashwini J., *BIMS, University of Mysuru, India*

Esha Jain, *The NorthCap University, Gurugram, India*

Danielle Kadlec, *Luiss Business School, Italy*

Fatma Sena Karal, *Turkish-German University, Turkey*

Bernice Kotey, *University of New England, Australia*

Jonika Lamba, *The NorthCap University, Gurugram, India*

Zakaria Lissaneddine, *National School of Business and Management, University of Moulay Ismail, Morocco*

Rajesh Many, *Mahatma Gandhi University, India*

Robert Marlin, *Queensland University of Technology, Australia*

Joana Maria Costa Martins das Dores, *University of Aveiro, Portugal*

Tlou Maggie Masenya, *Durban University of Technology, South Africa*

Diego Matricano, *Università degli Studi della Campania "L. Vanvitelli", Italy*

Zeynep Orman, *Istanbul University-Cerrahpasa, Turkey*

Fahri Özsungur, *Adana Science and Technology University, Turkey*

Samet Oztoprak, *Istanbul University-Cerrahpasa, Turkey*

Ranjith P. V., *CMS Business School, India*

Shailesh Palekar, *Queensland University of Technology, Australia*

Digvijay Pandey, *Department of Technical Education, India*

Nicholas Patterson, *Deakin University, Australia*

Francisco Xavier Pedro, *Universidade do Minho, Portugal*

Carla M. B. F. Pires, *CBIOS – Research Center for Biosciences & Health Technologies, Universidade Lusófona, Portugal & ISCTE, Instituto Universitário de Lisboa, Portugal*

Volkan Polat, *Yalova University, Turkey*

Sabyasachi Pramanik, *Haldia Institute of Technology, India*

Tansif Ur Rehman, *University of Karachi, Pakistan*

María-Mercedes Rojas-de-Gracia, *University of Málaga, Spain*

Debabrata Samanta, *Christ University, India*

Marisa Analia Sanchez, *Universidad Nacional del Sur, Argentina*

Deepak Saxena, *Birla Institute of Technology and Science, Pilani, India*

Sabrina Schork, *TH Aschaffenburg, Germany*

Plácido Sierra-Herrezuelo, *University of Malaga, Spain*

Mehmet Ali Şimşek, *Tekirdag Namik Kemal University, Turkey*

Murat Selçuk Solmaz, *Piri Reis University, Turkey*

Shahryar Sorooshian, *University of Gothenburg, Sweden*

Ayberk Soyer, *Istanbul Technical University, Turkey*

Halit Alper Tayali, *Istanbul University School of Business, Turkey*

Dhananjay Thiruvady, *Deakin University, Australia*

Aparna J. Varma, *GSSS Institute of Engineering and Technology for Women, India*

Nagarajan Venkatachalam, *Queensland University of Technology, Australia*

Rebecca Jen-Hui Wang, *Lehigh University, USA*

Atilla Wohllebe, *Szent István University, Kaposvár, Hungary*

Guy Wood-Bradley, *Deakin University, Australia*
Kamil Yagci, *Pamukkale University, Turkey*
Ibrahim Yikilmaz, *Kocaeli University, Turkey*
Mustafa Yılmaz, *Yalova University, Turkey*
Dina Ziadlou, *Colorado Technical University, USA*
Juana Ines Zuntini, *Universidad Nacional del Sur, Argentina*

Table of Contents

Detailed Table of Contents

the technique and method to fit the theory in a particular context. It also helps to bring modifications regarding the existing theories.

A series of necessary structural transformation has started to be implemented in Turkey with the new economic program described under the heading of "New Economy Program: Structural Transformation Steps 2019." In the field of tax transformation of these structural transformation steps, some studies have been carried out towards the creation of "New Tax Architecture." Within the scope of these studies, a new tax application under the name of "digital service tax" is designed. In fact, this step taken by the government of Turkey for the taxation of digital services is parallel to the developments in the world. In this study, for the better understanding of the necessity/importance of digital service tax and what kind of tax application is it, digital service tax planned to be implemented in Turkey is evaluated with its all aspects and in line with the developments in the world.

Digital transformation is progressing exponentially. Given the importance of this transformation, managerial strategies and practices need to be adapted to meet the new challenges. While countries are on a journey toward a process where human interactions and transactions—with the government, businesses—and consumption of goods, services, and ideas primarily conducted through the use of the internet and internet-based technologies, they are all traveling at different speeds. Based on the theory, drawing from the Global Innovation Index (GII) input-output framework and literature review on innovation, the chapter intends to answer the question: What is the impact of management and strategies for digital enterprise transformation on welfare?

Accounting is a discipline as old as human history, and with the last industrial revolution, it started to digitalize by taking a different dimension. It is important to know the ideas, the new order, and the new qualifications that employees should have, which are the basis of digital accounting, which has a quite new history in the world. In addition, mastering new developments and practices is important in order to continue the profession and apply it in its modern sense. This chapter was designed by author due to the lack of a comprehensive publication in the field of digital accounting and it is a fairly new concept. In this context, basic concepts were disclosed that subject and industrial revolutions. Later on, applications such as e-invoice, e-document, e-book, e-archive, which make up digital accounting by being separated from the traditional sense in the field of accountancy, are explained, and suggestions for the design new researches and diversification are presented.

Digital platform businesses challenge incumbents by utilizing an ecosystem of actors that provide benefits to customers like cost reduction, convenience, or complementary products and services. Traditional enterprises should transform in order not to lose market share. This transformation potentially induces drastic changes to business models, organizational strategy, business processes, and corporate culture, among others. This chapter aims to understand how incumbent software vendors adapt to digital platform-mediated settings. The research methodology is grounded in an in-depth case study. The work contributes with a description of practical implications exposing implementation challenges, strategic decisions regarding the multiple roles in an ecosystem, criteria to select alliances, the degree of openness, and how to go from idea to action. These findings therefore enrich the literature on digital platform management.

Scientific knowledge will be advanced in the need for the application of neuroeconomics focused on one of the services of the information and communication technologies (ICT) of companies that is e-commerce of exponential artisanal SMEs driven by women entrepreneurs, by developing a proposal for a business model to increase the possibility of growth of their companies at the level national and international level. The methodology used was deductive, exploratory, descriptive, correlational, and documentary. Neuroeconomics have the potential to explain the phenomena that are considered as a deviation from the prediction or behavioral bias of decision-making models in economic theory. The study up to this point is quantitative using primary and secondary sources of information for research.

Mobile services applications in digital transformation era have become increasingly important and providing business and customers with a diversity of services, quality, and values with no cost and to help banks' practitioners identify and improve their services. This chapter aims to explore and understand management and strategies of digital business transformation in banks' change through the use of digital technologies and business models to improve applications, practice, performance, and customer values. The digitization of bank services is aimed at reducing costs, improving services, and digitalization of an enterprise is necessary to increasing effectiveness, efficiency, and sustainability of its functioning through dramatic changes in the management quality, both technological processes and decision-making processes at all levels of management, based on modern methods of production and further use of information about the state and prediction of possible changes in managed elements and subsystems.

The term "big data" refers to the very large and diverse sets of structured, semi-structured, and unstructured digital data from different sources that accumulate and grow very rapidly on a continuous basis. Big data enables enhanced decision-making in various types of businesses. Through these technologies, businesses are able to cut operational costs, digitally transform business operations to be more efficient and effective, and make more informed business decisions. Big data technologies enable businesses to better understand their markets by uncovering hidden patterns behind consumer behaviors and introduce new products and services accordingly. This chapter shows the critical role that big data plays in businesses. Initially, in this chapter, big data and its underlying technologies are explained. Later, this chapter discusses how big data digitally transforms critical business operations for enhanced decision-making and superior customer experience. Finally, this chapter ends with the possible challenges of big data for businesses and possible solutions to these challenges.

Big data is presently considered integral to the management and strategies for digital enterprise transformation. Beyond being 'a lot of data', big data can be characterized in terms of seven Vs: volume, velocity, variety, variability, veracity, visualization, and value. Already being applied in private businesses, big data has immense potential for the digital transformation of public services in advancing the e-governance agenda. This chapter explores the nature of big data in public service and discusses its application in areas such as tax administration, transportation, energy, public health, and disaster management. Challenges and concerns are noted in terms of data quality, infrastructure cost, availability of suitable human resources, privacy, and security. Possible solutions such as shared services, cloud computing, open source software, open data framework, and regulatory compliance are noted. The chapter ends by noting future research directions to realize the full potential of Big data application in digital transformation of public services.

In addition to the development of social technology and the widespread use of the internet, the fact that people are getting used to sharing their goods and services has made the concept of sharing economy a popular issue. Sharing economy is "a potential new way for sustainability," and it is noted that it would disrupt the unsustainable hyper-consumption practices directing capitalist economies. In this regard, the importance of sharing economy becomes prominent. In this study, first of all, basic information was given about sharing economy and then the concepts about how it made progress were introduced. In the next step, the definitions of sharing economy were given, the importance of sharing was mentioned, and then the products used in sharing economy were mentioned. In the following stage, the benefits of sharing economy to nature were addressed, and the weaknesses and dark sides of sharing economy were revealed. Finally, the impact of the sharing economy on the service sector was emphasized, and opinions were presented for future research on this subject.

In a globalized world, tourist destinations must have a website containing accurate information for potential tourists. However, there is currently no model that serves as a guide to evaluate the usability of tourism websites. A web usability audit manual is presented in this work with the application of a case study methodology, which combines theoretical contributions with those of a real audit of a tourism institution. Apart from the description of the manual itself, the results of this work have made it possible to identify a series of actions to be taken into account, as well as others that should be avoided when a usability audit is being carried out in the tourism field.

This literature review presents a number of motives and opportunities for Supply Chain 4.0 transition with underlying pillars in focus that are IoT, AI, big data, and blockchain technology. All technologies and systems are described briefly concerning the existing literature, with an extensive focus on blockchain technology. It becomes apparent that we are standing in front of a massive supply chain transition, where connectivity and digital networks will create competitive advantages. Aspects like efficiency, traceability, visibility, transparency, auditability, and flexibility will play significant roles for organisations and their ability to successfully adapt to future supply chain transformations.

Emerging technologies have redesigned the financial services industry through innovative means to cater to evolving customer expectations of personalisation and ease. FinTech has been progressed as one of the most pioneering and cost-effective disruptive technologies. Initial adaptation of FinTech solutions has permitted several start-ups, financial service providers, and other assorted sectors to accomplish an augmented pace of growth. This chapter highlights how emerging technologies are altering the subtleties of doing business for financial services benefactors, possibility of emerging technologies, advantages and disadvantages, technology linked issues/challenges in financial services, and also highlights drivers of this revolution.

Preface

Disruptive Technologies have stimulated the digital transformation for business and government enterprises. In recent times many organisations of all sizes (e.g. small, medium, and large) are moving towards digital enterprise. The business landscape has changed in the year 2020 and into the future, with the far-reaching global impact of COVID-19 pandemic, the demand and the necessity for digital enterprise transformation have accelerated exponentially. Management and strategies for the adoption and wider usage of newer digital technologies for the transformation of an enterprise through digital tools such as real-time video communications (e.g., zoom, skype, google meet, and many others) through which physical distance has disappeared, which has shown enterprise and people no longer required to be physically present in the same place having face to face interaction rather can be spread far away geographically. Large scale applications of artificial intelligence is being harnessed and increasingly being used widely across different platforms and apps, robotics taking over tedious and difficult jobs from humans through automated machine learning. Cloud computing is easily making on demand computing accessible from anywhere, integrated with block chain technology in which computers are autonomously managing and updating records. Digital payment and banking which has eliminated the need for cash and replaced by digital transactions, and cloud data in which the information can be accessed by the user from anywhere in the world. Inclusion of all these newer technologies have shown the fast pace at which the digital enterprise transformation is rapidly evolving, and new eco-systems are reshaping the digital enterprise model.

Three prominent players are leading the transformation, which are: people (e.g., senior leaders, managers, employees & customers), digital technology (e.g. artificial intelligence, robotics, cloud computing & data, and others), and digital enterprise (e.g. dealing in products & services which are being transformed digitally). The important roles played by these players is also leading to innovation. This book focuses on all the three prominent players. The process for management and strategies for digital enterprise transformation is not straight forward and is rather complicated. This study unravels the underlying process for management & strategies to fully incorporate new digital tools and technologies across all aspects of an enterprise undergoing transformation. The chapters in this book presents interesting research in which the authors have in depth studied digital enterprise transformation at different stages and across different settings, identified key issues, analysed and made sense of vast variety of data, that provides deeper insights and for unravelling the core problems under investigation and developing solutions and recommendations and suggesting future research directions for digital enterprise transformation.

On the road to digital enterprise transformation there are many successes, difficulties, challenges, and failures that an enterprise can learn from. Failures are not an end, rather are turning points for discovering newer innovations that can stem from such setbacks. Humans are constantly driving and at the centre of solving real world problems and driving the digital enterprise transformation and making important contribution through strategic thinking and focusing on core problems facing the enterprise. This also means modernising the management and the strategies around digital workforce as well as customers, and to fully understand their different roles and to make the interaction seamlessly simple, through digital platform interface. Digital business is not clearly understood at different levels of management as it passes through a very complicated process. The key areas of digitalisation and global challenges as shown during COVID-19 pandemic period are new and unique and requires new knowledge that is gained from a deep understanding of complex issues (technical e.g. technology related, & non-technical e.g. people related) that have been examined and reported in this book.

The journey for developing and completing this book is a long one in which all authors have made a valuable contribution to the body of new research knowledge, and adopted new research techniques to study the problems, and found innovative solutions to address those complicated problems. This study will be very useful for many researchers to build on new findings that have been reported in this book. This book will also serve as a valuable tool for many students, practitioners, government, managerial staff and other professionals to learn about new developments in digital enterprise transformation of business systems from a global perspective. International studies have been presented with important new findings from America, Australia, Asia, Europe, Africa & the Middle east, which demonstrates the far-reaching impact for digital enterprise transformation, and suggests that digital businesses are global and are continuously evolving online faster than ever and into new ecosystems in different parts of the world via internet.

ORGANIZATIONOFTHEBOOK

A brief description of each of the chapters follows:

Chapter 1 proposes a three-ecosystems framework in the context of transnational digital entrepreneurship (TDE). It argues that the embeddedness and engagement within digital, host and home-country entrepreneurial ecosystems holistically affect TDE process, adoption of strategic activities and entrepreneurs. The research indicates that there is an increasing faith amongst researchers and policymakers in the vital position of TDE for socioeconomic development in transnational entrepreneurs' host and home countries, which has manifested as a result of the contribution to innovation, job creation, and income generation. This paper aims to contribute to the rapidly growing literature on transnational entrepreneurship (TE) and digital entrepreneurship (DE) by theoretically exploring the key-impacting components in the process of TDE. The paper offers an integrated theoretical framework/model supported by three ecosystems and a set of testable propositions for future empirical TDE research. This research will theoretically contribute to TE and DE literature

Chapter 2 describes scrum as an agile method for strategic organizational learning in digital enterprise transformation. In the context of managing digital enterprise transformation, the generation and distribution of knowledge across the entire organization is of great importance: Because existing processes are being questioned and activities are changing, the promotion of organizational learning should be part of the digital transformation strategy. This chapter uses the example of Scrum to show how organizational learning can be supported by agile working methods. After an introduction to organizational learning and to Scrum as a process of continuous improvement, the four elements of organizational learning are used and compared to the characteristic elements of Scrum. In addition, the author points out existing research gaps, especially in quantitative research, and gives practical advice for managers on how to use Scrum to promote organizational learning.

Chapter 3 explores a new entrepreneurship model for digital enterprises. Career management is an important and up-to-date issue in strategic human resources management. Career management has significant impacts on many topics such as entrepreneurship, leader-employee interaction, increasing competitiveness, organizational climate, application of innovative and creative ideas, the efficiency of organizational decisions, organizational performance and profitability, internationalization, teamwork, project and process management, is a concept regarding entrepreneurship. Career entrepreneurship which is introduced to literature for the first time is explained in this chapter. This concept is put forward with the topics of a theoretical framework, career entrepreneurship, digital career management system, entrepreneurial career behavior, ICT-career management, and digital enterprise transformation. In the conclusion section, suggestions are made to provide important insights for human resources managers, leaders, politicians, and academicians.

Chapter 4 aims to propose a conceptual framework for e-government risks identification through a literature review of papers specifically focusing on e-government risks. To achieve this objective, a content analysis of papers on e-government risks is made. This allows proposing a conceptual framework comprising a list of seven categories of risk factors, the negative consequences on the e-government project and their impacts on its stakeholders. This conceptual framework can be useful for both researchers and practitioners. It offers a first step to enhance awareness of the various risk factors, their negative consequences on the project deployment as well as their impacts on e-government stakeholders. Project managers can use it as a diagnostic tool of the risks of e-government projects, which will help better assessment and management of risks. For future research, it may be appropriate to investigate e-government risk factors using empirical research and draw conclusions about risk factors categories of e-government projects and their failure risk.

Chapter 5 explains the theoretical context of e-banking for digital enterprise transformation. E-banking offers an ever-alluring response to the pressures by its consumers for more products, services, and 24-hour access to accounts. Additionally, personal e-banking definitely made the banking process convenient as well as less time consuming than ever before. Therefore, no more standing in the lines or using an old check as well as stamp method to pay utility bills. Thus, facilitation has been extended in its true sense within the respective domain by banks across the globe. While, Digital Enterprise Transformation facilitates financial services organizations by enabling them to be more secure, compliant, as well as being digital. It modifies the experience of employees, partners, customers, and stakeholders. Theory and research both are important notions. The theory provides the basic structure of propositions and research provides the technique and method to fit the theory in a particular context. It also helps to bring modifications regarding the existing theories.

Chapter 6 reports on a new digital service tax for the transformation of the taxation architecture in Turkey. A series of necessary structural transformation has started to be implemented in Turkey with the new economic program described under the heading of "New Economy Program: Structural Transformation Steps 2019". In the field of tax transformation of these structural transformation steps, some studies have been carried out towards the creation of "New Tax Architecture". Within the scope of these studies, a new tax application under the name of "digital service tax" is designed. In fact, this step taken by the government of Turkey for the taxation of digital services is parallel to the developments in the world. In this study, for the better understanding of the necessity / importance of digital service tax and what kind of tax application is it, digital service tax planned to be implemented in Turkey is evaluated with its all aspects and in line with the developments in the World.

Chapter 7 examines the impact of management and strategies for digital enterprise transformation on welfare. Digital transformation is progressing exponentially. Given the importance of this transformation managerial strategies and practices need to be adapted to meet the new challenges. While countries are on a journey toward a process where human interactions and transactions—with the government, businesses—and consumption of goods, services, and ideas primarily conducted through the use of the internet and internet-based technologies, they are all traveling at different speeds. Based on the theory, drawing from the Global Innovation Index (GII) input-output framework and literature review on innovation, the chapter intend to answer the question: What is The Impact of Management and Strategies for Digital Enterprise Transformation on Welfare? Thus, deriving policy implications aimed at improving countries' innovative, management and strategies for digital enterprise transformation readiness to impact on welfare.

Chapter 8 investigates strategies for digital transformation in business and in particular the role of digital accounting strategy. Accounting is, a discipline as old as human history and technology developing today and with the last industrial revolution, it started to digitalize by taking a different dimension. It is important to know the ideas, the new order and the new qualifications that employees should have, which are the basis of digital accounting, which has a quite new history in the world. In addition, mastering new developments and practices is important in order to continue the profession and apply it in its modern sense. This chapter was designed by author due to the lack of a comprehensive publication in the field of digital accounting and it is a fairly new concept. In this context, firstly basic concepts were disclosed that subject and industrial revolutions. Later on applications such as e-invoice, e-document, e-book, e-archive, which make up digital accounting by being separated from the traditional sense in the field of accountancy are explained and suggestions for the design new researches and diversification are presented.

Chapter 9 provides insight to how incumbents respond strategically to emerging digital platform-mediated settings? Digital platform businesses challenge incumbents by utilizing an ecosystem of actors that provide benefits to customers like cost reduction, convenience or complementary products and services. Traditional enterprises should transform in order not to lose market share. This transformation potentially induce drastic changes to business models, organizational strategy, business processes, and corporate culture, among others. This chapter aims to understand how incumbent software vendors adapt to digital platform-mediated settings. The research methodology is grounded in an in-depth case study. The work contributes with a description of practical implications exposing implementation challenges, strategic decisions regarding the multiple roles in an ecosystem, criteria to select alliances, the degree of openness and how to go from idea to action. These findings therefore enrich the literature on digital platforms management.

Chapter 10 is an illustration of the utility of neuroeconomics in decision making and behavior. Scientific knowledge will be advanced in the need for the application of neuroeconomics focused on one of the services of the information and communication technologies (ICT) of companies that is e-commerce of exponential artisanal SMEs of women entrepreneurs, by developing a proposal for a business model to increase the possibility of growth of their companies at the level national and international level. Methodological approach. The methodology used was deductive, exploratory, descriptive, correlational and documentary. Findings. Neuroeconomics have the potential to explain the phenomena that are considered as a deviation from the prediction or behavioral bias of decision-making models in economic theory and explores practical implications. The study up to this point is quantitative using primary and secondary sources for research.

Chapter 11 explores the management and strategies for customers adoption of mobile banking services. Mobile services applications in digital transformation era have become increasingly and providing business and customers with a diversity of services, quality and values whit no cost and to help banks' practitioners identify and improve their positions. This Chapter aims to explore and understand management and strategies of Digital business transformation in banks' change through the use of digital technologies and business models to improve applications, practice, performance and customer values. The digitization of bank services is aimed at reducing costs, improving services, and digitalization of an enterprise is necessary to increasing effectiveness, efficiency and sustainability of its functioning through dramatic changes in the management quality, both technological processes and decision-making processes at all levels of management, based on modern methods of production and further use of information about the state and prediction of possible changes in managed elements and subsystems.

Chapter 12 articulates the role of big data in business with particular emphasis on digital transformation for enhanced decision making and superior customer experience. The term "Big Data" refers to the very large and diverse sets of structured, semi-structured, and unstructured digital data from different sources that accumulate and grow very rapidly on a continuous basis. Big data enables enhanced decision making in various types of businesses. Through these technologies, businesses are able to cut operational costs, digitally transform business operations to be more efficient and effective, and make more informed business decisions. Big data technologies enable businesses to better understand their markets by uncovering hidden patterns behind consumer behaviors, and introduce new products and services accordingly. This chapter shows the critical role that big data plays in businesses. Initially, in this chapter, big data term and its underlying technologies are explained. Later, this chapter discusses how big data digitally transforms critical business operations for enhanced decision-making and superior customer experience. Finally, this chapter ends with the possible challenges of big data for businesses and possible solutions to these challenges.

Chapter 13 demonstrates the application of big data for digital transformation of public services. Big data is presently considered integral to the management and strategies for digital enterprise transformation. Beyond being 'a lot of data', Big data can be characterized in terms of seven Vs - Volume, Velocity, Variety, Variability, Veracity, Visualization, and Value. Already being applied in private businesses, Big data has immense potential for the digital transformation of public services in advancing the e-Governance agenda. This chapter explores the nature of Big data in public service and discusses its application in areas such as tax administration, transportation, energy, public health, and disaster management. Challenges and concerns are noted in terms of data quality, infrastructure cost, availability of suitable human resources, privacy and security. Possible solutions such as shared services, cloud computing, open source software, open data framework, and regulatory compliance are noted. The chapter ends by noting future research directions to realize the full potential of Big data application in digital transformation of public services.

Chapter 14 exemplifies the opportunities for share or lose as a radical challenge for traditional economy. In addition to the development of social technology and the widespread use of the Internet, the fact that people are getting used to sharing their goods and services has made the concept of sharing economy a popular issue. Sharing economy is "a potential new way for sustainability", and is noted that it would disrupt the unsustainable hyper-consumption practices directing capitalist economies. In this regard, the importance of sharing economy becomes prominent. In this study, first of all, basic information was given about sharing economy and then, the concepts about how it made progress were introduced. In the next step, the definitions of sharing economy were given, the importance of sharing was mentioned, and then the products used in sharing economy were mentioned. In the following stage, the benefits of sharing economy to nature were addressed and the weaknesses and dark sides of sharing economy were revealed. Finally, the impact of the sharing economy on the service sector was emphasized and opinions were presented for future research on this subject.

Chapter 15 represents a usability audit model for destination websites management in the digital economy. In a globalized world, tourist destinations must have a website containing accurate information for potential tourists. However, there is currently no model that serves as a guide to evaluate the usability of tourism websites. A web usability audit manual is presented in this work with the application of a case study methodology, which combines theoretical contributions with those of a real audit of a tourism institution. Apart from the description of the manual itself, the results of this work have made it possible to identify a series of actions to be taken into account, as well as others that should be avoided when a usability audit is being carried out in the tourism field.

Chapter 16 embodies the motives for the new disruptive technologies with special focus on blockchain technology. . This literature review presents a number of motives and opportunities for Supply Chain 4.0 transition with underlying pillars in focus that are IoT, AI, Big Data and Blockchain Technology. All technologies and systems are described briefly concerning the existing literature, with an extensive focus on Blockchain Technology. It becomes apparent that we are standing in front of a massive supply chain transition, where connectivity and digital networks will create competitive advantages. Aspects like efficiency, traceability, visibility, transparency, auditability, and flexibility will play significant roles for organisations and their ability to successfully adapt to future supply chain transformations.

Chapter 17 demonstrates the impact of emerging technologies in financial services. Emerging technologies have redesigned the financial services industry through innovative means to cater to evolving customer expectations of personalisation and ease. FinTech has progressed as one of the most pioneering and cost-effective disruptive technologies. Initial adaptation of FinTech solutions has permitted several start-ups, financial service providers and other assorted sectors to accomplish an augmented pace of growth. This chapter highlights how emerging technologies are altering the subtleties of doing business for financial services benefactors, possibility of emerging technologies, advantages & disadvantages, technology-linked issues/challenges in financial services & also highlights drivers of this revolution.

Kamaljeet Sandhu
University of New England, Australia

Acknowledgment

I would like to acknowledge the help and contribution of all people, more specifically, to the authors and reviewers that took part in the review process. Without their support, this bookwould not have become a reality. All the authors have made valuable contribution by making many revisions to their chapters, presenting their interesting research to the readers of this book.

Reviewers provided continuous and important feedbacks to the authors for improvements in their chapters, coherence, and content presentation of chapters. I would like to personally thank all the authors and reviewers who have worked very hard to complete this book successfully. At every step we worked together as a highly coordinated and focused team.

In this journey we became very good and close colleagues, and this book has brought us all together from different parts of the world, and we have a valuable working relationship and I look forward to working with this great team again in another interesting book project to come soon. I would like to personally thank the staff at IGI-Global, development editors, who have provided the highest level of service and have been very helpful and supportive in this research at each stage of the book development process, without their persistent help this publication would not have been possible.

I would like to thank my family, including my father and mother who passed away leaving beautiful memories and the importance for higher education and new learning that was ingrained in my very early life and which later was built into my ability to provide this advanced scholarly work to the advancement of new scientific knowledge. This book is a tribute to my dear mum for all her love, support, belief, kindness, and trust, that I have received which transformed me into an author for scholarly research. I would not have achieved this book success without it. I also like to thank Jasper (my king charles spaniel puppy) for all the love, kisses, and support that I have received on writing this book. I also wish to thank Professor Brian Corbitt (RMIT University Melbourne, Australia), my research mentor and colleague, without him I would not have been here today writing this book.

Kamaljeet Sandhu
University of New England, Australia

Chapter 1
Ecosystem Strategies for Transnational Digital Entrepreneurship:
A Conceptual Framework of Three Ecosystems

Carson Duan
https://orcid.org/0000-0001-5459-9352
University of New England, Australia

Bernice Kotey
https://orcid.org/0000-0003-2287-7295
University of New England, Australia

Kamaljeet Sandhu
https://orcid.org/0000-0003-4624-6834
University of New England, Australia

ABSTRACT

This chapter proposes a three-ecosystems framework in the context of transnational digital entrepreneurship (TDE). It argues that the embeddedness and engagement within digital, host, and home-country entrepreneurial ecosystems holistically affect TDE process, adoption of strategic activities, and entrepreneurs. The research indicates that there is an increasing faith amongst researchers and policymakers in the vital position of TDE for socioeconomic development in transnational entrepreneurs' host and home countries, which has manifested as a result of the contribution to innovation, job creation, and income generation. This chapter aims to contribute to the rapidly growing literature on transnational entrepreneurship (TE) and digital entrepreneurship (DE) by theoretically exploring the key-impacting components in the process of TDE. The chapter offers an integrated theoretical framework/model supported by three ecosystems and a set of testable propositions for future empirical TDE research. This research will theoretically contribute to TE and DE literature.

DOI: 10.4018/978-1-7998-8583-2.ch001

INTRODUCTION

Transnational entrepreneurship (TE) has become predominant research streams in immigrant entrepreneurship study in the last two decades (Nkongolo-Bakenda & Chrysostome, 2020; Brown, Mawson, Lee, & Peterson, 2019; Ren & Liu, 2015; Portes & Yiu, 2013) along with growing international immigration, globalisation and development of international trades. A widely defined concept of transnational entrepreneurs refers to immigrant social actors "who enact networks, ideas, information, and practices for the purpose of seeking business opportunities or maintaining businesses within dual social fields, which in turn force them to engage in varied strategies of action to promote their entrepreneurial activities" (Drori, Honig, & Wright, 2009). They are "capable of bearing risks and taking strategic initiatives to establish, integrate, and sustain foreign operations" (Yeung, 2002).

Digital entrepreneurship, as a new subfield of entrepreneurship (Al Amoush & Sandhu, 2020; Elia, 2020; Satalkina & Steiner, 2020) started from the 1990s, is the process of finding or creating an entrepreneurial opportunity and pursue it through the use of ICT technology, digital platforms and other information and communication equipment (Zaheer, Breyer, & Dumay, 2019; European Commission, 2016). DE highlights digital transformations in entrepreneurship. Therefore, DE has been identified in many business categories: production, sale, logistic, trade, business management and operation from (Sussan and Acs 2017). DE also enhanced innovation in business processes and models. DE and digital transformation, as a critical pillar of the digital economy, has revolutionised the entrepreneurship environment and has been a vital force pushing the economy forwards.

Today, TE has been deeply transformed by the development of digital technologies. But there is a shortage of research on transnational digital entrepreneurship (TDE). Up to date, it lacks TDE definition, research framework, research methodologies development and investigation agenda. In this study, the cross-border economic activities conducted by entrepreneurs based on the usage of digital technology (i.e., cross-border e-commerce platforms) are defined as transnational digital entrepreneurship, and these entrepreneurs are transnational digital entrepreneurs. The paper addresses the gaps with the following key research questions: 1) What role do the three ecosystems (host-, home-country entrepreneurial systems and digital ecosystem) play in TDE? 2) How do transnational digital entrepreneurs exploit opportunities and leverage resources within three ecosystems? 3) How embeddedness and engagement with three ecosystems affect transnational digital entrepreneurs?

TDE is studied from the perspectives of entrepreneurial and digital ecosystems in this paper. Ecosystem strategies in this study are a series of techniques for controlling and directing business to achieve a set of predetermined goals in considering ecosystem effects. Ecosystem approach has become the latest fruitful instrument for entrepreneurship and digital technology studies for the last ten years (Sussan & Acs, 2017; WEF, 2013). These two recently matured frameworks, the entrepreneurship ecosystem (Isenberg, 2011) and digital ecosystem (Li, Du, & Yin, 2017), were merged conceptually by Sussan and Acs (2017) and revisited by Song (2019). The new concept of digital entrepreneurial ecosystems (DEE) provides the living and non-living digital ecosystem components, including "digital infrastructure governance…, digital user citizenship.., digital entrepreneurship and digital marketplace" in the digital economy (Song, 2019).

The objective of this paper is to conceptualise the relationship between transnational digital entrepreneurs and three ecosystems (host-country, home-country and digital) and provides an integrated theoretical framework. The paper emphasises the three ecosystems impacts while stressing the historical research findings regarding three ecosystems. Finally, the research provides a set of testable propositions for further empirical investigation. This theoretical study makes a number of contributions to TE and DE literature. Firstly, it highlights the limitations of conventional research frameworks on TE study. Secondly, the paper further extends the concept of the entrepreneurial ecosystem to cover the host and home-country context and argues that transnational entrepreneurs are determined by both of them. Thirdly, this paper conceptualises the process of TDE in an integrated framework with five constructs: entrepreneurs' characteristics, motivations, business strategies, outcomes and three ecosystems. The framework has the potential to enable the engagement of causal-effect research amongst these components. Fourthly, considering that understanding the critical factors for TDE success can favour the development of government policies and programs that affect all immigrants, the results will have significant implications to policymakers in TDE promotion (Kushnirovich, 2015). Finally, this research suggests four testable propositions for future research agenda.

The paper is organised into six sections: the second section presents the background and expected contributions and is followed by a review of the connected literature. The third section proposes an integrated conceptual framework for TDE research. The proposed research propositions are presented in the fourth section, while solutions and recommendations implications are presented in sections five and six.

BACKGROUND

Transnationalism, first used by Bourne in 1916, refers to migrants that maintain cultural ties with their home-country (Kerr & Kerr, 2019). The study of contemporary migrant transnational entrepreneurship started in the early 1990s (Vertovec, 2003; Schiller et al., 1995;) from sociocultural, political and economic transformation and adaptation perspectives following economic globalisation and an increasing number of international migrants since the 1970s. It became apparent that migrants were participating in socioeconomic and political activities in both their host and home countries. Schiller et al. defined transnationalism as "processes by which immigrants build social fields that link together their country of origin and their country of settlement" (Schiller et al., 1995).

After twenty years of development, TE has become a predominant research field in entrepreneurship study (Ren & Liu, 2015). Within the host-country entrepreneurship ecosystem, transnational entrepreneurs experience disadvantages in the exploitation of entrepreneurial opportunities and organisation of resources due to discrimination and blocked mobility (Collins, 2002). The key ecosystems factors which promote and hinder TE activities include socioeconomic, political-cultural (Brzozowski, Cucculelli, & Surdej, 2017) and institutional perspectives. Other identified factors are cultural background, the scale of co-ethnic community and transnational capabilities (Nkongolo-Bakenda & Chrysostome, 2019; Li, Isidor, Dau, & Kabst, 2018).

From the home-country ecosystems perspective, the studied factors include funding for start-ups (Kushnirovich, 2015), access to home-country markets and other resources (Brzozowski et al., 2017), changes in the home country's economic and politic status (Van Tubergen, 2005), and educational facilities (Hart et al., 2009; Sandhu, 2008/2009). The studies lack an ecosystem approach and exclusive findings (Duan, Sandhu, & Kotey, 2021). Once the home-country is treated as an entrepreneurial ecosystem, it is not yet clear how this ecosystem will impact TE (Brzozowski et al., 2017). Moreover, there is an absence of systematic study tools to analyse the collaborative effects of entrepreneurial factors from the host-country (including co-ethnic community), home-country, firm and the individual on TE.

Digital technology has dramatically transformed the way transnational entrepreneurs engaging in cross-border trade and other economic activities (Zhao & Collier, 2016). In today's digital economy era, there is a general acknowledgement of the importance of digital entrepreneurship (DE) to socioeconomic development among policymakers, researchers and society (Sahut et al., 2019). DE has rapidly become a new interdisciplinary research field (Nambisan, 2017); the field has been examined through information systems (Du, Pan, Zhou, & Ouyang, 2018), economics, management, innovation (Nambisan, 2017), policy, education (Li, Liu, Zhang, & Li, 2017), strategy and sociology standpoints in conjunction with entrepreneurship disciplines (Zaheer et al., 2019).

TE research is essential particularly in advanced countries because of the high percentage of foreign-born population, with a significant portion of them engaging in formal and informal entrepreneurial activities (Collins, 2002). Furthermore, the number of new immigrant businesses has a positive relationship with the number of non-immigrant firms in the host-country (Li et al., 2018). Evidence shows that Australia and New Zealand have experienced socioeconomic gains from international migration and IE (Collins, 2002).

LITERATURE REVIEW

TE has been researched from international entrepreneurship and IE perspectives (Nkongolo-Bakenda & Chrysostome, 2019). International entrepreneurship research originates from studies on MNC to understand the nature of the process of internationalisation (Vertovec, 2003). IE has focused on its traditional value of economic adaptation, social integration in the environments of immigrants' host and home country. The common approach for both perspectives of TE studies is transnationalism and dual embeddedness framework. Transnationalism and dual embeddedness, as an alternative perspective to assimilation and integration theories, have a background in transnational migrants and focus on reasons, evidence and implications (Schiller, Basch, & Blanc, 1995). The following will review current TE literature from these three aspects: IE, transnationalism, and entrepreneurial ecosystem.

Transnational Entrepreneurship

Transnational linkage and transnational social space are two perspectives in transnationalism research. Transnational linkage refers to settled new immigrants carrying out culture, language, social connections and market in both the host and home countries (Baltar & Icart, 2013). This linkage promotes TE as Portes et al. (2013, p80) state that immigrant entrepreneurs have always "represented a minority of their respective ethnic communities, the majority of them depend on transnational links" for their business success. The extant literature on the TE has shown enough evidence that 21st century is a multicultural era, featured by transnationalism and dual embeddedness, whereby ethnic minorities utilise their host and home-country resources to facilitate their transnational entrepreneurial activities (Brzozowski et al., 2017). These valuable resources might not available to native-born peers. Thus, TEs benefit from their dual embeddedness and their familiarity with the socioeconomic environment in both the host and home countries. The bifocality attribute led scholars to affirm that TE does have competitive advantages over other types of entrepreneurship (Nkongolo-Bakenda & Chrysostome, 2019).

Five types of transnational entrepreneurs have been identified (Sequeira, Carr, & Rasheed, 2009): circuit firm operators, who transfer goods and remittances; culture product operators, who rely on the demand and consumption of home-country culture goods by the co-ethnic community and mainstream market; co-ethnic service operators, who cater to immigrant communities in goods and services such as foodstuffs, clothing, religious products; diaspora entrepreneurs who rely on their host-country contacts, products, technologies; and elite expansion operators, who engage in company internationalisation from host-country to home-country or vice versa.

TE study has expanded exponentially for last twenty years, addressing questions such as: what drives immigrants to establish cross-border businesses; how does entrepreneurship environment impact TE; and what the different characteristics amongst entrepreneurs from various ethnic backgrounds (Kerr & Kerr, 2019). Up to now, several terms have been used to define TE, such as international and diaspora entrepreneurship. Scholars make use of these terms interchangeably or with a self-defined research target. The well-accepted definition of an transnational entrepreneur is "social actors who enact networks, ideas, information, and practices for the purpose of seeking business opportunities or maintaining businesses within dual social fields, which in turn force them to engage in varied strategies of action to promote their entrepreneurial activities" (Drori, Honig, & Wright, 2009, p1001) and they are "capable of bearing risks and taking strategic initiatives to establish, integrate, and sustain foreign operations" (Yeung, 2002, p37). A well-agreed viewpoint of transnational entrepreneurs is limited to migrants only.

It has been recognised that contemporary immigrants have a firm intention to pursue entrepreneurship with a high success rate (Kerr & Kerr, 2019). To explain this phenomenon, for the last two decades, researchers have developed new propositions beyond the theories mentioned above (Brzozowski et al., 2017). These propositions include brain circulation (Saxenian, 2005) or knowledge spillover (Li et al., 2018; OECD, 2010), cultural (ethnic) diversity (Acs, Åstebro, Audretsch, & Robinson, 2016), cross-border activities or transnationalism (Drori et al., 2009; Lin & Tao, 2012), and "social network" or "transnational ties" (Brzozowski et al., 2017; Sundararajan & Sundararajan, 2015). These new arguments have a consensus that TE is affected by both host and home countries.

Following this trend, some scholars suggested in-depth studies on the mechanisms of different entrepreneurial activities influenced by both home and host countries (You & Zhou, 2019; Li et al., 2018). Other scholars recommend that home-country influences should be studied from social, cultural and market perspectives (Collins & Low, 2010). You and Zhou (2019) state that immigrant enterprises are shaped not only by the local market in the host country but also by multiple layers of socioeconomic and politico-institutional circumstances in the home country. They found that individual characteristics and home-country interpersonal networks affect the processes of host-country economic adaptation and business formation. From home-country entrepreneurial ecosystem perspective, Duan, Kotey, & Sandhu (2020b) noticed that, depending on the home-country embeddedness, transnational entrepreneurs are influenced by every ecosystem domains.

The literature on TE is still relatively sparse (Brown et al., 2019). Predominate theories applied in the study are all related to resource dependence theories to explain the real advantages entrepreneurs take from cross-border economic business activities. More recently, scholars have been trying to understand the dual environments TEs operate in (Nkongolo-Bakenda & Chrysostome, 2019; Drori et al., 2009) through country-specific institutional and socioeconomic characteristics (Brzozowski et al., 2017), hostility or attitude towards the host or home-country (Chand & Tung, 2014), availability of financial support and other socio-political-economic factors. Brzozowski et al. (2017) conceptualised a theoretical framework for TE research from an economic adaptation standpoint, in which he proposed that TE is intervented by socioeconomic development factors from the host and home countries. He emphasised four important impact factors of TE which are entrepreneurs' personal motivations and development strategies, cultural value, socioeconomic systems in both host and home countries, and family supports and expectations.

Digital Entrepreneurship

DE includes all-new pathways of doing business based on three digital technology components: artefacts, infrastructures and platforms (Elia, 2020) in finding new customers, designing and offering products and services, generating revenue and reducing cost, collaborating with partners, creating opportunity, reducing business risk and increasing competitive advantage. A digital artefact is a digital component, an application or app, or media content that is offering a specific function or value to end-users. Duan, Kotey and Sandhu (2020) found Chinese transnational digital entrepreneurs utilise an App (WeChat) on the smartphone to recruit new customers and marketing products in their home country. Digital infrastructure is a set of digital technologies working individually or collaboratively to achieve digitalisation. Elia et al. (2020) recognised Amazon Web Services, Microsoft Azure and many more cases of digital infrastructure for cloud computing or other purposes. Finally, A digital platform is a shared set of services and required architectures that enable complementary offering, including digital artefacts (Elia et al. 2020). Scholars have investigated many of these well-known platforms (e.g. Uber, Airbnb, Alibaba). Millions of entrepreneurs started their DE journal based on these platforms (Song, 2019). Duan et al. (2020) illustrated how Alibaba digital platforms enable TDE by providing six transnational online trading business supporting services. The platforms like Uber, Airbnb, Alibaba have enabled an industry transformation in specific industry sectors and created "new foundations for industry leadership and ecosystem innovation (Elia et al., 2020, p2)."

Consequently, the impact of ICT technology on business innovation and entrepreneurship is multifaceted as they have been facilitators, mediators, business models and outcomes of entrepreneurship (Steininger, 2018). According to the intensity of ICT technologies, DE can be mild (improve), moderate (change) or extreme (Novel). Six steams of DE research were identified by Kraus et al. (2018), including digital business model, digital process, platform strategies, digital ecosystem, entrepreneurship education and social entrepreneurship. The utilised technology can also classify the DE, for example, internet-driven business model, internetworked business, business webs, etc. (Elia et al., 2020).

The success of a DE venture replies not only on the characteristics of the business model as aforementioned but also on the digital entrepreneurs and entrepreneurial ecosystems in which it is nurtured (Elia et al., 2020). The business model is one of four determinants of DE process; the other three are prerequisites for digitalisation, dynamic shifts in the business transformation and digital innovation affordances. Even the DE process is one of the determinants in the success of entrepreneurship, the characteristics of the entrepreneur are critical for entrepreneurial achievement. These characteristics include risk-taking attitude, personal ambition, social position, the capability of accessing entrepreneurial resources, professionalism and attributes to starting a digital business (Satalkina & Steiner, 2020). The personal motivation is another key success factor being recognised by most of the scholars (Sussan & Acs, 2017).

Transnational Digital Entrepreneurship

Drawing from the digital entrepreneurship definition from European Commission (2016), transnational entrepreneurs who crate new ventures or transform the existing organisations through novel ICT innovation

Figure 1. Transnational digital entrepreneurship (Own elaboration)

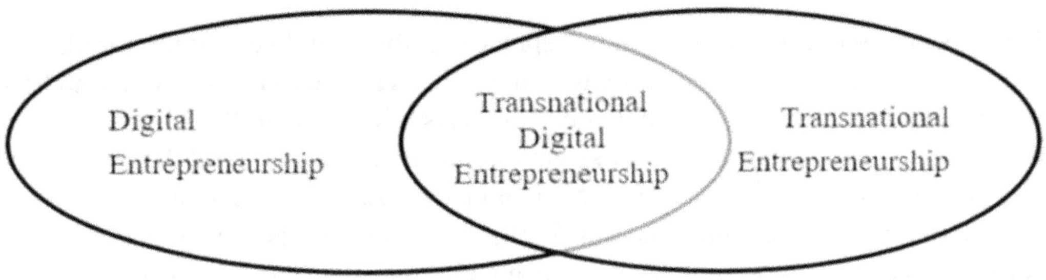

and/or novel usage of such innovation are transnational digital entrepreneurs. These entrepreneurs are the research target of this paper, and their transborder entrepreneurial activities based on digital technology (e.g. smartphone apps or cross-border e-commerce platforms) are transnational digital entrepreneurship.

Therefore, TDE contains characteristics of TE and DE. First, digital technology has encouraged entrepreneurs to develop their businesses beyond their domestic markets and become international. In the transnational context, this means the entrepreneurs extend their businesses from the host-country to home-country. Second, the home-country entry mode has been transformed from traditional B2B to both B2B and B2C. Third, the information flows regarding customer preference and product features have been become meaningful from contextual material. Forth, the cross-nation transactions have become comfortable and instant. The latest offers from digital technologies also include services for accounting, marketing, logistic and more. With digital technology, the dual embeddedness entrepreneurs are capable of engaging in the opportunities and resources with removed barriers. These barriers can be air travel in the past.

TDE is characterised by a combination of entrepreneurs, transnational digital entrepreneurial strategies, entrepreneurial outcomes, digital and entrepreneurial ecosystem in bother entrepreneurs' host and home countries (Table 1) (Satalkina & Steiner, 2020; Brzozowski et al., 2017; Drori et al., 2009). The motivations of engaging in cross-border activities are crucial for the transnational business venture creation (Shinnar & Nayi, 2019; Portes & Yiu, 2013). The combined strategies from TE and DE play a key role in the success of TDE. Within these strategies, traditional immigrant entrepreneurial activities are still valid due to transnational entrepreneurs are still maintaining all the characteristics of immigrants. As an immigrant, they are still facing all obstacles and barriers in their host-country, and very often, they are forced to look for entrepreneurial opportunities in their home-country (Portes et al., 2002).

The processes of TDE relate primarily to the consequences of digital behaviour patterns, social effects and knowledge enhancement. The TDE development strategies cover the range from the entrepreneurial intentions in transnational digital context to start a new venture, and the decision-making process to knowledge integration (Satalkina & Steiner, 2020). The outcomes of TDE include financial and non-financial perspective in the context of personal, community and cross-country impacts.

TDE business environments include three ecosystems: boundaryless digital ecosystem, host-country entrepreneurial ecosystem and home-country entrepreneurial ecosystem. The functionalities and relationship between three ecosystems and TDE will be reviewed from the next section.

Digital Ecosystem

The business environment of the digital entrepreneur is the digital ecosystem. Similar to a biological ecosystem, the ideal digital ecosystem would overcome intricate internal problems through a self-evolving system. Digital ecosystem is a result of the developments achieved in ICT, web-powered social networks and virtual communities, business networks via sharing of knowledge and ICT-enabled service. Certain scholars highlight the significance of DE research in a broadened social network, taking in the flexible boundaries limiting the discipline (Liu et al. 2018). As per the European Commission, a digital ecosystem consists of barriers and driving factors which include the regulatory framework, market conditions, access to finance, entrepreneurial capabilities, immigrants and culture (Bogdanowicz 2015).

Digital service companies are likely to upright industries on a global scale (Sussan and Acs 2017). The digital service business models of YouTube, Amazon and other noteworthy companies have been exhaustingly analysed (Sahut et al. 2019) as an individual digital ecosystem. The development of such models has seen a shift in the business models, which initially focused on supplying products to providing services later defined as the service-dominant logic (SDL) (Sussan and Acs 2017). It is evident from SDL that service exchanges are the only form of economic transactions which occurs between economies and societies. According to Karmarkar (2015), there are two distinguishable trends: transition to a service economy and the progression towards an information economy. He adds that "More and more value will continue to accrue to services, to the information sector and to their intersection: information services". SDL considers services as a process, which is engaging in an activity for someone else, with a change in focus from "producer" to the unified process of co-relating between various induvial (Vargo, 2008).

An e-commerce platform can be a boundaryless, infinite and multifaceted and timeless digital ecosystem. E-commerce enhances the efficiency which in transactions occurring between the producers and the buyers, it minimises the cost of the transaction (He 2019) and eliminates the marketspace boundaries. Digital artefacts, platforms and infrastructures are the three most important and unique factors in the world of DE (Nambisan 2017). In the case of the platform firm, new value creation is done by users for all the other participants and develop a new stream of income by maintaining the advantage offered by the platform (He 2019).

Many cross-country e-commerce platforms can be treated as one digital ecosystem (Li et al., 2012). Duan et al., (2020) analysed Alibaba digital ecosystem in TDE context and found there are at least six pillars existing within Alibaba digital ecosystem. Ali-customer channels are (Taobao, Tmall, Aliexpress, 1688); e-startups (Registration, online training, personalised e-shop web site); Ali-logistic partners, claim system, delivery services, warehouse networks; E-shop scaling up services (cloud, API, Ali-university, online-offline services); Ali-finance and accounting service (Alipay, tax, refund); Business intelligent (big data, market, customer, product analysis). For the convenience of theoretical framework creation, in this research, a transnational digital ecosystem includes all digital components which enhance digital connections between entrepreneurs' host and home countries.

Entrepreneurial Ecosystem

An entrepreneurial ecosystem refers to a system of socioeconomic, political and infrastructural components which promote the development of innovative businesses and enhance their performance (Stam & Spigel, 2016). Several definitions of an entrepreneurial ecosystem have been developed over the last two decades (Stam & Spigel, 2016). Although each definition has considered different entrepreneurial

Table 1. Impact Factors of transnational digital entrepreneurship (Own elaboration)

Dimensions	Determinants
Transnational Digital Entrepreneurship Motivations	*Individual characteristics:* ► Having the desire to own a business ► Utilising own skills ► Attitude to change and risk *Personal experiences and circumstances:* ► Have business or industry sector experience ► Have support from family or friends *Personal values:* ► Improving personal social status ► To be financial freedom ► Want to secure family future and help others ► Live in a desirable lifestyle *Business ideas and opportunities:* ► Having products or ideas to meet market demand ► An opportunity appearing *Self-efficacies:* ► Perceived capabilities ► Perceived success and rewards
Transnational Digital Entrepreneurial Strategies	*Transnational Entrepreneurship Strategies* ► Immigrant entrepreneurship strategies ► Transnational embeddedness strategies ► Female entrepreneurship ► Formal/informal business strategies ► Ethnic enclave strategies ► Social network strategies ► Internationalisation strategies *Digital Entrepreneurship Strategies* ► Digital capabilities, digital adoption and digital facilities ► Digital features in operation activities ► Merging of value creation and revenue mechanism ► Knowledge acquisition and strategic learning ► Digital business tendencies, competition and leadership ► Digital business model configurations ► Intermediary role, enhancing the role and social influence
Transnational Digital Entrepreneurship Outcomes	► Financial outcomes ► Non-financial outcomes ► Personal outcomes ► Community outcomes ► Host-country outcomes ► Home-country outcomes
Host-country Entrepreneurial Ecosystems, Home-country Entrepreneurial Ecosystem Digital Ecosystem	*Host- and Home-country Entrepreneurial Ecosystems* ► Market accessibility ► Human capital ► Business support, infrastructure, professions, ► Culture and social norms ► Funding and finance ► Government policies and leadership *Digital Ecosystem* ► Resource availability/constraints ► Digital entrepreneurship attitudes ► Context effect on digital startup formation ► Digital cluster framework ► Facilitating conditions within the infrastructure ► Digital infrastructure architecture ► System of relationships ► Digital community and network patterns

factors that dynamically interact with one another, the consensus is that a functional EE provides capital (financial, knowledge, institutional, social, and so on) to enable entrepreneurs to discover, assess, exploit and take advantage of market opportunities (Nicotra, Romano, Giudice, & Schillaci, 2018). Recent studies have expanded the elements of an ecosystem to include additional dimensions such as culture, market, human, research institute, government and institutional (Isenberg, 2011). Each dimension is weighted differently in a specific EE. The World Economic Forum (WEF) argues that funding, workforce and market are the most critical factors to a functional EE (WEF, 2013).

Various studies show that TE is influenced by personal attributes, host-country entrepreneurial environment, co-ethnic community characteristics and immigrants' home-country factors (Brzozowski et al., 2017; Lin & Tao, 2012; Oliveira, 2010; Van Tubergen, 2005). Host-country key influential factors identified in the literature include financial support, labour market, consumers, suppliers, professional services, social reception, regulation and political context. Personal attributes are savings, education, work experience, age, legal status, language skills, migratory experience and ambitions. Others factors including gender, marital status, the purpose of migration, length of stay in a host-country, risk appetite and more are added to the list. From a community perspective, the community size, entrepreneurial culture, willingness to share knowledge, and acceptance of low paying jobs contribute to IE (Li et al., 2018). Researched home-country factors include finance, education, economic development, corruption status and government policies (You & Zhou, 2019).

Empirical research shows that there is a high percentage of immigrants engaging in cross-border business activities and operating their business in host- and home-country entrepreneurial ecosystems (Bagwell, 2018). Wang et al. (2015) found immigrant entrepreneurs have a higher tendency to be involved in transnational economic activities because of an established linkage with the home-country. Therefore, Wang et al. argue that immigrants involved in cross-border business activities are more likely to establish a business out of perceived opportunity rather than necessity (Wang & Liu, 2015). Immigrants acquire information by different techniques such as language, social media platforms (Taylor, 2017), *guanxi* in Chinese communities (Zhang, 2013) and Internet trading sites (He, 2019). For some time, immigrant entrepreneurs have been able to locate business opportunities by searching in places where their counterparts do not. These opportunities not only exist in the marketplace for ethnic products and services but in the non-ethnic or mainstream market as well. Based on the resource-based view (RBV) and opportunity structure theory, the differences in resources and opportunities cause disparities in entrepreneurial activities and business performances between IEs and their native-born peers.

Although both TE and EE disciplines have gained worldwide acceptance among scholars in recent entrepreneurship studies, IE research under the framework of EE is almost neglected (Von Bloh, Mandakovic, Apablaza, Amoros, & Sternberg, 2019). Furthermore, the EE framework can be equally applied at the city/regional level and national level (Isenberg, 2011), even though the original concept of EE is location-specific. Isenberg's (2010) often-cited article is a national-scale view of EEs. Similarly, the boundary of ecosystem studies has shifted from the local community or region to country or even multi-country studies (Legros, Karuranga, Lebouc, & Mohiuddin, 2013).

In summary, TE has not been holistically explored within the ecosystem framework. It would be more valuable for this to be examined under the framework of DEEs, considering the dual embeddedness of IEs (Bagwell, 2018). Up until now, most TE determinants studies are at the factor-level, instead of the system-level. As Motoyama and Knowlton (2017) identified, the connections and interconnections amongst the factors of the ecosystem, and how these factors affect businesses, are significant research gaps.

Digital Entrepreneurial Ecosystem

Entrepreneurial ecosystem centres on the fact that new ventures emerge and grow not only because of talented and visionary individuals but the business environment by which entrepreneurs facilitate their activities to achieve success (Zaheer et al., 2019). The framework of entrepreneurial ecosystem encourages scholars to research the entrepreneurship environment as a system of interconnected socioeconomic and political-cultural elements instead of studying a single or a few factors. As an actor, entrepreneurs play a key role in the ecosystem. It is believed that the entrepreneurial ecosystem enhances entrepreneurship by providing entrepreneurial opportunities and resources, hence creating productive firms (Nicotra et al., 2018; Kotey, 2006). Despite the acceptance of EE, the framework has not been holistically examined in the context of IE and TE. There is a lack of an existing framework which links TE with EE. Developing new theoretical frameworks which can be accepted by academics and policymakers to maximise immigrant business performance can be fundamental to promoting and supporting the prosperity of the immigration economy (Chand & Rosalie, 2011).

One of the key players in digital ecosystems is e-commerce platforms which are enablers of the economic activities in an environment of borderless, infinite, multifaceted and timeless. It increases efficiency between producers and buyers, reduces transaction costs (He, 2019) and removes the boundaries of marketspace. Digital artifacts, platforms and infrastructures are three distinct and related factors in the realm of DE (Nambisan, 2017). The platforms from Alibaba, Tencent and Amazon are the business ecosystems. The business models of those platforms operate differently with a traditional pipeline and hierarchy business structure (He, 2019); its value proposition has been created through connectivity and network traffic. In those firms, users co-create values for all participants and foster new revenue streams by sustaining the advantage of the platform.

Li et al. (2012) defined DE as "…a self-organising, scalable and sustainable system composed of heterogeneous digital entities and their international focusing on interactions among entities to increase system utility, gain benefits, and promote information sharing, inner and inter cooperation and system innovation (p119)." Some scholars emphasised the importance of DE research at an extended social network area, drawing from the concept of the loose geographic boundary character of the discipline (Liu, Nandhakumar, & Zachariadis, 2018). As expressed, digital service companies are likely to upright industries on a global scale (Sussan & Acs, 2017). The European Commission draws a seven-pillar digital ecosystem framework with barriers and drivers to DE, and these are the regulatory frameworks, market conditions, access to finance, entrepreneurial capabilities, immigrants and culture (Bogdanowicz, 2015).

RESEARCH METHODOLOGY

This research followed McGaghie, Bordage and Shea's (2001) four-step new theory creation process to build up the required conceptual framework. The steps are 1) choose the topic, 2) conduct a literature review, 3) isolate the critical variables, and 4) generate the conceptual framework and research propositions. First, the topic is fixed on what are the potential growth management strategies could be adopted by transnational digital entrepreneurs. Second, the research utilised existing knowledge by synthesising current TE and DE literature in addition to the entrepreneurial ecosystem and digital ecosystem. The research paper collection process was mainly depending on ProQuest and Web of Science databases and reports from international organisations such as OECD, World Economic Forum. Third, the authors

Figure 2. Framework for Transnational Digital Entrepreneurship Research (Own elaboration)

Dimensions	Determinants
Transnational Digital Entrepreneurship Motivations	*Individual characteristics:*
	▶ Having the desire to own a business
	▶ Utilising own skills
	▶ Attitude to change and risk
	Personal experiences and circumstances:
	▶ Have business or industry sector experience
	▶ Have support from family or friends
	Personal values:
	▶ Improving personal social status
	▶ To be financial freedom
	▶ Want to secure family future and help others
	▶ Live in a desirable lifestyle
	Business ideas and opportunities:
	▶ Having products or ideas to meet market demand
	▶ An opportunity appearing
	Self-efficacies:
	▶ Perceived capabilities
	▶ Perceived success and rewards
Transnational Digital Entrepreneurial Strategies	*Transnational Entrepreneurship Strategies*
	▶ Immigrant entrepreneurship strategies
	▶ Transnational embeddedness strategies
	▶ Female entrepreneurship
	▶ Formal/informal business strategies
	▶ Ethnic enclave strategies
	▶ Social network strategies
	▶ Internationalisation strategies
	Digital Entrepreneurship Strategies
	▶ Digital capabilities, digital adoption and digital facilities
	▶ Digital features in operation activities
	▶ Merging of value creation and revenue mechanism
	▶ Knowledge acquisition and strategic learning
	▶ Digital business tendencies, competition and leadership
	▶ Digital business model configurations
	▶ Intermediary role, enhancing the role and social influence
Transnational Digital Entrepreneurship Outcomes	▶ Financial outcomes
	▶ Non-financial outcomes
	▶ Personal outcomes
	▶ Community outcomes
	▶ Host-country outcomes
	▶ Home-country outcomes
Host-country Entrepreneurial Ecosystems, **Home-country Entrepreneurial Ecosystem** **Digital Ecosystem**	*Host- and Home-country Entrepreneurial Ecosystems*
	▶ Market accessibility
	▶ Human capital
	▶ Business support, infrastructure, professions,
	▶ Culture and social norms
	▶ Funding and finance
	▶ Government policies and leadership
	Digital Ecosystem
	▶ Resource availability/constraints
	▶ Digital entrepreneurship attitudes
	▶ Context effect on digital startup formation
	▶ Digital cluster framework
	▶ Facilitating conditions within the infrastructure
	▶ Digital infrastructure architecture

followed Yin's (2002) guidance to select unique research papers. By reading through the empirical and theoretical research papers, the fragmented evidence and knowledge were summarised, and six constructs were created. Finally, after revision processes, the theoretical frameworks and propositions were established. The results of theoretical creation reveal that TDE holistically depends on three ecosystems: digital ecosystem, host-country and home-country entrepreneurial ecosystems (Figure 2). The constructs and the relationship among them will be explained further in the next section. For discussion convenience, the following paper will refer to the framework as three ecosystems framework or transnational digital entrepreneurial ecosystem.

THREE ECOSYSTEMS FRAMEWORK AND PROPOSITIONS

The concepts of TE, DE, digital and entrepreneurial ecosystem are theoretical foundations of the development of the transnational digital entrepreneurship research framework. The framework is built on Stam's (2015) causal relationships among ecosystem inputs, outputs and outcomes. The relationship between the digital ecosystem and entrepreneurial ecosystems is consistent with Sussan and Acs' (2017) theory of digital entrepreneurial ecosystems. The proposed framework expresses that, in the context of TDE, the ecosystem construct is actually three ecosystems comprising the host and home-country entrepreneurial ecosystems and cross-border digital ecosystem. Empirical studies have confirmed that new immigrants are embedded in the host and home country socioeconomic and politico-cultural societies (Ren & Liu, 2015) and digital ecosystem (Xie, Xie, & Martinez-Climent, 2019).

This framework is consistent with few theoretical frameworks as well. Brzozowski's (2017) economic adaptation framework illustrates that TDE is driven by the host and home-country socioeconomic, cultural norms; personal motivations, skills, experiences and migration strategy; and family support and expectations. The framework is an enhancement of the conceptual framework of digital entrepreneurship for immigrant (Duan et al., 2020). The framework emphasises the importance of three ecosystems. It recommends that the ecosystem impacts are of significant effects and suggests that future TDE research can be based on this framework.

Transnational Digital Entrepreneurship and Three Ecosystems

TDE studies are about how transnational digital entrepreneurs "actively engage and develop business activities in an actual business environment" (Drori et al., 2009, p1006) by engaging in novel digital technologies. In addition to access resources, there are other drivers from "relational, financial and institutional aspects of specific entrepreneurial ecosystems that promote migration and transient relocation" (Brown et al., 2019). TDE can be conceptualised as a process starting from entrepreneurs' motivation within a specific circumstance to the interaction within three ecosystems to entrepreneurial activities, and consequently to business outcomes.

Three ecosystems refer to the host-country, home-country entrepreneurial ecosystems bridged by a transnational digital ecosystem such as e-commerce platforms. Three ecosystems not only provide opportunities and resources to TDE activities but the facilities to organise them. Three ecosystems are an agglomeration of various entrepreneurial resources to nurture entrepreneurial activities (Stam, 2015) which leads to new venture creation and expected outcomes. Each factor of three ecosystems directly or indirectly affect TDE decision-making and strategies in different mechanism (WEF, 2013).

Transnational business performances are determined by a combined of entrepreneurs' attributes, activities and effects of three ecosystems. Well-functional three ecosystems foster high productivity, high-profit enterprises (Nicotra et al., 2018; Stam & Spigel, 2016; Kotey & Meredith, 1997). Therefore, one research scheme can be proposed.

P1: TDE is holistically affected by the host-country entrepreneurial ecosystem, home-country entrepreneurial ecosystem and digital ecosystems which bridges the two entrepreneurial ecosystems. The successes of TDE rely on the effectiveness of these three ecosystems.

Transnational Digital Entrepreneurs and Three Ecosystems

Early studies of immigrant entrepreneurs who have a goal to survive in a new settlement country dominated traditional IE and TE research (Portes et al., 2002), and there was a consensus that immigrants' transnational ventures were meant as the way of survival for immigrants (Aldrich, & Waldinger, 1990). They relied on the mobilisation of their social networks in both host and home countries. Currently, however, the TE concept is heterogeneous. It refers to many IEs who start their own businesses, not because of obstacles in the host country, but as a result of eagerness to exploit a business opportunity and pursue a personal goal (Lin, Zheng, Lu, Liu, & Wright, 2019). One stream and TE is business people who migrate to a new country for lifestyle or family purposes (Drori et al., 2009) and maintain enterprises in more than one county.

An individual's socioeconomic profile, personality and perception of the entrepreneurial environment are the critical determinants of engagement in TE (van der Zwan, Thurik, Verheul, & Hessels, 2016). TEs typically have innovative ideas, resources and market opportunities before starting their business ventures. Scholars argue that some immigrants become these TEs because of lack of business or employment opportunity in the host country, and therefore, they are forced into creating the transnational ventures (Portes et al., 2002). Portes (2002) and his colleagues' empirical studies show a large portion of transnational entrepreneurs are in fact pushed into the engagement of cross-border economic activities. Their findings are partially supported by the study by Lin et al. (2012), whose result shows employment status is the most important driver for immigrants to become transnational entrepreneurs. It indicates that immigrants without a full-time job are more likely to becomes transnational entrepreneurs. They conclude the pursuit the TIEs by engaging business activities with home-country has become a way of overcoming the obstacles they are facing in the host-country (Lin & Tao, 2012).

There is a lack of research on the associations between entrepreneurs' embeddedness and engagement in three ecosystems, and the relationship between entrepreneurs and the effect of three ecosystems have not yet been researched. There is a need to research these relationships in TDE settings. Thus, the paper proposes:

P2: The three ecosystems embeddedness and engagement of transnational digital entrepreneurs holistically affect the process and success of TDE. Entrepreneurs less embedded and engaged in three ecosystems have fewer capabilities to access and use opportunities and resources from the ecosystems, and consequently results in lower entrepreneurial outcomes.

Transnational Digital Entrepreneurs' Strategic Activities and Three Ecosystems

Strategic business activities have challenged transnational entrepreneurs because the host-country ecosystem could be fundamentally different from that of their home-country (Yeung, 2002). These entrepreneurial activities include 1) introducing new (or improved) goods, 2) introducing new processes of production, 3) opening new markets, 4) exploiting new sources of supplies and 5) creating new ventures (Schumpeter, 1943). Activities also include opportunity identification and development, resource accumulation and organisation, and responding to the government and society (Gartner, 1985) and individuals who start business ventures regardless of the firm's profitability (Drucker, 1985). Drucker's specification was widely accepted and utilised by organisations (GEM, 2017/2018) and scholars (Von Bloh et al., 2019; van der Zwan et al., 2016).

Entrepreneurial activities are processes in which individuals access resources, exploit opportunities and create businesses for innovation (Stam, 2015; Gartner, 1985). The activities undertaken in an immigrant firm are determined by the entrepreneurs' characteristics and entrepreneurial ecosystems. The strategic activities undertaken by transnational entrepreneurs are fundamentally shaped by ecosystem factors such as social, institutional, markets, human capitals, both in their host and home countries (Yeung, 2002). Once embedded in these ecosystems, transnational digital entrepreneurs can take advantage of their entrepreneurial endowments and additional resources to enhance their newly created ventures and business activities.

Entrepreneurial strategic activities drive the TDE process to develop new goods, services, methods of production, markets and organisations (Gartner, 1985). It also includes routine business activities such as income generation and servicing a co-ethnic community. Entrepreneurs search for resources in three ecosystems in order to combine them in new and creative manners and to meet unmet market demands, but the successes of innovative activities depend on the available resources and support from the three ecosystems. These activities lead to superior prospects for entrepreneurial firm growth, acquisition of profit and better firm performance. Opportunity entrepreneurial activities are influenced mainly by entrepreneurs' motivations and three ecosystems, and survival activities are actions to keep income creation and business afloat.

Although the literature shows that the host-country ecosystem can promote or hinder all types of immigrant entrepreneurs, home-country ecosystem factors could be in favour of transnational entrepreneurs because opportunities and resources from the home-country are additional capitals which can only be obtained through greater experiences, knowledge and network resources (Von Bloh et al., 2019). Having these extra capitals, transnational entrepreneurs could open up new markets, approach new suppliers, improve firm productivity and reduce production cost with new technologies from their home-country (Von Bloh et al., 2019).

Many factors in the three ecosystems play an essential role in fostering the TDE (Brzozowski, 2019; You & Zhou, 2019). Transnational human capital and social capital, including networks, families and relatives, help TEs navigating in an international context (Brzozowski et al., 2017). Transnational institutions and governments simultaneously promote and hinder TE performance (You & Zhou, 2019). Working on a transnational marketplace, entrepreneurs increase transnational trading, boost immigrant incomes and enhance community cohesion (Lin & Tao, 2012). Later research shows infrastructures and business supports encourage TE, particularly through e-commerce platforms and improved logistic services (Duan et al., 2020; Song, 2019).

Most recently, Nkongolo-Bakenda and Chrysostome (2019) empirically studied diasporic transnational entrepreneurs in the Canadian context by separating the business environments of TE into a host and home-country settings. Their framework comprises host-country facilitating factors (attitude and institutional support) and facilitating and impeding factors from home-country (formal and inform legal system, socioeconomic, human and financial, cultural, attitude, regulation and institution). The results show Canadian transnational entrepreneurs' perceive factors such as taxes, regulations, corruption, scarcity of finance and qualified human resources, and cultural value in the home-country as primary obstacles for startup and growing ventures. By contrast, government support and local attitude towards the entrepreneurs play a moderate impact.

Existing literature has provided different, and contrasting in some cases, perspectives on the activities and performances of transnational businesses (Wang & Liu, 2015). Wang and Liu. (2015) found that immigrant firms have a significantly higher tendency to be involved in transnational economic activities when compared to native firms, even after removing controlled firm-level and owner-level characteristics. They believe that personal networks with their home-country could play a significant role in fostering transnational economic activities for immigrant-owned firms. They further considered that, while limited labour market opportunities may have pushed immigrants to turn to TDE, these immigrants are more likely to establish businesses out of opportunity backed by their transnational ties with the home country.

Digital ecosystem and digital transformation have lowered the bars for engaging in entrepreneurship. New digital technology brought about by the application of e-technologies have stimulated entrepreneurship to benefit the micro-entrepreneur and SME owner (Duan et al, 2020). E-commerce platforms have designed a business environment for micro, small and medium enterprises (MSEMs), and they describe the development as the platform business ecosystem (He, 2019). These platforms bring multisided marketplaces, including producers, e-shop owners, buyers and logistics partners, with Alibaba e-commerce platforms to co-create value. It acts as a one-stop business center for MSEMs owners by providing operation and management services. Evidence shows digital ease business establishment.

Entrepreneurial activities convert entrepreneurial motivation, resources and opportunities to organised economic performance under the support of three ecosystems. Previous studies have focused on individual-level determinants. There is less investigation into the effect of ecosystem factors in the context of TDE activities. While existing research on three ecosystems provides content-rich factors related to entrepreneurial activities, the causal relationship between ecosystem factors with entrepreneurial activities has not been studied sufficiently and holistically (Nicotra et al., 2018). Therefore, the subsequent propositions are offered:

P3a: The traditional immigrant and transnational entrepreneurship approaches in the host-country are still major strategies affecting the success of transnational digital entrepreneurs.

P3b: Host-country entrepreneurial ecosystem affects TDE strategies adopted by transnational digital entrepreneurs. The entrepreneurs benefit from each host-country entrepreneurial ecosystem pillar.

P3c: Home-country entrepreneurial ecosystem affects TDE strategies adopted by transnational digital entrepreneurs. The entrepreneurs benefit from each home-country entrepreneurial ecosystem pillar.

P3d: Digital ecosystem affects TDE strategies adopted by transnational digital entrepreneurs. The entrepreneurs benefit from boundary-less digital ecosystem to bridge host-country and home-country entrepreneurial ecosystems, consequently to ease transnational business creation and increase transnational economic activities between entrepreneurs' host and home countries.

SOLUTIONS AND RECOMMENDATIONS

This paper proposed a conceptual framework for the study of TDE process. It developed a set of testable propositions for future empirical studies regarding transnational digital entrepreneurs exploiting entrepreneurial opportunities, deploying strategic activities and enhancing TDE outcomes. The research perspective has focused on the significance of theories of the host- and home-country entrepreneurial ecosystem and digital ecosystem. All ecosystem elements need to be taken into account while researching the TDE phenomenon from this three ecosystems perspective.

This paper argues that, because of three ecosystems effects, in comparison to traditional entrepreneurs, transnational digital entrepreneurs have additional tangible and intangible resources which facilitate new opportunity recognition, innovative activities and new venture creation. In the case of undertaking cross-border economic activities, transnational digital entrepreneurs are able to organise entrepreneurial resources from both host and home countries relying on available digital ecosystems. The difference among these leverageable resources from three ecosystems create a higher rate of entrepreneurship and better firm performance in immigrant groups. It is one of the answers to the question of why immigrants are more eager to pursuit transnational entrepreneurship activities, and also partially explains why firms with cooperation between immigrants and natives perform better than a single ethnicity (Kerr & Kerr, 2019).

There are significant shortages in research, both theoretically or empirically, on the impact factors for transnational digital ventures from three ecosystems (Bazhair, & Sandhu, 2015), and this research will fill a few theoretical gaps. The propositions in this study demonstrate that three ecosystems have positive effects on cross-nation business opportunity actualisation. This paper has focused on the identification and conceptualisation of (1) integrating the TE and DE theories within digital ecosystem framework, (2) providing a conceptual/theoretical framework to encourage causal-effect study between three ecosystems and TDE, and (3) building up propositions for future empirical studies. It implies that (1) policymakers need to take note of encouraging immigrants' socio-economic ties with their country of origin, (2) transnational entrepreneurs need to enable viable resources from both home and host countries by utilising digital technologies to build high growth competitive businesses, (3) economists and scholars can help policymakers and entrepreneurs to identify resources and advantages existed in the home-country of an immigrant group, and 4) more user-friendly digital ecosystems, particularly cross-border e-commerce platforms, are required to encourage transnational trades.

FUTURE RESEARCH DIRECTIONS

This is the first attempt paper, by authors' understanding, to conceptually analyse the association between TDE and influential factors of the host-country, home-country and digital entrepreneurial ecosystems. The research findings would lead to the development of TDE field through the empirical evidence with regards to the relationship found among motivation, strategic activities and outcomes of entrepreneurs and three ecosystems. The complete understanding of three ecosystem effects can lead to the formation of government policies and programs which influences all entrepreneurs.

The research on the digital and entrepreneurial ecosystem for TDE is in its infant stage. Some conceptual studies can only be found in some technology sectors, such as ICT and biology (Ginsberg, Horwitch, Mahapatra, & Singh, 2010). This paper integrates the entrepreneurial ecosystem and digital ecosystem frameworks to conceptualise TDE process, and proposed potential strategies could be adopted by transnational digital entrepreneurs. Further development of ecosystem strategies in TDE field is of importance for enhancing international trades, increasing socioeconomic prosperity in entrepreneurs' host- and home-countries and improving interconnections among nations.

This research has focused on the conceptualisation of the relationship among three ecosystems and TDE process, and there is a need to empirically assess the theoretical constructs that enable assessment of the conceptual framework. Further research could examine whether transnational digital entrepreneurs who embedded in three ecosystems perform better over a long period of time, with firms focused on one or two ecosystems. More importantly, researching the digital ecosystem effects on transnational digital entrepreneurs can help to promote international trade, and consequently contribute to host-country socioeconomic development and job creation.

CONCLUSION

This paper argues that TDE should be studied in three ecosystems. In the study, the authors conceptualise that transnational digital entrepreneurs operate in three ecosystems that are distinct from the existing literature in which transnational entrepreneurs are believed to operate in dual entrepreneurial ecosystems (host and home countries). Transnational digital entrepreneurs have the potential to access three ecosystems, which provides more opportunities for them to exploit, and more resources to reorganise. The key functionality of digital ecosystem is to bridge entrepreneurs' host and home-country ecosystems. However, three ecosystems and their factors may not equally impact each individual. It is reasonable to conceptualise that some transnational digital entrepreneurs have less capability to utilise these resources due to their reduced embeddedness within the three ecosystems, in particular, the digital ecosystem engagement. On the other hand, more embedded and engaged transnational digital entrepreneurs will have more access to opportunities and resources.

Regarding transnational entrepreneurs facing obstacles and barriers in taking host-country ecosystem benefit, the paper argues these entrepreneurs have advantages to take home-country ecosystem benefits. In regard to cross-border digital ecosystems, the paper also claims that transnational entrepreneurs benefit more from it than born-natives because all digital ecosystems are with cultural elements such as language, customs, preferred products or brands. Social-and cultural cognitive effects exist in all social spaces regarding business.

This research proposes that some of the distinctive advantages existing in three ecosystems are specifically only available for transnational digital entrepreneurs who proactively engage in three ecosystems to develop opportunities. Although the initial entrepreneurial motivation may, to a greater extent, be driven by demographic and psychological drivers, to convert such motivations to activities still require an optimal external entrepreneurial environment. Therefore, an entrepreneur's proactive embeddedness are preconditions for the effectiveness of three ecosystems. One potential practical implication for entrepreneurs is to seek opportunities and required resources on a larger geographic scale to cover these three ecosystems. Those to-be entrepreneurs need to extend their mindset to accumulate network resources and explore more opportunities in the ecosystems and to recognise the "differentiation" competitive advantages when deeply embedded in them.

ACKNOWLEDGMENT

The Commonwealth of Australia funded this research.

REFERENCES

Acs, Z., Åstebro, T., Audretsch, D., & Robinson, D. T. (2016). Public policy to promote entrepreneurship: A call to arms. *Small Business Economics*, *47*(1), 35–51. doi:10.100711187-016-9712-2

Aldrich, E. H., & Waldinger, R. (1990). Ethnicity and Entrepreneurship. Annual Review of Sociology, 16, 25.

Bagwell, S. (2018). From mixed embeddedness to transnational mixed embeddedness An exploration of Vietnamese businesses in London. *International Journal of Entrepreneurial Behaviour & Research*, *24*(1), 104–120. doi:10.1108/IJEBR-01-2017-0035

Baltar, F., & Icart, I. B. (2013). Entrepreneurial gain, cultural similarity and transnational entrepreneurship. *Global Networks-a Journal of Transnational Affairs*, *13*(2), 20. doi:10.1111/glob.12020

Bazhair, A., & Sandhu, K. (2015). Factors for the Acceptance of Enterprise Resource Planning (ERP) Systems and Financial Performance. *Journal of Economics, Business and Management, 14*(7).

Beckers, P., & Blumberg, B. F. (2013). Immigrant entrepreneurship on the move: A longitudinal analysis of first- and second-generation immigrant entrepreneurship in the Netherlands. *Entrepreneurship and Regional Development*, *25*(7-8), 654–691. doi:10.1080/08985626.2013.808270

Bogdanowicz, M. (2015). *Digital Entrepreneurship Barriers and Drivers.* Retrieved from: https://ec.europa.eu/jrc/en/publication/digital-entrepreneurship-barriers-and-drivers-need-specific-measurement-framework

Brown, R., Mawson, S., Lee, N., & Peterson, L. (2019). Start-up factories, transnational entrepreneurs and entrepreneurial ecosystems: Unpacking the lure of start-up accelerator programmes. *European Planning Studies*, *27*(5), 885–904. doi:10.1080/09654313.2019.1588858

Brzozowski, J., Cucculelli, M., & Surdej, A. (2017). The determinants of transnational entrepreneurship and transnational ties' dynamics among immigrant entrepreneurs in ICT sector in Italy. *International Migration (Geneva, Switzerland)*, *55*(3), 105–125. doi:10.1111/imig.12335

Chand, M., & Ghorbani, M. (2011). National culture, networks and ethnic entrepreneurship: A comparison of the Indian and Chinese immigrants in the US. *International Business Review*, *20*(6), 13. doi:10.1016/j.ibusrev.2011.02.009

Chand, M., & Tung, R. L. (2014). Bicultural identity and economic engagement: An exploratory study of the Indian diaspora in North America. *Asia Pacific Journal of Management*, *31*(3), 763–788. doi:10.100710490-014-9375-y

Chand, M. T., & Rosalie, L. (2011). Global competitiveness, consumer choice and 'country of origin' effect: An exploratory East-West study. *Asia Pacific Journal of Management*, *17*(3), 15.

Collins, J. (2002). The Chinese diaspora in Australia. *International Journal of Entrepreneurial Behaviour & Research*, 8.

Drori, I., Honig, B., & Wright, M. (2009). Transnational Entrepreneurship: An Emergent Field of Study. *Entrepreneurship Theory and Practice*, *33*(5), 1001–1022. doi:10.1111/j.1540-6520.2009.00332.x

Drucker, F. P. (1985). Innovation and Entrepreneurship. *Routledge Classic 2015*.

Du, W. Y., Pan, S. L., Zhou, N., & Ouyang, T. H. (2018). From a marketplace of electronics to a digital entrepreneurial ecosystem (DEE): The emergence of a meta-organisation in Zhongguancun, China. *Information Systems Journal*, *28*(6), 1158–1175. doi:10.1111/isj.12176

Duan, C., Kotey, B., & Sandhu, K. (2020a). *Digital Entrepreneurship for Immigrants: Motivation, Strategies, Ecosystems, and Performance*. IGI Global. doi:10.4018/978-1-7998-2799-3.ch009

Duan, C., Kotey, B., & Sandhu, K. (2020b). Transnational immigrant entrepreneurship: effects of home-country entrepreneurial ecosystem factors. International Journal of Entrepreneurial Behavior & Research, (ahead-of-print). doi:10.1108/IJEBR-05-2020-0300

Duan, C., Kotey, B., & Sandhu, K. (2021). *Understanding immigrant entrepreneurship: home-country entrepreneurial ecosystem perspective*. New England Journal of Entrepreneurship., doi:10.1108/NEJE-05-2020-0013

European Commission, (2016). *Digital Entrepreneurship Scoreboard 2015*. Directorate-General for intermarket, Industry, Entrepreneurship and SMEs.

Gartner, B. W. (1985). A Conceptual Framework for Describing the Phenomenon of New Venture Creation. *Academy of Management Review, 10*(4), 12.

GEM. (2017/2018). *GEM Global Report 2017/18*. Retrieved from https://www.gemconsortium.org/report/gem-2017-2018-global-report

Ginsberg, A., Horwitch, M., Mahapatra, S., & Singh, C. (2010, 18-22 July 2010). *Ecosystem strategies for complex technological innovation: The case of smart grid development*. Paper presented at the Picmet 2010 Technology Management for Global Economic Growth.

He, X. H. (2019). Digital entrepreneurship solution to rural poverty: Theory, practice and policy implications. *Journal of Developmental Entrepreneurship*, *24*(1), 32. doi:10.1142/S1084946719500043

Isenberg, D. (2011). The entrepreneurship ecosystem strategy as new paradigm for economic policy: principles for cultivating entrepreneurship: The Babson entrepreneurship ecosystem project. Babson College.

Kariv, D., Menzies, T. V., Brenner, G. A., & Filion, L. J. (2009). Transnational networking and business performance: Ethnic entrepreneurs in Canada. *Entrepreneurship and Regional Development*, *21*(3), 239–264. doi:10.1080/08985620802261641

Kerr, S. P., & Kerr, W. (2019). *Immigrant entrepreneurship in America: Evidence from the survey of business owners 2007 & 2012*. Retrieved from https://www.nber.org/papers/w22385

Kotey, B. (2006). Entrepreneurship and Regional Development: A Theoretical Frame Work. *Small Enterprise Research, 14*(2), 25. doi:10.5172er.14.2.20

Kotey, B., & Meredith, G. G. (1997). Relationships among Owner/Manager Personal Values, Business Strategies, and Enterprise Performance. *Journal of Small Business Management*, *1997*(April), 27.

Kotey, B., Sharma, B., & Gao, K. (2013). The Configuration of Entrepreneurial Strategy in Chinese Small Textile Manufacturing Firms. *Journal of New Business Ideas and Trends, 11*(1).

Kushnirovich, N. (2015). Economic Integration of Immigrant Entrepreneurs. *Entrepreneurial Business and Economics Review, 3*(3), 9–27. doi:10.15678/EBER.2015.030302

Lan, T., & Zhu, S. J. (2014). Chinese apparel value chains in Europe: Low-end fast fashion, regionalisation, and transnational entrepreneurship in Prato, Italy. *Eurasian Geography and Economics, 55*(2), 156–174. doi:10.1080/15387216.2014.948471

Legros, M., Karuranga, E. G., Lebouc, M.-F., & Mohiuddin, M. (2013). Ethnic Entrepreneurship In OECD Countries: A Systematic Review Of Performance Determinants Of Ethnic Ventures. *The International Business & Economics Research Journal (Online), 12*(10), 1199. doi:10.19030/iber.v12i10.8131

Li, C. G., Isidor, R., Dau, L. A., & Kabst, R. (2018). The More the Merrier? Immigrant Share and Entrepreneurial Activities. *Entrepreneurship Theory and Practice, 42*(5), 698–733. doi:10.1177/1042258718795344

Li, P., Liu, S. W., Zhang, S. B., & Li, C. H. (2017). A Study on Factors Affecting Students' Entrepreneurial Intentions in HIT. In M. A. Tao (Ed.), *2017 24th Annual International Conference on Management Science & Engineering* (pp. 358-362). New York: IEEE.

Lin, D. M., Zheng, W., Lu, J. Y., Liu, X. H., & Wright, M. (2019). Forgotten or not? Home-country embeddedness and returnee entrepreneurship. *Journal of World Business, 54*(1), 1–13. doi:10.1016/j.jwb.2018.08.003

Lin, X., & Tao, S. (2012). Transnational entrepreneurs: Characteristics, drivers, and success factors. *Journal of International Entrepreneurship, 10*(1), 50–69. doi:10.100710843-011-0082-1

Liu, J. Y., Nandhakumar, J., & Zachariadis, M. (2018). When guanxi meets structural holes: Exploring the guanxi networks of Chinese entrepreneurs on digital platforms. *The Journal of Strategic Information Systems, 27*(4), 311–334. doi:10.1016/j.jsis.2018.10.003

Motoyama, Y., & Knowlton, K. (2017). Examining the Connections within the Startup Ecosystem: A Case Study of St. Louis. *Entrepreneurship Research Journal, 7*(1). Advance online publication. doi:10.1515/erj-2016-0011

Nambisan, S. (2017). Digital Entrepreneurship: Toward a Digital Technology Perspective of Entrepreneurship. *Entrepreneurship Theory and Practice, 41*(6), 1029–1055. doi:10.1111/etap.12254

Nicotra, M., Romano, M., Giudice, D. M., & Schillaci, E. C. (2018). The causal relation between entrepreneurial ecosystem and productive entrepreneurship: A measurement framework. *The Journal of Technology Transfer, 43*(3), 33. doi:10.100710961-017-9628-2

Nkongolo-Bakenda, J.-M., & Chrysostome, V. (2019). Dual environments of home and host countries of diasporic transnational entrepreneurs: an empirical study in the Canadian context. *International Journal of Entrepreneurship and Small Business.*

Oliveira, R. C. (2010). The determinants of immigrant entrepreneurship and employment creation in Portugal: Chapter 4 of Migrant Entrepreneurship in OECD Countries. Academic Press.

Portes, A., Guarnizo, L. E., & Haller, W. J. (2002). Transnational entrepreneurs: An alternative form of immigrant economic adaptation. *American Sociological Review*, *67*(2), 278–298.

Portes, A., Guarnizo, L. E., & Landolt, P. (1999). The study of transnationalism: Pitfalls and promise of an emergent research field. *Ethnic and Racial Studies*, *22*(2), 237. doi:10.1080/014198799329468

Portes, A., Haller, W. J., & Guarnizo, L. E. (2002). Transnational entrepreneurs: An alternative form of immigrant economic adaptation. *American Sociological Review*, *67*(2), 278–298. doi:10.2307/3088896

Portes, A., & Yiu, J. (2013). Entrepreneurship, transnationalism, and development. *Migration Studies*, *1*(1), 20. doi:10.1093/migration/mns036

Portes, A., & Zhou, M. (1996). Self-employment and the earnings of immigrants. *American Sociological Review*, *61*(2), 219. doi:10.2307/2096332

Ren, N., & Liu, H. (2015). Traversing between transnationalism and integration: Dual embeddedness of new Chinese immigrant entrepreneurs in Singapore. *Asian and Pacific Migration Journal*, *24*(3), 298–326. doi:10.1177/0117196815594719

Reynolds, D. P., Bygrave, D. W., Autio, E., Cox, W. L., & Hay, M. (2002). *Global Entrepreneurship Monitor: 2002 Executive Report*. Academic Press.

Sahut, J.-M., Luca, I., & Frédéric, T. (2019). The age of digital entrepreneurship. *Small Business Economics*, •••, 1–11.

Sandhu, K. (2008). E-Services Acceptance Model (E-SAM). In SAdvances in Computer and Information Sciences and Engineering. Springer.

Sandhu, K. (2009). Measuring the performance of the electronic service acceptance model (E-SAM). *International Journal of Business Information Systems*, *4*(5), 13. doi:10.1504/IJBIS.2009.025205

Saxenian, A. (2005). From Brain Drain to Brain Circulation: Transnational Communities and Regional Upgrading in India and China. *Studies in Comparative International Development*, *40*(2), 26. doi:10.1007/BF02686293

Schiller, N. G., Basch, L., & Blanc, C. S. (1995). From immigrant to transmigrant - Theorising transnational migration. *Anthropological Quarterly*, *68*(1), 48–63. doi:10.2307/3317464

Schumpeter, A. J. (1943). Capitalism, Socialism and Democracy (3rd ed.). Harperperennial Modernthought.

Sequeira, J. M., Carr, J. C., & Rasheed, A. A. (2009). Transnational Entrepreneurship: Determinants of Firm Type and Owner Attributions of Success. *Entrepreneurship Theory and Practice*, *33*(5), 1023–1044. doi:10.1111/j.1540-6520.2009.00333.x

Shinnar, S., & Nayir, Z. (2019). Immigrant Entrepreneurship in an Emerging Economy: The Case of Turkey. *Journal of Small Business Management*, *57*(2), 559–575. doi:10.1111/jsbm.12408

Song, A. K. (2019). The Digital Entrepreneurial Ecosystem-a critique and reconfiguration. *Small Business Economics*, *53*(3), 569–590. doi:10.100711187-019-00232-y

Stam, E. (2015). Entrepreneurial Ecosystems and Regional Policy: A Sympathetic Critique. *European Planning Studies*, *23*(9), 10. doi:10.1080/09654313.2015.1061484

Sussan, F., & Acs, Z. J. (2017). The digital entrepreneurial ecosystem. *Small Business Economics*, *49*(1), 55–73. doi:10.100711187-017-9867-5

van der Zwan, P., Thurik, R., Verheul, I., & Hessels, J. (2016). Factors influencing the entrepreneurial engagement of opportunity and necessity entrepreneurs. *Eurasian Bus Rev*, *6*.

Van Tubergen, F. (2005). Self-Employment of Immigrants: A Cross-National Study Study of 17 Western Societies. *Social Forces*, *84*(2), 23. doi:10.1353of.2006.0039

Vertovec, S. (2003). Migration and other modes of transnationalism: Towards conceptual cross-fertilisation. *The International Migration Review*, *37*(3), 641–665. doi:10.1111/j.1747-7379.2003.tb00153.x

Von Bloh, J., Mandakovic, V., Apablaza, M., Amoros, J. E., & Sternberg, R. (2019). Transnational entrepreneurs: Opportunity or necessity driven? Empirical evidence from two dynamic economies from Latin America and Europe. *Journal of Ethnic and Migration Studies*. Advance online publication. doi:10.1080/1369183X.2018.1559996

Wang, Q., & Liu, C. Y. (2015). Transnational activities of immigrant-owned firms and their performances in the USA. *Small Business Economics*, *44*(2), 345–359. doi:10.100711187-014-9595-z

Wang, Y. R., & Warn, J. (2019). Break-out strategies of Chinese immigrant entrepreneurs in Australia. *International Journal of Entrepreneurial Behaviour & Research*, *25*(2), 217–242. doi:10.1108/IJEBR-03-2017-0108

WEF. (2013). *Entrepreneurial Ecosystems Around the Globe and Company Growth Dynamics*. Retrieved from: https://www.weforum.org/reports/entrepreneurial-ecosystems-around-globe-and-company-growth-dynamics

Yeung, H. W. C. (2002). Entrepreneurship in International Business: An Institutional Perspective. *Asia Pacific Journal of Management*, 19.

Yin, R. K. (2002). *Case study research: Design and methods*. SAGE Publications.

You, T., & Zhou, M. (2019). Simultaneous Embeddedness in Immigrant Entrepreneurship: Global Forces Behind Chinese-Owned Nail Salons in New York City: PROD. *The American Behavioral Scientist*, *63*(2), 166–185. doi:10.1177/0002764218793684

Zaheer, H., Breyer, Y., & Dumay, J. (2019). Digital entrepreneurship: An interdisciplinary structured literature review and research agenda. *Technological Forecasting and Social Change*, *148*, 148. doi:10.1016/j.techfore.2019.119735

Chapter 2
Scrum as an Agile Method for Strategic Organizational Learning in Digital Enterprise Transformation:
Applying the Four Elements of Organizational Learning

Atilla Wohllebe
https://orcid.org/0000-0001-5848-3453
MATE Hungarian University of Agriculture and Life Sciences, Kaposvár Campus, Kaposvár, Hungary

ABSTRACT

In the context of managing digital enterprise transformation, the generation and distribution of knowledge across the entire organization is of great importance. Because existing processes are being questioned and activities are changing, the promotion of organizational learning should be part of the digital transformation strategy. This chapter uses the example of Scrum to show how organizational learning can be supported by agile working methods. After an introduction to organizational learning and to Scrum as a process of continuous improvement, the four elements of organizational learning are used and compared to the characteristic elements of Scrum. In addition, the author points out existing research gaps, especially in quantitative research, and gives practical advice for managers on how to use Scrum to promote organizational learning.

INTRODUCTION

Increasingly, many markets have become faster moving and more complex, customer requirements are constantly changing. In this environment, classic "waterfall"-based project management functions less and less. Agile working methods and frameworks such as Scrum and Kanban have become more and

DOI: 10.4018/978-1-7998-8583-2.ch002

more relevant in recent years and can be found especially as a part of digital enterprise transformation strategies.

At the same time, digitalization is now presenting enterprises of all sizes and in all industries with major challenges. While in some cases it is "only" a matter of process innovations, other companies are even rethinking entire business models, partly because new competitors are constantly emerging and customers have higher expectations. The increasingly rapid technological development associated with digitization and the associated shortening of product life cycles also reduces the half-life of knowledge. The acquisition of new, up-to-date knowledge is increasingly becoming a central challenge for enterprises.

The introduction of agile working methods can be seen as a consequence of the need for faster, more output-focused product development and is now part of strategies for managing the digital enterprise transformation. As an agile working method Scrum plays a central role in this development.

Against the background of the decrease in the half-life of knowledge described above, the question arises as to what extent agile methods can also help here. With a focus on Scrum this chapter therefore examines how Scrum can support the learning process of organizations and their individuals and thus contribute to mastering the challenges of the digital enterprise transformation.

The research question of the contribution of Scrum to organizational learning as a core challenge of the digital enterprise transformation is methodically examined through a literature review.

The chapter first introduces the concepts of organizational learning and agile working and presents Scrum as a method of agile working. The four elements of organizational learning are introduced as a model for the presentation of organizational learning. Existing findings of the literature on both topics are reviewed. In the following synthesis it will be shown to what extent Scrum supports organizational learning and thus can contribute to a successful transformation process as a component of the digital enterprise transformation strategy.

Background

Organizational learning has been discussed in the scientific community for many years and is particularly relevant to the economic sciences, with links to psychology and sociology. An organization can be regarded as learning if it is able to draw conclusions from past experiences for action in the present (Levitt & March, 1988). In the context of this chapter, organizational learning is especially understood as the ability of an organization to learn continuously and as a whole. The aim is to distribute knowledge of individual members of the organization from the past to others who may (also) need this knowledge for (better) fulfilling their tasks in the present and in the future. In this sense organizational learning can also and especially be understood as a process of continuous improvement through knowledge and understanding (Fiol & Lyles, 1985). Research from different contexts shows that the ability to organizational learning can be an important component in improving organizational performance (Ali, Peters, Khan, Ali, & Saif, 2020; Gachanja, Nga'nga', & Kiganane, 2020; İpek, 2019; Qureshi & Kashif, 2009; Tortorella, Cawley Vergara, Garza-Reyes, & Sawhney, 2020).

Before the question can be discussed how far Scrum can support the development of a (continuously) learning organization, agile working and Scrum in particular must first be briefly introduced: The idea of agile working has also been known for several years. Originally coming from software development, "The Agile Manifesto", first published in 2001, describes the principles on which many methods of agile working are based (Beck, Beedle, van Bennekum, Cockburn, & Cunningham, 2001).

These four principles are:

- Individuals and interactions over processes and tools
- Working software over comprehensive documentation
- Customer collaboration over contract negotiation
- Responding to change over following a plan

In this respect, the term agility in the sense of agile working is to be understood primarily as the ability to adapt by a combination of feedback loops and transparency (Lethmate, 2016). Current research therefore emphasizes that agile working methods are particularly suitable for use in dynamic competitive and market environments (Stormi, Laine, & Korhonen, 2019).

As an agile working method many elements of Scrum reflect the principles of the agile manifesto by Beck et al. (2001). In the case of Scrum these principles are reflected by short (often two-weeks), iterative development and feedback cycles, so-called sprints, with the release of a functional product increment at the end of each cycle (Roock & Wolf, 2016, p. 141). Also, because customers (i.e. requesters of software functionalities) are thus able to see first results quickly, Scrum probably has a positive effect on customer satisfaction (Khalid, Butt, Jamal, & Gochhait, 2020).

Essential for Scrum is the work in cross-functionally composed teams. The team members are empowered decision-makers, who are enabled to make their own decisions concerning their work. This self-responsibility of each individual and the team as a whole for their product is characteristic for Scrum. A Scrum team typically consists of three roles working together:

- Product Owner
- Development Team
- Scrum Master

Both the Scrum team as a whole and the development team are cross-functional. Depending on the application, the development team is a combination of frontend, backend and database development, if necessary in combination with user experience experts.

The product owner is the product manager, who usually combines business and development viewpoints, is responsible for the product vision and defines the tasks for product development (often as tickets) and prioritizes them in the product backlog.

The development team is responsible for the actual development of the software or product. It works in (often) two-week cycles, the sprints, and decides independently how to handle the tasks at hand. In particular, this implies that the development team decides in the sprint planning process how many of the pending tickets will make it through the upcoming sprint.

In many transformation projects, the scrum master is often perceived with the role of the project manager, a role that is familiar in practically all organizations. In fact, however, the scrum master is not technically involved in the product. The role of the scrum master is to support the development team and the product owner in adhering to the Scrum process and to ensure that the Scrum process is followed. It is also important to understand that the Scrum Master is responsible for the adherence to the Scrum process, but does not act as a disciplinary leader of a team and therefore should not be a manager in the classical sense.

It can be assumed that the Scrum process followed by the Scrum team leads to an increase in quality of the software development (Arcos-Medina & Mauricio, 2020; Kendall, Kong, & Kendall, 2010; Roock

& Wolf, 2016, p. 10). Also, agile management has a positive effect on organizations to focus more on creating value for customers and end users (Denning, 2019).

Scrum in particular has established itself in practice in recent years and is practiced in many companies often as part of an overarching strategy for digital transformation. Scrum is not always used in its original form, but can also be found in practice in modified form. Scrum and its derivatives are now used in many different environments (Landaeta, Viscardi, & Tolk, 2011; Säisä, Tiura, & Matikainen, 2019).

MAIN FOCUS OF THE CHAPTER

The chapter provides practitioners in the areas of digital transformation, management and organization with valuable information on whether and how organizations can use Scrum to increase their organizational learning capacity as one part of a sustainable digital enterprise transformation strategy.

First, existing literature on organizational learning is reviewed. In addition to the model of the four elements of organizational learning, the influence of the organizational structure on the ability of an organization to learn will be considered. The challenges in this context are also addressed.

After having introduced Scrum as a method of agile working in the background, it will be shown how Scrum can be understood as a process of continuous improvement and how knowledge and learning is handled in cross-functional teams and beyond the boundaries of teams. The role of leadership in the context of Scrum is also discussed.

In the subsequent synthesis, the elements of organizational learning are brought together with the components of Scrum. The following practical recommendations are made on how Scrum can support the process of organizational learning as an element of the digital enterprise transformation strategy.

First, however, a common understanding of the terms "digital enterprise", "transformation" and "strategy" used in this context must be achieved:

For the term "digital enterprise" there are different definitions in the literature. For example, Xu (2014, p. 5) defines a digital enterprise in a relatively broad sense as a company that (also) uses digital technologies in the various stages of its value creation or in its activities. This also corresponds to the view of Huber (2013), who defines the completion of the digitization of all value-added processes as the completion of the transformation to a digital enterprise. This rather broad definition contrasts with the approach of Skilton (2015), according to which a digital enterprise is an organization that provides physical or virtual products or services in one or more digital ecosystems. The definition from Skilton (2015) thus refers less to the value-added process and more to the environment in which services or products are delivered. In this chapter, the digital enterprise, especially against the background of transformation, is understood as a company that makes substantial use of digital technologies in its value creation process or to generate competitive advantages.

Based on Deuringer (2000, p. 38), the term "transformation" refers to a profound, fundamental, holistic and lasting change in a company. This transformation includes aspects of changing attitudes, restructuring, revitalization and renewal, with the aim of ensuring the continued existence of entrepreneurial success. In particular, the "digital transformation" goes far beyond simple digitization, but also implies changes in bureaucratic and organizational culture. Mergel, Edelmann, and Haug (2019) emphasize that the digital transformation can only be measured in the short term through the increased use of digital services, while in the long term, above all, a gain in effectiveness and customer satisfaction must be measurable.

Based on Müller-Stewens (n.d.), the term "strategy" is understood in this chapter as a fundamental and long-term oriented behavior of a company or organization to implement long-term goals. From this, the strategy for digital enterprise transformation is derived accordingly as the fundamental, long-term behavior of a company with the goal of digitizing the value-adding processes of a company, its bureaucratic and organizational culture, in order to achieve higher effectiveness and higher (customer) satisfaction (derived from the definition approaches of Xu (2014, p. 5), Huber (2013), Deuringer (2000, p. 38), Mergel, Edelmann, and Haug (2019) and Müller-Stewens (n.d.)).

Issues, Controversies, Problems

In this chapter several issues are critically discussed:

- The introduction to organizational learning will also highlight the corresponding challenges for organizations and their individuals.
- With regard to Scrum, the challenge of whether and how team knowledge can be transferred into organizational knowledge is discussed.
- Scrum also requires managers to have a new understanding of leadership, which is also discussed.
- Finally, suggestions are made on how managers can meet the challenge of organizational learning in the context of digital enterprise transformation in practice.

ORGANIZATIONAL LEARNING

Learning as an Organizational Challenge

Regardless of the size or industry of a company, the generation, storage and distribution of knowledge can be considered one of the core tasks of a sustainable existing organization. Against this background, the term "learning organization" or, analogously, the term "organizational learning" has developed. Organizational learning can be understood as the ability of an organization to continuously distribute the knowledge of its individuals within the organization in a process - with the goal of continuous improvement or adaptation to changing circumstances based on the knowledge from the past (Fiol & Lyles, 1985; Levitt & March, 1988).

Accordingly, members of a learning organization strive to generate, share and apply new knowledge or to check existing knowledge for its continuing validity (Hitt, 1995). In fact, in many organizations, knowledge distribution already takes place naturally, for example through social interactions - but there are usually no defined, formal processes for a structured and consciously controlled distribution of knowledge (Shah, Maitlo, Jones, & Yusuf, 2019). Companies try to remedy this situation, for example through their own initiatives, coaching and mentoring and a culture of empowerment (Wiewiora, Chang, & Smidt, 2020). In the following, the term organization is used in the context of companies, where an organization consists of several individuals who (classically) belong to a team.

Companies that promote organizational learning thus contribute positively to the development of the organization (Qureshi & Kashif, 2009). Also, with the ability of organizations to learn improves their business performance (Ali et al., 2020). Furthermore, an organization in which knowledge is distributed proactively is less dependent on individuals and potentially keeps its knowledge more up-to-date - an important aspect in the fast-paced digital enterprise transformation (Santos, Goldman, Shinoda, & Fisher, 2011).

The Impact of an Organizational Structure

The organizational structure must be seen as an important factor influencing how strongly organizational learning is lived in companies: If an organization is classically functionally structured (e.g. in production, logistics, marketing, sales) the distribution within the respective functionally oriented organizational unit works better than between two organizational units. This can also be observed in a similar way when an organization is structured according to sales markets or strategic business units (SBUs).

The organizational structure classically isolates members of the organization according to a given system within organizational units (e.g. teams, departments or divisions). Thus, organizational structure has a strong effect on the level of organizational learning in the overall organization.

In summary, it can be said that a high degree of organizational learning is usually accompanied by a low degree of centralization and a high degree of socialization (Turi & Sorooshian, 2019).

The Four Elements of Organizational Learning

In their work "The Challenge of Organizational Learning", Milway and Saxton (2011) examine how non-profit organizations learn or attempt to develop learning organizations. The authors define a total of four dimensions to the concept, which they consider to be central if an organization wants to ensure the ability to learn. Table 1 shows the four elements of organizational learning.

The first critical element they identify is the leadership within an organization: Leaders should support organizational learning with a clear vision and objectives and act as role models in the sense of the project - for example by participating in learning activities.

The second element is to establish a culture of continuous improvement, not only measuring but also rewarding (not necessarily monetary) organizational learning. In particular, however, aligned beliefs and values are mentioned here. In particular, a culture of error, in which errors are not understood as failures but as opportunities for learning together, can be an important component here.

Table 1. Four elements of organizational learning acccording to Milway & Saxton (2011)

Supportive Leaders	Culture of Continuous Improvements	Defined Learning Structure	Intuitive Knowledge Processes
Valuing leaders: • Vision and goals for organizational learning • Champions and role models	Appreciative culture: • Aligned beliefs and values • Reinforcing incentives • Commitment to measurement of results	Aligned structure: • Defined roles and responsibilities to capture, distill, apply and share knowledge • Networks and coordination	Embedded processes: • Process defined to support organizational learning • Technology platforms supporting the process

The third element outlined by the authors is the "defined learning structure". Thus, defined roles and clear responsibilities in organizational learning, for example with regard to the collection or distribution of knowledge, help with implementation. The authors also stress the importance of networks and the coordination of learning activities. The task of the structure is especially the facilitation of a knowledge flow - towards those people within an organization who need a certain knowledge.

Intuitive knowledge processes are defined as the fourth and final element. This is about integrating organizational learning into existing work processes in the best possible way, with the aim of avoiding additional effort for employees as far as possible. Technological support, for example through knowledge management applications, also plays an important role here in order to increase acceptance among employees.

There are also other frameworks for describing organizational learning. For example, a process-related consideration with the elements knowledge acquisition, information distribution, information interpretation and organizational memory could also be possible (Ke & Wei, 2006).

Challenges Implementing Organizational Learning

With the four elements of organizational learning, Milway & Saxton (2011) provide an important framework for the success factors in creating a learning organization. Particularly in the context of digitization, current research also shows that the ability for organizational learning can have a positive effect on the implementation of digital transformation (Tortorella et al., 2020). Nevertheless, the learning of an organization must be preceded by the willingness of its individuals to learn individually. In this respect, the ability of an organization to learn depends to a large extent on its human resources (Antunes & Pinheiro, 2020). In this respect, the organizational learning process must be preceded by an individual learning process (Santos et al., 2011). Companies must also actively support the learning process on different levels through various measures (Wiewiora et al., 2020).

Furthermore, Milway & Saxton (2011) identify three main challenges that they repeatedly encounter in their research in different organizations if organizational learning is to be more strongly established:

1. Many organizations lack clear objectives and metrics to measure the success of their learning activities.
2. Leaders often fail to establish incentive systems that stimulate the individual members of the organization, the teams within the organization and the organization as a whole.
3. There is a so-called process gap: organizations often lack a defined process that allows employees to share their knowledge within a clearly defined framework.

All in all, it has to be said that although the various aspects of establishing organizational learning are well known, many companies are experiencing difficulties, especially in the management of the same.

SCRUM IN THE CONTEXT OF ORGANIZATIONAL LEARNING

Scrum as a Process of Continuous Improvement

At the core of Scrum are the so-called sprints, in which the product increments are developed iteratively. Sprints are usually between one week and one month long, although in practice there are often two-week cycles. Each sprint begins with sprint planning, in which the development team pulls the tasks from the product backlog prioritized by the product owner. These product backlog items go into the sprint backlog, which is a collection of those tasks for which the development team is committed to work on in the next sprint. The tasks should be defined by the product owner in such a way that they can be processed within a sprint. Usually the team estimates the effort of the tasks in so-called story points during the sprint planning meeting (Roock & Wolf, 2016, p. 25). Research has shown that these sprint planning meetings can have a positive effect on the delivered product quality (Liu, Ho, Chang, & Tsai, 2019).

Within the sprint, the development team then works on the tasks, agreeing on the progress and possible problems and challenges in the daily scrum meeting. At the end of each sprint there is at best a potentially releasable increment, so that the sprint has developed real added value for the customer or user (Roock & Wolf, 2016, p. 25). This stronger focus on value creation can be seen as a particular strength of agile working methods in general (Denning, 2019).

Furthermore, at the end of each sprint there is a review and a retrospective. These two meetings are central to Scrum as a process of continuous improvement:

At the review meeting, the development team presents the results to all interested parties - including, at best, those who have requested certain functions from the product owner. The development team receives direct, immediate feedback from the requesters and has the opportunity to ask questions in order to further improve the product (increment), for example, in the context of an upcoming sprint (Roock & Wolf, 2016, pp. 24, 83). Through such mechanisms, agile methods can help to identify misunderstandings regarding communicated requirements at an early stage (Amorim, Mira da Silva, Pereira, & Gonçalves, 2020; Solli-Sæther & Karlsen, 2014). Through mechanisms like the review meeting in Scurm, the use of agile methods in software and product development can lead to a higher customer orientation(Ashmore & Wedlake, 2016).

In the retrospective meeting, which is moderated by the Scrum Master, the development team and the product owner discuss aspects of the collaboration during the past sprint. The goal of the retrospective meeting is - in contrast to the review meeting, which is of a content nature - to improve the collaboration and to remove possible obstacles and difficulties in the collaboration. The retrospective meetings are moderated by the Scrum Master and are a central part of Scrum. Often these meetings follow a standardized agenda, where at the end concrete tasks are derived for specific members of the team to effectively solve the problems addressed in retrospective (Derby & Larsen, 2006). In this respect the Retrospective Meeting can probably be seen as the most important, even if very time-consuming, meeting in the whole Scrum process (Gaikwad et al., 2019). Some authors even assume that the lack of implementation of the improvements from the retrospective meeting will result in a complete failure of Scrum (H. Wolf, Solingen, & Rustenburg, 2011, p. 124f.).

In principle, the entire Scrum process follows the principle of "Inspect & Adapt", as Roock & Wolf (2016, p. 25) emphasize. In this respect Scrum also functions according to the Plan-Do-Check-Act (PDCA) cycle, as it was developed many years before by Shewhart and Deming (1986). Also in the PDCA cycle new improvements are iteratively developed and implemented and then reviewed and adjusted. In this respect the successful use of Scrum also represents the continuous improvement of the product, which the team is responsible for. This is probably one of the reasons why agile working methods and process models are regarded as a positive influencing factor on the motivation and satisfaction of employees (Qureshi & Kashif, 2009).

The review meeting and especially the retrospective meeting in Scrum can be understood as an important feature of a process of continuous learning and improvement. This institutionalized promotion of continuous learning is particularly important in dynamic environments such as the sustainable digital transformation of an enterprise.

Functional Learning in Cross-Functional Teams

Characteristic for many agile working methods - and so also for Scrum - is the cooperation in cross-functional teams. In this respect, it is particularly important to note that these theoretical considerations on the adaptation of structures also take place in practice: The introduction of agile methods is often accompanied by far-reaching changes in the organizational structure (Van Ruler, 2019). In addition, existing professional role models and existing process chains are often questioned and dissolved (Lee & Chen, 2019).

Because the employees of different functions are organized together in a team that plans and carries out its work together, there are fewer dependencies on people outside the team: All functions relevant for the creation of a product are united within a team. It is therefore not surprising that a study has shown that the use of agile working methods can improve collaboration (Noguera, Guerrero-Roldán, & Masó, 2018). The literature emphasizes, for example, that in the case of Scrum the intended meetings have a positive effect on knowledge sharing and thus contribute to organizational learning (Solli-Sæther & Karlsen, 2014).

At the same time, this cross-functional organization of self-organized teams presents a decisive challenge in functional learning: Because the daily work in a team is cross-functional, employees with the same function from different teams have theoretically no and practically only few points of contact with each other. These and other reasons can be seen as a challenge in the daily cooperation of self-organized teams, which may also not work in a sufficiently focused way, as Gjøystdal and Karunaratne (2020) find out in a case study in the oil and gas industry.

At the same time, however, learning within a function is extremely important, not despite but because of cross-functional cooperation: It is not uncommon for an employee in a particular function to be the only one in a cross-functional team who can fulfill this function. This is probably one of the reasons why finding suitable employees for agile teams or Scrum teams in particular is considered an important challenge for the successful implementation of Scrum and ensuring functional and cross-functional learning (Almeida, Almeida, & Figueiredo-Braga, 2018).

Scrum makes no explicit suggestions about this challenge, although the agile method is nevertheless considered in the literature to support communication (Sievi-Korte, Richardson, & Beecham, 2019). Especially in large projects and complex organizations Scrum has its weaknesses (Khalid et al., 2020). In this respect, Scrum, similar to many other agile methods, does not necessarily lead to mutual promotion of organizational learning, because these methods often do not have explicit processes and functions in this regard (Annosi, Martini, Brunetta, & Marchegiani, 2020).

At the same time, the approach of so-called "communities of practice" (CoPs) has been established in the literature. Here employees of the same function from different teams meet, learn from each other and thus jointly build up new, functionally oriented knowledge (Milway & Saxton, 2011). The approach of these CoPs is based on tacit knowledge and the ability of employees and teams to self-organize (Chau & Maurer, 2004).

Transferring Team Knowledge Into the Organization

In practice, CoPs can be designed very differently: From moderated events enriched with impulse lectures and presentations to casual coffee rounds, there are many conceivable variations. The important thing is not so much how a COP takes place, but rather how it helps the participants to progress - and thus the members of an organization can learn and develop beyond team structures.

CoPs are thus a way of counteracting the distribution of knowledge at organizational level. This is regarded as the central challenge of organizational learning - even with agile team structures (Santos & Goldman, 2011). It should be noted that agile methods do not per se lead to the promotion of organizational learning (Annosi et al., 2020).

In addition to cross-team, functional learning, it is also important to further develop the organization in its cooperation, i.e. to a certain extent to let the retrospective meetings take place not only on the level of the teams but also on the level of the overall organization. For this purpose a transition team can be established to improve the cooperation of the organization as a whole. This transition team is practically the Scrum Master of the organization and solves such problems in cooperation that a Scrum Master on team level alone could not solve (Roock & Wolf, 2016, p. 184).

In addition, the Transition Team also has the task of distributing the existing knowledge. For example, it would be conceivable to make the knowledge of individual (Scrum) teams available to the other teams in the organization (Roock & Wolf, 2016, p. 191). In this respect, the approach of continuous development also differs from the more project-oriented approach of change management and is better suited to the constant changes in the environment of an organization (Laloux, 2015, p. 128).

Leadership and Measuring Learning in Scrum

After this chapter has introduced Scrum as a process and shown how Scrum teams and employees can learn functions from each other, the focus is now on understanding leadership in the Scrum environment. Because Scrum is based on the idea that experts work together in cross-functional teams, the role of professional guidance of a classic management approach clearly recedes into the background. At the same time, the idea of distributed leadership or shared leadership is clearly coming to the fore: leadership is divided into different functions (Moe, Dingsøyr, & Kvangardsnes, 2009). This is why the commitment of top management in the introduction of agile working methods such as Scrum plays a central role in success (Lee & Chen, 2019).

In an agile context, leadership focuses on providing employees with the right information and skills and the right environment for an effective impact. Because the integration of agile methods into the existing work processes of employees requires a high degree of flexibility and the willingness to engage in such forms of cooperation, it is especially the task of leadership to encourage the employees here (Hidalgo, 2019). Managers who promote an agile corporate culture are characterized above all by the fact that they foster the collaboration of employees and organizational units and can thus make an important contribution to the individual and overall success of the organization (Cleveland & Cleveland, 2020).

Because the question of "what" is determined by the product owner anyway, while the team decides on "how", there is no need to break down from overall goals to subgoals (Roock & Wolf, 2016, p. 196). In this respect Scrum assumes a high intrinsic motivation of the employees, whereby the Scrum process drives the employees and the team to learn and improve on their own initiative (Roock & Wolf, 2016, p. 132).

In fact, Scrum also provides no clear, unambiguous instructions how to measure the performance of teams. Also the performance measurement of individual employees is only indirectly addressed. However, it should also be stressed that classical forms of retrospective performance measurement may contradict the basic idea of agile working as a continuous process: Van Ruler (2019) points out in this context that evaluations in agile environments should be a continuous activity rather than one-off measurements. For example, Wannes and Ghannouchi (2019) suggest measuring the hours previously estimated and ultimately actually spent on a task.

The sprint velocity can be considered essential for the performance of a Scrum team - and thus also for its ability to learn and improve. This metric measures how many story points a team can handle per sprint. These story points reflect how complex a certain task is, whereby the points are usually awarded by the team itself in the sprint plannings. In this respect the sprint velocity is a way to measure the performance of a Scrum team, but usually only stabilizes with the experience of a team (Roock & Wolf, 2016, p. 154).

SYNTHESIS: SCRUM IN THE FOUR ELEMENTS OF ORGANIZATIONAL LEARNING

Theory and practice show that Scrum can in many ways support both individual learning and the learning of organizations in its entirety (Santos et al., 2011). The ability of organizations to learn is also and especially in the context of the digital enterprise transformation a central ability: Continuous learning helps to keep up with the rapid developments on the market and in technology in order to be able to persist in the long run.

After this chapter has introduced the four elements of organizational learning and roughly sketched elements and working methods in Scrum, the different facets of Scrum will now be compared with the four elements of organizational learning.

With regard to the first element, the need for supportive leaders, Scrum does not provide explicit answers here, but requires managers to have a new understanding of leadership: Instead of static goals, managers must offer the right setup for the Scrum process - which may then result in a learning process. An important role in this learning process can certainly be seen in the Scrum Master: Because he is supposed to ensure that the Scrum process is followed, he implicitly supports the learning process. For example, his role in the context of a retrospective meeting can be understood as a form of supportive leadership, although the Scrum Master has no disciplinary leadership responsibility.

The extent to which Scrum supports a culture of continuous improvement is particularly evident in retrospective and review meetings. Because the agile method of working works iteratively, a recurring form of improvement is created here, because the team can remove its impediments bit by bit and increase its sprint velocity. Scrum is therefore not only a method that promotes or welcomes learning, it is even anchored as a clear component in many elements of the process, whereby at the core of this culture is also assumed intrinsic motivation of the team.

This is one reason why the Scrum Master and the intrinsically motivated teams have a clearly defined learning structure as the third of the four elements of organizational learning. Also the introduction of a transition team and the establishment of communities of practice show a clearly defined learning structure, because through these networks and coordination activities knowledge is actively distributed and the organization can learn. Although these structures are not explicitly part of Scrum, they often go hand in hand in literature and practice.

When it comes to intuitive knowledge processes, Scrum provides a clear structure of processes and elements when and how to work on organizational learning. The retrospectives and reviews at the end of every sprint are essential here. Looking at technology platforms, Scrum does not give explicit guidelines here.

Table 2. Characteristics of Scrum corresponding to the four elements of organizational learning

Four elements of organizational learning	Corresponding Scrum elements
Supportive Leaders (Valuing leaders) Vision and goals for organizational learning Champions and role models	• Understanding leadership as a service for employees to empower them to contribute to the success of the company • Assuming employees to be intrinsically motivated • Scrum master role to ensure team keeping to the Scrum process
Culture of Continuous Improvements (Appreciative culture) Aligned beliefs and values Reinforcing incentives Commitment to measurement of results	• Trusting the team as being intrinsically motivated • Working in iterations including retrospective and reviews • Actively clearing away impediments to increase velocity and collaboration • Actively demanding for customer feedback to improve the product
Defined Learning Structure (Aligned structure) Defined roles and responsibilities to capture, distill, apply and share knowledge Networks and coordination	• Scrum master as a defined role to keep to the Scrum process • Transition team to discuss impediments across the organization • Communities of practice to spread functional knowledge
Intuitive Knowledge Processes (Embedded processes) Process defined to support organizational learning Technology platforms supporting the process	• Clear structure, roles and processes within the Scrum framework • Freedom of choice in terms of exact methods and technical support

With regard to an intuitive learning process as the fourth element of the four elements of organizational learning, it can be stated that Scrum with its elements, roles and processes provides clear structures to promote individual learning and organizational learning in the best possible way. The retrospectives and reviews at the end of the iterative sprints are an essential feature. With regard to the required technology platforms, Scrum does not demand any concrete systems, instead Scrum users can decide freely.

SOLUTIONS AND RECOMMENDATIONS

This chapter focuses on the question to what extent Scrum as an agile working method supports organizational learning and thus can contribute to the long-term success of digital business transformation in a constantly changing environment with ever new technologies and developments.

In this sense, the literature points out that organizational learning begins with individual learning and the acquired knowledge must be made available not only within teams but also within the entire organization. With the help of the four elements of organizational learning the chapter shows that different aspects have to be considered, whereas Scrum can cover many of these aspects:

The introduction of Scrum can have a positive effect on the output orientation and the generation of added value for customers. Due to the better adaptability of a company to its constantly changing environment, agile methods such as Scrum also help to react to such changes better, faster and more flexibly. Furthermore, Scrum can also contribute to improving individual learning, team learning and organizational learning.

For the successful management of the digital enterprise transformation the introduction of Scrum can therefore be a potential building block of the strategy. With regard to a positive effect on organizational learning three things have to be considered from the author's point of view:

1. The introduction of Scrum must be accompanied by a new understanding of leadership that allows for the self-responsible investment of working time in retrospectives, reviews and other forms of learning.
2. Communities of practice and similar formats must continue to enable functional learning beyond the boundaries of cross-functional teams.
3. Opportunities must be created to transfer team knowledge into organizational knowledge. This applies in particular to improvements of a process-related and organizational nature beyond functional knowledge.

FUTURE RESEARCH DIRECTIONS

Research into the effect of agile working methods on organizational learning provides, in addition to the findings from literature and practice presented here, many other potential topic areas and questions. Especially the quantitative consideration of individual and organizational learning in different forms of work and organization can still be considered in many facets.

Also, in the context of Scrum there are always movements and advances such as the "No-Estimate" movement, where in the context of planning the complexity of tasks is no longer estimated in story points or similar measures, but not at all. However, because the agile environment in practice changes quite quickly, documented practical research on such developments is rare.

Especially interesting and of high practical relevance could be comparative observations of classical and different agile working methods with regard to organizational learning. Occasionally, research has already been conducted into how learning can be implemented using agile methods - precisely for the purpose of learning (Budu, 2018; Moses, 2015).

CONCLUSION

The aim of this chapter was to show how the different aspects of Scrum - elements, work processes and roles - correspond to the four elements of organizational learning, in order to find out whether Scrum can potentially support organizational learning, but also individual learning.

After an introduction to the topic of organizational learning, the four elements of organizational learning were introduced and challenges were pointed out. In particular it was pointed out that the starting point of organizational learning is individual learning and both are influenced by the organizational structure. In particular, however, there is often a lack of clear goals and metrics for organizational learning, of commitment on the part of managers or of concrete incentive systems and process-related structures to ensure that learning actually takes place within the organization.

With regard to Scrum, the role of the Scrum Master, the understanding of employees as self-responsible individuals who are willing to learn and the task of retrospectives and reviews in the learning process were discussed. Thus, learning in the context of Scrum is especially to be understood as process improvement, while functional learning takes place mainly via communities of practice. Both were discussed intensively, as well as the need for a new understanding of leadership if Scrum is to be introduced.

In summary, it can definitely be said about Scrum as an agile working method that it pays off in many ways on the four elements of organizational learning. In addition, the framework has been expanded in practice by many aspects beyond its pure form in the literature and thus supports the learning process of individuals, teams and the organization as a whole. Particularly in the context of digital transformation, in which entire enterprises are subject to change in a dynamic environment, this ability for organizational learning can be an important part of the strategy.

One can certainly consider it a challenge that Scrum is only in a few places explicitly and concretely designed for organizational learning and therefore does not provide any concrete metrics or guidelines for this dedicated purpose. At the same time many aspects of Scrum can be found that at least indirectly contribute to organizational learning: For example, the measurement of a sprint velocity can be used as an indicator for the measurement of a learning process.

As a central difference between Scrum and the learning process in a classical organization there's at least one very essential assumption: Scrum assumes that employees have a high intrinsic motivation and want to improve themselves, the team they work in and their work process. Therefore Scrum intends that employees in Scrum teams are empowered to make decisions on their own responsibility. Any manager who as part of a digital enterprise transformation anchors the introduction of Scrum in his or her strategy should consider this assumption. Otherwise working in cross-functional, technically self-sufficient teams with little relevance of disciplinary leadership can hardly work. If a leader is willing to hand over responsibility and leave technical decisions to the teams, Scrum can therefore achieve important advantages for the digital enterprise transformation.

REFERENCES

Ali, S., Peters, L. D., Khan, I. U., Ali, W., & Saif, N. (2020). Organizational Learning and Hotel Performance: The Role of Capabilities' Hierarchy. *International Journal of Hospitality Management, 85*, 102349. doi:10.1016/j.ijhm.2019.102349

Almeida, A. M. P., Almeida, H. S., & Figueiredo-Braga, M. (2018). Mobile solutions in depression: Enhancing communication with patients using an SMS-based intervention. *Procedia Computer Science, 138*, 89–96. doi:10.1016/j.procs.2018.10.013

Amorim, A. C., Mira da Silva, M., Pereira, R., & Gonçalves, M. (2020). Using agile methodologies for adopting COBIT. *Information Systems, 101496*, 101496. Advance online publication. doi:10.1016/j.is.2020.101496

Annosi, M. C., Martini, A., Brunetta, F., & Marchegiani, L. (2020). Learning in an agile setting: A multilevel research study on the evolution of organizational routines. *Journal of Business Research*, *110*, 554–566. doi:10.1016/j.jbusres.2018.05.011

Antunes, H. de J. G., & Pinheiro, P. G. (2020). Linking knowledge management, organizational learning and memory. *Journal of Innovation & Knowledge*, *5*(2), 140–149. doi:10.1016/j.jik.2019.04.002

Arcos-Medina, G., & Mauricio, D. (2020). The Influence of the Application of Agile Practices in Software Quality Based on ISO/IEC 25010 Standard. *International Journal of Information Technologies and Systems Approach*, *13*(2), 27–53. doi:10.4018/IJITSA.2020070102

Ashmore, S., & Wedlake, M. (2016). Developing the Product Your Customer Really Wants: The Value of an Agile Partnership. *Information Resources Management Journal*, *29*(3), 1–11. doi:10.4018/IRMJ.2016070101

Beck, K., Beedle, M., van Bennekum, A., Cockburn, A., & Cunningham, W. (2001). *Manifesto for Agile Software Development.* Retrieved July 19, 2020, from Manifesto for Agile Software Development website: https://agilemanifesto.org/

Budu, J. (2018). Applying Agile Principles in Teaching Undergraduate Information Technology Project Management. *International Journal of Information and Communication Technology Education*, *14*(3), 29–40. doi:10.4018/IJICTE.2018070103

Chau, T., & Maurer, F. (2004). Tool Support for Inter-team Learning in Agile Software Organizations. In G. Melnik & H. Holz (Eds.), *Advances in Learning Software Organizations* (pp. 98–109). Springer Berlin Heidelberg., doi:10.1007/978-3-540-25983-1_10

Cleveland, M., & Cleveland, S. (2020). Culturally Agile Leadership: A Relational Leadership Development Approach. *International Journal of Public and Private Perspectives on Healthcare, Culture, and the Environment*, *4*(1), 1–9. doi:10.4018/IJPPPHCE.2020010101

Denning, S. (2019). Lessons learned from mapping successful and unsuccessful Agile transformation journeys. *Strategy and Leadership*, *47*(4), 3–11. doi:10.1108/SL-04-2019-0052

Derby, E., & Larsen, D. (2006). *Agile retrospectives: Making good teams great*. Pragmatic Bookshelf.

Deuringer, C. (2000). *Organisation und Change-Management: Ein ganzheitlicher Strukturansatz zur Förderung organistorischer Flexibilität*. Dt. Univ.-Verl. doi:10.1007/978-3-322-81381-7

Fiol, C. M., & Lyles, M. A. (1985). Organizational Learning. *The Academy of Management Review*, *10*(4), 803–813. doi:10.2307/258048

Gachanja, I. M., Nga'nga', S. I., & Kiganane, L. M. (2020). Influence of organization learning on innovation output in manufacturing firms in Kenya. *International Journal of Innovation Studies*, *4*(1), 16–26. doi:10.1016/j.ijis.2020.02.001

Gaikwad, P. K., Jayakumar, C. T., Tilve, E., Bohra, N., Yu, W., & Spichkova, M. (2019). Voice-activated solutions for agile retrospective sessions. *Procedia Computer Science*, *159*, 2414–2423. doi:10.1016/j.procs.2019.09.416

Gjøystdal, S., & Karunaratne, T. (2020). Effect of Inadequate Self-Organized Teams in Agile Project Management: A Case Study From the Oil and Gas Industry. *International Journal of Information Technology Project Management*, *11*(3), 95–106. doi:10.4018/IJITPM.2020070106

Hidalgo, E. S. (2019). Adapting the scrum framework for agile project management in science: Case study of a distributed research initiative. *Heliyon*, *5*(3), e01447. doi:10.1016/j.heliyon.2019.e01447 PMID:30976706

Hitt, W. D. (1995). The learning organization: Some reflections on organizational renewal. *Leadership and Organization Development Journal*, *16*(8), 17–25. doi:10.1108/01437739510097996

Huber, A. S. (2013). Das Ziel Digital Enterprise: Die professionelle digitale Abbildung von Produktentwicklung und Produktion. In U. Sendler, G. Baum, H. Borcherding, M. Broy, M. Eigner, H. K. Kohler, ... M. Stümpfle (Eds.), *Industrie 4.0: Beherrschung der industriellen Komplexität mit SysLM*. Springer Vieweg. doi:10.1007/978-3-642-36917-9_7

İpek, İ. (2019). Organizational learning in exporting: A bibliometric analysis and critical review of the empirical research. *International Business Review*, *28*(3), 544–559. doi:10.1016/j.ibusrev.2018.11.010

Ke, W., & Wei, K. K. (2006). Organizational Learning Process: Its Antecedents and Consequences in Enterprise System Implementation. *Journal of Global Information Management*, *14*(1), 1–22. doi:10.4018/jgim.2006010101

Kendall, K. E., Kong, S., & Kendall, J. E. (2010). The Impact of Agile Methodologies on the Quality of Information Systems: Factors Shaping Strategic Adoption of Agile Practices. *International Journal of Strategic Decision Sciences*, *1*(1), 41–56. doi:10.4018/jsds.2010103003

Khalid, A., Butt, S. A., Jamal, T., & Gochhait, S. (2020). Agile Scrum Issues at Large-Scale Distributed Projects: Scrum Project Development At Large. *International Journal of Software Innovation*, *8*(2), 85–94. doi:10.4018/IJSI.2020040106

Laloux, F. (2015). *Reinventing organizations: Ein Leitfaden zur Gestaltung sinnstiftender Formen der Zusammenarbeit* (M. Kauschke, Trans.). Verlag Franz Vahlen. doi:10.15358/9783800649143

Landaeta, R. E., Viscardi, S., & Tolk, A. (2011). Strategic management of scrum projects: An organizational learning perspective. In *First International Technology Management Conference*, (pp. 651–656). San Jose, CA: IEEE. 10.1109/ITMC.2011.5996039

Lee, J.-C., & Chen, C.-Y. (2019). Investigating the environmental antecedents of organizations' intention to adopt agile software development. *Journal of Enterprise Information Management*, *32*(5), 869–886. doi:10.1108/JEIM-06-2018-0119

Lethmate, R. (2016). *Auf einen Kaffee mit Ralf Lethmate* (N. Wolf, Interviewer) [Agile Review]. Retrieved from https://www.itagileshop.de/lesen/agile-review/2016-sonderausgabe-kunden-begeistern/#cc-m-product-10651914598

Levitt, B., & March, J. G. (1988). Organizational Learning. *Annual Review of Sociology, 14*, 319–340. Retrieved from https://www.jstor.org/stable/2083321

Liu, J.-W., Ho, C.-Y., Chang, J. Y. T., & Tsai, J. C.-A. (2019). The role of Sprint planning and feedback in game development projects: Implications for game quality. *Journal of Systems and Software*, *154*, 79–91. doi:10.1016/j.jss.2019.04.057

Mergel, I., Edelmann, N., & Haug, N. (2019). Defining digital transformation: Results from expert interviews. *Government Information Quarterly*, *36*(4), 101385. doi:10.1016/j.giq.2019.06.002

Milway, K. S., & Saxton, A. (2011). *The Challenge of Organizational Learning*. Retrieved July 19, 2020, from Stanford Social Innovation Review website: https://ssir.org/articles/entry/the_challenge_of_organizational_learning

Moe, N. B., Dingsøyr, T., & Kvangardsnes, O. (2009). Understanding Shared Leadership in Agile Development: A Case Study. In *2009 42nd Hawaii International Conference on System Sciences*, (pp. 1–10). Waikoloa, HI: IEEE. 10.1109/HICSS.2009.480

Moses, J. (2015). Agile Writing: A Project Management Approach to Learning. *International Journal of Sociotechnology and Knowledge Development*, *7*(2), 1–13. doi:10.4018/IJSKD.2015040101

Müller-Stewens, P. D. G. (n.d.). *Definition: Strategie*. Retrieved July 19, 2020, from Https://wirtschaftslexikon.gabler.de/definition/strategie-43591

Noguera, I., Guerrero-Roldán, A.-E., & Masó, R. (2018). Collaborative agile learning in online environments: Strategies for improving team regulation and project management. *Computers & Education*, *116*, 110–129. doi:10.1016/j.compedu.2017.09.008

Qureshi, M. R. J., & Kashif, M. (2009). Seamless long term learning in agile teams for sustainable leadership. In *2009 International Conference on Emerging Technologies*, (pp. 389–394). Islamabad, Pakistan: IEEE. 10.1109/ICET.2009.5353140

Roock, S., & Wolf, H. (2016). Scrum—Verstehen und erfolgreich einsetzen (1. Auflage). Heidelberg: dpunkt.verlag.

Säisä, M. E. K., Tiura, K., & Matikainen, R. (2019). Agile Project Management in University-Industry Collaboration Projects. *International Journal of Information Technology Project Management*, *10*(2), 8–15. doi:10.4018/IJITPM.2019040102

Santos, V., & Goldman, A. (2011). An Approach on Applying Organizational Learning in Agile Software Organizations. In A. Sillitti, O. Hazzan, E. Bache, & X. Albaladejo (Eds.), *Agile Processes in Software Engineering and Extreme Programming* (pp. 324–325). Springer Berlin Heidelberg. doi:10.1007/978-3-642-20677-1_27

Santos, V., Goldman, A., Shinoda, A. C. M., & Fisher, A. L. (2011). A view towards Organizational Learning: An empirical study on Scrum implementation. In *Proceedings of the 23rd International Conference on Software Engineering & Knowledge Engineering*, (pp. 583–589). https://www.researchgate.net/publication/221391284_A_view_towards_Organizational_Learning_An_empirical_study_on_Scrum_implementation

Shah, M., Maitlo, A., Jones, P., & Yusuf, Y. (2019). An investigation into agile learning processes and knowledge sharing practices to prevent identity theft in the online retail organisations. *Journal of Knowledge Management, 23*(9), 1857–1884. doi:10.1108/JKM-06-2018-0370

Shewhart, W. A., & Deming, W. E. (1986). *Statistical method from the viewpoint of quality control*. Dover.

Sievi-Korte, O., Richardson, I., & Beecham, S. (2019). Software architecture design in global software development: An empirical study. *Journal of Systems and Software, 158*, 110400. doi:10.1016/j.jss.2019.110400

Skilton, M. (2015). *Building the digital enterprise: A guide to constructing monetization models using digital technologies*. Palgrave Macmillan. doi:10.1057/9781137477729

Solli-Sæther, H., & Karlsen, J. T. (2014). Enablers and Barriers of Knowledge Sharing for Offshore Outsource ISD Project: A Case Study. *International Journal of Information Technology Project Management, 5*(2), 44–59. doi:10.4018/ijitpm.2014040104

Stormi, K. T., Laine, T., & Korhonen, T. (2019). Agile performance measurement system development: An answer to the need for adaptability? *Journal of Accounting & Organizational Change, 15*(2), 231–256. doi:10.1108/JAOC-09-2017-0076

Tortorella, G. L., Cawley Vergara, A. M., Garza-Reyes, J. A., & Sawhney, R. (2020). Organizational learning paths based upon industry 4.0 adoption: An empirical study with Brazilian manufacturers. *International Journal of Production Economics, 219*, 284–294. doi:10.1016/j.ijpe.2019.06.023

Turi, J. A., & Sorooshian, S. (2019). The impact of organisational structure on organisational learning. *Middle East J. of Management, 6*(2), 204. doi:10.1504/MEJM.2019.097817

Van Ruler, B. (2019). Agile communication evaluation and measurement. *Journal of Communication Management (London), 23*(3), 265–280. doi:10.1108/JCOM-12-2018-0136

Wannes, A., & Ghannouchi, S. A. (2019). KPI-Based Approach for Business Process Improvement. *Procedia Computer Science, 164*, 265–270. doi:10.1016/j.procs.2019.12.182

Wiewiora, A., Chang, A., & Smidt, M. (2020). Individual, project and organizational learning flows within a global project-based organization: Exploring what, how and who. *International Journal of Project Management, 38*(4), 201–214. doi:10.1016/j.ijproman.2020.03.005

Wolf, H., van Solingen, R., & Rustenburg, E. (2011). *Die Kraft von Scrum: Eine inspirierende Geschichte über einen revolutionären Projektmanagementansatz*. Addison-Wesley.

Xu, J. (2014). *Managing digital enterprise*. Springer. doi:10.2991/978-94-6239-094-2

KEY TERMS AND DEFINITIONS

Agile Methods: Agile methods are forms and models of cooperation that are designed to respond better to changing requirements during the planning and working process than classic, waterfall-like working models, where detailed rough and fine concepts are often developed. A decisive factor for agile methods is the alignment with the principles of the agile manifesto.

Community of Practice: A community of practice is a meeting of employees of the same function (e.g. marketing) from different cross-functional teams (e.g. product-related strategic business units). The purpose of this meeting is to exchange functional knowledge as a form of individual and organizational learning.

Culture of Continuous Improvement: The term Culture of Continuous Improvement describes an organizational culture in which improvements are not project-related and one-time oriented, but where opportunities for improvement flow directly into the work process.

Increment: The term "increment" originates from product development and in this case refers to a small but finished and usable component of a product. Conceivable here would be, for example, a partial functionality of a large software, whereby this partial functionality as such should potentially already be usable for the end user.

Organizational Learning: The term organizational learning refers to the learning of an organization as a whole, rather than just its individual members. It is primarily about making the knowledge of individual employees and the knowledge of individual teams available to other parts of the organization in order to develop the organization as a whole.

Scrum: Scrum is an agile method of project management and is used especially in software development. Scrum works according to a defined work process, in which different, defined roles are involved at certain points in time.

Sprint: Sprint in the sense of Scrum refers to an iteration of the Scrum process in which a product increment is developed and implemented. The Sprint begins with Sprint Planning and ends with Review and Retrospective. During the sprint (often lasting two weeks) the team exchanges information about the current progress of work in the Daily.

Chapter 3
A New Entrepreneurship Model for Digital Enterprises:
Career Entrepreneurship

Fahri Özsungur
https://orcid.org/0000-0001-6567-766X
Mersin University, Turkey

ABSTRACT

Career management is an important and up-to-date issue in strategic human resources management. Career management has significant impacts on many topics such as entrepreneurship, leader-employee interaction, increasing competitiveness, organizational climate, application of innovative and creative ideas, the efficiency of organizational decisions, organizational performance and profitability, internationalization, teamwork, project and process management, is a concept regarding entrepreneurship. Career entrepreneurship, which is introduced to literature for the first time, is explained in this chapter. This concept is put forward with the topics of a theoretical framework, career entrepreneurship, digital career management system, entrepreneurial career behavior, ICT-career management, and digital enterprise transformation. In the conclusion section, suggestions are made to provide important insights for human resources managers, leaders, politicians, and academicians.

INTRODUCTION

Today's technology has become a global structure with the development of the information network. The Internet accelerates the distribution and transmission of information and has improved information technology. The combined development of the Internet and technology has made its technological devices compatible with each other (Davidson, & Vaast, 2010). This adaptation has revealed many applications. Smartphones, social media, information technology applications, computers, and technologies where information has been adapted with innovation have also raised many ideas of entrepreneurial (Ghezzi, & Cavallo, 2018). Developing information technology through constant innovation and adaptation enabled new initiatives, creative ideas, and innovative actions to develop (Giones, & Brem, 2017).

DOI: 10.4018/978-1-7998-8583-2.ch003

Developing countries have begun to provide incentives to adapt to this development (Hafezieh, Akhavan, & Eshraghian, 2011). Developing countries increase the importance given to technology to ensure economic development, to enter international markets, to increase the competitiveness of national enterprises, to add information technology to companies' value chains, and to create new initiatives (Hair et al., 2012). The free market economy that emerged with globalization has triggered competition between countries with the development of information technology (Ziyae, Sajadi, & Mobaraki, 2014). Entrepreneurs looking for new markets in the face of unlimited consumer needs can reach consumers in different countries via the internet (Hull et al., 2007).

Thanks to the information processing, storage, transmission, and transformation of information technology, new initiatives have been paved to meet evergrowing consumer needs (Kelestyn, & Henfridsson, 2014). The Internet is an important factor that enables continuous renewal for these initiatives (Sussan, & Acs, 2017). With the Internet, businesses can enter new markets, gain different customers, and advertise on social media (Richter, Kraus, & Syrjä, 2015). On the other hand, the most important factor in the emergence and implementation of new entrepreneurial ideas in the information age is human (Richter et al., 2015). Entrepreneur-customer interaction in the digital environment enables different innovations to emerge. This free and competitive environment has raised the problem of the efficient use of human resources by businesses in developing countries.

The efficient use of human resources in enterprises will enable new initiatives, innovations, and creative ideas to be realized (Mtima, 2009). The ease of interaction and communication requirements of the information society with technological innovations necessitates the development of knowledge, skills, and abilities in employee-leader, entrepreneur-customer relations (Nambisan, 2017). It is necessary to gain a sustainable competitive advantage in the digital world and focus on human resources management, career development, workforce planning, talent management for new initiatives (Ngoasong, 2018). These elements reveal career management.

Career management is an important type of management that provides efficient management of human resources, regulates the relations of individuals with the organization, and increases commitment to the organization (Greenhaus, Callanan, & Godshalk, 2010). This type of management has gained considerable momentum today through information and communication technology (ICT) (Scholarios et al., 2008). The increase of virtual applications and computer networks helps employees to develop a career and an intra-organizational career development strategy (Benson, Morgan, & Filippaios, 2014). ICT helps to define the requirements of a task or job, obtain technical information, and determine the qualification and competence criteria according to the characteristics of the job (Singh, 2020). Besides, this technology enables the efficient use of the network, access, interaction, and communication, which are important requirements of the digital world (Almeida, Fernandes, & Viollaz, 2020). For this reason, career development and management are more functional with ICT (Omar & Tajudeen, 2020).

In this chapter, career development and entrepreneurship issues related to the human resources necessary for providing innovative and creative products and services to global consumers of the digital world are explained. The concept of career entrepreneurship has been introduced to the literature to give entrepreneurship a different impetus through information technology that enables them to adopt new customers by adapting to the digital world (Kautonen, Kibler, & Minniti, 2017; Kerr, & Armstrong-Stassen, 2011; Korotov, Khapova, & Arthur, 2010). Previous studies have focused on the individual aspect of career entrepreneurship. Besides, these studies do not reveal the theoretical basis and are far from explaining the entrepreneurial behavior models. In particular, ensuring the adaptation of developing countries to information technology, and gaining a career understanding of entrepreneurship will provide important contributions to provide a sustainable competitive advantage in the global world. On the other hand, this study aims to develop entrepreneurship theories by revealing career entrepreneurship with conceptual and theoretical frameworks. This chapter will provide important insights for instructors, researchers, policymakers in developing countries, academicians, and students.

RESEARCH METHODOLOGY

This book chapter was formed by a systematic review method (Komba & Lwoga, 2020). In this method, the research question is determined and an extensive literature review is made on the subject. The research findings obtained are classified according to the content of the subject (Petticrew & Roberts, 2008). Classified information is included in the study by organizing it as headings (Pawson et al., 2005). The flow of the study is formed by evaluating classified information and titles (Rahi, 2017). Thus, integrity is ensured by evaluating the researched subject with its contents (Victor, 2008). As a result, this method was adopted and these procedures were followed respectively. The research questions were determined as follows: What is the conceptual and theoretical framework of career entrepreneurship, what is its relationship with the digital career management system? What is an entrepreneurial career behavior and what are its elements? The information and data obtained from the literature review related to the research question were coded. The coded information was combined under the related topics. After classification and combining, the topics were sorted according to their level of relationship.

Conceptual Framework

Career Entrepreneurship

Entrepreneurship is the transformation of innovative and creative ideas into action and the transformation of risks into opportunities (Wilson, Kickul, & Marlino, 2007). Creative ideas emerge as a result of cognitive coding and information transformation process, which results from the experience and interpretation of the acquired information in the cognitive process. Innovation occurs as a result of integrating new knowledge with existing knowledge (Scott, & Twomey, 1988). As a result of these actions, the idea of entrepreneurship is put forward by the entrepreneur. For this reason, entrepreneurship is the creation and implementation of ideas. Entrepreneurs can put forward the entrepreneurial spirit in process management as well as implement the idea put forward.

Revealing the idea for innovation turns into entrepreneurship by developing knowledge, skills, and talents. Therefore, the individual can continue the idea of an entrepreneur to the extent that he/she can manage his / her knowledge, skills, and talents. The entrepreneur has also a good manager, researcher, and productive features. These features can become sustainable through career management (Henderson, & Robertson, 2000). In the context of obtaining and implementing career opportunities, it is necessary to provide the necessary actions, to exhibit proactive behaviors, to develop a process for personal development, and to formulate strategies for achieving positive outcomes for the future (Davey, Plewa, & Struwig, 2011). Thus, a competitive advantage is achieved. These characteristics are combined with the aim of entrepreneurship. Entrepreneurship has the aim of achieving a competitive advantage by constantly introducing creative and innovative ideas. When both concepts are combined, the concept of career entrepreneurship emerges.

Career entrepreneurship is a type of entrepreneurship in which entrepreneurship is constant development in an individual context, exhibiting information acquisition behavior to benefit from opportunities, benefiting from the experience, sustaining innovative actions through the development of knowledge, skills, and talents. Career entrepreneurs have proactive, flexible, developmental, researching, and self-renewing characteristics. The entrepreneur avoids temporary actions to be superior in the context of the competition within the organization. Sustainable, future-oriented, positive, value-added, and synergistic actions take priority for these entrepreneurs.

ICT and Career Management

ICT is an important tool in the realization of these plans. Organizational career management benefits from the convenience of the digital world (Kettunen, & Makela, 2019). Web pages, smartphone applications, face recognition systems have brought significant innovations for companies. The use of social media and virtual applications in the recruitment process increases interaction and communication and creates a corporate culture.

Career management is a planning model including the achievement of individual success, acquisition of professional skills, development of adaptation behavior, and development of business-related skills and competencies (Kettunen, & Sampson, 2019). These plans can be transformed into strategies when they are long-term (Rajenderan, & Zawawi, 2019).

THEORETICAL FRAMEWORK

Mind Mapping Approach

Information and communication technology is a type of technology that enables the acquisition of information through technological tools and includes "Adoption, Diffusion, Use and Impact" processes (Kuťák et al., 2019). The information obtained through technological context can be adopted, distributed to different communication channels, and can be used and effected by individuals accessing information as a result of this distribution. All these processes reveal an important communication network. Mind mapping plays an important role in explaining and developing this network. Mind mapping is the classification of an idea by transforming it into information (Anas et al., 2019). It plays an important role in the classification and functionalization of complex ideas. The information obtained in the individual's learning stage is used in decision-making with this technique.

The coding and classification of complex information through keywords and figures is essential to reach the right information and disseminate information in today's digital age (Sun, Wang & Wegerif, 2019). Computer systems have become more functional with the rapid development of the internet by classifying complex information into related concepts (Ma'ruf, Syafii, & Kusuma, 2019). This approach is also important for individuals' career development. Training provided in the digital environment, consultancy services for personal development, the realization of leader-employee interaction in the workplace in the digital environment, notifications via e-mails, corporate career development programs, online career courses can become functional through mind mapping. With this technique, managers can improve their subordinates' competencies and learning skills.

Interaction Theories

Technology Interaction

Theory of Reasoned Action (Davis et al., 1989) suggests that human behavior is influenced by emotions and the people around it. The Technology Acceptance Model (Venkatesh and Davis, 2000) is a theory that includes perceived usefulness, perceived ease of use, and subjective norm functions. It aims to improve the acceptance and adaptation behavior that results from the interaction of information technology with the individual. Theory of Planned Behavior (Taylor and Todd, 1995) is based on intention and attitudes in individual interaction with technology.

Model of PC Utilization (Taylor and Todd, 1995) is a theory based on predicting expected outcomes by adapting the shaping of behaviors to computer use. According to this theory, adaptation problems and emotions related to use as a result of the interactions of the employees in the workplace affect individual behaviors. Another theory based on the influence of the digital world on human behavior is the Innovation Diffusion Theory (Moore and Benbasat, 1991). This theory assumes that innovation is continuous and the continuity of technological developments affects the social system. The diffusion effect of innovation serves as an intercultural bridge. Innovation affecting social systems through communication shows the effect of diffusion as a result of individual and social acceptance. According to Rogers and Shoemaker (1971), the diffusion of innovation depends on the characteristics of compatibility, complexity, testability, relative advantage, and observability.

The social cognitive theory explains the causal link between an individual's interaction with technology and the resulting behavior with internal and external environmental factors (Compeau and Higgins, 1995). Individual factors such as emotions, expectations, anxiety, self-efficacy, and motivation constitute internal factors, social environment for adaptation to social formations and physical environment for adaptation to the physical environment constitute external environmental factors. The individual performs harmony or non-compliance behaviors by being influenced by these factors in interaction with technology. Performance, expectations, and perceptions are three important factors in the development of behaviors.

Theory of Acceptance and Use of Technology (UTAUT), which seeks a causal relationship in the interaction between technology and the individual, was developed by Venkatesh et al. (2003), and Unified Unified Theory of Acceptance and Use of Technology (UTAUT2), which evaluates the same relationship in the context of individual being consumer, was developed by Venkatesh et al. (2012). UTAUT is a theoretical structure consisting of Performance Expectancy, Effort Expectancy, Attitude towards Technology Use, Social Impact, Facilitating Conditions, Self-Efficacy, Anxiety, Behavioral Intention for the Use of the System. UTAUT2 consists of Performance Expectancy, Effort Expectancy, Social Impact, Facilitating Conditions, Hedonic motivation / Perceived Pleasure, Price Value, Attitude / Habit, Behavioral Intention. Both theories are based on the idea that internal and external factors influence the individual's interaction with information and communication technology.

Learning Theories

The learning theories of social, constructivist, behaviorist, cognitive, connectivism are the theories that try to explain the learning processes of the individual. The rapid realization of information and communication through the internet brings many problems. The source of the information, the distribution channels, and the last access point that the information reaches raises reliability issues. Despite these problems, learning is essential for access to the innovations of the digital world, for the source and transmission of information. The first of the learning theories is the social learning theory. The thought based on this theory is that the information obtained as a result of the interaction of individuals with social factors is shared in the social environment and this sharing provides a continuous transfer of information (Bandura & Walters, 1977: 38).

Although constructivist learning theory is based on the fact that learning is a social activity, it involves the personal and social acquisition of information that emerges after the interaction (Padirayon, Pagudpud, & Cruz, 2019; Rieger, 2019). Behaviorist learning theory focuses on behavior patterns that result from reactions to environmental influences (Kawai, 2019).

Cognitive learning theory is based on the assumption that an individual gains and transmits information obtained from the external world through a process that occurs as a result of organizing, storing, coding, recalling, and transmitting through the brain and nervous system (Mowrer & Klein, 2019). This process is complicated by the fact that emotions, experiences, and new knowledge involve reasoning. Whether the information held in memory is permanent or temporary is determined by the criteria for future benefit.

The connectivism learning theory is based on the idea of where the need for information can be met (Huang, Spector & Yang, 2019). According to this theory, the linking of information sources accelerates the learning process and decision making is an important learning process. Complexity is based on the basic ideas of network, chaos, and self-organization. Once the information is obtained, it must be communicated through connections. It must also be capable of providing access after it is forwarded. The Internet is an important digital service provider based on the logic of the thought on which this theory is based. The information in the system is transmitted via the internet, and the transmitted information is stored in the target systems where access is possible (Brown, 2000).

Entrepreneurship Theories

Resource Based Theories

The use of resources in organizations is essential for gaining competitive advantage and sustainability (Alvarez & Barney, 2017). Entrepreneurship theory based on the thought that resources are heterogeneous values (Kellermanns et al., 2016). It is important for entrepreneurship practices to mobilize the resources that are owned to reveal new ideas and processes. On the other hand, obtaining new resources and channeling the existing resources appropriately for the implementation of the entrepreneurial idea is among the requirements of the resource-based theory (Barney, 2018). The resource-based theory adopted for entrepreneurship is about the value attached to resources (Nason & Wiklund, 2018). Resources in entrepreneurship are not accepted as a means of satisfying needs and sustainable competition (Korobov et al., 2017). The entrepreneur adopts a set of important values to create and implement new ideas using resources. In entrepreneurship, the resource assists the management of the process, ensures the emergence of new ideas, inspires by knowledge and experience (Day & Jean-Denis, 2016).

According to the resource-based theory, resource is an essential factor for opportunities. In entrepreneurship, the resource is an essential element in turning risks into opportunities (Rydehell, Isaksson, & Löfsten, 2019). This element can be material or spiritual. For this reason, according to the resource-based theory, these resources are needed to develop and implement the idea of entrepreneurship (Lo, Huarng, & Rey-Martí, 2019). However, the theory does not focus on the career element that is important to humans in the use, management, and acquisition of resources. The necessary tools for career development and the outputs to be obtained are important resources for entrepreneurship. The theory is generally based on resources related to the organization. However, it does not focus on human career development.

Opportunity Based Theories

Opportunity is the time or conditions that provide revealing an idea. These opportunities are the key to success, a whole set of possibilities for promotion or employment (He et al., 2020). The key to success is a whole set of opportunities for promotion or employment (Amorós et al., 2019). Therefore, opportunity-based behavior provides an efficient and profitable output. The realization of entrepreneurship through the exploitation of opportunities enabled the opportunity-based theory to emerge. Contrary to what Schumpeter claims, the proponents of this theory have revealed that the entrepreneur is not the source of change, but the beneficiary (Dimitratos et al., 2012). This idea argues that the act of creativity is not directly related to the action of entrepreneurship (Brown, Davidsson, & Wiklund, 2001). The idea put forward in the resource-based theory was completed with the opportunity based theory.

Opportunities create new opportunities and resources. Thus, the individual seeks opportunities to reveal and implement the entrepreneurial idea. Entrepreneurial opportunities are transformed into entrepreneurial practices by channeling available resources to these opportunities. This theory put forward by Peter Drucker is based on the idea of transforming opportunities created by technology, technical, social, and cultural changes into entrepreneurial ideas and practices (Oyson & Whittaker, 2010). Although this theory concerns a wide field in the context of entrepreneurship, its most important shortcoming is that it does not involve an idea integrated with the idea of career entrepreneurship (Baptista & Karaöz, 2006). There is a need for an integrative idea for the employees to present their innovative ideas with cooperation with the organization (Kamaludin, Saad, & Aziz, 2012). Career entrepreneurship is an important shortcoming of this theory.

CAREER ENTREPRENEURSHIP

Career and Entrepreneurship

Career consists of activities that are essential to self-actualization behavior to gain expertise, develop competence for an existing profession, and achieve success and expertise. Career is a process involving time, labor, economic requirements. This process includes psychological and behavioral subjects. An individual's self-development in a workplace, his / her expertise, adaptation to change, and the necessary initiatives foreseeing opportunities lead to be perceived differently by the others (Vance, & Bergin, 2019). These actions herald a possible success.

Entrepreneurship is an action in which risks are turned into opportunities, innovative and creative ideas are put forward and implemented, and innovative and process-oriented actions are conducted (Rosa, 2019). The entrepreneur not only presents his/her new ideas but also acts to become a good manager. It creates a positive organizational climate by managing the organization it creates with innovative actions. This organizational climate helps employees create innovative and creative ideas for the organization, creating a corporate identity. In this way, transparency in management and individual development becomes more possible.

While the career is a set of behaviors that an individual demonstrates for self-improvement, entrepreneurship is an individual's behavior to put forward his/her innovative and creative actions (Rider, Thompson, Kacperczyk, & Tåg, 2019). Both can be realized for individual development. Career development is realized for increasing competitiveness within the organization or professional development (Venkataraman, 2019). Entrepreneurship puts the concept of "self" to the forefront in the act of creativity to gain a competitive advantage (Huda et al. 2019; Schenkel, Farmer, & Maslyn, 2019). The "self" is important for both concepts. In entrepreneurship, the idea and the implementation of the idea are predominant, while career management is focused on process management. For this reason, the concept of career entrepreneurship will make important contributions in terms of differences and similarities of both concepts to contribute to each other.

Digital Career Management System

The digital world is progressing in the rapid and efficient development of individual skills. If we ignore information pollution on the Internet, the speed and possibilities of access to information also positively affect personal development (Oliver, & Williams-Duncan, 2019). In today's world where access to the right information is becoming increasingly difficult and information is becoming more complex, the realization of career management in the digital environment makes it difficult to apply some systematic methods. Information security becomes increasingly difficult due to cyber-attacks and digital security gaps (Staunton, 2019). Besides, the complexity of information, problems in access to information, problems related to the systematic classification of information are among the problems of today's digital world. Therefore, the career management system needs to be adapted to the requirements of the digital world.

Workforce planning and development strategies, career counseling, executive coaching, organizational career development programs, teamwork development, professional development coaching, skills, and competency development are among the career management systems (Figueroa-Armijos, & Motta Veiga, 2019). These systems are influenced and developed by the innovations of information and communication technology.

Workforce Planning and Development Strategies

Workforce planning is the strategy implemented within the scope of human resources management. The selection of human resources in the recruitment process, adaptation to the job, job placement in accordance with career characteristics, orientation is related to workforce planning and development strategies. These strategies are important for the placement and training of the appropriate human resources in the work and organization. This process can also be performed in a digital environment. The realization of recruitment and placement via the web page is necessary for access to more human resources. It is possible to give job descriptions, the organizational identity of the organization, and opportunities of individuals to develop a career within the organization as a message to the external environment with these strategies.

Career Counseling and Executive Coaching

Career counseling is a counseling service that facilitates employees within the organization to develop their careers (de Haan, 2019). This service can also be provided through outsourcing (Rathmell, Brown, & Kilburg, 2019). If the organization allows its employees to develop their careers, this is the output of a human resources strategy. Executive coaching is carried out if the employee is an executive candidate. This system is used in order to meet the needs of the managers in the future and to ensure the placement of the employees according to the merit system. These strategies that can be determined in the digital environment can be realized via online surveys, online training services, online counseling, video conference coaching to improve the competencies of individuals.

Professional Development Coaching

Professional development helps employees within the organization perform the work that meets their job descriptions (Lemons, & Toste, 2019). Professional development coaching services are among the services that will be provided to transfer professional experiences to experienced employees by experienced managers, to provide professional information to employees through research on the internet, and to inform them about the mission and vision of the organization. These services aim to eliminate the lack of professional knowledge and experience by revealing the importance that the employee attaches to his / her profession. ICT is an important tool in this development. Professional knowledge and experience can be researched, and communicated to employees through ICT at an international level.

Skills and Competency Development

The transfer of knowledge and experience to individuals may sometimes not be sufficient. Skills and competency are important for productivity in the works to be performed. A low level of skills and competency increases individuals' risk of errors, reduces productivity, and leads to loss of time and effort. The skills and competencies of individuals need to be improved for efficiency and quality in manufacturing and service outputs, increase employee performance within the organization (Magsamen-Conrad, Dillon, Hanasono, & Valdez, 2020). This development involves the acquisition of the necessary skills to adapt and fulfill the characteristics of the work to be performed by the individual. Skills are related to the individual's business predisposition, the application of the learned knowledge, accomplishing the work, and finalizing it under the purpose. Competency is related to the training of suitable employees for work. ICT can be used to develop both features.

Organizational Career Development Programs

Ensuring continuous learning, sustainable productivity in the internal information flow, strengthening communication in the organization's external environment and relations with its stakeholders are the main objectives of organizational career development programs (Bagdadli, & Gianecchini, 2019). In addition to these objectives, it is aimed to develop individuals' careers within the organization and to provide added value to the organization with the success to be achieved through career development. Generally, educational opportunities, financial aids, and incentives are among these programs. The success of the programs enables the formation of organizational culture and makes them adopted by the employees. Thus, workforce migration is prevented by planning employee career development within the organization (Edo, 2019; Vézina, & Bélanger, 2019). The image of the organizational culture adopted by the workers leads to positive predictions about the institutionality of the organization in the external environment. These programs can be performed through ICT. Samples of career development programs are the announcement of career development activities in social media accounts on smartphones, cooperation programs with universities, activities, and training with professional organizations, and career development applications on smartphones.

Team Work Development

Intra-organizational harmony occurs through the joint work and interaction of individuals. This adaptation significantly affects organizational performance (Howe et al., 2019). Sharing ideas, making mutual comments on the information obtained, brainstorming help to create creative and innovative ideas. Teamwork is one of the activities that allow this harmony and creative ideas (Gao, Huang, Su, & Xie, 2019). Online working groups are creative activities that can be realized in multinational companies. Bringing together different opinions about business or professional information, teamwork has become functional with virtual applications (eg WhatsApp or Facebook groups). The rapid circulation of the information is possible through ICT. Thus, the necessary knowledge and experiences for career development, project-based shares contribute to employees through teamwork.

Entrepreneurial Career Behavior

Career management is an entrepreneurial behavioral model for organization leaders and employees. The individual performs entrepreneurial behavior by including process, innovation, creative actions and practices, training, programs, and projects that will contribute to career development (Vondracek, Lerner, & Schulenberg, 2019). This behavior emerges as research of opportunities, development of knowledge obtained, selection of appropriate business and organization, strategy development, planning a sustainable career development (Taber, 2019). When these behaviors coupled with entrepreneurial behavior, form the behaviors of the career entrepreneur. In career entrepreneurship, creating a new job or developing an existing job is put forward by individual career development. A career entrepreneur has behavioral patterns based on innovative, developmental, creative, proactivity, and digital thinking.

Innovative Behavior Model

Innovative behavior refers to an action and process. Actions include alteration, restyling, rearrangement, restructuring, renovation, transformation, reorganization (Williamson, Battisti, Leatherbee, & Gish, 2019). These actions occur in a specific process. Innovation in the process is related to management skills (Ng, & Wang, 2019). Technological, technical, and service-oriented innovations can be the subject of sustainable as well as innovative processes in entrepreneurship. Introducing individual skills and competencies through innovative actions constitutes an innovative behavioral model. Career development Through ICT can provide innovative contributions to the professional development of individuals. The Internet, social media, and information technology provide information on creative ideas that will be the source of innovative actions.

Developmental Behavior Model

Individual development in career entrepreneurship is the outputs of the features of self-assertion, self-criticize, self-confidence, self-realization, self-respect, self-identification self-improvement, self-satisfaction, self-consciousness, self-assessment, and self-awareness (Ford, 2019; Briley et al. ., 2019).

The fact that the individual's characteristics are directed towards development in the context of career triggers developmental behavior. This behavioral model enables activities within the organization to provide important insights for individuals to be aware of their characteristics. This behavior can also be performed by the leader or the employee. The fact that individual characteristics are based on career development triggers the realization of programs, activities, and training appropriate to the developmental behavior model. ICT can only be used as a tool for the development of this behavioral model.

Creative Behavior Model

The creative behavior model allows the entrepreneur to find the application area of the creative ideas that s/he desires to turn into action (De Clercq, & Belausteguigoitia, 2019). Original ideas, which have not been proposed before, are the product of imagination (Zhang, & Lee, 2019). The key concepts in these ideas are imaginative, original, inventive. In career development, creative behavior can be developed when the innovations of the virtual world are combined with imagination. In this behavioral model, individual outcomes are aimed to realize career development. Creative behavior is the first step for entrepreneurship. Career development programs can be realized to gain professional skills and to put forward the creative ideas of the employees within the organization. These programs also promote the development of entrepreneurial behavior.

Proactive Behavior Model

Proactive behavior is the prediction of opportunities, assuming risks, creating or controlling a situation to take action (Varela, Bande, Del Rio, & Jaramillo, 2019). If innovative actions are involved in a process, controlling behavior is performed (Xu, Zhang, & Chan, 2019). Proactive behavior is demonstrated by anticipation without waiting for problems to occur. This model of behavior is important for the implementation of creative ideas and opportunities in entrepreneurship (Parker, Wang, & Liao, 2019; Wu et al., 2019). Career development plays an important role in realizing the corporate culture and corporate image of the individual and the organization. ICT enables the creation of a database of employee characters and job predispositions in career management. The information obtained is recorded in the digital environment and it is provided to identify suitable candidates for the placement of suitable personnel.

Digital Behavioral Model

Digital opportunities are increasingly influencing individuals' behavior (Allen, 2019). ICT elements such as smartphone applications, social media, and the internet can predetermine the behavior patterns of individuals (Degadt, Lambrecht, & Broekaert, 2019). The implementation of creative ideas becomes possible using technology and the Internet (Beliaeva, Ferasso, Kraus, & Damke, 2019). Digital behavior is a model that influences the formation of behavior by digital elements (Geissinger et al., 2019; Steininger, 2019). New initiatives, innovative ideas can be turned into action through digital elements. The high level of followers of an event that is popular in social media is likely to attract the attention of the entrepreneur and integrate them into products and services and exhibit creative innovative behaviors.

ICT has the characteristics of bringing together people with different cultural characteristics, which enable the integration of social groups. This situation causes social formations that come together in a virtual environment to create their own culture and social pressure. These cultural formations affect the behavior of individuals. Thus, the digital behavior model is formed.

Digital Transformation Behavior Model

When enterprises/businesses start to implement their entrepreneurial actions, they have to cope with some difficulties in the face of developing technology. When innovative behaviors are technology-oriented, the digital age can be adapted (Maropoulos et al., 2007). For this reason, entrepreneurs need to identify the requirements of the digital age, evaluate opportunities and threats, and turn risks into benefits. However, not every technological or digital innovation may be an opportunity for the entrepreneur. For this reason, the digital needs of the consumer group, where the idea of entrepreneurship will benefit, should be determined. Especially in the context of career entrepreneurship, digital requirements/needs, and digital satisfaction should be considered in the context of consumers.

Digital satisfaction is about the consumer's expectations, needs, and wishes about a particular digital product. Furthermore, satisfaction requires hedonic motivation. On the one hand, consumer perception about digital innovation comes to the fore, and on the other hand, needs come to the fore. Digital transformation is an important action that satisfies this perception and meets satisfaction needs. When the entrepreneur performs this action, s/he follows the process below:

Stage 1 Behavior Intention: Digital transformation behavior intention,
Stage 2 Determination:

- Determination of 'consumer/customer needs' regarding digital innovation,
- Determination of consumer/customer wishes regarding digital innovation,
- Determination of consumer/customer expectations regarding digital innovation,
- Setting international standards for digital innovation,
- Identifying needs, wishes, and expectations for future customers,

Stage 3 Transformation: Transformation of digital innovation to the needs, wishes, and expectations of current and future customers,
Stage 4 Sustainability: Feedback "Feedback" for the sustainability of digital transformation behavior.

Digital transformation behavior takes place in four basic processes (figure 1). After the intention of entrepreneurship is revealed, this process steps are followed and digital transformation behavior occurs. "Behavior intention" is a mandatory factor. On the other hand, "feedback" is also an essential element for the sustainability of digital transformation behavior. Behaviors for sustainability are necessary for new digital transformation behaviors. Because digital transformation is necessary for the implementation of digital innovations. Besides, sustainability is an important element in creating a strategy in digital transformation.

Career Entrepreneurship and Digital Enterprise Transformation

Career entrepreneurship involves opportunities for progress, the advancement of the organization or business in the context of the career, the development of a particular vocation/profession, the creation of new professions and career opportunities, innovations in the career development process, ensuring the balance and harmony of work-career-employee, developing a career culture and creating a strategy

Figure 1. Digital transformation behavior process

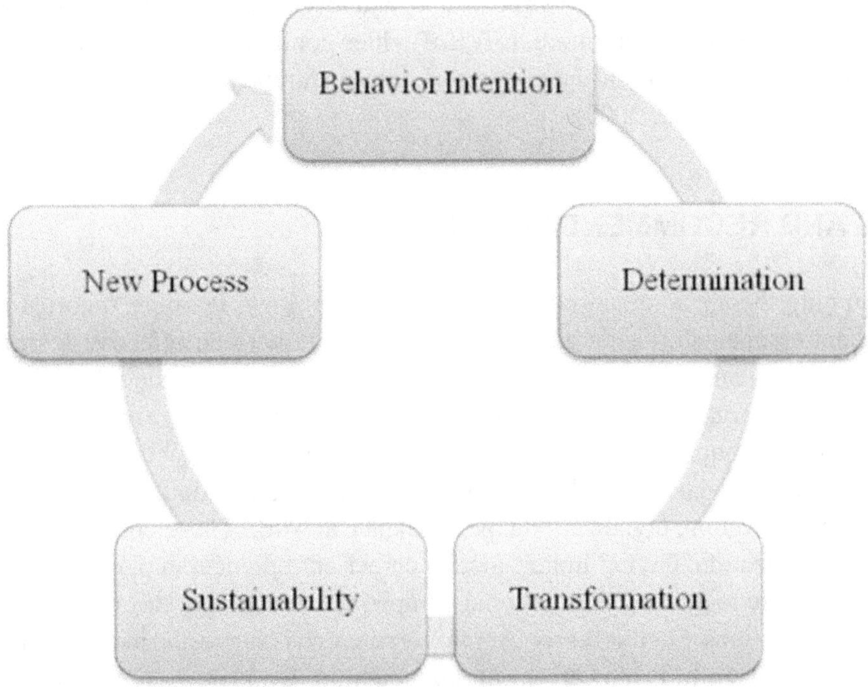

in this direction. Career development is essential in career entrepreneurship. Although individuals develop behavior to develop their careers, enterprises are the entities that create opportunities for career development. Digital enterprises help individuals in this context by transforming the innovations of the digital world into opportunities.

Digital enterprises provide digital resources to consumers through design, planning, presentation, and transformation. consumers' needs are met through information and communication technology (Passerini, El Tarabishy, & Patten, 2012). Digital enterprise transformation in career initiative is performed through the process of harmonizing innovative applications for career development and entrepreneurial behavior with digital technology. On the other hand, the new applications needed are brought to the digital enterprise with entrepreneurial actions (Baiyere, Salmela, & Tapanainen, 2020). Digital transformation is performed in two ways: To harmonize existing applications (resources) with digital innovations, to apply digital innovations directly to the enterprise.

In career entrepreneurship, workforce planning and development strategies, career counseling and executive coaching, professional development coaching, skills and competency development, organizational career development programs, teamwork development are evaluated in the context of digital innovation and compatibility. Programs/systems that do not comply with digital innovations are replaced with new ones. In this case, the digital enterprise will replace the career-oriented business infrastructure with a new one. On the other hand, harmonization is a difficult process. Enterprise's technological infrastructure must be compatible with harmonization and have sufficient financial resources (Hirschheim, Heinzl, & Dibbern, 2020). Financial resources and liquidity ratio should be taken into consideration in digital enterprise transformation. If the benefit to be obtained as a result of the transformation is less than possible losses, the process of transition to new technology (digital transformation process) to be harmonized or transformed may be prolonged. On the other hand, customer and consumer expectations, needs, political barriers, cultural effects, market status, and level of competition/rivalry should be taken into account in transformation. Furthermore, IoT, IIoT, video conferencing, smartphones have important functions in digital transformation in the context of career entrepreneurship (Monostori et al., 2010; Sandhu, 2008; Sandhu & Corbitt, 2002).

SOLUTIONS AND RECOMMENDATIONS

When mind mapping theory, interaction theories with technology, learning theories are considered together, career entrepreneurship is an entrepreneurship model with an effective learning ability that benefits from technology and digital opportunities through mapping technique. Developing this model with ICT is important for organizational strategy and career planning. Because revealing or implementing the career development through entrepreneurship enables the development of corporate culture, increases the commitment of the stakeholders and the employees to the organization, enhances the productivity, service and product innovation, organizational performance at work. These outputs will ensure the sustainability of the organization. Giving importance to career entrepreneurship, especially in developing countries, will contribute to gaining international competitive advantage, sustainability, and economic development of organizations. For this reason, empirical research is suggested in different cultures revealing the relationship between ICT and career entrepreneurship. Besides, it is recommended that career development plans of the organizations and employees in developing countries should be improved in the context of career entrepreneurship and the necessary training should be provided.

FUTURE RESEARCH DIRECTIONS

Since Career entrepreneurship has an important role in today's business life, it is recommended to increase the qualitative and quantitative researches. Besides, studies performed in samples with different cultural characteristics should be compared. Developing a scale for this new type of entrepreneurship is recommended for future studies. The relationship between career entrepreneurship, and intrapreneurship, and organizational climate should be investigated.

CONCLUSION

Advances in technology and ICT have also affected human resource management. Career entrepreneurship is a type of entrepreneurship in which entrepreneurship is constant development in an individual context, exhibiting information acquisition behavior to benefit from opportunities, benefiting from the experiences, sustaining innovative actions through the development of knowledge, skills, and talents. Bringing this type of entrepreneurship to the literature is important for strategic human resource management, efficient use of ICT, and career planning. Sustainability, future orientation, positivity, and synergies are important in this entrepreneurship. Therefore, career behavior in this entrepreneurship includes innovative, developmental, creative, proactive, and digital behavior models. The realization of the necessary training, projects, and programs for the development of these behavioral models of individuals enables the creation of innovations in entrepreneurship.

Career entrepreneurship is a type of entrepreneurship required by human resources in the 21st-century information society. Career-oriented entrepreneurship is crucial in the effective management of human resources, business performance, developing relations with stakeholders, and creating an organizational culture. Since this type of entrepreneurship is a multidisciplinary and multi-factor issue, managing employees, executives, leaders, stakeholders in a common vision are the requirements of the 21st century.

To gain a sustainable competitive advantage of the organization, to ensure the trust of its stakeholders in the organization, and to adopt the mission and vision of the organization to all stakeholders are possible by digital innovations. Providing coaching, consulting services in a virtual environment, and performing office and file management with the smartphone and digital applications can ensure that the work is carried out efficiently outside the office. The planning of projects and the digitalization of work-related warnings provide proactive behavior. In addition, data stored in the digital environment can be interpreted and predictable for the organization. Accounting records and the rate of change of the organization's financial data by years provide important information about profitability and productivity. Thus, the entrepreneurial actions of the organization can be guided according to these data. On the other hand, the personal characteristics of the employees, demographic information, employee error rates, and digitizing the problems of the employees through feedback are important for career development. Utilizing ICT for orientation, counseling, coaching, training, professional development, skills, and talent development provides an important strategy in human resource management.

The new knowledge added to the literature is developing the entrepreneurship theories by revealing the issues of career entrepreneurship, entrepreneurial career behavior models, digital career management system. The study contributes to the development of resource and opportunity based theories in the entrepreneurship literature.

ACKNOWLEDGMENT

This research received no specific grant from any funding agency in the public, commercial, or not-for-profit sectors.

REFERENCES

Allen, J. P. (2019). *Digital Entrepreneurship*. Routledge. doi:10.4324/9780429506567

Almeida, R. K., Fernandes, A. M., & Viollaz, M. (2020). Software Adoption, Employment Composition, and the Skill Content of Occupations in Chilean Firms. *The Journal of Development Studies*, *56*(1), 169–185. doi:10.1080/00220388.2018.1546847

Alvarez, S. A., & Barney, J. B. (2017). Resource-based theory and the entrepreneurial firm. *Strategic entrepreneurship: Creating a new mindset*, 87-105.

Amorós, J. E., Ciravegna, L., Mandakovic, V., & Stenholm, P. (2019). Necessity or opportunity? the effects of State fragility and economic development on entrepreneurial efforts. *Entrepreneurship Theory and Practice*, *43*(4), 725–750. doi:10.1177/1042258717736857

Anas, N., Zulkipli, S. N., Noor, M. S. M., Noh, A. M. M., Ariff, M. I. M., Ghazali, Z. M., ... Rosli, H. M. (2019). *Usefulness and Effectiveness of Mind Mapping: An Analysis of CTU101 and CTU151*. Academic Press.

Bagdadli, S., & Gianecchini, M. (2019). Organizational career management practices and objective career success: A systematic review and framework. *Human Resource Management Review*, *29*(3), 353–370. doi:10.1016/j.hrmr.2018.08.001

Baiyere, A., Salmela, H., & Tapanainen, T. (2020). Digital transformation and the new logics of business process management. *European Journal of Information Systems*, *29*(3), 1–22. doi:10.1080/0960085X.2020.1718007

Bandura, A., & Walters, R. H. (1977). *Social learning theory* (Vol. 1). Prentice-hall.

Baptista, R., & Karaöz, M. (2006). Entrepreneurial human capital and the early survival chances of new start-ups: Opportunity-based vs. necessity-based entrepreneurship. *Small Business Economics*, *36*(3), 249–270. doi:10.100711187-009-9226-2

Barney, J. B. (2018). Why resource-based theory's model of profit appropriation must incorporate a stakeholder perspective. *Strategic Management Journal*, *39*(13), 3305–3325. doi:10.1002mj.2949

Beliaeva, T., Ferasso, M., Kraus, S., & Damke, E. J. (2019). Dynamics of digital entrepreneurship and the innovation ecosystem. *International Journal of Entrepreneurial Behaviour & Research*, *26*(2), 266–284. doi:10.1108/IJEBR-06-2019-0397

Benson, V., Morgan, S., & Filippaios, F. (2014). Social career management: Social media and employability skills gap. *Computers in Human Behavior*, *30*, 519–525. doi:10.1016/j.chb.2013.06.015

Briley, D. A., Livengood, J., Derringer, J., Tucker-Drob, E. M., Fraley, R. C., & Roberts, B. W. (2019). Interpreting behavior genetic models: Seven developmental processes to understand. *Behavior Genetics*, *49*(2), 196–210. doi:10.100710519-018-9939-6 PMID:30467668

Brown, J. S. (2000). Growing up: Digital: How the web changes work, education, and the ways people learn. *Change: The Magazine of Higher Learning*, *32*(2), 11–20. doi:10.1080/00091380009601719

Brown, T. E., Davidsson, P., & Wiklund, J. (2001). An operationalization of Stevenson's conceptualization of entrepreneurship as opportunity-based firm behavior. *Strategic Management Journal*, *22*(10), 953–968. doi:10.1002mj.190

Compeau, D. R., & Higgins, C. A. (1995). Computer Self-Efficacy: Development of a Measure and Initial Test. *Management Information Systems Quarterly*, *19*(2), 189–211. doi:10.2307/249688

Davey, T., Plewa, C., & Struwig, M. (2011). Entrepreneurship perceptions and career intentions of international students. *Education + Training*, *53*(5), 335–352. doi:10.1108/00400911111147677

Davidson, E., & Vaast, E. (2010). Digital entrepreneurship and its sociomaterial enactment. In *2010 43rd Hawaii International Conference on System Sciences* (pp. 1-10). IEEE. 10.1109/HICSS.2010.150

Davis, F. D., Bagozzi, R. P., & Warshaw, P. R. (1989). User Acceptance of Computer Technology: A Comparison of Two Theoretical Models. *Management Science*, *35*(8), 982–1003. doi:10.1287/mnsc.35.8.982

Day, S. W., & Jean-Denis, H. (2016). Resource Based View of social entrepreneurship: Putting the pieces together. *Journal of Strategic Innovation and Sustainability*, *11*(2).

De Clercq, D., & Belausteguigoitia, I. (2019). Coping and laughing in the face of broken promises: Implications for creative behavior. *Personnel Review*, *49*(4), 993–1014. doi:10.1108/PR-11-2018-0441

de Haan, E. (2019). *Critical Moments in Executive Coaching: Understanding the Coaching Process Through Research and Evidence-based Theory*. Routledge. doi:10.4324/9781351180764

Degadt, J., Lambrecht, J., & Broekaert, W. (2019). Business Modelling of Digital Entrepreneurship and Digital Collaboration Solutions to Increase Global Growth in Businesses Owned by Happy Women Entrepreneurs. In *Conference Proceedings Chapters* (pp. 241-264). Bulgarian Association for Management Development and Entrepreneurship.

Dimitratos, P., Voudouris, I., Plakoyiannaki, E., & Nakos, G. (2012). International entrepreneurial culture—Toward a comprehensive opportunity-based operationalization of international entrepreneurship. *International Business Review*, *21*(4), 708–721. doi:10.1016/j.ibusrev.2011.08.001

Edo, A. (2019). The Impact Of Immigration On The Labor Market. *Journal of Economic Surveys*, *33*(3), 922–948. doi:10.1111/joes.12300

Figueroa-Armijos, M., & da Motta Veiga, S. (2019). Predictors of Early-Career Self-Employment among Millennials in the Digital Economy: The Role of The Great Recession. *Proceedings of the 52nd Hawaii International Conference on System Sciences*. 10.24251/HICSS.2019.546

Ford, D. H. (2019). *Humans as self-constructing living systems: A developmental perspective on behavior and personality*. Routledge.

Gao, J., Huang, C., Su, J., & Xie, Q. (2019). Examining the Factors Behind the Success and Sustainability of China's Creative Research Group: An Extension of the Teamwork Quality Model. *Sustainability*, *11*(4), 1195. doi:10.3390u11041195

Geissinger, A., Laurell, C., Sandström, C., Eriksson, K., & Nykvist, R. (2019). Digital entrepreneurship and field conditions for institutional change–Investigating the enabling role of cities. *Technological Forecasting and Social Change*, *146*, 877–886. doi:10.1016/j.techfore.2018.06.019

Ghezzi, A., & Cavallo, A. (2018). Agile business model innovation in digital entrepreneurship: Lean Startup approaches. *Journal of Business Research*.

Giones, F., & Brem, A. (2017). Digital technology entrepreneurship: A definition and research agenda. *Technology Innovation Management Review*, *7*(5), 44–51. doi:10.22215/timreview/1076

Greenhaus, J. H., Callanan, G. A., & Godshalk, V. M. (2010). Career management. *Sage (Atlanta, Ga.)*.

Hafezieh, N., Akhavan, P., & Eshraghian, F. (2011). Exploration of process and competitive factors of entrepreneurship in digital space: A multiple case study in Iran. *Education, Business and Society*, *4*(4), 267–279. doi:10.1108/17537981111190051

Hair, N., Wetsch, L. R., Hull, C. E., Perotti, V., & Hung, Y. T. C. (2012). Market orientation in digital entrepreneurship: Advantages and challenges in a Web 2.0 networked world. *International Journal of Innovation and Technology Management*, *9*(06), 1250045. doi:10.1142/S0219877012500459

He, J., Nazari, M., Zhang, Y., & Cai, N. (2020). Opportunity-based entrepreneurship and environmental quality of sustainable development: A resource and institutional perspective. *Journal of Cleaner Production*, *256*, 120390. doi:10.1016/j.jclepro.2020.120390

Henderson, R., & Robertson, M. (2000). Who wants to be an entrepreneur? Young adult attitudes to entrepreneurship as a career. *Career Development International*, *5*(6), 279–287.

Hirschheim, R., Heinzl, A., & Dibbern, J. (2020). *Information Systems Outsourcing: The Era of Digital Transformation*. Springer Nature. doi:10.1007/978-3-030-45819-5

Howe, J. L., Penrod, J. D., Gottesman, E., Bean, A., & Kramer, B. J. (2019). The rural interdisciplinary team training program: A workforce development workshop to increase geriatrics knowledge and skills for rural providers. *Gerontology & Geriatrics Education*, *40*(1), 3–15. doi:10.1080/02701960.2018.1454917 PMID:29583103

Huang, R., Spector, J. M., & Yang, J. (2019). Learning in the Context of Technologies. In *Educational Technology* (pp. 33–48). Springer. doi:10.1007/978-981-13-6643-7_2

Huda, M., Qodriah, S. L., Rismayadi, B., Hananto, A., Kardiyati, E. N., Ruskam, A., & Nasir, B. M. (2019). Towards Cooperative with Competitive Alliance: Insights into Performance Value in Social Entrepreneurship. In Creating Business Value and Competitive Advantage with Social Entrepreneurship (pp. 294-317). IGI Global.

Hull, C. E., Caisy Hung, Y. T., Hair, N., Perotti, V., & DeMartino, R. (2007). Taking advantage of digital opportunities: A typology of digital entrepreneurship. *International Journal of Networking and Virtual Organisations*, *4*(3), 290–303. doi:10.1504/IJNVO.2007.015166

Kamaludin, I. A. M. M. H., Saad, M. M., & Aziz, N. A. (2012). Sustainability–Driven Entrepreneurship: The Mediating Effect of Opportunity-Based Management Structure on the Relationship between Entrepreneurial Orientation and Environmental Sustainability Management of SMEs: A Conceptual Framework. *European Jounrla of Business and Management*, *4*(13), 148–156.

Kautonen, T., Kibler, E., & Minniti, M. (2017). Late-career entrepreneurship, income and quality of life. *Journal of Business Venturing*, *32*(3), 318–333. doi:10.1016/j.jbusvent.2017.02.005

Kawai, N. (2019). Historical Transition of Psychological Theories of Fear: The View of Fear in Behaviorism. In *The Fear of Snakes* (pp. 1–18). Springer. doi:10.1007/978-981-13-7530-9_1

Kelestyn, B., & Henfridsson, O. (2014). *Everyday digital entrepreneurship: The inception, shifts, and scaling of future shaping practices*. Academic Press.

Kellermanns, F., Walter, J., Crook, T. R., Kemmerer, B., & Narayanan, V. (2016). The resource-based view in entrepreneurship: A content-analytical comparison of researchers' and entrepreneurs' views. *Journal of Small Business Management, 54*(1), 26–48. doi:10.1111/jsbm.12126

Kerr, G., & Armstrong-Stassen, M. (2011). The bridge to retirement: Older workers' engagement in post-career entrepreneurship and wage-and-salary employment. *The Journal of Entrepreneurship, 20*(1), 55–76. doi:10.1177/097135571002000103

Kettunen, J., & Makela, J. P. (2019). Practitioners' conceptions of ethical practice in social networking in career services. *International Journal for Educational and Vocational Guidance, 19*(3), 345–362. doi:10.100710775-018-9383-4

Kettunen, J., & Sampson, J. P. Jr. (2019). Challenges in implementing ICT in career services: Perspectives from career development experts. *International Journal for Educational and Vocational Guidance, 19*(1), 1–18. doi:10.100710775-018-9365-6

Komba, M. M., & Lwoga, E. T. (2020). Systematic Review as a Research Method in Library and Information Science. In *Handbook of Research on Connecting Research Methods for Information Science Research* (pp. 80–94). IGI Global. doi:10.4018/978-1-7998-1471-9.ch005

Korobov, S. A., Moseyko, V. O., Novoseltseva, E. G., Epinina, V. S., & Marusinina, E. Y. (2017). Socio-economic Development of Small and Medium Entrepreneurship: Potential of Resource-Based Approach. In *Russia and the European Union* (pp. 453–459). Springer. doi:10.1007/978-3-319-55257-6_58

Korotov, K., Khapova, S., & Arthur, M. (2010). Career entrepreneurship. *Published in Organizational Dynamics, 40*(2), 127–135. doi:10.1016/j.orgdyn.2011.01.007

Kuťák, D., Doležal, M., Kerouš, B., Eichler, Z., Vašek, J., & Liarokapis, F. (2019). An Interactive and Multimodal Virtual Mind Map for Future Workplace. *Frontiers in ICT (Lausanne, Switzerland), 6*, 12. doi:10.3389/fict.2019.00014

Lemons, C. J., & Toste, J. R. (2019). Professional Development and Coaching: Addressing the "Last Mile" Problem in Educational Research. *Assessment for Effective Intervention, 44*(4), 300–304. doi:10.1177/1534508419862859

Lo, F. Y., Huarng, K. H., & Rey-Martí, A. (2019). Entrepreneur subsidiary of business groups from emerging markets: A multi-level perspective. *The International Entrepreneurship and Management Journal, 15*(2), 471–483. doi:10.100711365-019-00563-y

Ma'ruf, A. H., Syafii, M., & Kusuma, A. P. (2019). Pengaruh Model Pembelajaran Mind Mapping Berbasis HOTS terhadap Motivasi dan Hasil Belajar Siswa. *Mosharafa: Jurnal Pendidikan Matematika, 8*(3), 503–514.

Magsamen-Conrad, K., Dillon, J. M., Hanasono, L. K., & Valdez, P. A. (2020). Developing an intergroup communication intervention curriculum: Enhancing workforce skills across generations. In *Five Generations and Only One Workforce: How Successful Businesses Are Managing a Multigenerational Workforce* (pp. 148–176). IGI Global. doi:10.4018/978-1-7998-0437-6.ch008

Maropoulos, P. G., Zhang, D., Chapman, P., Bramall, D. G., & Rogers, B. C. (2007). Key digital enterprise technology methods for large volume metrology and assembly integration. *International Journal of Production Research, 45*(7), 1539–1559. doi:10.1080/00207540600942326

Monostori, L., Erdős, G., Kádár, B., Kis, T., Kovács, A., Pfeiffer, A., & Váncza, J. (2010). Digital enterprise solution for integrated production planning and control. *Computers in Industry, 61*(2), 112–126. doi:10.1016/j.compind.2009.10.008

Moore, G. C., & Benbasat, I. (1991). Development of an Instrument to Measure The Perceptions of Adopting an Information Technology Innovation. *Information Systems Research, 2*(3), 192–222. doi:10.1287/isre.2.3.192

Mowrer, R. R., & Klein, S. B. (2019). A contrast between traditional and contemporary learning theory. *Contemporary Learning Theories: Volume II: Instrumental Conditioning Theory and the Impact of Biological Constraints on Learning*, 1.

Mtima, L. (2009). Copyright Social Utility and Social Justice Interdependence: A Paradigm for Intellectual Property Empowerment and Digital Entrepreneurship. *West Virginia Law Review, 112*, 97.

Nambisan, S. (2017). Digital entrepreneurship: Toward a digital technology perspective of entrepreneurship. *Entrepreneurship Theory and Practice, 41*(6), 1029–1055. doi:10.1111/etap.12254

Nason, R. S., & Wiklund, J. (2018). An assessment of resource-based theorizing on firm growth and suggestions for the future. *Journal of Management, 44*(1), 32–60. doi:10.1177/0149206315610635

Ng, T. W., & Wang, M. (2019). An actor–partner interdependence model of employees' and coworkers' innovative behavior, psychological detachment, and strain reactions. *Personnel Psychology, 72*(3), 445–476. doi:10.1111/peps.12317

Ngoasong, M. Z. (2018). Digital entrepreneurship in a resource-scarce context: A focus on entrepreneurial digital competencies. *Journal of Small Business and Enterprise Development, 25*(3), 483–500. doi:10.1108/JSBED-01-2017-0014

Oliver, K. M., & Williams-Duncan, S. (2019). Faith Leaders Developing Digital Literacies: Demands and Resources across Career Stages According to Theological Educators. *The Journal of Media Literacy Education, 11*(2), 122–145. doi:10.23860/JMLE-2019-11-2-7

Omar, S., & Tajudeen, F. P. (2020). The Influence of Career Adaptability and Career Commitment to Minimize Intention to Leave Among ICT Professionals. *International Journal of Human Capital and Information Technology Professionals, 11*(2), 23–38. doi:10.4018/IJHCITP.2020040102

Oyson, M., & Whittaker, D. H. (2010). *An opportunity-based approach to international entrepreneurship: Pursuing opportunities internationally through prospection*. Academic Press.

Padirayon, L. M., Pagudpud, M. V., & Cruz, J. S. D. (2019). Exploring constructivism learning theory using mobile game. *IOP Conference Series. Materials Science and Engineering, 482*(1), 012004. doi:10.1088/1757-899X/482/1/012004

Parker, S. K., Wang, Y., & Liao, J. (2019). When is proactivity wise? A review of factors that influence the individual outcomes of proactive behavior. *Annual Review of Organizational Psychology and Organizational Behavior*, *6*(1), 221–248. doi:10.1146/annurev-orgpsych-012218-015302

Passerini, K., El Tarabishy, A., & Patten, K. (2012). *Information technology for small business: managing the digital enterprise*. Springer Science & Business Media. doi:10.1007/978-1-4614-3040-7

Pawson, R., Greenhalgh, T., Harvey, G., & Walshe, K. (2005). Realist review-a new method of systematic review designed for complex policy interventions. *Journal of Health Services Research & Policy*, *10*(1, suppl), 21–34. doi:10.1258/1355819054308530 PMID:16053581

Petticrew, M., & Roberts, H. (2008). *Systematic reviews in the social sciences: A practical guide*. John Wiley & Sons.

Rahi, S. (2017). Research design and methods: A systematic review of research paradigms, sampling issues and instruments development. *International Journal of Economics & Management Sciences*, *6*(2), 1–5. doi:10.4172/2162-6359.1000403

Rajenderan, M., & Zawawi, D. (2019). Leaky Pipeline Syndrome in Information and Communication Technology (ICT) Industry of Malaysia: A Conceptual Study on Female Career Barriers and Retention Management. *International Journal of Academic Research in Business & Social Sciences*, *9*(2). Advance online publication. doi:10.6007/IJARBSS/v9-i2/5672

Rathmell, W. K., Brown, N. J., & Kilburg, R. R. (2019). Transformation to academic leadership: The role of mentorship and executive coaching. *Consulting Psychology Journal*, *71*(3), 141–160. doi:10.1037/cpb0000124 PMID:31787830

Richter, C., Kraus, S., Brem, A., Durst, S., & Giselbrecht, C. (2017). Digital entrepreneurship: Innovative business models for the sharing economy. *Creativity and Innovation Management*, *26*(3), 300–310. doi:10.1111/caim.12227

Richter, C., Kraus, S., & Syrjä, P. (2015). The shareconomy as a precursor for digital entrepreneurship business models. *International Journal of Entrepreneurship and Small Business*, *25*(1), 18–35. doi:10.1504/IJESB.2015.068773

Rider, C. I., Thompson, P., Kacperczyk, A., & Tåg, J. (2019). Experience and entrepreneurship: A career transition perspective. *Industrial & Labor Relations Review*, *72*(5), 1149–1181. doi:10.1177/0019793919852919

Rieger, K. L., Chernomas, W. M., McMillan, D. E., & Morin, F. L. (2019). The arts as a catalyst for learning with undergraduate nursing students: Findings from a constructivist grounded theory study. *Arts & Health*, 1–20. doi:10.1080/17533015.2019.1608569 PMID:31038419

Rogers, E. M., & Shoemaker, F. F. (1971). *Communication of Innovations: A Cross- Cultural Approach*. The Free Press.

Rosa, P. (2019). Entrepreneurial Growth Through Portfolio Entrepreneurship: The Entrepreneurial Career Ladder. In The Family Business Group Phenomenon (pp. 111-144). Palgrave Macmillan.

Rydehell, H., Isaksson, A., & Löfsten, H. (2019). Effects of internal and external resource dimensions on the business performance of new technology-based firms. *International Journal of Innovation Management, 23*(01), 1950001. doi:10.1142/S1363919619500014

Sandhu, K. (2008). E-services acceptance model (e-sam). In *Advances in Computer and Information Sciences and Engineering* (pp. 224–229). Springer. doi:10.1007/978-1-4020-8741-7_40

Sandhu, K., & Corbitt, B. J. (2002). *Assessing web-based electronic services adoption model (E-SAM)*. Deakin University School of Information Systems.

Schenkel, M. T., Farmer, S., & Maslyn, J. M. (2019). Process improvement in SMEs: The impact of harmonious passion for entrepreneurship, employee creative self-efficacy, and time spent innovating. *Journal of Small Business Strategy, 29*(1), 64–77.

Scholarios, D., Van der Heijden, B. I., Van der Schoot, E., Bozionelos, N., Epitropaki, O., Jedrzejowicz, P., Knauth, P., Marzec, I., Mikkelsen, A., & Van der Heijde, C. M. (2008). Employability and the psychological contract in European ICT sector SMEs. *International Journal of Human Resource Management, 19*(6), 1035–1055. doi:10.1080/09585190802051337

Scott, M. G., & Twomey, D. F. (1988). The long-term supply of entrepreneurs: Students' career aspirations in relation to entrepreneurship. *Journal of Small Business Management, 26*(4), 5.

Singh, J. S. K. (2020). Social Competencies, Job Performance and Cultural Adjustment Among Expatriate Assignees In Malaysia. *Malaysian Management Journal, 21*, 17–32.

Staunton, T. (2019). Icarus, Grannies, Black Holes and the death of privacy: Exploring the use of digital networks for career enactment. *British Journal of Guidance & Counselling*, 1–12. doi:10.1080/03069885.2019.1698007

Steininger, D. M. (2019). Linking information systems and entrepreneurship: A review and agenda for IT-associated and digital entrepreneurship research. *Information Systems Journal, 29*(2), 363–407. doi:10.1111/isj.12206

Sun, M., Wang, M., & Wegerif, R. (2019). Using computer-based cognitive mapping to improve students' divergent thinking for creativity development. *British Journal of Educational Technology, 50*(5), 2217–2233. doi:10.1111/bjet.12825

Sussan, F., & Acs, Z. J. (2017). The digital entrepreneurial ecosystem. *Small Business Economics, 49*(1), 55–73. doi:10.100711187-017-9867-5

Taber, B. J. (2019). Career Counselling Interventions to Enhance Career Adaptabilities for Sustainable Employment. In *Handbook of Innovative Career Counselling* (pp. 103–115). Springer. doi:10.1007/978-3-030-22799-9_7

Taylor, S., & Todd, P. A. (1995). Understanding Information Technology Usage: A Test of Competing Models. *Information Systems Research, 6*(2), 144–176. doi:10.1287/isre.6.2.144

Vance, C. M., & Bergin, R. (2019). The Social Expat-Preneur: Examining a Growing International Career Model Supporting Global Social Entrepreneurship. In Creating Business Value and Competitive Advantage With Social Entrepreneurship (pp. 186-204). IGI Global.

Varela, J. A., Bande, B., Del Rio, M., & Jaramillo, F. (2019). Servant Leadership, Proactive Work Behavior, and Performance Overall Rating: Testing a Multilevel Model of Moderated Mediation. *Journal of Business-To-Business Marketing*, *26*(2), 177–195. doi:10.1080/1051712X.2019.1603417

Venkataraman, S. (2019). The distinctive domain of entrepreneurship research. In *Seminal Ideas for the Next Twenty-Five Years of Advances* (pp. 5–20). Emerald Publishing Limited. doi:10.1108/S1074-754020190000021009

Venkatesh, V., & Davis, F. D. (2000). A theoretical extension of the Technology Acceptance Model: Four Longitudinal Field Studies. *Management Science*, *46*(2), 186–204. doi:10.1287/mnsc.46.2.186.11926

Venkatesh, V., Morris, M. G., Davis, G. B., & Davis, F. D. (2003). User Acceptance of Information Technology: Toward a Unified View. *Management Information Systems Quarterly*, *27*(3), 425–478. doi:10.2307/30036540

Venkatesh, V., Thong, J. Y. L., & Xu, X. (2012). Consumer Acceptance and Use of Information Technology: Extending The Unified Theory of Acceptance and Use of Technology. *Management Information Systems Quarterly*, *36*(1), 157–178. doi:10.2307/41410412

Vézina, S., & Bélanger, A. (2019). Impacts of education and immigration on the size and skills of the future workforce. *Demographic Research*, *41*, 331–366. doi:10.4054/DemRes.2019.41.12

Victor, L. (2008). Systematic reviewing. *Social Research Update*, *54*(1), 1–4.

Vondracek, F. W., Lerner, R. M., & Schulenberg, J. E. (2019). *Career development: A life-span developmental approach.* Routledge. doi:10.4324/9781315792705

Williamson, A. J., Battisti, M., Leatherbee, M., & Gish, J. J. (2019). Rest, zest, and my innovative best: Sleep and mood as drivers of entrepreneurs' innovative behavior. *Entrepreneurship Theory and Practice*, *43*(3), 582–610. doi:10.1177/1042258718798630

Wilson, F., Kickul, J., & Marlino, D. (2007). Gender, entrepreneurial self–efficacy, and entrepreneurial career intentions: Implications for entrepreneurship education. *Entrepreneurship Theory and Practice*, *31*(3), 387–406. doi:10.1111/j.1540-6520.2007.00179.x

Wu, X., Lyu, Y., Kwan, H. K., & Zhai, H. (2019). The impact of mentoring quality on protégés' organization-based self-esteem and proactive behavior: The moderating role of traditionality. *Human Resource Management*, *58*(4), 417–430. doi:10.1002/hrm.21968

Xu, Q., Zhang, G., & Chan, A. (2019). Abusive supervision and subordinate proactive behavior: Joint moderating roles of organizational identification and positive affectivity. *Journal of Business Ethics*, *157*(3), 829–843. doi:10.100710551-017-3691-3

Zhang, J. H., & Lee, J. H. (2019). Beyond the Hawthorne Research: Relationship Between IT Company Employees' Perceived Physical Work Environment and Creative Behavior. In *International Conference on Software Engineering Research, Management and Applications* (pp. 147-159). Springer.

Ziyae, B., Sajadi, S. M., & Mobaraki, M. H. (2014). The deployment and internationalization speed of e-business in the digital entrepreneurship era. *Journal of Global Entrepreneurship Research*, *4*(1), 15. doi:10.118640497-014-0015-2

ADDITIONAL READING

Maree, K. (2019). *Shaping the story: A guide to facilitating narrative career counselling*. BRILL.

Nagy, N., Froidevaux, A., & Hirschi, A. (2019). Lifespan perspectives on careers and career development. In *Work across the lifespan* (pp. 235–259). Academic Press. doi:10.1016/B978-0-12-812756-8.00010-4

Özsungur, F. (2019). *The Effects of Technology Acceptance and Use Behaviour on Women's Entrepreneurship Motivation Factors*. Asia Pacific Journal of Innovation and Entrepreneurship., doi:10.1108/APJIE-09-2019-0070

Ponterotto, J. G., & Park-Taylor, J. (2019). Careerography: Introducing a New Tool for Research, Theory Development, Practice, and Training in Career Psychology. *Journal of Career Development*. doi:10.1177/0894845319867429

Zacher, H., Rudolph, C. W., Todorovic, T., & Ammann, D. (2019). Academic career development: A review and research agenda. *Journal of Vocational Behavior*, *110*, 357–373. doi:10.1016/j.jvb.2018.08.006

KEY TERMS AND DEFINITIONS

Career Entrepreneurship: A type of entrepreneurship in which entrepreneurship is constant development in an individual context, exhibiting information acquisition behavior to benefit from opportunities, benefiting from the experiences, sustaining innovative actions through the development of knowledge, skills, and talents.

Career Management: A system that includes workforce planning and development strategies, career counseling, executive coaching, organizational career development programs, teamwork development, professional development coaching, skills, and competency development.

Digital Behavioral Model: A behavioral pattern that influences the formation of behavior by digital elements.

Digital Satisfaction: A perceptual state regarding the consumer's expectations, needs, and wishes about particular digital products.

Digital Transformation Behavior Model: A behavior model that meets the consumer's expectations, needs, and wishes, adapts digital innovations to existing innovations and enables them to be applied to the existing system, and consists of behavior intention, determination, transformation and sustainability process.

Entrepreneurial Career Behavior: An entrepreneurial behavioral model for organization leaders and employees that emerges as research of opportunities, development of knowledge obtained, selection of appropriate business and organization, strategy development, planning sustainable career development.

Opportunity-Based Theory: A theory that the creation of entrepreneurship ideas is based on the approach of benefit from opportunities.

Proactive Behavior Model: A behavior model based on the implementation of creative ideas and benefiting from opportunities in entrepreneurship.

Resource-Based Theory: A theory based on the idea that entrepreneurship ideas and practices are based on the use of existing resources and obtaining new resources.

Chapter 4
E-Government and Digital Transformation:
A Conceptual Framework for Risk Factors Identification

Fatma Bouaziz
Faculty of Economics and Management, University of Sfax, Tunisia

ABSTRACT

This chapter aims to propose a conceptual framework for e-government risks identification through a literature review of papers specifically focusing on e-government risks. To achieve this objective, a content analysis of papers on e-government risks is made. This allows proposing a conceptual framework comprising a list of seven categories of risk factors, the negative consequences on the e-government project, and their impacts on its stakeholders. This conceptual framework can be useful for both researchers and practitioners. It offers a first step to enhance awareness of the various risk factors, their negative consequences on the project deployment, as well as their impacts on e-government stakeholders. Project managers can use it as a diagnostic tool of the risks of e-government projects, which will help better assessment and management of risks. For future research, it may be appropriate to investigate e-government risk factors using empirical research and draw conclusions about risk factors categories of e-government projects and their failure risk.

INTRODUCTION

In recent years, government organizations, over the world, have attempted to embrace the potential of digital technologies, included as a key objective in political agendas and strategic programs of government transformation. This use of digital technologies by government organizations is labeled as digital government. It corresponds to "the use of digital technologies, as an integrated part of governments' modernization strategies, to create public value" (OECD, 2014, p. 6).

DOI: 10.4018/978-1-7998-8583-2.ch004

Several authors have regarded digital government as a strategic imperative for government organizations to improve service performance, enhance customer experience, streamline operations, and create new business models (Glyptis et al., 2020; Gong et al., 2020). Accordingly, digital government creates opportunities for enhancing efficiency, effectiveness, accountability and transparency, and improving communication, interaction, as well as collaboration between citizens and government organizations (Glyptiset al., 2020; Peharda et al., 2011), which are a sine qua non for co-production (Falco & Kleinhans, 2018). In addition, digital government leads to the transformation of government organizations and their interrelationships with stakeholders.

However, despite high expectations regarding digital government and its transformational potential, high failure rates, cost and time overruns, and unmet functional specifications are reported (Choudhari et al., 2007; Gong et al., 2020; Heeks, 2003). Gong et al. (2020) justified failures in transforming government organizations by the lack of understanding the complexity of digital transformation and the relationships among technologies, information use, organizational contexts, and institutional arrangements. Other researchers attribute this failure to the many risk factors that hinder the successful implementation of digital government projects (Bouaziz, 2006; Evangelidis, 2004; Weerakkody et al., 2015).

According to Gomes et al. (2020), risk management in project allows, through corrective actions, to direct the manager to the intended objective, without the risk spread being of great relevance. When applied to the management of e-government projects, risk management and risk assessment techniques would reduce the threats, which stem from the various risks of these projects (Choudhari et al., 2007). In fact, appropriate risk assessment methodologies are able to enhance decision-making by turning threats into opportunities. However, although digital government projects suffer from high failure rates, risk is not properly addressed by researches (Weerakkody et al., 2015).

Thus, in this chapter, the author aims to respond to the following question: what are the risk factors of e-government projects?

Studying e-government projects risks by focusing on the identification of the risk factors of these projects will contribute to narrow the research gap revealed by Weerakkody et al. (2015). In fact, these authors have proposed that risk factors in the context of e-government projects deserve more attention to reduce the research gap. Moreover, this reveals a paramount importance with the exponential and continuous evolution of information and communication technologies (ICTs) covering new trends such as Social Media Networks, Cloud Computing, Internet of Things, Big Data Analytics and Artificial Intelligence. It will help develop a dynamic knowledge base to take new e-government risk factors in account and successfully lead to digital transformation of government organizations.

This chapter is organized as follows: in the first section, the concept of digital government is defined. Then, digital government is investigated as a means for digital transformation strategy of government organizations. Finally, risk of failure of e-government projects and risk management are discussed. The second section focuses on the research methodology. The third section examines the literature devoted to the risk factors in the specific context of e-government to propose a framework of e-government risk factors, project performance and impacts on stakeholders. The fourth, fifth and sixth sections are respectively devoted for solutions and recommendations, future research directions and conclusion.

BACKGROUND

Digital Government: a Bi-dimensional Concept

Digital government corresponds to "the use of digital technologies, as an integrated part of governments' modernization strategies, to create public value" (OECD, 2014, p. 6). The OECD (2014) evokes an ecosystem of digital government that includes several stakeholders: government actors, non-governmental organizations, businesses, citizens' associations and individuals. The actors of this ecosystem contribute, each according to its prerogatives and needs, to the production of data, services and content through interactions with the government. All of these interactions rely on the use of ICTs to provide information and services and to realize internal administrative activities, management and decision-making. These technologies are introduced into government processes to support internal functioning and operations and external relationships.

Digital government is a broad concept that includes two dimensions: e-democracy and e-government (Zwass, 2006). E-democracy corresponds to "the use of ICTs to support the process of broad participation of citizens and of those who represent others, in debates, political discourses, surfacing and elaboration of societal issues, emergence of representation, polling, and voting" (Zwass, 2006). Over time, researchers become interested in the use of advanced technologies, social media and web 2.0 tools to support democracy. They focus on the role of these technologies in enhancing formal political processes, two-way communication and information of citizens to effectively participate in decision-making about public issues.

E-government refers to "the use by the governments of ICTs, and particularly the Internet, as a tool to achieve better government" (OECD, 2014, p. 6). It is a key objective in political agendas and governmental strategic programs. It is also a central part of the process of modernizing the government organizations (Alcaide–Muñoz et al., 2017; Meijer et al., 2018). The aim is to improve services provided by government organizations, and interaction between government and citizens (Peharda et al., 2011).

E-government includes four application types. The first type is Government to Government (G to G). This application has to do with internal interaction among governments at various levels and in different places. It allows joining government organizations and sharing their information and skills. It improves government organizations' work before interacting with external stakeholders (citizens, businesses and civil society).The second type of e-government applications is Government to Business (G to B). This aims to serve the business sector. Development of this application promotes information transparency and procedures simplification. Government to Citizen (G to C) is the third type of applications. It allows interaction between citizens and the government organizations to facilitate access to government information via websites, save time and effort in government transactions, enhance government services delivery, reduce costs and build trust between government and citizens. The last application is Government to Employees (G to E). It concerns the relationships and interaction between government organizations and public sector employees. It covers their needs for information, accomplishment of administrative procedures and development of competencies through e-learning applications.

Based on the aforementioned developments, digital government can be viewed as a generic concept that relies on four major ideas:

- The use of digital technologies by the government organizations as a means for information, communication, transaction and decision-making processes. Digital technologies are used to ensure administrative, managerial (e-government) and governance (e-democracy) activities.
- The involvement of several stakeholders: government organizations, public and private companies, citizens, and civil society. These stakeholders constitute the ecosystem of digital government (OEDC, 2014).
- The potential of transforming the government organizations as well as internal and external relationships, even if this potential is not always exploited.
- The search for benefits realization at individual and organizational levels, and at internal and external levels. This refers to the creation of public value through digital government (OECD, 2014).

The figure 1 illustrates these ideas about the digital government.

Figure 1. Digital government: e-government and e-democracy dimensions

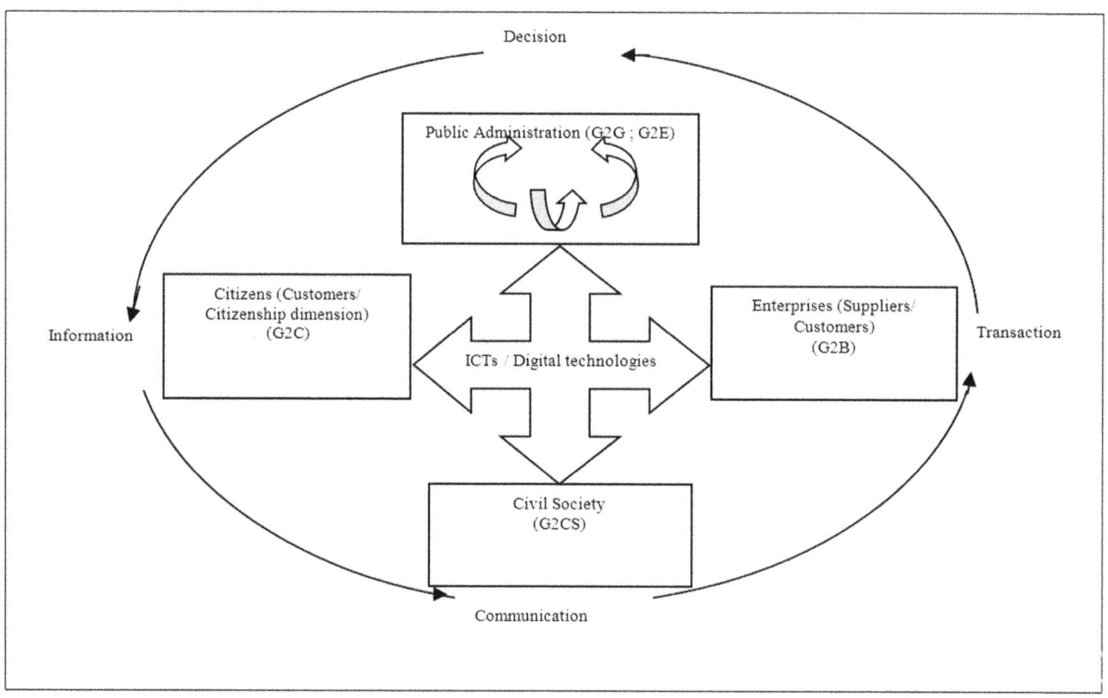

Accordingly, digital government refers to the use of ICTs internally between both government organizations functions and departments and externally with several stakeholders (citizens, business, NGO, civil society). This use is to accomplish activities of information, communication, transaction and decision-making at administration, management and governance processes levels.

In this chapter, the author focus is on e-government. All of the e-government applications take advantage of the digital technologies' new trends, namely Cloud Computing, Big Data, Data analytics, Internet of Things, Artificial Intelligence, Social Media, etc. Digital technologies improve ICT infrastructures and create big databases and digital applications. They lead to new ways of governing, functioning and serving the community.

Thanks to digital technologies, e-government reduces costs, improves transparency, accountability and citizens' trust in government organizations. Peharda et al. (2011) cited five zones of improvements due to e-government implementation. Accordingly, e-government leads to better collaboration between citizens and government agencies as well as better citizens' life quality and public sector services quality. It reduces efforts and costs through provision of products and services electronically. It enhances efficiency and effectiveness of public sector services. Finally, it leads to higher availability and easier accessibility to services and information. Falco and Kleinhans (2018) cited the example of social media as a means for creating opportunities for two-way communication and collaboration between governments and active citizens, both offline and online, which is sine qua non for co-production. Therefore, government organizations and citizens make "better use of each other's assets and resources to achieve better outcomes and improved efficiency" (Falco & Kleinhans, 2018, p. 20). Moreover, Alcaide–Muñoz et al. (2017) summed the benefits of e-government as follows:

- Improving information accessibility and transparency,
- Improving public service delivery,
- Increasing interaction and improving citizens' participation in public affairs,
- Improving democratic models,
- Increasing trust in governments,
- Increasing organizational flexibility and agility in a dynamic environment.

Digital Government: A Means for Digital Transformation of the Government Organizations

Several definitions of digital transformation have been proposed in the extant literature. However, authors acknowledged that consensus has not been achieved regarding a common definition of this notion (Gong et al., 2020; Vial, 2019). Considering that digital transformation is a multidimensional phenomenon driven by technology that impacts society, politics and economy, Vial (2019) proposed a summative definition based on the analysis of 23 definitions. The author described it as a continuous process "that aims to improve an entity by triggering significant changes to its properties through combinations of information, computing, communication, and connectivity technologies" (Vial, 2019, p. 121). Heilig et al. (2017, p. 3) use "the term digital transformation to exclusively refer to the required transformations driving the digitalization in and between organizations based on a digital strategy". They added that "more specifically, a digital transformation refers to a broader process of transforming an organization or a network of organizations at different levels (e.g., strategy, governance, leadership, culture, people, technology, etc.) by making use of digital technologies and concepts, to which we refer as enablers".

Three key components are at the core of the aforementioned definitions. These are digital technologies, significant changes and digital strategy. **Digital technologies** are a central driver for digital transformation (Bouaziz, 2020b; Gong et al., 2020; Peter et al., 2020; Vial, 2019). They are viewed as combinations of information, computing, communication, and connectivity technologies (Vial, 2019). They encompass social network technologies, mobile technologies, (big) data analytics, cloud computing, Internet of Things, artificial intelligence, block chain, robotics, and virtual reality. By digital technologies, OECD (2014, p. 6) refers to all "ICTs, including the Internet, mobile technologies and devices, as well as data analytics used to improve the generation, collection, exchange, aggregation, combination, analysis, access, searchability and presentation of digital content, including for the development of services and apps".

Digital technologies are sine qua non of **significant changes** that involve transformation of business strategies, business processes, firm capabilities, products and services, organizational structures, management concepts, and key inter firms relationships in extended business networks (Bouaziz, 2020b; Gong et al., 2020; Matt et al., 2015; Vial, 2019). Indeed, digital transformation is perceived as an ongoing process of using new digital technologies in everyday organizational life, which recognizes agility as the core mechanism for the strategic renewal of an organization's business model, collaborative approach, and eventually culture (Warner & Wäger, 2018). Furthermore, digital transformation is about structuring new business operations to facilitate and fully leverage firms' core competence through digital technology in order to attain competitive advantage (Liu et al., 2011). It goes far beyond functional thinking and holistically considers the "comprehensiveness of actions" that must be taken to exploit the opportunities or avoid the threats that stem from digital technologies (Singh & Hess, 2017, p. 124).

According to Matt et al. (2015), organizations need to establish management practices to govern digital transformation. They propose to formulate a **digital transformation strategy** that serves as a central concept to integrate the entire coordination, prioritization, and implementation of digital transformation within an organization. Matt et al. (2015) noted that digital transformation strategies build on a business- centric perspective to focus on the transformation of products, processes, and organizational aspects owing to new technologies. They include changes and implications for products, services, and business models as a whole. They have a cross-functional character and need to be aligned with other functional and operational strategies. According to the same authors, digital business strategies often discuss the possibilities and the effects of digital technologies for organizations. However, Peter et al. (2020) revealed that managers lack the knowledge and the know-how as for the development and implementation of digital strategies, which has been behind the inability of organizations to implement digital transformation plans. The authors identified two views on how a digital transformation strategy should be addressed. The first view emphasizes the need for a digital strategy dedicated to digital transformation requiring more than just a chapter in an overarching corporate strategy, as proposed by Matt et al. (2015). On the contrary, the second view proposes a fusion of organizational strategy and information systems strategy. This leads to the concept of digital business strategy, defined as organizational strategy, formulated and executed by leveraging digital resources to create differential value (Vial, 2019).

When discussing digital government and digital transformation in government organizations, several authors (Bouaziz, 2020a; Gil-Garcia et al., 2018; Glyptis et al., 2020) argued that digital government involves new styles of leadership, new decision-making processes, different ways of organizing and delivering services, and new concepts of citizenship, which requires rethinking existing processes and changing organizational behaviors (Glyptis et al., 2020). A strategy of government organizations' transformation based on the abilities of digital technologies and digital government is thus to be defined (Bouaziz, 2020a; Glyptis et al., 2020). In this case, digital government should be perceived as a tool to transform administrative processes and service delivery. It requires an implementation strategy based on an integrated approach so that the whole government is transformed (Glyptis et al., 2020). Bouaziz (2020a) noted that digital government relies on the idea that the alignment between digital government strategy and modernization strategy focusing on the public value creation is required to lead to the creation of public value, and that the digital government should be inscribed in a strategy of government organizations transformation based on the abilities of digital technologies. The author added that the evolution towards the digital government fits more under a paradigm shift of government organizations modernization, and change of management than an automatic application of digital technologies to existent processes, structures, and operational modes. However, Gong et al. (2020) noted that for many governments, adopting these technologies constitutes a new journey, as the scale and scope of the changes associated with their use are unclear. In fact, these technologies are disruptive in organizations and nations, changing traditional forms and altering the status quo. Gong et al. (2020) precise that "transformation in the public sector involves changes in the quality of certain social structures. Rather than a simple improvement in performance, it entails a fundamental change in the structures, processes, and/or culture of public sector organizations, which may involve the organizational structures of agencies, the administrative relationships between citizens using public services and the organizations providing them, or changes in the bureaucratic culture and external relationships between agencies". Therefore, the governments' use of digital technologies should be combined with organizational changes to improve the structures and operations of government organizations. To do so, an isolated view of these changes without considering the complex institutional setting of the public sector will underestimate the challenges throughout the digital transformation of government organizations (Gong et al., 2020). Glyptis et al. (2020) added that e-government implementation is not a straightforward process but a more complex procedure necessitating a mix of micro and macro factors: technological, institutional and organizational, social and cultural, economic, as well as legal and political. Accordingly, the reformation of the government organizations and their transformation into digital governments are required in order to enhance efficiency, effectiveness, accountability and transparency, improving communication and access to information. This will require a management of the government organizations' digital transformation that take into account uncertainties and failure risks of these endeavors. In fact, despite all the benefits that result from transforming the government organizations into digital organizations, in practice, this transformation remains a difficult task (Glyptis et al., 2020) prone to failure (Gong et al., 2020). Furthermore, it is not certain to achieve the e-government benefits due to the risky nature of e-government initiatives and the many risk factors that impediment their implementation (Bouaziz, 2006; Choudhari et al., 2007; Evangelidies, 2004; Heeks, 2003; Peharda et al., 2011; Weerakkody et al., 2015).

Risk and Failure Risk in E-Government Projects

Based on the literature on project management and information systems, Bouaziz (2006) defined e-government projects as temporary organizations, designed and set up to meet specific objectives' change within the government organizations by the introduction of ICTs. As in all types of projects, financial resources, technical means and human skills are deployed to lead these projects under constraints related to schedule, budgets and quality. Conducting these endeavors is not always successful. Choudhari et al. (2007) revealed that e-government suffers from cost and time overruns and unmet functional specifications due to inherent risk in it. Accordingly, e-government projects are unique undertakings that involve a degree of uncertainty, and are inherently risky (Choudhari et al., 2007). The complexity and broad scope of these projects make that risks are found in many areas.

Heeks (2003) divided e-government initiatives into three main situations:

- *Total failure*: the initiative is never implemented or is implemented but immediately abandoned.
- *Partial failure*: the initiative's major goals are not attained and/or there are significant undesirable outcomes.

- *Success*: most stakeholder groups attained their major goals and did not experience significant undesirable outcomes.

According to the same author, "major goals are the main objectives a group wanted to achieve with the initiative", whereas "undesirable outcomes are unexpected outcomes that a group did not want to happen but which did happen». Thus, an e-government project is successful if it is completed within budget, within schedule, and conforms to stakeholders' requirements.

Two categories of criteria to assess the success of e-government are in use (Bouaziz & Chaabouni, 2013; Choudhari et al., 2007). These criteria are related to the success of the project (Product Performance) and the success of the project management process (Process Performance).

The success of the project is synonymous to the success of the product delivered, which should meets stakeholders' expectations (project team, users of systems from public employees and external users, project sponsors). Choudhari et al. (2007) proposed using six items to measure product performance: the system meets functional specifications, the system design conforms to the specified standards, the developed application is reliable, the system meets intended through put and response time, the system meets user expectation with respect to ease of use and the system meets security requirements.

The success of the project management process assesses the degree of development process' success in completion to the project. Four measures are used (Choudhari et al., 2007): the developed system is flexible to support new product and user needs, the developed application is reliable, the project is completed on schedule, the system is developed within budget.

The implementation of e-government projects is a daunting task, since they involve many factors of risk that hinder their success. Risk is investigated in several fields. It is interpreted from two perspectives (March & Shapira, 1987; Lyytinen et al., 1998), namely the economic perspective and the managerial perspective. From the economic perspective, risk is the variation in the distribution of possible outcomes, their probabilities and their subjective values. Risk is a probabilistic concept that can have both negative and positive consequences. It is defined as "a discrete occurrence that may affect the project for better or worse and it consists of two components: probability and impact on the project. Accordingly, risk can be written as function of these two variables risk=f (probability, impact)" (Peharda et al., 2011).

From the managerial perspective, risk is rather associated with the magnitude of poor results or losses (March & Shapira, 1987). For managers, only the threat of negative consequences is taken into account, while uncertainty about the positive consequences is not considered as an important aspect of risk (March & Shapira, 1987).

The managerial perspective of risk is adopted in the case of e-government projects. For example, Bouaziz (2006) defined risk as a negative gap between the projects' objectives and the real situation. This gap results from negative consequences that act on the process of project realization, and lead to impacts generating a cost for the organization. Recent studies defined risks of social media use, as referring to the possible threat or damage or insecurity of using the social media services. They are the negative or unwanted consequences that arise after the government has started using these tools (Falco & Kleinhans, 2018; Khan et al., 2014).

The negative consequences include budget and schedule overruns, poor quality systems, user's dissatisfaction, and systems abandon (Bouaziz, 2006). For Willcocks and Margetts (1994), risk refers to exposure to such consequences as failure so as to obtain some or all of anticipated benefits due to implementation difficulties, implementation time much longer and/or costs much higher than expected, technical systems performance significantly below the estimate and incompatibility of the system with selected hardware and software. These negative consequences induce negative impacts or losses supported by e-government project stakeholders. Willcocks and Margetts (1994) insisted on the fact that the risk of a negative consequence becomes a salient problem only when it is relevant to stakeholder concerns and interests. Different settings and stakeholders will see different outcomes as salient. The OECD (2014) mentions an ecosystem that includes several stakeholders: government actors, non-governmental organizations, businesses, citizens' associations and individuals. All of them are threatened by negative impacts once an e-government project fails. Barki et al. (1993) enumerated eleven impacts / losses that the organization would support when an information system is not implemented or has operational problems (Table 1). Heeks (2003) identified six categories of potential costs of e-government failure, which are direct and indirect financial costs, opportunity costs, political costs, beneficiary costs and future costs (Table 1).

Table 1. Impacts of e-government failure

<table>
<tr><th>Impacts on the organization when a developed IS is not implemented or it has operational problems (Barki et al., 1993)</th><th>Potential costs of e-government failure
Heeks (2003)</th></tr>
<tr><td>• Financial health</td><td>• Direct Financial Costs. The money invested in equipment, consultants, new facilities, training programs, etc.
• Indirect Financial Costs. The money invested in the time and effort of public servants involved.</td></tr>
<tr><td>• Organizational efficiency</td><td rowspan="2">• Beneficiary Costs. The loss of benefits that a successful e-government project would have brought.</td></tr>
<tr><td>• Profitability</td></tr>
<tr><td>• Reputation of the information system department</td><td rowspan="3">• Political Costs. The loss of 'face' and loss of image for individuals, organizations and nations involved in failure.</td></tr>
<tr><td>• Reputation of the user department</td></tr>
<tr><td>• Organizational image</td></tr>
<tr><td>• The survival of the organization</td><td rowspan="5">• Future Costs. An e-government failure increases the barriers for future e-government projects. It does this in two main ways. First, through loss of morale of stakeholders, particularly e-government champions, who may 'defect' to the private sector or overseas. Second, through the loss of credibility and loss of trust in e-government as an approach to change. This increases risk aversion in some stakeholders; and provides support for others with vested interests in the status quo.</td></tr>
<tr><td>• Market share</td></tr>
<tr><td>• Customer relations</td></tr>
<tr><td>• Competitive position</td></tr>
<tr><td>• Ability to carry out current operations</td></tr>
<tr><td></td><td>• Opportunity Costs. The better ways in which that money could have been spent, if it were not spent on the e-government failure</td></tr>
</table>

The negative consequences arise due to risk factors. They induce negative impacts supported by e-government project stakeholders. Risk factors are those factors that act negatively on the result of e-government projects and hinder their success (Bouaziz, 2006). They comprise all the factors that reduce the chances of success of an e-government project. These are the key elements to control in order to reduce the risk of projects' failure.

To summarize the previous developments, the figure 2 is elaborated. It proposes a conceptualization of the concept of e-government risk according to the managerial perspective.

Figure 2. The concept of risk according to the managerial perspective

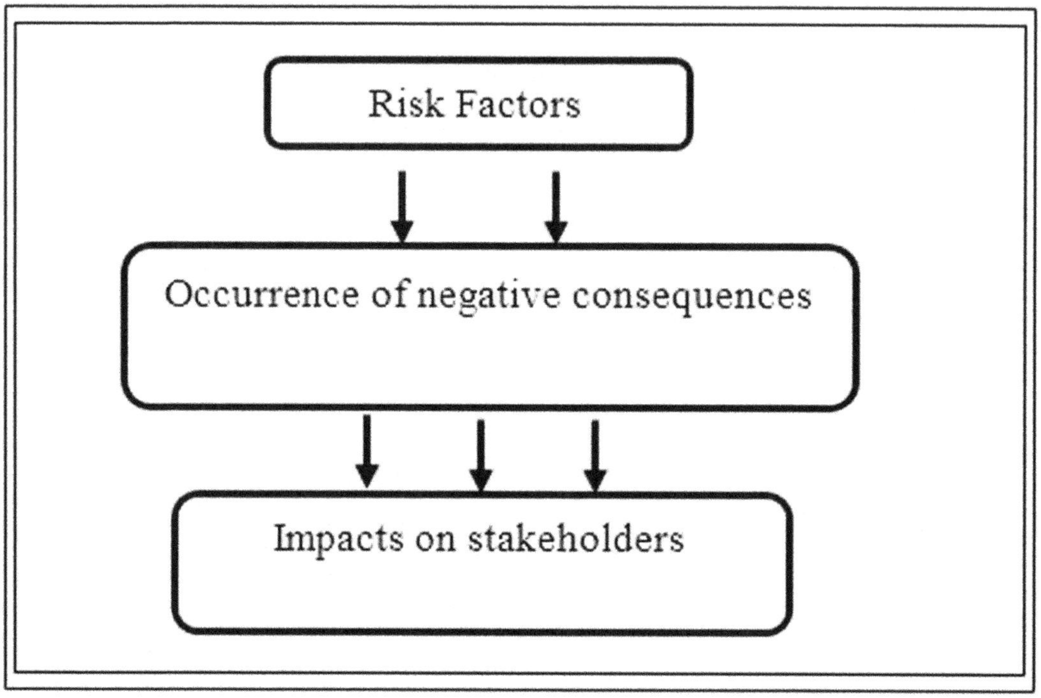

Risk Management and Risk Assessment in E-Government

Risk management is one of the most important steps in the process of project management (Gomes et al., 2020). It must be done during the project's whole life cycle, from planning and design to implementation and maintenance. It is an iterative process including several steps notably, risk identification and analysis, assessment and prioritization, risk treatment, risk monitoring and control, and capitalization as well as risk documentation.

Gomes et al. (2020) noted that risk management in project allows, through corrective actions, to direct the manager to the intended objective, without the risk spread being of great relevance. According to these authors, identifying and assessing risk factors in a project is the most important risk management step. Thus, identifying risk factors and adopting measures to mitigate them is decisive in the course of this process since risk factors are the key elements to be controlled by projects managers and are subject to counter measure strategies. Kefallinos et al. (2009) have described several methodologies for risk assessment. These methodologies are based on:

- Qualitative methodologies: e.g. preliminary risk analysis or hazard analysis (PHA), Hazard and operability (HAZOP).
- Tree-based methodologies: e.g. management oversight risk tree (MORT), Safety management organization review technique (SMORT).

- Dynamic systems methodologies: e.g. Go method; Digraph matrix / fault graph analysis.

Other methodologies for e-services risk assessment include the Consultative, Objective and Bi-functional Risk Analysis (COBRA), the End-to-End Security Assessment (EESA) and the Operationally Critical Threat, Asset and Vulnerability Evaluation (OCTAVE) (Kefallinos et al., 2009).

Along all of these methodologies for risk assessment, risk factors identification is a fundamental step. However, based on a systematic literature review on costs, opportunities, benefits and risks that influence the implementation of e-government, Weerakkody et al. (2015) found that a moderate number of studies have examined e-government risks and that not many of them have considered risks in an empirical form of research. The authors explained their findings by the lack of a focused approach on risk-related issues since measuring risk was not the ultimate aim of most studies.

METHODOLOGY

This research aims to identify the risk factors of e-government projects. To achieve this aim, a literature review on risk and risk factors assessment of e-government is made. Papers that have a clear focus on risk of e-government or concern risks related to the implementation of ICTs in the government organizations are sought after being based on key words such as: e-government risks, failure risk, e-government risk assessment, risk management methodology, information systems and public/ government organizations. This allows finding in the literature some frameworks specifically dedicated to e-government risk factors identification and assessment. Although they are low in number, they have been generated based on different theoretical perspectives and empirical methodologies to propose methods, checklists as well as toolkits and to assist e-government risk factors identification and risk assessment. Then, a content analysis of the selected works is done to bring out all the risk factors and risk factors categories mentioned by authors. Nvivo Software is used to identify the most cited risk factors categories and to place the risk factors under these categories. In fact, redundancies and similarities among these factors have been found. This allows elaborating, in a final step, a synthesis by proposing a list of risk factors categories and their components in terms of risk factors. This leads to the proposition of a framework of e-government risk factors, exposed in the following section.

PROPOSITION OF A FRAMEWORK OF E-GOVERNMENT RISK FACTORS, PROJECT PERFORMANCE AND IMPACTS ON STAKEHOLDERS

To analyze information systems projects risks, Willcocks and Margetts (1994) deployed an analytical framework based on organizational change perspective by Pettigrew et al. (1985, 1991, 1992). Six conceptual, interplaying categories are brought by the authors to investigate information systems risk factors. History, internal and external contexts directly or indirectly affect IT related change in terms of content and processes. Together, they lead to various outcomes that include cost, time, technical performance, operational efficiency, stakeholder impact, user acceptance, satisfaction and/or usage. Heeks (2003) suggested that central to e-government success and failure is the amount of change between "where we are now" and "where the e-government project wants to get us". "Where we are now" means the current realities of the situation. "Where the e-government project wants to get us" means the model or conceptions and assumptions built into the project's design. According to the author, e-government success and failure depends on the size of gap that exists between "current realities" and "design of the e-government project". The larger this design-reality gap, the greater the risk of e-government failure, and vice versa. Heeks (2003) proposed a model based on the notion of gaps and the seven dimensions: Information, Technology, Processes, Objectives and values, Staffing and skills, Management systems and structures, and other resources. These dimensions are summarized by the "ITPOSMO". They are used to understand the design-reality gaps and success or failure of e-government. Evangelidis (2004) proposed "FRAMES" as a framework for risk assessment and modelling in e-government services. He accepted that any electronic government transaction service should be seen as a socio-technical system that comprises three socio-technical subsystems interconnecting four main modules of the transaction service project. These four main modules are the customers, the e-service, the organizational level, and the intra-organizational service. FRAMES provide a way of implementing risk assessment in e-services. For the purpose of his study, Evangelidis (2004) proposed a classification of risk factors that surround e-government projects based on five categories, which are the Societal, Technical, Economical, Political and Security. Bouaziz (2006) made a comparison between the risk factors of software projects and the failure or success factors of e-government. She revealed similarities in factors between the two streams of research. In addition, the author introduced the insufficiency of organizational capabilities as another category of risk factors. Thus, she proposed three categories of risk factors in government-to-government projects. The first category includes the risk factors related to the project (size and complexity that can be associated with the content of technological change). The second category includes the risk factors related to the insufficiency of organizational capabilities in the alignment between the organizational strategy and the e-government strategy, in expertise and competencies, in the ICT infrastructure and in the engagement of the project stakeholders. The third category is composed by the risk factors related to the relationship among public agencies, and includes collaboration absence and information retention. Choudhari et al. (2007) proposed a risk assessment model of risk dimensions that surround e-governance projects. Factors related to bureaucracy, political leadership support and government organization culture are some of the important aspects that require close investigation and understanding. Identified categories of risk factors include System Specification, Planning, Technology and Technical Aspects, e-Governance Organization, and Stakeholders. Kefallinos et al. (2009) presented a model of a tool tailored risk measurement specifically for e-government projects. The model included a wide range of relevant risk factors and seven associated dimensions to compute risk. They proposed a Risk–Impact–Probability–CSF–Counter measures–Cost–Coverage (RIPC[4]) matrix that serves as a checklist assessment tool aimed to be used by key ICTs and security governance actors, during the planning, design and implementation phases, in a periodic and iterative manner. According to the authors, risk areas in e-government projects are situated at several levels, including Political level; Managerial level; Service staff level; Contactor(s) level; End-users level; Social level; Existing operational policies/procedures; Legal/regulatory level, Financial level, Procurement level, and Interoperability level. Peharda et al. (2011) introduced a methodology for risk assessment and corresponding costs in e-government projects based on Bayesian network. According to this author, Bayesian network or belief network is a powerful tool for knowledge representation and reasoning under uncertainty conditions. The purpose of this methodology is to assess probability of risk occurrence and corresponding costs in e-government. In order to identify risks, the authors have used challenges for e-government initiatives. The primary challenges were grouped into five categories according to their core aspect: information and data, information technology, organizational and managerial, legal and regulatory, as well as institutional and environmental. Loukis and Charalabidia (2011) presented an empirical study of risk factors of large government information systems projects in the Greek public sector. The analysis identified 21 risk factors that influenced information systems related to e-government project implementation. 'Incomplete-Problematic-Vague' request for proposals and insufficient information systems personnel were identified as the two highest relative frequency risk factors.

With the evolution of digital technologies, government organizations is more and more oriented to adopt social media networks and web 2.0 applications to implement two-way communication channels with citizens. Researchers have in turn investigated the risks, challenges, problems, and other issues associated to social media use by government organizations. Thus, Picazo-Vela et al. (2012) have studied the perceived risks and benefits of social media among public servants from Mexico, and especially the strategic elements to include social media in e-government policy as a communication channel with citizens. In order to understand the risks and benefits associated with social media, they apply an existing conceptual framework used to understand key dimensions influencing digital government applications (Gil-Garcia, et al., 2007; Luna-Reyes, et al., 2010). The layers included in the framework are general context, institutional framework, inter-organizational collaboration and networks, organizational structures and processes, information and data, and ultimately technology. Zheng (2013) investigated through a qualitative inductive approach the risk factors of micro blogging. They distinguished five dimensions: social and economic, political, legal and policy, organizational and managerial, information related, and technological. Sivarajah and Irani (2013) also built a conceptual framework including the risks of web 2.0 applications. Five categories of risk factors were adopted, which are political and legal, reputational, security, societal, and technical. Khan et al. (2014) have developed and tested a risk–benefit model of social media use in the public sector. The considered risk factors were time, psychological, social, and privacy. Falco and Kleinhans (2018) employed a snowball approach to search in literature the challenges associated with social media communication with citizens. They distinguish between challenges and risks since risks arise at a later stage in default of addressing challenges. Examples of risks include intellectual property or copyright infringement, psychological consequences, identity theft, public criticism, the time amount spent by government employees on social media while at work, system failures and downtime. The authors think that the ability to address challenges would reduce and mitigate risks. After literature review, they identify the following challenges/ risk factors:

- Internal/ Direct and Indirect challenges: Availability of social media strategy and policy guidelines, Data management, technology and proper understanding of benefits, Organizational reputation, Organization structure and culture, Availability of trained personnel, expertise, cost justification.
- External Direct and Indirect challenges: Digital divide and inaccessibility, Complexity and speed of social media change (data protection, privacy and ownership), Accuracy, completeness, and format of social media data coming from the public, Institutional framework, laws and regulations.

In summary, the following conclusions are advanced:

- There is not much research specifically dedicated to risk and risk factors identification of e-government;
- Despite research scarcity, there is a steady interest of researchers in these issues over time: the works having been exposed above span since 1994 to date;
- The investigated studies rely on different theoretical perspectives (e.g. sociotechnical perspective; organizational change perspective) and empirical approaches-if there is. This adds difficulties

when comparing these works' results. However, authors have proposed risk factors and risk factors categories that overlap.

- With the evolution of digital technologies, risk factors are extended to include factors related to external issues like Digital divide and inaccessibility, Complexity and speed of social media change (data protection, privacy and ownership), Accuracy, completeness, format of social media data coming from the public, and ultimately privacy and security.
- Table 2 shows a summary of the findings concerning risk factors and proposes risk factors categorization. Risk factors are aggregated into seven categories: Managerial and Organizational; Technology and Technical Aspects; Political, Legal and Regulatory; Project Characteristics; Information and Data, Stakeholders risks factors and Environmental, Social/ societal. These categories are described in Figure 3, elaborated with the help of Nvivo Software. The number of encoded elements designs the areas in this figure. A larger area indicates a higher number of encoded elements. Thus, it appears that the most referenced risk factors in the analyzed papers belong respectively to the category of organizational and managerial risk factors, then technology and technical, as well as political, legal, and regulatory categories. The risk factors, which belong to the categories named stakeholders, project characteristics, and environmental, social and societal are mentioned in an equal manner. The information and data risks are the least cited category of risk factors.

Figure 4 exposes a framework for risk factors categories, negative consequences on project performance and negative impacts on e-government stakeholders. Through this framework, the author formulates five propositions, as follows:

- Proposition 1: Risk factors induce negative consequences on the performance of the e-government project management process.
- Proposition 2: Risk factors induce negative consequences on the e-government product performance.
- Proposition 3: Negative consequences on the performance of the e-government project management process lead to negative impacts on the stakeholders of e-government projects.
- Proposition 4: Negative consequences on the e-government product performance lead to negative impacts on the stakeholders of e-government projects.
- Proposition 5: the risk of e-government projects failure can be mitigated if countermeasures to treat risk factors are adopted in advance.

SOLUTIONS AND RECOMMANDATIONS

From the above sections, it appears that, despite the various benefits that e-government offers, it is not always successful. The author thinks that the deployment of a risk management process allowing a proactive analysis that anticipates problems and implements actions to avoid them needs to be performed. Risk management is a standard practice in the management of any project. It ensures the achievement of projects' objectives and contributes to reduce their failure risk. A risk assessment to identify risk factors, negative consequences on project performance (process management and product), and impacts

Figure 3. Risk factors categories by number of encoded elements

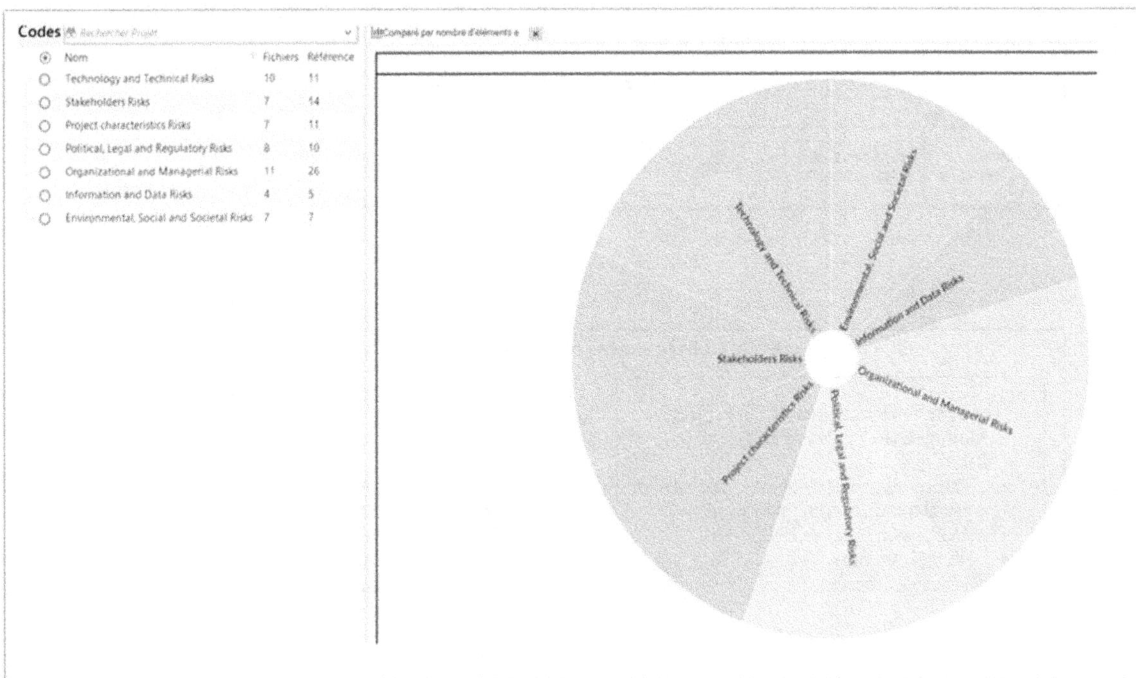

on stakeholders should highlight the potential risks and their impacts. Through this theoretical chapter, the author recommended that risk management of e-government should be integrated through the whole life cycle of the project since the stapes of feasibility, design, implementation, and maintenance. It should be considered as a critical activity in the process of digital government development and digital transformation of government organizations. Moreover, risk factors identification should concern all the stakeholders of e-government projects, particularly with the adoption of social media networks and other digital devices in the activities of interaction and communication of the government organizations with business, citizens, and civil society. For this reason, the risk-factors stakeholders category is identified independently from other categories of risk factors.

Moreover, analysis showed that the most referenced risk factors in the analyzed papers belong respectively to the category of organizational and managerial risk factors, then technology and technical, and political, legal, and regulatory categories. The risk factors, which belong to the categories named stakeholders, project characteristics, and environmental, social and societal are mentioned equally. The information and data risks are the least cited category of risk factors. Finding that organizational and managerial risk factors are the most cited by authors corroborates the idea that the transformation of government into e-government is not only a technical issue and that digital technologies must not be the objective in themselves. Yet, they are to be considered as an enabler of the digital transformation of the public sector. This digital transformation is not a straightforward process. However, it should be holistically approached as a more complex 'journey' of organizational changes that includes a factors' mix: organizational, managerial, institutional and technological, social and cultural, economic, as well as legal and political.

Figure 4. A framework of e-government risk factors, project performance and impacts on stakeholders

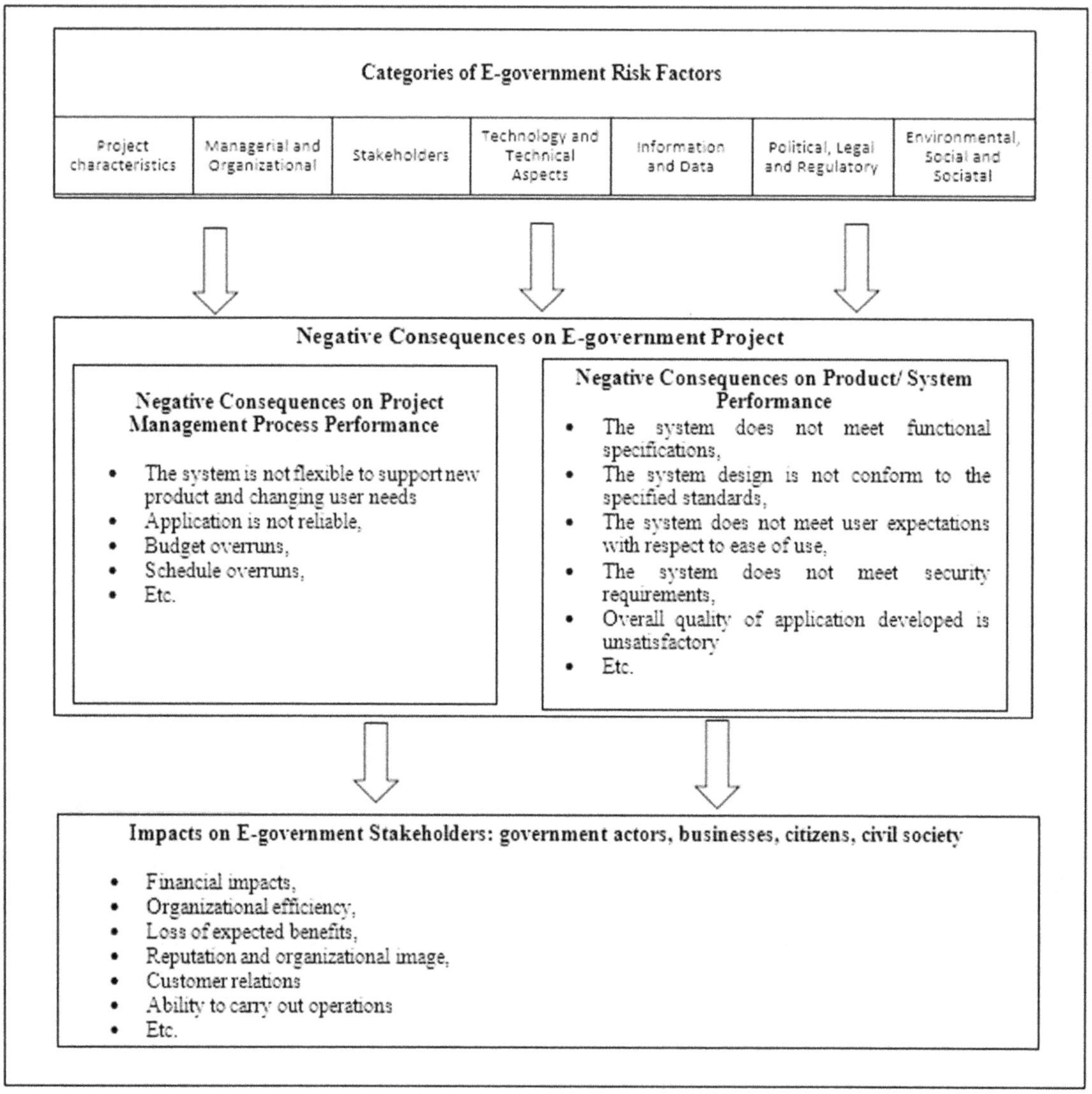

Gong et al. (2020) ascertained that understanding and predicting the development of digital transformation is important for policymakers, government executives, researchers, and all individuals who prepare, make, implement, or evaluate digital government decisions. This chapter draws attention to a particular aspect in which digital government and digital transformation of government organizations should rely on a digital transformation strategy that is aligned with an overall strategy of government organizations reformation. However, previous researchers reported the difficulty to obtain this alignment due to the complexity of digital transformation endeavors and unclear impacts of digital technologies as enablers of organizational changes that occur on different organizational levels. Based on case studies of e-government projects carried out by Tunisian government organizations, Bouaziz and Chaabouni (2012) revealed that a dynamic approach to e-government alignment was adopted in the case of the projects that

Table 2. Risk factors categories

Risk factors categories	Definitions and Examples	Authors
Project characteristics	The risk factors related to the project: size and complexity that can be associated with the content of technological change: • Large size of the project • Project complexity • System Specification • Many heterogeneous technologies in the project • Problematic – obsolete technical specifications • Problematic - vague project scope • Financial (Very high cost of the project)	• Willcocks and Margetts (1994) • Evangelidis (2004) • Bouaziz (2006) • Choudhari et al. (2007) • Kefallinos et al. (2009) • Loukis and Charalabidis (2011) • Peharda et al. (2011)
Managerial and Organizational risk factors	Managerial: refers to factors as • Planning (referring to the risks that erupt from estimation of cost, schedule and milestones) • Availability of social media strategy and policy guidelines • Incomplete - problematic - vague project implementation plan • Lack of alignment of organizational goals and project • Inappropriate project team • Insufficient users involvement • Lack of proper change management	• Willcocks and Margetts (1994) • Heeks (2003) • Bouaziz (2006) • Choudhari et al. (2007) • Kefallinos et al. (2009) • Loukis and Charalabidis (2011) • Peharda et al. (2011) • Picazo-Vela et al. (2012) • Sivarajah and Irani (2013) • Zheng (2013) • Falco and Kleinhans (2018)
	Organizational (structures and procedures): includes characteristics of the organization itself such as strategy, structure, rewards system, management, and human resources. They include factors as: • Organization structure and culture • Lack of processes and organizational structures redesign • Lack of clear general and IS strategy of the organization, creating problems as to the orientation of the project • Lack of organizational readiness and capabilities • Lack of knowledge • Lack of resources • Manager's attitudes and behavior • Users or organizational diversity, • Multiple or conflicting goals • Resistance to change • Turf and conflicts	
Stakeholders risk factors	End-users: factors that are related to government employees, such as • Availability of trained personnel • Expertise • User point of view • Meet expectations of users • Time risk • Psychological risk	• Willcocks and Margetts (1994) • Bouaziz (2006) • Choudhari et al. (2007) • Kefallinos et al. (2009) • Loukis and Charalabidis (2011) • Peharda et al. (2011) • Picazo-Vela et al. (2012) • Khan et al. (2014) • Flaco and Kleinhans (2018)
	Staff level includes: • Friendliness of the system to the staff • Communication skills of the staff • Suitable technical background • Incentives for effective and secure use of the system by the staff • Shift of power due to use of new technologies and knowledge (can create barriers, closed groups, competition) • Change of duties which may be required by organizational or procedural modifications • Fears for job loss by the adoption of new technologies and procedures • Staff-to-end-user interface (procedures, ease of access) – staff point of view	
	Inter-organizational / interagency Risks: • Information retention • Absence of inter-agency collaboration • No exploitation of the IS that will be developed in the project by other public organizations • Intergovernmental relationships • Inter-organizational collaborations and networks	
	Contractors: • Incomplete - problematic -vague RFP – Contract • Networks with low performance and/or very high operating cost • Contactor(s) level ICT skills and technology expertise	
	Procurement: • Timely procurement procedures • Warehousing and asset management	

continued on following page

Table 2. Continued

Risk factors categories	Definitions and Examples	Authors
Technology and Technical Aspects	Security and Privacy • Lack of critical - personal data protection • Low emphasis on the security of the IS to be developed • Inappropriate behavior • Loss of control and vulnerability to hackers • Security issues • Privacy risk • Hackers and "water army"	• Heeks (2003) • Evangelidis (2004) • Choudhari et al. (2007) • Kefallinos et al. (2009) • Loukis and Charalabidis (2011) • Peharda et al. (2011) • Picazo-Vela et al. (2012) • Sivarajah and Irani (2013) • Zheng (2013) • Falco and Kleinhans (2018)
	Technology: • Complexity and speed of social media change (data protection, privacy and ownership) • Inadequate maintenance and support of the IS after the end of the project • Many heterogeneous technologies in the project • Usability • Technological incompatibility • Technology complexity • Technology newness • Technological substitution	
	Interoperability: • Lack of interoperability with existing or under development IS infrastructure • Technology integration planning • Lack of standards • Backwards compatibility with existing systems	
Information and Data	• Data management • Accuracy, completeness, and format of social media data coming from the public • Information and data quality • Dynamic information needs • Repetition of content in several platforms • Reliability of the information published by governments • Dispersion of a message in the different channels • Lack of information or updated information • Access to data • Integrity and validity of the information • Some information is sensitive and cannot be distributed • Setting of a process to organize, structure, and distribute the data in the network	• Heeks (2003) • Peharda et al. (2011) • Picazo-Vela et al. (2012) • Falco and Kleinhans (2018)
Political, Legal, Regulatory	Political level: these risks highlight the implications that government policies or decisions could have on the government organization. Risk may also arises from the leadership at political and managerial level. • Supporting resolve and decision making • Long-term, unified support • Technology culture of political leadership • Project familiarization of political leadership (high-level) • Funds allocation (high-level) Jurisdiction conflict resolution between government agencies • Policy and political pressures	• Willcocks and Margetts (1994) • Evangelidis (2004) • Kefallinos et al. (2009) • Peharda et al. (2011) • Picazo-Vela et al. (2012) • Sivarajah and Irani (2013) • Zheng (2013) • Falco and Kleinhans (2018)
	Legal and Regulatory: • Institutional framework, laws and regulations • Restrictive laws and regulations • One year budgets • Intergovernmental relationships • Existing procedures (department or local government guidelines, procedures and funding arrangements)	
Environmental, Social/ Societal	Environmental risk: this refers to risks that usually affect the way individuals live and interact in society with the use of technology. • Environmental context (social, economic, demographic)	• Evangelidis (2004) • Kefallinos et al. (2009) • Peharda et al. (2011) • Picazo-Vela et al. (2012) • Sivarajah and Irani (2013) • Khan et al. (2014) • Falco and Kleinhans (2018)
	Digital Divide: • Technological and digital illiteracy impacts the understanding of web and social networks • Digital divide and inaccessibility	

involve different government organizations. In fact, the difficulty of aligning e-government projects for all stakeholders has led Tunisian government organizations to choose, as a first step, partial alignment built around key stakeholders. Doing so, the key stakeholders created "islands of alignment" and passed beyond others ("islands of non-alignment") for which the alignment hasn't yet been built. Therefore, the alignment of digital government projects is to ensure under a digital transformation strategy, which in turn should take into account the risks and uncertainties surrounding digital government projects through a detailed section dedicated to e-government risk management.

FUTURE RESEARCH DIRECTIONS

In this chapter, the author has chosen to focus only on studies emphasizing e-government risk factors to elaborate a conceptual framework of e-government risk factors, the negative consequences on projects and the negative impacts on their stakeholders. The limitation of this chapter is that it is only theoretical and the number of the analyzed papers is small. However, given the gap in the area of e-government research on e-government risk factors, the conceptual framework proposed here can be considered as a first step to enhance awareness on the various risk factors, their negative consequences on the project deployment and impacts on e-government stakeholders. Thus, for future research directions, it may be appropriate that researchers investigate e-government risk factors using empirical research. A qualitative approach based on multiple case studies allows testing the formulated propositions and drawing conclusions about risk factors categories of e-government projects and their failure risk.

Alternatively, researchers can investigate further studies on e-government barriers and success/ failure factors and the literature on ICTs' projects risks in economic enterprises so as to elaborate a sounder list of the e-government risk factors and categories. Digital strategy for digital government transformation and its alignment with business strategy is another direction for research. How to build such alignment-is a question that merits to be studied particularly that digital government projects imply several stakeholders.

CONCLUSION

The aim of this chapter was to propose a conceptual framework for e-government risk assessment through a literature review of papers specifically focusing on e-government risks. It builds on the statement by Weerakkody et al. (2015) highlighting research gaps in this field. To achieve this objective, a literature review on digital government, digital transformation and digital strategy is firstly carried out. It shows that digital government is a bi-dimensional concept that encompasses e-democracy dimension and e-government dimension. Moreover, it reveals that digital government should be inscribed in a strategy of government organizations transformation that takes advantages of the abilities of digital technologies perceived as a tool to transform administrative processes and service delivery. It requires an implementation strategy based on an integrated approach so that the whole government can be transformed.

Then, papers on e-government risk factors were analyzed. Although limited in number, a list of seven categories of risk factors was identified: Managerial and Organizational; Technology and Technical Aspects; Political, Legal and Regulatory; Project Characteristics; Information and Data, Stakeholders risk factors, and Environmental, Social/ Societal. The negative consequences on the e-government project and their impacts on the stakeholders were also highlighted. At a theoretical level, this work reveals the criticality of the risk factors' category named Managerial and Organizational. Consequently, this highlights the necessary management of digital transformation of government organizations and the subsequent organizational and managerial changes. In addition, Stakeholders risk factors' category was proposed independently of other categories of risk factors. This will allow better assessment of this risk factors category and better identification of appropriate counter measures to deal with it, especially that digital government projects require the collaboration of several stakeholders.

At a managerial level, policy makers and managers of digital government projects can use the developed conceptual framework as a diagnostic tool of the risks involved in e-government projects, which will help in better risk identification and management. The list of risk factors, negative consequences on the project deployment and impacts on e-government stakeholders will help in developing a dynamic knowledge base to take new e-government risk factors in account and successfully lead digital transformation of government organizations.

REFERENCES

Alcaide–Muñoza, L., Rodríguez–Bolívara, M. P., Cobob, M. J., & Herrera–Viedmac, E. (2017). Analysing the scientific evolution of e-Government using a science mapping approach. *Government Information Quarterly*, *34*, 545–555. doi:10.1016/j.giq.2017.05.002

Barki, H., Rivard, S., & Talbot, J. (1993). Toward an Assessment of Software Development Risk. *Journal of Management Information Systems*, *10*(2), 203–225.

Bouaziz, F. (2006). Managing e-government projects failure and risks. *7th International Business Information Management (IBIMA) Conference.*

Bouaziz, F. (2020a). From E-government to Digital Government: the Public Value Quest in the Tunisian Public Administration. In V. Ponnusamy, K. Rafique, & N. Zaman (Eds.), *Employing Recent Technologies for Improved Digital Governance* (pp. 107–127). IGI Global.

Bouaziz, F. (2020b). Digital government competences for digital public administration transformation. In K. Sandhu (Ed.), *Leadership, Management, and Adoption Techniques for Digital Service Innovation* (pp. 244–263). IGI Global.

Bouaziz, F., & Chaabouni, J. (2012). A framework to analyze the alignment of e-government projects. *International Journal of Electronic Government Research*, *8*(2), 75–90. doi:10.4018/jegr.2012040104

Bouaziz, F., & Chaabouni, J. (2013). Criteria for assessing the success of e-government projects. In E-Government Success Factors and Measures: Concepts, Theories, Experiences, and Practical Recommendations. Centro de Investigacin y Docencia Econmicas, Mexico.

Choudhari, R. D., Banwet, D. K., & Gupta, M. P. (2007). Identifying Risk Factors in for E-governance Projects. In A. Agarwal & V. V. Ramana (Eds.), *Foundations of E-government* (pp. 270–277). Computer Society of India.

Evangelidis, A. (2004). FRAMES-A Risk Assessment Framework for e-Services. *Electronic. Journal of E-Government*, *2*(1), 21–30.

Falco, E., & Kleinhans, R. (2018). Beyond Information-Sharing. A Typology of Government Challenges And Requirements For Two-Way Social Media Communication With Citizens. *The Electronic. Journal of E-Government*, *16*(1), 18–31.

Gil-Garcia, J. R., Dawes, S. S., & Pardo, T. A. (2018). Digital government and public management research: Finding the crossroads. *Public Management Review*, *20*(5), 633–646. doi:10.1080/14719037.2017.1327181

Gil-Garcia, J. R., Pardo, T. A., & Baker, A. (2007). Understanding context through a comprehensive prototyping experience: A tested research strategy for emerging technologies. In *Proceedings of the 40th. Hawaii International Conference on System Sciences*. Waikoloa, HI: IEEE Computer Society

Glyptis, L., Christofi, M., Vrontis, D., Del Giudice, M., Dimitriou, S., & Michael, P. (2020). E-Government implementation challenges in small countries: The project manager's perspective. *Technological Forecasting and Social Change*, *152*, 1–11. doi:10.1016/j.techfore.2019.119880

Gomes, D. F., da Eira Dias, A. S. M., da Costa Abreu, A. J. F. P., & Guitiss Navas, H. V. (2020). Organizational and Methodological Influence of Risk Management in Projects. *International Congress on Engineering - Engineering for Evolution*, 209-221. DOI 10.18502/keg.v5i6.7035

Gong, Y., Yang, J., & Shi, X. (2020). Towards a comprehensive understanding of digital transformation in government: Analysis of flexibility and enterprise architecture. *Government Information Quarterly*, *37*, 1–13. doi:10.1016/j.giq.2020.101487

Heeks, R. (2003). Most eGovernment-for-Development Projects Fail: How Can Risks be Reduced? *iGovernment Working Paper Series*. http://idpm.man.ac.uk/publications/wp/igov/index.shtml

Heilig, L., Lalla-Ruiz, E., & Voß, S. (2017). Digital transformation in maritime ports: Analysis and a game theoretic framework. *NETNOMICS: Economic Research and Electronic Networking*, *18*(2-3), 227–254.

Kefallinos, D., Lambrou, M. A., & Sykas, E. D. (2009). An Extended Risk Assessment Model for Secure E-Government Projects. *International Journal of Electronic Government Research*, *5*(2), 72–92.

Khan, G. F., Swar, B., & Kon Lee, S. (2014). Social Media Risks and Benefits: A Public Sector Perspective. *Social Science Computer Review*, *32*(5), 606–627. doi:10.1177/0894439314524701

Liu, D., Chen, S., & Chou, T. (2011). Resource fit in digital transformation: Lessons learned from the CBC Bank global e-banking project. *Management Decision*, *49*(10), 1728–1742. doi:10.1108/00251741111183852

Loukis, E., & Charalabidis, Y. (2011). Why Do e-Government Projects Fail? Risk Factors of Large Information Systems Projects in the Greek Public Sector: An International Comparison. *International Journal of Electronic Government Research*, *7*(2), 59–77. doi:10.4018/jegr.2011040104

Luna-Reyes, L. F., Gil-Garcia, J. R., & Celorio-Mansi, J. A. (2010). *Reporte de Resultados de Talleres con Directores de Informática Municipales*. Universidad de las Américas Puebla-INFOTEC.

Luna-Reyes, L. F., Gil-Garcia, J. R., & Cruz, C. B. (2007). Collaborative digital government in Mexico: Some lessons from federal web-based interorganizational information integration initiatives. *Government Information Quarterly*, *24*(4), 808–826.

Lyytinen, K., Mathiassen, L., & Ropponen, J. (1998). Attention shaping and software risk- a categorical analysis of four classical risk management approaches. *Information Systems Research*, *9*(3), 233–255.

March, J. G., & Shapira, Z. (1987). Managerial perspectives on risk and risk taking. *Management Science*, *33*(11), 1404–1418.

Matt, C., Hess, T., & Benlian, A. (2015). Digital Transformation Strategies. *Business & Information Systems Engineering*, *57*(5), 339–343. doi:10.100712599-015-0401-5

Meijer, A., Rodríguez Bolívar, M.P., & Gil-Garcia, J.R. (2018). From E-Government to Digital Era Governance and Beyond: Lessons from 15 Years of Research into Information and Communications Technology in the Public Sector. *Journal of Government organizations Research and Theory*, 1-6.

OECD. (2014). *Recommendation of the Council on Digital Government Strategies*. Retrieved from http://www.oecd.org/gov/digital-government/Recommendation-digital-government-strategies.pdf

Peharda, P., Munđar, D., & Vrček, N. (2011). Methodology for risk assessment and corresponding costs in e-government projects. *Proceedings of the 22nd Central European Conference on Information and Intelligent Systems*, 335-342.

Peter, M. K., Kraft, C., & Lindeque, J. (2020). Strategic action fields of digital transformation: An exploration of the strategic action fields of Swiss SMEs and large enterprises. *Journal of Strategy and Management*, *13*(1), 160–180. doi:10.1108/JSMA-05-2019-0070

Picazo-Vela, S., Gutiérrez-Martínez, I., & Luna-Reyes, L. F. (2012). Understanding risks, benefits, and strategic alternatives of social media applications in the public sector. *Government Information Quarterly*, *29*, 504–511. doi:10.1016/j.giq.2012.07.002

Singh, A., & Hess, T. (2017). How Chief Digital Officers Promote the Digital Transformation of their Companies. *MIS Quarterly Executive*, *16*(1), 1–17.

Sivarajah, U., & Irani, Z. (2013). A theoretical model for the application of web 2.0 in e-government. *European, Mediterranean & Middle Eastern Conference on Information Systems (EMCIS2013)*, 1-18.

Vial, G. (2019). Understanding digital transformation: A review and a research agenda. *The Journal of Strategic Information Systems*, *28*(2), 118–144. doi:10.1016/j.jsis.2019.01.003

Warner, K. S. R., & Wäger, M. (2018). Building dynamic capabilities for digital transformation: An ongoing process of strategic renewal. *Long Range Planning*, *52*(3), 326–349. doi:10.1016/j.lrp.2018.12.001

Weerakkody, V., Irani, Z., Lee, H., Osman, I., & Hindi, N. (2015). E-government implementation: A bird's eye view of issues relating to costs, opportunities, benefits and risks. *Information Systems Frontiers*, *17*, 889–915. doi:10.100710796-013-9472-3

Willcocks, L., & Margetts, H. (1994). Risk assessment and information systems. *European Journal of Information Systems*, *3*(2), 127–137.

Zheng, L. (2013). Social media in Chinese government: Drivers, challenges and capabilities. *Government Information Quarterly*, *30*, 369–376. doi:10.1016/j.giq.2013.05.017

Zwass, V. (2006). The web-internet compound as the infrastructure of digital government. *Business Process Management Journal*, *12*(1), 7–12. doi:10.1108/14637150610643715

ADDITIONAL READING

Aichholzer, G. (2004). Scenarios of e-Government in 2010 and implications for strategy design, *Electronic. Journal of E-Government*, *2*(1), 1–10.

Bertot, J. C., & Jaeger, P. T. (2008). The E-Government paradox: Better customer service doesn't necessarily cost less. *Government Information Quarterly*, *25*, 149–154.

Ebrahim, Z., & Irani, Z. (2005). E-government adoption: Architecture and barriers. *Business Process Management Journal*, *11*(5), 589–611.

Hamid, B., Jhanjhi, N. Z., & Humayun, M. (2020). Digital Governance for Developing Countries Opportunities, Issues, and Challenges in Pakistan. In V. Ponnusamy, K. Rafique, & N. Zaman (Eds.), *Employing Recent Technologies for Improved Digital Governance*. IGI Global.

Kutsch, E., Denyer, D., Hall, M., & Lee-Kelley, E. (2012). Does risk matter? Disengagement from risk management practices in information systems projects. *European Journal of Information Systems*, *22*(6), 637–649.

Siddiquee, N. A. (2016). E-government and transformation of service delivery in developing countries: The Bangladesh experience and lessons, Transforming Government: People. *Process and Policy*, *10*(3), 368–390. doi:10.1108/TG-09-2015-0039

Smith, H. A., McKeen, J. D., & Staples, D. S. (2001). Risk Management in Information Systems: Problems and Potentials. *Communications of AIS*, (7), 1–29.

Sundberg, L. (2019). Electronic government: Towards e-democracy or democracy at risk? *Safety Science*, *118*, 22–32. doi:10.1016/j.ssci.2019.04.030

Twizeyimana, J. D., & Andersson, A. (2019). The public value of E-Government – A literature review. *Government Information Quarterly*, *36*(2), 167–178. doi:10.1016/j.giq.2019.01.001

Wallace, L., Keil, M., & Rai, M. (2004). Understanding Software Project Risk- A Cluster Analysis. *Information & Management*, *42*, 115–125.

KEY TERMS AND DEFINITIONS

Digital Government: A concept that has broadened in scope from an early focus on the use of ICTs for government administration to the more recent notion that information and technology influence administration, management, and governance.

Digital Technologies: These are mobile technologies, social media, the Internet of things, wireless technology, sensor networks, artificial intelligence, Big Data, nanotechnology, biotechnology, cognitive systems, renewable energy technologies and biometric software.

Digital Transformation: An ongoing process of using new digital technologies in everyday organizational life, which recognizes agility as the core mechanism for the strategic renewal of an organization's business model, collaborative approach, and eventually the culture.

Digital Transformation Strategy: Builds on a business-centric perspective to focus on the transformation of products, processes, and organizational aspects owing to new technologies. It has a cross-functional character and needs to be aligned with other functional and operational strategies.

E-Democracy: The use of ICTs to support the process of broad participation of citizens, and of those of them who represent others, in the debate, political discourse, surfacing and elaboration of societal issues, emergence of representation, polling, and voting.

E-Government: Refers to services provision and information dissemination through ICTs by government organizations to their stakeholders (other government organizations, citizens, businesses, and civil society). It is the use of ICTs by government organizations in their processes of information, communication, transaction, and decision-making.

Negative Consequences: Include budget and schedule overruns, poor quality systems, user's dissatisfaction, and systems abandon. They induce negative impacts or losses supported by e-government project stakeholders.

Risk Factors: Factors that act negatively on the result of e-government projects and hinder their success.

Risk Management: An iterative process including the steps of risk identification and analysis, risk assessment and prioritization, risk treatment, risk monitoring and control, and risk capitalization and documentation.

Undesirable Outcomes: Unexpected outcomes that a group did not want to happen but which did happen.

Chapter 5
Theoretical Context of E-Banking for Digital Enterprise Transformation

Tansif Ur Rehman
https://orcid.org/0000-0002-5454-2150
University of Karachi, Pakistan

ABSTRACT

E-banking offers an ever-alluring response to the pressures by its consumers for more products, services, and 24-hour access to accounts. Additionally, personal e-banking definitely made the banking process convenient as well as less time-consuming than ever before. Therefore, no more standing in the lines or using old check as well as stamp method to pay utility bills. Thus, facilitation has been extended in its true sense within the respective domain by banks across the globe. Digital enterprise transformation facilitates financial services organizations via enabling them to be more secure, compliant, as well as being digital. It modifies the experience of employees, partners, customers, and stakeholders. Theory and research both are important notions. Theory provides the basic structure of propositions and research provides the technique and method to fit the theory in a particular context. It also helps to bring modifications regarding the existing theories.

INTRODUCTION

The respective work focuses on exploring the theoretical context of e-banking for Digital Enterprise Transformation in contemporary era. The objective of respective study is to highlight as well as critically analyze the significant role of e-banking for Digital Enterprise Transformation with a theoretical perspective. To an extent, this study will facilitate in filling gaps of other studies as it focuses on exploring multifaceted theoretical aspects of respective phenomena.

Theory and research both are important notions (Collins, 2019). Theory provides the basic structure of propositions and research provides the technique and method to fit the theory in a particular context (Gottdiener, 2019). It also helps to bring modifications regarding the existing theories (Robbins et al.,

DOI: 10.4018/978-1-7998-8583-2.ch005

2018; Sarantakos, 2013). Theories guide our observations of the world (Lemert, 2019). A theory is never proven, though; the research can only provide support for a theory (Szakolczai, & Thomassen, 2019). However, research also can reveal weakness in theory and force researchers to modify the theory or develop a new and more comprehensive one (Inglis, & Thorpe, 2018; Cozby, 1997).

Theory refers to a logically interrelated set of propositions from which scientific uniformities are derived (Schroeder, 2018). A theory incorporates a handful speculation from which scientific generalizations have themselves been a derivative (Benzecry et al., 2017; Merton, 1967). Similarly, theory makes way to ease the understanding of the observation in an organized manner (Scott & Marshall, 2005). Moreover, theories are inherently based on facts, and it facilitates to trace the respective patterns. It not only gives a clear idea about a phenomenon, but it is diverse in nature (Jones, & Bradbury, 2017).

This means, that research also clarifies and reformulates theories and there remains interconnection between the two (Abrutyn, 2016). It is imperative that the researcher is well oriented simultaneously with theoretical and conceptual aspects of the respective research problem. By following an approach of the 'pertinence of theory' the pursuit of research problem becomes systematic and fruitful (Outhwaite, 2016).

MAIN FOCUS OF THE CHAPTER

Research encompassing e-banking for Digital Enterprise Transformation is an important area to investigate, as society has evolved in being more dependent on technology. The presented research has incorporated a theoretical context of e-banking for Digital Enterprise Transformation. Thus, the respective research builds a context around these aspects.

RESEARCH METHODOLOGY

The respective work focuses on exploring the theoretical context of e-banking for Digital Enterprise Transformation in contemporary era. The objective of respective study is to highlight as well as critically analyze the significant role of e-banking for Digital Enterprise Transformation with a theoretical perspective. To an extent, this study will facilitate in filling gaps of other studies as it focuses on exploring multifaceted theoretical aspects of respective phenomena. In this regards, the respective study type is qualitative and its nature is explanatory. Secondary academic sources have been used, i.e. past researches, reports, policy manuals, as well as dictionaries.

THEORETICAL CONTEXT OF E-BANKING

"Electronic banking is a form of banking in which funds are transferred through an exchange of electronic signals rather than through an exchange of cash, checks, or other types of paper documents (Encyclopedia, 2020). According to Banka Ekonomike (2020), "E-banking is a product designed for the purposes of online banking that enables you to have easy and safe access to your bank account". According to Sergey Yablonsky (2016), "All forms of banking services and transactions performed through electronic means. E-banking includes the systems that enable financial institution customers, individuals or businesses, to access accounts, transact business, or obtain information on financial products and services through a public or private network, including the internet".

According to various researches, new technology adopters generally earned higher incomes, worked longer hours, moved more frequently (i.e. more mobility) and also possessed more positive attitudes towards the change as compared with the non-adopters (Nazaritehrani & Mashali, 2020). The core issues that prevents the adoption of e-banking includes, the convenience aspects of service along with its compatibility with the customers existing lifestyle (Chao et al., 2019; Suh, 2002). A beneficial starting point in an attempt to resolve these issues is to obtain the customer's willingness towards new as well as emerging technology based delivery channels (Mahmood, 2019).

A significant number of researches have already identified the issues that affect consumers' attitudes and acceptance of new technology in financial service industry and types of consumers most likely to use these aspects (Rabiu et al., 2019). A significant factor for non-use, especially among older consumers was the preference for conducting financial affairs through a human (Sharma et al., 2019; Zeithaml & Gilly, 1987).

The comparisons between ATM usage in various European countries evidently found that the main concern of users included, fears over its security, possibility of machine breakdown, as well as running out of cash (Singanamalla et al., 2019). New technology requires complex understanding as well as mental capability. Thus, the technology may be difficult to manipulate due to limited capability of the firm employees (Dannenberg & Kellner, 1998). Technology readiness of firm also plays a significant role in their attitudes towards the technology itself (YuSheng & Ibrahim, 2019). Technology readiness is conceptualized as being a combination of both the positive as well as negative feelings towards technology (Agwu, 2018; Walker et al., 2002).

People's confidence sometimes improve their lives, or simply makes things more difficult as well as less secure (Hanafizadeh & Zare-Ravasan, 2018). Other researches have indicated that customer's attitude and beliefs about technology are correlated with their intention to use it (Chircu & Kauffman, 2002). Customers as well as banks are concerned about technical as well as technological issues for commercial usage of the internet (Khan et al., 2018). Zugelder, Flaherty, and Johnson (2000) have mentioned that customer protection is the major technical issue associated with e-marketing. Among other various things, the customer's protection issues can cover unfair and deceptive trade practices by the suppliers, unauthorized access, and usage by others, such as hacker, or system failures (Sakhdari & Burgers, 2018).

Customer's protection is very important for building online customer confidence (Shen & Cheung, 2018). Because, as there is no face to face contact and there is a great possibility, at least in customer's perception of the phenomenon, for having problems or making mistakes via the World Wide Web (Westland, 2002). One important factor that determines the level of demand for internet banking services is the number of people having access to the internet (Ahanger, 2011). Various other account's security related issues would affect customer preferences as well as loyalty towards the adoption of internet banking (Li et al., 2017).

Marketing as well as social psychology researches indicate that customers differ in type of relationship they wish to maintain with the service providers, such as the banks (Davcik & Grigoriou, 2016). This clearly implies that customers who desire social as well as psychological benefits by establishing personal relationships with the banks will prefer face to face interactions (Kajuju, 2016). Internet banking environment thus will have a detrimental effect on such customers (Kashmari et al., 2016). On the other hand, for those customers whose relationship is based on efficiency of the services, internet banking environment will be an ideal situation undoubtedly (Laukkanen et al., 2009).

Customers differ in type of relationships they intend to maintain with their service providers (Mahmoodi & Naderi, 2016). Reynolds, Chelazzi, and Desimone (1999) suggest that relationships have functional as well as social benefits. Another study concluded that customers vary on the value they place on these related benefits (Gwinner, Gremler, & Bitner, 1998). Various other theories related to customer's satisfaction affect the rate of adoption along with the degree of acceptance of any innovative service, like e- banking.

Rogers, Everett, and Shoemaker (1974) state that customers go through several stages in knowledge conviction and decision confirmation before they finally adopt any product or a service. Guiltinand and Donnelly (1983) emphasized on the very importance of awareness before adoption of any such innovative product. Contemporary banks appeared to have taken a cue from this aspect as the strategy of most of the banks have been to create wide spread awareness via its informational websites before launching onto a full scale transaction websites, as it helps a lot (Felix, 2014).

More focused research in the pertinent area of customer satisfaction and internet indicated that the product information content on web design along with web layouts were one of the major factors that affect customer's satisfaction (Nazaritehrani & Mashali, 2020; Doll et al., 1995; Doll, Xia, & Torkzadeh, 1994). Customer's confidence on internet banking would also largely depend on how the banks would deal with any false transaction and security concerns that may occur during e-banking (Chao et al., 2019). Stewart (1999) claimed that failure of the internet in retail banking is largely attributable due to lack of trust the consumers have in e-channels.

The opportunities from implementing web technology could be restricted, if there is a lack of customer's trust in the respective system (Rabiu et al., 2019). As, they view trust as an expectation of the ability to perform, reliability, and intention of a partner (Singanamalla et al., 2019). In this sense, trust has to be viewed as a behavioral intention or behavior that reflects dependence on other partner respectively (Mahmood, 2019). Morgan and Hunt (1994) defined trust as the very perception of confidence in exchange of partner's reliability as well as integrity. Both of the notions clearly underline the significance of confidence as well as reliability regarding the conception of the phenomenon 'trust'.

ADVANTAGES AND DISADVANTAGES OF E-BANKING

According to Nazaritehrani and Mashali (2020); Chao et al., (2019); Mahmood (2019); Rabiu et al., (2019); and YuSheng & Ibrahim (2020) the advantages as well as disadvantages of e-banking are enlisted.

Advantages

1. **Convenience:** Unlike a physical bank, online banking websites are never closed. As, they are available 24 hours a day, seven days a week, and they are only a mouse click away from the customer.
2. **Effectiveness:** Many of online banking websites now offer sophisticated tools, including account aggregation, portfolio managing programs, rate alerts, as well as stock quotes to facilitate customers to manage their assets more effectively than ever before.
3. **Efficiency:** Accessing and managing all bank accounts, including CDs, IRAs, and even securities are now reachable from one secure website.
4. **Pervasiveness:** Even if a customer is abroad, he can easily log on instantly to his online bank and take care of his business, whenever he needs it.

5. **Transaction speed:** Now, the online banks' websites execute and confirm the carried out transactions at or even swifter pace as compared to ATM processing speed.

Disadvantages

1. **Banks' website modifications:** Even the largest banks periodically upgrade their online programs to add new features in unfamiliar places. In some of the cases, the customer has to re-enter account information and it is a bit of inconvenient for the customer to do so.
2. **Learning curve:** Banking websites can be a bit difficult to navigate at first time. As, customers become familiar with these with the passage of time.
3. **Start-up time consumption:** In order to register for the bank's online program, the customer has to provide her/his ID and sign a form at a bank branch they have an account in.
4. **Trust factor:** The biggest hurdle to online banking is learning to trust it for many people. Questions that usually bother customers are; Is my transaction carried out? Did I push the transfer button twice?, etc.

ADOPTION ISSUES OF E-BANKING

Perceived (Anticipated) Risk

Perceived risk is very significant, as it can also force the customer to reject new internet banking services being offered (Nazaritehrani & Mashali, 2020). It is also related closely to reliability as well as system failure. Customers are always worried that technology-based service delivery systems will not work, as they expect them to do so (Mahmood, 2019). They also lack confidence that their problems will not be be solved quickly (Walker et al., 2002). Westland (2002) revealed that the transaction risk occurs when online markets fail to assure that service will be delivered with adequate quality and slow response time. After the internet interaction leads to a delay of service delivery, it causes customers to be unsure that their transaction was completed (Jun & Cai, 2001).

Registration Process Complexity

Conventional wisdom suggests that the account opening process at many banks seems to have become burdensome, due to heightened regulatory demands and compliance and control pressures. Banks today collect more customer information than ever before, follow a greater number of steps while on boarding, and ensure strict controls throughout the customer service life cycle (Temenos, 2017). Registration process is also an important aspect (Chao et al., 2019). As, it influences the customers to adopt internet banking services (Rabiu et al., 2019). It should be very simple as well as easy for the customer. As, the customer can reject or avoid e-banking due to the complex registration process of e-banking services.

Security of the System

Strong concerns about the security is one of the most common issue with regards to refraining from the usage of internet banking services (Sharma et al., 2019; Madu, 2002). Security's violation can lead to various other problems, such as destruction of operating systems, and even disruption of the information access (Min & Galle, 1999). Mostly, the customers are not satisfied with the infrastructure of the web security systems (YuSheng et al., 2019; Rotchanakitumnuai & Speece, 2003; Black et al., 2001). In the sphere of e-banking, security is one of the most significant future challenges as the customers fear higher risk in using the web for their financial transactions (Gerrard and Cunningham, 2003).

Internet users are very much concerned about their privacy issues, including transparency, collection, usage as well as disclosure of their personalized information (Singanamalla et al., 2019). This very concern primarily relates to the notion of authentication. Banking and finance industries report highest incidence of misuse directly related to these industries, as possessing one of the highest dependencies on computers at their workplaces (Agwu, 2018; Hutchinson, 2001).

Transaction's Reliability

Reliability involves the consistency of performance as well as dependability (Hanafizadeh & Zare-Ravasan, 2018). It means that the firm performs the service right the first time. It also means the firm honors its promises that are made (Khan et al., 2018). It involves (especially) the accuracy in billing and information, keeping correct records, and performing services at the designated time (McKinney, Yoon, & Zahedi, 2002; Zeithaml, Parasuraman, & Malhotra, 2002, 2000). Reliability is very much associated with the technical functioning of e-banking website. Particularly, the extent to which it is available and functioning properly, i.e. hassle free (Sakhdari& Burgers, 2020).

PERCEIVED RISKS IN E-BANKING

There is a higher-level of compliance risk, because of the ever-changing technology, i.e. amount of replicated errors and other pertinent issues (Kuak et al., 2019; Khan, 2009; Florina, Liliana, & Viorica, 2008). E-banking usually fails when customers perceive its services as unreliable and slow (Pedro et al., 2018; Furst et al., 2000).

According to Yang, Whitefield, and Boehme (2007), senior citizens also face problems while using e-banking because of the lack of confidence and familiarity with it. While, Kumar, Sareen, and Barquissau (2012) stress that the level of trust is directly associated with the adoption of e-banking.

In 1962, Everett Rogers presented 'Diffusion of Innovation Theory', and it stands as one of the oldest theories regarding adoption. He stressed that an individual must comprehend the thought, behaviour, and product as well as service as being innovative. Roger also believed that only through this diffusion is possible, which acts as a key to adoption (Rogers, 2003).

Baker (1999) states that because of fraud most of the people refrain from the adoption of e-banking. While, Attaran (1999) and Kawai (2019) claims that scams are the reason behind it. In Acohido and Swartz (2008) view, cyber hackers are the real threat to customers on the internet.

BACKGROUND OF MOBILE BANKING

Mobile Banking

It is a term associated with performing balance checks, account's transaction, and payments via mobile device (Nazaritehrani & Mashali, 2020). For more than 30 years, financial institutions have used different modes to satisfy their customers' need more conveniently. Automated teller machine (ATM) came, in New York's Chemical Bank (USA) on 2nd October, 1969 (Kirkpatrick, 2009).

Internet banking was launched in the mid-1990s, and it enabled customers to access their accounts by using a home computer with a simple internet connection. But, it faced slow as well as tentative growth as banks had to work out on technology issues and by building customer trust at instance. Mobile phones can be carried anywhere and by majority of people. Web-enabled functions further broadened its scope. Thus, making mobile phones an ideal medium by which various services by banks can be rendered (Sharma et al., 2018).

Short Message Service (SMS)

To some extent, mobile banking and SMS banking are synonymous terms, because SMS-banking uses text (content) messaging and it works in 'push' or a 'pull' mode (Chao et al., 2019; Rabiu et al., 2019). As in pull mode, the bank sends one-way text for alerting a mobile user of specific account and even for promoting new bank services. While, in push mode, the mobile user sends a text via a predefined code to a specific number and the bank responds back with a text message possessing the required information (Laudon & Traver, 2001).

WORLD OF CHANGING TECHNOLOGY AND MOBILE BANKING

The idea that technology has brought a lot of knowledge, economic benefits along with the freedom to masses is now an established fact (Ford, 2019). Experience to remain in connection and exchanging information about markets as well as quick learning to change business arrangements and techniques are now making business more profitable and attractive (Huang et al., 2019). It has enabled traders towards wide markets and has eased the efforts of doing any business, and it all has a positive impact on people's life (Timmers, 1999).

With the penetration of mobiles, new economic benefits are realized by markets by using them for the purpose of banking (Pedro, 2018). There is an immense need for venturing a banking model that works on the branchless banking concept, i.e. e-banking. The extent of customer reach through the mobile banking platform is enormous. It is directly linked to the number of customers that start using the mobile phone. The mobile industry is still expanding and the telecom companies have a long way to go and sell through aggressive pricing and new package offerings (Abdou, English, & Adewunmi, 2014).

The convenience offered through mobile banking is an even bigger driver for the use of this service. The most interesting trend is that even people who are unfortunately not educated are quite capable and smart about using cell phones and readily accept new features (Zhang & Lee, 2019). This interest of the new and undaunted task of getting used to the features on the mobile phone alone would be the real force behind the take up of mobile banking across the globe (Pedro, 2018).

There exists various devices on which e-banking is available, such as smartphones, tablets, laptops, desktops, smart LED TV, etc. While, "Cybersecurity is the protection of computer systems and networks from the theft of or damage to their hardware, software, or electronic data, as well as from the disruption or misdirection of the services they provide" (Schatz et al., 2017). The respective field of cybersecurity has also became more essential because of an enhanced dependency on internet, computer, as well as wireless networking like Wi-Fi and Bluetooth. In contemporary world, because of its complex nature, i.e. in terms of technology and politics, cybersecurity has also been a crucial challenge (Stevens, 2017).

In contemporary era, digital skills required by customers for interacting with e-banking have been made more convenient by the process of continuous improvements. Anyone who uses an android device can now easily carry out an online transaction. Online tutorials are also available along with printed brochures of banks to further facilitate e-banking. According to Digital Skills Global (2020), respective digital skills are required by employers regarding e-banking. Data science and data analytics, digital marketing, digital project management, element of uniqueness, digital business analysis, programming, web and app development, digital design and data visualization, social media, digital product management, and decision making for leaders. While, in accordance with Digital Marketing Institute (2020), six digital skills that will be needed to secure employees in future are advanced social selling, expert data analysis, multi-platform UX design, mobile expertise, creative thinking, network and information security.

THEORETICAL CONTEXT OF DIGITAL ENTERPRISE TRANSFORMATION

Stephanie Overby (2020) stated, "Ongoing digital transformation across industries became a given in 2019. At the same time, digital transformation fatigue also became very real." While, President of ISG (a global technology advisory as well as research organization), Steve Hall (2020) is of the view "2020 will still see the rapid scaling of digital initiatives across industries. In many areas, chief information officers and organizations have prepped their organizations for change but haven't made the full leap to transforming their culture to fully embrace the change."

Digital Enterprise Transformation is the incorporation of computerized technology into the domain of business. In a general sense, changing how a firm manages as well as deliver value to its consumers. In addition, it is the effect of ongoing sociocultural changes that require firms to repetitively challenge the existing parameters, experimentation, and become more comfortable with malfunctioning and even failure (The Enterprisers Project, 2020).

EIGHT ESSENTIALS IN DIGITAL ENTERPRISE TRANSFORMATION

According to The Enterprisers Project (2020), there exists eight essential Digital Enterprise Transformation trends that IT as well as business leadership should be aware of:

1. A shakeout (because of the investments in big data governance and analytic progression by competitors).
2. Swift adoption of digital operating models, that includes integrated cross-functional units.
3. New Digital Enterprise Transformation success metrics.
4. Ongoing acquisitions and mergers in the information technology outsourcing sector.

5. New digital partnerships should be formed by consultancies.
6. Enlargement of public cloud adoption.
7. Attention to long-term value of digital initiative.
8. Enhance use of machine learning and artificial intelligence.

ICTS AND DIGITAL ENTERPRISE TRANSFORMATION

Information and Communication Technologies-enabled transactions like, telemedicine, e-shopping, and social media that facilitates its consumers to have additional selection in how they interact, communicate, and shop (Rouse, 2019). For business organizations, progression within the domain of Information and Communication Technologies have surely provided ample opportunities, conveniences as well as cost savings (Allen, 2019).

Internet technologies are now even being utilized in higher education by digital learning management systems and have become a crucial as well as indispensable tool regarding educational learning activities (Al-Amoush & Sandhu, 2019). Enterprise Resource Planning (ERP) systems and their link with financial performance has also been discussed in great detail by scholars like Ayman Hassan Bazhair and Kamaljeet Sandhu (2015). While a user's experience is strongly related to perceived ease of usage as well as perceived usefulness to user motivation in user acceptance of Web-based eServices (Sandhu, 2008). Web-based electronic service, end-user adoption, as well as implementation necessitate an assessment of consumer contextual factors (Sandhu, 2009).

These benefits are cost cutting in highly automated businesses processes, data revolution in firms which are turning data generated by Information and Communication Technologies into insights that drive new services and products.

BANKING SECTOR AND DIGITAL ENTERPRISE TRANSFORMATION

Boston Consulting Group suggests that in order to build a digital transformation strategy, credit unions as well as banks should focus on respective pillars:

1. Leveraging the power of data
2. Reinventing a consumer's digital journey
3. Building an organization that is digitally driven
4. Redefining the existing operating model

(The Financial Brand, 2018).

Digital transformation is basically beyond just facilitating mobile as well as online functionality (Allen, 2019). Providers of traditional banking need to combine convenience along with digital speed that is compatible with human interaction (Pedro et al., 2018). It should be contemplative and protective at critical points in a consumer's journey.

While, four out of five financial organizations have a firm belief that digital transformation will essentially modify banking sector and completely transform the respective competitive landscape. According to the Boston Consulting Group 43% admit that their organization has not even formulated a digital strategy. Surprisingly, when it comes to digital transformation one-in-five executives of banking sector consider their credit union as well as organization as "market leading" (The Financial Brand, 2018).

CONTEMPORARY ERA AND DIGITAL ENTERPRISE TRANSFORMATION

Those banks which utilize Digital Enterprise Transformation can possibly attain competitive advantages to a great extent:

1. It unleashes innovation at scale and speed level.
2. Customer's upcoming needs are fulfilled.
3. Changing marketplace expectations are met by operational agility.

Digital Enterprise Transformation facilitates financial services organizations via enabling them to be more secure, compliant, as well as being digital (Allen, 2019). It modifies the experience of employees, partners, customers, and stakeholders (Schenkel, 2019).

SOLUTIONS AND RECOMMENDATIONS

After critically analyzing the subject matter under evaluation and going through previous researches the respective suggestions are proposed for strengthening the aspects encompassing e-banking for digital enterprise transformation in contemporary era. Security protections offered by banks should include the respective spheres, careful reference to authorized websites (in their publications), effective firewall implementation, minimum 128-bit encryption, padlock icon usage, i.e. evidence of security protection displayed on screens, secured protection of PINs and passwords, stated limits to the customer's liability for unauthorized use of the access codes, strong virus protection, verification via usage of digital certificates, etc. The respective governments should invite foreign investors via engaging them in bilateral contracts and investment plans encompassing e-banking. Banks should install hardened operating systems, i.e. the system's software as well as firewalls should be configured to the highest security settings in consistency with the level of protection as per the customer's requirement. Banks should conduct regular system as well as data integrity checks. Banks also need to implement more security to minimize the associated risks as to increase their customer's authentication, such as personal identification number and audit trial for transactions. Customers who are not be technologically sophisticated should be appealed by banks, as services should be simple enough to use. Private banks should develop a strong liaison with the respective government regarding the swiftness of their internet approach. More customized and featured mobile banking services should be introduced.

FUTURE RESEARCH DIRECTIONS

Significant areas for conducting future research encompassing e-banking for Digital Enterprise Transformation via engaging qualitative, qualitative, or eclectic approach can be, computer-focused as well as computer-assisted crimes, customer's preferences, consumer psychology, cyber security, perceived and actual risks, identification of e-banking related issues, issues in e-commerce sector, cyber security issues in e-commerce, gender adaptability of technology, perceived and actual risks in e-commerce, ease of doing business and the dilemma of cybercrime, foreign investments in ICT sector and its effect on cyber behavior, identification of ICTs related issues and e-fraud, issues encompassing online crimes and role of remittances in contemporary era.

CONCLUSION

Internet banking channel offers less waiting time with higher spatial convenience along with lower cost structure than traditional distribution channels used. The success of the internet banking can be gauged by identifying the number of current as well as the anticipated registered users. Internet banking allows customers to carry out financial transactions on a secure website operated by their retail or virtual bank. The onset of internet and the popularity of personal computers presented both an opportunity and a challenge for the banking industry. While, perceived risk can force the customer to reject e-banking services being offered. It is also related closely to reliability as well as system failure. The customer can also reject or avoid e-banking due to the complex registration process of e-banking services.

Strong concerns about the security are also one of the most common issues with regards to refraining from the usage of internet banking services. Reliability is very much associated with the technical functioning of e-banking website. All these respective factors can be an obstacle for an individual to associate with e-banking. Fierce competition among existing banks and technological innovation have truly enabled a wide range of banking services and products. Now the banks are in the forefront to improve product and efficiency via harnessing technology.

Technology itself is modifying relationships among banks along with its internal as well as external customers. With the advent of technology, barriers faced by many industries have been removed. Technology has brought superior products and channel's management with specialized focus on customer relationship in its true sense. The reason for rapid growth of internet and mobile banking is basically its acceptance as being an extremely cost-efficient delivery channel and access to accounts from anytime and anywhere thus required.

REFERENCES

Abdou, H. A., English, J., & Adewunmi, P. O. (2014). An investigation of risk management practices in electronic banking: The case of the UK banks. *Banks and Bank Systems, 9*(3).

Abrutyn, S. (2016). *Handbook of contemporary sociological theory*. Springer International Publishing. doi:10.1007/978-3-319-32250-6

Acohido, P., & Swartz, J. (2008). *Zero-day threat: The shocking truth of how banks and credit bureaus help cyber crooks steal your money and identity*. Union Square Press.

Agwu, E. (2018). The role of e-banking on operational efficiency of banks in Nigeria. *Basic Research Journal of Business Management and Accounts*, *6*(1), 1–10. doi:10.2139srn.3122498

Ahanger, R. G. (2011). An investigation into the determinants of customers' preferences and satisfaction of internet banking. *Journal of Applied Sciences*, *11*(3), 426–437. doi:10.3923/jas.2011.426.437

Al-Amoush, A. B., & Sandhu, K. (2019). A new model for acceptance of analytics in learning management systems at Jordanian universities (JLMS). In Modern Technologies for Teaching and Learning in Socio-Humanitarian Disciplines (pp. 138-161). IGI Global.

Allen, J. P. (2019). *Digital entrepreneurship*. Routledge. doi:10.4324/9780429506567

Attaran, M. (1999). Internet-based business opportunities: Buyers beware of scams. *Information Management & Computer Security*, *7*(4), 176–178. doi:10.1108/09685229910292682

Baker, C. R. (1999). An analysis of fraud on the internet. *Internet Research*, *9*(5), 348–360. doi:10.1108/10662249910297750

Bazhair, A. H., & Sandhu, K. (2015). Factors for the acceptance of enterprise resource planning (ERP) systems and financial performance. *System*, *14*(7), 16.

Benzecry, C. E., Krause, M., & Reed, I. A. (Eds.). (2017). *Social theory now*. University of Chicago Press. doi:10.7208/chicago/9780226475318.001.0001

Black, N. J., Lockett, A., Winklhofer, H., & Ennew, C. (2001). The adoption of Internet financial services: *A qualitative study. International Journal of Retail & Distribution Management*, *29*(8), 390–398. doi:10.1108/09590550110397033

Chao, X., Kou, G., Peng, Y., & Alsaadi, F. E. (2019). Behavior monitoring methods for trade-based money laundering integrating macro and micro prudential regulation: A case from China. *Technological and Economic Development of Economy*, *25*(6), 1–16. doi:10.3846/tede.2019.9383

Chircu, A. M., & Kauffman, R. J. (2002). Limits to value in electronic commerce- related I. T investments. *Journal of Management Information Systems*, *19*.

Collins, P. H. (2019). Intersectionality as critical social theory. *Duke University Press Books*.

Cozby, P. C. (1997). *Methods in behavioral research*. Mayfield Publishing Company.

Dannenberg, M., & Kellner, D. (1998). The bank of tomorrow with today's technology. *International Journal of Bank Marketing*, *16*(2), 90–97. doi:10.1108/02652329810206743

Davcik, N. S., & Grigoriou, N. (2016). How dynamic marketing capabilities affect market share performance output: An innovative brand oriented approach. In Groza M., Ragland, C. (Eds.), *Marketing challenges in a turbulent business environment. Developments in marketing science: Proceedings of the academy of marketing science*. Springer. 10.1007/978-3-319-19428-8_37

Digital Marketing Institute. (2020). *6 digital skills that will future-proof a workforce*. Retrieved from https://digitalmarketinginstitute.com/blog/6-digital-skills-that-will-future-proof-a-workforce

Digital Skills Global. (2020). *The top 10 digital skills tech companies are looking for today*. Retrieved from https://digitalskillsglobal.com/blog/the-top-10-digital-skills-tech-companies-are-looking-for-today

Doll, W. J., Raghunathan, T. S., Lim, J., & Gupta, Y. P. (1995). A confirmatory factor analysis of the user information satisfaction instrument. *Information Systems Research*, *6*(2), 177–189. doi:10.1287/isre.6.2.177

Doll, W. J., Xia, W., & Torkzadeh, G. (1994). A confirmatory factor analysis of the end-user computing satisfaction instrument. *Management Information Systems Quarterly*, *18*(4), 453–461. doi:10.2307/249524

E-Banking. (2020). In *Banka Ekonomike.* Retrieved from https://www.bekonomike.com/en/%C3%87ka-eshte-E-Banking-Inidividet

E-Banking. (2020). In *Encyclopedia.* Retrieved from https://www.encyclopedia.com/finance/encyclopedias-almanacs-transcripts-and-maps/electronic-banking

Felix, P. (2014). Prospects and challenges of electronic banking in Ghana: The case of Zenith Bank, Sunyani. *International Journal of Advances in Management. Economics and Entrepreneurship*, *1*(1), 6–14.

Florina, V., Liliana, M., & Viorica, I. (2008). *Risk management of e-banking activities.* Retrieved December 1, 2019, from http://steconomice.uoradea.ro/anale/volume/2008/v3-financesbanksaccountancy/160.pdf

Ford, D. H. (2019). *Humans as self-constructing living systems: A developmental perspective on behavior and personality*. Routledge.

Furst, K., Lang, W. W., & Nolle, D. (2000). *Internet banking: Developments and prospects.* Economic and Policy Analysis Working Paper, 1-58. Retrieved June 11, 2016, from http://199.83.40.54/publications/publications-by-type/economics-working-papers/2008-2000/wp2000-9.pdf

Gerrard, P., & Cunningham, B. (2003). The diffusion of internet banking among Singapore consumers. *International Journal of Bank Marketing*, *21*(1), 16–28. doi:10.1108/02652320310457776

Gottdiener, M. (2019). *The new urban sociology* (6th ed.). Routledge. doi:10.4324/9780429244452

Guiltinand, J. P., & Donnelly, J. H. (1983). The use of product portfolio analysis in bank marketing planning. In Management Issues for Financial Institutions. Academic Press.

Gwinner, K. P., Gremler, D. D., & Bitner, M. J. (1998). Relational benefits in services industries: The customer's perspective. *Journal of the Academy of Marketing Science*, *26*(2), 101–114. doi:10.1177/0092070398262002

Hall, S. (2020). *What is digital transformation?* https://enterprisersproject.com/what-is-digital-transformation

Hanafizadeh, P., & Zare-Ravasan, A. (2018). A model for selecting IT outsourcing strategy: The case of e-banking channels. *Journal of Global Information Technology Management*, *21*(2), 111–138. doi:10.1080/1097198X.2018.1462070

Huang, R., Spector, J. M., & Yang, J. (2019). Learning in the context of technologies. In *Educational Technology* (pp. 33–48). Springer. doi:10.1007/978-981-13-6643-7_2

Hutchinson, D., & Warren, M. (2001). *A framework of security authentication for internet banking.* Paper presented at the 3rd International Conference on Information Integration and Web-based Applications & Services, Linz, Austria.

Inglis, D., & Thorpe, C. (2018). *An invitation to social theory* (2nd ed.). Polity.

Jones, P., & Bradbury, L. (2017). *Introducing social theory* (3rd ed.). Polity.

Jun, M., & Cai, S. (2001). The key determinants of Internet banking service quality: A content analysis. *International Journal of Bank Marketing*, *19*(7), 276–291. doi:10.1108/02652320110409825

Kajuju, N. K. (2016). *The effect of electronic banking on liquidity of commercial banks in Kenya* (Unpublished doctoral thesis). School of Business, University of Nairobi, Kenya.

Kashmari, A., Nejad, A. H. G., & Nayebyazdi, A. (2016). Impact of electronic banking innovations on bank deposit market share. *Journal of Internet Banking and Commerce*, *12*(1), 1–12.

Khan, H. H., Ahmad, R. B., & Chan, S. G. (2018). Market structure, bank conduct and bank performance: Evidence from ASEAN. *Journal of Policy Modeling*, *40*(5), 934–958. doi:10.1016/j.jpolmod.2018.02.001

Khan, S. (2009). *Adoption issues of internet banking in Pakistani' firms* (Unpublished master thesis). Lulea University of Technology, Lulea.

Kirkpatrick, R. (2009). *1969: The year everything changed.* Skyhorse Publishing Inc.

Kuak, D., Dolezal, M., Kerous, B., Eichler, Z., Vasek, J., & Liarokapis, F. (2019). An interactive and multimodal virtual mind map for future workplace. *Frontiers in ICT (Lausanne, Switzerland)*, *6*, 12.

Kumar, M., Sareen, M., & Barquissau, E. (2012). Relationship between types of trust and level of adoption of internet banking. *Problems and Perspectives in Management*, *10*(1), 82–92.

Laudon, K. C., & Traver, C. G. (2001). *E-commerce: Business, technology, society*. Addison-Wesley.

Laukkanen, T., Sinkkonen, S., & Laukkanen, P. (2009). Communication strategies to overcome functional and psychological resistance to Internet banking. *International Journal of Information Management*, *29*(2), 111–118. doi:10.1016/j.ijinfomgt.2008.05.008

Lemert, C. (2019). *Social theory: The multicultural, global, and classic readings* (6th ed.). Routledge.

Li, Y., Spigt, R., & Swinkels, L. (2017). The impact of FinTech start-ups on incumbent retail banks' share prices. *Financial Innovation*, *3*(1), 26. doi:10.118640854-017-0076-7

Madu, A. A., & Madu, A. A. (2002). Dimension of e-quality. *International Journal of Quality & Reliability Management*, *19*(3), 246–258. doi:10.1108/02656710210415668

Mahmood, Y. N. (2019). The impact of quality service factors on banking service sector case study in Erbil banks. *Tikrit Journal of Administration and Economics Sciences*, *2*(42).

Mahmoodi, S., & Naderi, H. (2016). Assessment of modern banking services to achieve and realization of e-commerce and its impact on the profitability of banks listed on the Tehran stock exchange. *Modern Applied Science*, *10*(9), 263. doi:10.5539/mas.v10n9p263

McKinney, V., Yoon, K., & Zahedi, F. M. (2002). The measurement of web-customer satisfaction: An expectation and disconformation approach. *Information Systems Research*, *13*(3), 296–331. doi:10.1287/isre.13.3.296.76

Merton, R. K. (1967). *On theoretical sociology*. Free Press.

Min, H., & Galle, W. P. (1999). Electronic commerce usage in business-to-business purchasing. *International Journal of Operations & Production Management*, *19*(9), 909–921. doi:10.1108/01443579910280232

Morgan, R. M., & Hunt, S. D. (1994). The commitment-trust theory of relationship marketing. *Journal of Marketing*, *58*(3), 20–38. doi:10.1177/002224299405800302

Nazaritehrani, A., & Mashali, B. (2020). Development of e-banking channels and market share in developing countries. *Financial Innovation*, *6*(12), 12. Advance online publication. doi:10.118640854-020-0171-z

Outhwaite, W. (2016). *Social theory: Ideas in profile*. Profile Books.

Overby, S. (2020). *What is digital transformation?* https://enterprisersproject.com/what-is-digital-transformation

Pedro, C. P., Ramalho, J. J. S., & Silva, J. V. (2018). The main determinants of banking crises in OECD countries. *Review of World Economics*, *154*(1), 203–227. doi:10.100710290-017-0294-0

Rabiu, I. D., Ladan, S., Usman, H. A., & Garba, M. (2019). Impact of e-banking on the operational efficiency of banks in Nigeria. *International Journal of Academic Research in Business & Social Sciences*, *9*(2). Advance online publication. doi:10.6007/IJARBSS/v9-i2/5527

Reynolds, J. H., Chelazzi, L., & Desimone, R. (1999). Competitive mechanisms subserve attention in macaque areas V2 and V4. *The Journal of Neuroscience: The Official Journal of the Society for Neuroscience*, *19*(5), 1736–1753. doi:10.1523/JNEUROSCI.19-05-01736.1999 PMID:10024360

Robbins, S. P., Chatterjee, P., Canda, E. R., & Leibowitz, G. S. (2018). *Contemporary human behavior theory: A critical perspective for social work practice (What's new in social work)* (4th ed.). Pearson.

Rogers, E. M. (2003). *Diffusion of innovations* (5th ed.). Simon and Schuster.

Rogers, E. M., & Shoemaker, F. (1974). Communication of innovations: A cross-cultural approach. *Man*, *9*(2).

Rotchanakitumnuai, S., & Speece, M. (2003). Barriers to internet banking adoption: A qualitative study among corporate customers in Thailand. *International Journal of Bank Marketing*, *21*(6/7), 312–323. doi:10.1108/02652320310498465

Rouse, M. (2019). *ICT (Information and Communications technologies)*. https://searchcio.techtarget.com/definition/ICT-information-and-communications-technology-or-technologies

Sakhdari, K., & Burgers, J. H. (2018). The moderating role of entrepreneurial management in the relationship between absorptive capacity and corporate entrepreneurship: An attention-based view. *The International Entrepreneurship and Management Journal*, *14*(4), 927–950. doi:10.100711365-017-0477-0

Sandhu, K. (2008). E-services acceptance model (E-SAM). In *Advances in Computer and Information Sciences and Engineering* (pp. 224–229). Springer. doi:10.1007/978-1-4020-8741-7_40

Sandhu, K. (2009). Measuring the performance of the electronic service acceptance model (E-SAM). *International Journal of Business Information Systems*, *4*(5), 527–541. doi:10.1504/IJBIS.2009.025205

Sarantakos, S. (2013). *Social research*. Palgrave Macmillan. doi:10.1007/978-1-137-29247-6

Schatz, D., Bashroush, R., & Wall, J. (2017). Towards a more representative definition of cyber security. *Journal of Digital Forensics, Security and Law, 12*(2).

Schenkel, M. T., Farmer, S., & Maslyn, J. M. (2019). Process improvement in SMEs: The impact of harmonious passion for entrepreneurship, employee creative self-efficacy, and time spent innovating. *Journal of Small Business Strategy*, *29*(1), 64–77.

Schroeder, R. (2018). Social theory after the internet: Media, technology, and globalization. *UCL Press*. doi:10.2307/j.ctt20krxdr

Scott, J., & Marshall, G. (2009). *A dictionary of sociology* (3rd ed.). Oxford University Press. doi:10.1093/acref/9780199533008.001.0001

SharmaM.SharmaC.KhanA. (2019). *Smart ATM: Technology acceptance modeling and analysis*. doi:10.2139srn.3356363

Shen, L., & Cheung, S. O. (2018). How forming joint ventures may affect market concentration in construction industry? *International Journal of Construction Management*, *18*(2), 151–162. doi:10.1080/15623599.2017.1301026

Singanamalla, S., Potluri, V., Scott, C., & Medhi-Thies, I. (2019). PocketATM: Understanding and improving ATM accessibility in India. In *Proceedings of the Tenth International Conference on Information and Communication Technologies and Development*. ACM. 10.1145/3287098.3287106

Stevens, T. (2018). Global cybersecurity: New directions in theory and methods. *Politics and Governance*, *6*(2), 1–4. doi:10.17645/pag.v6i2.1569

Stewart, K. (1999). Transference as means of building trust in World Wide Web sites. *Proceedings of the 20th ICIS*.

Suh, H., & Han, I. (2002). Effect of trust on customer acceptance of internet banking. *Electronic Commerce Research and Applications*, *1*(4), 7–63. doi:10.1016/S1567-4223(02)00017-0

Szakolczai, A., & Thomassen, B. (2019). *From anthropology to social theory: Rethinking the social sciences*. Cambridge University Press.

Temenos. (2017). Top 5 regulatory burdens faced by banks. Retrieved from https://www.temenos.com/en/blog/2015/august/regulation-headaches/#

The Enterprisers Project. (2020). What is digital transformation? https://enterprisersproject.com/what-is-digital-transformation

The Financial Brand. (2018). *The four pillars of digital transformation in banking*. https://thefinancialbrand.com/71733/four-pillars-of-digital-transformation-banking-strategy/

Timmers, P. (1999). *Electronic commerce: Strategies and models for business-to-business trading*. Wiley and Sons Ltd.

Walker, R. H., Craig-Lees, M., Hecker, R., & Francis, H. (2002). Technology- enabled service delivery: An investigation of reasons affecting customer adoption and rejection. *International Journal of Service Industry Management, 13*(7), 91–106. doi:10.1108/09564230210421173

Westland, C. (2002). Transaction risk in e-commerce. *Decision Support Systems, 33*(1), 187–103. doi:10.1016/S0167-9236(02)00010-6

Yablonsky, S. (2016). *Intermediaries in E-Commerce. Encyclopedia of E-Commerce Development.* Implementation, and Management., doi:10.4018/978-1-4666-9787-4.ch005

Yang, J., Whitefield, M., & Boehme, K. (2007). New issues and challenges facing e-banking in rural areas: An empirical study. *International Journal of Electronic Finance, 1*(3), 336. doi:10.1504/IJEF.2007.011503

YuSheng, K., & Ibrahim, M. (2019). Service innovation, service delivery and customer satisfaction and loyalty in the banking sector of Ghana. *International Journal of Bank Marketing, 37*(5), 1215–1233. doi:10.1108/IJBM-06-2018-0142

Zeithaml, V. A., & Gilly, M. C. (1987). Characteristics affecting the acceptance of retailing technologies: A comparison of elderly and non-elderly consumers. *Journal of Retailing, 63*(1), 49–68.

Zeithaml, V. A., Parasuraman, A., & Malhotra, A. (2000). *A conceptual framework for understanding e-service quality: Implications for future research and managerial practice.* Marketing Science Institute, Working paper report no. 00-115.

Zeithaml, V. A., Parasuraman, A., & Malhotra, A. (2002). Service 1uality delivery through websites: A critical review of extant knowledge. *Academy of Marketing Science Journal, 30*(4), 3620–3675. doi:10.1177/009207002236911

Zhang, J. H., & Lee, J. H. (2019). Beyond the Hawthorne research: Relationship between IT company employees' perceived physical work environment and creative behavior. In *International Conference on Software Engineering Research, Management and Applications* (pp. 147-159). Springer.

Zugelder, M. T., Flaherty, T. B., & Johnson, J. P. (2000). Legal issues associated with international Internet marketing. *International Marketing Review, 17*(3), 253–271. doi:10.1108/02651330010331651

ADDITIONAL READING

Akhlaq, M. A. (2011). Internet banking in Pakistan: Finding complexities. *Journal of Internet Banking and Commerce, 16*(1), 1–14.

Allen, J. P. (2019). *Digital entrepreneurship.* Routledge. doi:10.4324/9780429506567

Anas, N., Zulkipli, S. N., Noor, M. S. M., Noh, A. M. M., Ariff, M. I. M., Ghazali, Z. M., & Rosli, H. M. (2019). *Usefulness and effectiveness of mind mapping: An analysis of CTU101 and CTU151.*

Benson, V., Morgan, S., & Filippaios, F. (2014). Social career management: Social media and employability skills gap. *Computers in Human Behavior, 30*, 519–525. doi:10.1016/j.chb.2013.06.015

Briley, D. A., Livengood, J., Derringer, J., Tucker-Drob, E. M., Fraley, R. C., & Roberts, B. W. (2019). Interpreting behavior genetic models: Seven developmental processes to understand. *Behavior Genetics, 49*(2), 196–210. doi:10.100710519-018-9939-6 PMID:30467668

Chavan, J. (2013). Internet banking - Benefits and challenges in an emerging economy. *International Journal of Research in Business Management, 1*(1), 19–26.

Chen, S. (2001). *Strategic management of e-business*. Wiley and Sons.

Eisenmann, T., & Trispas, M. (Eds.). (2002). *Internet business models: Text and cases*. McGraw-Hill Irwin.

Ford, D. H. (2019). *Humans as self-constructing living systems: A developmental perspective on behavior and personality*. Routledge.

Government of Pakistan. Ministry of Finance. (2018). *Economic Survey of Pakistan 2017-18*. http://www.finance.gov.pk/survey/chapters_18/overview_2017-18.pdf

Guiltinand, J. P., & Donnelly, J. H. (1983). The use of product portfolio analysis in bank marketing planning. In Shanmugam and Burke (Eds.). Management Issues for Financial Institutions, p. 50.

Hamel, G. (2000). *Leading the revolution*. Harvard Business School Press.

Huang, R., Spector, J. M., & Yang, J. (2019). Learning in the context of technologies. In *Educational Technology* (pp. 33–48). Springer. doi:10.1007/978-981-13-6643-7_2

Hutchinson, D., & Warren, M. (2001). *A framework of security authentication for internet banking*. Paper presented at the 3rd International Conference on Information Integration and Web-based Applications & Services. Linz, Austria: Austrian Computer Society.

Kawai, N. (2019). Historical transition of psychological theories of fear: The view of fear in behaviorism. In *The Fear of Snakes* (pp. 1–18). Springer. doi:10.1007/978-981-13-7530-9_1

Kettunen, J., & Makela, J. P. (2019). Practitioners' conceptions of ethical practice in social networking in career services. *International Journal for Educational and Vocational Guidance, 19*(3), 345–362. doi:10.100710775-018-9383-4

Kirkpatrick, R. (2009). *1969: The year everything changed*. Skyhorse Publishing Inc.

Komba, M. M., & Lwoga, E. T. (2020). Systematic review as a research method in library and information science. In *Handbook of Research on Connecting Research Methods for Information Science Research* (pp. 80–94). IGI Global. doi:10.4018/978-1-7998-1471-9.ch005

Krishnamurthy, S. (2003). *E-commerce management: Text and cases*. Thompson Learning.

Kuak, D., Dolezal, M., Kerous, B., Eichler, Z., Vasek, J., & Liarokapis, F. (2019). An interactive and multimodal virtual mind map for future workplace. *Frontiers in ICT (Lausanne, Switzerland), 6*, 12.

Nupur, J. M. (2010). E-banking and customers' satisfaction in Bangladesh: An analysis. *International Review of Business Research Paper, 6*(4), 145–156.

Omar, S., & Tajudeen, F. P. (2020). The influence of career adaptability and career commitment to minimize intention to leave among ICT professionals. *International Journal of Human Capital and Information Technology Professionals, 11*(2), 23–38. doi:10.4018/IJHCITP.2020040102

Pedro, C. P., Ramalho, J. J. S., & Silva, J. V. (2018). The main determinants of banking crises in OECD countries. *Review of World Economics, 154*(1), 203–227. doi:10.100710290-017-0294-0

Rajenderan, M., & Zawawi, D. (2019). Leaky pipeline syndrome in information and communication technology (ICT) industry of Malaysia: A conceptual study on female career barriers and retention management. *International Journal of Academic Research in Business & Social Sciences, 9*(2). Advance online publication. doi:10.6007/IJARBSS/v9-i2/5672

Rayport, J. F., & Jaworski, B. (2001). *Electronic commerce.* McGraw-Hill.

Schenkel, M. T., Farmer, S., & Maslyn, J. M. (2019). Process improvement in SMEs: The impact of harmonious passion for entrepreneurship, employee creative self-efficacy, and time spent innovating. *Journal of Small Business Strategy, 29*(1), 64–77.

Vondracek, F. W., Lerner, R. M., & Schulenberg, J. E. (2019). *Career development: A life-span developmental approach.* Routledge. doi:10.4324/9781315792705

Zeithaml, V. A., Parasuraman, A., & Malhotra, A. (2000). *A conceptual framework for understanding e-service quality: Implications for future research and managerial practice.* MA: Marketing Science Institute, Working paper report no. 00-115.

Zhang, J. H., & Lee, J. H. (2019). Beyond the Hawthorne research: Relationship between IT company employees' perceived physical work environment and creative behavior. In *International Conference on Software Engineering Research, Management and Applications* (pp. 147-159). Springer.

KEY TERMS AND DEFINITIONS

Adoption Issues: The act of embracing ideas or technology.

Banking: The services offered by a bank.

Digital Enterprise Transformation: Strategies by which organizations take advantage of information technology to develop digital capabilities.

E-Banking: Online banking, i.e. via the internet.

Enterprise: A business or company.

ICTs: Technologies that provide access to information through telecommunications.

Perceived Risks: Uncertainty a consumer has while using electronic services.

Reliability: The quality of being trustworthy.

Strategy: A plan of action designed to achieve a long-term or overall aim.

Theory: An idea or set of ideas that is intended to explain facts or events.

Transformation: A marked change in form, nature, or appearance.

Chapter 6
A New Digital Service Tax for the Transformation of the Taxation Architecture in Turkey

Deniz Şahin Duran
Economic and Administrative Sciences Faculty, Gaziosmanpaşa Üniversity, Turkey

ABSTRACT

A series of necessary structural transformation has started to be implemented in Turkey with the new economic program described under the heading of "New Economy Program: Structural Transformation Steps 2019." In the field of tax transformation of these structural transformation steps, some studies have been carried out towards the creation of "New Tax Architecture." Within the scope of these studies, a new tax application under the name of "digital service tax" is designed. In fact, this step taken by the government of Turkey for the taxation of digital services is parallel to the developments in the world. In this study, for the better understanding of the necessity/importance of digital service tax and what kind of tax application is it, digital service tax planned to be implemented in Turkey is evaluated with its all aspects and in line with the developments in the world.

INTRODUCTION

We are the witnesses to an age in which the existing tax systems are inadequate for the taxation of novel business and trade models arising from the sweeping and day-to-day changes and advancements in the digital economy, which has become a topical issue as a result of the integration of technology and economics. The inability to duly tax the income generated by digital economic activities despite the fact that this income has reached significant levels has forced institutions and organizations like the OECD and the EU as well as national governments to take action. In this respect, there are efforts to regulate national and international taxation guidelines and taxation practices suitable for novel business and trade models. One of the topics coming to the fore as a result of these efforts is the digital services tax (DST). The reason behind the prominence of the issue is that in parallel with the digitalization of

DOI: 10.4018/978-1-7998-8583-2.ch006

economies in the present day, many countries in the world have sought to tax digital services as they have significant tax potential.

On the other hand, a series of necessary structural transformations have started to be implemented in Turkey within the scope of a new economic program delineated under the title "The New Economic Program: Steps for Structural Transformation 2019". Concerning the issue of tax transformation within these steps for structural transformation, there have been certain initiatives to establish the "New Taxation Architecture". Within the scope of said initiatives, a brand-new taxation practice called the "digital services tax (DST)" is envisaged. Essentially, this step taken by the Turkish government to introduce taxes on digital services is in parallel to global developments.

Taking the intensive use of digital services in the economy of Turkey into consideration, one might argue that the taxation of digital services may lead to the realization of considerable tax potential. In order to clarify the necessity/importance and nature of the digital services tax, the present study aims to evaluate the digital services tax envisaged to be implemented in Turkey in light of global developments, taking the subject, basis, rate, and exceptions of the tax into account, and considering all its aspects. In this respect, the study initially puts forward a general overview of global developments regarding digital services and their taxation. Then, it continues by providing detailed information about and an assessment of the taxation transformation in Turkey within the scope of "The New Economic Program: Steps for Structural Transformation 2019" and the digital services tax to be levied as a part of these steps.

GLOBAL DEVELOPMENTS CONCERNING DIGITAL SERVICES AND THEIR TAXATION

The Concept of Digital Services and the Issue of the Taxation of Digital Services

Emerging with the World Wide Web (WWW) only 25 years ago, the concept of digitalization has brought about the nature of innovativeness and product development in addition to the interaction between producers and consumers, triggering a profound transformation in existing industries. As of 2020, the number of connected devices in the world is expected to reach 30 billion. According to the World Economic Forum (WEF), the approximate value of this digital transformation is estimated to reach US$ 100 trillion by 2025. The EU is also expected to reap the benefits resulting from this transformation upon taking its strategic connection goals for 2025 within the framework of its Digital Single Market strategy. As the value of 5G and the EU data market exceeds US$ 106 billion in 2020, it is estimated that European industries such as production, energy, automobile, and healthcare might optimize their infrastructures and services for the "Internet of Things" (cited in Bozdoğanoğlu & Kaya, 2019: 1650). The digital transformation stemming from the development of digital means such as analytical tools, mobile devices, and cloud computing has resulted in the emergence of novel needs and new business domains, gave speed to economic activities, and established the digital economy (Yüce & Akbulut, 2018: 105). In other words, the influence of the process of digitalization on the content and functioning of the economy through various channels has brought about the concept of "digital economy". In his book titled "The Digital Economy: Promise and Peril in the Age of Networked Intelligence" in which he coins the term, Tapscott (1996) identified 12 distinctive features of the digital economy. Looking at the emergence of the concept of the digital economy, the process was triggered with the notional elimination of the distance between individuals and the change in the nature of goods and services as a result of the advancements in information and communication technologies in recent years. In addition to these advancements, issues such as the ways of corporate organization, production methods, and marketing strategies have been redefined and the digital transformation has become a reality owing to the proliferation of digital goods and e-commerce. The digital economy has emerged as a result of this transformation process (cited in Karabulut, 2020: 265).

If one attempts to give an overall definition of the digital economy, they might encounter various arguments as there is no consensus in this regard. However, according to the International Monetary Fund (IMF), the digital economy is sometimes defined narrowly as online platforms and the activities mainly arising from these platforms as well as any activity using digitalized data are components of the digital economy; in modern economies, however, the concept encompasses the entire economy (cited in Bozdoğanoğlu & Kaya, 2019: 1651). Looking at the changes in the share of the digital economy in the world economy, one notices that the importance of the digital economy for the global economy increases rapidly with each passing day. In fact, the top 10 companies in the world in terms of market value were financial institutions in 1990; by contrast, technology companies have come to the fore in 2019, making up 7 out of the 10 top companies with the highest market values (Ekinci & Pala, 2020: 114). Particularly, the changes in the e-commerce sector, which has the largest share in the digital economy, prove the rapid increase in the significance of the digital economy on a global scale.

The chapter containing the Action 1, Tax Challenges Arising from Digitalization, within the Base Erosion and Profit Shifting (BEPS) framework published by the OECD defines the digital economy as the outcome of the period of change brought about by information and communication technologies (ICT). One of the basic concepts one encounters with the development of the digital economy is "digital services". Any medium on which the online activity takes place without needing face-to-face contact is called a "*digital service medium*". Therefore, all activities taking place on the said platform are defined as "*digital services*".

Today's technology allows companies to develop novel business models and to engage in commercial activities without a "brick-and-mortar workplace". Some examples of such services include AirBnB allowing one to rent a space without owning property, Alibaba selling a wide range of products without having an inventory, Booking.com selling hotel rooms without owning a hotel on its own right, social networking sites like Facebook and Instagram that have become a sharing platform of user-made content without creating their own content, and companies offering agency and advertising services on the digital medium without having a physical office. These companies are *digital companies* offering *digital services*.

With their numbers increasing each day, digital companies attain market values worth billions of dollars owing to their digital services, which begs the question of how to tax companies offering digital services. This is because the digital economy has certain intrinsic difficulties in terms of national and international taxation systems. Traditional tax laws regulate new ways of conducting commercial activities, yet the existing international tax laws and taxation principles cannot keep up with the changes in types of global activities. The fundamental problem in this regard is that the decline in the importance of physical presence in the digital economy, the rise of the significance and mobility of non-tangible assets, and the new business models emerging from digitalization allow businesses to generate substantial profits without being physically present in a given country. Taxing such profits under the international taxation system has become quite challenging since it functions on the basis of physical presence in a country (Olbert & Spengel, 2017: 4; Tax Journal, 2018: 8). In other words, as it is not quite common in the digital economic model to own a traditional workplace or company, it becomes extremely difficult for tax offices to inspect digital companies on the basis of existing legislative regulations. Therefore, the "taxation rules depending on physical presence" regulated and implemented prior to the rise of the digitalized economy (based on the traditional economic structure) makes it difficult to tax the companies in question as these rules do not function effectively in the novel economic context. Furthermore, on one hand, national tax authorities have difficulties in identifying the tax situation of transactions taking place in the digital economy and finding the real identity of related taxpayers; on the other hand, another problem arises from the inability to establish a single tax-related measure about the digital economy due to the variety of digital business models. The legislation concerning formal and tangible tax-related obligations and tax-raising powers is detailed and allows for the relatively easy monitoring of the taxpayer; however, the digital economy has given rise to many issues and discussions about the tax-raising powers in international taxation. In brief, national tax laws and international tax regulations structured in alignment with the traditional economic structure are not suitable for the digital economy, therefore, existing taxation rules do not meet contemporary needs and bring about the significant issue of base erosion (tax revenue losses of countries) on a global scale. This entails the digital transformation of taxation rules as well (cited in Birinci, 2019; Tax Journal, 2018: 8; Öz & Kara, 2016; Yüce & Akbulut, 2018).

In a sense, the impossibility to tax digital services within the framework of existing tax-related regulations has brought about the need for separate legislation suitable for the digital economic structure (Akçura, 2019); in this regard, governments have been obliged to act at both national and international level in order to meet the requirements for public spending and to ensure tax justice.

There are two main underlying objectives of the effective taxation of the digital economy. The first objective is to tax the activities of big markets allowing the online sales of goods and services as well as the markets oriented to search-based advertising made use of in search engines. As for the second objective, it concerns the taxation of e-commerce, the entire range of activities of which deals with online services. The former is about the effective taxation of digital services.

Global Developments Concerning the Taxation of Digital Services

In order to eliminate the uncertainties about the taxation of the digital economy and the division of the tax or, in more technical terms, to overcome the confusion regarding tax-raising powers, the OECD published, following the request and demand by the G20, the Base Erosion and Profit Shifting (BEPS) Action Plan in July 2013. Consisting of 15 actions, the BEPS Action Plan starts by addressing the tax challenges arising from the digital economy as the first chapter. Within this scope, a new commission under the title of "the Task Force on the Digital Economy" was established within the Committee of Fiscal Affairs (CFA) of the OECD with the objective of examining tax-related issues arising from digital economic activities in an in-depth manner and focusing on solutions to these issues. The participation of non-member countries of the OECD and G20 was ensured under equal terms and the commission was assigned with the task of drafting a report outlining digital economy-based taxation problems and proposed solutions. Having had undertaken the efforts for this assigned task, the commission published the final version of the report it drafted and updated with improvements in October 2015. The report in question consists of detailed explanations concerning the digital economy, BEPS issues and tax problems arising from them, and suggestions. Therefore, rather than proposing a new taxation method, the Action Plan No. 1 published as a part of the BEPS package in October 2015 is a report on the tax challenges (problems) of the digital economy, mainly covering the digital economic model and its functioning (OECD, 2018: 18; OECD, 2015: 5).

Then, during the meeting of Finance Ministers in March 2017, it was decided that the OECD draft a report on the taxation of digitalization by April 2018. Following this decision, the OECD published a report titled "Interim Report: Tax Challenges Arising from Digitalization" in March 2018. Taking tax-related issues into account, the report analyses the features of digitalized business models as well as their ways to and potentials of value creation while assessing a series of options regarding the taxation of the digital economy. However, the report fails to reach a decisive conclusion. It underlines that the distribution of taxation rights among countries shall be determined pursuant to the tax nexus and profit distribution principles. Additionally, the report also evaluates the interim measures taken by some countries concerning the structure of the taxes to be levied on certain e-services and indicates that some countries are against such interim measure on the grounds that they entail risks and negative outcomes. It also emphasizes the BEPS action plans have taken effect, that multinational corporations have changed their tax regulations in this regard, and that governments have reported increases in their tax revenues. The final version of the report on which there are differences of opinion among 113 OECD member states is planned to be published (following the efforts to achieve a conciliation-based solution) by 2020 (Dutilh, 2018; OECD, 2018; Ber, 2018). In brief, the interim report published by the OECD in March 2018 elaborates on short-term national practices; one can infer from this report that the primary goal of the OECD is to lay the foundations of progress towards a "long-term, multilateral solution" at the next stage. Essentially, the efforts of the OECD so far has solely aimed to provide guidance for countries. There is no doubt that the consensus-based solution will take some time, yet there is pressure on governments to act urgently concerning data problems arising from digitalization. However, there is no agreement among countries regarding interim solutions.

It is a known fact that in addition to the efforts undertaken by the OECD, many entities and countries like the EU, the US, China, India, and Russia also make certain endeavors to reduce tax losses caused by the digital economy (Tamer, 2018: 62). The efforts by the OECD have raised awareness among EU countries regarding the necessity of adopting measures to tax the digital economy (Uricchio, 2016: 88). Therefore, the EU has also taken similar steps to the OECD concerning the taxation of the digital economy. The European Commission made two comprehensive legal proposals (issued draft directives) for "fair taxation of the digital economy" on 21.03.2018, right after the Finance Ministers meeting of the G20. The first of these two proposals is reforming the corporation tax rules for digital activities. As for the second, it suggests the implementation of an interim tax on certain revenues generated from digital activities (Marinobu, 2018). In other words, one of the endeavors made by the EU is the draft directive on rules governing the definition of a significant digital presence concerning corporate tax. The second endeavor is the directive on the rules concerning the digital services tax to be imposed on the revenues generated by digital services. The essential provisions of the directive taking effect as of 1 January 2020 can be summarized as follows:

The directive on the rules concerning a significant digital presence (a digital permanent establishment) regarding corporate taxation states that the European Commission adopted the communication on "A Fair and Efficient Tax System in the European Union for the Digital Single Market" on 21 September 2017 and that there is a need for novel international rules on where the business value is created in the digital economy and where this value should be assigned to for taxation against the difficulties arising from the digital economy. These rules should reform existing international taxation guidelines concerning the definition of a permanent establishment and profit distribution applicable for digital activities, expand the definition of the permanent establishment, and define the concept of taxable nexus for a significant digital presence (a virtual permanent establishment) within the jurisdiction of each country.

To provide an accurate definition of a taxable nexus for a digital business operating in a given country, one must take the revenues of the service provider, the number of users, and the number of the business contract for the digital service into consideration (Ber, 2018). In this regard, the said directive sets forth a series of criteria for a digital platform to be considered to have a taxable digital presence or a digital permanent establishment in one of the member states. This is because the legislative directive aims to allow member states to tax the revenues of a company generated within its jurisdiction even if the said company is not physically established in the member state concerned (Birinci, 2019: 514). The said criteria that might establish a real connection between the places in which the digital profit is generated and taxed were identified as follows (European Commission, 2018):

- The digital platform exceeds the threshold of €7 million in terms of annual revenues from the provision of digital services in a member state in a taxable year
- It has more than 100,000 people using its digital services in a Member State in a taxable year
- Over 3,000 business contracts for digital services are created between the platform and business users in a taxable year.

"For an enterprise to be taxed on the basis of its significant digital presence in another country, the profit distribution principle must be built on a significant digital presence. One must pay particular attention to the fact that value creation in the digital business model occurs in the place where the users are located and the data on the users are collected as well as at the location where the digital service is provided. Therefore, the digital business model built on a significant digital presence must distribute profits fairly. However, the taxpayer must not be prevented from using an internationally-recognized alternative method, provided that the taxpayer can prove it. As digital businesses can carry out its cross-border transactions without having a physical presence in other countries, countries must act in unison concerning the profit payments of businesses and come up with harmonious regulations" (Ber, 2018).

The draft directive on the rules regarding the digital services tax to be imposed on the revenues generated from certain digital services concerns the implementation of an interim tax to be levied on certain revenues obtained from digital activities. Named the "Digital Services Tax", the tax in question is proposed to be imposed on gross revenues at a fixed rate. The digital services tax is envisaged to be abolished if an international solution in the presence of the OECD or the UN is achieved (European Commission, 2018). "The Digital Services Tax (DST) denotes the taxation of revenues arising from the provision of certain digital services stemming from user value creation. DST is applied when user participation is the basic input in the digital activity and the business generates its activities and revenues from this instance. DST is not applicable when the good or service, the digital interface is provided directly to users and it is the users who collect the revenue. Similarly, DST does not cover revenues generated by undertaking retail sales activities arising from the provision of goods or services over the Internet page of the company. Revenues accumulated through a digital interface used as a payment and communication service are also not included within the scope of DST. For example, when Mr (X), resident in Spain, books a one-week stay on the website of the Hotel (Y) in Paris and makes the payment via Paypal, his transaction is not within the scope of DST. However, if Mr (X) books a one-week stay in Hotel (Y) in Paris on Booking.com, the revenues of Booking.com arising from this transaction are subject to DST" (Ber, 2018). The directive in question outlines some of the details concerning the proposed application of DST as follows (European Commission, 2018):

- The Digital Services Tax (DST) shall be imposed on certain digital services including the provision of advertising space, the offering of market spaces facilitating direct transactions between users, and the transfer of collected user data while providing digital content and payment services.
- Businesses attaining certain thresholds cumulatively shall be subject to DST. DST shall apply to companies with total annual worldwide revenues of €750 million and EU revenues of €50 million arising from digital services. If this economic entity belongs to a consolidated group, the thresholds in question shall be considered at the group level.
- The rate for DST shall be 3%. For each taxable month, the DST payer has to deliver the tax return and make the payment within 30 days following the last day of the taxable period.
- DST shall apply to the member states where the users are present. If the users are in different member states, the proposal shall also allow member states to calculate the tax base to be attributed based on certain distribution criteria. The directive also envisages collaboration between member states and a single contact point for taxpayers to fulfil all administrative requirements concerning the new tax.

The opinions of EU member states about the EU directives are rather complex. While the UK, France, Spain, Portugal, Italy, and Hungary are in favour of the draft directives of the European Commission; Ireland, Belgium, the Netherlands, and Greece are against them. As for Sweden, Austria, Germany, and Finland, these countries are undecided with regard to the draft directives. Ireland is concerned about the negative impacts of the directives on the investments of international corporations in Ireland and argues that the solution must come from the G20 and the OECD. As for Germany, it remains neutral for it is concerned about the automobile industry becoming a target of the US as a retaliation. This is because the US expressed its concerns regarding the said regulations and stated that it would take counter-measures if these draft directives entered into force during the G20 summit in Buenos Aires. Differences of opinion within the EU regarding DST resulted in France and Germany adopting different practices (Ber, 2018). Even though the said directive could not be entered into force within the EU due to differences in opinion (i.e. although the digital services tax could not become a common taxation practice in the EU), the scope of and application suggestions for the tax as well as the way it is addressed is significant as it clarifies and guides the evaluations on the subject matter. In fact, following the proposal package mentioned above, around 20 EU member states led by France (e.g. Spain, Italy, the UK, France, Germany, Austria, Hungary, Belgium, Czechia etc.) adopted digital tax laws or proposed laws to adopt unilateral practices with their special regulations and mentioned the issue during the efforts to establish the budget, as seen from the relevant press coverage.

It is a known fact that many international organizations like the OECD and the EU as well as many countries devote efforts to the taxation of the digital economy in the general sense and to the issue of digital services taxes in the narrower sense. In fact, the most recent endeavor is the collaboration of the G7, the G20, the Council of the EU, and the OECD with 129 countries in order to come up with a global digital taxation framework. The final draft is expected to be prepared in 2020 (Ulusoy, 2019). However, as digital transactions are quite complex and difficult (since they concern non-tangible goods and services, therefore they entail cross-border activities without physical presence), a common ground is yet reached among countries regarding the taxation of the digital economy. Thus, we observe unilateral measures taken by individual countries rather than common steps at the international level. The table below demonstrates some examples of the unilateral measures adopted by individual countries.

Table 1. Unilateral Measures

COUNTRY	DIGITAL ECONOMY TAX MEASURE	SITUATION
US	No federal-level digital economy measures State sales tax collection	n/a Active
Austria	Equalization tax (advertisement tax)	Draft
Australia	Diverted profits tax Goods and services tax	Active Active
China	Value-added tax	Active
India	Equalization tax Digital establishment	Active Draft
United Kingdom	Diverted profits tax Withholding tax (concerning certain intellectual property rights of those settled abroad)	Active Draft
Israel	Digital establishment Value-added tax	Active Active
Italy	Withholding tax (web tax) / digital services tax Digital establishment	Active Active
Kuwait	Digital establishment	Active
Hungary	Equalization tax (advertisement tax)	Active
Saudi Arabia	Digital establishment	Active
Taiwan	Digital establishment Value-added tax	Active Active
Turkey	Withholding tax Electronic establishment Value-added tax	Active Active Active
New Zealand	Goods and services tax	Active

(Data Source: Tax Journal, 2018)

As seen in the table, some countries have taken initiatives to adopt unilateral national tax measures targeting the digital economy. International bodies avoid such an approach due to several reasons; for instance, the approach in question might result in double taxation, may entail administrative costs for businesses, and can result in inconsistent rules. However, the delay at the international level has made such unilateral measures inevitable considering the political, social, and income-raising pressures at the national level (Tax Journal, 2018: 9). Nevertheless, it has become an obligation for the subject matter to be dealt with at the international to develop common solutions as digital transactions go beyond country borders and cause problems regarding the tax-raising powers of multiple countries.

EFFORTS FOR DIGITAL SERVICES TAX IMPLEMENTATION IN TURKEY

Since 2016, there have been certain steps and initiatives undertaken in Turkey regarding the taxation of the digital economy. In this respect, various adjustments have been made in the Turkish digital taxation system (e.g. the introduction of an obligation to pay a withholding tax covering e-commerce and payments made through other online activities, the expansion of the definition of the "electronic establishment", the regulation of the rules concerning the information transfer of Internet service providers and online advertising agencies regarding their monthly transactions with their Turkish clients etc.). Today, the regulation concerning the digital services tax, which has come to the fore with the tax transformation realized within the scope of "The New Economic Program: Steps for Structural Transformation 2019", is another significant initiative.

Tax Transformation in Turkey Within the Scope of "The New Economic Programme: Steps for Structural Transformation 2019"

Prepared with the objective of attaining the level of a grand and powerful country and published under the title of "The New Economic Program: Steps for Structural Transformation 2019" as of 10 April 2019, the new economic program of Turkey actualizes a series of structural reforms in the economy. One of the envisaged reforms within these structural transformations is, without any doubt, the tax transformation.

The section of the structural transformation steps dealing with the tax transformation has a tripartite structure. The first part is the new tax architecture, the second part concerns dealing with the black economy, and the third part is about taxpayer rights.

Under the section of "New Tax Architecture", the goals defined are reducing exceptions and exemptions, decreasing corporate tax gradually, extending the practice of tax returns, spreading the tax to the base, accomplishing taxation increasing based on income levels, and facilitating entrepreneurship and establishing new businesses. The section titled "Dealing with the Black Economy" underlines the objectives of voluntary tax compliance, dealing with counterfeit and fallacious documents, effective enforcement in this respect, technical solutions, e-invoicing, and tracking of merchandise movements through unique codes. As for the objectives included under the title "Taxpayer Rights" aiming to protect and improve these rights, they include the creation of the Executive Board on Taxpayer Rights, the establishment of the procedures and principles of the right of hearing, regular and orderly assessment of taxpayer satisfaction, and making the declaration of taxpayer rights a binding document (Republic of Turkey Ministry of Treasury and Finance, 2019).

The draft of the new taxation system prepared by the Ministry of Treasury and Finance within the scope of the establishment of the novel tax architecture and mentioned frequently in the press under the names of "new tax draft" or "new tax obligations draft" can be summarized as follows:

1. *Corporate Tax Rates*: The President acquires the authority to lower the rate of the tax that publicly-traded corporations need to pay under certain circumstances in order to encourage corporations to go public. The corporate tax rate is reduced by 18%. The rate, which is set to be 22% for 2020, is planned to be reduced to 20%. The rate will remain at 20% for financial institutions. However, the corporate tax rate will be applied as 20% in 2020.
2. *Income Tax Tables*: The tax table included in the Income Tax Law will have 7 tax brackets instead of 4. The aim of this increase is to collect more taxes from higher income levels. Therefore, new brackets and rates are added to the table to increase the taxes levied from those with higher revenues. Maintaining the first four brackets in the existing table, the plan does not include any changes in the tax liabilities of groups with revenues up to TL 500,000. The regulation removes the fees paid to sports referees from the list of exceptions while envisaging an increase in the withholding tax rates to be applied to athletes playing in the top league.

3. *Valuable Residence Tax*: A new tax named "Valuable Residence Tax" is introduced for residences valued over TL 5 million. It is envisaged that the tax rate shall be 1%, that the tax shall enter in force with the returns to be given in February 2020, and that it shall be paid in two equal instalments in February and August. Public residences, residences of diplomatic staff, single residences of those with no income or only with pensions, and residences considered as commercial goods belonging to those involved in building construction business are identified as categories exempted from the tax.
4. *Accommodation Tax Draft*: A new tax is introduced for services provided in hotels, motels, holiday camps, hostels, apart-hotels, guest houses, and camping sites. The taxpayer will be the entity providing the accommodation service. The tax base is the total fee for overnight stays and other services. The tax rate is 2%. The President will be able to increase this rate up to three times the actual rate or decrease it down to 1%. The tax will be applied with a rate of 1% in 2020. The returns of the tax can be declared in monthly intervals and paid in this respect. The services to be exempted from the tax are those provided in public guest houses, student residences and camps, and services provided for diplomatic representatives, consuls, and members of international bodies.
5. *Digital Services Tax Draft*: The tax is envisaged to be applied to services provided on digital platforms, all advertising services, content sales (games, music, videos, in-app purchases etc.), (paid) services provided on social networking websites, and agency services provided on web sites acting as intermediaries during the sales of goods and services. The Digital Services Tax is planned to be declared and paid on a monthly basis. The tax rate will be 7.5%. The taxpayer will be the "digital service provider". If the revenues of the digital service provider in Turkey are below % TL 20 million or if its global revenues are below €750 million or the equivalent amount in any foreign currency in TL terms, the service provider will be exempted from the tax. The base of the digital services tax will be the revenues generated from the services included within the scope of the tax during the relevant taxable period. The proposal lists the cases in which exceptions are made as follows: Services subject to the special communication tax, services for which a treasury share is paid in accordance with the Telegram and Telephone Law, services provided under the Banking Law, payment services provided under the law governing electronic monetary institutions, sales of products developed in R&D centers and the services provided through these products.
6. *Extension of Exceptions*: The new plan envisages the taxation of sports referees, removing them from the list of exceptions. If the revenues within the scope of self-employment revenue exemptions regulated under the Income Tax Law exceed TL 500,000, these revenues will be declared and taxed. The withholding tax rate applied to the fees paid to athletes playing in the top league, for sports played in leagues, will be increased. Furthermore, in cases these incomes exceed TL 500,000, they will be declared and taxed. The new plan also introduces expense limitations concerning private cars in the identification of commercial profits and self-employment profits.
7. *Other issues*: Taxpayers with a solid record (with regular payments) are rewarded with a 5-point discount. In court cases (at the final stage of appeals), if the taxpayer withdraws the lawsuit, a discount (tax discount) shall be applied to their debt. The scope of exceptions in self-employment profits will be narrowed down and self-employment revenues exceeding TL 500,000 will be subject to taxation. Employee benefits for transport, provided that they do not exceed TL 10 per day, in the form of transport cards or tickets will be exempted from income tax. The plan also clarifies the issue of identifying those who are liable for deductions during the payment of solicitor's fees to lawyers. Provided that the real estate values to be established by the Directorate of Land Registry are also

taken into consideration, the title deed fees are planned to be set in accordance with the real value during property transfers. New powers are introduced concerning the increase of withholding tax rates applied to securities in foreign currency terms and revenues generated from foreign currency accounts. The Banking and Insurance Transaction Tax applied to foreign exchange sales will be increased and the President will have the authority to further increase the tax.

To sum up, one might say that the "New Tax Draft" entails major regulations. Some prominent features of the plan include the introduction of new taxes such as the "Valuable Residence Tax" and the "Digital Services Tax", the further reduction of the corporate tax, which already has an insignificant share in the overall tax revenues, the increase of the maximum income tax rate from 35% to 45%, and the introduction of a discount for those who withdraw their legal proceedings (Batı, 2019). The following chapter deals with the details of the digital services tax, coming to the fore with the new tax draft and then signed into law, as it is the subject matter of this study.

Digital Services Tax in Turkey

With the adoption of the "Legislative Proposal on the Digital Service Tax Law and the Amendments to Certain Tax Laws" dated 24.10.2019 within the Committee on Planning and Budget of the Grand National Assembly of Turkey", the digital services tax was adopted as a new tax in Turkey. Governed under articles 1-7 of the Law Dated 5 December 2019 and dated 7194 on the Digital Service Tax and the Amendments to Certain Laws and to the Decree-Law (hereinafter, "Law") No. 375, the digital services tax entered into force in accordance with Article 52, Paragraph 1, sub-paragraph (a) on 1 March 2020. Within this scope, the law was published on the Official Gazette dated 20 March 2020 and No. 31074 under the General Declaration on the Implementation of the Digital Services Tax (hereinafter, "Declaration"), indicating the procedures and principles concerning the application of the tax. The regulations within the framework of the digital services tax are as follows:

Subject of the Tax: The following services provided in Turkey comprise the subject of the digital services tax:

- All advertising services provided on the digital media (including advertising control and performance assessment services, services regarding the transfer and management of user data, and technical services dealing with the provision of the advertisement), **(e.g. Adsense, Admob, Adwords etc.)**.
- Services provided on the digital platform concerning the digital sales of any auditory, visual, or digital content (including computer software, applications, music, videos, games, in-game applications etc.) and allowing one to listen to, watch, play, save, or use this content on electronic devices **(i.e. iTunes, Spotify, Netflix etc.)**.
- Services regarding the provision and management of digital media through which users can interact with one another (including services for the sales or the facilitation of sales of goods or services among users) **(e.g. Facebook, LinkedIn, Instagram etc.)**.

Furthermore, agency services provided for the services indicated above are also subject to the digital services tax.

Taxpayer and Entities Obliged to Pay of the Tax: The taxpayers of the digital services tax are digital service providers. (One does not consider the questions of whether the taxpayer has the full obligation regarding the tax in accordance with the Income Tax Law dated 31.12.1960, no. 193 and the Corporate Tax Law dated 13.06.2006, no. 5520 and whether the entity, in case of limited tax liability, performs its activities through an establishment or permanent representatives in Turkey in terms of digital services tax obligation).

If the taxpayer does not reside in Turkey and does not have an establishment and legal and commercial centers in Turkey and in other relevant cases, the Ministry of Treasury and Finance may deem the parties to the activities subject to taxation and those acting as intermediaries to the transaction and payment to be liable for the tax to secure tax claims. In other words, a tax responsible was identified regarding the payment of the digital services tax to ensure tax security. Those acting as intermediaries for the payment within the borders of Turkey are considered responsible for the payment of the tax.

Tax Exemptions and Exceptions: Those who are exempted from the digital services tax or have exceptions are as follows:

- Those Exempted from DST: Entities whose revenues in Turkey generated from services included within the scope of DST in the accounting period before the one in question are below TL 20 million in Turkey or below €750 million or equivalent amounts in foreign currency in TL terms globally are exempted from the digital services tax. If the taxpayer is a member of a consolidated group in terms of financial accounting, the total revenues of the group generated from the activities included within the scope of the tax are taken into consideration during the application of these margins. If both of the margins indicated within the accounting period in question are exceeded, the exemption is rendered invalid and the entity becomes liable to pay the digital services tax as of the fourth taxable period following the taxable period during which the margin is exceeded. The cumulative revenues generated within the relevant taxable period as of the three-month periods of the accounting period are taken into consideration while identifying the excess in terms of the margins concerned. The tax exemption of those whose revenues remain below one of the indicated margins for two consecutive accounting periods is reapplied as of the following accounting period. Furthermore, the President will have the power to decrease the amounts of exemptions down to zero or to increase them up to three times the indicated amount.
- Exceptions for DST: The revenues generated from the following services provided on the digital medium are an exception to the digital services tax, and the said revenues are not taken into consideration during the identification of the margins indicated above.
    - Services for which a treasury share is paid within the scope of the Additional Clause No. 37 of the Telegram and Telephone Law dated 04.02.1924, no. 406,
    - Services subject to the special communication tax within the scope of Article 39 of the Income Tax Law dated 13.07.1956, no. 6802,
    - Services covered by Article 4 of the Banking Law dated 19.10.2005, no. 5411,
    - Sales of products developed as a result of R&D activities performed at R&D centres as defined in Article 2 of the Law on Supporting Research, Development and Design Activities dated 28.02.2008, no. 5746 as well as the services exclusively provided over these products,
    - Payment services within the scope of Article 12 of the Law on Payment and Security Settlement Systems, Payment Services and Electronic Money Institutions dated 20.06.2013, no. 6493.

Tax Base, Rate, and Calculation: The tax base for the digital services tax is the revenues generated from the services covered within the scope of the tax during the relevant taxable period. The rate for the digital services tax is 7.5%. The digital services tax is calculated by applying the rate to the tax without any discounts on the calculated amount. Furthermore, the President has the power to reduce this rate down to 1% or increase it up to two times the actual rate, either separately or jointly in terms of service types.

Taxation Period, Declaration, Levy, and Payment: The taxation period for the digital services tax is the monthly periods within the calendar year. The revenues are converted to TL terms if generated in foreign currency terms. However, the Ministry of Treasury and Finance has the authority to identify three-month taxable periods instead of monthly ones depending on service types and operating volume of the taxpayer. The digital services tax is levied by the declaration of the taxpayers. However, in cases where Article 3 § 2 of the Law is applied, this declaration can be made by those who are made responsible for making tax deductions.

Taxpayers and those responsible for tax deductions are obliged to submit the digital service tax returns to the relevant tax office until the end of the month following the taxable period. The digital services tax is levied by the tax office of the service provider subject to value-added tax; if the service provider is not obliged to pay value-added tax, the DST is levied by a tax office to be determined by the Ministry of Treasury and Finance. It is levied on behalf of the taxpayer or the natural or legal person responsible for the tax. In case of ordinary partnerships, the levy is made on behalf of one of the partners, provided that the said partner shall be severally responsible for the payment of the tax. Taxpayers obliged to submit tax returns and those responsible for tax deductions pay the digital services tax for one taxable period within the declaration period.

Tax Security: The draft in question also includes provisions ensuring the safety of DST. These provisions are as follows:

- Digital service providers or their authorized representative in Turkey who do not fulfil their declaration and payment obligations concerning the taxes within the scope of the Tax Procedure Law dated 04.01.1961, no. 213 might be notified by the tax office authorized to levy the digital services tax for the fulfilment of these duties through the means of notification indicated under the Law no. 213, electronic mail, or any other communication tool using the information gathered from the means of communication indicated on their website, domain name, IP address, and similar sources and this notification is declared on the website of the Revenue Administration.
- If these obligations are not fulfilled within thirty days following the notification, the access to the services provided by the digital service providers in question are blocked until the obligations are fulfilled as per the request of the Ministry of Treasury and Finance and this decision is then submitted to the Information Technologies and Communications Authority to notify access providers. The decision to block access is applied by access providers within 24 hours following the notification.
- The procedures and principles concerning the implementation of this article are determined by the Ministry of Treasury and Finance in consideration of the opinions of the Ministry of Transport and Infrastructure.

EVALUATIONS OF THE DIGITAL SERVICES TAX IMPLEMENTED IN TURKEY

Upon examining the regulations concerning DST, one sees that the primary purpose of DST is to tax the revenues of digital and social platforms resident abroad but earning profits in Turkey. More clearly, international service providers such as Google, Apple, Instagram, YouTube, Facebook, Amazon, Twitter, Linkedln, Netflix, Spotify, App Store, Yandex, and Steam will be taxed based on the revenues they generate in Turkey. In this regard, it would be accurate to say that DST mainly concerns big technology companies prominent in Turkey (particularly digital giants based in the US). Furthermore, one might also argue that DST has the potential to generate considerable amounts of tax revenues since digital services are frequently used within the economy of Turkey.

The steps taken by the Turkish government to tax digital services seem sensible considering the developments in the rest of the world. On the other hand, it might not be a good idea to compare DST regulations in Turkey with other countries as DST is also a novel practice in other countries (i.e. they remain as a proposal in some countries while recently legalized in others; in some other countries, the works are still underway). Making such comparisons and assessments considering various aspects would produce more accurate results after the global practices gain more ground and are improved and once the DST-related outcomes in Turkey start to emerge. Yet one might still argue that the provisions concerning DST that passed into law show similarities with many other national practices. One of the significant aspects concerning the provisions is the tax rate differing from other practices. When compared to the rates averaging at around 2 or 3% in other countries, the rate of 7.5% in Turkey is quite elevated. Another important point is the "prevention of access" within the scope of tax security.

This high tax rate might result in various decisions, outcomes or access preventions affecting the daily lives of citizens in Turkey. Above all, payment of the tax by means of deduction signifies that the persons and businesses receiving services in Turkey are the ones paying the tax. This is because technology giants, whose expenditures will increase as a result of the new regulations, might adjust their pricing policies in Turkey based on the new tax; therefore, DST would mean mark-ups for consumers. In other words, the objective would be to have the end-user to pay the new tax to the maximum extent possible. In this case, as underlined by Bingöl (2019), beneficiaries of digital services will now be obliged to receive these services with mark-ups up to 7.5%. Considering that digital services are already subject to a transaction and expenditure tax, one might argue that the payment of this latest tax would be borne by end-users.

Another concern regarding the DST rate is the competitive disadvantages for persons resident in Turkey and the potential risk of the tax to make it harder for international corporations to invest in Turkey. The Turkish Industry and Business Association (TÜSİAD) made a statement underlining these concerns. Emphasizing that Turkey works on an approach at the OECD level, TÜSİAD indicated that imposing a high rate of DST and planning sanctions like blocking access in case the tax obligation is not met is wrong and made the following statement: "*The new proposal entails significant costs and competitive disadvantages, either directly or indirectly, for persons resident in Turkey who are already taxpayers while posing an important obstacle to the investments of international corporations in Turkey. This would have a negative impact on the recently-emerging digital ecosystem and the development of our SMEs. Reducing the rate of the digital services tax to a sensible level and underlining that it is an interim regulation to remain in force until an OECD-based solution is achieved*".

On the other hand, the provisions concerning DST may result in the access to services provided by digital service providers being blocked if they do not submit their tax returns and fulfil their obligations. This might cause businesses and citizens in Turkey to encounter problems such as access prohibition while soliciting digital services. In fact, Dr Bumin Doğrusöz, an expert of tax law, made the following statements to DW Türkçe (the Turkish version of DW) also indicating the risks: "*No company based abroad would give their consolidated financial statements to Turkey. Therefore, access prohibition would be inevitable*" (Ünker, 2019). Additionally, there are also concerns regarding the possibility of access issues leading to other negative discourses in Turkey. One consideration is that technology giants, whose services are blocked because they failed to pay their taxes, would associate the prohibition to the lack of press freedom and to human rights infringements instead of addressing their failure to pay taxes, taking the tax practice out of its context with criticisms of democracy and modernity (İleri, 2019).

In brief, it is more than likely that DST, implemented quite recently within the framework of existing provisions, may give rise to various issues and arguments and trigger reactions. Naturally, the issues, shortcomings, and faults of the DST practices would be addressed with various steps in order to make its foundations more reliable. This is because DST is inevitable in Turkey as it is in the rest of the world since digital activities proliferate and pose a significant potential for taxation, considering the issues of tax justice and the need to address significant base (revenue) losses.

SOLUTIONS AND RECOMMENDATIONS

Digital service tax is a new tax regulation around the world. Most countries are working diligently on this regulation. Digital services tax regulations in Turkey have been identified over its counterparts worldwide. But, ın conclusion, there are some differences between implementations. Especially, Turkish digital service tax is so high than other countries. Although the high rate seems good in terms of increasing tax collection, it may lead to different ways to avoid tax in the future. Other than that due to such a large proportion invested in Turkey, which will also be able to block the way for international companies. In this framework, it will be more effective to reduce the rate to reasonable levels as in other country practices. In addition, the issue of determining taxpayer is one of the controversial areas. Law No. 7194 on the criteria for obtaining income in Turkey is incomplete. In the taxation of the service to be provided in the digital environment, the regulations for determining the taxpayer using traditional methods will not be effective. This deficiency should be corrected with legal regulations.

FUTURE RESEARCH DIRECTIONS

The digital services tax is important in order to get a larger share from the digital economy on a global scale. Therefore, it is very important in the academic studies to be carried out on digital services tax. Future research can be focused on:

- Practice results relating to digital services tax in Turkey and in the world.
- Problems encountered in digital services tax applications and solutions.
- Behavioral Responses to the digital services tax.
- Standard or different implementation and evaluation from all states.

For future research, the research methods could involve quantitative, qualitative and mixed methods approaches. The participants should consist of all administrators, taxpayers, policy makers, academics.

CONCLUSION

Under existing laws, the revenues generated by institutions are essentially taxed by countries in which they are residents and which hosts their headquarters. However, activities within the digital economy have expanded as a result of the integration of technology with the economy, leading to a surge in the revenues gained from such activities. In spite of these developments, the inability of existing laws and taxation guidelines to tax the revenues in question in a due manner and the issue of base losses have come to the fore. This is because international corporations like Google, Facebook, Spotify, Amazon, Apple, and Instagram providing global services being taxed only in their own countries entails significant tax losses for countries in which these corporations offer services and generate revenues. Such tax (base) losses obliged institutions and organizations like the G7, the G20, the OECD, and the EU as well as national governments to take action; in this respect, one of the issues dealt with within this scope has been the practice of "digital services tax". With the digital services tax, it becomes possible to tax companies offering digital services on a global scale based on a rate of their revenues generated from their services offered in relevant countries.

In alignment with global developments, the Turkish government have also drafted and adopted a law on the taxation of digital services. Upon examining the regulations concerning DST in the law in question, one sees that the primary purpose of DST is to tax the revenues of digital and social platforms resident abroad but earning profits in Turkey. More clearly, international service providers such as Google, Apple, Instagram, YouTube, Facebook, Amazon, Twitter, Linkedln, Netflix, Spotify, App Store, Yandex, and Steam will be taxed based on the revenues they generate in Turkey. Since the global and Turkish efforts in this regard are quite recent, it is still too early to make detailed assessments and interpretations of the practices. However, in light of the information given to the public through press outlets, one might say that DST provisions in Turkey are generally similar to the practices in many other countries. Yet the tax rate differs from the rest of the world significantly. The rate of 7.5% planned to be implemented in Turkey is quite high when compared with the average rates of around 2 to 3% in other countries. Another important point is the "prevention of access" within the scope of tax security.

REFERENCES

Akçura, A. (2019). *Global Practices In the Taxation of The Digital Economy and The Position of Turkey.* Retrieved From https://www.verginet.net/dtt/1/dijital-ekonomi-vergilendirilmesi-dunya-Turkiye-uygulamalari.aspx

Batı, M. (2019). *The New Tax Draft with All Its Articles.* Retrieved From https://t24.com.tr/haber/doc-dr-murat-bati-yazdi-madde-madde-yeni-vergi-taslagi,845205

Ber, H. (2018). *An Overview of the Issue of Taxing the Digital Economy.* Retrieved From https://vergialgi.net/dijital-ekonominin-vergilendirilmesi-sorunsalina-genel-bir-bakis

Bingöl, O. (2019). *On Taxation: Digital Services Tax on the Horizon.* Retrieved From https://vergiyedair.com/2019/10/24/dijital-hizmet-vergisi-geliyor/

Birinci, N. (2019). The Effect of Digitalization on Tax Base and Unilateral Measures. *Finance Journal*, (176), 505–527.

Boccia, F. (2016). Introduction: The Digital Economy and Fiscal Policy In The Age of E-Commerce. In Francesco Boccia, Robert Leonardi (Ed.), The Challenge of the Digital Economy, Market, Taxation and Appropriate Economic Models (pp. 1-17). Academic Press.

Bozdoğanoğlu, B., & Haspolat Kaya, I. (2019). Opportunities and Challenges Created by Digitalization for Tax Administrations: The Digitalization Process of Tax Administrations While The Economy Is Digitalized. *MHD*, *15*(176), 1647–1676.

Budak, T. (2018). *Taxing the Digital Economy*. On İki Levha Publishing.

Dutilh, N. (2018). *Taxation and the Digital Economy: European and International Initiatives to Create a Fair Tax System*. Retrieved From https://www.lexology.com/library/detail.aspx?g=5b609b46-77bb-4061-b091-11333b1f5f9e

Ekinci, E., & Pala, O. (2020). Reflections of the Developments In The Digital Economy on Taxation: Evaluating Tax Audits Within Digital Companies Resident Abroad. *Tax World Journal*, *39*(462), 113–130.

European Commission. (2018). *Digital Taxation: Commission Proposes New Measures to Ensure That All Companies Pay Fair Tax In the EU*. European Commission Press Release. Retrieved From https://ec.europa.eu/commission/presscorner/detail/en/IP_18_2041

Hayvalı, A. (2019). *New Taxes, New Rates*. Retrieved From https://www.habergazetesi.com.tr/yazarlar/19605/yeni-vergiler-yeni-oranlar

İleri, Y. (2019). *The Danger Posed by Google, Facebook, Twitter, and Instagram for Digital Taxation*. Retrieved From https://odatv.com/dijital-vergide-google-facebook-twitter-ve-instagram-tehlikesi-30101959.html

Journal, T. (2018). Taxation of the Digital Economy: Unilateral Measures. *Insight and Analysis for the Business Tax Community*, *1389*, 7–13.

Karabulut, Ş. (2020). Financial Implications of theDigital Age: Digital Service Tax. *Finance Journal*, *178*, 263-288.

Legislative Proposal on the Digital Service Tax Law and The Amendments to Certain Tax Laws Dated 24. From https://www2.tbmm.gov.tr/d27/2/2-2312.pdf doi:10.2019. Retrieved

Morinobu, S. (2018). *Strategies for Taxing the Digital Economy*. The Tokyo Foundation for Policy Research. Retrieved From https://www.tkfd.or.jp/en/research/detail.php?id=24

OECD. (2013). *Action Plan on Base Erosion and Profit Shifting*. OECD Publishing. Retrieved From https://www.oecd.org/ctp/BEPSActionPlan.pdf

OECD. (2015). Addressing the Tax Challenges of the Digital Economy, Action 1-2015 Final Report. In *Series: OECD/G20 Base Erosion and Profit Shifting Project, French*. OECD Publishing.

OECD. (2015). *OECD/G20 Base Erosion and Profit Shifting Project: Executive Summaries 2015 Final Reports*. OECD Publishing. Retrieved From https://www.oecd.org/ctp/beps-reports-2015-executive-summaries.pdf

OECD. (2018). *Tax Challenges Arising From Digitalization- Interim Report 2018: Inclusive Framework on BEPS*. OECD/G20 Base Erosion and Profit Shifting Project, OECD Publishing. Retrieved From https://www.oecd.org/tax/beps/brief-on-the-tax-challenges-arising-from-digitalisation-interim-report-2018.pdf

Olbert, M., & Spengel, C. (2017). International Taxation In The Digital Economy: Challange Accepted? *World Tax Journal*, (February), 3–46.

Öz, E., & Kara, M. C. (2016). A Global Look at Digital Taxation. *Tax World Journal*, *36*(424), 30–37.

Sayın, A. (2019). *What Provisions Does the New Tax Proposal Include?* Retrieved From https://www.habergazetesi.com.tr/yazarlar/19605/yeni-vergiler-yeni-oranlar

T.C. Ministry of Treasury and Finance. (2019). *Ministry of Treasury and Finance of the Republic of Turkey, New Economic Programme: Steps for Structural Transformation*. Retrieved From https://ms.hmb.gov.tr/uploads/2019/04/Yeni-Ekonomi-Program%C4%B1-2019-v5.pdf

TÜSİAD. (2019). *The Legislative Proposal on New Tax Provisions Include Items that Need to be Reconsidered for All Segments of Society*. Retrieved From https://tusiad.org/tr/basin-bultenleri/item/10459-yeni-vergi-duzenlemesine-i-liskin-kanun-teklifi-tum-toplum-kesimleri-i-cin-yeniden-degerlendirilmeye-muhtac-duzenlemelere-sahiptir

Ulusoy, A. (2019). *Digital Services Tax On The Horizon*. Retrieved From https://www.yenisafak.com/yazarlar/ahmetulusoy/dijital-hizmet-vergisi-geliyor-2053220

Ünker, P. (2019). *How Will the New Taxes Affect the Consumer?* Retrieved From https://www.dw.com/tr/yeni-vergiler-t%C3%BCketiciyi-nas%C4%B1l-etkileyecek/a-51090228

Uricchio, A. (2016). A Few Ideas for Reforming Internet Taxation. In F. Boccia & R. Leonardi (Eds.), *The Challenge of the Digital Economy, Market, Taxation and Appropriate Economic Models* (pp. 83–96). Academic Press. doi:10.1007/978-3-319-43690-6_6

Yüce, M., & Akbulut, N. (2018). Measures Adopted Concerning the Taxation of the Digital Economy within the Scope of the BEPS Action Plan. *Academic View Journal*, *68*, 105-123.

ADDITIONAL READING

Tapscott, D. (1996). The Digital Economy: Promise and Peril. In *The Age of Networked Intelligence*. McGraw-Hill.

KEY TERMS AND DEFINITIONS

Digital Company: Companies that offer digital brokerage services and advertising services without a fixed workplace.

Digital Economy: The new economic model born as a result of today's technological and information revolution.

Digital Service Environment: Any environment where online activity takes place, without confrontation.

Digital Services: All activities carried out in digital services environment or services offered by digital companies.

Digital Services Tax: A tax on income from certain digital services or the taxation of income from the provision of certain digital services resulting from user value creation.

Digital Transformation: The intensive use of information technologies and the transfer of business processes and information to digital (electronic) environment by saving money and time.

E-Commerce: It is the production, promotion, sales, insurance, distribution and payment transactions of goods and services through computer networks.

Chapter 7
The Impact of Management and Strategies for Digital Enterprise Transformation on Welfare

Francisco Xavier Pedro
https://orcid.org/0000-0001-8947-8980
Universidade do Minho, Portugal

Joana Maria Costa Martins das Dores
https://orcid.org/0000-0001-7514-9836
University of Aveiro, Portugal

ABSTRACT

Digital transformation is progressing exponentially. Given the importance of this transformation, managerial strategies and practices need to be adapted to meet the new challenges. While countries are on a journey toward a process where human interactions and transactions—with the government, businesses—and consumption of goods, services, and ideas primarily conducted through the use of the internet and internet-based technologies, they are all traveling at different speeds. Based on the theory, drawing from the Global Innovation Index (GII) input-output framework and literature review on innovation, the chapter intends to answer the question: What is the impact of management and strategies for digital enterprise transformation on welfare?

INTRODUCTION

This chapter aims to analyze and describe the *impact of management and strategies for digital enterprise transformation on welfare.*

Several revolutions have happened in the past. The Information Technology (IT) Industry is multiplying and transforming the business standards of tomorrow. First Industrial Revolution (1.0, 1700) drove the discovery of the use of steam engines to optimize the production process in the industry. Second Industrial Revolution (2.0, 1800) was the precursor of electricity for mass production. Third Industrial

DOI: 10.4018/978-1-7998-8583-2.ch007

Revolution (3.0, 1900) was the hallmark of the use of Information and Communication Technology (ICT), the internet, and electronic elements that automated production processes; Fourth Revolution - better known as 4.0, (intelligence – digital enterprise transformation) - is the junction of Technologies and Speed. IT industry has already gained much traction at the global level shifting towards the fourth industrial revolution (4.0) by adhering to cutting-edge technologies through digital enterprise transformation. The Fourth Industrial Revolution (4.0) on the digitization of all its processes, allowing the interaction between physical and digital systems, thereby achieving the use of real-time information for making timely decisions (Riola, J.M. et al. 2020). The Fourth Industrial Revolution involves several changes in the workforce's key features. The fourth revolution catalyzes welfare, socio-economic changes and cross-sector boundaries (e.g., water service, health, business), new business models that will influence the job market. Such progress will impact the academic sector as new forms of research based on massive amounts of data will be possible, and the industrial technology sector will request new research needs (Garrido-Baserba, M. et., 2020). With the Fourth Industrial Revolution, the management and strategies of companies are disruptive, at a time when the world manages the pandemic crisis of COVID-19, with no time for the preparation of these companies to absorb the impact of the accelerated digital transformation on welfare. Digital technologies have dramatically changed the world and, as a consequence, there is an urgent need to redefine the impact of management and strategies for digital enterprise transformation on welfare. Companies are experiencing significant transformations in management and in their strategies to absorb the inevitable acceleration of digital transformation. The management and strategies for digital enterprise transformation need to plan and produce disruptive innovations for traditional business management tools and poses a challenge for the integration of the digital transformation of companies' management processes and strategies at present.

Based on theory and conceptual model, the study developed a panel data, grouped on the *Global Innovation Index*, encompassing 50 countries during 2019, and analyzed it through a series of multiple regression techniques. The conceptual model assumes institutions, human capital, research, infrastructure, market sophistication and business sophistication as inputs. Furthermore, it assumes the *education (knowledge and technology)*, and improvement of *goods and services (creative)* as the output of welfare.

Through data analysis, model creation, multiple linear regressions and from the empirical analysis, the chapter has a threefold objective:

1. Analyze the *Impact of Management and Strategies for Digital Enterprise Transformation on Welfare.*
2. Investigate the *Impact of Management and Strategies for Digital Enterprise Transformation on education.*
3. To discuss the *Impact of Management and Strategies for Digital Enterprise Transformation* on *goods and services (creative outputs).*

Such instruments provide policymakers with a panoply of relevant information on managerial strategies and practices need to be adapted to meet the digital *enterprise transformation* new challenges.

The chapter covers the *Introduction, Background* (Literature Review), *Research Methodology* (Theory, Methods and Model Specification), *Solutions* and *Recommendations* (Results and Discussions), *Future Research Directions, Conclusions and References.*

The management and strategies for digital transformation framework rely on the distinction between technological *inputs* and *outputs to measure the absorption of technological intensity and deriving policies for welfare.* Thus, "*inputs*" are the elements of the national economy that allow innovatively and *management and strategies for digital enterprise transformation* activities and "*outputs*" the results of innovative activities in the economy, which results in welfare.

The indicators aggregate in a total of 21 sub-pillars, which, in turn, are aggregated in seven pillars. Five of them are *input* pillars, consisting of *Institutions, Human Capital and Research, Infrastructure, Market Sophistication and Business Sophistication,* and here taken as a proxy for *Management and Strategies for Digital Enterprise Transformation*. At the same time, two are *outputs* pillars, that is, referring to *knowledge and technology outputs* and *creative outputs,* here taken as *welfare* embodied in *education* and the supply of goods and services. The *inputs* and *outputs* pillars aggregated to form the *input and output sub-indices* (Figure 1).

BACKGROUND

Background and Basic Understanding

The definition of the term strategy (or strategies) implies a common theme: the deliberate and conscious set of guidelines that determine decisions for the future. For example, in Game Theory, strategy corresponds to the set of rules that is to govern the moves of the players (Mintzberg, H., 1979). In military theory, a strategy is the science or art of combining and employing the means of war in planning and directing large military movements and operations (dictionary.com/browse/strategy). Moreover, in management theory, the definition of strategy is the determination of the primary long-term goals and objectives of an enterprise, and the adoption of courses of action and the allocation of resources necessary for carrying out these goals (Chandler, A. D., 1990).

All these definitions treat strategy as (a) explicit, (b) developed consciously and purposefully, and (c) made in advance of the specific decisions to which it applies.

Enterprise is (1) a project that is difficult, complicated, or risky, (2) a unit of economic organization or activity, especially a business organization, (3) a systematic, purposeful activity, (4) and readiness to engage action (merriam-webster.com/dictionary/enterprise).

Digital Transformation (DT) **is** the adoption of digital technology to transform goods, services or businesses, through replacing older digital technology with newer digital technology (Lankshear, C., & Knobel, M., 2008).

Digitization (the technical conversion), digitalization (the business process) and the digital transformation (the effect) therefore accelerate and illuminate the already existing and ongoing processes of change in the enterprise (Khan, S., 2016).

Welfare ensures that members of a society can meet basic needs, such as goods (food) and services (education) (Williams, W., & Elmore, R. F., 2014).

According to GII index, (1) education (knowledge and technology outputs), in terms of welfare, corresponds to knowledge creation, knowledge impact and knowledge diffusion. Furthermore, (2) good and services (creative outputs) imply intangible assets, creative goods and services, online creativity and health care (Duarte, M. P., & Carvalho, F. M.,2020).

In recent years, companies in almost every industry have conducted a series of initiatives to explore management and strategies for new digital enterprise transformation and explore their impact on welfare. The digital transformation of companies involves products, processes and organizational structures.

Companies need to establish management practices and strategies to govern this ecosystem of digital enterprise transformation.

A critical approach is to formulate management and strategies that serves as a central concept to integrate all coordination, prioritization and implementation of digital transformations within a company. (Matt, C., Hess, T., & Benlian, A., 2015).

Regardless of the sector or company, management and strategies for digital enterprise transformation have some aspects in common. These elements have four essential dimensions: use of technologies, changes in value creation, structural changes and financial aspects. The use of technologies addresses a company's attitude towards new technologies, as well as its ability to exploit these technologies. From a management and strategies perspective, the use of new technologies often implies changes in value creation. They concern the impact of digital enterprise transformation strategies on companies' value chains, that is, the extent to which new digital activities deviate from the traditional core business - often still analogue. Structural changes refer to variations in a company's organizational configuration, especially concerning the placement of new digital activities within corporate structures. Moreover, finally, its ability to finance a digital enterprise transformation effort (Matt, C., Hess, T., & Benlian, A., 2015).

The impact of management and strategies for digital enterprise transformation on welfare requires aligning the use of technologies, changes in value, structural changes and financial aspects (Matt, C., Hess, T., & Benlian, A., 2015). At the same time, there are studies on the digital enterprise transformation such digitization and welfare, digital transformation strategies (Frennert, S., 2018), Industry 4.0, digitization, and opportunities for sustainability (Ghobakhloo, M., 2020), digital transformation and public services (Larsson, A., & Teigland, R.,2019). However, there is a gap in the study of management and strategies for digital enterprise transformation and welfare, based on indices of technological intensity and innovation inputs-outputs. Therefore, no studies in management and strategies for digital enterprise transformation relating to welfare, based on GII indices. This chapter will try to close this gap in the available literature. To allow a range of options for managers, policymakers and researchers, ways to promote welfare derived from the current digital acceleration in the post-pandemic era of COVID 19.

Literature Review

Digital Enterprise Transformation

Digitization essentially refers to taking analogue information and encoding it into zeroes and ones so that computers can store, process, and transmit such information. *Digitalization*, it is the process that highlights a digital business (Bloomberg, J., 2018). *Digital enterprise transformation* strategies focus on the transformation of products, processes, and organizational aspects owing to new technologies. Their focus includes digital activities at the interface. Digital enterprise transformation strategies go beyond the process paradigm and include changes and implications for welfare (Matt, C., Hess, T., & Benlian, A., 2015), (Table 1).

Digital Enterprise Transformation and Management Strategies

Larsson, A., & Teigland, R. (2019), investigate how strategies for digital transformation process impacts on welfare.

Table 1. Digitization, digitalization and digital enterprise transformation

Reference	Concept	Definition	Example
Bloomberg, J. (2018). Digitization, digitalization, and digital transformation. Gartner's IT Glossary	Digitization	Encoding it into zeroes, store and process.Process of changing from analogue to digital form.	Converting handwritten or typewritten text into digital (LP or video off of a VHS tape).
	Digitalization	Digital technologies change a business model and provide new revenue and value-producing opportunities.	As such interactions move away from analogue technologies (snail mail, telephone calls) to digital ones (email, chat, social media), both work and leisure domains become digitalized.
	Digital Enterprise Transformation	In contrast, is not something that enterprises can implement as projects. Refer to customer-driven strategic business transformation requiring cross-cutting organizational change and implementation of digital technologies.	Uber Platform; ebay Digital Enterprise Transformation Platform; Facebook Enterprise, Digital Trasnformation Platform.

Source: Authors

Organisation for Economic Co-operation and Development (OECD, 2016) establishes strategies for digital enterprise transformation, focusing on specific public service areas in which government needs to impact on welfare, emphasising the focus on digitalisation of health care, education, and protection services, including the use of assistive technologies referred to as "digital welfare".

Strategies for educational technology has a disruptive or transformative influence on the educational environment today. These strategies then proceed by looking at what is happening now with the increasing impact of digital technologies and finally examining the potential futures in terms of what lies ahead for this public good in particular (Larsson, A., & Teigland, R. (2019).

Regarding education as welfare, the emphasis falls on EdTech and adoption of strategies for digital enterprise transformation. The improvement of goods and services, it highlights the relationship between strategies for digital enterprise transformation and social care, telemedicine, and blockchain in health care. The strategies for digital enterprise impact on welfare through the improvement of health services, the real-time response and the simplification of processes. (Larsson, A., & Teigland, R. (2019).

Other studies investigate the implemented comparative measures and the challenges faced by higher education institutions (HEIs) dealing with the strategies for digital enterprise transformation of their processes. The research results show a significant change in the particular interest in the use of strategies for digital technologies at HEIs. (Limani, Y., Hajrizi, E., Stapleton, L., & Retkoceri, M., 2019). With these strategies for digital enterprise transformation, the machine will not replace the teacher. Nevertheless, the teacher will replace another teacher whom fewer masters the technologies to put them at the service of welfare.

Duarte, M. P., & Carvalho, F. M. (2020) developed strategies for digital enterprise transformation using a panel dataset, based on the global innovation index framework, and analysed it through a series of multiple regression techniques. Their results suggest a strong, positive influence of Business Sophistication on innovation outputs in countries of the Eurozone, derived mainly from the capacity of domestic firms to absorb strategies for knowledge of the environment.

Faghin, N., and Sazegar, M. (2019) proposes strategies for a taxonomy of country performance based on GDP and innovation indicators within G20 economies and considered the impact of GDP on welfare and investigates how the development of G20 economies relates to the innovation promotion factors extracted from the Global Innovation Index (GII). Several indicators are used, such as population (in millions), GDP (in USD billion), and seven indicators extracted from the GII data. Through the evaluation process, the seven indicators divided into input and output data; five of them are the input data (institutions, human capital and research, infrastructure, market sophistication, and business sophistication), and the other two are the output data (knowledge and technology output and creative output). The taxonomy provides the identification of country performance and presents relevant information to policymakers, who seek to apply effective economic strategies for digital transformation and develop global policies.

The present literature review theorises the impact of management and strategies for digital enterprise transformation on welfare. However, the gap in the literature persists. The available literature does not seem to clarify an accurate study that starts from the empirical data of the technological intensity and innovation index to gauge its impact on welfare, in this case, measured by the quality of education and the improvement in the offer of services.

Digital Enterprise Transformation and Welfare

Some authors (Mutanov, G., Mamykova, Z., Kopnova, O., & Bolatkhan, M., 2020) argue from theory and about data management strategies assessing the value of IT and ensure the adoption of practical decisions strategies —conceptualised the issues of data management strategies in higher education, using the example of the university. (Mutanov, G., Mamykova, Z., Kopnova, O., & Bolatkhan, M., 2020).

Other authors (Korachi, Z., & Bounabat, B., 2020) analyze various strategies for digital enterprise transformation and classify their common elements that frame and drive the formulation of management enterprise strategies. The analysis identified how IT governance and strategies for management could contribute to formulating strategies for digital enterprise transformation. Based on this empirical study several results proposed are strategic awareness, strategic business planning, IT organisational structure, steering committee, IT prioritisation process, IT investment decisions, IT strategic planning, IT budgeting, IT reporting, IT reaction capacity and management strategy (Korachi, Z., & Bounabat, B., (2020). According to Reis, D.A., et al. (2019), the strategies for creative expression combined with the protection of intellectual property stimulates and increases innovation. The authors identify innovation input and innovation output to the outcomes of innovation (products of knowledge and technology; innovative products).

Alkhaleefah, A. (2018) identify the factors and strategies that contributed positively to improve the international rank of Saudi Arabia. The analysis suggests that the most significant factor for digital enterprise transformation strategies is infrastructure, market sophistication, business sophistication, creative output.

Reis, D.A. et al. (2019) found that innovation input is related to innovation environment and innovation output, which in turn with proper innovation outcomes (products of knowledge and technology; innovative products).

Based on the GII metrics, the research aims to investigate the possible relationship between input and output in the innovation ecosystem. Using annual country data, they estimate a quantile regression model to identify the structural relationship between innovation input and output. The findings show that for digital enterprise transformation, innovation input has a significant and positive effect on innovation output. Besides, the more findings useful for national innovation policies since they emphasize the need to promote better innovation incentives strategies.

Crespo, N. F., and Crespo, C. F. (2016) indicate that strategies for the political decision-making processes required for improving the level of innovation.

On digital transformation strategies, Sohn, S.Y. et al. (2016), proposed a structural equation model (SEM) based on the hypothesis of the national innovation structure among seven factors representing inputs (institution, human capital and research, infrastructure, marketing sophistication and business sophistication) and outputs (knowledge and technology outputs, and creative outputs). Using GII data from 2013, they discovered that strategies for business sophistication and infrastructure have the most potent direct and indirect effects on creative output.

Strategies for digital transformation, - according to Aydin, E. et al. (2016) - deals with human capital and research, infrastructure, market sophistication, business sophistication and their effects on knowledge and technology output. Aydin, E. et al. (2016) found their results from studies on 17 developing countries during the period 2011. Using Pooled Ordinary Least Squares method, the authors showed that infrastructure, market sophistication, business sophistication are significant variables in explaining welfare - knowledge and technology output.

Nair, H. et al. (2014), focuses on innovation output of the United Arab Emirates or UAE. They observed that the output indicator improves from a value of 29.6 to about 42 when knowledge absorption input is considered individually, whereas the output increases to over 45 when all five indicators are simultaneously improved. So, strategies for digital enterprise transformation impacts on welfare.

Digital strategy in business aims to develop those activities that will support the main strategic goals namely:

1. efficient support of digital technology to the existing business model (run the business),
2. using digital technology to change existing business processes (change the business,
3. making innovative business models applying digital technology (reinvent the business). (Hasibović, A. Ć., & Tanović, A., 2019).

The tables below summarize the literature review, previous and recent research studies and how these findings impacted the present study. Thus, Tables 2 and 3 present the two trends underlying this research, namely, (1) digital enterprise transformation and management strategies and (2) digital enterprise transformation and welfare.

Despite these arguments, there is a substantial and often divergent gap regarding the impact of management and strategies for digital enterprise transformation on welfare, especially in education and in improving or not the supply of goods and services.

Table 2. Digital enterprise transformation and management strategies

Authors	Article Title	Digital Enterprise Transformation and Management Strategies
Castagna, F; Centobelli, P; Cerchione, R; Esposito, E; Oropallo, E; Passaro, R, 2020	Customer Knowledge Management in SMEs Facing Digital Transformation	Examine how "medium enterprises (SMEs) operating in creative industries in their customer knowledge management strategies". Their " finding showed the difficulties of SMEs operating in creative industries to be responsive to the rapid technological changes that are affecting CKM, as well as the lack of support from information technology vendors in the decision-making process for choosing adequate digital systems".
Mesas-Carrascosa, FJ; de Castro, AI; Torres-Sanchez, J; Trivino-Tarradas, P; Jimenez-Brenes, FM; Garcia-Ferrer, A; Lopez-Granados, F, 2020	Classification of 3D Point Clouds Using Color Vegetation Indices for Precision Viticulture and Digitizing Applications	"Remote sensing applied in the digital transformation of agriculture and, more particularly, in precision viticulture offers methods to map field spatial variability to support site-specific management strategies; these can be based on crop canopy characteristics such as the row height or vegetation cover fraction, requiring accurate three-dimensional (3D) information". "This methodology offers new capabilities for the use of sensors onboard platforms as a tool for precision viticulture and digitizing applications".
Meltzer, EO et al. 2020	Guidance to 2018 good practice: ARIA digitally-enabled, integrated, person-centred care for rhinitis and asthma	"AimsMobile Airways Sentinel NetworK (MASK) belongs to the Fondation Partenariale MACVIA-LR of Montpellier, France and aims to provide an active and healthy life to rhinitis sufferers and to those with asthma multimorbidity across the life cycle, whatever their gender or socio-economic status, in order to reduce health and social inequities incurred by the disease and to improve the digital transformation of health and care. The ultimate goal is to change the management strategy in chronic diseases.MethodsMASK implements ICT technologies for individualized and predictive medicine to develop novel care pathways by a multi-disciplinary group centred around the patients.StakeholdersInclude patients, health care professionals (pharmacists and physicians), authorities, patient's associations, private and public sectors". "Lessons learnt(i) Adherence to treatment is the major problem of allergic disease, (ii) Self-management strategies should be considerably expanded (behavioural), (iii) Change management is essential in allergic diseases, (iv) Education strategies should be reconsidered using a patient-centred approach and (v) Lessons learnt for allergic diseases can be expanded to chronic diseases".
Hasibovic, AC; Tanovic, A, 2020	PRINCE2 vs Scrum in digital business transformation	"Digital transformation or Industry 4.0 indicates new management strategies, for which right framework is almost mandatory".This "paper also emphasizes that digital transformation of an organisation can not be just an IT project".
Taneja, O., 2020	Leveraging Digital Transformation in Regional Economies with Concomitant Skills Development of People for More Efficient Operations & Resilience of Buildings over Their Life-Cycle	"Digital technologies are ubiquitous, but how digital transformation is applied to derive benefits for the built environment requires a critical assessment and execution". "The Challenge in regional economies lies in selecting the appropriate mix of technologies that can be reliably sustained and embraced by the community and workers without creating frustration and digital divide". "Digital Transformation & IoT facilitate cost-effective data gathering and analytics to deliver a comprehensive insight and management strategies for any sector". "A high performance building is founded on harmony of environment with human nature and integrates sensors, controls, measurements and automation to target optimization of how space is used, how equipment is operated, and how behavior modification is directed based on insights garnered through software analytics".

Source: Authors

RESEARCH METHODOLOGY

The scientific paradigm of this research fits into positivism. The authors use the inductive method, that starts from the particular and the secondary data of the GII, to generalize or universalize the results. Based

Table 3. Digital enterprise transformation and welfare

Authors	Article Title	Digital Transformation and Welfare
Hanelt, A; Bohnsack, R; Marz, D; Marante, CA, 2020	A Systematic Review of the Literature on Digital Transformation: Insights and Implications for Strategy and Organizational Change	"DT is moving firms to malleable organizational designs that enable continuous adaptation, and this move is embedded in and driven by digital business ecosystems"."The article derives a research agenda and provides managerial implications for strategy and organizational change, namely technology impact, compartmentalized adaptation, systemic shift and holistic co-evolution".
Correani, A; De Massis, A; Frattini, F; Petruzzelli, AM; Natalicchio, A, 2020	Implementing a Digital Strategy: Learning from the Experience of Three Digital Transformation Projects	"The rapid growth of digital technologies and the extraordinary amount of data that devices and applications collect each day are increasingly driving companies to radically transform the business architecture through which they create and appropriate value". "However, companies may fail to extract value from digital transformation due to the disconnection between strategy formulation and strategy implementation". "This article presents a framework than can help companies implement their digital transformation strategy and thereby renovate their business model".
Fischer, M; Imgrund, F; Janiesch, C; Winkelmann, A, 2020	Strategy archetypes for digital transformation: Defining meta objectives using business process management	"Digital transformation dominates practical and scientific discourse". "Still, many companies do not have a clear plan on how to approach it". "Particularly, small- and medium-sized enterprises struggle to initiate their digital journey as they lack resources and expertise". "In response, the authors examine how five companies use business process management (BPM) to implement digital transformation".
Wang, HC; Feng, JZ; Zhang, H; Li, X., 2020	The effect of digital transformation strategy on performance The moderating role of cognitive conflict	"The purpose of this study is to verify whether digital transformation strategy (DTS) could improve the organizational performance and provide a comprehensive analysis for enterprises on the necessity of implementing digital transformation in the context of China and draw on the perspectives of Skewed conflict, minority dissent theory and too-much-of-a-good-thing. To further reveal the micro-psychological mechanisms underlying the effect of DTS on organizational performance, this study confirmed the inverted U-shaped moderating effect of the top management team's cognitive conflict. Therefore, this research provides a new theoretical perspective for future research in the field of IT/IS, DTS and digital strategy".
Tekic, Z; Koroteev, D., 2019	From disruptively digital to proudly analog: A holistic typology of digital transformation strategies	"Recently booming academic interest in digital transformation aims to provide continuous support to managers in dealing with this important issue. However, as with all new fields, the scholarly literature is characterized by increased variability and diversity of topics covered, constructs used, and the relationships between them, resulting in an unclear and blurry understanding of the whole of digital transformation. The paper closes this gap by identifying distinctive digital transformation strategies in terms of two critical dimensions: usage of digital technologies and readiness of a business model for digital operation"

Source: Authors

on data from the GII, the authors intend to assess the strategies and management for digital enterprise transformation and their impact on welfare.

Research methodology follows steps: (1) literature review on management and strategies for digital enterprise transformation and welfare, (2) data selection from the Global Innovation Index (GII) input-output framework, (3) data analysis and (4) discussion of findings.

Regarding literature review - on management and strategies for digital enterprise transformation and welfare, - the research performed in the Scopus database allowed researchers access to the full-text content of more than 1,500 peer-reviewed journals in the fields of management and economics (e.g., Academy of Management Journal or Management Science).

Then a search was made on the Scopus using the following keywords: 'digital transformation' and 'welfare' and 'managerial strategies'. These keywords resulted in a sample of 560 articles. The authors next performed a backwards-forward search by reviewing the references of the articles.

Furthermore, for data selection, the authors chose the countries that occupy the first 50 places in the GII ranking on 2019 — in this way, trying to understand the impact of management and strategies for digital transformation on welfare. These countries are the ones that had the most significant capacity to absorb technological intensity and digital transformation and hence derive public strategies and policies with an impact on welfare.

The research analysis followed the construction of three explanatory models through multiple regressions, using the SPSS software. Furthermore, it was discussed and interpreted the results to gauge the contribution of each variable (input) on welfare (output). Then, it could be established the strategies and management in the context of the accelerated digital transformation that affects companies and entrepreneurs.

The Impact of Management and Strategies for Digital Enterprise Transformation on Welfare

Theory, Data and Methods Issues, Controversies, Problems

The models built in this chapter was based on theories, literature review, and tested from the GII database. Having perceived the first Top 50 GII ranking countries inside the overall countries in this section, the authors propose a conceptual model to study *The Impact of Management and Strategies for Digital Enterprise Transformation on Welfare.*

These models - tested on the GII data (released by INSEAD - European Institute of Business Administration)- served to build the research design.

The INSEAD - launched the GII in 2007 to improve measurement of innovation readiness as a component of strategies for digital enterprise transformation of countries and to find means of generating meaningful comparisons, - helps business leaders and public policymakers to adopt managerial strategies for the relative performance (Duarte, M. P., & Carvalho, F. M. P. O., 2020).

The GII report of 2019 covers 126 countries, compared along 80 indicators.

Its framework distinguishes inputs and outputs.

Inputs are elements of the national economy that enable digital transformation and innovative activities. Outputs results of the impacts of innovative economic activities on welfare.

Indicators aggregated in 21 sub-pillars, in turn, are aggregated under seven pillars. Five of those are input pillars, consisting in institutions, human capital and research, infrastructure, market sophistication, and business sophistication, while two are output pillar, namely knowledge and technology outputs, and creative outputs. Both input and output pillars then aggregated to form the input and the output sub-indices.

Theory, previous literature, and empirical studies show, in most cases, the existence of a positive correlation between, digital *enterprise transformation and welfare and digital enterprise transformation and management strategies.* However, this study aims to understand *The Impact of Management and Strategies for Digital Enterprise Transformation on Welfare, particularly on* education and supply of goods and services. That is, after analyzing the relationship between *Technological Inputs* on strategies for digital enterprise transformation and *Technological Outputs on* Welfare, the chapter intends to understand how *Digital Enterprise Transformation impacts on welfare.*

Figure 1 shows the proposed conceptual model, in which arrows represent the hypothesis developed below.

Figure 1. Conceptual model
Source: Authors

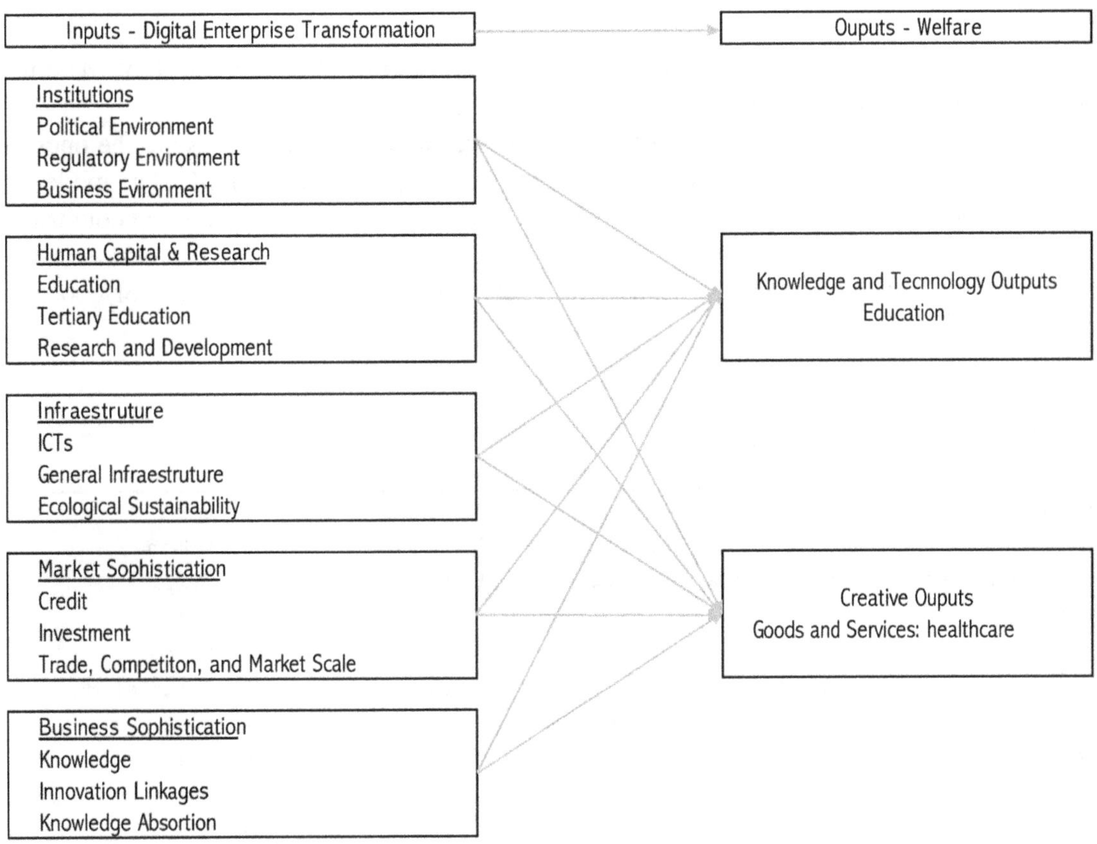

Duarte M.P. et al. (2007), argues that there is a positive impact of innovation inputs on creative outputs in every income group.

However, *The Impact of Management and Strategies for Digital Enterprise Transformation on Welfare* (education and supply of goods and services) is unclear. Hence the starting point is: What is *The Impact of Management and Strategies for Digital Enterprise Transformation on Welfare* (education and supply of goods and services)?

Therefore, we propose the following hypothesis:

H1: Management and Strategies for Digital Enterprise Transformation has a positive impact on Welfare.
H2: Management and Strategies for Digital Enterprise Transformation has a positive impact on education.
H3: Management and Strategies for Digital Enterprise Transformation has a positive impact on improving the supply of Goods and Services.

Based on the longitudinal GII framework, we have developed a pooled OLS regression models in order to test the proposed hypothesis. We then applied the models to a sub-sample composed exclusively by top 50 ranking countries in order to understand *The Impact of Management and Strategies for Digital Enterprise Transformation on Welfare* (education and supply of goods and services).

Data and sample

As mentioned above, we have developed a panel dataset composed of 50 countries (Table 4) during 2019. The study uses GII data exclusively.

The authors chose the first 50 countries in the GII ranking. Since these countries are the ones that have the best indicators of the absorption of technological intensity, according to GII. The models assume that there is no heterogeneity because our goal is not to explore differences between countries or possible fixed or variable effects, but from the database to try to understand *The Impact of Management and Strategies for Digital Enterprise Transformation on Welfare* (education and supply of goods and services).

Table 4. Sample

1°	Switzerland	11°	Republic of Korea	21°	Austria	31°	Slovenia	41°	Greece
2°	Sweden	12°	Ireland	22°	Australia	32°	Portugal	42°	VietNam
3°	United States of America	13°	Hong Kong, China	23°	Belgium	33°	Hungary	43°	Thailand
4°	Netherlands	14°	China	24°	Estonia	34°	Latvia	44°	Croatia
5°	United Kingdom	15°	Japan	25°	New Zealand	35°	Malaysia	45°	Montenegro
6°	Finland	16°	France	26°	Czech Republic	36°	United Arab Emirates	46°	Russian Federation
7°	Denmark	17°	Canada	27°	Malta	37°	Slovakia	47°	Ukraine
8°	Singapore	18°	Luxembourg	28°	Cyprus	38°	Lithuania	48°	Georgia
9°	Germany	19°	Norway	29°	Spain	39°	Poland	49°	Turkey
10°	Israel	20°	Iceland	30°	Italy	40°	Bulgaria	50°	Romania

Source: Authors

Variables and Code Book

Tables 5 and 6 show the variables and the code *book.*

We reconstructed the database from the individual reports of each country, generated by the GII in 2019, taking into account the score in a ranking of 1-100 points. Then we developed a *Code Book,* to allow a better clarification of the relationship between the variables, always based on the reports and database of the GII for the year 2019.

Code Book and Dependent Variables

To analyze the relationship between *innovation inputs* and *outputs,* we used two dependents variables in the model (*Knowledge and Technology Outputs* (OX6)) and Technological *Innovation Outputs (OX8*

Table 5. Code book - independent variables

Indepentent Variables: Technological Inputs	Code	Description / Proxy
Institutions	InX1	Discrete variable form 1-100
Political Environment	InX1,1	Measurement Political Environment score
Regulatory Environment	InX1.2	Measurement Regulatory Environment score
Business Evironment	InX1.3	Business Evironment
Human Capital & Research	InX2	Discrete variable form 1-100
Education	InX2.1	Measurement Education score
Tertiary Education	InX2.2	MeasurementTertiary Education score
Tertiary Education	InX2.3	MeasurementTertiary Education score
Infraestruture	InX3	Discrete variable form 1-100
ICT's	InX3.1	Measurement ICT's score
General Infraestruture	InX3.2	Measurement General Infraestruture score
Ecological Sustainability	InX3.3	Measurement Ecological Sustainability score
Market Sophistication	InX4	Discrete variable form 1-100
Credit	InX4.1	Measurement Ecological Sustainability score
Investment	InX4.2	Measurement Investment score
Trade, Competiton, and Market Scale	InX4.3	Measurement Trade, Competiton, and Market Scale score
Business Sophistication	InX5	Discrete variable form 1-100
Knowledge	InX5.1	Measurement Knowledge score
Innovation Linkages	InX5.2	Measurement Innovation Linkages score
Knowledge Absortion	InX5.3	Measurement score Knowledge Absortion score

Source: Authors

Code Book and Independent Variables

The explanatory variables used are the scores of the innovation *input sub-index (In)* and the five innovation input pillars, *Institutions (InX1), Human Capital and Research (InX2), Infrastructure (InX3), Market Sophistication (InX4), Business Sophistication (InX5),* and three sub-input pillars within *Market Sophistication (InX4),* namely Credit *(InX4.1), Investment (InX4.2), Trade, Competition, and Market Scale (InX4.3).*

Table 6. Code book - dependent variables

Dependents Variables : Ouputs	Code	Description / Proxy
Knowledge and Tecnnology Outputs	OX6	Discrete variable form 1-100
Knowledge creation	OX6.1	Measurement Knowledge creation score
Knowledge impact	OX6.2	Measurement Knowledge impact score
Knowledge diffusion	OX6.3	Measurement Knowledge diffusion score
Creative Ouputs	OX7	Discrete variable form 1-100
Intagible assessts	OX7.1	Intagible assessts score
Creative goods & services	OX7.2	Creative goods & services score
Online creativity	OX7.3	Online creativity score
(OX6+OX7)/2	OX8	Technologial Innovation Output score
(InX1+InX2+InX3+InX4+InX5)/2	InXO	Techonogical Innovation Input score

Source: Authors

Model Specification

Considering the available data and the conceptual model presented, the linear regressions with data, proposed above, using several estimators the most common the pooled ordinary least squares is the one that best fits (Baltagi, 2015; Wooldridge, 2016). So, we developed four models in both pooled OLS.

To build the models, we used the method based on theoretical reasons. So, we use the hierarchical method. Answering the initial research question, the authors formulated three hypotheses. The study developed three models corresponding to each hypothesis. Each model was built hierarchically using the software. The models were assembled by gradually inserting an explanatory variable.

Model 1

First, the authors perform a linear regression between *Digital Enterprise Transformation*, (innovation input pillars), namely, *Institutions (InX1), Human Capital and Research (InX2), Infrastructure (InX3), Market Sophistication (InX4), and Business Sophistication (InX5)* against Welfare (education) the output sub-index *Innovation Outputs (InX8)* to assess *The Impact of Management and Strategies for Digital Enterprise Transformation on Welfare* (education and supply of goods and services), measured by *Technological Innovation Outputs* (OX8).

Therefore, to test hypothesis H1, the authors developed the following models:

$$OX8_{it} = \beta_0 + \beta_1 InX_{1it} + \beta_2 InX_{2it} + \beta_3 InX_{3it} + \beta_4 InX_{4it} + \beta_5 InX_{5it} + \mu_{it};$$

$$i = 1,2,\dots 50; t = 2019 \quad (1)$$

Where, *Ox8it* is the dependent variable Welfare, measured by *Technological Innovation Outputs* (OX8) for each country (i=1,2....50) in the year 2019, *β0* is the intercept, *β1, β2, β3, β4, β5* are the slope of the variable of interest and the coefficients of *InX1, InX2, InX3, InX4,* and *InX5*, which stand for *Inputs of Institutions, Human Capital and Research, Infrastructure, Marketing Sophistication, Business Sophistication,* respectively, and μit as a stochastic error.

Table 7. Descriptive statistics and correlation matrix

Variables	Cod	Mean	S.D	N	OX8	InX1	InX2	InX3	InX4	InX5
Tecnological Innovation Ouputs	OX8	4.3	9.319	50						
Institutions	InX1	79.1	10.533	50	.611					
Human Capital & Research	InX2	47.1	10.503	50	.632	.700				
Infraestruture	InX3	57.4	7.242	50	.677	.824	.700			
Market Sophistication	InX4	57.2	10.215	50	.498	.632	.581	.498		
Business Sophistication	InX5	47.1	11.339	50	.900	.705	.761	.739	.510	

Source: Authors

Model 2

Secondly, we perform a linear regression between Digital *Enterprise Transformation*, measured by all input pillars, *Institutions (InX1), Human Capital and Research (InX2), Infrastructure (InX3), Market Sophistication (InX4), and Business Sophistication (InX5)* against education measured by the output sub-index *Knowledge and Technology Outputs (InX6)* to assess how Management *and Strategies for Digital Enterprise Transformation have a positive impact on Education* (OX6).

Therefore, to test hypothesis H2, we developed the following models:

$$OX6_{it} = \beta_0 + \beta_1 InX_{1it} + \beta_2 InX_{2it} + \beta_3 InX_{3it} + \beta_4 InX_{4it} + \beta_5 InX_{5it} + \mu_{it};$$

$$i = 1,2,\ldots 50; t = 2019 \qquad (2)$$

Where, *Ox6it* is the dependent variable *(Knowledge and Technology Outputs (OX6)* for each country (i=1,2…..50) in the year 2019, *β0* is the intercept, *β1, β2, β3, β4, β5* are the slope of the variable of interest and the coefficients of *InX1, InX2, InX3, InX4, and InX5*, which stand for *Inputs of Institutions, Human Capital and Research, Infrastructure, Marketing Sophistication, Business Sophistication,* respectively, and μit as a stochastic error.

Model 3

Third, we perform a linear regression between *Digital Enterprise Transformation*, measured by all input pillars, *Institutions (InX1), Human Capital and Research (InX2), Infrastructure (InX3), Market Sophistication (InX4), and Business Sophistication (InX5)* against *Creative Outputs* (Goods and Services) OX7.

Therefore, to test hypothesis H3, we developed the following models:

$$OX7_{it} = \beta_0 + \beta_1 InX_{1it} + \beta_2 InX_{2it} + \beta_3 InX_{3it} + \beta_4 InX_{4it} + \beta_5 InX_{5it} + \mu_{it};$$

$$i = 1,2,\ldots 50; t = 2019 \qquad (3)$$

Table 8. Coefficients and variance inflation factors (VIF)

Model 1 (a)	Unst. Coefficients B	Std. Error	St. Coefficients Beta	t	Sig	Collinearity Statistics Tolerance	VIF
Constant	3,249	5,218			0,623	0,537	
inX1-Institutions	-0,132	0,111	-0,149	-1,183	0,2243	0,246	4,066
inX2-Human Capital & Research	-0,155	0,095	-0,174	-1,633	0,109	0,341	2,932
inX3-Infraestruture	0,186	0,157	0,145	1,88	0,241	0,262	3,817
inX4-Market Sophistication	0,118	0,077	0,13	1,545	0,129	0,552	1,812
inX5-Business Sophistication	0,793	0,089	0,964	8,92	0,000	0,332	3,009
(a) dependent variable - Technological Outputs							

Source: Authors

Where *Ox7it* is the dependent variable *Creative Outputs – Goods and Services (OX7))* for each country (i=1,2….50) in the year 2019, $\beta 0$ is the intercept, $\beta 1, \beta 2, \beta 3$, *are* the slope of the variable of interest and the coefficients of *InX1, InX2, InX3, InX4, and InX5*, which stand for *Inputs of Institutions, Human Capital and Research, Infrastructure, Marketing Sophistication, Business Sophistication,* respectively, and μit as a stochastic error.

Table 9. Descriptive statistics and correlation matrix

Variables	Cod	Mean	S.D	N	OX8	InX1	InX2	InX3	InX4	InX5
Knowledge & Technology Outputs	OX6	39.33	12.458	50						
Institutions	InX1	79.088	10.533	50	.501					
Human Capital & Research	InX2	47.056	10.503	50	.634	.700				
Infraestruture	InX3	57.394	7.242	50	.568	.824	.700			
Market Sophistication	InX4	57.190	10.215	50	.498	.632	.581	.498		
Business Sophistication	InX5	47.071	11.339	50	.858	.705	.761	.739	.510	

Source: Authors

Table 10. Coefficients and variance inflation factors (VIF)

Model 2 (b)	Unst. Coefficients B	Unst. Coefficients Std. Error	St. Coefficients Beta	t	Sig	Collinearity Statistics Tolerance	Collinearity Statistics VIF
Constant	3,545	7,884	-0,325	0,450	0,655		
inX1-Institutions	-0,385	0,168	-0,325	-2,292	0,027	0,246	4,066
inX2-Human Capital & Research	-0,024	0,143	-0,02	-0,167	0,868	0,341	2,932
inX3-Infraestruture	0,042	0,237	0,025	0,179	0,859	0,262	3,817
inX4-Market Sophistication	0,248	0,116	0,203	2,143	0,038	0,552	1,812
inX5-Business Sophistication	1,078	0,134	0,981	8,032	0,000	0,332	3,009

(b) dependent variable - Knowledge and Technology Outputs

Source: Authors

Table 11. Descriptive statistics and correlation matrix

Variables	Cod	Mean	S.D	N	OX7	InX1	InX2	InX3	InX4	InX5
Creative Outuputs	OX7	41.302	8.269	50						
Institutions	InX1	79.088	10.533	50	.621					
Human Capital and Research	InX2	47.056	10.503	50	.469	.700				
Infraestruture	InX3	57.394	7.241	50	.670	.824	.700			
Market Sophistication	InX4	57.190	10.214	50	.371	.632	.581	.498		
Business Sophistication	InX5	47.0714	11.338	50	.735	.705	.761	.739	.510	

Source: Authors

Table 12. Coefficients and variance inflation factors (VIF)

Model 3 (b)	Unst. Coefficients B	Unst. Coefficients Std. Error	St. Coefficients Beta	t	Sig	Collinearity Statistics Tolerance	Collinearity Statistics VIF
(Constant)	2,953	6,856		0,431	0,669		
inX1 - Institutions	0,122	0,146	0,155	0,835	0,408	0,246	4,066
inX2 - Human Capital and Research	-0,286	0,124	-0,363	-2,297	0,026	0,341	2,932
inX3 - Infraestruture	0,33	0,206	0,289	1,602	0,116	0,262	3,817
inX4 - Marketing Sophistication	-0,011	0,101	-0,014	-0,112	0,911	0,552	1,812
inX5 - Business Sophistication	0,507	0,117	0,695	4,342	0,00	0,332	3,009

(b) dependent variable - Creative Outputs

Source: Authors

SOLUTIONS AND RECOMMENDATIONS

Results and Discussion

Tables 7 - 12 show the main descriptive statistics, the correlation matrix, and variance inflation factors (VIF). An analysis of the correlation matrix reveals the existence of significant correlations between the variables. The existing correlations between the variables could result in multicollinearity. However, the highest VIF value (4.066 for variable InX1) is below the standard rule of thumb of 10 (Wooldridge, 2016), which indicates that multicollinearity should not be a problem.

Model 1

Descriptive statistics, correlation matrix, and variance inflation factors (VIF): Tables 7 and 8 show the main descriptive statistics, the correlation matrix, and variance inflation factors (VIF). An analysis of the correlation matrix reveals the existence of significant correlations between the variables. The existing correlations between the five input pillars could not result in multicollinearity issues when regressed together. However, the highest VIF value (4.066 for variable InX1 - Institutions) is below the typical rule of thumb of 10 (Wooldridge, 2016), which indicates that multicollinearity should not be a problem.

It was found *The Impact of Management and Strategies for Digital Enterprise Transformation* measured by *Technological Innovation Inputs (Institutions, Human Capital & Research, Infrastructure, Marketing Sophistication, Business Sophistication)* can predict the *welfare* measured by *Technological Innovation Outputs* (Knowledge & *Technological and Creative Outputs).* The analysis resulted in a statistically significant model. Following that *Business Sophistication* described as follows: I F (5, 44) = 42,689; p< 0,001; = 0,911) I.

The model shows that *Business Sophistication (β=0,964; t=8,920; p<.001)* are able (strongly) to predict Technological *Innovation Outputs (Knowledge & Technology and Creative Outputs).* The exegesis of the results of this first model points to the confirmation of our initial hypothesis, according to which *Management and Strategies for Digital Enterprise Transformation have a positive impact on welfare.*

However, the excessive weight of *Business Sophistication* in the model is evident. This excessive weight may be an open path for policymakers to focus on measures aimed at changing or increasing *Business Sophistication* by increasing measures aimed at the *Knowledge Workers, Innovation Linkages, Knowledge Absorption* sub-pillars. In this model, we expected *Institutions and Human Capital and Research* to have a positive impact. This result does not happen since the impact of these variables is negative *(Institutions, β = -.149; Human Capital and Research β = -.179);* however, it is statistically insignificant with *p> .05.*

Then, from *Model 1, the equation (1) becomes*

$$OX8_{it} = \beta_0 + \beta_1 InX_{1it} + \beta_2 InX_{2it} + \beta_3 InX_{3it} + \beta_4 InX_{4it} + \beta_5 InX_{5it} + \mu_{it};$$

$$i = 1, 2, \ldots 50; t = 2019 \tag{1}$$

Welfare *(Knowledge & Technology and Creative Output) = 3,249 - 0,132 (Institutions) - 0,155(Human Capital & Research,) + 0,186 (Infrastructure)+0,118(Marketing Sophistication) +0,793 (Business Sophistication)* + µit .

Model 2

Carried out multiple regression to verify whether the impact of *Management and Strategies for Digital Enterprise Transformation* on *education (Knowledge & Technology).* Again, we confirm Hypothesis 2.

$$OX6_{it} = \beta_0 + \beta_1 InX_{1it} + \beta_2 InX_{2it} + \beta_3 InX_{3it} + \beta_4 InX_{4it} + \beta_5 InX_{5it} + \mu_{it};$$

$$i = 1, 2, \ldots 50; t = 2019 \tag{2}$$

Then, from Model 2, the equation (2) becomes:Education *(Knowledge & Technology) = 3,545 - 0,385 (Institutions) - 0,024(Human Capital & Research,) + 0,042 (Infrastructure)+0,248(Marketing Sophistication) +(1) (Business Sophistication)* + µit.

Model 3

Carried out multiple linear regression to verify whether *Management and Strategies for Digital Enterprise Transformation* impact on the improvement of the supply of Goods and Services (*Creative Output,* - intangible *assets, creative goods and services, and online creativity).*

The analysis resulted in a statistically significant model, (F (5, 44) = 14.683; p <0.001; = 0.625)).

The model shows that *Management and Strategies for Digital Enterprise Transformation, - Institutions (β = 0.155; t = 0.835; p> 0.001), Human Capital and Research (β = -0, 363; t = -0.297; p> 0.001), Infrastructure (β = 0.289; t = 1.602; p> 0.001), Marketing Sophistication (β = -014; t = -0.112; p> 0.001),* and *Business Sophistication (β = 0.695; t = 4.342; p <0.001),* - has a positive impact on *supply* of *Goods and Services (Creative Output, i.e., intangible assets, creative goods and services, and online creativity).*

Taking into account the available data and statistics, we emphasize that *Management and Strategies for Digital Enterprise Transformation* that occurs in *Business Sophistication* ($\beta = 0.695$; $t = 4.342$; $p < 0.001$), has the most powerful and most significant impact on *welfare,* namely in education and improving the supply of goods and services.

Then, from Model 3, the equation (3) becomes:

$$OX7_{it} = \beta_0 + \beta_1 InX_{1it} + \beta_2 InX_{2it} + \beta_3 InX_{3it} + \beta_4 InX_{4it} + \beta_5 InX_{5it} + \mu_{it};$$

$$i = 1, 2, \ldots 50; t = 2019 \quad (3)$$

Goods and Services (*Creative Outputs) = 2,953 + 0,122 (Institutions) - 0,286 (Human Capital & Research,) + 0,33(Infrastructure) – 0,011(Marketing Sophistication) + 0,507 (Business Sophistication)* + µit

Again, we confirm Hypothesis Nº. 3, according to which there is a positive impact of the management and strategy for digital enterprise transformation in the improvement of goods and services (creative outputs). If we analyze table nº 10, of the coefficients and the Variance Inflator Factors (VIF), we will notice that although the impact is positive, the contribution levels of each factor or variable differs. Thus, business sophistication that significantly explains the improvement of goods and services (creative outputs). Whether the management variable or for policymakers, it will be business sophistication, which in our codebook corresponds to knowledge, innovation linkages and knowledge absorption or the ability to absorb digital transformations.

The digital enterprise transformation strategies have been driven by companies, becoming the trend of social, economic and industrial development, affecting health and education. Health, education and social security have an impact on welfare.Therefore, the impact of digital transformation on welfare is not linear.

From theory and GII framework this study considers as indicators of digital enterprise transformation strategies, the degree of technology absorption and innovation that occurs in (1) institutions (political, legal and business environment), (2) in human capital, research and development (in education, tertiary education and research and development), (3) in infrastructures (ICTs, general infrastructure, ecological sustainability), (4) in the sophistication of the market (credit, investment, trade, competition and market of scale) and finally, (5) business sophistication (knowledge, innovation linkages, and absorption of knowledge). Therefore, welfare is measured by education indicators (knowledge and technology, i.e. (6) knowledge creation, knowledge impact and knowledge diffusion) and (7) creative outputs (i.e., intangible assets, creative goods and services, online creativity).

This study explored how digital enterprise transformation influences welfare, examining the impact of the digital transformation indicators of 50 countries that occupy the top ranking in the GII digital transformation index.

Theoretical Implications

The current results present several theoretical contributions to existing research:

Hanelt, A. et al. (2020) propose managerial implications for strategy and organizational change, namely technology impact, compartmentalized adaptation, systemic shift and holistic co-evolution.

Correani, A. et al. (2020) argue that companies fail to extract value from digital enterprise transformation due to the gap between managerial strategy formulation and managerial strategy implementation.

Tekic, Z. et al. (2020) defends that the gap persists by identifying differential digital variable transformation strategies by the usage of digital technologies and readiness of a business model for digital operation.

Practical Implications

Industrial policies to promote the development of the digital economy and the company's digital transformation experiences are beneficial to countries and organizations. Specifically, this research provides suggestions for managerial practice.

Given that digital enterprise transformation has a positive relationship to welfare, managers must undertake digital strategy immediately. The use of digital technologies, the redesign of the business model and the adjustment of the organizational structure need changes in order to achieve the digital strategy through continuous iteration and development.

Castagna, F. et al. (2020) showed the difficulties of SMEs operating in creative industries to be responsive to the rapid digital transformation changes.

Mesas-Carrascosa, F. J. et al. (2020) show how remote sensing applied in the digital transformation of agriculture and, more particularly, in precision viticulture offers methods to map spatial field variability to support site-specific management strategies and thereby increase the quality and quantity of goods and services.

Meltzer, E. O et al. (2020) showed how to provide an active and healthy life by improving the digital transformation of health and care.

However, the according to Taneja, O., (2020), the challenge in digital economies lies in selecting the appropriate mix of technologies that can be reliably sustained and embraced by the community and workers without creating frustration and the digital divide.

Digital transformation facilitates cost-effective data gathering and analytics to deliver a comprehensive insight and management enterprise strategies for any sector (Taneja, O., 2020).

FUTURE RESEARCH DIRECTIONS

Limitations and Future Directions of Research

Despite the importance of this research, our results have some limitations. First, the studies choice the top 50 countries of GII. A random selection of countries, regardless of their digital involvement, would likely lead to a different conclusion. The study was limited to the year 2019, and the study needed to cover a time horizon of 10 years to compare the results taking into account the fixed and variable effects over time.

Future studies should better explore the differences in the framework input-output technological intensity of countries and their ability to absorb knowledge regardless of their ranking and region.

CONCLUSION

In the era of accelerated digital enterprise transformation economy, and the post-pandemic COVID-19, digital technologies can significantly influence welfare through the absorption of digital transformations on education (knowledge and technology), improvement of goods and services (creative) and comprehensively change the organizational model, structure and business processes.

Furthermore, the impact of digital transformation on welfare has become a matter of strategic management for companies and policymakers.

Developing management and strategies help companies to have a well-defined path and benefit from digital enterprise transformation, enhancing education and creative outputs. A positive impact of management and strategies for digital enterprise transformation on welfare is not a self-standing process. This process is dependent on the technological intensity and innovation that a given country can absorb and managerial strategies for companies. The results showed that not all pillars – inputs - had the same impact; many of them had adverse effects and even insignificant contribution. Nevertheless, in aggregate, the study confirms that management and strategies for digital enterprise transformation explain welfare (education and the improvement in the offer of quality goods and services).

Therefore, it urges the policies directed at improving welfare and absorbing management strategies for digital enterprise transformation.

Management and strategies for digital enterprise transformation are strongly correlated with inputs innovation and outputs innovation technology. The hyperconnected and disruptive nature of digital technology has further highlighted the impact of management and strategies for digital enterprise transformation on welfare.

Therefore, the study confirms the hypotheses stated: *the impact of management and strategies for digital enterprise transformation on welfare.*

REFERENCES

Alkhaleefah, A. (2018). What to do to improve the international saudi innovation Rank/Score. *International Journal of Mechanical Engineering and Technology*, *9*(3), 435–442.

Aydin, E., Polat, A., & Ergene, L. T. (2016, November). Vector control of DFIG in wind power applications. In *2016 IEEE International Conference on Renewable Energy Research and Applications (ICRERA)* (pp. 478-483). IEEE. 10.1109/ICRERA.2016.7884383

Baltagi, B. H., Egger, P. H., & Kesina, M. (2016). Bayesian Spatial Bivariate Panel Probit Estimation', Spatial Econometrics: Qualitative and Limited Dependent Variables (Advances in Econometrics, Volume 37). Emerald Group Publishing Limited.

Bloomberg, J. (2018). Digitization, digitalization, and digital transformation: confuse them at your peril. *Forbes*.

Bousquet, J., Bedbrook, A., Czarlewski, W., Onorato, G. L., Arnavielhe, S., Laune, D., ... Morais-Almeida, M. (2019). Guidance to 2018 good practice: ARIA digitally-enabled, integrated, person-centred care for rhinitis and asthma. *Clinical and Translational Allergy*, *9*(1), 1–19.

Canonica, G. W., Antó i Boqué, J. M., Mullol i Miret, J., & Valero Santiago, A.MASK study group. (2019). Guidance to 2018 good practice: ARIA digitally enabled, integrated, person-centred care for rhinitis and asthma. *Clinical and Translational Allergy, 9.*

Cantú-Ortiz, F. J., Sánchez, N. G., Garrido, L., Terashima-Marin, H., & Brena, R. F. (2020). An artificial intelligence educational strategy for the digital transformation. *International Journal on Interactive Design and Manufacturing*, 1-15.

Castagna, F., Centobelli, P., Cerchione, R., Esposito, E., Oropallo, E., & Passaro, R. (2020). Customer Knowledge Management in SMEs Facing Digital Transformation. *Sustainability*, *12*(9), 3899. doi:10.3390u12093899

Chandler, A. D. (1990). *Strategy and structure: Chapters in the history of the industrial enterprise* (Vol. 120). MIT Press.

Correani, A., De Massis, A., Frattini, F., Petruzzelli, A. M., & Natalicchio, A. (2020). Implementing a digital strategy: Learning from the experience of three digital transformation projects. *California Management Review*, *62*(4), 37–56. doi:10.1177/0008125620934864

Crespo, N. F., & Crespo, C. F. (2016). Global innovation index: Moving beyond the absolute value of ranking with a fuzzy-set analysis. *Journal of Business Research*, *69*(11), 5265–5271. doi:10.1016/j.jbusres.2016.04.123

Duarte, M. P., & Carvalho, F. M. (2020). *Portugal in the Global Innovation Index: A panel data analysis* (No. 0144). Gabinete de Estratégia e Estudos, Ministério da Economia.

Faghih, N., & Sazegar, M. (2019). A Taxonomy of Country Performance Based on GDP and Innovation Indicators for the Group of Twenty (G20). In *Globalization and Development* (pp. 163–200). Springer. doi:10.1007/978-3-030-14370-1_7

Fischer, M., Imgrund, F., Janiesch, C., & Winkelmann, A. (2020). Strategy archetypes for digital transformation: Defining meta objectives using business process management. *Information & Management*, *57*(5), 103262. doi:10.1016/j.im.2019.103262

Frennert, S. (2018). Lost in digitalization? Municipality employment of welfare technologies. *Disability and Rehabilitation. Assistive Technology*. PMID:30264649

Garrido-Baserba, M., Corominas, L., Cortés, U., Rosso, D., & Poch, M. (2020). The fourth-revolution in the water sector encounters the digital revolution. *Environmental Science & Technology*, *54*(8), 4698–4705. doi:10.1021/acs.est.9b04251 PMID:32154710

Ghobakhloo, M. (2020). Determinants of information and digital technology implementation for smart manufacturing. *International Journal of Production Research*, *58*(8), 2384–2405. doi:10.1080/00207543.2019.1630775

Hanelt, A., Bohnsack, R., Marz, D., & Antunes, C. (2020). A systematic review of the literature on digital transformation: Insights and implications for strategy and organizational change. *Journal of Management Studies*, joms.12639. doi:10.1111/joms.12639

Hasibović, A. Ć., & Tanović, A. (2019, May). PRINCE2 vs Scrum in digital business transformation. In *2019 42nd International Convention on Information and Communication Technology, Electronics and Microelectronics (MIPRO)* (pp. 1514-1518). IEEE. 10.23919/MIPRO.2019.8756716

Khan, S. (2016). *Leadership in the digital age: A study on the effects of digitalisation on top management leadership*. Academic Press.

Korachi, Z., & Bounabat, B., (2020). *Towards a Frame of Reference for Smart City Strategy Development and Governance*. Academic Press.

Lankshear, C., & Knobel, M. (Eds.). (2008). *Digital literacies: Concepts, policies and practices* (Vol. 30). Peter Lang.

Larsson, Z. Y., Di Gangi, P. M., & Teigland, R. (2019). Sharing my way to success: A case study on developing entrepreneurial ventures using social capital in an OSS community. *Information and Organization*, *29*(1), 23–40. doi:10.1016/j.infoandorg.2018.12.001

Limani, Y., Hajrizi, E., Stapleton, L., & Retkoceri, M. (2019). Digital Transformation Readiness in Higher Education Institutions (HEI): The Case of Kosovo. *IFAC-PapersOnLine*, *52*(25), 52–57. doi:10.1016/j.ifacol.2019.12.445

Matt, C., Hess, T., & Benlian, A. (2015). Digital transformation strategies. *Business & Information Systems Engineering*, *57*(5), 339–343. doi:10.100712599-015-0401-5

Mesas-Carrascosa, F. J., de Castro, A. I., Torres-Sánchez, J., Triviño-Tarradas, P., Jiménez-Brenes, F. M., García-Ferrer, A., & López-Granados, F. (2020). Classification of 3D point clouds using color vegetation indices for precision viticulture and digitizing applications. *Remote Sensing*, *12*(2), 317. doi:10.3390/rs12020317

Mintzberg, H. (1979). Patterns in strategy formation. *International Studies of Management & Organization*, *9*(3), 67–86. doi:10.1080/00208825.1979.11656272

Mutanov, G., Mamykova, Z., Kopnova, O., & Bolatkhan, M. (2020). Applied research of data management in the education system for decision-making on the example of Al-Farabi Kazakh National University. In *E3S Web of Conferences* (Vol. 159, p. 09003). EDP Sciences. doi:10.1051/e3sconf/202015909003

Nair, H., Staat, H. J., Tran, T., van Houselt, A., Prosperetti, A., Lohse, D., & Sun, C. (2014). The Leidenfrost temperature increase for impacting droplets on carbon-nanofiber surfaces. *Soft Matter*, *10*(13), 2102–2109. doi:10.1039/C3SM52326H PMID:24651906

OECD. (2016). *Energy and Air Pollution: World Energy Outlook Special Report 2016*. OECD.

Reis, D. A., de Moura, F. R., & de Aragao Gomes, I. M. (2019, May). The Linkage between Intellectual Property and Innovation in the Global Innovation Ecosystem. In *European Conference on Intangibles and Intellectual Capital* (pp. 218-XIII). Academic Conferences International Limited.

Sohn, S. Y., Kim, D. H., & Yoon, J. H. (2016). Technology credit scoring model with fuzzy logistic regression. *Applied Soft Computing*, *43*, 150–158. doi:10.1016/j.asoc.2016.02.025

Tekic, Z., & Koroteev, D. (2019). From disruptively digital to proudly analog: A holistic typology of digital transformation strategies. *Business Horizons*, *62*(6), 683–693. doi:10.1016/j.bushor.2019.07.002

Vrooman, J. C. (2009). *Rules of relief: institutions of social security, and their impact*. Academic Press.

Wang, H., Feng, J., Zhang, H., & Li, X. (2020). The effect of digital transformation strategy on performance. *International Journal of Conflict Management*, *31*(3), 441–462. doi:10.1108/IJCMA-09-2019-0166

Williams, W., & Elmore, R. F. (Eds.). (2014). *Social Program Implementation: Quantitative Studies in Social Relations*. Academic Press.

Wooldridge, J. M. (2016). *Introductory econometrics: A modern approach*. Nelson Education.

Chapter 8
Strategies for Digital Transformation in Business:
Digital Accounting Strategy

Fatmanur Deniz
https://orcid.org/0000-0002-4291-8026
Nevşehir Hacı Bektaş Veli Üniversitesi, Turkey

ABSTRACT

Accounting is a discipline as old as human history, and with the last industrial revolution, it started to digitalize by taking a different dimension. It is important to know the ideas, the new order, and the new qualifications that employees should have, which are the basis of digital accounting, which has a quite new history in the world. In addition, mastering new developments and practices is important in order to continue the profession and apply it in its modern sense. This chapter was designed by author due to the lack of a comprehensive publication in the field of digital accounting and it is a fairly new concept. In this context, basic concepts were disclosed that subject and industrial revolutions. Later on, applications such as e-invoice, e-document, e-book, e-archive, which make up digital accounting by being separated from the traditional sense in the field of accountancy, are explained, and suggestions for the design new researches and diversification are presented.

INTRODUCTION

Businesses compete with their competitors by developing unique strategies in the sectors they operate. With the technological developments and digitalization experienced today, these strategies have started to differentiate. In this context, digital transformation in accounting, which is one of the basic functions of businesses, will be discussed and the subject will be explained in detail. Along with the information presented, an answer will be sought for the question of what digital strategies businesses should develop in the field of accounting.

In this section, the relationship between digital transformation and strategy will be explained through accounting, and the relationship between digital accounting and strategy will be explained. Therefore,

DOI: 10.4018/978-1-7998-8583-2.ch008

it is important to explain the concept of strategy first. Grant (2008) stated that the concept of strategy is not only a detailed plan or programmed set of instructions, but an integrative main idea that guides the decisions and actions of individuals or organizations. According to another definition, the strategy includes the ways and methods to achieve corporate goals determined by the resources available and all managerial decisions taken towards them (Johnsen, 2016).

Humanity has made continuous progress in the historical process. Since the first primitive weapons made of stone and wood, people have been in technological development. The goods produced during these periods were first bartering with one another and in this way, it was subjected to commercial activities. At this point, it can be mentioned that the accounting discipline existed in primitive until the years when the barter economy was made. Accounting discipline has developed with humanity and technological developments. Many innovations, from the use of water and steam power in production to today's internet-based applications, have been used in accounting and there has been a parallel development. In addition to the efforts to bring it into a national and international order, it has been widely was used in technology on accounting in time. Accounting, which was first used as a counting function in clearing transactions, later functioned as a systematic discipline in a certain order. With the development of technology and the use of it in the field of accounting, accounting processes have started to be made in electronic media. The concept of Industry 4.0, which was introduced in the recent past, has brought a separate point to the accounting studies and has turned to many different features by converting the accounting concept into a digital accounting concept. Accounting, where the bookkeeping period has been transferred to computers in the recent past, has become a very important function for businesses that directly affect the decision-making processes with Industry 4.0, shortly accounting has gone beyond the traditional understanding.

It is possible for businesses to determine effective strategies by following current developments and to make their activities continuous by providing a competitive advantage. For this reason, it is important for businesses to develop strategies and direct digital transformation using which innovations in the field of accounting in the digital transformation era. For this purpose, this book section has been designed. As the scope of the section, industrial revolutions are presented in order to understand the digitalization and transformation process. In light of this information, information was given about digital transformation and its applications in the field of accounting. Finally, information about how businesses can produce strategies using this information is given.

Within the scope of this study, the concept of digital accounting, which is quite new, has been handled, explained in detail, and supported with current application examples. Before addressing the concept of digital accounting and developments, the explanation of the conditions and concepts such as accounting, digitalization, industrial revolutions, recent industrial revolutions, and their effects on accounting is important for understanding the subject. In this regard, the basic concepts of the study were explained first.

BACKGROUND

The concept of digital accounting is quite new. For this reason, the number of studies in the literature is very few. If limited literature is mentioned, the book by Deshmukh (2006) is an important resource. Additionally, Amidu et al. (2011), Güney (2014), Gan et al. (2017), and Relhan (2013) are the most cited e-accounting (digital accounting) articles. On the other hand, in order to have full knowledge of digital accounting, it is necessary to know about the recent industrial revolution. In this context, the main sources about the last industrial revolution: Lasi et al. (2014), Stock and Seliger (2016), Lee et al. (2015), Vaidya et al. (2018), and Roblek et al. (2016) are scientific studies. When the literature is examined, it is seen that studies on strategy and digital accounting are lacking. There are studies such as Naranjo-Gil (2004) and Bromwich (1999) dealing with the relationship between accounting and strategy in very limited literature. However, there is a great lack of studies on digital transformation, digital accounting, and strategy. This study was designed because of this shortcoming. First, digitalization and the last industrial revolution will be explained by using the mentioned literature. Then digital accounting and applications will be presented.

MAIN FOCUS OF THE CHAPTER

The concept of accounting is actually a concept dating back to the early ages in human history. Even if it starts with the first commercial activities, the counting work, which forms the basis, is also older than these activities. Initially, counting operations with fingers began to be performed on abacuses over time; With the development of technology, it was made with machines. It is important to explain the concept of accounting based on the counting system, which historically peers to humanity, in terms of understanding the subject.

Initially, the counting work done with the fingers of the hands was carried out with abacuses developed in Mesopotamia with the increase in the amounts over time and facilitating the counting of more quantities. This system was insufficient with the increase in the human population in the world, the start of commercial transactions, and technological developments. Scientists have been interested in the need to have machines to find a solution to this problem and have made long studies in this regard. As a matter of fact, Pascal invented the world's first calculator in 1642, where the first addition and subtraction can be performed. However, this was still insufficient, although it facilitated operations. At this point, Leibniz invented the first impact machine in 1671. These simple machines were revolutionary when they were invented, but they had to be used as a system to calculate error-free and large quantities. This was an innovation that could not be reached until the development of computers. The machines of Pascal and Leibniz could also be developed with the development of studies on computers, the foundation of which was laid with the connection of mathematics and logic, and the use of electricity with machines. The work done by Babbage in the 19th century was concluded and the first advanced calculator was obtained. Then, in 1947, with the invention of ENIAC, the world's first computer, calculators were transferred to computers. The relationship between accounting, counting, and computer can be easily understood from the fact that people who count and calculate in ancient times are called computers (McCartney, 2001; Woodford, 2017).

Accounting discipline, which has been modernized by inventing calculators and computers, has gained a different dimension with digitalization. At this point, the concept of digitalization becomes important. The starting point of the concept of digitalization is also based on the math and logic marriage, which forms the basis of computers and calculators. Because great scientists such as Leibniz, Boolean, Newton, and Pascal have associated the number 1 in logic with the number 1 in mathematics, and the number 0 with the no. All the technological developments and digitalization we experience today are based on these 0-1 figures. Technological products and software are produced by expressing everything in coding language with 0 and 1. Based on this relationship, the concept of digitalization can be defined as the digitization of data obtained while performing certain jobs with the help of technological tools.

In a broader sense, digitalization is the technological innovation that provides access to richer information in less time and with less human labor in connection with each other, as a result of technological developments (Bělohlávek et al., 2017).

When we look at the accounting history, it is seen that the accounting processes performed manually in the recent past have been rapidly digitized. First, cash register receipts can be given. Instead of manually writing a receipt, cash registers make the receipts by using the technological tools. Accountants, on the other hand, made manual calculations by using transaction slips or receipts for all these sales and purchases before going digital. It was very time- and labor-intensive to perform all the transactions such as making individual journal entries, creating temporary and definitive trials, keeping book-led. However, with digitalization, sales made by a big market are automatically transferred from cash registers to computers, and these transactions are carried out with a very short time and workforce by processing the transferred information in software developed for computers. In this respect, the discipline accounting and profession that is most affected by digitalization is accountancy.

It is a threat to accountants that computers and their applications quickly replace accountants and do almost all things perfectly. Of course, it is a threat to integrate robots that we see only in movies in our childhood and embellish them with humanoid features. However, there is a need for accountants to improve their ability to use digitalization and their reporting capabilities. At this point, digitalization should be perceived as an innovation that facilitates the profession and accountants should perform their jobs in this direction.

Technological development and digitalization have emerged as a result of many years of work with the industrial revolutions. In this respect, industrial revolutions need to be briefly explained before explaining how the digitalization in question, and what innovations it brings, its advantages and disadvantages.

INDUSTRIAL REVOLUTIONS AND INDUSTRY 4.0

Industrial and technological development started with the tools and tools made by stones and trees of the people called primitive. Later on, the processing of mines and natural resources continued its development as a result of the development of people's abilities. The needs have increased in parallel with the development of humanity and the increase in the population. People have become unable to respond to these increasing needs by manual processing, and it has been revealed that there must be some innovations. Over time, there has been a transformation from workshop-type production to mass production.

As a result of the developments in the history of humanity and technology, the first industrial revolution emerged in England in the last quarter of the 18th century and spread all over the world; It was realized by inventing the machines working with water and steam power that can be used in production. This development is considered the beginning of industrialization in the world history and forms the basis of all other industrial revolutions. With the first industrial revolution, the operations made with simple tools are now being carried out by machines in a shorter time and in a larger amount. As a result, there was a transition from the workshop production to the factories. The most important effect of the first industrial revolution is the complete separation from past periods in terms of production and economy. These developments continued until the end of the 19th century (Yin et al., 2018).

By the end of the 19th century, the use of sliding bands in production, which was adopted after World War II and led to the mass production of Henry Ford in automobile production, caused a new industrial revolution in America. With the creation of product lines based on bands and the use of electricity in production, it has now been passed from small production to mass production. If we talk about the production line and band at this point, it is the design and use of all production processes in factories or production sites, for example in the production of an automobile, with a system such as a walking belt located in the current shopping malls. The raw material is put on this tape, followed by a station for each job and the process is completed without people carrying these parts. This convenience has enabled mass production. But in the beginning, these mass productions were concerned with the production of uniform products. The black Model Ts produced by Ford are the best examples and this production caused the period to be called Fordism (Ford et al., 2017; Tomac et al., 2019).

With the effect of the first and second industrial revolution, while mass production was emphasized all over the world, a new industrial revolution appeared on the horizon with the introduction of ENIAC, which was the first computer in 1947, and started to be used industrially in 1951. As a result of the development of the computer industry and the acceleration of technological studies in Silicon Valley in America, the 3rd Industrial Revolution or Industry 3.0 was introduced as a new industrial revolution. Computers were started to be used in production, and the realization of the works called automation with the help of machines started. It is an industrial revolution that still has an effect on the world and is widely used in many places. Even so, Industry 3.0; officially ended with the introduction of Industry 4.0 in Germany in 2011, and actually started to be implemented in 2015 (Köhler and Schimanovich, 2017).

In the period up to Industry 4.0, the important issues to be taken into consideration in the first three industrial revolutions, revolutions, and reasons were realized simultaneously. For example, the first revolution, mass production, and the second revolution, the use of computers and the third revolution took place together with mechanization and steam power, and these were simultaneous. In the last industrial revolution, all the premises emerged spontaneously with technological development, while the industrial revolution emerged as a result. First of all, computers were developed very quickly, smartphones and tablets were invented, the internet became widespread, and all kinds of information and data were accessible every second. In addition, flash disks, which are a physical product, have begun to leave their place in virtual environments called a cloud, the use of cameras in every area of our lives has increased, the vending machines we have received have become widespread, and when there is a malfunction in the factories, the sensor has detected a signal called a sensor. All this was a revolution and was eventually called Industry 4.0. It is obvious that the latest industrial revolution emerged naturally as a result of these developments. However, a new industrial revolution has emerged in the recent past, especially for reasons such as the Far East countries such as China, Japan, and South Korea dominating the product markets. As a result of this requirement, Germany introduced Industry 4.0 as a new revolution in the Hannover technology fair in 2011. The main purpose here was the thought of ending Far Eastern domination in production (Doğan & Derici, 2019).

Towards the end of the last century, the increase in international trade and the increase in the amount and variety of production created a competitive environment between enterprises and countries. Now businesses had to make low-cost productions in addition to quality products. Increasing quality is a topic that takes a long time and is still being studied in the field of accounting, as in every field. However, the increase in both raw material, technology, and labor costs in production in the early 2000s led to cost management. At this point, the use of machines in production areas with Industry 4.0 causes a decrease in labor cost, which is the biggest cost item in production (Strandhagen et al., 2017).

If a definition of Industry 4.0 is made, a vision is developed for the technology to be used in production areas and this vision is realized as a system. According to another definition, by establishing a new and future-oriented technological infrastructure in a production area, this directional transformation is achieved. Industry 4.0 is a holistic and visionary concept that integrates all processes with developments in information and communication fields, sensors as automation, data collection tools, and sharing function. Considering the definitions mentioned in general, Industry 4.0 is a new situation emerging with the intense influence and transformation of IT, communication, internet, sensor, automation, artificial intelligence, and robotic technologies. As it is a new concept, the basic features and components of Industry 4.0 need to be explained in terms of understanding this industrial revolution (Batth et al., 2018).

BASIC FEATURES OF INDUSTRY 4.0

Industry 4.0 enters not only production areas but also every moment of our lives with its content and components. In this regard, our entire life is in a transformation. In order to experience this transformation process and to be able to implement and manage it flawlessly, the characteristics of Industry 4.0 that reveal the differences from other revolutions must be known. Undoubtedly, there are differences from other industrial revolutions based on what has been described so far, and these differences, which are also expressed as the basic features of Industry 4.0, can be expressed as follows (Monizza et al., 2018; Rauch et al., 2020):

- It uses value networks to facilitate collaboration between businesses and provides horizontal integration in this way.
- Achieves vertical integration by accepting manufacturing systems in a flexible and editable way.
- Provides end-to-end engineering integration throughout the entire production process to produce personalized products or different products.
- It provides a forward acceleration in production thanks to the exponential technologies used.

With Industry 4.0, production areas are now designed for flexible production. Because in the new generation marketing, the concepts of producing personalized and different products come to the fore. Accepting that there is no limit in the world, commercial activities such as a single market and shopping according to consumers made it necessary for businesses to produce personalized products, which was only possible with a flexible production line. At this point, businesses now compete with their competitors and have to cooperate. With this situation, which is called collaborative competition, companies that operate in a similar manner cooperate and become an ecosystem by entering into a horizontal integration. On the other hand, it creates an ecosystem in vertical integration between the companies' own suppliers and suppliers, and in these cases, the data flow must be fast and accurate. This is all about Industry 4.0 and its components. In this respect, it is necessary to explain the basic components of Industry 4.0, which we often hear in our lives and which we are even a data source.

BASIC COMPONENTS OF INDUSTRY 4.0

There have been many technological developments that necessitated the last industrial revolution that emerged as a concept introduced by Kagerman in Germany in 2011. These developments are expressed in the literature as the main components of Industry 4.0. These components, which must be known in

Figure 1.

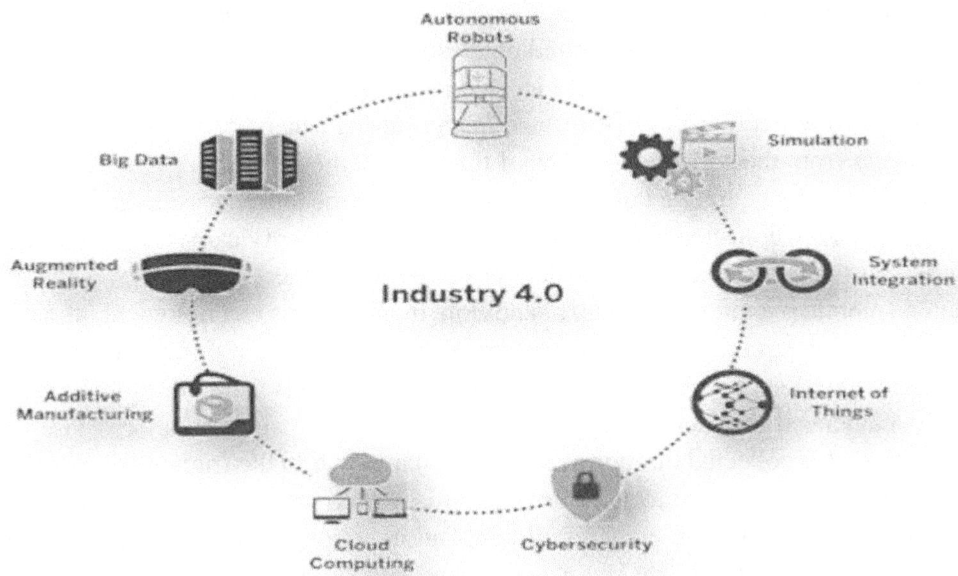

order to understand Industry 4.0 and its effects on our lives, are shown on the given figure and explained later (Tarassov, 2018; Garay-Rondero et al., 2020).

It is accepted in many sources that the first application of Industry 4.0 took place in Cambridge University at the beginning of 1990's. Researchers working at the University of Cambridge were making great strides when using a coffeemaker outside the study room. When there was no coffee left in the coffee machine, they would go to no avail. To prevent this situation, employees placed a camera in a place that saw the coffee machine and developed a software. Thanks to this software, the camera shot the camera every half minute and the employees were monitoring whether there was coffee by looking at this screen. This simple mechanism is accepted as the first example of the internet of objects that we hear everywhere and which is one of the basic components of Industry 4.0.

There are a number of concepts in all applications and examples of Industry 4.0, and these concepts need to be explained first, as they play a role in understanding the components of Industry 4.0. In this regard, the concept of object is any physical asset that can contain information or communication hardware and software embedded within Industry 4.0. The sensor is a data collection device from objects that interact with each other over the internet network. Objects with hardware and software collect data using sensors associated with it to identify events in and around them. For example, the temperature of the machine, the humidity of the environment, the intensity of the wind, etc. Data such as are obtained with sensors. Smart objects cannot use each of the data it obtains with sensors. In this regard, the relevant data should be transferred to the relevant machines or departments. For this reason, an internet network is created between the objects and the related data is shared. Sharing information among smart objects in an internet network is called communication and connectedness (Hakima, 2010; Minoli, 2013; Karvinen and Karvinen, 2014; Francesco, 2017).

One of the most important components of Industry 4.0 is the internet of things. The Internet of Things is a new system that allows physically found objects in the real world to connect to the Internet through wireless and wired connections to sensors located inside or adjacent to them. It is often used in the English language as "Internet of Things (IoT)" and many sources accept it. It is a networked system that includes the process from the collection of data of the objects, the internet of which is physical, to the communication. Thanks to the Internet of Things, we are collecting and accessing new data at every moment of our lives. Data are collected every second with sensors, security cameras or mobile phones located in a machine in the workplace, and this data is shared with other machines over the internet, again, via computers, mobile phones and tablets. In addition, thanks to this technological infrastructure, we reach at any time and make examinations. It is an example of the internet of things where we perform the operations such as fire sensors or remote light control in smart homes from our mobile phones and monitor the security cameras of our home (Felipe et al., 2020).

The amount of data that is collected through sensors and shared within the framework of the Internet of Things is so large that it is important to store them and make them useful by processing. Think, we used to know how many people used to enter a building. But now how many people pass by the door every second, their gender, height, etc. we can access many data such as features. Well, what should be done in a professional sense should be mentioned. A business wants to access the data it gets every second, so it is important to access it on the internet. For this, cloud systems have been developed and these big data from sensors are automatically transferred to these repositories on the internet. Thus, it is possible to reach this data every second. For businesses' decision makers, processing of big data is just as important. A decision maker wants to look at a report based on as many different criteria as possible before deciding on an event. For this reason, big data is important. Data is obtained simultaneously from many machines operating in a factory. Then they are separated and analyzed according to the machines. Another benefit of this is that production is not required to stop or hinder production areas. The machines send a problem signal via sensors. In this way, engineers understand that there will be a problem and they intervene without causing production to stop. It is possible to give an unlimited number of examples in all similar areas (Erl et al., 2015; Murugesan and Bojanova, 2016).

The acquisition of big data through sensors and the storage of this data stack in cloud systems reveals the concept of cyber security within the scope of Industry 4.0. In other words, ensuring the privacy and security of these data is an important problem. In this context, cyber security covers all activities related to the protection of business data by preventing access to, disclosure, destroying, modifying and damaging an information without the permission and authorization of an information. According to Industry 4.0, both a system must be safe and each machine is responsible for protecting the data it produces (Vacca, 2013).

Robots are an important concept that entered our lives with Industry 4.0 and which we used to see as a dream on television. The robots, which are called autonomous robots in the industrial sense, are smart machines that can perform processes that contain artificial intelligence thanks to their hardware and software features, can create decision options in order to help the decision processes of managers, and implement them when necessary, collect data from the environment, and interact with other similar objects. Another fact that needs to be explained at this point is the concept of smart machine. Smart machines monitor their status. In this way, they provide the data needed for preventive maintenance themselves and forward them to the required units. Autonomous robots have begun to enter our lives with the latest industrial revolution and movie scenes have become real. We can now see applications such as the use of robots in surgeries, cashier-free safes, lawyer robots, promotional worker robots (Mataric, 2007; Farbod, 2009).

Another component of Industry 4.0 is physical systems or simulation. In the industrial sense, the physical system is a mechanism designed in integration with the software included in its content and followed by the algorithms it contains. These systems use information technology to communicate, manage and track. In this context, an environment that exists in the real world can be designed in the virtual world. In this way, possible improvements, possible mistakes, designing the most suitable production line and investments are designed in a virtual environment. These processes, which require a lot of time, labor and cost in the real world, are designed and run through simulation in a computer environment and all resources are saved. In this way, designing a new production area will be more efficient and effective as it will be based on more solid foundations (Jeschke, 2017).

Integration of businesses with resources and functions within themselves is vertical, and integration with stakeholders outside of it is horizontal integration. With this versatile system integration, rapid decisions can be made by preventing communication disruption within the enterprise. In this way, it operates a more efficient production and management process. The best example of horizontal integration outside the enterprise is a supply chain. If a prefix outside the production is given, a product sold in a market falls from the stock of the enterprise through a cash register. The company, which is a supplier at the same time, makes preparations by seeing this situation. From the opposite point of view, the enterprise can determine its suppliers' stocks, the status of their orders, delivery time, etc. can easily see the information. In this respect, a versatile system integration is an important component for all internal and external stakeholders (Kagermann et al., 2013; Deloitte, 2015).

Another popular component that has entered our lives with the latest industrial revolution is the three-dimensional printers. It is called layered, that is, additive production with the production made with three-dimensional printers. Through these machines, it is quite easy for a printer to produce articles such as writer on a text or official paper, to produce a human limb or to produce spare parts for an industry, and the most important feature of this process is that the machines themselves can be produced in a short time and at a reasonable cost thanks to software without the need for people. With these machines, product designs are now processed into the machine system without the need for system design and modification, and it takes only minutes to make a prototype, ie, an example (Chrisopher, 2016; Gibson et al., 2015).

One of the important components that make Industry 4.0 feel in our lives is augmented reality. We can now see the environments simulated by computers in real world simulated environments with wearable technological products. This can be exemplified by situations such as cinemas and computer games where multidimensional films are shown with special glasses (Brett, 2016).

This revolution in the industrial world has expanded the limits of digitalization and caused changes in many professions with these components. One of the important changes in data collection, storage, separation and analysis was in the field of accounting. After Industry 4.0 and its innovations, its effects on the accounting world and digital accounting concepts are now possible to be mentioned on a solid basis.

EFFECTS OF INDUSTRY 4.0 ON ACCOUNTING

Accounting is a discipline that exists almost as old as its age. The accounting profession, which is based on the principle of keeping books manually, from the counting processes made by primitive methods to the invention of calculators, was transferred to the electronic environment with the invention of computers. The development of artificial intelligence applications, the introduction of smart machines and autonomous robots and their use started to cause changes in the requirements and content of the accountancy profession. In this respect, before talking about the digital accounting and applications that are gaining importance and associated with digitalization, it is necessary to know what effects the last industrial revolution has had in the field of accountancy.

With the development of computers and the widespread use of the Internet, the introduction of information technologies in the field of accounting over time started digitalization in accounting. The digital transformation in this context has forced the accounting field and accountants to change in terms of their way of working, practices and structure. Many transactions have been started to be carried out in digital media, from transactions held by businesses to issuance of invoices and creation of books. The developments require that the employees operating in this field should be closely related to information technologies and the Internet as well as their professional knowledge. Understanding the effects of digital transformation in the accounting field to employees is important for understanding the concept and can be explained as follows (Dengler and Matthes, 2018; Moll and Yigitbasioglu, 2019; Meske and Junglas, 2020):

- Efficiently and efficiency are increased by saving time in transactions.
- Registrations and transactions can be carried out easily and fairly quickly.
- Access to the records kept has become easier and these records have become quite simple.
- Thanks to the control mechanism of computers, errors are reduced.
- Labor costs, which are the biggest cost item, decreased because fewer employees were required.
- Employees' development was monitored.
- The transactions are simple, clear and fast, facilitating customer satisfaction.
- Being able to make transactions easily has a positive effect on employee motivation.

Today, developments in the field of accounting discipline are taking place very quickly and the requirements of the profession change with these innovations. Accountants no longer need to keep a manual book in the digital world. In other words, there is no need to create trials and keep the Notebook. These are already done through software developed for computers. At this point, the most important task of accountants emerges as reporting. Information of a product sold through an autonomous robot containing artificial intelligence can be given to senior management and supplier; buying and selling figures can be transferred to the accounting program with data such as customer information and payment method. After that, computers that use software in digital media can make records and calculations concerning the accounting department. Up to this point, an accountant's duty can be made with artificial intelligence in a machine and computer resulting from Industry 4.0. However, the most important feature that accountants should have in our age emerges at this point: reporting. Accountants should provide a comprehensive and professional report to top management, from sales, purchases, demographic structures of consumers, profitability rates, new investment advice and new supplier information. These programs can provide these figures, but the ability to interpret belongs to accountants and should use it. In this regard, Industry 4.0 and its applications are an important revolution that facilitates the work of accountants.

In times when technology was not used effectively, the main problem of accounting systems and businesses was the existence of non-transparent, distorted and modified information. It is an obvious fact that any comments made with wrong information and every decision taken will be erroneous. In this respect, the most important effect on accountancy and businesses is that the information is up-to-date, transparent, accurate and reliable. Analyzes made with these data are real and prevent erroneous decisions. At the same time, this allows businesses to perform reliable analysis while performing the current situation and SWOT analysis. Similar situation is valid in the country's economies and since the qualified data reflect the real data, it enables the economic structure to be strengthened by preventing the applications that harm the economy such as tax evasion, fraud and informal economy. In this way, stakeholders of the enterprises also benefit. Because data is published instantly in a stock market company and is not hidden due to the principle of transparency. When evaluated from these aspects, it is inevitable to perform more effectively for accountants (Petrova, 2018; Liakhovych et al., 2019).

With the electronic transformation in accounting, the new system created for the creation, transferring, and recording of transactions, records, and edited books recorded in electronic media, in a shorter time, easier, more effective, and efficient in other matters, in addition to reducing costs. makes it possible to carry out inspections. With digitalization, accountants and advisors will now quit their classic duties. In this context, new roles will be in the form of reporting, auditing, and consultancy. In this regard, the reporting and auditing skills developed, which are adapted only to digital accounting, have a good command of the profession; There will be a need for accountants who can obtain reports from large amounts of data, support the management by providing information with benefits (Kruskopf et al., 2019; Pan and Seow, 2016).

These developments as a result of Industry 4.0 are directly related to the basic concepts of accounting. In this respect, it is important in terms of its effects on accounting by reminding the basic concepts of accounting with Industry 4.0. At this point, accounting has basic concepts such as social responsibility, the essence of the essence, periodicity, the personality of the business and the transactions expressing monetary value, again being consistent in the records of the transactions, prudence and finally the thought that the life of the company is continuous.

In order to understand the digital transformation in accounting, the basic concepts of accounting and its relationship with the last industrial revolution should be examined. In this context, the concept of social responsibility will be discussed first. Social responsibility implies that the interests of the society should be taken into consideration rather than personal interests in the accounting transactions carried out in the enterprises, and the transactions should be carried out in an objective, fair, clear and understandable manner. Thanks to robots and instant data transmission, this principle has been achieved automatically by making an important contribution. It is very difficult to have misleading information without human intervention in the system to be created and used. In this respect, Industry 4.0 provides serious support to the accounting discipline in terms of the concept of social responsibility.

The Priority of Essence concept states that while focusing on the essence of the transactions, the operations should be focused on while accounting and evaluating the transactions that the companies have made regarding financial events. It is the medium that the programming language will be carried out in accordance with the concept of the priority of the essence, if the processes made by the autonomous robots containing the software developed in Industry 4.0 result comply with the procedures and legal regulations, as well as standards such as the uniform accounting standard. In addition to these, it is seen that accounting is supported by reinforcing the latest industrial revolution in cases such as which transaction belongs to which period, consistency, importance and impartiality of numbers. In summary, the basic concepts of accounting, the functioning, reliability of these concepts, and the structure and performance of the accounting system have strengthened along with the innovations brought by the recent industrial revolution.

DIGITAL ACCOUNTING

The e-transformation process that started with e-government applications in countries has also shown itself in accounting applications over time. An integrated accounting system based on information technologies is now being designed. These structures, which contain software equipped with information technologies, provide important contributions to accountancy. These developments made by the Ministries of Finance started a transformation process by directly affecting the accounting systems of the companies. At first, this transformation was in the form of transferring records, books, documents, and archives to electronic media. The effects of digitalization on the accounting system can generally be expressed as titles as follows (Knudsen, 2020; Möller et al., 2020):

- Effect on Records
- Impact on documentation
- Archive effect
- Impact on reporting
- Impact on staff

In the accounting system, daily transactions are recorded in electronic media along with e-transformation, classified, and prepared for analysis. In this way, daily records are transferred directly to the general ledger. In addition, the digital signature of the person making the records is taken and who made this record is recorded. In terms of documents, a document about a transaction subject to accounting is prepared digitally between the parties and digitally signed and transmitted to the parties in a digital environment (mail, etc.). Another transformation in the field of accounting is about archives and documents are archived in cloud systems instead of physical environments. This includes advantages and disadvantages such as safe storage, easy access, and easy classification of documents. From another point of view, saving all financial data in digital media makes it easy to make financial statements and analyzes easily and to submit them to digital media. In terms of personnel, more educated, internet and technology-oriented personnel are required than classical accountants.

While personal intuition is important to carry out transactions in traditional accountancy; an intuitive approach no longer has a place in today's accountancy. In accounting with artificial intelligence, without the influence of accounting employees, the artificial intelligence applications used will be able to detect customer transactions in a very short period of time from information about the transactions of the business customer. This situation gave an advantage to the financial sector, in particular banks, in addition to accountants. In many processes such as credit risk valuation, credit card issuance, investment, risk factors are made in a short time by means of artificial intelligence machines and the risk is minimized. This allows diversification of bank strategies and products and increasing their profitability. It is evident that the same situation has an advantage over the accounting department's business and operations, comments or reports. Manual data entry, which used to be used in accounting, is now automated with artificial intelligence applications and provides time advantage. The contributions of these artificial intelligence applications and thus digitalization to accounting can be expressed as items (Smith, 2018; Fettry et al., 2019; Knudsen, 2020):

- Increasing the amount and quality of data analysis,
- To increase the observation and perception power,

- Combining cognitive capacity,
- Increasing consistency,
- Reducing repetitive tasks,
- Reducing errors,
- Transactions related to invoices are made much faster,
- Fast data analysis,
- Real-time audits to ensure compliance.

Accountants operating in today's conditions have to improve themselves in the face of artificial intelligence, because technological advances will cause many accountants to work. In the face of this situation, only accountants who accept, adopt and use artificial intelligence and innovations will be able to continue their business by making a difference.

Technological innovations in the world and the increase in the usage areas of artificial intelligence and emerging trends have revealed the necessity of redesigning accounting. For this reason, it is important that accountants prepare for the future and develop themselves in line with the requirements of the age. The accounting industry, like all areas, is developing and involves more digital or electronic applications. It is important for professionals to adapt to this change and development, and should receive training on digitalization. Because all these developments bring digital applications and accounting closer together. With the technologies developed and put into practice in the field of accounting, today, businesses have been able to perform more efficient and efficient transactions with lower costs than in the past. All these developments in the industrial field and technology are called Accounting 4.0 or Digital Accounting, inspired by Industry 4.0 and the digital applications used. If a broad definition of this phenomenon is to be made, it can be expressed as recording the financial transactions and events of the organizations in cash, classifying, summarizing and reporting and analyzing the results and doing their work in digital media. Now, within the framework of this concept, the accounting sector is being redesigned and electronic, digital media are being used. This situation provides faster, reliable and transparent record keeping, in this case, eliminates situations such as costs and data security (Kruskopf et al., 2019).

The e-accounting system or digital accounting (Accounting 4.0) that emerged in the e-transformation process in the field of accounting differs from the classical accounting system in terms of many features. The most important innovations of the new system emerging today are the electronic invoice registration system, e-invoice, e-ledger and e-archives. In addition to these traditionally used applications in accounting, situations such as delivery notes, calculators, written documents, declarations and statements, face-to-face communication are now being carried out digitally. In our country, e-government application and the use of electronic document management systems in public institutions and organizations are the most important examples of digitalization. If it is examined in the field of accounting, the digital applications to be applied today can be collectively expressed as follows (Deshmukh, 2006; Tsai, 2007; Gullkvist, 2011):

- E-billing
- E-waybill
- E-archive
- E-book
- Software instead of physical tools
- Mails

- Electronic statements and documents
- Electronic declarations
- Meetings in mail and virtual environment

It is named as e-registration with digital transformation in the records that form the basis of these applications. According to this information, e-registration includes the smallest transactions that can be accessed and processed by keeping them in digital media. The e-document, on the other hand, is the whole of digital records with the features that it should have according to the Tax Procedure Law. The Electronic Invoice (e-invoice) Registration System is an application that eliminates the archiving of the invoices issued according to the specified standards to the Revenue Administration system and eliminates the archiving with a paper, and allows the consumers to be created and delivered electronically in a secure environment and has the same legal binding. With these digital applications, which have entered our lives with the digital transformation in the field of accounting, it has started to be integrated into the internet area, and thus more efficient and efficient activities are carried out at lower costs. Electronic production of documents; By increasing the speed of the transaction, it makes it possible to carry out transactions in a short time and all transactions are documented with very low errors and costs compared to the printed documents. This makes it easier to archive documents such as invoices for the transactions, and the archiving of digital media in the form of e-archives also facilitates the flow and access of information. In addition to all these benefits, replacing printed documents in electronic form are environmentally friendly practices. In this context, less paper and printing materials will be used. These practices contribute to the operating profit by reducing the cost of such activities of businesses.

E-ledger, in a similar manner to e-invoices, expresses that the mandatory books that businesses are required to keep for their transactions related to accounting are arranged in digital media in the same format, in accordance with the same rules and standards. All transactions regarding the books prepared as a requirement of e-books are stored and stored securely in digital media. Developments in the world made it compulsory to organize these books of the enterprises, which concern accounting. There are many benefits of e-book application to businesses such as e-invoice application, and businesses make these books in electronic media for a number of purposes. These purposes are generally; Facilitating the revision of kept books against changing factors when needed, getting rid of a serious cost by making printing processes electronically, acting honestly against tax, ensuring the formation of a structure suitable for auditing, facilitating the process of compliance with international auditing and accounting standards (McDonald et al., 2018).

E-archive application, on the other hand, is an application that does not need a place like any physical warehouse, which ensures that documents such as invoices and books are securely stored, presented and reported when necessary in parallel with the legal obligations and standards developed by the Revenue Administration. Today, in order to benefit from these applications, first of all, it is necessary to be registered in the e-invoice registration system. It is aimed to understand the issue more clearly by giving the digital accounting applications that express the accountancy transactions in electronic environments under the next heading (Xu, 2020).

SOLUTIONS AND RECOMMENDATIONS

- Keeping the data completely in virtual environments and recording them,
- All calculations are made in a virtual environment with artificial intelligence,
- Making all declarations and notifications through automatic and multiple thinking systems between institutions,
- Financial consultancy to be replaced by consultancy,
- End of accountancy face to face and through documents,
- Making widespread operations such as robots such as cashless safes in accounting,
- Instant data entry and analysis,
- Creating instant electronic audit and audit reports,
- Stock counts with robots and machines such as drone.

The accounting system with Industry 4.0, like the rest of the world, shifts to virtual environments and develops with artificial intelligence applications. In the face of this change, accountants need to improve themselves in accordance with the requirements of the electronic accounting concept. Turkey to increase the awareness of e-accounting practices and the application must be done correctly and conscious educational institutions in theoretical and / or transfer through the use of intelligent technology is of great importance. In terms of academic and practice, the use of smart technologies should not be considered as e-transformation. Because benefiting from advanced technologies through computers is only a tool to fulfill that process. Within the e-Government e-Transformation in Turkey it is experienced as a process. It is clear that the application can be realized with the help of smart technologies, and e-Transformation is an extremely comprehensive phenomenon and formation. For this reason, it would be appropriate to bring the issue to the agenda, understand the transformation correctly and convey it both nationally and internationally.

FUTURE RESEARCH DIRECTIONS

Digital accounting, discussed within the scope of this section, brings a different perspective to the traditional strategies of businesses. Many transactions are now made over the internet. As a result of these processes taking place in virtual environments, managers can easily access useful information. As a result, new questions arise. How will new, continuous and updated information be used? How will strategies be developed based on these data?

Managers use these data and reports to see their strengths and weaknesses in the strategy formulation process. As there are constantly changing consumer preferences, it is important to constantly update information in digital environments today. Only in this way can managers develop dynamic strategies. Because in changing market conditions, long-term strategies will not be valid. Businesses that use long-term strategies determined by traditional methods will fail. Therefore, today's strategies must be dynamic and can change quite quickly. This is only possible with reliable and well-analyzed data. The task of transforming existing data into useful information now belongs to the accounting departments.

CONCLUSION

As a result of the developments experienced, many new situations have emerged. Each of these emerging situations is a candidate for a new research topic. For example; Studies can be conducted on what the new features that accountants should have. The problems experienced by employees in the digital transformation process can be examined. Changes in the strategy determination and implementation processes of the managers can be investigated. Similar studies can be carried out, as well as studies that compare the results obtained by businesses that implement the strategies taken in the old system with the results of businesses using digital methods. It is a fact that businesses that act in accordance with the requirements of the digital age and can use artificial intelligence correctly will develop more effective strategies. In this way, businesses can gain serious advantages over their competitors and achieve very successful results.

REFERENCES

Batth, R. S., Nayyar, A., & Nagpal, A. (2018, August). Internet of robotic things: driving intelligent robotics of future-concept, architecture, applications and technologies. In *2018 4th International Conference on Computing Sciences (ICCS)* (pp. 151-160). IEEE. 10.1109/ICCS.2018.00033

Bělohlávek, R., Dauben, J. W., & Klir, G. J. (2017). *Fuzzy logic and mathematics: a historical perspective*. Oxford University Press.

Bromwich, M. (1999). Thoughts on management accounting and strategy. *Pacific Accounting Review*, *11*(1/2), 41–48. doi:10.1108/eb037925

Dengler, K., & Matthes, B. (2018). The impacts of digital transformation on the labour market: Substitution potentials of occupations in Germany. *Technological Forecasting and Social Change*, *137*, 304–316. doi:10.1016/j.techfore.2018.09.024

Deshmukh, A. (2006). *Digital accounting: The effects of the internet and ERP on accounting*. IGI Global. doi:10.4018/978-1-59140-738-6

Doğan, N. Ö., & Derici, S. (2019). Project Management and Efficiency of the Projects in the Industry 4.0 Era. In Agile Approaches for Successfully Managing and Executing Projects in the Fourth Industrial Revolution (pp. 188-209). IGI Global.

Dutia, T. (1995). The restructuring of the system of accounting in Romania during the period of transition to the market economy. *European Accounting Review*, *4*(4), 739–748. doi:10.1080/09638189500000047

Felipe, L., Beukes, E. W., Fox, B. A., & Manchaiah, V. (2020). Quality and readability of English-language internet information for vestibular disorders. *Journal of Vestibular Research*, (Preprint), 1-10.

Fettry, S., Anindita, T., Wikansari, R., & Sunaryo, K. (2019, July). The future of accountancy profession in the digital era. In *Global Competitiveness: Business Transformation in the Digital Era: Proceedings of the First Economics and Business Competitiveness International Conference (EBCICON 2018), September 21-22, 2018, Bali, Indonesia* (p. 8). Routledge. 10.1201/9780429202629-2

Garay-Rondero, C. L., Martinez-Flores, J. L., Smith, N. R., Morales, S. O. C., & Aldrette-Malacara, A. (2019). Digital supply chain model in Industry 4.0. *Journal of Manufacturing Technology Management, 31*(5), 887–933. doi:10.1108/JMTM-08-2018-0280

Grant, R. M. (2008). *Contemporary Strategy Analysis*. Wiley.

Gullkvist, B. (2011). Drivers of diffusion of digital accounting practice. *Contributions to Accounting, Auditing and Internal Control, 25*.

Johnsen, A. (2016). Strategic Planning and Management in Local Government in Norway: Status After Three Decades. *Scandinavian Political Studies, 39*(4), 333–365. doi:10.1111/1467-9477.12077

Knudsen, D. R. (2020). Elusive boundaries, power relations, and knowledge production: A systematic review of the literature on digitalization in accounting. *International Journal of Accounting Information Systems, 36*, 100441. doi:10.1016/j.accinf.2019.100441

Köhler, E., & Schimanovich, W. (2017, February). Kurt Gödel: A Godfather of Computer Science. In *International Conference on Computer Aided Systems Theory* (pp. 49-65). Springer.

Kruskopf, S., Lobbas, C., Meinander, H., Söderling, K., Martikainen, M., & Lehner, O. M. (2019). Digital accounting: Opportunities, threats and the human factor. *ACRN Oxford Journal of Finance and Risk Perspectives, 8*, 1–15.

Liakhovych, G., Bezruchuk, S., Ivanenko, V., & Laichuk, S. (2019). SWOT-analysis of accounting outsourcing. *European Cooperation, 3*(43), 7–19. doi:10.32070/ec.v3i43.50

McCartney, S. (2001). *ENIAC: The triumphs and tragedies of the world's first computer*. Berkley Publishing Group.

McDonald, I. J., Mcphee, A. D., Haldenby, P. A. J., Chan, P. M. W., & Lee, J. J. S. (2018). *U.S. Patent Application No. 15/287,815*. US Patent Office.

Meske, C., & Junglas, I. (2020). Investigating the elicitation of employees' support towards digital workplace transformation. *Behaviour & Information Technology*, 1–17. doi:10.1080/0144929X.2020.1742382

Moll, J., & Yigitbasioglu, O. (2019). The role of internet-related technologies in shaping the work of accountants: New directions for accounting research. *The British Accounting Review, 51*(6), 100833. doi:10.1016/j.bar.2019.04.002

Möller, K., Schäffer, U., & Verbeeten, F. (2020). *Digitalization in management accounting and control: an editorial*. Academic Press.

Monizza, G. P., Bendetti, C., & Matt, D. T. (2018). Parametric and Generative Design techniques in mass-production environments as effective enablers of Industry 4.0 approaches in the Building Industry. *Automation in Construction, 92*, 270–285. doi:10.1016/j.autcon.2018.02.027

Naranjo-Gil, D. (2004). The role of sophisticated accounting system in strategy management. *International Journal of Digital Accounting Research, 4*(8), 125–144.

Pan, G., & Seow, P. S. (2016). Preparing accounting graduates for digital revolution: A critical review of information technology competencies and skills development. *Journal of Education for Business*, *91*(3), 166–175. doi:10.1080/08832323.2016.1145622

Petrova, P. (2018). Industry 4.0 and Accounting: Challenges and Opportunities. *Nauchni trudove*, (3), 135-144.

Rauch, E., Linder, C., & Dallasega, P. (2020). Anthropocentric perspective of production before and within Industry 4.0. *Computers & Industrial Engineering*, *139*, 105644. doi:10.1016/j.cie.2019.01.018

Smith, S. S. (2018). Digitization and financial reporting–how technology innovation may drive the shift toward continuous accounting. *Accounting and Finance Research*, *7*(3), 240–250. doi:10.5430/afr.v7n3p240

Strandhagen, J. W., Alfnes, E., Strandhagen, J. O., & Vallandingham, L. R. (2017). The fit of Industry 4.0 applications in manufacturing logistics: A multiple case study. *Advances in Manufacturing*, *5*(4), 344–358. doi:10.100740436-017-0200-y

Tarassov, V. B. (2018, September). Enterprise total agentification as a way to industry 4.0: Forming artificial societies via goal-resource networks. In *International Conference on Intelligent Information Technologies for Industry* (pp. 26-40). Springer.

Tomac, N., Radonja, R., & Bonato, J. (2019). Analysis of Henry Ford's contribution to production and management. *Pomorstvo*, *33*(1), 33–45. doi:10.31217/p.33.1.4

Tsai, C. F. (2007). On Classifying Digital Accounting Documents. *International Journal of Digital Accounting Research*, *7*(13).

Tsiatsis, V., Karnouskos, S., Holler, J., Boyle, D., & Mulligan, C. (2018). *Internet of Things: technologies and applications for a new age of intelligence*. Academic Press.

Woodford, C. (2017). *A brief history of computers*. Academic Press.

Xu, X. (2020). Application Research of Accounting Archives Informatization Based on Big Data. In *Data Processing Techniques and Applications for Cyber-Physical Systems (DPTA 2019)* (pp. 55–62). Springer. doi:10.1007/978-981-15-1468-5_9

Yin, Y., Stecke, K. E., & Li, D. (2018). The evolution of production systems from Industry 2.0 through Industry 4.0. *International Journal of Production Research*, *56*(1-2), 848–861. doi:10.1080/00207543.2017.1403664

ADDITIONAL READING

Abed, S. (2014). A review of e-accounting education for undergraduate accounting degrees. *International Business Research*, *7*(2), 113. doi:10.5539/ibr.v7n2p113

Amidu, M., Effah, J., & Abor, J. (2011). E-accounting practices among small and medium enterprises in Ghana. *Journal of Management Policy and Practice*, *12*(4), 146–155.

Deshmukh, A. (2006). *Digital accounting: The effects of the internet and ERP on accounting*. IGI Global. doi:10.4018/978-1-59140-738-6

Durmuş, A. F. (2018). *"Opinions and Expectations of Members of Accounting Profession About Digital Accounting a Research in Malatya Province", Reading on Technology and Knowledge Management*. Arad publications.

Ghaffar, A. M., Mokhtar, M. Z., Ismail, W. N. S. W., & Othman, M. R. (2019). Determinant of e-accounting (EA) adoption among Malaysian maritime SMES. *International Journal of Engineering & Technology, 8*(1.8), 102-105.

Kagermann, H., Lukas, W., & Wahlster, W. (2011). Industry 4.0: with the internet of things on the way to the 4th industrial revolution. *VDI news, 13*.

Noronha, M. R., & Kulkarni, A. R. (2012). E-Accounting in India. *Indian Journal of Accounting*, *42*(2), 1–10.

Popkova, E. G., Ragulina, Y. V., & Bogoviz, A. V. (Eds.). (2019). *Industry 4.0: Industrial revolution of the 21st century* (p. 253). Springer. doi:10.1007/978-3-319-94310-7

Relhan, A. (2013). E-accounting practices of SMEs in India. *International Journal of Technical Research*, *2*(1), 1–10.

Velankar, N., Gupta, R. C., & Garud, U. (2013). E-Accounting practices among SMEs: A study of MP Region. *Journal of Management Value and Ethics*, *3*, 94–106.

KEY TERMS AND DEFINITIONS

Digital Accounting: It manufactures information technologies, namely software and objects that will allow the artificial intelligence applications to manage processes, by minimizing the impact and presence of people working in accounting.

E-Document: It is the whole of the digital records with the features that should have according to the Tax Procedure Law.

E-Ledger: Similar to e-invoices, it refers to the compulsory books, which are required to be kept by the enterprises for the transactions related to accounting according to the provisions of the Tax Procedure Law and the Commercial Code, arranged in digital media in the same format, in accordance with the same rules and standards.

E-Registration: It includes the smallest transactions that can be accessed and processed by keeping them in digital media.

Industry 4.0: IT is a new situation that occurs when IT, communication, internet, sensor, automation, artificial intelligence and robotic technologies affect and transform production processes intensely.

Internet of Things: It is a networked system that includes the process of physical objects from data collection to communication.

Object: Any physical entity that can contain information or communication hardware and software embedded in it.

Sensor: It is a data collection device from objects that interact with each other over the internet network.

Chapter 9
How Incumbents Respond Strategically to Emerging Digital Platform-Mediated Settings?
Analysis of Enterprise Software Vendors

Marisa Analia Sanchez
Universidad Nacional del Sur, Argentina

Juana Ines Zuntini
Universidad Nacional del Sur, Argentina

ABSTRACT

Digital platform businesses challenge incumbents by utilizing an ecosystem of actors that provide benefits to customers like cost reduction, convenience, or complementary products and services. Traditional enterprises should transform in order not to lose market share. This transformation potentially induces drastic changes to business models, organizational strategy, business processes, and corporate culture, among others. This chapter aims to understand how incumbent software vendors adapt to digital platform-mediated settings. The research methodology is grounded in an in-depth case study. The work contributes with a description of practical implications exposing implementation challenges, strategic decisions regarding the multiple roles in an ecosystem, criteria to select alliances, the degree of openness, and how to go from idea to action. These findings therefore enrich the literature on digital platform management.

INTRODUCTION

The root of our problems is not that we're in a Great Recession, or a Great Stagnation, but rather that we are in the early throes of a Great Restructuring. Our technologies are racing ahead but many of our skills and organizations are lagging behind. So it's urgent that we understand these phenomena, discuss their implications, and come up with strategies that allow human workers to race ahead with machines instead of racing against them. (Brynjolfsson & McAfee, 2011)

DOI: 10.4018/978-1-7998-8583-2.ch009

Cross boundary technologies such as the Internet, mobile, cloud computing and social media, have reduced the need of holding a physical infrastructure. This has given rise to platform businesses such as Amazon, Uber, or eBay. These platforms challenge incumbents by utilizing an ecosystem of actors that provide benefits to customers like cost reduction, convenience or complementary products and services. Thus, new business models emerge creating a new demand and traditional enterprises should transform in order not to lose market share. The digital enterprise transformation goes far beyond internal process optimization as they potentially induce drastic changes to organizational strategy, business models, and business processes and information systems that support value creation. Any of these changes is more painful in traditional enterprises that have established ways of doing things that may constrain their response. Venkatraman (2017) discusses some traps that prevent incumbents to recognize and size the opportunities posed by digital transformation. For example, historical competencies that worked in industrial-age economies but might run their course; or the reliance on networks of relationships without incorporating new relations that might bring value such as technological start-ups or digital giants. The literature reflects an increasing interest on platform concepts and is prolific on issues related with platform-based business models and strategies (Parker, Van Alstyne, & Choudary, 2016), (Gawer & Cusumano, 2014), (Cusumano, Gawer, & Yoffie, 2019), (Tura, Kutvonen, & Ritala, 2017), (Weill & Woerner, 2015), (Zheng, 2015). However, most research considers entrepreneurs or digital giants organizations and there is a lack of research on how traditional organizations adapt to emerging digital platforms (Garud, Kumaraswamy, Roberts, & Xu, 2020), (de Reuver, Sorensen, & Basole, 2018), (Altman, 2015). In particular, for the case of the software industry there is a market driven scenario that requires a business model adaptation. For example, consider an Enterprise Resource Planning (ERP) system vendor whose customers are mainly retailers. Many retailers have an eBay store, transactions data should be integrated with the ERP system, and customers prefer a particular payment processing system. The solution requires strategic choices such as belonging to a platform, enabling interoperability, or including new partners (retailer, e-commerce platform, digital financial service provider). As a whole, a rebooting of the digital enterprise model is required. Moreover, companies (in particular digital natives) may decide to expand into related products or services broadening industry boundaries. Therefore, established firms are exposed to other players' expansion. On the other hand, the incumbent has the opportunity to exploit network effects by belonging to a platform player (for example, the ERP vendor joining eBay by integrating the ERP with eBay transactions). The research question for this study is how incumbent software vendors adapt to emergent platform-mediated settings in their business models.

In order to approach the problem of incumbents' adaptation within the context of digital platforms many issues should be addressed. Both internal and external factors contribute to the complexity of the business transformation. A transition does not occur instantly and may take many forms depending, for example, on the degree of product control the firm is willing to yield. An organizational transformation may not be realized by becoming a platform player or complementor but by a firm's capability to engage in different networks (Bosh-Sijtsema & Bosch, 2015). In this research work, we intend to analyze incumbents' transformation in the software sector. The results aim to provide a management guide for those traditional organizations that are on the way of redefining their business models to compete in an ecosystems setting.

The research methodology is based on an in-depth case study. First, we provide a theoretical background of business ecosystems and platforms. Second, the business model concept provides a framework to reason about the product-based to platform transition. Third, we present the main issues of the chapter emerging from a case study. Then, a section is devoted to explore recommendations for traditional enterprises. Future research directions are briefly described. Finally, a conclusion stressing the main contributions closes the chapter.

BACKGROUND

The aim of the work is to understand how traditional companies respond in their business models to operate and integrate into a platform-mediated setting. This section provides a brief introduction of what is meant by business ecosystem and platforms.

Business Ecosystems and Platforms

In the literature there are different approaches to defining a business ecosystem. Gawer (2014) observes that research on platforms and ecosystem has been developed from two disciplines: industrial economic and the engineering design. The works based on economic theories define platforms as markets (two-sided markets, multi-sided markets) that enable transactions between different types of consumers. A platform provides the infrastructure and rules for a marketplace, bringing together producers and consumers. The owners of the platform control their intellectual property and governance. Providers serve as the platforms' interface with users. Producers deliver, develop or add components to a platform and enhance the value of the platform, and consumers use them (Van Alstyne, Parker, & Choudary, 2016). These markets exploit network effects. Due to network effects, a large number and range of stakeholders accumulate around the platform, which forms the business ecosystem (Rong, et al., 2018). Direct network effects arise when the benefit of network participation to a user depends on the number of other network users with whom they can interact. This benefit can be augmented by indirect network effects, whereby different sides of a network can mutually benefit from the size and characteristics of the other side (Van Alstyne, Parker, & Choudary, 2016). Indirect network effects arise if there is a complementarity between the demands of two or more types of consumers.

The stream of works that adopts an engineering design perspective views product platforms as technological architectures that facilitate innovation through modularity and structured around a core and periphery (Gawer, 2014). Modularity is a very well-known concept in the software system development landscape because is the main design principle to reduce complexity. Designers achieve modularity by partitioning a system model into independent components and standard interfaces. In order to develop complements of a product, developers use Application Programming Interfaces (APIs) or Software Developer Kits (SDKs). APIs refers to digital control points that set the terms for which data and services can be efficiently shared or "called" over the Internet (Basole, 2016). A SDK is a collection of software development tools in one installable package. Hence, APIs and SDKs are fundamental to support open innovation.

Cusumano *et al.* (2019) classifies platforms based on their primary function. The "innovation platforms" usually consist of common technological building blocks that the owner and ecosystem partners can share in order to create new complementary products and services. The "transaction platforms" are intermediaries or online marketplaces that make it possible for people and organizations to share information or to buy, sell, or access a variety of goods and services. The authors use the term "hybrid" to refer to the combination of innovation and transaction platforms within the same company or within the same platform infrastructure.

Software Ecosystems

Software companies can no longer compete in terms of product excellence. Enterprise applications not only depend on the operating system but on e-commerce platforms or social networks that are immersed in the business operating processes. A software ecosystem is defined as a set of actors functioning as a unit and interacting with a shared market for software and services, together with the relationships among them ((Jansen, Finkelstein, & Brinkkemper, 2009) as cited in (Angeren, Kabbedijk, Popp, & Jansen, 2013)). The paradigm of software ecosystems is useful and poses challenges within a single organization (Schultis, Elsner, & Lohmann, 2014), (Andreo & Bosch, 2019). Schultis *et al.* (2014) coin the term "internal software ecosystems" to refer to internal organizational units with own business objectives, organizational independent with own product management, and have relative autonomous processes and software-engineering life cycles.

Jansen *et al.* (2009) observes that software vendors cope with challenges that may be analyzed from three different perspectives: the software ecosystem level, the software supplier network level, and the software vendor level. Decisions at the ecosystem level refer to strategic choices on how to behave in the ecosystem to maximize profitability. A software supply network is a series of linked software, hardware, and service organizations cooperating to satisfy market demands (Jansen, Brinkkemper, & Finkelstein, 2009). At this level, decisions are related to who will be suppliers, governance of relationships with buyers and suppliers and cross-organizational quality assurance. Finally, at the software vendor level, decisions refer to portfolio and product line planning, knowledge management and design for extensibility, portability and variability. We will come back to this when discussing results.

The digital transformation, in particular the availability of cloud computing, have changed the way software is delivered. Native cloud computing software companies emerged as rivals of traditional enterprises. Basole and Park (2019) consider legacy and cloud software vendors to assess the influence of volume and diversity of relationships on firm value. They have found that legacy vendors need to redefine their ecosystem partner portfolio, including new ones and reconsidering existing partners that can prevent transitioning. The authors observe that partner diversity may not increase firm value since partners from different sectors may have different processes that can make collaboration difficult (Basole & Park, 2019).

Due to the relevance of software ecosystems, its governance has attracted the attention of both academics and practitioners. Governance in software ecosystems refer to managerial tools of players in software ecosystems that have the goal of influencing an ecosystem's health (Alves, Oliveira, & Jansen, 2017). A comprehensive proposal regarding this topic is the software ecosystem governance maturity model (SEG-M^2) proposed by Jansen (2020). The maturity model presents a set of areas of focus, which contain capabilities, which in turn contain a set of practices, within maturity levels and result in functional domain capabilities. The SEG-M^2 identifies seven areas: associate models, ecosystem health, open markets, open platforms, intellectual property, open innovation, and software development governance. Each focus area demands skills for software development utilizing an ecosystem model. These skills encompass both technical and management ones. The latter includes skills such as management and coordination of partners; partner health analysis, sharing of market data, making strategic choices regarding competing ecosystems, creating shared innovations and ecosystems standards, among others (Clear, 2019).

Because of the digital transformation, information technology is becoming an integral part of the product itself. The evolution to smart, connected products requires a traditional manufacturer to build what is essentially an internal software company (Porter & Heppelmann, 2015). Digital servitization refers to the transition from products to smart product-service-software systems that enable value creation and capture through monitoring, control, optimization, and autonomous function (Kohtamäki, Parida, Oghazi, Gebauer, & Baines, 2019). However, building software related characteristics is not usually part of the traditional product engineering process. Kohtamäki *et al.* (2019) address the digital servitization in manufacturing firms' business models. The authors observe that implementation of digital servitization business models extends operations beyond the boundaries of a single firm and hence an ecosystems perspective is essential. Consequently, new forms of collaboration surrounding hardware and software ecosystems appear.

BUSINESS MODELS IN PLATFORM-MEDIATED SETTINGS

In this section, we examine the literature regarding business models definitions and elaborate on how they are defined in a platform-mediated setting. As a starting point, we consider a conceptualization of technological platforms as evolving organizations or meta-organizations as proposed by Gawer (2014). Gulati *et al.* (2012) use the term meta-organization to define the network of firms or individuals not bound by authority based on employment relationships, but characterized by a system-level goal. Gawer puts the focus on agents of the platform and posited five hypothesis about platform competition and innovation. This focus on organizations leads to the strategic management question of how to create value (Porter, 1991). Organizations define business models to describe how they create value (Osterwalder & Pigneur, 2010). The business model concept was conceived from a firm-centered perspective (Fehrer, Woratscheck, & Brodie, 2018). This means that a model definition is based on a value-proposition that does not consider the firm as being part of an ecosystem in which the way of creating value does not restrict to the inside of the organization. In this work, we adopt the unified framework of the business model concept proposed by Al-Debei and Avison (2010) which is comprehensive and appropriate to the complex nature of digital business. The framework provides the dimensions that need examining when adapting a business model from product to a platform-based organization: that is strategy, business model components and business processes. In the following paragraphs, we organize the analysis of the transformation following the structure of the business model framework as defined by Al-Debei and Avison (2010).

Al-Debei and Avison (2010) observe that strategy is the first stage that pours into the business model components. Since a long time, firms have recognized the value of defining a strategy with focus on customers (Zeng, 2018). However, platform-based organizations are oriented to serve both end users and complementors that create products that complement the core product (Altman, 2015). Other authors present the same idea when they put emphasis on that the platform leader should define a strategy to foster ecosystem value (Van Alstyne, et al., 2016), (Adner & Kapoor, 2010), (Bosh-Sijtsema and Bosch, 2015). This strategy transition to compete in a platform-mediated setting may be challenging. Many scholars have reported that it is strategy and not technology that drives digital transformation (Kane, Palmer, Phillips, Kiron, & Buckley, 2015), (Ross, Sebastian, & Beath, 2016). Kane (2017) refers to digital transformation as the response of an organization to compete effectively in an increasing digital world.

In what follows, we describe the business model components: the value proposition, architecture, network and finance.

Value Proposition

This dimension of the business model describes the products or services the firm offers and the market segments. In line with a strategy that fosters ecosystem value, the value proposition should be attractive to end users, producers and complementors (Parker, Van Alstyne, & Choudary, 2016). Incumbent software vendors should certainly include the end users in their strategy but many of them should add third party application developers. Complementors should perceive an opportunity to offer their products or services.

Value Architecture

This component includes the technological architecture and the organizational infrastructure (comprising assets, resources and core competencies). In the industrial era, a source of competitive advantage is the ownership and control of physical resources and consequently many incumbent firms directs their investments based on that logic. In platform-mediated settings, competitive advantage is strongly dependent on the ability of platform firms to stimulate value co-creation with their network of complementors (Adner & Kapoor, 2010), (Libert, Beck, & Wind, 2016) and exploit the ensuing positive feedback dynamics. Opening up the platforms provide more benefits to the owner, by creating a greater volume and variety of contributions, motivations and ideas than the owner alone could have mustered (McAfee & Brynjolfsson, 2017) and hence facilitating innovation (Boudreau, 2010), (Al-Debei & Avison, 2010), (Basole, 2016), (Brenk, 2020). However, organizations should decide to what extent they will enable complementors to join. Firms may apply a collaborative approach for innovation and a competitive approach of complements building (Bosh-Sijtsema and Bosch, 2015). Openness may raise the risk of decreasing the platform quality or the owner may lose control on functions or data. As mentioned earlier in this work, the technical mechanism to open platforms is offering APIs and/or SDKs and firms define the type and quantity of these mechanisms to control openness. In addition, pricing strategies can be used to control openness. Openness may also threat entrepreneurs because of the platform firm's ability to appropriate their complementary innovations (Nambisan, Siegel, & Kenney, 2018), (Hannah & Eisenhardt, 2018), (Wen & Zhu, 2019). Eisenmann *et al.* (2007) observe that some resource-based view of the firm papers mention that customer bases can be valuable resources, and hence argue that the process of managing platform envelopment can be viewed as a dynamic capability (e.g. the process of recombining user bases into multi-platform bundles). Platform envelopment refers to the strategy through which a provider in one platform market can enter another platform market, and combine its own functionality with that of the target in a multi-platform bundle that leverages shared user relationships (Eisenmann, Parker, & Van Alstyne, 2007). Parker *et al.* (2016) recommend absorbing the functions and the user base of an adjacent platform when it represents a competitive threat.

Technical solutions such as APIs or SDKs enable software developers to contribute with their applications. However, software tools and protocols are not enough to attract and retain complementors. In platform-based organizations, the capability to manage relationships with complementors and external partners becomes extremely important.

Since the value of a platform depends on the number of interactions, a core competence is the ability to grow the users and complementors base (to exploit direct and indirect network effects). Pricing decisions regarding whom to charge and ways of monetize also have impact on the size of the platform user base (Van Alstyne, Parker, & Choudary, 2016), (Cusumano, Gawer, & Yoffie, 2019).

The transition from being a product-based to being a platform-based organization has implications for organizational identity (Altman, 2015). Altman conceptualizes organizational identity as a shared understanding on the part of organizational members about "what business are we in?" For example, Amazon changed identity from "bookseller" to "marketplace". Altman explains that a change in organizational identity has effects on the business sector the company is in; placing value on serving end-users, developers and complementors; and awareness about informing software innovations to complementors before release because changes may have effects on other dependent applications.

Value Network

This dimension depicts the position of an organization in the value system and its relationship with different stakeholders (Al-Debei & Avison, 2010). Angeren *et al.* (2013) refer to software ecosystem subsystems or clusters as "associative models" and describe the structure of this model. The associative model consists of multiple levels or roles. Every participant has one of more roles with predefined requirements, benefits and costs. For example, benefits for SAP software solution partners range from marketing benefits, revenue sharing or access to SAP customer ecosystem. The platform owner may define requirements that have to be met in order to participate (Angeren, Kabbedijk, Popp, & Jansen, 2013) and allow controlling the quality of participants' contributions. In addition, pricing strategies can be used to control third party developer entrance.

Pellizzoni *et al.* (2019) analyse the impact of strategic alternatives in a platform-based environment with particular reference to the decision to become a platform provider or to join an existing platform. The authors use social network analysis to study the relationships between different apps providers in the health and fitness industry while performance is measured by the number of mobile applications downloads. Their findings show that it is possible to reach the performances of platform providers working as complementors and that even though the position in the network can help companies to reach a high number of users, it does not mean that they are going to use or like their apps.

Decisions regarding the network coordination depend on the governance of the platform. For innovation platforms, governance issues relate to the degree of openness and the extent to which a platform company competes with complementors (Cusumano, Gawer, & Yoffie, 2019). Transaction platforms should also consider minimizing low-quality transactions, facilitating returns and avoiding fraud (Cusumano, Gawer, & Yoffie, 2019).

Product centered firms can transition to play a more central role in a digital ecosystem by easing their software products integration with vertical partners. Then, organizations that aim to enable transactions through the coordination and collaboration among enterprises in a network offer APIs to partners.

Concerning software ecosystems, the customer is perceived as supporting innovation and software development in terms of user-driven innovation (Bosh-Sijtsema & Bosch, 2015). Hence, firms should invest in customer relationship management and provide means discover and monitor customers' needs.

Value Finance

This dimension depicts information related to costing, pricing methods, revenue structure and value proposition arrangements (Al-Debei & Avison, 2010), (Osterwalder, Pigneur, & Tucci, 2005). Traditional software vendors rely on license-based business models. More recently, license-based model transition to pay-per-use models in which customers purchase software on a subscription basis, paying only form what they need when they need it (Peng & Gala, 2014). Moreover, the internet and digital technologies in general enabled other forms of making profits. Based on a comprehensive research over 300 companies, Gassmann *et al.* (2014) introduce 55 generic business model patterns. For example, "add-on" (the core product has a competitive price but there are additional services that increase the price); "crowdfunding"; "freemium" (the basic version of an offer is given for free and premium services are priced); "leverage customer data" (customer data is collected and profits are generated by selling it or by developing new offering from it), "pay-per-use" (the actual usage of a service is charged).

The business processes and information systems contain the activities that create products or services. According to Al-Debei and Avison (2010) the business model should be the baseline from where processes and systems are derived. At the same time, these processes should enable the business model. Concerning the transition to platform-based enterprise, new processes are defined or become more relevant (*e.g.* complementors relationship management, quality control of third-party applications); and other processes are redefined to satisfy requirements such as open innovation.

Figure 1 depicts the business model framework summarizing the issues and challenges for incumbent software vendors transitioning from product-centered company to one operating in an ecosystem.

MAIN FOCUS OF THE CHAPTER

In this chapter, we focus on how incumbents adapt to emergent platform-mediated settings that lead to new forms of competition, collaboration and mutual co-existence. Khanagha *et al.* (2020) address the problem of how incumbents respond strategically to dominant platforms in which they are not leaders. A possible strategy is joining the platform to capture value with the risk of not having influence on the platform architecture (Zhu & Liu, 2018). Another strategy is creating a new platform by either acquiring a platform or establishing its own platform with the risk of failing to compete with the rival platform (Cusumano, Gawer, & Yoffie, 2019). Khanagha *et al.* (2020) describe how an established technology firm (Cisco) responded by creating a new platform without undermining the dominant platform. Cisco was a hardware complementor of leading cloud platforms ecosystems based on centralized computing architecture. The growth of the Internet of Things demanded decentralized data processing closer to devices to increase speed and security. Cisco created a decentralized technology platform (Fog) managing data via distributed clouds near the physical devices (differentiated functionality). At the same time, Fog platform provides a connection with dominant cloud platforms. Once the platform was established, a scaling phase followed and Cisco shifted strategy promoting standardization and co-development that reflects competition with leading platforms (Khanagha, Ansari, Paroutis, & Oviedo, 2020). The authors illustrate a dynamic strategy departing from offering non-overlapping value to competing with dominant platforms. The proposal is relevant to large incumbents that are losing market share to platforms competitors.

In this chapter, we focus on software vendors that are willing to take nonrivalrous approaches. The business model provided a framework to reason about possible effects of transitions from a product-based to a platform-based organization. The identified issues and challenges are the foundation to approach an in-depth case study. The topics guide the aspects that should be studied for the case when studying secondary data and during the interviews. We developed an in-depth case study to analyze the transformation of the business model of an incumbent software company. Generalization is not the goal of this research. In order to answer how and why decisions are made of an unexplored research topic and

Figure 1. Business model framework summarizing issues and challenges for incumbent software vendors transitioning from a product-based to a platform-based business
Source: own elaboration

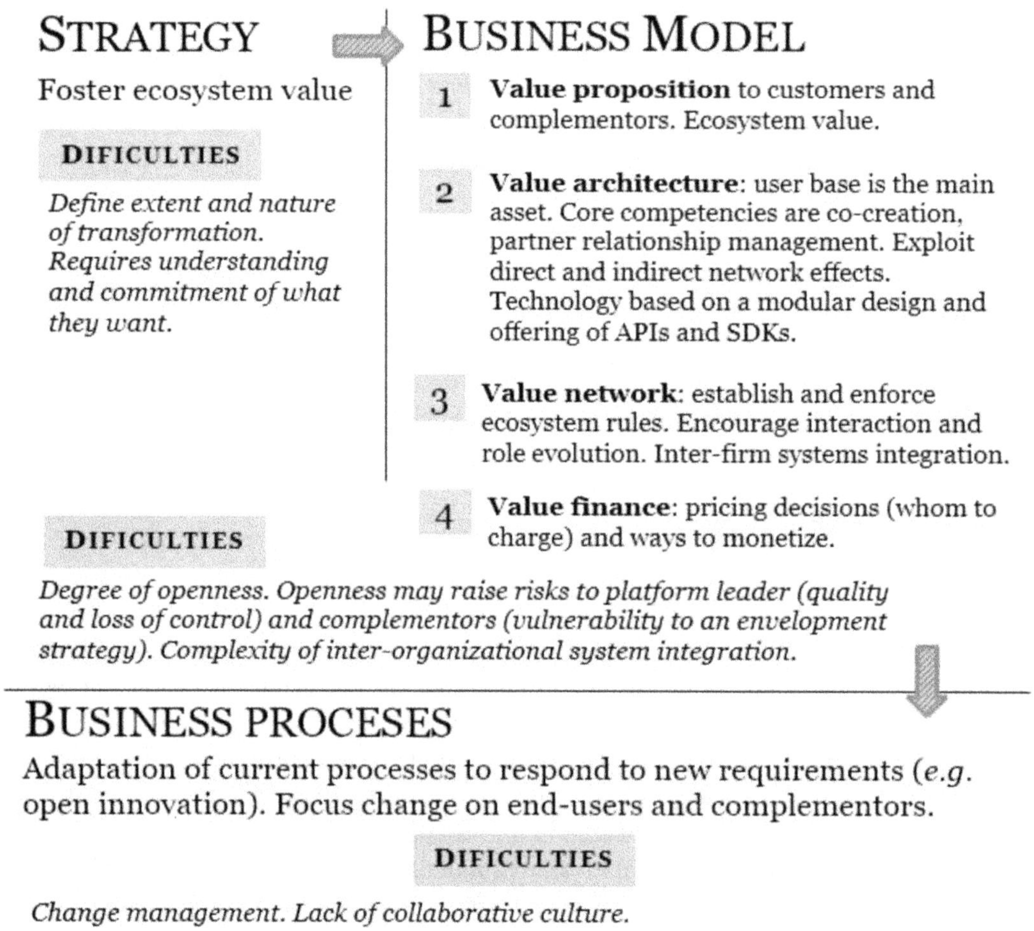

setting, a single case study approach is adequate (Eisenhardt & Graebner, 2007). Single case allows a more precise understanding of the circumstances in which the phenomena occurred and therefore tend to be more reliable than comparison of two cases (Stake, 2000) (as cited in (Mariotto, Zanni, & Salati, 2014)). The unit of analysis is a software company. The company has a very well-known brand of an ERP product and can undoubtedly be regarded a traditional enterprise for which the challenge of transformation is more defying. Data from the company website, articles published in domain specific magazines were used to develop a description of the case. Then, an interview with a Commercial Manager and an Account Executive were performed in order to gather additional information and insights from the company. The interviews were guided by the questions included in the Appendix. Time was given to the interviewees to discuss the proposed topics and add all the information that they consider germane. The duration of interviews was approximately of 40 minutes, and they took place at the work-place.

The preparation of the interview included an explanation of the purpose and structure of the interview, a presentation of a brief definition of platforms and examples (Android, Windows, Uber, Mercado Libre), confidentiality terms, and the method of recording (taking notes and taping). The openness to allow interviews was essential to facilitate triangulation purposes. Data analysis was then carried out to understand key decisions regarding the business model.

Before proceeding to present the findings, we briefly comment on platforms in Argentine. By the end of 2016, there were five national capital platforms operating in the country. In this year, a change of government favored an environment for the income of international investments and global firms such as Uber, Airbnb, Glovo, Freelancer, and Cabify started their operations in the country (Madariaga, Buenadicha, Molina, & Ernst, 2019). The most important platform is Mercado Libre, Inc. that engages in the provision of online commerce platform with focus on e-commerce and its related services (Johnson, Mekikian, & Barnett, 2020). It is the largest online auction site in Latin America. The firm provides users a mechanism for buying, selling and paying as well as collecting, generating leads, and comparing lists through e-commerce transactions. Mercado Libre, founded by Marcos Galperín in 1999 in Buenos Aires operates in twelve Latin American countries and in the first quarter of 2019 enabled the sale of more than 82,8 million items (Cronista, 2019). NASDAQ market stock valuation exceeds $12.7 billion.

Issues Revealed by the Analysis of Axoft Argentina S.A

Axoft Argentina S.A. is a national player within the enterprise software market (Axoft Argentina S.A., 2019). The company was settled in 1988. The core product is an Enterprise Resource Planning (ERP) software named Tango for which the company is a keystone player in the market. The main ERP software rivals are MaxiRest, Lince, Dragonfish, Bejerman and Buenos Aires Software. In 1993, Tango for Windows was developed and it was the first ERP working over Windows in the country. The company is ISO 9001 certified since 2006.

With the aim of assessing the extent and form of the transition unfolding in Axoft, we first determine the actors in the ecosystem and how they are related. The company sells both directly to end-users and through software distributors. There are 200 sales centers alongside the country operated by distributors. Distributors perform pre-sales activities, sales, and post sales activities like support and answering product-related questions. They provide support services to their customers and to those who have bought directly to Axoft. Axoft has application platforms for different market segments: on premise applications, on demand applications and mobile applications. The company has approximately 65,000 customers, and 16,000 of them are "registered" (the business model is based on an annual fee) (Prensario TI Latin America, 2016). Customers may belong from "Evolución", "Plus", "X-Plus" or "Gold" categories depending on the paid resources (for example, number of work stations or size of database).

Axoft offers a variety of cloud based solutions which are mostly free for those acquiring the basic ERP and renew the annual fee (Axoft Argentina S.A., 2019), (Prensario TI Latin America, 2016). Some of the on premise solutions include Gestión, Punto de Venta, Estudios Contables, and Restŏ. Axoft has an alliance with the telecommunications company Claro to provide Tango Nube that is the cloud Tango solution. Claro provides a virtual server to each customer. Examples of cloud-based solutions are Clientes (customers), Tiendas (integrates Tango applications with e-commerce stores), Tablero (scorecard), and Fichadas (employee in/out board software). Tango Factura is a cloud-based solution offered to professionals and mono-tax (taxpayer under the simplified tax regime). Table 1 depicts Axoft's solutions. For each product, we include the market and revenue model. The column entitled "Examples of product integration" lists organizations and solutions integrated with Tango applications.

Table 1. Axoft's solutions. Source: own elaboration

Name	Market	Pricing method	Examples of product integration
Applications			
Tango Gestión	Enterprises	License-based	Mercado pago, Mercado Libre, Prestashop, Mercado Shop, Tienda Nube, oh! Gift Card, Lapos, Posnet, AFIP, ARBA.
Tango Nube	Enterprises	License-based	AFIP, ARBA.
Tango Estudios Contables	Accounting firms	License-based	AFIP, ARBA.
Tango Punto de Venta (point of sales, works with fiscal printers)	Enterprises	License-based	Mercado pago, Mercado Libre, Mercado shop, Tienda Nube, oh! Gift Card, Lapos, Posnet, AFIP.
Tango Restŏ	Restaurant, delivery	License-based	Pedidos Ya, Lapos, Posnet, AFIP, Pedidos móviles.
Tango Factura (cloud-based)	Professionals and mono-tax	License-based	Mercado pago, Mercado Libre, Mercado shop, AFIP, Tango Estudios Contables.
Tango (educational version of Punto de Venta, Restŏ, Gestión, and Estudios contables)	Universities, colleges and schools.	Free for educational institutions	
Tango Punto de Venta Alquiler	Enterprises	License-based	Mercado pago, Mercado Libre, Mercado shop, Tienda Nube, oh! Gift Card, Lapos, Posnet, AFIP.
Tango Estudios Contables Alquiler	Accounting firms	License-based	AFIP, ARBA.
Ecosystem hub			
Tango Nexo (includes applications such as Clientes, Tango tiendas, and Scorecard)	Tango community (distributors and customers)	Free for Tango users	Access data generated by Tango applications.
Integration software			
Tango Tiendas	Enterprise/Restŏ	License-based	Mercado Libre, Tienda Nube, Pedidos Ya, Tango
Training			
Tango University	Open	Feed	Training on Tango products.

Based on the interviews with the Commercial Manager and Account Executive, it is clear that Axoft understands that the firm's community goes beyond distributors and end-users. Most customers are enterprises and Axoft includes in its community these enterprises' customers (even if they do not owe Tango) and educational institutions in its strategy.

Respondents agreed on that the following are part the firm's strategy: improve customers' experience, innovation, decision taking and efficiency. They emphasized that current investments aim to transform product-oriented processes to customer-oriented processes. A major effort is on course to change the focus from product-based to a solution-based strategy.

Table 2. Brief description of organizations related with Axoft. Source: Own elaboration.

Organization	Brief description
Mercado Libre	Online commerce platform with focus on e-commerce and its related services.
Mercado Pago	A company that operates an online payments system that supports online money transfers.
Prestashop	Provider of software resources to create an e-commerce store (open source).
Tienda Nube	Provider of software resources to create an e-commerce store.
Pedidos Ya	On-line delivery provider.
Mercado shop	Provider of software resources to create an e-commerce store integrated with Mercado Libre.
oh! Gift Card	Gift card provider.

In order to understand the degree on that Axoft opens Tango, respondents were asked about complementors' incentives and openness issues. Respondents mentioned that Tango databases are in a non-proprietary format and Axoft provides APIs that connects Tango Ventas with any e-commerce portal (GitHub, Inc., 2019), (Axoft Argentina S.A., 2019). Nexo applications can be downloaded from the Android or iOS store and both Tango customers (enterprises) and these enterprises' customers are able to access their account status. For this purpose, Axoft took a fundamental step: the migration of the software to the web. The web-based solution (Tango Delta) and APIs will be available to distributors who may be encouraged to develop applications. The purpose of Tango Delta is to increase connectedness. For confidential reasons it is not yet possible to provide further details of this solution. In addition, with the aim of understanding and discovering the needs of different actors, the firm re-designed the knowledge management process to take into account all actors (personnel, distributors, end-users, third-party developers). When asked about the level of knowledge of customers, respondents mentioned that direct sell allowed them to have a representative sample of users' experience. In addition, the company always performs surveys aimed at distributors to gather information about general and specific topics. Surveys' results provide insights to prioritize Axoft's development projects.

Respondents were asked what described best the firm's attitude towards risk. The interviewers mentioned that anything that they do entails a risk because it may affect the brand "Tango". They added that the business model is defined by the active customers and those that renew the license subscription. If customers do not perceive value in Tango products then they would decide not to renovate. The forthcoming release Tango Delta represents a huge risk because if customers are not satisfied then the company may experience a customer leak. There are some traditional customers used to do what they have always done and are reticent to change. Respondents added that the company has a risk area focused on determining risks and defining actions to minimize it consequences in case of occurrence. Regarding Tango Delta they aim to motivate and persuade distributors so they can successfully communicate the product's benefits to their customers. On the other hand, they observed that it is also risky to leave the product as it is since for the company not to innovate means to perish.

Concerning the value network, partnerships are developed to fulfil some goals such as extension of the partner ecosystem, and to develop new products and services. The Commercial Manager mentioned that they select the main vertical players in the software industry, and work on partnership agreements with them. For example, Producteca provides software integration solutions and is key in the integration of Tango with e-commerce portals or Mercado Libre. Another example is the partnership with Zoho which offers a CRM software solution designed to manage sales, marketing, contacts, customer support and other business functions. Axoft aims to focus on building a robust ERP system and the interviewees refer to Tango as the "motor" around which other applications run.

Interviewees were asked to describe requirements and benefits for companies related with Axoft. In general, companies provide APIs with full documentation. For example, the integration with Mercado Libre, Producteca, Prestashop, among others is using APIs through Tango Tiendas. Axoft benefits with the integration of its ERP with another software solutions, and companies also benefits because they access Axoft's customer base (network effect). Regarding Microsoft, Axoft's choice working over Windows operating system, allowed Axoft to be part a Microsoft platform ecosystem. There is an agreement with the cloud service provider Claro through which Axoft has a preferential price for using the infrastructure and services. The relationship with fiscal mark printers' providers like Epson and Hasar is also of mutual benefit: the companies provide printers before selling a new release so Axoft updates software, and these companies assure that their printers are going to work properly with Tango solutions. Respondents stressed the importance of having a fluid communication among partner companies. If there is a software change, systems' integration may fail and solutions will take longer to be ready for customers. Table 3 presents the main actors related with Axoft.

Table 3. Axoft's value network. Source: Own elaboration

Organization	Role	Comments on partner's benefits/costs
Software distributor	Software partner that resells Tango.	Marketing, revenue sharing agreements with Axoft, and derived from product support. Requirements to become a distributor are an initial investment and vendor lock-in.
Microsoft	Service providers	Marketing, access to Axoft's customer base.
Mercado Libre, Inc.	E-commerce web store platform provider	Mercado Libre platform integration with Tango Tiendas, access to Axoft's customer base.
Producteca,Vtex	E-commerce software solution provider	System integration with Tango Tiendas, access to Axoft's customer base
Prestashop, Tienda Nube	Provider of resources to create an e-commerce store	System integration with Tango Tiendas, access to Axoft's customer base.
Pedidos Ya	Online delivery provider	System integration with Pedidos Ya (Tango Restŏ), access to Axoft's customer base
Claro	Cloud provider (infrastructure and service)	A commercial agreement states preferential prices for Axoft (Claro's service plan for small and medium size enterprises). Access to Axoft´s customer base. Revenues based on infrastructure and service used.
Epson, Hasar, Posnet, Lapos	Fiscal mark printers providers and debit and credit card processing equipment	Mutual benefit derived from testing of software on devices assures the integration is working for users.
Government (AFIP, ARBA)	Define fiscal and tax regulations	Not applicable.

Finally, interviewees were provided with a list of 10 possible barriers that may hinder transformation and were asked to select all that apply. There was consensus that the main barriers are "lack of organizational agility", "economic crisis", "insufficient resources" and they added to the list "customers' adaptation to change". Respondents explained that with the expression "organizational agility" they refer to its capability to change focus toward customers and complementors and transform processes accordingly. For this aim, managers receive the support of a coach who performs a procedural coaching that articulates actions in all areas. With regard to the economic recession, one respondent observed that despite the recession the transformation will occur the same, although transformation time might be dilated. The lack of resources refers to software engineers because in the development lab there is

Figure 2. Summary of Axoft business model transformation from a product-based to a firm operating in a platform mediated setting
Source: own elaboration

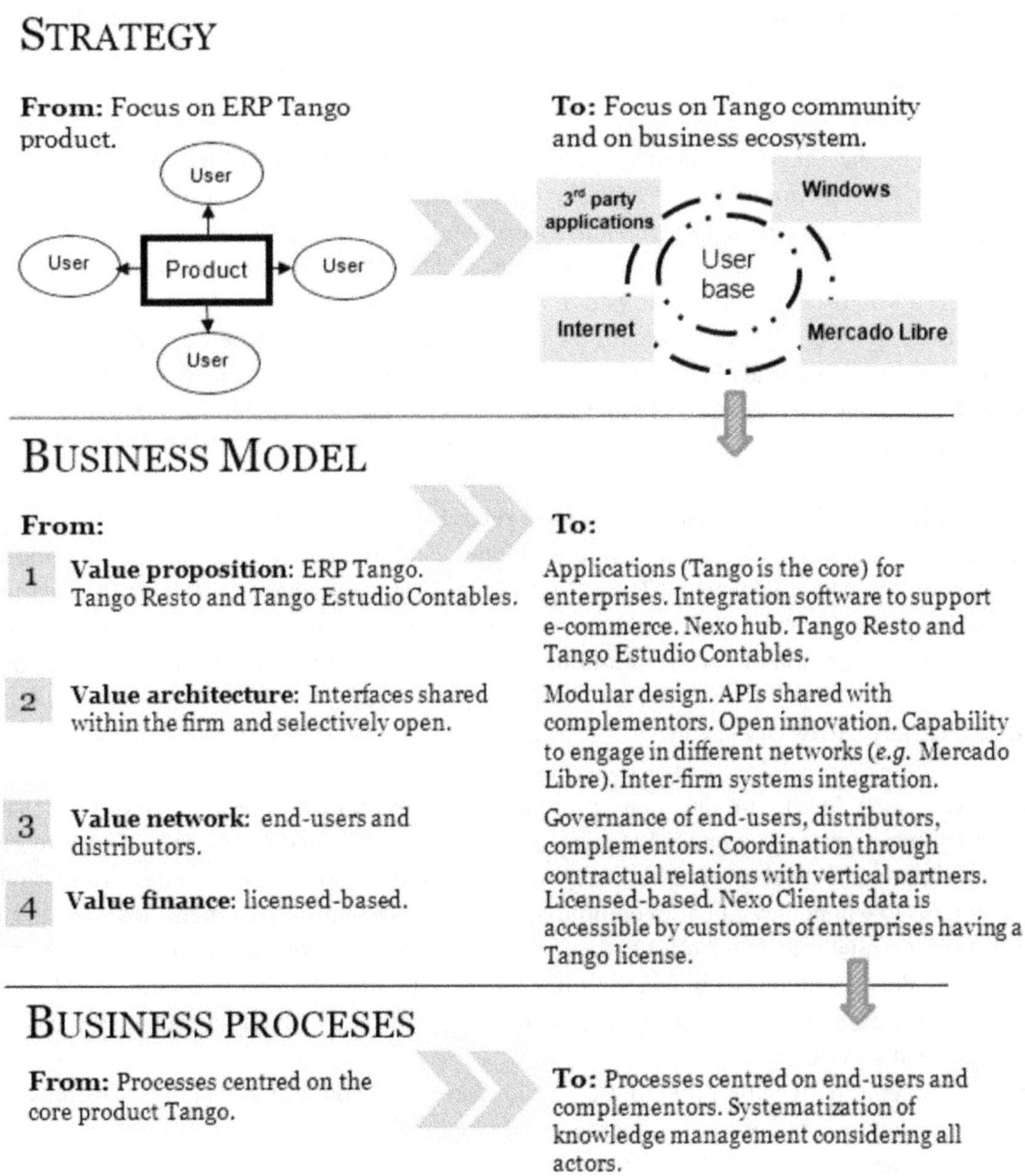

a lot of rotation since it is a sector in which there is full employment. They mentioned that customer's insufficient technological infrastructure used to be a problem that have been ameliorated with the cloud software solutions. Interviewees stressed the importance of their customers' capability to adapt to changes since their solutions are going through a strong innovation process. Figure 2 depicts the transformation of Axoft's business model.

SOLUTIONS AND RECOMMENDATIONS

In order to understand the transformation steps that help Axoft to thrive in a software ecosystem, we provide an analysis structured following the three perspectives, as defined by Jansen *et al.* (2009).

Software Ecosystem Level

Axoft is working on the Tango community, and consider the ERP software Tango as the "motor" integrated with other software solutions. As a product provider, we can regard Axoft a key player. At the same time, Axoft works in a market in which Microsoft and Mercado Libre are leading players. Tango was the first ERP working over Windows in the country and the choice of the operating system allowed Axoft to be part a Microsoft platform ecosystem. Axoft is a complementor in Windows platform. Mercado Libre is the biggest e-commerce store in the region and the integration between the ERP software and the customers' online portals increases the stickiness of the solution and may attract new customers considering the huge users base of Mercado Libre. Though the relationship is asymmetric, we may regard it as of collaboration. Hence, a key recommendation is defining the role that the company plays in each business ecosystem.

Another critical decision at the ecosystem level regards openness. Tango databases are in a non-proprietary format. Consequently, any software developer can build software extending functionalities of Tango. In addition, APIs that connect Tango Ventas with any e-commerce portal enable that the user base of Prestashop, Tienda Nube, Pedidos Ya, among others, are potential customers of Tango products. In addition, by the integration of partner solutions with Tango, Axoft maximize customers' retention.

Software Supply Network Level

Distributors (they sell Axoft's products and provide after-sales support) are key actors in the supply network. Distributors ensure a countrywide reach and strengthen the market presence. They are mainly attracted since they are exclusive representatives in their region, and Tango is a well-known brand that attracts customers to whom they can offer complimentary services or products. In the near future, a large set of APIs will be available to distributors to develop complementary applications of Tango. Sometimes, new business models put emphasis in fostering new kinds of relationships and question if old relations still add value. In this case, distributors remain as key actors as they provide confidence to customers who rely on a local service provider.

Claro is a strategic partner by providing cloud infrastructure and service. Axoft is increasing the offer of cloud-based products. With the emergence of cloud computing there is an increasing trend for companies to migrate their internal ERP application and databases into the cloud (Peng & Gala, 2014).

Cloud technology is a solution for customers because they do not need to make a big hardware investment and they are able to access applications from any place.

There are also software developers that are not commercially linked with Axoft but they develop software for Tango users to fulfil any particular requirement or functionality not provided by Tango. The support to these software developers by providing APIs is positive as they play the role of complementors.

Software Vendor Level

Decisions regarding the portfolio and product lines foster collaboration within the Tango community. Tango Nexo platform is an access portal of Tango web applications that can be accessed from any device. Tango Sync is a tool used to synchronize data from the desktop Tango system with Nexo applications. Nexo Clientes is a web application with which commercial and financial information can be made available to customers from the Tango Ventas module. This application provides Tango users a communication channel with their customers even if they not have a Tango license. That is, it connects customers with customers. This design decision may also lead to a positive network effect and customers of an existing customer might become an Axoft's customer as well. It is recommended to consider actions that nurture the product community because they are an opportunity to exploit network effects.

FUTURE RESEARCH DIRECTIONS

Axoft transitions from a product to platform-based business model to provide a solution for customers that operate in a platform-mediated setting. These customers typically have an e-commerce store at a retail portal (*e.g.* Mercado Libre) or use paying buttons provided by third parties and require that their ERP systems support these new operational processes. In this case, we refer to a customer participating in platforms and, from the point of view of digital maturity, no difficulties or resistance will arise to adopt the innovations proposed by Axoft. On the other hand, for customers who continue to operate according to a traditional product-centric business model, innovations represent a requirement to adapt to new rules that they do not need (or at least do not consider necessary). This poses a challenge in retaining and providing a satisfactory software solution to these customers. In the previous section, we mentioned that interviewees stressed the importance of their customers' capability to adapt to changes since their solutions are going through a strong innovation process. In this sense, it is of interest to research the impact that the transition from a product-centric business model to platforms has on traditional customers, and how to manage change for these customers. Change management should address cultural issues, technical risks reduction and effective communication on how a customer can enhance its business to be an active part of the digital ecosystem.

The results presented in the previous section highlight that the pain point of the transformation is defining the path of this transition in order to maintain a balance between opening up the software and not losing control of the software product developed by the company. Inherent in this objective is the issue on how to use APIs and SDKs to attract complementors, and the consequences of this use to platform users and platform owners. Scholars have extensively studied these topics for pure platform-based business models. However, in this chapter we consider software vendors that transition from product to platform based business models. In addition, as observed in the introduction of this work, a transition does not occur instantly and may take many forms depending, for example, on the degree of product control the firm is willing to yield. Then, potential research topics are how to use APIs and SDKs and define terms and conditions for different members of the business ecosystem.

CONCLUSION

The contributions of this work are twofold. First, the work contributes to management literature in terms of discussing how traditional digital enterprises transform to compete in an ecosystems setting. Based on a literature review the themes and strategy decisions arising when adapting to emerging business models are identified. The business model perspective allowed working out a comprehensive management discussion. The focus of this research is on traditional firms centered around a software product and that should transform to be able to offer a solution that adds value to customers. For customers, stand-alone applications are not enough since their processes are supported by the integration of many systems (*e.g.* online commerce store platform, ERP, CRM, payments processing system).

Second, based on the case study analysis we were able to infer strategic choices and concrete actions performed in order to pursue transformation. The first challenge is migrating products to market demands of cloud-based applications and integration with other systems to provide a solution that adds value to customers. A suggested strategy is to focus on the core product and motivate other actors to contribute with complementary applications (by opening APIs to promote systems' integration). Also, limit partnerships to those that add value to the customers. Two necessary actions are customer-oriented processes and systematization of knowledge management process including all actors in the ecosystem. For the case of a traditional firm, the fact of having customers who are using products since a long time may pose the risk of customers' aversion to change. Then, it may also be relevant to define actions to mitigate this risk. Even though the use of a single case poses a limit to generalize any result, the case provided valuable evidence on a Latin American setting where emergent technologies have more potential than is currently being realized and economic recession slows down market growth.

REFERENCES

Adner, R., & Kapoor, R. (2010). Value creation in innovation ecosystems: How the structure of technological interdependence affects firm performance in new technology generations. *Strategic Management Journal*, *31*(3), 306–333. doi:10.1002mj.821

Al-Debei, M., & Avison, D. (2010). Developing a unified framework of the business model concept. *European Journal of Information Systems*, *19*(3), 359–376. doi:10.1057/ejis.2010.21

Altman, E. (2015). *Platform and Ecosystem Transitions: Strategic and Organizational Implications. Doctoral dissertation.* Boston: Harvard Business School.

Alves, C., Oliveira, J., & Jansen, S. (2017). Software ecosystems governance-a systematic literature review and research agenda. *Proc. 19th Int. Conf. Enterprise Inf. Syst. (ICEIS)*, 1, pp. 215-226. 10.5220/0006269402150226

Andreo, S., & Bosch, J. (2019). API Management Challenges in Ecosystems. In S. Hyrynsalmi, M. Suoranta, A. Nguyen-Duc, P. Tyrväinen, & P. Abrahamsson (Eds.), *Software Business. ICSOB 2019. Lecture Notes in Business Information Processing* (Vol. 370). Springer. doi:10.1007/978-3-030-33742-1_8

Angeren, J., Kabbedijk, J., Popp, K., & Jansen, S. (2013). Managing software ecosystems through partening. In S. Jansen, S. Brinkkemper, & M. Cusumano (Eds.), Software Ecosystems: analyzing and managing business networks in the software industry (pp. 85-102). Edward Elgar Publishiing.

Axoft Argentina, S. A. (2019, November 8). *Tango nexo.* Retrieved November 8, 2019, from https://www.tangonexo.com/

Axoft Argentina, S. A. (2019, September 16). *Tango software.* Retrieved from https://www.axoft.com/

Axoft Argentina, S. A. (2019). *Tango Tiendas.* Retrieved November 11, 2019, from https://www.tangonexo.com/tiendas/

Basole, R. (2016, November/December). Accelerating Digital Transformation. Visual Insights from the API Ecosystem. *IT Pro*, 20-25.

Basole, R., & Park, H. (2019). Interfirm Collaboration and Firm Value in Software Ecosystems: Evidence From Cloud Computing. *IEEE Transactions on Engineering Management*, *66*(3), 368–380. doi:10.1109/TEM.2018.2855401

Bosh-Sijtsema, P., & Bosch, J. (2015). Plays nice with others? Multiple ecosystems, various roles and divergent engagement models. *Technology Analysis and Strategic Management*, *27*(8), 960–974. doi:10.1080/09537325.2015.1038231

Boudreau, K. (2010). Open platform strategies and innovation: Granting access vs. devolving control. *Management Science*, *56*(10), 1761–1777. doi:10.1287/mnsc.1100.1215

Brenk, S. (2020). Open Business Model Innovation – The Impact of Breadth, Depth, and Freedom of Collaboration. Academy of Management Proceedings, 1, 1-6. doi:10.5465/AMBPP.2020.19

Brynjolfsson, E., & McAfee, A. (2011). *Race against the machine: how the digital revolution is accelerating innovation, driving productivity, and irreversibly transforming*. Digital Frontier Press.

Clear, T. (2019). Software Ecosystems: What Do We Need to Know? *ACM Inroads*, *10*(2). Advance online publication. doi:10.1145/3395963

Cronista. (2019, May 3). *La crisis no pudo con MercadoLibre: vendió más en Argentina y ganó u$s 94 millones.* Retrieved November 11, 2019, from https://www.cronista.com/apertura-negocio/empresas/La-crisis-no-pudo-con-MercadoLibre-vendio-mas-en-Argentina-y-gano-us-94-millones-20190503-0004.html

Cusumano, M., Gawer, A., & Yoffie, D. (2019). *The Business of Platforms. Strategy in the Age of Digital Competition, Innovation, and Power*. HarperCollins publishers.

de Reuver, M., Sorensen, C., & Basole, R. (2018). The digital platform: A research agenda. *Journal of Information Technology*, *33*(2), 24–35. doi:10.105741265-016-0033-3

Eisenhardt, K., & Graebner, M. (2007). Theory building from cases: Opportunities and callenges. *Academy of Management Journal, 50*(1), 25–32. doi:10.5465/amj.2007.24160888

Eisenmann, T., Parker, G., & Van Alstyne, M. (2007). Platform envelopment. *Strategic Management Journal, 32*(12), 1270–1285. doi:10.1002mj.935

Fehrer, J., Woratscheck, H., & Brodie, R. (2018). A systemic logic for platform business models. *Journal of Service Management, 29*(4), 546–568. doi:10.1108/JOSM-02-2017-0036

Garud, R., Kumaraswamy, A., Roberts, A., & Xu, L. (2020). Liminal movement by digital platform-based sharing economy ventures: The case of Uber Technologies. *Strategic Management Journal, •••*, 1–29. doi:10.1002mj.3148

Gassmann, O., Frankenberger, K., & Csik, M. (2014). *The business model navigator: 55 models that will revolutionise your business*. Pearson.

Gawer, A. (2014). Bridging differing perspectives on technological platforms: Toward and integrative framework. *Research Policy, 43*(7), 1239–1249. doi:10.1016/j.respol.2014.03.006

Gawer, A., & Cusumano, M. (2014). Industry Platforms and Ecosystem Innovation. *Journal of Product Innovation Management, 31*(3), 417–433. doi:10.1111/jpim.12105

GitHub, Inc. (2019). *GitHub*. Retrieved November 11, 2019, from https://github.com/TangoSoftware/ApiTiendas

Gulati, R., Puranam, P., & Tushman, M. (2012). Meta-Organization Design: Rethinking Design in Interorganizational and Community Contexts. *Strategic Management Journal, 33*(6), 571–586. doi:10.1002mj.1975

Hannah, D., & Eisenhardt, K. (2018). How firms navigate cooperation and competition in nascent ecosystems. *Strategic Management, 39*(12), 3163–3192. doi:10.1002mj.2750

Jansen, S. (2020). A focus area maturity model for software ecosystem governance. *Information and Software Technology, 118*, 106219. doi:10.1016/j.infsof.2019.106219 PMID:32490064

Jansen, S., Brinkkemper, S., & Finkelstein, A. (2009). Business Network Management as a Survivial Strategy: A Tale of Two Software Ecosystems. In *Proceedings of the First Workshop on Software Ecosystems* (pp. 34-48). Falls Church: CEUR Workshop Proceedings.

Jansen, S., Finkelstein, S., & Brinkkemper, A. (2009). A sense of community: A research agenda for software ecosystems. In *31st International Conference on Software Engineering, New and Emerging Research Track* (pp. 187-190). Vancouver: IEEE Press. 10.1109/ICSE-COMPANION.2009.5070978

Johnson, C., Mekikian, G., & Barnett, W. (2020). The Rise of Mercado Libre. Case IB-109. Stanford Graduate School of Business.

Kane, G. (2017, April 17). Digital Maturity, Not Digital Transformation. *MIT Sloan Management Review*. Retrieved from https://sloanreview.mit.edu/article/digital-maturity-not-digital-transformation/

Kane, G., Palmer, D., Phillips, A., Kiron, D., & Buckley, N. (2015). *Strategy, not technology, drives digital transformation*. MIT Sloan Management Review.

Khanagha, S., Ansari, S., Paroutis, S., & Oviedo, L. (2020). Mutualism and the dynamics of new platform creation: A study of Cisco and fog computing. *Strategic Management Journal*, (Special issue), 1–31. doi:10.1002mj.3147

Kohtamäki, M., Parida, V., Oghazi, P., Gebauer, H., & Baines, T. (2019). Digital servitization business models in ecosystems: A theory of the firm. *Journal of Business Research*, *104*, 380–392. doi:10.1016/j.jbusres.2019.06.027

Libert, B., Beck, M., & Wind, J. (2016). *The Network Imperative. How to survive and grow in the age of digital business models*. Harvard Business Review Press.

Madariaga, J., Buenadicha, C., Molina, E., & Ernst, C. (2019). *Economía de plataformas y empleo: ¿cómo es trabajar para una app en Argentina?* CIPPEC - BID - OIT.

Mariotto, F., Zanni, P., & Salati, G. (2014). What is the use of a single-case study in management research? *Revista de Administração de Empresas*, *54*(4), 358–369. doi:10.1590/S0034-759020140402

McAfee, A., & Brynjolfsson, E. (2017). *Machine, Platform, Crowd. Harnessing our digital future*. W. W. Norton & Company Ltd.

Nambisan, S., Siegel, D., & Kenney, M. (2018). On Open Innovation, Platforms, and Entrepreneurship. *Strategic Entrepreneurship Journal*, *12*(3), 354–368. doi:10.1002ej.1300

Osterwalder, A., & Pigneur, Y. (2010). *Business Model Generation: A Handbook for Visionaries, Game Changers, and Challengers*. John Wiley & Sons, Inc.

Osterwalder, A., Pigneur, Y., & Tucci, C. (2005, July). Clarifying business models: Origins, present, and future of the concept. *Communications of the Association for Information Systems*, *15*, 1–25. doi:10.17705/1CAIS.01601

Parker, G., Van Alstyne, M., & Choudary, S. (2016). *Platform Revolution. How networked markets are transforming the economy and how to make them work for you*. W. W. Norton & Company.

Pellizzoni, E., Trabucchi, D., & Buganza, T. (2019). Platform strategies: How the position in the network drives succes. *Technology Analysis and Strategic Management*, *31*(5), 579–592. doi:10.1080/09537325.2018.1524865

Peng, G., & Gala, C. (2014). Cloud ERP: A New Dilemma to Modern Organisations? *Journal of Computer Information Systems*, *54*(4), 22–30. doi:10.1080/08874417.2014.11645719

Porter, M. (1991). Towards a Dynamic Theory of Strategy. *Strategic Management Journal*, *12*(S2), 95–117. doi:10.1002mj.4250121008

Porter, M., & Heppelmann, J. (2015). How Smart, Connected Products are Transforming Companies. *Harvard Business Review*, 1–19.

Prensario TI Latin America. (2016, October). Software ERP en América Latina. Nuevo perfil de negocio cambia el mercado. *Prensario TILA*, *14*(184), 4–12.

Rong, K., Lin, Y., Li, B., Burström, T., Butel, L., & Yu, J. (2018). Business ecosystem research agenda: More dynamic, more embedded, and more internationalized. *Asian Business & Management, 17*(3), 167–182. doi:10.105741291-018-0038-6

Ross, J., Sebastian, I., & Beath, C. (2016). How to Develop a Great Digital Strategy. *MIT Sloan Management Review.*

Schultis, K., Elsner, C., & Lohmann, D. (2014). *Architecture challenges for internal software ecosystems: A large-scale industry case study. In Proceedings of the 22nd ACM SIGSOFT International Symposium on Foundations of Software Engineering*. ACM. https://doi.acm.org/10.1145/2635868.2635876

Stake, R. (2000). The case study method in social inquiry. In N. Denzin & Y. Lincoln (Eds.), *The American tradition in qualitative research* (Vol. 2). Sage Publications.

Tura, N., Kutvonen, A., & Ritala, P. (2017). Platform design framework: Conceptualisation and application. *Technology Analysis and Strategic Management, 30*(8), 881–894. doi:10.1080/09537325.2017.1390220

Van Alstyne, M., Parker, G., & Choudary, P. (2016, April). Pipelines, Platforms, and the New Rules of Strategy. *Harvard Business Review*, 54–60, 62.

Venkatraman, V. (2017). *The Digital Matrix. New Rules for Business Transformation Through Technology*. LifeTree Media Ltd.

Weill, P., & Woerner, S. (2015). Thriving in an increasingly digital ecosystem. *MIT Sloan Management Review, 56*(4), 27–34.

Wen, W., & Zhu, F. (2019). Threat of Platform-Owner Entry and Complementor Responses: Evidence from the Mobile App Market. *Strategic Management Journal, 40*(9), 1336–1367. doi:10.1002mj.3031

Zeng, M. (2018). *Smart Business. What Alibaba's Success Reveals about the Future of Strategy*. Harvard Business Review Press.

Zheng, M. (2015). Economic and Business Dimensions. Three Paradoxes of Building Platforms. *Communications of the ACM, 58*(2), 27–29. doi:10.1145/2700343

Zhu, F., & Liu, Q. (2018). Competing with complementors: An empirical look at Amazon.com. *Strategic Management Journal, 39*(10), 2618–2642. doi:10.1002mj.2932

ADDITIONAL READING

Benlian, A., Hilkert, D., & Hess, T. (2015). How Open is this Platform? The Meaning and Measurement of Platform Openness from the Complementors' Perspective. *Journal of Information Technology, 30*(3), 209–228. doi:10.1057/jit.2015.6

Cozzolino, A., Verona, G., & Rothaermel, F. T. (2018). Unpacking the Disruption Process: New Technology, Business Models, and Incumbent Adaptation. *Journal of Management Studies, 55*(7), 1166–1202. doi:10.1111/joms.12352

Giessmann, A., & Legner, C. (2016). Designing business models for cloud platforms. *Information Systems Journal*, *26*(5), 551–579. doi:10.1111/isj.12107

Ricart, J., Snihur, Y., Carrasco-Farré, C., & Berrone, P. (2020). Grassroots Resistance to Digital Platforms and Relational Business Model Design to Overcome It: A Conceptual Framework. *Strategy Science*, *5*(3), 1–21. doi:10.1287tsc.2020.0104

Shi, X., Li, F., & Chumnumpan, P. (2020). Platform Development: Emerging Insights From a Nascent Industry. *Journal of Management*. Advance online publication. doi:10.1177/0149206320929428

Sköld, M., Freij, Å., & Frishammar, J. (2020). New Entrant or Incumbent Advantage in Light of Regulatory Change: A Multiple Case Study of the Swedish Life Insurance Industry. *European Management Review*, *17*(1), 209–227. doi:10.1111/emre.12345

Teixeira, T. (2019). *Unlocking the Customer Value Chain. How Decoupling Drives Consumer Disruption*. Currency.

Zhu, F. (2019). Friends or foes? Examining platform owners' entry into complementors' spaces. *Journal of Economics & Management Strategy*, *28*(1), 23–28. doi:10.1111/jems.12303

KEY TERMS AND DEFINITIONS

Application Programming Interfaces (APIs): An API is a software interface that allows the sharing of data or services.

Business Ecosystem: A network of stakeholders (*e.g.* suppliers, manufacturers, distributors, complementors) involved in the delivery of a product or service through both competition and collaboration.

Business Model: A description of how a business creates value.

Complementor: A firm (sometimes an entrepreneur) offering products or services that increase the value of another company offering.

Digital: Refers to the use of technology that generates, stores and processes data.

Digital Platform: A digital platform refers to the infrastructure and rules for a marketplace that enable and ease interactions between producers and consumers.

Enterprise: An organization made up of human, intangible and physical resources, and whose objective is to achieve some economic or commercial benefit, satisfying the needs of customers through the offer of goods or services.

Incumbent: A traditional enterprise in its sector. Enterprises are usually classified as digital natives, entrepreneurs or incumbents.

Software Developer Kits (SDKs): A SDK is a collection of software development tools in one installable package.

Software Ecosystem: A software ecosystem is defined as a set of actors (*e.g.* software developers, vendors, distributors, complementors) interacting on a shared software market to satisfy consumers' demands.

Strategy: A set of decisions with the aim of achieving a certain goal.

Transformation: Changes to organizational strategy, business models, and business processes and information systems that support value creation.

APPENDIX

1. Considering the increase of economies based on platforms, and the business models focus from products to platforms. In your opinion, should the firm reconsider its role in the business ecosystem?
2. If the answer to the previous question is affirmative, how does the firm mobilize to re-define its role?
3. In your opinion, does Axoft develop incentives to include different actors in the software ecosystem? (for example, the offer of APIs, SDKs)
4. To what extent do you consider that these are part of your organization's strategy? *Please, select all that apply and assign a priority.*

Innovation, Improve user experience, Decision making, Efficiency

5. In your opinion, Axoft's goals to extend partnerships are … *Please, select all that apply.*

Extension of partnership ecosystem, New products and services, Expand the market revenues through partnerships, Other (Please, specify)

6. Do the following companies define requirements to integrate their systems to Axoft's solutions?
    a. Microsoft
    b. Mercado Libre
    c. Prestashop, Tienda Nube, Pedidos Ya, Producteca, Vtex
    d. Claro
    e. (other) ……
7. Does Axoft define requirement to integrate its solutions with the following companies?
    a. Mercado Libre
    b. Prestashop, Tienda Nube, Pedidos Ya, Producteca, Vtex
    c. Claro
    d. (other) ……
8. To what extent Axoft's value proposition depends on new ways of collaboration with stakeholders (for example, customers, e-commerce portals, developers, distributors, government agencies)?

Not at all … Great extent

9. To what extent does the firm know customers' needs?

Sells through another company … Owner of customer relationship

10. In your opinion, Axoft fosters collaboration mechanisms inside the company and between different actors of the ecosystem (for example, through collaboration networks, communication channels).
11. In your opinion, what best characterizes Axoft's approach towards risks?

Minimize risks, avoid errors, access control to data, information not shared … Transparency, freedom to innovate, trial and error approach

12. In your opinion, which barriers are hindering Axoft to transform the business model from one based on products to one based on platforms? *Please, select all that apply.*

Lack of organizational strategy, Lack of collaborative culture, Many priorities that compete, Lack of organizational agility, Security concerns (data), Economic recession, Lack of leadership, Insufficient resources, Insufficient technological infrastructure, Other (Please, specify)

Chapter 10
Management and Strategies for Digital Enterprise Transformation:
Proposal for the Utility of Neuro-Economics in the Services of ICT of the Exponential SMEs of the Artisanal Industry of Women Entrepreneurs in Mexico

Jovanna Nathalie Cervantes-Guzmán
Centro Universitario de Ciencias Económico Administrativas, Universidad de Guadalajara, Mexico

ABSTRACT

Scientific knowledge will be advanced in the need for the application of neuroeconomics focused on one of the services of the information and communication technologies (ICT) of companies that is e-commerce of exponential artisanal SMEs driven by women entrepreneurs, by developing a proposal for a business model to increase the possibility of growth of their companies at the level national and international level. The methodology used was deductive, exploratory, descriptive, correlational, and documentary. Neuroeconomics have the potential to explain the phenomena that are considered as a deviation from the prediction or behavioral bias of decision-making models in economic theory. The study up to this point is quantitative using primary and secondary sources of information for research.

INTRODUCTION

Neuroeconomics is an emerging discipline that combines the findings and modeling tools of neuroscience, psychology and economics to explain the behavior of human choice (Glimcher, 2003).

The aspects in neuroeconomics that propose a new significant episode of change, according to Glimcher and Rustichini (2004) are:

DOI: 10.4018/978-1-7998-8583-2.ch010

- Integration of behavioral work carried out by economists, psychologists and neuroscientists, for the development of a unified theory of the choice of behavior.
- Technological advances that allow us to look at the brain will eventually replace the simple mathematical ideas of economics with more detailed neuronal descriptions.

Within the framework of the above considerations, SMEs in Mexico constitute 95% of established companies and contribute 23% to Gross Internal Product, but they have a series of problems that cause 75% to close their operations after 2 years in the market (INEGI, 2010), and its chance of success is on average from 25% to 30% below the world average that is 40% (Fernández, 2010). It is appropriate to highlight that 47% directed by the female gender, contributing 37% of GIP, also contribute 70% of GIP and allocate 70% of their income to the community and family (González, 2016). Despite this, Latin America has the highest rate of business failure run by women. In Mexico alone, 2.2 million formal companies 17.63% are directed by the female gender, in addition, that 50% have a profit of less than $ 50,000 USD compared to 25% of the companies that operate men (Power & Magnoni, 2010).

According to the United Nations Educational, Scientific and Cultural Organization (UNESCO, 2001), it states that the artisanal sector has a predominant role in economic development and the fight against poverty, but they lack a long way to go to achieve its maximum potential in generating employment and income to achieve greater economic growth in developing countries. The artisanal sector has great untapped potential in e-commerce that can generate a greater amount of income and jobs that produce a social and economic impact on entrepreneurs worldwide and especially women (Foote, 2015).

The purpose and scope in the research is the management and strategies for digital enterprise transformation by using neuroeconomics, a model proposal focused on understanding consumer decision-making on one of the services of the information and communication technologies of companies focus in electronic commerce of exponential artisanal SMEs of women entrepreneurs will be developed.

BACKGROUND

Statement of the Problem

According to the International Telecommunication Union (2015), internet is used by 43.3% of the world's population, which corresponds to 3,200 million Internet users. Companies use ICT as a new channel for the dissemination of products and/or services, appearing a second group of ICT services formed by the electronic commerce which is a mode of remote purchases through a network of telecommunication's that has increased its potential by adapting people with new technologies. The way in which internet has increased its penetration in the online market has caused changes in the way in which business interacts with consumers, developing e-commerce causing companies to increase the total number of sales and an increase in online retail interactions of consumers (VanderMeer, et al, 2001). The number of digital buyers worldwide is rapidly expanding from 1,32 billion in 2014 to 1,66 billion in 2017 and is expected to increase to 2,14 billion in 2021 (Statista, 2018). What translates into an increase in electronic sales of retailers globally from 2014 in 1.336 billion dollars to 2,290 billion dollars in 2017 and an increase in 4,479 billion dollars is forecast for 2021 (Statistica, 2018). With a participation in retail e-commerce 2016 in the Asia and the Pacific regions with 12.1%, Eastern Europe with 8.3%, North America with 8.1%, Central and Eastern Europe with 3.4% and Latin America with 1.9% (Statista, 2018).

Electronic commerce offers great potential for the expansion of companes to international markets by intensifying the sales power by creating a new distribution channel to reach new customers, develop their own marketing strategies and produce new business opportunities (Colvee 2013). In addition, e-commerce is a powerful tool that allows SMEs to move faster in the development phases by positioning the company in the world market (Hussain, 2013). The proper management of electronic commerce will allow artisanal SMEs to increase their competitiveness (Aragon & Rubio, 2005) in a sector where, despite their significant participation and their annual growth rate of over 4%, they have not been able to increase it (FONART, 2009).

One of the big problems for the integration of SMEs in e-commerce is to achieve efficiency in electronic platforms due to ignorance of customer behavior in decision making (Sacristan, 2013).

In the context of the above considerations, SMEs in Mexico constitute 95% of established companies and contribute 23% to GIP, but they have a series of problems that cause 75% to close their operations after 2 years in the market (INEGI, 2009), and its chance of success is on average from 25% to 30% below the world average which is 40% (Fernández, 2010). At the international level, the percentage of survival and the half-life of SMEs is similar in countries such as Spain, where more than 70% does not exceed 4 years of life and 80% of SMEs fail within the first 5 years, in the United States of America 30% of SMEs do not reach the third year and have an average life of 6 years and in the underdeveloped countries only the first 3 years of life survive between 50% and 75%.

Artisanal SMEs are a great engine of the economy where 47% are directed by the female gender, contributing 37% of GIP, they also allocate 70% of their income to the community and the family unlike men who contribute only between 30% and 40% (González, 2016). Despite this, Latin America has the highest rate of business failures managed by women. In Mexico, only 2,2 million formal companies 17.63% are directed by the female gender, in addition, that 50% have a profit of less than $ 50,000 USD against 25% of the companies that operate men (Power & Magnoni, 2010) .

The artisanal sector is a global creative economy, which represents what can be exemplified as a country that would symbolize the fourth largest economy and labor force in the world according to the Inter-American Development Bank (IDB). It is a global industry that generates revenues of $ 34 billion per year, and only developing countries provide 64% of global exports. According to the United Nations Organization for Education, Science and Culture (UNESCO, 2001), it states that the artisanal sector has a predominant role in economic development and in the fight against poverty. In addition, preferences in market consumption are changing because they care about the origin of the product, which they produce and how it was manufactured, changing their preferences for mass-produced products at hand, the only one of its kind and independent design (INDEGO Africa, 2016). They have a long way to go to achieve their full potential in employment and income generation to achieve greater economic growth in developing countries.

MAIN FOCUS OF THE CHAPTER

The artisanal sector has great untapped potential in electronic commerce that can generate a greater amount of income and jobs that produce a social and economic impact on entrepreneurs around the world and especially women (Foote, 2015). This can be achieved through the use of neuroeconomics, which is an emerging discipline that combines the findings and tools of modeling neuroscience, psychology and economics to explain the behavior of human choice; neuroscience provides tools to answer questions of economic models that cannot be explained; and economics contributes to neuroscience decision models to examine the mechanisms of communication between brain circuits (Glimcher, 2003).

Scientific knowledge will be advanced in the need for the application of neuroeconomics in the e-commerce of exponential artisanal SMEs of women entrepreneurs, having the potential to explain the phenomena that are considered as deviation from the prediction or behavioral bias of the models of decision making to achieve the increase of its market on a larger scale and its growth regardless of its size and location.

The study will be designed with the theme of women entrepreneurs of exponential artisanal SMEs certified internationally by the NGO "Women Owned". First, it will conduct a survey of young millennials that are 80% of the people who buy in e-commerce. The results will allow to improve electronic commerce through neuroeconomics techniques to increase the possibility of growing their businesses nationally and internationally.

The variables of the research were formed by the review of literature based on PhD thesis and an article focused on neuro-correlation in decision-making, the online consumer decision-making process, the intention to purchase the consumer in the online purchasing environment, neuroeconomic studies in decision-making and the role of emotions in decision-making through a cognitive approach to neuroeconomics.

Issues, Controversies and Problems

The increase in online shopping has transformed the internet into a powerful force, being a tool that has a great influence on consumer behavior (McGaughey & Mason, 1998), modified the way the individual acquires a product by the large amount of information that it provides, making it easier for the potential client to evaluate the products and services of different suppliers, which modifies the traditional buying behavior (Koufaris, 2003). Because it allows the purchase through crossed channels, this together with the development of technological characteristics such as the search for information, the evaluation of the different alternatives offered and the realization of the purchase (Constantinides, 2004).

In order to increase the number of consumers and their conversion rate, it is necessary to understand online consumer behavior to improve their shopping experience and satisfaction (Zhang, et al, 2011). Consumer behavior in the traditional market is different from its purchasing behavior in electronic commerce, with the information of this limited and poorly studied (Denis, et al, 2009) in terms of making the purchase decision (Brynjolfsson, et al, 2010) being the void of literature that focuses on this research. Increasing theoretical knowledge in the decision-making process in this area is crucial, and this can be explored by developing a new behavior model (Rickwood & White, 2009).

LITERATURE REVIEW

Artisanal SMEs in the Economic Context of the Countries

According to the United Nations Educational, Scientific and Cultural Organization (UNESCO), artisanal products have characteristics that define them as their usefulness, esthetic a, artistic, creative, link to culture, decoration, functionality, traditional, symbolic and significantly social (Etienne-Nugue, 2009).

Artisanal SMEs in Developing Countries

After agriculture, the artisanal sector is the second employer in developing countries, mostly made up of women who perform traditional handicrafts to obtain economic resources. These countries have a competitive advantage because of their cultural traditions, artisanal skills and specialized raw materials (Foote, 2015).

The artisanal sector is a global creative economy, it can be exemplified by representing it as a country that would symbolize the fourth largest economy and labor force in the world according to the Inter-American Development Bank (IDB). It is a global industry that generates revenues of $ 34 billion a year, with only developing countries providing 64% of exports worldwide. According to the United Nations Educational, Scientific and Cultural Organization (UNESCO, 2001), it states that the artisanal sector has a predominant role in economic development and the fight against poverty. In addition, preferences in market consumption are changing because they care about the origin of the product, who made it and how it was manufactured, changing their preferences for mass-produced products to the handmade, the only one of its kind and independent design (INDEGO AFRICA, 2016).

Handcrafts SMEs in Mexico

In Mexico, handicrafts are the main economic-cultural item in terms of production, the generation of renumbered work with 43% dedicated to the manufacture of handicrafts, and a total cultural expenditure of 37.7%, is an industry which generates 122 million pesos, which is represented in terms of a GIP 1.3 higher than that of agriculture (INEGI, 2012).

In the current economic context caused by the economic crisis and unemployment, the relevance of artisanal SMEs that produce garments, household goods and objects with various uses has increased (Sandoval & Guerra, 2010). These productions are integrated by the various fields of human, cultural, social, educational and economic development, the latter being the development of a business (Hernández-Girón, et al, 2007).

Challenges of Gender Equity in the Business World

Companies that have greater gender equity increase their results causing higher levels of growth and performance; this paradigm shift according to the report on the Principles of Empowerment of Women in Businesses published by the UN Women (2016) are:

- Women are key economic agents that produce prosperity, employment, innovation and are an engine of development. The greater the number of women belonging to the Economically Active Population (EAP) the economy increases because it leads to greater social mobility with benefit in the family, community and society.
- There is a positive correlation between business activity and GIP growth. Productivity in Latin America and the Caribbean could increase by 25% if female entrepreneurship is supported.
- The use of female talent would produce benefits for companies such as creativity, efficiency and business efficiency, and improvement of business management.

- Companies with a greater presence of women tend to develop corporate social responsibility and diversity schemes in philanthropic work, which leads to an improvement in the brand image, customer loyalty, recruitment of professional talent, and increased productivity.

In countries where there is a greater number of women entrepreneurs there is greater economic growth, in contrast to countries where it is restricted there is a stagnant economy, there is also an impact on the social environment (UNIDO, 2011). In spite of this, there are currently twice as much male as female entrepreneurship (Reynolds, et al, 2002).

The female gender decides to undertake to obtain their own income, develop an innovative idea, move up in their work careers, flexibility between work, family (Heller, 2010) and by necessity this being a factor that has a direct relationship between the level of development and the business development rate generating a correlation between the developing countries that have a higher rate as opposed to the more developed countries have a lower rate showing a concordance between the levels of low economic remuneration and the creation of a company developed by women (ECLAC, 2004).

Entrepreneurs From Developing Countries

Research in emerging countries by the National Foundation for Women Business Owners (NFWBO) found that women who own business have common characteristics regardless of the business, its establishment, administration, operation, and goals differs from that of the male gender since they are aimed at owning small businesses, making decisions based on diverse criteria, higher priority to quality of life instead of increasing business income, investments controlled by the lack of support for part of the institutions to obtain credit, limited capital, and mainly seek to reconcile the different aspects of their life; in contrast to their counterparts that focus on financial and economic aspects oriented towards profitability. They have similar problems for the growth of their companies, having common needs to achieve this as access to information, training, technological assistance and access to national and international markets.

The contribution of women in the economy of Latin America and the Caribbean had an increase of 35% in 1980 to 53% in 2007 promoting economic growth, financial security in the family, increase in consumption capacity and reduction in poverty of the region (Pages & Piras, 2010).

Despite the increase in female labor participation, this continues to have several problems, according to the World Economic Forum (WEF) according to the report on the Global Gender Gap 2016 that gender equality in economic activity and Labor will be possible in 170 years (Hernández, 2016). Similarly, the 2009 report indicates that the gender gaps with the greatest degree of relevance in Latin America and the Caribbean are in the sub-indices of economic and political participation.

The gender gap in the business sector increases in developing countries, these being the majority of the countries in the Latin American and Caribbean region, where only 22% of women work independently (Hellen, 2010).

SMEs that are led by 51% by women entrepreneurs generate an important contribution to the economy representing 31% to 38%, which constitutes 8 to 10 million, in formal SMEs in developing countries. Female entrepreneurship is composed of micro-sized SMEs 32% to 39%, small size 30% to 36%, medium-sized 17% to 21% (Shukla, 2011).

Despite these figures, according to a study by McKinsey of the IFC (2011), women-led businesses are restricted in their growth path with a reduction in their per capita income growth rate by 0.1 - 0.3percentage points.

Entrepreneurship in Mexico

Mexico where the economic participation of women is only 43% compared to 78% of men. Despite constituting 51.2% of people enrolled in postgraduates, only 29% have leadership positions in companies, 23% in intermediate positions and 5% in board of directors. They have a salary gap with respect to the same work performed by the male gender from 15% to 20% and in leadership positions up to 40% (UN Women, 2016).

According to the 2016 State Competitiveness Index composed of a statewide survey of 32,000 people, a sum was added to the weights of each indicator at the state level, defined as the normalized values from 2001 to 2014 multiplied by the weight of each indicator. The indicator that had an increase of 160 in its weight and has remained constant until 2014 was the index of labor informality between women and men. The indicator of economically active women only increased in their weight 60 staying relatively equal until 2014. The wage equity indicator had an increase of 30 in their weight and has only increased 30 until 2014.

Also, according to the World Economic Report Forum (2017) worldwide it can be seen that there was a stagnation in the progress of the global index of gender equity, but in contrast in Mexico this had a decrease

Theoretical Framework

The success of a company in e-commerce depends on various factors that are classified in 3 main categories:

1. Characteristics of the website
2. Characteristics of the consumer
3. Characteristics of the brand

Characteristics of the Website

They are integrated by the attributes of the website that have an influence on the consumer's intention to purchase. These include:

Aesthetic Appearance

In the online shopping environment, visual elements can be used through the use of images, videos and other interactive features (Kim, et al, 2005). Being considered aesthetic appearance as a positive sensory experience that being the element that has a greater influence on the emotional experience of the consumer (Nasermoadeli, et al, 2013).

The aesthetic appeal on websites directly influences the internal affective state causing a sense of connection through images (Wang, et al, 2011).

Experience Flow

It is defined by Kim, Suh & Lee (2013) as consumer behavior in the interaction of man and computer. That is, your attention is totally focused on the activity you are doing online. This state of immersion is integrated by emotional and cognitive factors, and its interrelation with the flow components necessary to have skills and controls to interact with the website (Rose, et al, 2012).

Consumer Characteristics

In addition to the computer factors, the specific characteristics of the consumer also influence the decision of online purchases through the attitude towards the website (Hausman & Siekpe, 2009). Cowart & Goldsmith (2007) mention that the intention to participate in purchases through the internet is related to the styles in the decision making of consumers, where the objectives of the consumer are the drivers that allow him to experience the pleasure of acquired assets (Balaji, et al, 2007).

One of the factors that affect consumer decision-making is gender, this was demonstrated in a study conducted by Hui & Wan (2007) who evaluated the purchase of clothes online, discovering that in the female gender there is a certain degree of uncertainty due to the lack of satisfaction caused by the experience of buying the product that was generated physically by trying on clothes, generating a lower degree of cognitive and affective attitudes in the intention to buy online unlike men. For the male gender where interactivity has a positive impact, a friendly interface, and sufficient information in web design, which leads to a faster purchase decision (Ganguly, et al, 2010).

Likewise, the consumer culture has a vital role in decision-making in e-commerce, for the mitigation of its effects the design of the website must allow simple navigation, greater interactivity and have the necessary information to facilitate the purchase decision (Cowart & Goldsmith, 2007). For example, trust has a great value for the consumer in the West (Chen, et al, 2012).

Behavior

In consumer behavior, the emotional state related to enjoyment has a relationship similar to pleasure and excitement (Penz & Hogg, 2011). Enjoying purchases has an important impact on the flow status of buyers, generating an intention to revisit the websites (Kim, et al, 2013), exposing a direct relationship between flow and affection (Novak, et al, 2000) .

When a decision is made, the emotional and cognitive state of an individual guides him to the evaluation of the perceived risks and benefits of the decision that leads him to a final decision, later said process works as a feedback mechanism that will affect future decisions (Gutnik, et al, 2006).

Both emotional systems for decision making are integrated by:

- The analytical system is defined by Epstein (1994) as the involvement of conscious cognitive process that uses various algorithms and normative rules to generate logical behaviors that are oriented to reason.
- The experiential system being conceptualized by Slovic, Finucane, Peters & MacGregor (2004) as the use of past experiences, associations related to emotion when making decisions, taking into account to a greater extent the unconscious process than the conscious one.

Emotions have an influence on decision making, it also has indirect effects on the behavior of the individual through the implicit configuration of cognitive representations and this has positive or negative effects depending on the type of emotion such as anger, fear, happiness or the pleasure (Forgas, 2001).

Characteristics of the Brand

The intention to make an online purchase depends on the characteristics of the brand and the type of goods offered on the website, those that present a greater ease for sale online are the search products compared to the goods of experience (Moon, et al, 2008). The characteristics also influence the presentation in the former, which can lead to positive consumer participation in online purchases (Won Jeong, et al, 2009). In addition, offering sensory information generates pleasure and a positive perspective on consumers (Lian & Lin, 2008).

Products and Attributes of the Company

The purchase decision of consumers is faster when they have enough product and company information (Davidson, et al, 2000), showing a directly proportional relationship between the attitude of the buying behavior with the level of information of the good (Chiou, 2000).

In the purchase intention when a consumer acquires products via online, the predictive factor that has a greater relevance is the search for information, in addition to having an impact on the perceived risk of behavior, increasing their tendency to buy the product (Nowlis & McCabe, 2000; Phau & Poon, 2000).

Perceived Utility

Perceived utility is defined as the degree to which a person believes that using a particular system will accelerate their personal growth and improve performance in their work (Davis, 1989).

It is one of the factors with a greater degree of relevance in behavior when a decision is made and is related to convenience and ease of use (Davis, Bagozzi & Warshaw, 1989).

RESEARCH METHODOLOGY

Based on the needs of the study based on the information obtained from research files, the methodology used in the work was as follows:

- Documentary research. The research is documentary, depending on what was proposed by Pasteur (2013) uses documents, collects information, analyzes and presents results. It was used in the study in order to collect the documents that may be essential to understand and contextualize the study.
- Correlational Research. Allows to relate the variables of the problem in a particular context (Baptista, et al, 2010). One of its main characteristics is that it allows examining the relationship between the variables looking for their association but it is not necessary to find their causal relationships (Bernal, 2010).
- Quantitative Approach It is defined by Tamayo (2010) as the measurement of the variables and their relationship through a verification to test the hypothesis and validate their theories, offering the possibility of having a broader approach to women in developing countries.

Table 1. Matrix for the Operationalization of the Variables

Theme	General objective	General research question	Specific objectives	Research questions	Variables	Hypothesis	Methodological analysis
Proposal for the utility of neuro-economics in the services of ICT of the exponential SMES of the artisanal industry of women entrepreneurs in Mexico.	Develop a proposal for a theoretical model that evaluated the behavior in the decision making of the consumer in e-commerce of exponential Mexican artisanal SMEs directed by women entrepreneurs	How can we develop a theoretical model that evaluated the behavior in the decision making of the consumer in the e -Commerce of exponential Mexican artisanal SMEs run by women entrepreneurs?	Examine the factors that expose the relationship between decision making and consumer behavior in e-commerce	What are the factors that expose the relationship between decision making and consumer behavior in e-commerce?	Characteristics of the website	The characteristics of the website have a positive relationship with the intention to purchase	Descriptive and inferential statistics
			Expose the economic context of artisanal SMEs and the challenges of gender equity in developing countries	How is the economic context of artisanal SMEs and the challenges of gender equity in developing countries?	ConsumerConsumer	characteristicscharacteristics have a positive relationship with the intention to purchase	Descriptive and inferential statistics
			Analyze from a quantitative perspective the point of view of millennial consumer, their behavior for decision-making in the e-commerce of exponential Mexican artisanal SMEs directed by enterprising women	How is a millennial consumer point of view from a quantitative perspective, their behavior for decision making in the e-commerce of exponential Mexican artisanal SMEs directed by enterprising women?	Characteristics of the brand	The characteristics of the brand have a positive relationship with the intention to purchase	Descriptive and inferential statistics
					Purchase intention		Statistics inferential

Source: Own elaboration

- The sample was millennials, who are women and men born between 1989 and 2000, with an age range between 18 and 25 years. They were selected as digital natives make 80% of online purchases.

The instrument of the present investigation is a questionnaire, it is integrated by the variable characteristics of the web page, which was carried out through the information adapted from the thesis investigations of: Anen (2007), Karimi (2003) and Cheung (2015).

The second variable characteristics of the consumer, was generated with the information adapted from the thesis research of: Anen (2007), Karimi (2003), Gutnik, Forogh, Yoskowitz & Patel (2005), and Rohan (2013).

The third variable characteristics of the brand, was carried out with the information adapted from the thesis research of: Anen (2007), Karimi (2003) and Leelayouthayotin (2004). (See figure 1)

Once the information is collected in a database in Microsoft Excel, the SPSS statistical program was applied to perform the processing and analysis of the results.

The analysis comprised two stages:

1. Statistical representation of data
2. Method for sorting and presenting data

For the analysis, the inferential statistics that are responsible for organizing and summarizing the data (Munch & Angeles, 2006).

Figure 1. Proposed model
Source: Own elaboration

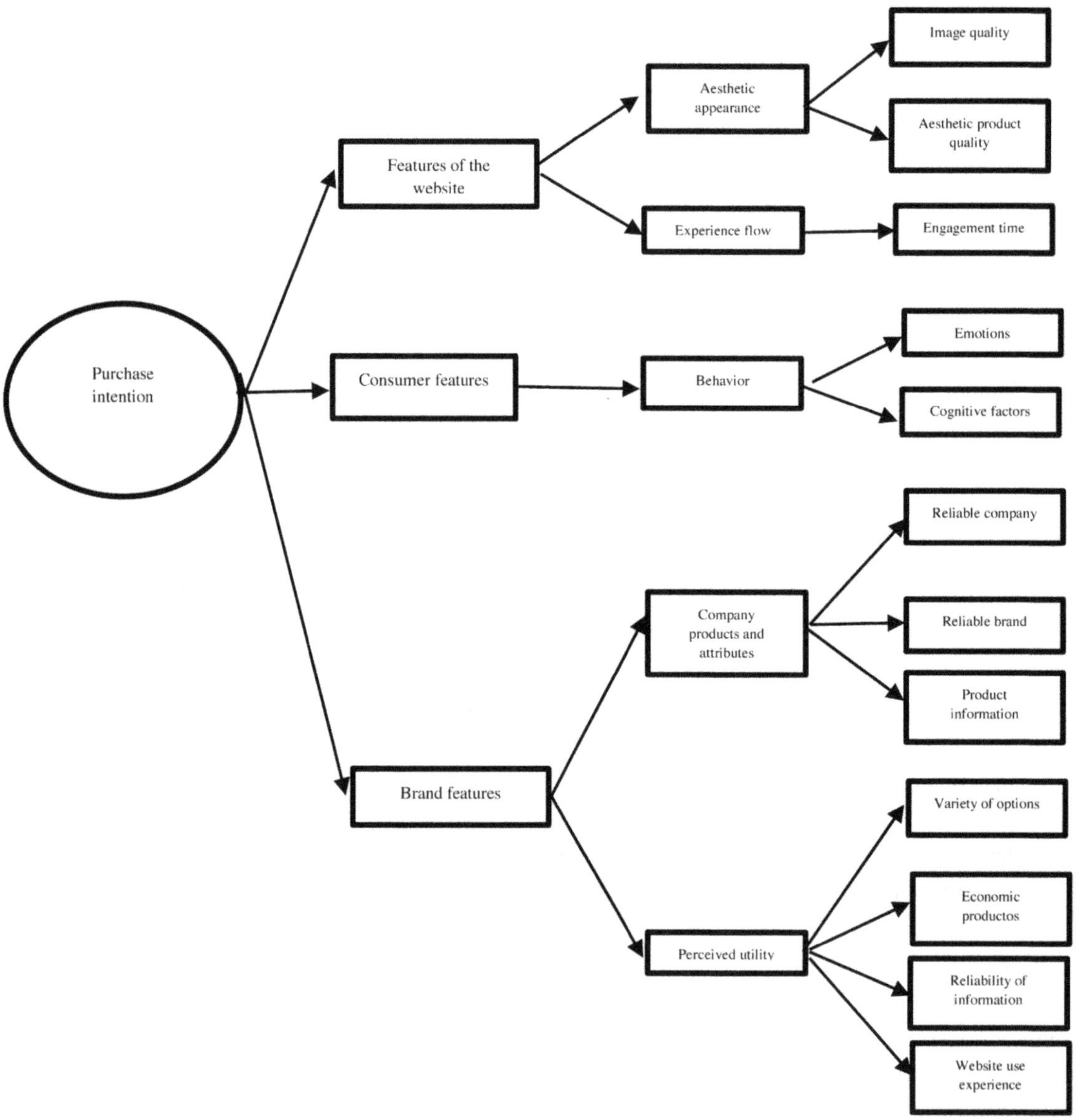

SOLUTIONS AND RECOMMENDATIONS

The reliability of the design of the data collection instrument was verified through a reliability analysis in the SPSS software calculating the Cronbach Alpha where the items measure the same construct and are highly correlated (Castañeda, at el, 2010). Of the elements analyzed, a reliability of 83.0% was obtained, which is considered high according to the classification of Anastasi & Urbina (1998) (See Annex 1).

In addition, the Kaiser-Meyer-Olkin (KMO) test was performed for the Analysis of the components with Varimax rotation that between closer to 1 has the value obtained implies that the relationship between the variables is high (Benavente, et al, 2011). The value of KMO is 0.807 which is considered remarkable. Likewise, the Bartlett sphericity test was carried out, where, if it is less than 0.05, it is accepted as a null hypothesis so that the factor analysis can be applied (ibid, 2011). Its significance is 0.000, so factor analysis can be applied. (See annex 2)

For the evaluation of the applicability of the questionnaire, it begins with the factor analysis with varimax rotation defined as the simplicity of a factor by the variance of the squares of its factor loads in the observable variables (Pérez, et al, 2004), this is for the interpretation of the factors in a faster way, because examining the characteristics of the variables of a group associated with a certain factor allows to find the common features that allow the identification of the factor and provide the denomination that respond to common features (Pérez, et al, 2004)

In addition, the ANOVA test was performed, this type of analysis will allow measuring the level of cause and effect that exists between an independent and a dependent variable, thus explaining which hypotheses are tested and which are rejected (Hernández, Fernández and Baptista, 2010). The F or F-test statistic is obtained from the estimation of the variation of the means between the groups of the independent variables and their division by the estimation of the variation of the means within the groups, if the means between the groups have a great variation and the average within a group varies little, that is, there is a heterogeneity between the groups and an internal similarity, the value of F will be high and the variables will be related; in terms of the ANOVA analysis of a factor that has a higher F will indicate a greater difference and therefore there is a stronger relationship between the variables, also the more the average of the dependent variable differs between the groups of the variables The higher the independent value will be the value of F. Following the 95% confidence level when its significance is less than 0.05 the two variables will be related (Cárdenas, 2015).

Subsequently, for the evaluation of the model, linear regression was used, being defined by Pérez (2011) as the explanatory determination of the functional that relates the variables. R^2 is an index that describes whether the data fit well in a straight line; Pearson r indicates the strength and direction of the relationship between two variables, varies between -1 (a perfectly negative relationship between the two variables) and 1 (a perfectly positive relationship between the two variables), a negative relationship, indicates that as that one variable increases and the other decreases. Its descriptive interpretation according to Gilford (1954) adapted according to Mejía (2009): (See table 2)

Table 2. Pearson's descriptive interpretation r

Value	Range	Descriptive interpretation of the correlation.
r	<20	Slightly insignificant
r	0.21 - 0.40	Low. Defined but low
r	0.41 - 0.70	Moderate, substantial
r	0.71 - 0.90	Marked, high
r	0.90 - 1.00	Very high, very significant

Source: Guilford (1954). Adaptation Mejía (2009)

In addition, the Beta coefficient (standardized) was analyzed, which indicates the explanatory hierarchy of the independent variables based on the explanatory weight in relation to the dependent variable. Having a significance of less than 0.05, it is assumed that 95% confidence of the independent variables contribute significantly to the model. The Beta coefficient (not standardized) indicates for each unit that the independent variable increases as the dependent variable increases (Santana, sf).

Finally, to analyze the relationship between the different variables for testing the hypothesis, a non-parametric analysis was carried out using the Kruskal Wallis test. It was used to test the hypotheses when exposing if there is a difference between the medians, when the value of the probability associated with the statistic is above the level of significance of 5% or 0.05 the null hypothesis is accepted when the theoretical value exceeds statistical. (Reidl, at el, 2010). (See table 3, 4 and 5)

Table 3. Independent variable analysis

Dimension	Confidence interval 95%	Cronbach's alpha	KMO	Barlett test
Web page characteristics	The intervals are represented by normal distribution. The confidence interval for the averages are quite robust and not very sensitive to the violation of the assumption	0.704	0.765	0.000
Consumer characteristics	The intervals are represented by normal distribution. The confidence interval for the averages are quite robust and not very sensitive to the violation of the assumption	0.828	0.781	0.000
Brand characteristics	The intervals are represented by normal distribution. The confidence interval for the averages are quite robust and not very sensitive to the violation of the assumption	0.753	0.803	0.000

Source: Own elaboration

FUTURE RESEARCH DIRECTIONS

In this article the use of any neuroscience technique was not involved, which cannot fully illustrate this particular aspect of the model regarding our current study.

Within the limitations of the thesis are that it is not a parametric statistic, because to perform a parametric analysis it must start from the following assumptions:

1. The population distribution of the dependent variable is normal: the universe has a normal distribution.
2. The level of measurement of the dependent variable is interval or ratio.
3. When two or more populations are studied, they have a homogeneous variance: the populations in question have a similar dispersion in their distributions.

Parametric statistics need to meet four requirements to apply:

1. The dependent variable must be distributed normally or very similar.

Table 4. Simple

regression Simple regression			
	1	2	3
Tests	**Website**	**features Consumer**	**characteristics Brand characteristics**
Value P e 95% Confidence	Interval 95.0% confidence intervals for the average: 0.0 +/- 0.198422 [-0.198422.0.198422		
Constant	- 1.10	- 0.01	- 8.39
B	0.599 ***	0.351 ***	0.750 ***
ANOVA (F)	17,526 ***	16,082 ***	20,842 ***
R2	71.1%	94%	85.9%
Pearson r	0.843	0.969	0.927

Source: Own elaboration

2. The homogeneity of the variances when comparing groups should have the same dispersion with respect to the average of the dependent variable.
3. Assignment and random selection of groups (completely random sampling)
4. The dependent variable is measured at the interval or ratio level (Reidl, et al, 2010).

CONCLUSION

The factors that affect decision making are different, may be affected by some particular characteristics such as gender, environmental factors and age. Gender in decision-making women have a greater risk aversion due to the high cortisol index, while men have a greater propensity to trust due to the high testosterone index. The environmental factors in the decision making that cause the decrease in sales and price reduction are influenced by various aspects such as lunar cycles, light intensity and geomagnetic storms (BBVA, 2011). Age influences decision-making since the reduction in the production of dopamine

Table 5. Multiple

regression Multiple regression			
	1	2	3
Tests	**Website**	**features Consumer**	**characteristicsbrand**
Constant	-1.51		
B	0.221 ***	0.154 ***	0.887 ***
ANOVA (F)	69.547 ***		
R2	77.1%		
Pearson r	0.878		
Kruskal Wallis	89.2%	90.4%	90.3%

Source: Own elaboration

and serotonin decreases when a person is aging, having less effect on the appreciation and reception of the reward, in addition to the assumed risk (Mohr, et al, 2010).

Neuroeconomics can provide the enrichment of specific economic models with the option of neuropsychological penetration.

It is necessary to implement in the e-commerce consumers of the exponential SMEs of the artisanal industry the knowledge of the discipline of neuroeconomics because the brain activity represents ¾ of the decisions taken, likewise each process involves the neurons that influence a particular behavior, In addition, the network of neural connections in the brain changes as the person acquires knowledge and experience. Therefore, neuroeconomics plays an important role in achieving the objective of better operational efficiency to accelerate market reactions and increase consumer expectations

Practical implications of the study were conducted using a study group: millenials.

REFERENCES

Anen, C. (2007). *Neural correlates of economic and moral decision-making* (Tesis doctoral).

Balaji, S., Babu, M. M., & Aravind, L. (2007). Interplay between network structures, regulatory modes and sensing mechanisms of transcription factors in the transcriptional regulatory network of E. coli. *Journal of Molecular Biology*, *372*(4), 1108–1122. doi:10.1016/j.jmb.2007.06.084 PMID:17706247

Baptista, P., Fernández, C., & Hernández, R. (2006). *Metodología de la investigación* (6th ed.). Editorial McGraw Hill.

Baptista, P., Fernández, R., & Sampieri, C. (2010). *Metodología de la investigación*. Editorial Mc Graw Hill.

Brynjolfsson, E., Dick, A., & Smith, M. (2010). A nearly perfect market? *Quantitative Marketing and Economics*, *8*(1), 1-33.

CEPAL. (2004). Novena conferencia regional sobre la mujer de América Latina y El Caribe. *Consenso de México*.

Chen, T., Drennan, J., & Andrews, L. (2012). Experience sharing. *Journal of Marketing Management*, *28*(13-14), 1535–1552. doi:10.1080/0267257X.2012.736876

Cheung, J. (2015). *Exploring Consumers' Experiential Responses and Shopping Intentions toward Visual User-Generated Content in Online Shopping Environments* (PhD Thesis). The University of Manchester, Manchester UK.

Chiou, J. (2000). Antecedents and Moderators of Behavioral Intention:Differences between US and Taiwanese Students. *Genetic, Social, and General Psychology Monographs*, *126*(1), 105–124. PMID:10713903

Constantinides, E. (2004) Influencing the online consumer's behavior: the Web experience. *Internet Research*, *14*(2), 111-126.

Cowart, K. O., & Goldsmith, R. E. (2007). The influence of consumer decision-making styles on online apparel consumption by college students. *International Journal of Consumer Studies*, *31*(6), 639–647. doi:10.1111/j.1470-6431.2007.00615.x

Davidson, R. J., Jackson, D. C., & Kalin, N. H. (2000). Emotion, plasticity, context, and regulation: Perspectives from affective neuroscience. *Psychological Bulletin, Vol, 126*(6), 890–909. doi:10.1037/0033-2909.126.6.890 PMID:11107881

Davis, F. (1989). Perceived Usefulness, Perceived Ease of Use, and User Acceptance of Information Technology. *Management Information Systems Quarterly, 13*(3), 319–339. doi:10.2307/249008

Davis, F., Bagozzi, R., & Warshaw, P. (1989). User Acceptance of Computer Technology: A Comparison of Two Theoretical Models. *Management Science, 35*(8), 982–1003. doi:10.1287/mnsc.35.8.982

Epstein, S. (1994). Integration of the cognitive and the psychodynamic unconscious. *The American Psychologist, 49*(8), 709–724. doi:10.1037/0003-066X.49.8.709 PMID:8092614

Etienne-Nugue, J. (2009). *Hablame de las artesanias*. UNESCO.

FONART. (2009). *Manual de Diferenciación entre Artesania y Manualidad*. Recovered from https://www.fonart.gob.mx/web/pdf/DO/mdma.pdf

Foote, W. (September 29, 2015). Tapping the potential of the artisan economy. *Forbes*. Recovered from https://www.forbes.com/sites/willyfoote/2015/09/29/tapping-the-potential-of-the-worlds-fourth-largest-economy/#3ea27e3f1aa2

Forgas, J. P. (Ed.). (2001). *Feeling and thinking: The role of affect in social cognition*. Cambridge University Press.

Glimcher, P. (2003). *Decisions, Uncertainty and the Brain: The Science of Neuroeconomics*. The MIT Press. doi:10.7551/mitpress/2302.001.0001

Glimcher, P. W., & Rustichini, A. (2004). Neuroeconomics: The Consilience of Brain and Decision. *Science, 306*(5695), 447–452. doi:10.1126cience.1102566 PMID:15486291

González, M. (2016). 31% del PIB nacional es aportado por mujeres empresarias. *Informa BTL*. Recovered from https://www.informabtl.com/31-del-pib-nacional-es-aportado-por-mujeres-empresarias/

Gutnik, L., Forogh, A., Yoskowitz, N., & Patel, V. (2006). The role of emotions in decision making: a cognitive neuroeconomic approach towards understanding sexual risk behavior. *Journal of Biomedical Information*. doi:10.1016/j.jbi.2006.03.002

Hausman, A., & Siekpe, J. (2009). The effect of web interface features on consumer online purchase intentions. *Journal of Business Research, 62*(1), 5–13. doi:10.1016/j.jbusres.2008.01.018

Heller, L. (2010). Mujeres emprendedoras en América Latina y el Caribe: realidades, obstáculos y desafíos. Santiago de Chile: United Nations.

Hernández-Girón, J., Yexcas, M., & Domínguez-Hernández, M. (2007). Factores de éxito en los negocios de artesanía en México. *Estudios Gerenciales, 23*(104), 77–99. doi:10.1016/S0123-5923(07)70018-9

Hussain, A. (2013). El potencial del comercio electrónico: oportunidades para las PYME de los países en desarrollo. *Revista del centro de comercio internacional*. Recovered from http://www10.iadb.org/intal/intalcdi/PE/2014/14253.pdf

Indego Africa. (2016). How the artisan sector can change the world. *ONE.* Recovered from https://www.one.org/us/2016/05/13/how-the-artisan-sector-can-change-the-world/

INEGI. (2009). *Censo Económico.* Micro, pequeña, mediana y gran empresa. Recovered from https://www.inegi.org.mx/est/contenidos/espanol/proyectos/censos/ce2009/default.asp?s=est&c=14220

INEGI. (2012). *Conociendo México.* Análisis de la demografía de los establecimientos 2012. Recovered from http://buscador.inegi.org.mx/search?tx=analisis+de+la+demografia+de+los+establecimientos&q=analisis+de+la+demografia+de+los+establecimientos&site=sitioINEGI_collection&client=INEGI_Default&proxystylesheet=INEGI_Default&getfield

International Telecommunication Union. (2015). Measuring the Information Society Report. Ginebra: ITU.

Karimi, S. (2013). *A purchase decision-making process model of online consumers and its influential factor a cross sector analysis* (PhD thesis). Manchester Business School.

Kim, H., Suh, K., & Lee, U. (2013). Effects of collaborative online shopping on shopping experience through social and relational perspectives. *Information & Management, 50*(4), 169–180. doi:10.1016/j.im.2013.02.003

Kim, J., Park, J., Kim, J., & Park, J. (2005). A consumer shopping channel extension model: Attitude shift toward the online store. *Journal of Fashion Marketing and Management, 9*(1), 106–121. doi:10.1108/13612020510586433

Leelayouthayotin, L. (2004). *Factors influencing online purchase intention: the case of health food consumers in Thailand* (PhD thesis). Universidad Southern Queensland, Australia.

McGaughey, R., & Mason, K. (1998). The Internet as a marketing tool. *Journal of Marketing Theory and Practice, 6*(6), 1–11. doi:10.1080/10696679.1998.11501800

Moon, B.J. (2004). Consumer adoption of the internet as an information search and product purchase channel: some research hypotheses. *International Journal of Internet Marketing and Advertising, 1*(1), 104-118.

Nasermoadeli, A., Ling, K. C., & Severi, E. (2013). Exploring the Relationship between Social Environment and Customer Experience. *Asian Social Science, 9*(1), 130–141.

Nowlis, S., & McCabe, D. (2000). The effect of the inability to touch merchandise on the likelihood of choosing products online. In *American Marketing Association. Conference Proceedings.* (Vol. 11, p. 308). American Marketing Association.

Pasteur, L. (2013). *Características y diferencias de la investigación documental, de campo y experimental.* Formación de competencias para la investigación.

Penz, E., & Hogg, M. (2011). The role of mixed emotions in consumer behaviour: Investigating ambivalence in consumers' experiences of approach-avoidance conflicts in online and offline settings. *European Journal of Marketing, 45*(1/2), 104–132. doi:10.1108/03090561111095612

Phau, I., & Poon, S. (2000). Factors influencing the types of products and services purchased over the Internet. *Internet Research, 10*(2), 102–113. doi:10.1108/10662240010322894

Powers, J., & Magnoni, B. (2010). *Dueña de tu propia empresa: identificación, análisis y superación de las limitaciones a las pequeñas empresas de las mujeres en América Latina y el Caribe.* Fondo Multilateral de Inversiones, BID.

Reidl, L., Cuevas, C., & López, R. (2010). *Métodos de Investigación en Psicología.* Universidad Nacional Autónoma de México. Recovered from https://www.rua.unam.mx/objeto/7987/metodos-de-investigacion-en-psicologia

Rickwood, C., & White, L. (2009). Pre-purchase decision-making for a complex service: retirement planning. *Journal of Services Marketing, 23*(3), 145-153.

Rohan, D. (2013). *Neuroeconomic Studies on Personality and Decision-Making* (Tesis doctoral). The University of Minessota, Minessota EUA.

Rose, S., Clark, M., Samouel, P., & Hair, N. (2012). Online Customer Experience in e-Retailing: An empirical model of Antecedents and Outcomes. *Journal of Retailing, 88*(2), 308–322. doi:10.1016/j.jretai.2012.03.001

Sacristan, J. (2013). La pyme tiene problema para lanzar su e-commerce. *El economista.* Recovered from https://www.eleconomista.es/catalunya/noticias/4766122/04/13/La-pyme-tiene-problemas-para-lanzar-su-ecommerce.html

Sandoval, E., & Guerra, E. (2010). *Migrantes e indígenas: acceso a la información en comunidades virtuales interculturales.* Recuperado de www.eumed.net/libros/2010b/684/

Shukla, M. (2011). *Entrepreneurship and small business management.* Kitab Mahal.

Slovic, P., Finucane, M. L., Peters, E., & MacGregor, D. G. (2004). Risk as analysis and risk as feelings: Some thoughts about affect, reason, risk, and rationality. *Risk Analysis, 24*(2), 311–322. doi:10.1111/j.0272-4332.2004.00433.x PMID:15078302

Statista. (2018a). *E-commerce share of total global retail sales in 2016, by region.* The Statistics Portal. Recovered from https://www.statista.com/statistics/239300/number-of-online-buyers-in-selected-countries/

Statista. (2018b). *Number of digital buyers worldwide from 2014 to 2021 (in billions).* The Statistics Portal. Recovered from https://www.statista.com/statistics/251666/number-of-digital-buyers-worldwide/

Statista. (2018c). *Retail e-commerce sales worldwide from 2014 to 2021 (in billions US dollars).* The Statistics Portal. Recovered from https://www.statista.com/statistics/379046/worldwide-retail-e-commerce-sales/

UNESCO. (2001). *Artesanías creadoras.* París: Unesco, Sección de Artesanías y Diseño.

United Nations Industrial Development Organisation (UNIDO). (2001). *Women Entrepreneurship Development in Selected African Countries.* Working Paper No. 7, United Nations Industrial Development Organisation.

VanderMeer, D., Dutta, K., & Datta, A. (2012). A Cost-Based Database Request Distribution Technique for Online e-Commerce Applications. *Management Information Systems Quarterly, 36*(2), 479–507. doi:10.2307/41703464

Wang, Y., Minor, M., & Wei, J. (2011). Aesthetics and the online shopping environment: Understanding consumer responses. *Journal of Retailing*, *87*(1), 46–58. doi:10.1016/j.jretai.2010.09.002

WeConnect International. (n.d.). *Prospere como mujer empresaria*. Recovered from https://weconnectinternational.org

Won Jeong, S., Fiore, A., Niehm, L., & Lorenz, F. (2009). The role of experiential value in online shopping: The impacts of product presentation on consumer responses towards an apparel web site. *Internet Research*, *19*(1), 105–124. doi:10.1108/10662240910927858

Zhang, T., Agarwal, R., & Lucas, H. (2011). The value of IT-enabled retailer learning: personalized product recommendations and customer store loyalty in electronic markets. *MIS Quarterly-Management Information Systems*, *35*(4), 859.

Chapter 11
Management and Strategies for Customers Adoption of Mobile Banking Services:
An Empirical Study for Digital Enterprise Transformation

Fouad Omran Elgahwash
University of Wollongong, Australia

ABSTRACT

Mobile services applications in digital transformation era have become increasingly important and providing business and customers with a diversity of services, quality, and values with no cost and to help banks' practitioners identify and improve their services. This chapter aims to explore and understand management and strategies of digital business transformation in banks' change through the use of digital technologies and business models to improve applications, practice, performance, and customer values. The digitization of bank services is aimed at reducing costs, improving services, and digitalization of an enterprise is necessary to increasing effectiveness, efficiency, and sustainability of its functioning through dramatic changes in the management quality, both technological processes and decision-making processes at all levels of management, based on modern methods of production and further use of information about the state and prediction of possible changes in managed elements and subsystems.

INTRODUCTION

The digital transformation phenomenon has been explored widely in different academic domains, resulting in a crude overview of the field. Management and Strategies of Digital transformation affects all sectors of society, in particular business. Banks as example, now are given an opportunity to radically change their systems, ideas and models by adoption a new digital technology through using social networks, mobiles, big data, Internet of things and blockchain. This mostly involves changes of the core business

DOI: 10.4018/978-1-7998-8583-2.ch011

operations and modifies products and processes, as well as business' structures, as banks ought to set up management practices to conduct these complex transformations (Lobschata, Muellerb et al. 2019, Ziyadin, Suieubayeva et al. 2020).

The purpose of management and strategies digital transformation is to provide more facilities, enhance exchange processes among banks and customers, and manage information These activities are important because they impact on the ability of banks to growth and achieve value for their customers, such as reduce transaction costs and enhance customer experiences (Lobschata, Muellerb et al. 2019, Zhao, Tsai et al. 2019).

Even banks that are well down the digital transformation path face tough ongoing hurdles, like make financial arrangements, talent struggles, and culture change. Because of digital transformation is different for every business. Digital transformation as the integration of digital technology into all areas of a business resulting in fundamental changes to how businesses operate and deliver value to customers. It means that management and strategies digital transformation closes the gap between what digital customers already expect and what businesses actually deliver (Ziyadin, Suieubayeva et al. 2020).

However, in Libya as example the bank mortgage processes have not yet embraced a full and using a comprehensive digital technology. The new wave of digitization inherent in banking services therefore calls for more empirical and scientific research studies to enhance understanding of the impact of technology on the mortgage industry and how this expertise and knowledge can be used to advice bank leaders and other stakeholders involved (Morales and Trinidad 2019).

There are many approaches and definitions of management and strategies digital transformation in the literature. Digital transformation is how to use and manage internet; smart phones; tablets and computers to create effective customers value with respect to traditional pathways. This explanation is absolutely circumstances change of new technology in operation; interaction; configuration and creation of value with respect to comprehensive sense, so digital transformation include networking business, customer values, pieces and all requires data analysis to reach information used and evaluated options that increase business performance to reach greater customers collaboration and interaction fir all the success of digital transformation (Nuri 2019).

Study by Osmundsen (2018) Identified management and strategies digital transformation activities that banks naturally engage in before, or during, digital transformation. One activity that seemed to be important was improving the bank's digital channels, that is, setting up, operating, and improving the channels, moving toward a multichannel strategy for reaching customers; value. In specific, banks pointed out the importance of managing the initiation and set-up of simplified processes and updated infrastructures.

Management and strategies digital transformation refers to a value creation process changing how banking industry could system operated, interacted and configured by using digital technology especially smart phones. Furthermore, it makes the banking industry improvements such as enhancing customer experience, customer expectations, customers value, operation effectiveness and creating digital business model by the impact of digital technologies. The use of advanced digital technologies as fundamentally improve business performance and to enhance customer experience, value creation activities and value propositions. Banks use of new digital technologies, such as mobile phones, artificial intelligence, cloud computing, blockchain, and the Internet, to enable major business improvements and to enhance customer experience, reorganize operations, or create new business models (Yang 2020).

Management and strategies digital transformation is an evolutionary process that influences digital technologies and capabilities to enable business models, operational processes and new customer relationships, customer experiences to create value, speedy development and adoption of emerging digital technologies. This requires banks to authority these technologies to keep up with changing competitive playing field and evolving requirements of today's digital perception customer and to increase and develop the digital opportunities and transform (Resego Morakanyane, Reilly et al. 2020)

Consequently, the new market dynamics require banks to shift their focus from developing internal banking processes to creating valuable interactions with customers (Haapio, Hannelo et al. 2019). Thus, the power of digit customer data, it's possible to make easy and understand customer "approaches, attitude, moods, motivation, desires and objectives that generate innovative actions and expectations. The huge diversity of technology prepares banks with opportunities and business access to challenge of the market position and redefine the market boundaries because of customer innovative behaviours and following traditional customer interaction and business performance and model, so It is to reach customer expectation and to respond changes in digital economy and competitions (Yang 2020).

All definitions of management and strategies digital transformation above have considered all the ways banks may need to correct their existing practices, involves a change in leadership, different thinking, encouragement of innovation, new business models, integrating digitisation of assets and an increased use of technology to improve the experience of bank's employees, customers values, suppliers and services quality. For example, mobile services have dramatically changed the preconditions for service delivery in recent years, heavily impacting on service options and services support and on accomplishing competitive advantages. Service providers in banks are now starting to employ M-services at various stages in the service delivery processes and in-service support operations to improve the quality, privacy and competitive advantages of their service offerings. Smartphones as new technology-enabled changes are changing the way service providers and their customers interact with each other and it allow customers to access their data and services remotely using mobile-enabled devices (Yeboah and Ewur 2014).

Mobile banking concept is acquisition currency electronic banking channel to be offered by banks, evaluating their performances is crucial for bank owners, customers, shareholders and service providers. Determining the performance of M-banking services helps bank owners, policy makers, and service providers (Ecer 2018). Furthermore, mobile banking working as a banking channel whereby the customer interacts with a bank via a mobile device, such as a mobile phone or personal digital assistant (Mutahar, Daud et al. 2018).

Mobile banking is offered through short message service, phone call, mobile phone Internet application, and certain specifically designed 'Apps' in mobile data application systems. While accessibility is an advantage of mobile banking, susceptibility to privacy risks may considerably inhibit its success (Shareefa, Baabdullahb et al. 2018). For example, mobile banking is an internet-based service, which enables customers to access bank accounts through mobile devices and conduct as well as complete bank-related transactions such as checking account status, transferring money and selling stocks (Kim, Jin et al. 2009).

BACKGROUND

Recent management and strategies digital transformations in banking industry have enabled the start of new access methods for services (Amin 2008). For instance, smartphone provided a significant opportunity for banking institutions to introduce new kinds of services to customers. Numerous studies have determined that M-services have had a positive influence in relationships between banks and customers via cell phones, SMSs and voice messaging. It has been strongly established as the most important distribution and communication channel for retail banking. As a result, mobile banking has significantly changed the way in which many customers access their bank account (Elgahwash 2016).

M-Services digitization is a term used for performing check balances, account transactions, payments and so on via a smartphone. It is most often presented via SMS, mobile voice and mobile banking applications. M-banking services have the potential role to save money, and provide an overview of accounts, loans and other available opportunities for customers. For example, according to the mobile banking usage statistics for Thailand published by the Bank of Thailand, the number of customer transactions conducted via mobile banking services has rapidly increased in the last few years (Boonsiritomachaia and Pitchayadejanant 2017).

However, customer actions towards service providers can be enhanced via digitalized strategies whilst web-based life is a strategic avenue for such initiations Social Customer Relationship Management in contemporary digital era. Business having considered the potential to work closely with customers and enabling them where ever they live it is a social channel or physical environment combination of Big Data analytics, robotics, artificial intelligence and internet of thing (Bultum 2014, Fairooz and Wickramasinghe 2019).

Mobile services are a powerful way to use customer's communication channels offer greatly expanded services, for example, checking an account balance, receiving information on previous money dealings and checking credit card information by telephone, face to face or SMS (Laukkanen and Pasanen 2008). Indeed, digital transformation can offer services such as: access to loan statements, monitoring of term deposits, one to one payment, bill payment processing, domestic and international fund transfers, status of requests for credit, mortgage approval, insurance coverage, loyalty-related offer-based services, exchange of data messages and emails, complaint submission and tracking, significant information (Islam, Mustafi et al. 2018).

Management and strategies digital transformation has a significant and positive impact in banking service. Actually, this may help the customers to access their banks at any time through banking system. Digital banking refers to the use of a smartphone or other cellular device to perform online banking tasks while away from the home computer, such as monitoring account balances, transferring funds between accounts, bill payment and locating an ATM (Islam, Mustafi et al. 2018).

Therefore, the objectives are:

I. Identify the factors affecting the customers' experience in management and strategies digital transformation era.
II. To provide some suggestions for the improvement and successful of the management and strategies digital transformation banking system and services.

The study by Islam, Mustafi et al. (2018) discovered that, each factor measured had some level of significant effect on consumer intention to adopt and use digital strategy. Additionally, the study shown that, perceived credibility and perceived financial cost were the major setback with regards to customers adoption of mobile services and as a result of this.

As result of M-services are easy to use and most customers are already becoming familiar with it. Otherwise, A mobile service allows banks to interact directly with customer base, so it is by using push notifications, chat and other features to create a rich customer experience. With a well-designed and executed mobile application, you can reach out and let your customers know you care to serve and provide (Zhao, Tsai et al. 2019).

Banking Management Transformation Digital Transformation

Management and strategies digital transformation is imperative for all enterprises and businesses can remain customers, competitive and appropriate system as increasingly digital. Most world banking is finding paths to deliver the digital services by offering interactive websites, customer service and improve the customer experience in various channels. Successful digital transformation could occur depending on strategic objectives of the organization, industry context, peer pressure and expectations of the customers. (Fairooz and Wickramasinghe 2019).

In order to succeed in management and strategies digital transformation, leading financial services focus on two balancing activities such, (1) redesigning customer value propositions and, (2) transforming their operations using digital technologies for greater customer interaction and collaboration. Digital transformation of Banking industry reflective significant change in the design of business model and the mechanism for innovation and create customers' value. This would change the business to adopt innovative business model and position customer at the centre of the business process to stay in the market with competitive field for Banking and Financial industry and value chain as well as introduce new channel to attract the existing and new customer by using active management digital transformation Resulted of Digital transformation technology changes in any kind of industry resulted in brand awareness, increase process efficiencies, privacy, competitive advantages and improve customer experience (Fairooz and Wickramasinghe 2019).

Nevertheless, this includes systems and activities such money deposits, withdrawals, and transfers. digital technologies are qualifying and completely new ways to deliver value to customers, altering competitive landscapes, and changing the underlying banks' markets (Annacone 2019).

Management and strategies digital transformation in banking largely entails the shift to offering online and digital services, as well as the massive number of backend changes required to support this transformation. Many banks make mistakes by taking on a series of separate digital initiatives, which struggle to succeed because they don't have the support or coordination to compete with digital-native solutions. Instead, digital transformation in banks must entail a top-down approach, integrating digital systems, customer experience platforms, apps, and infrastructure of big data, and blockchain technologies in systems (Haapio, 2019).

This kind of digital transformation in banking means understanding customer wants, needs and exceptions and investing in those wants and needs. However, it will save money in the long-term as it improves customer satisfaction, trust, loyalty and value-added, activities efficiently such as relationship building, and saves time by automating processes (Fairooz, 2019).

One of the most important aspect is readiness and ability to adapt to change. Banks are often held back by security, legislation, and strict frameworks intended to protect customer data and privacy. At the same time, new digital-native banking solutions and money apps are outpacing traditional banking in terms of growth and customer acquisition. Adapting policies to meet changing consumer demand, to quickly adapt to new technologies, and to respond as the market changes is essential to digital transformation in banking (Peter Marc, Kraft et al. 2020).

However, as technical capabilities and customers' comfort with technology continues to improve, more of these more complex interactions will move to digital. Interestingly, regarding customer satisfaction, customers who have had negative experiences that have been positively resolved report higher satisfaction than customers who have never had such experiences(Peter Marc, Kraft et al. 2020). Customers are trusted banking systems and technology for financial transactions because they have a lot of experience and deep relationships with these banks to receive services such sending money to family, paying bills – frequent, lower-amount, lower-risk transactions. Management and strategies digital transactions are expected to increase as technology and customer relationships 's comfort and higher net worth customers by using it (Biewener 2019).

Customers will be the ones deciding what kind of interface they prefer to connect with the bank and avail a service. banks are starting to redesign some platforms and processes based on an end-to-end digital approach. The goal is to speed up the product and service delivery while taking into consideration client feedback and needs in the design and building phases. The bank can respond quickly to external events and better internalize changes in the market, increase the value of the service with recommendations about potential new products, measure performance and adjust based on this knowledge. Digital transfer improves the capabilities of products and services to bring it closer to customers. It also helps the bank gain a better understanding of performance and, ultimately, increase the true value it adds to customers (Obukhova, Merzlyakova et al. 2020).

METHODOLOGY

Qualitative research is especially effective in obtaining culturally-specific information about values, opinions, behaviours, populations and information and communication technologies. It is also useful for gaining extensive information on how banking / customers can adapt to use digital transformation and smartphones applications and facilities (Murphy, Dingwall et al. 1998).

This investigation is conducted through a systematic literature review that focuses on empirical contributions of digital transformation in the Information Systems (IS) field. By reviewing dominant empirical contributions on digital transformation, and provide insight into banks' services undergo digital transformation to accomplish it is transformation, and adoption of digital transformation into banking system.

By using fifteen Semi-structured interviews were conducted to collect data from a sample of customers who have banking experience The results provide useful insight for banks in developing appropriate and real strategies to meet customer's needs, and further, to maintain and increase the degree of awareness and adoption with M- services and it had positive influence on evolution to digitization of bank services because it had sufficient knowledge and experience in using M- Services. Semi-structured interviews are ideal as they can be specifically targeted to investigate and understand suggested views of customers who use technologies in the banking sector (Kaplan & Maxwell 1994).

The value of interviewing is its ability to collect rich qualitative data about particular processes from the viewpoint of selected individual customers. Actually, it allows the interviewee to express their opinions, concerns and feelings as well as to build rapport, because they allow interaction between the interviewer and the interviewee (Leek, Turnbull et al. 2003).

FINDINGS AND RESULTS

In this section the analysis provides information about each respondent's demographic information in terms of five characteristics collected. Table 1, below shows interviewees' demographics summarised according to five major characteristics collected.

Overall analysis of the data in below table, the interviewees were from a background with a high level of education. It was expected that this sample would be able to clearly articulate their ideas of mobile services in the Libyan banking sector. Furthermore, the analysis provides information in terms of gender, age and education level, which is a typical analysis used in most studies (Selamat and Jaffar 2011). Interviewees can be summarised as below table: -

Table 1. Interviewee Characteristics

Interviews	Gender	Age	Education Level	Using Smartphones	Libyan Bank
C1	Male	25-34	Postgraduate	1-2 Years	GB
C2	Female	25-34	Postgraduate	1-2 Years	NCB
C3	Male	35-44	Postgraduate	Over 5Years	GB
C4	Male	25-34	Postgraduate	Less 1 Year	NCB
C5	Male	25-34	Postgraduate	1-2 Years	CDB
C6	Male	25-34	Postgraduate	1-2 Years	UB
C7	Male	25-34	Postgraduate	Less 1Years	SB
C8	Female	35-44	Undergraduate	2-5 Years	GB
C9	Male	25-34	Postgraduate	Less1 Years	GB
C10	Male	35-44	Postgraduate	1-2 Years	SB
C11	Male	35-44	Postgraduate	1-2 Years	GB
C12	Male	35-44	Postgraduate	Never	WB
C13	Male	25-34	Postgraduate	Never	NBC
C14	Male	35-44	Postgraduate	Never	GB
C15	Female	25-34	Postgraduate	Never	GB

Source: *Prepared by the Author (2020).*

As shown in Table 2, below, all interviewees had gender responses, and their age and education level responses seemed consistent. As shown in the table above 80% of respondents were male and 20% were females. This heavily skewed sample towards male respondents may reflect a greater interest in or exposure to interactions with the M- services for males.

In regard to age, Table 2, shows that only six (40%) of the respondents were in the age group 35 - 44 years. The majority of the respondents (60%) were 25-34 years old. The sample distribution of respondents' ages potentially supports the previously reported conclusion that older customers are usually less willing to adopt new technology than are younger customers (Yiu, et al. 2007). With respect to the level of education shows that the vast majority of respondents had done or were undertaking postgraduate studies (93%).

Respondents' Profile in relation to Usage of smartphones Services The profile covers respondents' gender, age, level of income and whether or not they have a bank account. Mobile Technology is important part of the digital transformation technologies. Mobile technologies (smartphones / tablets) understand the goal of digital transformation and provide seamless interaction with the customer at all touch points with business. The benefits of mobile technologies include greater productivity, 26 percent more profitable than normal result of mobile technologies in business is the current level of integration between technologies totally caused by the needs of the enterprise and focused on greatest business processes management (Schwertner 2017).

Table 2. Interviewee Demographics

Measure	Item	Frequency
Gender	Male Female	12 3
Age	25 – 34 35 – 44	60% 40%
Education Level	Undergraduate Postgraduate	7% 93%

Source: *Prepared by the Author (2020).*

With regards to smartphones services usage in table 3 below, fifty-two percentages of respondents who use mobile services in digital transformation era there were males and they are than females who is used M-Services which is 17%. These findings correlate with those of FinScope (2013), which indicate that 17.9% percent of males had used bank products against only 10.1 percent of females. This suggests that males are more likely to use phones than females (Feher, Szabo et al. 2017).

Table 3. Gender and Mobile Services Usage

Gender	Usage smartphones Services	Do not use
Male Female	52% 17%	33 18

Source: *Prepared by the Author (2020)*

Study by Schwertner (2017) mentioned that business benefits included more effective mobile working (46%), for higher productivity (41%), more use of standard processes (35%), better ability to enter new business areas (33%) and the ability to open up in new account, or known locations (32%).

Results of study by Motiwala and others (2018); indicated that the influence of success factors significantly varies among user segments for intention to use, which makes an important contribution to enhance interpretation of the Information Systems success models by M- Services. Mobile Services in digital transformation involves the use of mobile devices to access bank accounts for conducting financial transactions has grown rapidly with users. Banks realizes the strategic role of user's satisfaction and the importance of systems in their business models.

Digital Transformation Privacy

Privacy concerns have often been revealed as one of the key reasons customers aggravates to go online for transactions and to do purchases over the digital transformation. The privacy issue has also resulted in great concerns from both banks and their customers. The convenience with a large number of customers can access M-services has resulted in high concerns among customers. Actually, Customers' perceive a higher perception of privacy risk of banking system and services, the less customers propose to use this new channel (Ecer 2018).

privacy concerns in banking as the level of consumer worries regarding the possibility that their privacy might be violated, and the possibility that personal information might be revealed to other companies or to cross sell other banking products (Maya 2018).

Perceived privacy represents the ability of individuals to control the manner in which their personal information is collected and used in transactions. Identifying the reality of exchanging information in the online environment, customers become increasingly concerned every time their private information is given out in the process of information exchange. As a result, the Privacy attributable to facilitating technology adoption influences customers' willingness to use the technology for consumption purposes. In the banking industry, mobile technology users' perceived privacy is closely related to the innate characteristics of the mobile technology. Therefore, a consistent online system with protection of privacy is a great importance to enhance customers' perceptions of trust in the bank facilitating the services and consumption. (Zhang, Lu et al. 2018).

Privacy is defined as "the claim of individuals, groups, and institutions to determine for themselves, when, how, and to what extent information about them is communicated to others". Privacy generally includes the right of individuals to determine for themselves when, how, and to what extent information about them is communicated to others. Thus the more privacy provided in online banking the more chance to enhance banking technology and it can be trusted and accepted by all customer (Mohamed 2013).

M- Services allows easy access to banking services via mobile handsets, typically through modified versions of the internet banking services. Five interviewees are referred to the concept of m- Services in their interviews when discussing the benefits associated with M-service technologies. For example, C3 stated that: *My m-banking provides simple and brief messages about banking accounts and other critical information, so it gives flexibility in communication with banks' employees so I can know everything at any time by using M-* Services.

The respondents C12, C7 or C13 stated that: *I can receive private SMS from my bank about my account transactions and any other important information. This gives me, as a customer, flexibility in interacting and communicating with employees at my bank to know everything with a complete care of privacy processes.*

C12 stated that: *My bank provided a number of channels to manage my money and accounts anytime through modern electronic channels to serve my needs. In my opinion, those services by electronic tools will be supported by my interactions with the bank. This is related to many advantages, such as my ability to find out about my account and receive bank statements without wasting time going to the bank. I can receive enough information about the operation of my accounts with low risk and little cost in a private way.*

Sound electronic privacy protection can create a virtuous circle in which both the business and its customers benefit. If customers trust the business, in return they will provide better quality personal information. This allows the business to address customer needs more accurately and more cost-effectively. It means produce greater trust through sound protection of privacy are more likely to get closer to customers. Therefore, privacy is at the heart of the business and customer relationships, so It involves crucial issues about power, value and the use of personal information (Leek, 2003; McPhail, 2003)

C3 and C6 are stated that: *M-* Services *can be reduced overcrowding at the bank teller and lead to an increased degree of services, anywhere, because I can complete bank procedures from my home or office without the need to go to the branch, so it saves my time and my effort especially when I need to pay bills or transfer money with a complete protecting of my privacy with my bank.*

Interviewees commonly expressed their support for a program with rules to protect their accounts (such as developing a complex password) so increased protection procedures would be in place to address security concerns.

Digital Transformation and Service Quality

Service quality can be defined as economic activities that create value and positive benefits for customers at specific times and place as result of bringing about a desired change in services (Sadek, Zainal et al. 2010). An alternative definition is that service quality is the difference between the dimensions in customers' perceived service and opportunity of service (Wei 2009). When the banks provide services of poor quality, they will not be able to perform their work effectively. Moreover, as products and customer services within the banking industry become more similar and substitutable, switching costs become lower and more affordable for customers (Vogel 2005).

Customers often evaluate quality of service via groups of criteria. One common criterion is reliability, which means achievement in a manner that is what the customer wants. The second common criterion is the speed of response when the customer needs help. It refers to the access time needed by a customer in order to complete the required bank service. Customers are considered key for any business to survive; the ability of banks to deliver their products and services appropriately defines their success within the industry (Spathis and Georgakopoulou 2007).

system quality as example affects continuing to use M-services. System quality impacts not only adoption behaviour, but also customer satisfaction when the M-banking services are reliable, flexible, accessible, accurate and speedy, consumers will perceive them to be useful (Ecer 2018).

Most respondents in this study agreed that M-Services adoption has been enhancing their interactions with banking systems, as it has helped banks to conduct their activities more effectively and efficiently. For example, digital banking system has a strong ability to enhance the experience and quality of interactions with banks. Twelve interviewees believed that mobile applications could be a driver for increased quality of interaction opportunities between themselves and their bank.

From C1, C5 and C12 the comment was received: *I think there are some factors that help, such as employees' efficiency in interactions and providing quick answers for any questions. Additionally, good skills and a good impression are reflecting a good quality. Service speed, ease of use and response time for customers leads to positive interactions.*

Customers were looking for an improvement in their feelings towards their banks. There were many factors of importance that were identified for quality support such as increasing the trust, satisfaction of customers, and a smiling face from the employee in the branch when meeting customers. The interviewees indicated that this leads to increased honesty which is important for customers with their bank.

C12 stated that: *The bank can increase numbers of customers and profits by using Mobile applications to serve customers and add high value with low cost. Digital services strategy is a new tool which creates the ease of quality interaction between the bank and customers without the need for meeting face to face with tellers. Also, the website of my bank has adequate information which relates to loans and money transfers and also other important information for all customers.*

C7 and C8 are mentioned: *we have positive feelings towards the information, advantages and services which are supplied by my bank, as a result of their good quality website. Otherwise can send my queries to my bank via their website and I can receive answers from them straight way.*

Information quality is defined the degree to which the mobile system provides relevant, sufficient, and accurate information. Since customers may struggle to find their banking information because of the small screen size, how information is organized and presented in M-services can influence their level of satisfaction. Therefore, System quality is described the degree to which the mobile system is visually appealing and easy to use and navigate. System quality reflects the easy access of different and trustworthy services. For example, mobile services' system that enables reliable and flexible banking services can enhance customers' satisfaction level (Motiwalla, Albashrawi et al. 2018)..

Service quality is designated the degree to which the mobile system provides timely, responsive, and personalized services to users. Service quality emerges in the dimensions of assurance, reliability, empathy, and responsiveness, infrastructure and/or appearance over the past 20 years. (Motiwalla, Albashrawi et al. 2018).

Digital Transformation and Sustaining Competitive Advantages

Competitive advantage usually occurs when banks build long term customer relationships that can leverage information about specific customers to better understand their requirements and serve them. Some banks are able to become close enough to customers to suitably judge and serve their needs more effectively; customers join with banks with which they enjoy a good relationship (Ahmed, 2007).

Competitive advantage is sustained by adopting digital banking system with internet. Competitive advantage has importance as it influences and builds great value for both banks and customers. Indeed, e-banking has presented competitive advantages via cost reduction, positive word-of-mouth communication, better satisfaction, trust and customer loyalty. In reality, it has led to an increase in service efficiency of banks, with lower costs of operations towards customers and avoiding losing customers who probably would have switched to another bank (Elgahwash 2016).

A Study by Mnjala (2014) definition of competitive advantage included the resources, capabilities, competencies, assets and processes that supply banking services with a distinct attraction to its customers and unique advantage over its competitors. In this definition, activities are used to attract and maintain customers. Competitive advantage activities include: banks providing services to customers at the lowest cost in the shortest time; value adding to create a service that offers highly desirable and distinct quality; speed that permits operational processes to be executed in a faster and superior manner; speed that permits banks to adapt to changing requirements of the market and being quicker than competitors; banks having continuous flow of creative services, which is valued by the customer; and customer service that has superior responsiveness to customers. These activities should work together to create competitive advantages above and beyond activities that will positively reflect banking services to be increased (Mnjala 2014).

Competitive advantage is sustained when other businesses are unable to duplicate the benefits of one's strategy. The definition of competitive advantage as 'deceptively simple idea of assessing a bank's capabilities and market position by how they give it advantage relative to competitors. According to it definition, competitive advantages are brief and only worth as much as the value that the market places when its actions in services created value (Yeboah and Ewur 2014).

Competitive advantage means superior performance relative to other competitors in the same industry or superior performance relative to the industry average. Approximately everything can be considered as competitive edge, e.g. higher profit margin, greater return on assets, valuable resource such as brand reputation or unique competence in producing jet engines. In digital transformation strategy competitive advantage is thus when an organization outperform its competitors from a wide range time to gain it productivity (Owusu and Duah 2018).

All of the participants in interviews stated that they would prefer to recommend a Libyan bank that used M-banking to others (for example family, friends, colleagues and neighbours). There are many reasons for the recommendation of a bank that employs Digital technologies. For example, each one of C2, C5 and C10 stated that: *I would provide a recommendation for those M – services applications as a result of saving time, enhancing relationship operations and the ease of access, more convincing and speedy use of mobile services and really useful way for all.*

The use of digital technologies in the Libyan banking sector is slowly becoming commonplace. As the Libyan interviewees were living in Australia, they had become accustomed to using these technologies to conduct their banking. In Libya, technology is becoming more important for business processes, particularly in banks. A question was asked to explore interviewees' knowledge about digital system. The majority of interviewees [C1 – C6 and C8 - 15] agreed that these technologies created benefits / advantages for both banks and customers from the customer perspective.

C3 and C11 stated that: *we think services can reduce overcrowding and deliver the best services for customers, so it creates customer satisfaction about those services because the mobile provides services 24 hour per days and 7 days per week, so there are no holidays.*

C12 commented: *mobile services are a great chance for anyone to manage money with confidence from home or work office any time. It is easy to transfer money internally or to another country. This is an alternative channel for easy money management. It means M-service can save customers' time to finish financial procedures with their bank. Also, banks can create competitive advantage in their local market because they have already achieved customers' support against any future competitors.*

Digital Transformation Awareness Level

Awareness of innovation defined as "innovations existed and gain some understanding of how function". While, the awareness of innovation as" understanding whether the customer is aware or not of service itself and its benefits" because the awareness is a critical factor in causing customers to adopt digital banking. Awareness is the degree to which a consumer is aware of electronic banking channels. awareness on adoption of mobile financial services (Abdinoor and Mbamba 2017).

Customer awareness of digital banking services as represented by the amount of information they have about the services because individuals seem more likely to avoid uncertainty than to maximise the value and benefits of services. The awareness is to use and benefits of technology is most likely to reduce the level of the risk perceived. This factor is highly applicable to the mobile banking market in Yemen as example because it is a relatively new service and clients must thus be educated about its use and benefits. This implies that client adoption of mobile banking is highly dependent on how the banks market mobile banking services. Awareness plays a role affecting a clients' intention to use mobile banking services (Mutahar, Daud et al. 2018).

C12 stated that: *I prefer to increase the degree of awareness of electronic banking, so all customers know they can be targets and will protect their private information and keep their password strong and secure.* However, awareness for mobile banking is rooted in the appropriate design of the technology through the protection privacy of consumers (Shareefa, Baabdullahb et al. 2018).

Customer awareness is positively influence on usage of digital banking services and Customer awareness has the greatest influence on usage of mobile banking because of customers understanding of how mobile banking and mobile-related transactions operate as well as perceived privacy. Consumer awareness of mobile banking services is essential in promoting usage of mobile banking. Furthermore, people use digital banking services when they are perceived to be easy to use (Richard and Mandari 2018).

Customers' experiences with a technology influence their awareness of similar technologies and hence can increase their intention to adopt the digital banking services. Libyan banks have the potential to create a positive attitude towards their customers through increased adoption of m-banking. This can increase relationship quality, trust and satisfaction, and promote the value of the banking services (Gurau, 2011; Khatri, 2011).

From the interviewees' statements above, we can summarize that digital transformation technologies have the ability to share benefits between customers and banks. For example, sharing information among customers and banks in privacy in the Libyan banking sector will lead to increased trust and the reduction of daily routines and stress for employees in the banking system. Mobile applications as example can enhance customers' service quality, thereby increasing the number of new customers when a bank provides a high-quality and low-cost service. Mobile applications enable banks to create competitive advantages through the provision of good services to customers, as well as the ability to communicate and correct any errors. Digital transformation therefore has advantages for completing all processes by creating comfortable online interactions for customers with their bank, so it leads to the creation of customers' satisfaction about those services.

Digital Transformation Value

The concepts of value-in-use and value-in-context are essential pillars of the providers. In other words, value is created for the customer through a unique combination of the customer's and the provider's resources such as customer's knowledge and skills to use digital banking applications. The customers are the ones who determine value by integrating the bank's offering into their own lives. based in different customers experience and, in consequence. The term "value"-in context reflects the phenomenological perspective of value and requires that value is always co-created, contextually specific, and contingent on the integration of M- services (Scherer, Wünderlic et al. 2015, Pichelr, Summer et al. 2019).

Perceived value is a useful way to understand customer behaviour which is determined by customers' value perceptions for services that are offered by the financial market Perceived value is the trade-off between perceived benefit or quality and the perception of disadvantage or cost of using a service However, value involves interactions between the service and the customer and varies from one customer to another since a customer's motives and judgment of services Offering to be better value for consumption. (Omigie, Zo et al. 2017).

Perceived value is necessary to understand the perceived benefits relative to the cost of what a service offers, which influences a customer's decision to use the service A customer that has never used digital financial services, for example, may find it difficult to comprehend and appreciate the real value that the service offers to its customers. Perceived value provides a more robust measurement of customers' complete evaluation of the value for any service offering M-Services' value is the perceived effectiveness received in the form of reduced stress, lightened negative moods, reduced tension from a service in this case. Customers use such services because they are feeling better, allow the customer to get their mind off their problems, and help the customer to overcome stress. Of digital financial services strategy (Fairooz and Wickramasinghe 2019, Pichelr, Summer et al. 2019).

SOLUTIONS AND RECOMMENDATIONS

The financial services are facing a lot of challenges in management and strategies digital transformation era as they continue to create satisfaction; quality; and value for customers, so this is maybe significance of complex adaptive system in addressing many kinds of inside or outside digital solutions strategies. A digitized solutions strategy aims to rebuild a bank's value proposition by integrating a combination of products, services system rules and data. A digital strategy is valuable only if it drives resource allocation solutions and capital investments because banks leaders are believed that digital success involves both customer engagement and digitized solutions by provide value to achieved greater customer satisfaction and loyalty.

The main recommendation in this regard would be to discover such banks possibilities, opportunities, advantages and implement them in order to remember and attract more customers with easily accessible and efficient service. Banks would use of online banking and mobile banking applications is growing among banking customers. If banks were to introduce agreement confirmation online with the help of a mobile banking application, it would bring benefits to both banks and customers.

Banks have to invest mostly in digitization and innovative solutions, such as automation of services' system, new payment infrastructure, and analysis of big data to generate ideas, achieve goals of banks and customers, so Banks had better analyse and using the information they own about their customers and their transactions, not only on a known-your-customer basis, but in general. Use of such data will improve the understanding of customer needs and behavioural patterns and also drive operational efficiency and effectiveness throughout the organization.

Actually, the recommendations, about findings and areas requiring further investigation, are made to the Libyan banking sector in particular, and to the banks of other developing countries that are seeking the adoption of digital transformation in customer-facing systems to enhance bank interaction with customers: Further study is needed to develop a comprehensive view of determinants that influence individuals' attitudes and decisions around digital applications adoption. This requires an understanding of how to best integrate the concepts of consumer relationships, banking, and digital transformation. To achieve this, research must go beyond the theoretical and conceptual bases of financial field, and join forces with other experts and researchers from related areas (such as consumer attitude and customer relationships management) to establish outcomes that are useful for practitioners.

Another interesting area for further research could be a detailed study on online banking usage, measuring online banking acceptance along with other possible factors derived from various sources of literature. Testing of acceptance in conjunction with innovation theories may yield interesting outcomes for customer relationships.

Future research could be conducted to better understand how banks can facilitate greater commitment of customers to effectively use new mobile systems, particularly customer-focused knowledge of digital technologies.

LIMITATIONS

There are several limitations that are should be considered as potential future research opportunities and areas of future improvement when researching digital service technologies and their adoption in the developing world. Actually, it is almost impossible for any single study to cover every aspect within the research field of digital transformations. The author has been used a sampling (interview) of Libyan citizens who were aged between 18 – 54, they were educated. However, the sample respondents are limited to customers in the financials field who were willing to be interviewed. Although every effort was made to make this study as comprehensive as possible, certain limitations were present. The response rate was lower than was hoped for, and this is mainly attributed to difficulties in locations of interviewees.

CONCLUSION

With management and strategies digital transformation, the role of the information technology and information System management and function in the banks tends to become increasingly strategic, and the traditional expectations of the Information System function are challenged. As information system management is becoming a more integral part of the banks with new leadership roles and changes in responsibilities and cultures, so banks often need to redesign the relationship between the customers and the business by maxims the positive effects of digital transformation on large of customers. Management and strategies digitally transformed banks need to manage traditional activities and customers' approach in combination with a new digital ways and activities (Osmundsen, Lden et al. 2018).

Management and strategies digital transformation has ceased to be an alternative distribution channel and become the main channel. Hence, they are expected to improve self service quality from their banks (Ecer 2018). The majority of the respondents had employed the use of digital transformation technologies when they were available. Thus, the sample has sufficient knowledge of these technologies tools used in the banking sector to be suitable candidates for participation in this study.

Management and strategies digital transformation has come to be considered highly effective banking services methods because they process many advantages that traditional banking channels cannot offer. These advantages refer to the benefits that customers can enjoy by using digital transformation. For example, customers can benefit from a wider range of financial services encouragements, faster transaction speed, and increased information transparency, lower transaction handling fees, higher deposit rates, and extra credit card bonus points (Pousttchi and Schurig 2004). The interviewees in this study identified all of these benefits, suggesting that customers of banks are aware of the possibilities available even when their primary bank does not offer and promote such services.

The interviewees believe that digital transformation is easy and useful for interacting with their banks and saves them time, because they can use this technology tool anywhere (for example cafe, meeting, bed and bus) and at any time. The interviewed Libyans believed that digital- Services as example would be best for Libyan customers because it allows them to always interact with their banks, overcoming the restrictions of the still popular arrangement of in-branch banking using cheque books. Customers generally perceive M-banking as secure (Gurau 2011). However, theft of access codes, finances and personal data is a significant concern. This is especially problematic when customers move from access on fixed internet devices to m- Services, where devices are more easily lost or stolen (Sannes, 2001).

In table 3 above, it is clearly that Mobile services usage above that males show a high percentage of acceptances of digital banking-services use (80%), whereas female participation is lower (20%). The studies by Wu (2018) also reported that female respondents so far had a lower rate of adoption for M-banking than males. There are similar rates in studies by Al-Sukkar (2005), so all had a higher percentage of male respondents; however, these studies identified that males have a greater interest and preference than females for using m-services.

Most of the participants in the interviews were aged similarly; thus sixty percent (60%) of interview participants were in the 25-34 years age group. This demographic grouping may have been due to the convenient sample population used in this study (i.e. Libyans who were living in Australia, most of whom were studying at university). These age demographics are similar to the sample used in Ab-Hamid (2006). Furthermore, these results may suggest that the mobile money services markets are about to mature. The majority of the respondents who use mobile banking services were males aged between 25 and 34. This was expected because it is the working friendships and majority of those in informal employment use mobile banking services.

With respect to the level of education of the participants, all were highly educated, as was expected due to the convenient sample population of the research. Ninety three percent (93.3%) of the interviewees were engaged in postgraduate studies. The responses support the literature that claims highly-educated customers have more widely adopted Mobile services within the banking sector, such as the study by Khatri and Kurnia (2011). Additionally, educated consumers tend to have higher requirements of service in their quest for trust and satisfaction and seek more advanced quality services than less educated users.

The demographics and technology use analysis of the participants found that this younger generation of Libyans, who were students studying to further their education, were more likely to adopt newer technologies. These are individuals with the potential to drive M-service technology adoption in the banking sector on their return to Libya. Prior research has supported this argument, identifying that the younger generations are usually more interested in adopting mobile services than older generations (Twati 2008).

Management and strategies digital transformation were believed to increase the privacy of banking activities towards customers (such as paying bills) through reduced travel time to a physical branch, reduced paper work and 24 / 7 services access (Elgahwash and Freeman 2013).

Management and strategies digital transformation offerings are mostly value-added services, with the mobile phone acting as a new channel to operating an existing bank account, it is necessary to modify the delivery of such services to include rural customers and those who are not already using M-services. While M-services are growing in popularity, banks have yet to shift the access frontier in order to 'transform money' (Amin 2008, Donner and Tellez 2008).

Management and strategies digital transformation is often trying to provide customers with new ways of communicating responsibly in their current activities. This chapter enables banks to know the key drivers influencing M-services adoption and, therefore, what aspects to highlight in their strategies to focus on. Young and educated customers are heavy Mobile-services users - both males and females. However, banks have to be able to offer new types of e-services with added value to improve consumers' adoption of the M-services in their sector especially female bank customers who, so far, have shown a slower uptake in this and other studies (Simon, 2007).

Management and strategies digital transformation has appeared as significant distribution channel because M- service is able to satisfy the needs of the customer and provide benefits that make the service worth to accept. Actually, the findings indicate that the m- Services adoption are privacy, services quality, awareness and competitive advantages, so there are the most significant items of intentions to adopt m-services in developed and developing countries.

REFERENCES

Abdinoor & Mbamba. (2017). Factors influencing consumers' adoption of mobile financial services in Tanzania. *Cogent Business & Management, 4*(1392273).

Al-Sukkar, A. S. (2005). *The application of information systems in the Jordainan banking sector: A study of the acceptance of the Internet.* Doctoral Universty of Wollongong.

Amin, H. (2008). Factors affecting the intentions of customers in Malaysia to use mobile phone credit cards. *Management Research News Journal, 31*(7), 493–503. doi:10.1108/01409170810876062

Banerjee, M. (2009). *Internet banking: An interaction building channel for bank customer relationships. In Self-Service in the Internet Age.* Springer-Verlag.

Boonsiritomachaia, W., & Pitchayadejanant, K. (2017). Determinants affecting mobile banking adoption bygeneration Y based on the Unified Theory of Acceptance andUse of Technology Model modified by the TechnologyAcceptance Model concept. *Journal of Social Sciences, 1*(10).

Bultum, A. G. (2014). Factors Affecting Adoption of Electronic Banking System in Ethiopian Banking Industry. *Journal of Management Information System and E-commerce, 1*(1).

Cavusoglu, H. (2003). *The economics of information technology investments.* Doctoral Degree University of Texas at Dallas.

Donner, J., & Tellez, C. A. (2008). Mobile banking and economic development: Linking adoption. *Asian Journal of Communication, 18*(4), 318–322. doi:10.1080/01292980802344190

Ecer, F. (2018). An Integrated Fuzzy AHP and ARAS Model to Evaluate Mobile Banking Services. *Technological and Economic Development of Economy, 24*(2), 670–695. doi:10.3846/20294913.2016.1255275

Elgahwash, F. O. (2013). *The Role of Information and Communication Technologies in Enhancing Customer Relationships in the Libyan Banking Sector.* UOW.

Elgahwash, F. O. (2016). Factors have affected Mobile Services adoption in Libyan banking system: A qualitative evidence. *Journal of Al-Haqiqah in University of Adrar,* (38), 1–30.

Elgahwash, F. O., & Freeman, M. B. (2013). Self-Service Technology Banking Preferences: Comparing Libyans' Behaviour in Developing and Developed Countries. *International Journal of Intelligent Information Technologies, 9*(2), 7–20. doi:10.4018/jiit.2013040102

Fairooz & Wickramasinghe. (2019). Innovation and Development of Digital Finance: A Review on Digital Transformation in Banking & Financial Sector of Sri Lanka. *Asian Journal of Economics, Finance and Management, 1*(2), 69-78.

Feher, P., Szabo, Z., & Varga, K. (2017). *Analysing Digital Transformation among Hungarian Organizations. In 30th Bled E-Conference: Digital Transformation – From Connecting Things To Transforming Our Lives. Academic Press.*

Gurau, G. (2011). *Online Self-Services: Investigating the Stages of CustomerSST Systems Interaction.* www.igi-global.com/e-resources/library-recommendation/?id=1

Haapio, H., & Karjaluoto, H. (2019). Antecedents of Market Orientation in The Banking Sector During Its Digital Transformation. In 32nd Bled eConference. Humanizing Technology for a Sustainable Society. University of Maribor.

Islam, N., Mustafi, M. A. A., Rahman, N., Nower, N., Rafi, M. A., Natasha, M. T., Hassan, R., & Afrin, S. (2018). *Factors Affecting Customers' Experience in Mobile Banking of Bangladesh.* 13th Annual International Conference - Convergence, Bengaluru, India. 10.2139srn.3305925

Ivatury, G., & Pickens, M. (2006). *Mobile phone banking and low-income customers -evidence from South Africa: Consultative Group to Assist the Poor, The World Bank and United Nations Foundation. U. N. F.* CGAP.

Khatri, A., & Kurnia, K. (2011). *Mobile banking adoption: In Australian rural areas.* The Pacific Asia Conference on Information Systems (PACIS). Brisbane, Australia.

Kim, Jin, & Swinney. (2009). The role of etail quality, e-satisfaction and e-trust in online loyalty development process. *Journal of Retailing and Consumer Services, 16*(4), 239-247.

Laukkanen, T., & Pasanen, M. (2008). Mobile banking innovators and early adopters: How they differ from other online users. *Journal of Financial Services Marketing, 13*(2), 86–94. doi:10.1057/palgrave.fsm.4760077

Leek, S., Turnbull, P. W., & Naude, P. (2003). How is information technology affecting business relationships? Results from a UK survey. *Industrial Marketing Management Journal, 32*(2), 119–126. doi:10.1016/S0019-8501(02)00226-2

Lobschata, Muellerb, Eggersd, Brandimartee, Diefenbachf, Kroschkea, & Wirtzh. (2019). Corporate digital responsibility. *Journal of Business Research.*

Mashat, Ritchie, Lovatt, & Pratten. (2005). The Social Role of Accounting: Views and Perceptions of the Accounting Community in Libya towards Corporate Social Responsibility and Accountability. *M. M. U. s. Research*, 1-24.

Maya, F. F. (2018). Mobile-banking adoption: Empirical evidence from the banking sector in Pakistan. *International Journal of Bank Marketing, 36*(7), 1386–1413. doi:10.1108/IJBM-10-2017-0215

Mnjala, D. M. (2014). The Challenges of Creating Sustainable Competitive Advantage in the Banking Industry in Kenya. *IOSR Journal of Business and Management, 16*(4), 82-87.

Mohamed, A. (2013). Improving the Libyan customers' trust and acceptance for online banking technology (PhD). University of Salford.

Morales, D., & Trinidad, F. (2019). Predictors of acceptability of digital mortgage service of universal banks in the Philippines: An empirical study. *International Journal of Modern Trends in Business Research, 2*(8), 79–92.

Motiwalla, L., Albashrawi, M., & Kartal, H. (2018). Understanding Mobile Banking Success through User Segmentation *Proceedings of the 51st Hawaii International Conference on System Sciences.* 10.24251/HICSS.2018.110

Murphy, E., Dingwall, R., Greatbatch, D., Parker, S., & Watson, P. (1998). Qualitative Research Methods in Health Technology Assessment: A Review of the Literature. *Health Technology Assessment, 2*(16). Advance online publication. doi:10.3310/hta2160 PMID:9919458

Mutahar, A. M., Daud, N. M., Ramayah, T., Isaac, O., & Aldholay, A. H. (2018). The effect of awareness and perceived risk on the technology acceptance model (TAM): Mobile banking in Yemen. *Int. J. Services and Standards, 12*(2), 27. doi:10.1504/IJSS.2018.091840

Nuri, M. (2019). An empirical study on measurement of efficiency of digital transformation by using data envelopment analysis. *Management Science Letters, 9*, 549–556.

Obukhova, Merzlyakova, Ershova, & Karakulina. (2020). Introduction of digital technologies in the enterprise. In *E3S Web of Conferences*. EDP Sciences.

Omigie, N. O., Zo, H., Rho, J. J., & Ciganek, A. P. (2017). Customer pre-adoption choice behavior for M-PESA mobile financial services Extending the theory of consumption values. *Industrial Management & Data Systems, 117*(5), 910–926. doi:10.1108/IMDS-06-2016-0228

Osmundsen, K., Lden, J., & Bygstad, B. (2018). *Digital Transformation: Drivers, Success Factors and Implications*. The 12th Mediterranean Conference on Information Systems MCIS, Corfu, Greece.

Owusu, P. A., & Duah, H. (2018). Evaluating total quality management as a competitive advantage tool in mobile telecommunication services in Ghana. *European Journal of Research and Reflection in Management Sciences, 6*(1).

Peter Marc, K., Kraft, C., & Lindeque, J. (2020). Strategic action fields of digital transformation: An exploration of the strategic action fields of Swiss SMEs and large enterprises. *Journal of Strategy and Management, 13*(1), 160–180. doi:10.1108/JSMA-05-2019-0070

Pichelr, P., Summer, M., Weber, B., & Goodhart, C. (2019). *Does digitalization require Central Bank Digital Currencies for the general publ*. Monetary Policy & The Economy – First View.

Pousttchi, K., & Schurig, M. (2004). *Assessment of today's mobile banking applications from the view of customer requirements. 37th Hawaii International Conference on System Sciences (HICSS)*, Big Island, HI. 10.1109/HICSS.2004.1265440

Resego Morakanyane, R., Reilly, P. O., & McAvoy, J. (2020). Determining Digital Transformation Success Factors. *Proceedings of the 53rd Hawaii International Conference on System Sciences*. 10.24251/HICSS.2020.532

Richard & Mandari. (2018). *Factors influencing usage of mobile banking services: The case of ilala district in Tanzania*. Academic Press.

Sadek, D., Zainal, N., Taher, M., & Yahya, A. (2010). Service quality perceptions between Cooperative and Islamic Banks of Britain. *American Journal of Economics and Business Administration*, *2*(1), 1–5. doi:10.3844/ajebasp.2010.1.5

Scherer, N. W., & Wangenheim, V. (2015). The Value of Self-Service: Long-Term Effects of Technology based Self- Services usage on Customer Retention. *Journal of MIS Quarterly*, *39*(1), 177–200. doi:10.25300/MISQ/2015/39.1.08

Schwertner, K. (2017). Digital transformation of business. *Trakia Journal of Sciences in Trakia University*, *15*(1), 388–393. doi:10.15547/tjs.2017.s.01.065

Selamat, Z., & Jaffar, N. (2011). Information technology acceptance: From the perspective of Malaysian bankers. *International Journal of Business and Management*, *6*(1), 207–217.

Shareefa, M. A., Baabdullahb, A., Duttac, S., Kumard, V., & Dwivedie, Y. K. (2018). Consumer adoption of mobile banking services: An empirical examination of factors according to adoption stages. *Journal of Retailing and Consumer Services*, *43*, 54–67. doi:10.1016/j.jretconser.2018.03.003

Spathis, C., & Georgakopoulou, E. (2007). The adoption of IFRS in South Eastern Europe: The case of Greece. *International Journal of Financial Services Management*, *2*(1), 50–63. doi:10.1504/IJFSM.2007.011671

Twati. (2008). The influence of societal culture on the adoption of information systems: The case of Libya. *Communications of the IIMA Journal, 8*(1), 1-12.

Vogel, M. A. (2005). *Leveraging information technology competencies and capabilities for a competitive advantage. Doctoral Degree*. University of Maryland.

Wei, K. (2009). Service quality index: A study on Malasian banks. *Journal of Contemporary Management Research*, *5*(2), 109–124. doi:10.7903/cmr.1179

Wu, Y.-L., & Li, E. Y. (2018). Marketing mix, customer value, and customer loyalty in social commerce. *Internet Research*, *28*(1), 74–104. doi:10.1108/IntR-08-2016-0250

Yang, R. (2020). *Analysing the impact of digital transformation on corporate travel management* (Master Thesis). University of Vaasa.

Yeboah, J., & Ewur, G. D. (2014). Quality Customer Service as a Competitive Advantage in the Telecommunication Industry in the Western Region of Ghana. *Journal of Education and Practice*, *5*(5), 11.

Zhang, Lu, & Kizildag. (2018). Banking "on-the-go": examining consumers' adoption of mobile banking services. *International Journal of Quality and Service Sciences*, 1-19.

Zhao, Tsai, & Wang. (2019). *Improving Financial Service Innovation Strategies for Enhancing China's Banking Industry Competitive Advantage during the Fintech Revolution: A Hybrid MCDM Model*. Academic Press.

Ziyadin, Suieubayeva, & Utegenova. (2020). *Digital Transformation in Business*. Springer Nature Switzerland AG.

Chapter 12
Big Data in Business:
Digital Transformation for Enhanced Decision-making and Superior Customer Experience

Farid Huseynov
https://orcid.org/0000-0002-9936-0596
Gebze Technical University, Turkey

ABSTRACT

The term "big data" refers to the very large and diverse sets of structured, semi-structured, and unstructured digital data from different sources that accumulate and grow very rapidly on a continuous basis. Big data enables enhanced decision-making in various types of businesses. Through these technologies, businesses are able to cut operational costs, digitally transform business operations to be more efficient and effective, and make more informed business decisions. Big data technologies enable businesses to better understand their markets by uncovering hidden patterns behind consumer behaviors and introduce new products and services accordingly. This chapter shows the critical role that big data plays in businesses. Initially, in this chapter, big data and its underlying technologies are explained. Later, this chapter discusses how big data digitally transforms critical business operations for enhanced decision-making and superior customer experience. Finally, this chapter ends with the possible challenges of big data for businesses and possible solutions to these challenges.

INTRODUCTION

The term "Big Data" refers to the very large and diverse sets of structured, semi-structured and unstructured digital data from different sources that accumulates and grows very rapidly on continuous basis. Big data is so huge that traditional computational methods are incapable of processing it. Gartner, the world's leading research and advisory company, defines big data as "*high-volume, and high-velocity or high-variety information assets that demand cost-effective, innovative forms of information processing that enable enhanced insight, decision making, and process automation*". According to IBM, big data

DOI: 10.4018/978-1-7998-8583-2.ch012

is a term applied to data sets whose size or type is beyond the ability of traditional relational databases to capture, manage, and process the data with low latency. On the other hand, big data analytics is the use of advanced analytic techniques against these huge data sets. Big data analytics enables to uncover hidden patterns, correlations and other insights from huge data sets. From these two definitions it can be understood that big data term not only requires data-gathering strategies but also involves a wide range of analytical capabilities and skills. The big data is not a new concept and it has been around for years, however only recently it has gained popularity due to technology advancements which have enabled large sets of data to be analyzed faster and efficiently. Thanks to the recent developments in artificial intelligence and data analytics, extracting critical insights from big data and smart decision-making based on this processed data have become more and more possible. According to Statista (2020a), the global big data market (i.e., relevant software, hardware and services segment revenues) is forecasted to grow to 103 billion U.S. dollars by 2027, more than double its expected market size in 2018.

According to IBM, every single day 2.5 quintillion bytes of digital data is created in various types of digital platforms. That rate accelerates even more with the proliferation of the Internet of Things (IoT) and artificial intelligence technologies. The current daily data creation rate is so high that 90 percent of existing data in the world has been created in the last two years. As of 2019, 59 percent of world's population is online which means that more than 4.5 billion people are connected to the Internet via various types of computing devices (Statista, 2020b). These online users are actively using diverse type of platforms such as social networking, entertainment, e-commerce, education, health, etc. On these online platforms, huge amount of data is generated by users in every given second. For example, in a single minute more than 4 billion Youtube videos are watched, nearly half million tweets are sent, nearly 47.000 Instagram photos are posted, nearly half million Facebook comments are posted, and more than hundred million spam emails are sent (Forbes, 2018). In today's highly competitive online business environment, ignoring that amount of data would be a very big mistake for businesses. A very high number of businesses have understood that this huge amount of accumulating data is invaluable source for improving their operations and offerings. Therefore, a lot of businesses have started to invest considerable amount of money to the big data technologies. Thanks to low cost of data storage online business owners are able to store all of these data generated by online users on various platforms. However, for online businesses, being able to store huge amount of digital data is only small stage in the long big data journey. What is important in big data is that how to process it with advanced analytical techniques and derive useful insights and take right actions at the right time in order to stay ahead in the competition.

Big data technologies enable enhanced decision making in businesses. Through these technologies, businesses are able to allocate their scarce resources efficiently, cut operational costs, improve business operations, and increase the productivity of human capital. Big data technologies also enable businesses to better understand their markets. That is, big data enable businesses to uncover hidden patterns behind consumer behaviors and introduce new products and services accordingly. Furthermore, big data also enables businesses to offer personalized products and services that are appealing to each individual customer. Besides providing personalized products and services, big data also enables businesses to carry out scalable and personalized marketing campaigns aimed at the right users, at the right time and in the right form.

This chapter starts by discussing the main challenges faced by today's businesses in highly dynamic and competitive business environments. Later, this chapter shows how businesses can utilize big data technologies to digitally transform their business processes for enhanced decision making and superior customer experience.

RESEARCH METHODOLOGY

In this subsection the research methodology of this study is stated. The specific procedures and techniques used to identify, select, process, and analyze necessary information about the topic under question is stated in this part. The main objective of this chapter is to understand the critical role that big data technologies play in digitally transforming today's businesses to make enhanced business decisions and to deliver superior customer experience. In line with this objective necessary academic and reliable non-academic resources have been retrieved and analyzed. Resources used in this chapter include academic journals, books, conference papers, surveys of market search companies, statistical reports, etc. While collecting necessary literature on this topic, the more weight has been given to publications of the last five years. While retrieving necessary resources the combinations of following keywords have been used: big data analytics, data science, operational excellence, decision-making quality, customer experience. Full text of each retrieved resource was reviewed in detail in order to eliminate the unrelated ones. Resources that were not included in this chapter mainly focused on the technical and implementation aspects of big data technologies. The remaining resources have been discussed in line with the purpose of this chapter. Within the framework of all collected resources the chapter structure has been formed and presented as follows. Initially, in this chapter big data term and its underlying technologies are discussed in detail. Following that, main challenges faced by businesses today are stated. Later, this chapter discusses how critical big data is in overcoming challenges faced by business. This specific subsection discusses how online businesses gain operational excellence through big data technologies and also shows how big data technologies are used to provide superior online customer experience. Finally, in addition to the positive sides, this chapter concludes with challenges of big data for business, possible solutions to these challenges, and future research suggestions.

BACKGROUND: DEFINING BIG DATA AND ITS TECHNOLOGIES

Big data is the collection of structured, semi-structured, and unstructured data. Structured data is data that have a predefined format and structure. More specifically, structured data is easily searchable in databases due to its highly organized and formatted structure. Online shopping transaction record can be given as an example to the structured data. Every record will have its own timestamp, order number, order amount, item(s) purchased, payment details, and etc. Structured data is usually stored in relational databases. In relational databases data is maintained in relational tables which makes it efficient, intuitive, and flexible to store and access structured information. SQL, also known as Structured Query Language, is the language used to work with structured data stored in relational databases. In contrast to structured data, unstructured data has no pre-defined format or organization. Unstructured data cannot be organized in relational databases. Therefore, non-relational or NoSQL databases are used to manage unstructured data. Unstructured data can also be stored in data lakes which can hold a vast amount of raw data in its native format until it is needed. Unstructured data can be textual or non-textual and can be generated by humans or machines. Human generated unstructured data includes presentations, reports, spreadsheets, social media data, photos, audios, videos, etc. Machine generated unstructured data includes satellite imagery, various types of sensor data, digital surveillance, etc. Between structured and unstructured data there exist third category which is called semi-structured data. Semi-structured data is defined as "data that is neither raw data, nor very strictly typed as in conventional database system" (Abiteboul, 1997).

Although semi-structured data resembles structured data by its format, it is not organized with the same restrictive rules as structured data. Semi-structured data does not reside in a relational database, but it possesses some organizational properties that make it easier to analyze. Examples of semi structured data are: Email, CSV, XML and JSON documents, Resource Description Framework (RDF), Electronic data interchange (EDI), etc. According to the most experts, while structured data accounts only for about 20 percent, unstructured and semi-structured data accounts for about 80 percent of the digital data that is out there (Hurwitz, Nugent, Halper, & Kaufman, 2013).

In 2001, Gartner analyst Doug Laney introduced the 3Vs framework to describe big data. These 3Vs are; volume, velocity and variety. More recently, three more Vs have been proposed for addition to the previous framework, including variability, veracity, and value. The following paragraphs explains each V respectively.

- Volume is the measure of how much data is being generated. Every second large volumes of digital data are generated by billions of system users as well as by billions of smart computing devices and applications. As a result, digital data generated each second is very enormous and continuously growing. If not handled properly, this huge volume of data could pose challenges to the existing information systems infrastructures in terms of storage and processing.
- Velocity is the measure of how fast data is being generated. For example, in various type of social networking the speed at which digital data is created is very big. It is important that businesses manage the very fast incoming flow of data effectively and process it so fast that data does not lose its value. For example, in various social networking platforms the speed at which digital data is created is so high that it is difficult to express with numbers. This enormous data creation speed is also present in various IoT applications (e.g., smart home, smart city, smart retail, wearable technologies).
- Variety refers to the diversity of data being generated. Big Data is generated from various sources and in various forms such as structured, semi-structured, and unstructured. It may include videos, audios, imagery, documents, sensor data, logs, and many others. Each of these data types requires specialized storage and processing capabilities.
- Variability is the measure of up to what extent, or how fast, is the structure, meaning and shape of the data changing. If the meaning and shape of the data is constantly changing, then it will be very difficult to derive useful insights from it.
- Veracity refers to the biases, noises and abnormality in the gathered data. Veracity measures whether the data has something useful to offer? That is, it tries to ensure whether the data is clean and accurate. The quality of the gathered data can vary greatly. Accuracy of analysis depends on the veracity of the gathered data.
- Value refers how worthy the gathered data is of positively impacting a company's business. Big data should not be collected for the sake of collecting it. If big data do not have any potential to add any value to company's business, then investing time and effort in it will not make any sense.

Big data technologies can be classified into 4 sub-domains. These sub-domains are data storage, data mining, data analytics, and data visualization. Table 1 lists some well-known free, open source and commercial innovative big data solutions offered to business under each category. Most of these products listed in Table 1 provide solutions in more than one category.

MAIN CHALLENGES FACED BY BUSINESSES TODAY

Table 1. Big Data Technologies

	Technology	Description
Data Storage	Apache Hadoop	Apache Hadoop which is an open source software library that can effectively store large amount of data. By using simple programming models, this framework allows distributed processing of large data sets across clusters of computers. Apache Hadoop is designed in such a way that it can scale up from single servers to thousands of machines each of which provides local computation and storage. Therefore, it can deliver a highly available service on top of a cluster of computers. Instead of relying on hardware to provide high availability, in this framework failures are detected and handled at the application layer.
	Cloudera	Through cloud or on premises basis Cloudera provides a platform on which data engineering, data warehousing, machine learning, and data analytics can be carried out. Data management and analytics platform of Cloudera is built on top of Apache Hadoop and contemporary open source technologies. By using Cloudera platform users can efficiently capture, store, process and analyze enormous amounts of data. This platform empowers its users to use advanced analytics to make smart business decisions faster.
	MongoDB	MongoDB is a free document-oriented NoSQL database used for high volume data storage. It stores data in JSON-like documents. Instead of using tables and rows as in the traditional relational database management systems, MongoDB makes use of collections and documents. In MongoDB sd hoc queries, indexing, and real time aggregation provide powerful ways to access and analyze business data. At its core MongoDB is a distributed database. Therefore, it has high availability and horizontal scaling capabilities.
	Apache Cassandra	Apache Cassandra is a free and open source. The Apache Cassandra database provides scalability and high availability without degrading performance. In Apache Cassandra data is automatically replicated to multiple nodes for fault-tolerance. Failed nodes can be replaced with no downtime. Its linear scalability and fault-tolerance capability make it good choice for mission-critical data. Thanks to its architectural choices Cassandra consistently outperforms well-known NoSQL alternatives in benchmarks and real applications. Cassandra can be adopted for applications which cannot accommodate data loss, even if an entire data center goes down.
Data Mining	RapidMiner	This software package enables users to carry out data mining, text mining and predictive analytics. RapidMiner unifies the entire data science lifecycle from data prep to machine learning to predictive model operations. RapidMiner provides a group of products to build new data mining processes and setup predictive analysis. Its robust graphical user interface, RapidMiner Studio, accelerates the prototyping and validation of models. Among features of this software package there are clustering, data partitioning, data access and management, Bayesian modeling, market basket analysis, similarity calculation, data exploration, weighting and selection, data sampling and others.
	Sisense	Commercial business intelligence platform provided by Sisense includes everything that are required to get insights from multiple and large data sets. Sisense simplifies complex data preparation and analysis. For ultra-fast performance, Sisense technology uses parallel processing, compression, and an in-memory columnar database. Sisense has both on-premises and cloud solutions. Sisense works with Hive which is a data warehouse system designed for Big Data analytics.
	Tanagra	Tanagra is a free and open source data mining software for academic and research purposes. Tanagra aims to be an easy-to-use data mining platform for researchers and students. It has several data mining methods which includes exploratory data analysis, statistical learning, machine learning, and databases area. In addition to its supervised learning paradigms, Tanagra also includes other techniques such as clustering, factorial analysis, parametric and nonparametric statistics, association rule, feature selection, construction algorithms, and others.
	KNIME	KNIME platform provides end to end data science solutions for better decision making. KNIME Analytics Platform is the open source software for creating data science solutions. On the other side, KNIME Server is the enterprise software that enables team-based collaboration, automation, management, and deployment of data science workflows. KNIME software enable businesses to gather and wrangle their data, and later enable them to make sense of their data through modeling and visualization tools. The deployment and management functionalities of KNIME make it easy to put data science applications and services into action, and deliver usable, reliable, and reproducible insights for the business.
Data Analytics	Azure HDInsight	Microsoft's Azure HDInsight is a fully managed, full-spectrum, open-source cloud-based service for big data analytics. Through this platform organizations can process large amounts of streaming or historical data. Azure HDInsight can be utilized for machine learning applications, Internet of Things (IoT) environments, and ETL (extract, transform, load) scenarios. HDInsight allows to develop big data applications by utilizing open source frameworks such as Apache Hadoop, Apache Spark, Apache Hive, Apache Kafka, Apache LLAP, Apache Storm, and Microsoft Machine Learning Server.
	Splunk	Splunk is a software platform to search, analyze and visualize the machine-generated data gathered from the websites, applications, sensors, devices, etc. Business Process Analytics of Splunk enable to reduce delays in business processes with process mining and interactive observability. Some prominent features of Splunk are being able to visualize the performance of actual business process from event data, to find patterns in business processes that may indicate anomalies, to use data-driven insights to objectively investigate bottlenecks and problems, and others.
	Apache Spark	For large-scale data processing Apache Spark comes forward as a unified analytics engine. By using a state-of-the-art DAG scheduler, a query optimizer, and a physical execution engine, Apache Spark achieves high performance in batch and streaming data. Spark offers more than 80 high-level operators that which make it very easy to build parallel applications. It can be used interactively from the Scala, Python, R, and SQL shells. It runs on Hadoop, Apache Mesos, Kubernetes and can access diverse data sources.
	R-Language	It is free software environment for statistical computing and graphics. It possesses effective data handling and storage facilities. It also has a suite of operators to carry out calculations on arrays and matrices. In addition, R provides a wide variety of statistical (linear and nonlinear modelling, classical statistical tests, time-series analysis, classification, clustering, etc.) and graphical techniques, and it is also highly extensible. R is designed around a true computer language, and it allows users to add additional functionality by defining their own functions.

continued on following page

Table 1. Continued

	Technology	Description
Data Visualization	Tableau	Tableau help organizations visualize and understand their data. Tableau can interface with almost any database, spreadsheets, OLAP (Online Analytical Processing), and so on. Tableau simplifies transforming raw data into the very easily understandable format. Tableau has drag and drop features to create visualizations, and it also enable to share outputs with a few clicks. Tableau also allows to create interactive real-time visualization in the form of dashboards that provide actionable insights to decision makers.
	Plot.ly	Plotly is an analytics tool that lets users create charts and dashboards based on their data and easily share it online with interested parties. Plotly provides various online graphing, analytics, and statistics tools. Dashboards created with Plotly run advanced analytics such as machine learning, natural language processing (NLP), forecasting, computer vision, and others. Plotly also provides scientific graphing libraries for Python, R, MATLAB, Perl, Julia, Arduino, and REST.
	DataHero	DataHero is an online data visualization and data dashboard software platform which makes it easy for organizations to share critical business insights within organization and as well as with their external entities. DataHero makes it very easy to create various types of charts, reports, and KPI (key performance indicators) dashboards that can be easily understood. Intuitive drag-and-drop chart creation feature of DataHero enables users to generate insightful, intuitive, and great looking data visualizations in minutes. Through DataHero it is possible to connect all data sources (sales, marketing, customer success data, etc.) and see everything in a single place.
	Looker	Looker is a big data analytics platform that enable businesses to explore, analyze and share real-time business analytics easily. No desktop software is required to use Looker. More specifically, Looker's entirely browser-based experience eliminates the need for desktop client software installation and maintenance. Looker is mobile, tablet, and desktop friendly and the same time it is very easy to learn how to use it. Visualization types in Looker includes cartesian charts, pie and donut charts, progression charts, text and tables, maps, and others. Each of these visualization types has different settings which makes it possible to customize its appearance.

In today's global and competitive environment, businesses face numerous challenges which have significant impacts on business performance and continuity. These challenges include, but not limited to, achieving excellence in business operations, meeting frequently changing customer needs and expectations, making improved business decisions, and maintaining good relationship with business partners (Moktadir et al., 2020, Laudon & Laudon, 2020).

The first challenge is about operational excellence. In order to achieve higher profitability, businesses continuously try to find new ways to gain operational excellence and improve the efficiency of their business operations (Laudon & Laudon, 2020). Operational Excellence can be simply defined as execution of business strategies more consistently and reliably than competitors. Businesses with operational excellence will have lower operational risk, lower operating costs, and increased revenues relative to its competitors. Businesses share market space with other competitors and new market entrants who are continuously trying to attract each other's customers by introducing new and more efficient ways to produce products and services, and serve customers well. Now businesses are in such a situation that they must constantly struggle to gain new customers and not to lose existing customers to competitors.

The second challenge is that today, customers have diverse and constantly changing needs and expectations, and there are many businesses out there who are continuously trying to meet these diverse needs and expectations. It is now a matter of time to lose customers, which have been gained by great efforts, to direct competitors and new market entrants. If businesses want to keep their existing customers and attract potential ones with innovative products and services, they need to have 360-degree customer view. Having complete view of customer requires collection and analysis of critical customer data from the various customer touch points such as social media, mobile app, website, online shopping, and call center.

The third challenge is about improved decision-making. Many managers do not have the right information at the right time to make an informed business decisions (Laudon and Laudon, 2020). Therefore, most of the time they rely on forecasts, best guesses, and even luck. Not having the right information at the right time results in either overproduction or underproduction of goods and services. Not having timely and right information also results in misallocation of limited resources, slow response time to emerging opportunities, unsatisfied business partners, and loss of existing and potential customers. The biggest challenge for today's businesses is finding ways to provide continuous, reliable and real-time information to support business decision-making.

The final challenge is about developing and maintaining good relationships with business partners. It is very important that businesses maintain good relations with their business partners. Business partners' role in value creation process is vital. Maintaining good relationships with business partners requires mutual trust and should be in the interest of both parties. It is very important that information, which has a significant impact on the process of creating value for the customer, is mutually and continuously shared with the businesses and their partners. Most of today's businesses collaborate with many business partners. The biggest challenge which businesses face today is how to maintain good relationships and effectively share information with so many business partners for mutual benefit.

Overcoming all these challenges mentioned above has become a matter of survival for today's businesses. In the following section, how big data technologies turn these challanges into opportunities for businesses is explained with real examples.

SOLUTIONS AND RECOMMENDATIONS

By processing big data, businesses can digitally transform business processes, gain operational excellence, make improved business decisions, and build good relationship with their business partners and customers (Gunasekaran, 2017; Bag, Wood, Xu, Dhamija, & Kayikci, 2020; Sestino, Prete, Piper & Guido, 2020). Companies that successfully extract business value from data which they collect from multiple sources not only outperform their competitors in their respective markets but also put barriers in front of new market entrants. Analysis of big data enables businesses to make better and faster decisions using various forms of data from various sources that was once ignored due to technological shortcomings. In various types of businesses sources of big data include but not limited to IoT data, enterprise applications (ERP, CRM, SCM, etc.) data, website traffic, mobile digital platform data, e-commerce transaction records, social media interactions, and call center data. Data from these given sources can be in various forms and in various sizes. Thanks to the advancements in artificial intelligence and data analytics, processing of these diverse types of data have become more possible and faster. Today businesses have discovered the power of big data analytics and started to implement it in innovative ways to gain edge in the competition in their respective markets. Nowadays, businesses use advanced analytics techniques such as machine learning, text analytics, data mining, natural language processing, and many more to gain new insights from big data sets. Businesses are well aware of the fact that if they can successfully generate business value from their data, they will outperform their competitors. Analysis of big data not only can help any given business to improve its internal operations but also can help businesses to improve its relationship with its business partners and customers. Through big data technologies, traditional business operations are transforming and becoming more efficient and effective. These technologies enable businesses to make smarter and faster decisions by carrying out advanced analytics on all forms of business data including structured, semi-structured and unstructured data. It is possible to see implementation of big data in various type of sectors such as e-commerce, finance, production, retail, logistics, etc. Through real examples, the following paragraphs discusses how big data is being implemented successfully in different sectors to transform business operations and deliver superior customer experience.

Big data analytics can help in detecting and mitigating frauds in various types of businesses. It can help in monitoring business transactions in real time and proactively recognizing the abnormal patterns and behaviors within enormous amount of business data. The power of big data can be joined with four different types of advanced analytical techniques which are diagnostic, descriptive, predictive, and prescriptive. The use of big data along with diagnostic analytics (data analysis techniques to answer why problem is occurring), descriptive analytics (analysis of historical data to understand trends and evaluate metrics over time), predictive analytics (statistical models and forecasting techniques to understand the future), and prescriptive analytics (optimization and simulation algorithms to test the likely outcome of different actions) can help businesses to predict and mitigate fraud before they occur. Among other businesses, especially financial institutions come first in the use of big data. Everyday millions of financial transactions are carried out over financial institutions' systems. Nowadays, financial institutions rely on big data analytics to distinguish between real and counterfeit transactions. More specifically, big data analytics enable financial institutions to analyze enormous amount of financial data and create predictive models to identify and prevent fraudulent transactions in real time basis. Machine learning algorithms combined with big data enable to understand and interpret buying patterns of customers of financial institutions. When customer's credit card information is stolen and used, financial institutions can instantly understand abnormal activities and based on this they can freeze the card and transaction and notify the customer about this event. In addition to fraud detection and prediction, financial institutions also utilize big data to obtain real time stock market insights, to predict share prices, to predict foreign exchange rates, to make investment decisions, to decide on loan applications, etc. In all of these decision-making activities there are many dynamic factors that should be taken into consideration and it is impossible for a human to do it manually or through traditional computational techniques. Therefore, as other business financial institutions rely on big data technologies to uncover hidden patterns, correlations and other insights from huge financial data sets.

Big data technologies can be used to improve the management of supply chain in businesses. Big data generated in supply chain operations can be used to carry out real-time monitoring over supply chain activities. Big data can be analyzed to determine inefficiencies and take necessary measures to save cost, time, and effort. Improved demand planning, enhanced order optimization, accurate planning and scheduling, and improved responsiveness are just few of the many benefits of using big data in supply chain management (Medium, 2019). Amazon, world's largest online retailer and a prominent cloud services provider, is one of the many companies that successfully utilize big data analytics in its inventory management. Amazon's big data system collects and processes all the necessary information about its vendors and customers. Later, in order to reduce distribution costs, Amazon selects warehouses by taking into consideration the proximity of its vendors and customers. That is, big data analytics enables the warehouse closest to the vendors and customers to be selected for the sake of reducing shipping costs. Amazon successfully utilizes big data analytics in distribution of inventories according to customer preferences in particular areas. In 2011, Amazon's patented anticipatory shipping model which is powered by big data. Anticipatory shipping model uses historical orders and customer data to predict the future orders (Viet, Behdani, & Bloemhof, 2020). Based on these predictions, the products are sent to the nearest distribution centers so they will be ready for shipping once customers order them. Through anticipatory shipping model, company increases its product sales and customer satisfaction and at the same time decreases its delivery time and overall expenses. Amazon also successfully utilizes the power of big data to optimize its prices. Big data analytics enable Amazon to set prices according to the activity of a customer on the website, pricing of competitors, availability of products, item preferences, historical orders, expected profit margin, and other factors (Investopedia, 2020). Prices of items change dynamically as big data is analyzed and updated. According to the Business Insider, well-known financial and business news platform, Amazon changes its product prices more than 2.5 million times in a day which means that average product listed in Amazon changes prices every 10 minutes. As a result of this price optimization process, Amazon generally offers discounts on bestselling items, while generating more profits on less-popular items. Big data driven dynamic pricing strategy of Amazon helps company to increase profits by 25 percent each year. Amazon also utilizes big data in making personalized product recommendations to its customers. Amazon collects enormous amount of data about its customer behaviors such as purchase histories, items in shopping carts, items rated and liked, and what other customers have viewed and purchased. Later, all of these collected data are used in generating personalized product recommendations. More than 30 percent of Amazon's page views occurs as a result of big data enabled recommender systems. Such kind of personalized recommender systems have been found to increase impulse purchases by consumers in online shopping platforms (Hostler, Yoon, Guo, Guimaraes, & Forgionne, 2011; Ying, Caixia, Wen, & Xiaogang, 2018).

Similarly, UPS, one of the world's largest parcel delivery companies, successfully utilizes big data analytics to optimize its logistics operations. To ensure UPS drivers use the most optimized delivery routes in regard to distance, fuel and time, UPS developed On-Road Integrated Optimization and Navigation (ORION) system. ORION routing system uses broad fleet telematics and advanced algorithms to gather and calculate vast amount of data to provide optimized routes about more than 250 million locations to nearly 60.000 UPS drivers. In addition to providing optimal routes, ORION system ensures that in countries that drive on the right, UPS vans do not make a left turn unless it is necessary. ORION system showed that left turns made in the routes mean idling, which increases the time a route takes (UPS, 2016). Left turns mean going against traffic, which increases exposure to oncoming cars. On the other hand, right turns are faster and save fuel. ORION is expected to save between 300 and 400 million U.S. dollars annually. By reducing the total miles driven it is predicted to decrease the fuel consumption annually by 10 million gallons, and carbon dioxide (CO2) production by 100,000 metric tons (Informs, 2016).

In order to provide superior customer experience, companies rely on big data technologies which enable them to gain a 360-degree view of customers' behavior and motivations. Netflix, the world's leading streaming entertainment service with 183 million paid memberships, successfully utilizes the power of big data in improving the quality of their services as well as enhancing the experience of its subscribers. As subscribers stream contents on Netflix, vast amount of data (i.e., big data) are being generated. This big data includes, what subscribers watch, how they watch (e.g., the device, time of the day, day of the week, watching intensity), where each content was discovered, the recommendations that were shown but not played in each session, content ratings, and others (Gomez-Uribe & Hunt, 2015). Netflix is very successful at discovering hidden patterns behind its subscribers' behaviors which subscribes might not even aware of it. In fact, Netflix knows more about its subscribers viewing habits than subscribers do actually know about their own habits. With the help of big data analytics, Netflix can tell you what you want to watch next. According to the consumer research, a typical Netflix user loses interest after perhaps 60 to 90 seconds of choosing, having reviewed 10 to 20 titles (perhaps 3 in detail) on one or two screens (Gomez-Uribe & Hunt, 2015). Within that duration the user either finds something of interest or the risk of the user abandoning Netflix service increases substantially. Therefore, Netflix is well aware of the fact that it has only seconds to convince its viewers to stay with their services before it loses them. Netflix developed a big data fueled complex personalized recommendation system which provides personalized experiences and recommendations to its millions of viewers. Netflix estimates that big data driven complex recommender engine in total influences choice for nearly 80 percent of streamed hours. The remaining 20 percent streamed video hours comes from the search functionality. According to the Netflix, personalization and recommendation system helps company to save more than 1 billion U.S. dollars each year. That is, company states that it could lose more than 1 billion U.S. dollars every year from subscribers quitting its service if there was not such kind of personalized recommendation engine within their platform.

Coca-Cola, world's largest beverage company operating in more than 200 countries, is a very nice example to show how a non-tech company can harness the power of big data analytics in transforming its critical business operations to gain competitive edge in its market. With more than 100 million Facebook fans, and millions of Twitter and Instagram followers from different nations, social media is very important source of data for Coca-Cola. The company determined that its products were mentioned online once every two seconds in 2015. These enormous amount of social media data gives clues about who is consuming company's drinks, where customers are located, and what situations make them to talk about the company's brand. Coca-Cola also uses AI-based image recognition technology to determine when photographs of its and its competitors' products are uploaded to the internet, and later uses algorithms to determine the best way to serve them advertisements (Forbes, 2017). According to Coca-Cola, advertisement targeted in this way have a four times greater chance of being clicked by viewers on than other methods of targeted advertising. Coca-Cola also successfully introduces new products by utilizing the insight its gains from processing big data. In 2009, Coca-Cola introduced Freestyle fountain machine, which allows users to select from mixtures of flavors of Coca-Cola branded products. Later, company introduced Coca-Cola Freestyle mobile app which enable users to find Coca-Cola freestyle near them, get special offers at their favorite locations, save their favorite drinks for future consumptions, create and share their own mixes, check in and earn badges, complete challenges, and more. Data collected from these newly introduced machines and its mobile app provides invaluable insights about its customer preferences. Based on these huge amounts of collected data, Coca Cola was able to launch Cherry Sprite as a new flavor. Coca-Cola also utilizes big data to manage the quality of its products. For example, producing orange juice with a consistent taste year-around despite the inconsistent quality of the orange supply is very complex task. To deal with this complexity, Coca-Cola introduced very complex and sophisticated "Black Book" model. The Black Book model combines and processes various data sets for smart decision-making. Data sets include various types of data such as weather, expected crop yields, satellite imagery, regional consumer preferences, cost pressures, 600 different flavors that make up an orange, and many other variables such as acidity or sweetness details (Turban, Pollard, & Wood, 2018). Later, this model advises Coca-Cola on how to blend the orange juice to create the consistent taste. Developers of this model indicates that such kind of complex model requires analyzing up to 1 quintillion decision variables to consistently deliver the optimal blend.

All of the above-mentioned examples from well-known companies have clearly showed that the role of big data in transforming business operations should not be underestimated. Ignoring the power big data analytics can be a nonrecoverable mistake for businesses. Real business examples showed that big data analytics allows companies to quickly access and analyze their data to make smarter and faster business decisions which in turn yield more efficient operations, higher profits, and loyal customers.

FUTURE RESEARCH DIRECTIONS

The benefits of big data technologies for business entities are very apparent. On the other side, big data technologies have several challenges for businesses. These challenges are as follows: lack of understanding of big data technologies, the existence of too many big data technologies to select among, significant costs of deploying big data solutions, lack of skilled personal required to derive value from big data solutions, and security issues of big data technologies. It is important that businesses clearly understand these challenges and take necessary measure to come over these challenges before confronting negative impacts of them. The following paragraphs discuss each challenge one by one and recommend possible solutions. These listed challenges also guide future studies on what issues to focus on in the field of big data and come up with more effective solutions.

The first challenge is lack of understanding of what big data and its related technologies can do for company in the value creation process. Investments in big data technologies is a strategic level decision and therefore it is important that its potential firstly be clearly understood and accepted by top management and later be accepted throughout the organization with the help of top management. Similarly, organizations also do not understand how to get the most benefit from the big data technologies. It is very important that businesses understand information technology (IT) investments alone cannot bring desired effects unless these technological investments are accompanied by several complementary assets such as supportive values, organizational structures, and new behavioral patterns in the organization (Laudon and Laudon, 2020). Researches in the relevant domain states that organizations that support their IT investments with associated complementary assets (e.g., new business models, new business processes, training programs, management behavior, organizational culture) receives superior returns in contrast to the organizations that fail to do so (Laudon and Laudon, 2020). Therefore, any given company that aims to digital transform its business operations with the power of big data technologies should also plan in parallel to make necessary investments in above mentioned complementary assets. It is suggested that future studies focus on the acceptance and adoption issues of big data technologies by businesses. Most business managers are not even aware of the potential of these technologies.

The second challenge is that there exist too many big data technologies that provide innovative solutions in data storage, mining, analytics and visualization. Availability of too many options in the market initially may appear as an advantage; however, for businesses it may be confusing to make selection among many varieties of big data technologies. It is important that firms clearly define their business goals, objectives and strategies and select big data solutions which will help them to achieve their goals effectively and efficiently. That is, it is important that businesses select big data solutions that will help them to achieve their goals rather than selecting what is trendy in the market. There exist many big data consulting services and experts in the market which help business to select solutions that will help them to achieve their unique needs. Business firms are recommended to get consulting service in selecting suitable solutions before signing contract with big data service providers. It is recommended that future research should create a roadmap on how businesses should invest in big data technologies, taking into account their current and future needs.

The third challenge is related to the significant costs of deploying big data solutions in business firms. These significant costs are incurred as a result of new hardware, new software, new personnel, maintenance, new physical spaces, power, cooling, security, etc. In order to reduce costs of big data deployment process, business firms have several options. They have an option to adopt one of free and open source big data platforms. Preferring free and open source solutions will significantly reduce software licensing costs. Open source software will also allow business firms to customize software according to their specific needs. Furthermore, in free and open source software there will not be vendor lock-in issues. Vendor lock-in occurs when a customer becomes dependent on a vendor for products and services cannot easily switch to another vendor without a significant switching cost. Another way of reducing hardware, software, maintenance, personnel, and other related costs, business firms can go after cloud-enabled big data solutions instead of using on-premises solutions. Public cloud-based big data solutions enable organizations to use scalable and on-demand storage and computing resources for their analytics initiatives without incurring hardware and software costs of on-premises deployments solutions. Business firms also have an option to go after hybrid model which is another cost-effective solution in which parts of data are stored and processed in cloud and parts – on-premises. Public cloud solutions not only remove hardware and software maintenance costs but also costs of skilled labor required to manage these resources. It is recommended that future studies focus on the cost management issues of big data technologies for businesses.

The fourth challenge is that there is a worldwide shortage of professionals with data science skills. If not big companies, medium and small companies, encounter difficulties in recruiting skilled employees who can use big data technologies to meet unique needs of companies. If companies cannot easily find skilled employees in this field, one of the possible solutions is that instead of only considering searching and recruit talented employees, companies can save their time, effort and resources by taking advantage of the potential employees currently working in the company. More specifically, companies can consider setting up necessary training and development programs for employees who are eager to learn and develop new skill in data science to meet the existing gap within the company. Preferring cloud-enabled big data solutions can also eliminate existing skill gap to some extent. In cloud-enabled solutions companies do not need to install in-house hardware, software as result skilled employees required to oversee and maintain big data technologies are shifted toward cloud solution providers. It is suggested that future studies focus on training qualified personnel in the field of big data.

For businesses data security is another important challenge of big data deployment project. Big data can be considered among very valuable asset of business firms. Owning valuable data assets makes businesses open to numerous third-party attacks. Valuable and sensitive business data can be stolen and used for bad purposes. This situation will not only put businesses into difficult situation but also threatens users of their products and services. Once data breach occurs it may be very difficult or impossible to recover the situation and compensate individuals who might be adversely affected from the given event. Therefore, it is very important that businesses plan and take rigorous security measure before it is too late. Business firms should not consider security measures as a cost. Instead, they should approach it as a complementary asset which is required to derive value from big data solutions. If businesses cannot ensure big data security in-house, they can outsource these services from reliable third-party data security firms. It is suggested that future studies focus on information security and privacy issues in the field of big data.

CONCLUSION

This chapter discussed the critical role that big data plays in various types of businesses. Through real examples, this chapter showed that big data analytics enable businesses to make better and faster decisions by gaining new and useful insights from various data sources which have never used before. In this chapter, it is also shown that the amount of digital data has been growing and will continue to grow even faster, and for businesses being able to successfully analyze large data sets will become a key basis of competition. In the very near future, being able to analyze big data and being able to derive useful business insights from it will be matter of survival not an option in the highly competitive business environments. Business firms which become late to adapt themselves according to big data technologies will be gradually pushed out of market by firms which successfully adopted these technologies. Therefore, it is very important that businesses clearly understand how big data analytics can transform their business operations to be more efficient and effective, and at the same notice how big data solutions can help them to create new values for their customers. Businesses which have adopted or will adopt big data solutions should understand that as any other technologies, big data also have its own challenges. It is also important that businesses clearly understand these challenges and make sure that they are doing what they should do to address them appropriately before it become too late.

REFERENCES

Abiteboul, S. (1997). Querying semi-structured data. In *International Conference on Database Theory* (pp. 1-18). Berlin: Springer

Bag, S., Wood, L. C., Xu, L., Dhamija, P., & Kayikci, Y. (2020). Big data analytics as an operational excellence approach to enhance sustainable supply chain performance. *Resources, Conservation and Recycling*, *153*, 104559. doi:10.1016/j.resconrec.2019.104559

Forbes. (2017). *The Amazing Ways Coca Cola Uses Artificial Intelligence and Big Data To Drive Success*. Retrieved May, 2020, from https://www.forbes.com/sites/bernardmarr/2017/09/18/the-amazing-ways-coca-cola-uses-artificial-intelligence-ai-and-big-data-to-drive-success/#61b4504a78d2

Forbes. (2018). *How Much Data Do We Create Every Day? The Mind-Blowing Stats Everyone Should Read.* Retrieved May 2020, from https://www.forbes.com/sites/bernardmarr/2018/05/21/how-much-data-do-we-create-every-day-the-mind-blowing-stats-everyone-should-read/#514a5ebb60ba

Gomez-Uribe, C. A., & Hunt, N. (2015). The Netflix recommender system: Algorithms, business value, and innovation. *ACM Transactions on Management Information Systems*, *6*(4), 1–19. doi:10.1145/2843948

Gunasekaran, A., Papadopoulos, T., Dubey, R., Wamba, S. F., Childe, S. J., Hazen, B., & Akter, S. (2017). Big data and predictive analytics for supply chain and organizational performance. *Journal of Business Research*, *70*, 308–317. doi:10.1016/j.jbusres.2016.08.004

Hostler, R. E., Yoon, V. Y., Guo, Z., Guimaraes, T., & Forgionne, G. (2011). Assessing the impact of recommender agents on on-line consumer unplanned purchase behavior. *Information & Management*, *48*(8), 336–343. doi:10.1016/j.im.2011.08.002

Hurwitz, J. S., Nugent, A., Halper, F., & Kaufman, M. (2013). *Big data for dummies*. John Wiley & Sons.

Informs. (2016). *UPS On-Road Integrated Optimization and Navigation (ORION) Project*. Retrieved May 2020, from https://www.informs.org/Impact/O.R.-Analytics-Success-Stories/UPS-On-Road-Integrated-Optimization-and-Navigation-ORION-Project

Investopedia. (2020). *7 Ways Amazon Uses Big Data to Stalk You*. Retrieved May 2020, from https://www.investopedia.com/articles/insights/090716/7-ways-amazon-uses-big-data-stalk-you-amzn.asp

Laudon, K. C., & Laudon, J. P. (2020). *Management information systems: Managing the Digital Firm*. Pearson.

Medium. (2019). *Benefits of Using Big Data in Supply Chain Management*. Retrieved May 2020, from https://medium.com/@erpsolutionsoodles/benefits-of-using-big-data-in-supply-chain-management-1bcc1f6c915f

Moktadir, M. A., Dwivedi, A., Rahman, A., Chiappetta Jabbour, C. J., Paul, S. K., Sultana, R., & Madaan, J. (2020). An investigation of key performance indicators for operational excellence towards sustainability in the leather products industry. *Business Strategy and the Environment*, *29*(8), 3331–3351. doi:10.1002/bse.2575

Sestino, A., Prete, M. I., Piper, L., & Guido, G. (2020). Internet of Things and Big Data as enablers for business digitalization strategies. *Technovation*, *98*, 102173. doi:10.1016/j.technovation.2020.102173

Statista. (2020a). *Big Data Market Size Revenue Forecast Worldwide From 2011 to 2027*. Retrieved May 2020, from https://www.statista.com/statistics/254266/global-big-data-market-forecast/

Statista. (2020b). *Internet Usage Statistics: The Internet Big Picture*. Retrieved May 2020, from https://www.internetworldstats.com/stats.htm

Turban, E., Pollard, C., & Wood, G. (2018). *Information Technology for Management: On-demand Strategies for Performance, Growth and Sustainability*. John Wiley & Sons.

UPS. (2016). *ORION: The algorithm proving that left isn't right.* Retrieved May 2020, from https://www.ups.com/us/en/services/knowledge-center/article.page?kid=aa3710c2

Viet, N. Q., Behdani, B., & Bloemhof, J. (2020). Data-driven process redesign: Anticipatory shipping in agro-food supply chains. *International Journal of Production Research*, *58*(5), 1302–1318. doi:10.1080/00207543.2019.1629673

Ying, Z., Caixia, C., Wen, G., & Xiaogang, L. (2018). Impact of recommender systems on unplanned purchase behaviours in e-commerce. In *2018 5th International Conference on Industrial Engineering and Applications (ICIEA)* (pp. 21-30). IEEE. 10.1109/IEA.2018.8387066

ADDITIONAL READING

Chaves, A., Moura, Í., Bernardino, J., & Pedrosa, I. (2020). The privacy paradigm: An overview of privacy in Business Analytics and Big Data. In 2020 *15th Iberian Conference on Information Systems and Technologies (CISTI)* (pp. 1-6). IEEE.

Choo, K. K. R., & Dehghantanha, A. (2020). *Handbook of Big Data Privacy*. Springer International Publishing. doi:10.1007/978-3-030-38557-6

Marr, B. (2016). *Big data in practice: how 45 successful companies used big data analytics to deliver extraordinary results*. John Wiley & Sons. doi:10.1002/9781119278825

Marr, B. (2017). *Data strategy: How to profit from a world of big data, analytics and the internet of things*. Kogan Page Publishers.

Stephenson, D. (2018). *Big Data Demystified: How to use big data, data science and AI to make better business decisions and gain competitive advantage*. Pearson.

KEY TERMS AND DEFINITIONS

Big Data: Big data refers to the very large and diverse sets of structured, semi-structured and unstructured digital data from different sources that accumulate and grow very rapidly on continuous basis. Big data technologies enable enhanced decision making in various types of businesses.

Big Data Analytics: Big data analytics is the use of advanced analytic techniques against these huge data sets. Big data analytics enables to uncover hidden patterns, correlations and other insights from huge data sets.

Digital Transformation: Digital transformation is the process of using information systems and technologies to create entirely new or enhance existing business processes to meet changing business and market requirements.

Telematics: Telematics is a method of gathering, storing, and transmitting information about specific remote objects for tracking and reporting purposes. Telematics utilizes GPS, sensors, and other onboard diagnostics.

Chapter 13
Big Data for Digital Transformation of Public Services

Deepak Saxena
https://orcid.org/0000-0002-9331-3799
Birla Institute of Technology and Science, Pilani, India

ABSTRACT

Big data is presently considered integral to the management and strategies for digital enterprise transformation. Beyond being 'a lot of data', big data can be characterized in terms of seven Vs: volume, velocity, variety, variability, veracity, visualization, and value. Already being applied in private businesses, big data has immense potential for the digital transformation of public services in advancing the e-governance agenda. This chapter explores the nature of big data in public service and discusses its application in areas such as tax administration, transportation, energy, public health, and disaster management. Challenges and concerns are noted in terms of data quality, infrastructure cost, availability of suitable human resources, privacy, and security. Possible solutions such as shared services, cloud computing, open source software, open data framework, and regulatory compliance are noted. The chapter ends by noting future research directions to realize the full potential of Big data application in digital transformation of public services.

INTRODUCTION

Digital enterprise transformation may be defined as end-to-end value creation for the enterprise via management and application of digital technology aligned with business strategy. Big data is presently considered integral to the management and strategies for digital enterprise transformation. However, it is not entirely a new term. In the context of data and storage management, the term Big data was already in use in computing circles (e.g. Bourgoin & Smith, 1995; Mashey, 1997) even before the dawn of the new millennium. However, the term became well-known at the start of the decade when popular business research outlets such as McKinsey Global Institute (Brown, Chui, & Manyika, 2011) and Har-

DOI: 10.4018/978-1-7998-8583-2.ch013

vard Business Review (McAfee & Brynjolfsson, 2012) started publishing about it. By 2015, Gartner dropped the term from the hype cycle, noting that Big data has become so prevalent that it is now part of multiple emerging technologies (Heudecker, 2015) such as business intelligence, data science, social media analytics, enterprise information management or machine learning. The central role of Big data in digital enterprise transformation reflects in wide availability of technological solutions such as Apache Hadoop, Spark, Microsoft HDInsight, NoSQL, or Hive. In fact, Apache Hadoop has emerged as a best in-class Big data ecosystem, supporting data processing capabilities and system connectivity across heterogeneous databases and systems. However, since the focus of this chapter is on management and strategies for the transformation of digital enterprises, specific technologies are not discussed in this chapter. The interested reader is directed towards some recent works (Luengo, García-Gil, Ramírez-Gallego, García, & Herrera, 2020; Rao, Mitra, Bhatt, & Goswami, 2019) for a discussion on Big data ecosystem, technology and tools.

The key role of Big data in digital enterprise transformation and value creation may be inferred from the fact that KPMG / Harvey Nash CIO survey (2019) identifies Big data analytics as the most important (and the scarcest) skillset required in organizations. Big Data capabilities are found to be an important predictor of value creation and firm performance (Wamba, Gunasekaran, Akter, Ren, Dubey, & Childe, 2017; Mikalef, Boura, Lekakos, & Krogstie, 2019), especially in the private sector. However, the scope of Big data is not just limited to the private sector firms. Big data is frequently noted (Joseph & Johnson, 2013; Gaardboe, Svarre, & Kanstrup, 2015; Patel, Roy, Bhattacharyya, & Kim, 2017; Shukla & Mathur, 2020) as a key element in the management and strategies of digital public service transformation. This chapter explores the potential of Big data in advancing the e-Governance agenda via digital transformation of public services. Hence, the research question for this study is: *How does Big data contribute towards the digital transformation of public services?*. The research approach is exploratory in nature and thus relies on secondary data and studies. The remainder of the chapter is as follows. The next section provides a general background to Big data and outlines seven Vs that underpin the Big data revolution. This is followed by a discussion on how seven Vs are applicable to Big data in public service. Key application areas from the public service that may be transformed by Big data applications are discussed in detail. Thereafter. challenges and concerns associated with the development of Big data capabilities in the government are also noted. This is followed by offering solutions and recommendations to the problems raised earlier. Future research directions are noted before concluding the chapter.

Background

McAfee and Brynjolfsson (2012) note that Big data is more than ‘a lot of data’ owing to three key factors – Volume, Velocity and Variety – a categorization originally introduced by Laney (2001) to characterize e-Commerce data management. *Volume* refers to the generation of large chunk of data. It is estimated that the volume of digital data would be around 50 Zettabytes (1 Zettabyte equals 10^{21} bytes) in 2020, reaching a staggering 175 Zettabytes by 2025. *Velocity* refers to the speed with which data is generated. Correct and rapid processing of data in the real time has become extremely crucial for companies. For instance, Chinese retailer Alibaba processed around 544,000 orders per second on Singles day 2019. Similarly, Amazon US processed 20.2 million transactions during its Prime Day, a three-day event, in 2019. *Variety* refers to various forms of data in disparate formats that are combined to generate a holistic picture. For instance, Google collects and combines data from various sources (Android operating system, Chrome browser, Gmail, Maps, Search history, Voice, and YouTube activity to name a few) to personalize its offerings to the users.

It was soon realized that three Vs do not adequately capture the nature and potential of Big data. Noting its increasing importance, some additional Vs are suggested (Van Rijmenam, 2013; Khan, Uddin & Gupta, 2014) in relation to Big data – Variability, Veracity, Visualization, and Value. *Variability* refers to the variability in the meaning when processing natural language data. For example, the term 'great service' would differ in meaning depending on being preceded by 'got the reply within two hours' or 'still waiting for reply since last 15 days'. *Veracity* refers to the authenticity and truthfulness of the data (Rubin & Lukoianova, 2013). This is more relevant in case of unstructured data, for instance making sure that service reviews are coming from authentic users and not from automated bots. *Visualization* primarily relates to the appropriation of data as opposed to its inherent nature. Since Big data is unstructured and comes from a variety of sources, visualization of the trends helps in making sense of the vast tapestry of data. Therefore, all Big data applications include a dashboard (Pauwels, 2014) to assist top management in the decision-making. These dashboards include features like trend analysis or scenario planning, thereby extending the strategy toolbox (Woerner & Wixom, 2015). Finally, *Value* refers to the outcomes, for instance efficiency or reputational gains, made possible by Big data analytics. Beyond operational gains, however, Big data capabilities may act as an enabler of digital enterprise transformation (Dremel, Wulf, Herterich, Waizmann, & Brenner, 2017).

However, it may be noted that not all Vs are of equal importance at all times. For instance, Davenport and Dyche (2013) report that, compared to the volume alone, managing a variety of data sources in an integrated manner and developing analytical capabilities is more valuable for the companies. In contrast, managing large volume of transactions at a high velocity becomes crucial during events like Singles' Day or Black Friday sale. In this regard, Wamba et al. (2017) propose a Big Data Analytics Capability model consisting of three core areas – infrastructure flexibility, management capabilities, and personnel expertise capabilities. Big data infrastructure flexibility refers to modularity, connectivity and compatibility of various systems. Big data management capability requires planning, investment, coordination, and control of Big data resources. Finally, personnel expertise capabilities in the Big data context include technology, business and relational knowledge, along with technology management capability.

While Big data capabilities matter for all types of organizations from the perspective of digital enterprise transformation, it may be argued that not all Vs are important for all types of organizations. The factors that are significant for private companies may not exactly be the same as those relevant for digital public services. Similarly, short-term profit motive of the private sector is usually less relevant for public services that focus on creating public value (Saxena & McDonagh, 2019) in the long run. Next section highlights these differences and discusses how Big data may propel digital transformation of public service across diverse domains.

BIG DATA IN PUBLIC SERVICE

This section begins by outlining the nature of big data in public service by highlighting how seven Vs noted earlier relate to the government and public service. This is followed by discussion on public service applications from diverse areas such as tax administration, transportation, energy, public health, and disaster management. Thereafter challenges and concerns associated with Big data applications in the public service are discussed.

Nature of Big Data in Public Service

Mergel, Rethemeyer, and Isett (2016) define Big data for the public affairs as *high volume data that frequently combines highly structured administrative data actively collected by public sector organizations with continuously and automatically collected structured and unstructured real-time data that are often passively created by public and private entities through their Internet interactions* (p. 931). This definition touches upon many Vs discussed earlier. With help of specific examples, this section notes how each V relates to public services.

Volume

Governments usually deal with entire population for many departments such as revenue or social security. Public service data tends to be exhaustive (Kitchin, 2014) as compared to their private sector counterparts who have the liberty of focusing only on their intended customer base. With the exception of global corporate giants such as Amazon, Google or Facebook, the data processed by populous countries such as China, India or US easily surpasses the volume of data processed by companies.

Velocity

Depending on the time of the year, public systems may need to deal with very high velocity of data. There are often reports of tax systems being overloaded closer to the deadline of tax assessment and filing. As another example, the Covid-19 pandemic provides multiple instances of such high velocity data – from testing results to contact tracing, and registration for unemployment payments – that need to be quickly processed by the public services.

Variety

This is perhaps the most crucial element for the Big data for public services. Government systems collect data from a wide variety of sources at various levels (city level to federal government level), across departments (from health to education to agriculture) and across diverse systems. Enormous amount of data is stored in silos (Kim, Trimi, & Chung, 2014; Rajagopalan & Vellaipandiyan, 2013) across numerous systems within the government with data integration being a main challenge. Goldstein (2019) suggests that, owing to the variety of data being stored and processed by the governments, data lakes are a useful strategy for Big data utilization in public services. As opposed to data warehousing that relies on structured data, data lakes allow for centralized storage of any type of structured and unstructured data in raw form. This is a crucial requirement for public services since different government departments often find it difficult to agree upon their data needs.

Variability

Traditionally, governments used to collect opinions and suggestions from the interest groups by meeting with their representatives or by inviting suggestions. Social media has given them a great tool for not only directly interacting with the public, but also acting as a barometer of public reaction (Mergel et al., 2016) to a policy announcement. While the governments are yet to formally adopt this approach, scholars have already conducted sentiment analysis on key government decisions (Singh, Sawhney, & Kahlon, 2018) and citizen involvement with local government (Zavattaro, French, & Mohanty, 2015). With the growing importance of public opinion on the social media, it is an imperative that governments include social media sentiment analysis in their consideration.

Veracity

Quite often, the fraud with the government services (tax evasion, for example) happen due to the siloed nature of government data. To curb this tendency, governments have moved towards joined-up governance (Klievink & Janssen, 2009; Carey & Crammond, 2015) to ensure the veracity and consistency of data across departments. This is often done by linking the data via national identity mechanisms such as Social Security Number is the US, National Insurance Number in the UK, and Aadhaar in India. Once again, this takes us back to the variety element of the Big data, making it the most important factor in utilizing Big data in government.

Visualization

Since the data in Big data is often in unstructured form, possibly the most profound application of Big data is visualization (Davenport & Dyche, 2013) to aid in decision-making. Leaders in the government are often short on time and need condensed information to make quick decisions. For instance, Geographical Information Systems (GIS) and mapping data may be used to visualize the distribution of resources or requirements across the country. Such data visualization would help the leaders in quickly understanding the situation and taking evidence-based policy decisions (Höchtl, Parycek, & Schöllhammer, 2016).

Value

Value is the desired outcome of the Big data application and processing (Van Rijmenam, 2013; Khan et al., 2014). While the notion of value is often captured in terms of greater efficiency and increased revenue for private businesses, the notion of public value is more complex. Economic logic, such as cost savings or increased economic activity, is still applicable (Munné, 2016) to public services. However, public agencies also need to cater for equity and effectiveness (Boyle, 2006) apart from economic efficiency, for instance in deciding the location of schools to ensure accessible education. In addition, public agencies may also need collated Big data from different sources to fulfill the auditing requirements.

Big Data Applications in Public Service

To illustrate to potential of Big data in public service, this section discusses various Big data applications with illustrative examples from around the globe. These applications include, but not limited to, areas such as tax administration, transportation, energy, public health, and disaster management.

Tax Administration

Taxes, especially indirect taxes, form the core of government revenue. However, there is always some gap between expected tax liabilities and actual taxes paid. Internal Revenue Service (2019) estimates that gross annual tax gap in US during 2011-13 was more than $440 billion, around 16.4 percent of the taxes due. In contrast, that the tax gap in UK (HMRC, 2018) for 2017-18 was around £35 billion or 5.6 percent of taxes due. A major reason for the relative efficiency of the UK tax authorities is the use of Big data. Big data helps them in two major ways. First, they collate data from data aggregators and merchant service providers, including those from overseas. This way they can triangulate the sales and revenue data furnished by the companies and infer any relationships between the entities. Second, UK authorities identify high risk individuals and companies based on tax data analytics. Similar exercise is being conducted by Australian taxation office (Walker-Munro, 2020) that is developing a Big data network analytics solution called ANGIE to identity multi-layer complex relationship between its clients, in order to assist its tax avoidance taskforce. Atanasijević, Jakovetić, Krejić, Krklec-Jerinkić and Marković (2019) also report a similar project in the Republic of Serbia that employs Big data analytics (based on the weighted norm distance between the average income distribution of the industry sectors and the income distribution of the business) to identify low-risk and high-risk entities. High risk entities are then investigated further to ensure that there is no tax evasion or fraud (Campbell, 2014).

Transportation

Big data can be used for the management of intelligent transport for efficient public services. This is applicable both to the freight transport and public transport. The area of freight transport is no longer applicable only to the big companies like Amazon or DHL, it has become equally important for the governments across the world, for instance in planning and tracking medical supplies amid the coronavirus pandemic. Reflecting the variety element of Big data, data from the GPS trackers, satellite, sensors, and mobile devices (Zhu, Yu, Wang, Ying, & Tang, 2018) can be used to plan and optimize the route as well as for real-time tracking of the shipments. In the area of public transport, public service utilities may apply big data for operational improvements as well as for strategic planning. For instance, *HTM Personenvervoer*, a tram operator from Hague in Netherlands, uses smartcard data to predict ridership behavior and to plan the services across the tram network (Van Oort & Cats, 2015). At the operational level, *Stockholmstag*, the train operator in Stockholm in Sweden, uses Big data to ensure the reliability of its service (Kepes, 2015). The system forecasts and visualizes the train operations for next two hours. If it detects any potential delays (e.g. a train is delayed between stations X and Y, thereby introducing delay at station Z), it alerts the operator. To ensure the reliability of the service, a new train is then introduced from station Z so that there are no delays for the passengers waiting at the station. Heaphy (2019) reports similar application in Irish capital Dublin, where Dublin Bus services use visualization tools based on a variety of data – bus timetables, GPS-based vehicle location, CCTV footage, smartcard scans – to drill down on specific issues and offer traffic-calming measures to reduce congestion. Apart from traditional transport means, Big data analytics may play a crucial role in providing electric mobility as a service (Jnr, Petersen, Ahlers, & Krogstie, 2020), by allowing for the sharing of high velocity data on electric vehicles and the utilization of charging infrastructure in smart cities. Apart from the improvement in transport service delivery, such initiatives would also contribute towards the sustainability of the planet. With the advent of self-driving cars in the future, the importance of Big data in transport would become more important than ever.

Energy

Big data could be an enabler of intelligent energy management. Zhou, Fu, and Yang (2016) discuss the application of Big data across energy lifecycle – power generation, power transmission, power distribution, and demand side management. Based on the data collected from power grid equipment, GIS data, weather data etc., power generation companies run simulations and forecast power requirements. At times, they need more complex simulation for load balancing if they generate power from diverse sources (e.g. coal, nuclear, hydro or wind energy). During power transmission and distribution, data collected from sensors may be used for fault detection, electric device health monitoring, predictive maintenance, and power quality monitoring (Zhang, Huang, & Bompard, 2018). In situations where granular data is not available or customer privacy is prioritized, big data may still be used to generate clusters (Ushakova & Mikhaylov, 2020) for efficient energy management. At the same time, Big data also enables effective demand-side management primarily via smart meters. Smart meters provide feedback to the end users on their energy consumption so that they can adjust their usage. Italy provides the best example of the smart metering system installed by the state-controlled energy provider *Enel* (now rebranded as *e-distribuzione*). These meters provide data on daily, weekly, and monthly usage and help the consumers in reducing cost and the power company in increasing efficiency. Italy is well-ahead of the curve and has commenced the installation of second-generation smart meters (Stagnaro & Leoni, 2019) that would provide more real-time data to the consumers and make the process more interactive. Among Scandinavian nations, Sweden and Finland are also gearing up for the rollout of second-generation smart meters in 2021.

Public Health

Big data in healthcare (Pastorino et al., 2019) can include data from wearable devices, electronic health records, patient summaries, pharmaceutical data, telemedicine, health apps, social media, and socio-economic indicators, among others. Big data in healthcare can be used at multiple levels. At the clinical level, patient summary and electronic health records can provide an aid to the doctors for predicting the onset of disease and in designing the most appropriate treatment for a patient. Moreover, wearable devices contribute towards the patient-centered health monitoring to facilitate self-management of the chronic health condition (Chiauzzi, Rodarte & DasMahapatra, 2015), also supporting social distancing during the coronavirus pandemic. Big data also helps in patient-centered design in healthcare. For instance, MARIO project from Ireland has developed caring service robots for older people with dementia. With customized applications and user interface, the service robot helps the patients in fighting loneliness and isolation. At the institutional level, Big data can help is effective planning and cost optimization by using predictive analysis on disease occurrence and patient treatment. The eHealth project from Estonia has digitalized the patient information and prescriptions, thereby developing high-quality health services based on data and process analytics. However, the biggest application of Big data is apparent in the monitoring and surveillance of infectious disease (Hay, George, Moyes & Brownstein, 2013) such as the coronavirus pandemic that started in late 2019. Disease data can be clubbed with other environmental variables (e.g. population density, people movement, average age) to prepare a real-time map of the spread of the disease and to prepare containment strategies. Although having some privacy concerns, China (Health Code app) and Ireland (Covid Tracker app) have successfully used location-infection data and have applied Big data analytics to alert its population and public health officials on the spread of the disease. Moreover, Big data may also help in preventing further outbreaks. For instance, Chen et al (2020) report a case in Taiwan where a Covid-19 patient was identified based on their travel history, even before they could enter the general hospital.

Disaster Management

Apart from ongoing coronavirus crisis, there is always a possibility of natural and man-made disasters such as earthquake, flood or fire. A key element of effective disaster management is the availability of accurate and timely information (Akter & Wamba, 2019). Once a disaster occurs, emergency teams are often saddled with a barrage of information from multiple sources such as – telephone calls, news footage, social media posts, and satellite images. In this situation, Big data analytics may facilitate timely and targeted response. In the past, satellite images and GIS mapping have been used post-facto to delineate affected areas. However, with the ubiquitous availability of geolocation data and social media posts, Big data analytics can help in providing a real-time picture of the ongoing disaster, for instance in locating areas that require immediate assistance and identifying roads that are still approachable. Moreover, open source platforms like Ushahidi or OpenStreetMap allow volunteers across the world to pool data and capabilities to map the disaster in real time. Such form of crowdsourcing has been used, for instance, during earthquakes in Haiti (Norheim-Hagtun & Meier, 2010) and Nepal (Poiani, Rocha, Degrossi & Albuquerque, 2016), and flood relief in India (Anbalagan & Valliyammai, 2016). Once the disaster is over, machine learning can be applied on the Big data to accurately predict the next hotspots of fire or flood. For instance, analyzing data from three different sources, Dutta, Das and Aryal (2016) provide highly accurate (around 91 percent accuracy) estimate on bush-fire incidence in Australia. Such estimates can be used in planning early evacuation and mitigation. Thus, Big data analysis can help both in real-time response as well as in predictive planning.

Challenges and Concerns

While there is immense potential of Big data for the for digital transformation of public service, its management and strategic use is not without challenges. Across the domains outlined above, four key challenges could be identified for Big data application in the public service context.

Data Quality

A lot of historical data in public agencies is either in non-digital format (e.g. printouts, hardbound reports) or in cumbersome digital formats (e.g. scans). Even when digital data is present in information systems, it often exists in silos (Kim et al., 2014; Rajagopalan & Vellaipandiyan, 2013) across different units/departments. Consequently, there is little consistency and structure across disparate systems in the government (Joseph & Johnson, 2013). Data ownership may also become an issue (Pradhan & Shakya, 2018) if a system links dataset from different departments. Moreover, there is often resistance from public services in changing their legacy systems and data formats, further complicating Big data integration.

Infrastructure Costs

Due to technological limitations, quite often the most efficient way for the public service is to build state of the art infrastructure from scratch to support Big data applications. Hence, there is often a huge upfront infrastructure cost (Joseph & Johnson, 2013; Pradhan & Shakya, 2018) in terms of systems, servers, network, and data warehousing. Due to political urgency of other functions, government may not be interested in investing much in information technology. For instance, coronavirus crisis has resulted in budget deficits, with an increasing focus on investment in health and social services. However, as noted earlier, in the long term, investment in Big data infrastructure would be useful for public health in terms of disease tracing and epidemiological management.

Human Resource

Big data is not just about technology – one also needs skilled data scientists to make full use of the data. Due to their limited exposure of public service systems, outside consultants are often not able to appreciate the complexity and subtlety of government data. At the same time, there is often a lack of technological expertise in public service agencies. Due to inflexible nature of the hiring and salary scale, public agencies often find it difficult to attract suitable human resources (Pradhan & Shakya, 2018; Sarker, Hossin, Frimpong, & Xiaohua, 2018) with relevant information technology skills. The problem is exacerbated for Big data capabilities since finding human resources with relevant skillset is reported (KPMG, 2019) as a key issue even for the private sector. Taken together, limited domain knowledge among consultants and a lack of technological capabilities in government departments, create a barrier in the exploitation of Big data in public service.

Privacy and Security

Key benefits of Big data emerge from the standardization and integration of a variety of data sources. For public service agencies, this often means collecting and collating data on its citizens. This results in some privacy concerns in terms of potential state surveillance and right to privacy. For instance, Walker-Munro (2020) discusses concerns associated with privacy, inaccuracy, opacity and bias associated with Big data driven tax administration in Australia. Similar concerns are often raised on the Aadhaar project from India in terms of its failure to protect the privacy of its citizens (Dixon, 2017), especially when analyzed from the point of view of privacy frameworks in the west. Security of Big data is also an issue (Kitchin, 2016) since there is always a risk of hacking of government data. In fact, a rationale often advanced by government departments for not integrating their datasets with other departments is that it may undermine the security of their own database.

SOLUTIONS AND RECOMMENDATIONS

For any system, there would always be a tradeoff between the gains and the risks of using the system. Despite the challenges and concerns noted earlier, the benefits of Big data utilization in public service are manifold and potentially outweigh the risks. This section outlines some solutions and recommendations that may be adopted to ease the concerns and to mitigate the challenges of Big data management in public service transformation.

Shared Services

Considering the infrastructure cost, public agencies may invest in developing shared services (Richter & Brühl, 2020) that provide common service (e.g. human resources, payroll, citizen interface) across public agencies. For instance, Estonian public authorities are using two shared services – one for county councils and the other for central government – that have resulted in overall cost savings (Tammel, 2017) for the government. The shared services model may be applied to Big data management in government. This also aligns with the vision of Big data as an integrated data application. This may take the form of an autonomous public data agency that would benefit from resource pooling and would be able to attract suitable human resources with required competencies.

Cloud Computing

Recently, software firms have moved from providing from software-as-a-product to software-as-a-service. Moreover, the infrastructure is also being provided as a service over the internet. Taken together, this trend is marketed as cloud computing model for providing information systems services, including Big data (Lnenicka & Komarkova, 2019; Yang, Huang, Li, Liu & Hu, 2017). Adoption of cloud computing has the benefits of higher efficiency (since the processing is optimized at the level of the vendor) and lower cost (since many clients share the services provided by the cloud vendor). Moreover, cloud vendors heavily invest on the security of the system so that they do not loose their market due to possible security breaches. However, since the services are shared across clients, there is very little room for the customization. Hence, public agencies may use this architecture mainly for the services that are standard across departments, such as payroll or human resource management.

Open Source/Data

If a public agency wishes to have the in-house implementation requiring a high degree of customization, it may use open source Big data frameworks (Davenport & Dyche, 2013) such as Apache Hadoop, Cassandra or MongoDB. Moreover, using open source platforms allows for crowdsourcing (Anbalagan & Valliyammai, 2016; Norheim-Hagtun & Meier, 2010; Poiani et al., 2016) in areas such as disaster management or in public health management. In fact, now there is an increasing movement towards open data in government (Bertot, Gorham, Jaeger, Sarin & Choi, 2014) where public agencies share standardized datasets not only with other public agencies but also with the general population. Provision of open data helps towards fulfilling the obligations under the Freedom of Information acts enacted in various countries. This may also completement the cloud computing initiatives (Lnenicka & Komarkova, 2019) discussed earlier.

Regulatory Compliance

Irrespective of the solutions used, a key requirement for public agencies is regulatory compliance (Walker-Munro, 2020) in terms of government audit and towards ensuring the privacy of its citizens. Frameworks like *General Data Protection Regulation* in the European Union or *Australian Privacy Principles* support public agencies in ensuring regulatory compliance. In fact, such regulations may indirectly support the cause of Big data as data formats need to be standardized to fulfil regulatory requirements. This would, for instance, involve structuring data according to its sensitivity and implementing privacy preserving techniques (Gruschka, Mavroeidis, Vishi & Jensen, 2018) as per regulations. Such privacy preserving techniques would not only ensure Big data integration in a legally accepted way, it would also help in accurate data mining (Chamikara, Bertók, Liu, Camtepe & Khalil, 2020).

FUTURE RESEARCH DIRECTIONS

Based on the recommendations, there are two distinct research directions that apply to the management and application of Big data in public service transformation. The first direction relates to research on management strategies and architectural approaches (for instance, use of shared services and cloud computing) to exploit the potential of Big data in government. While a lot of evidence is available from the private sector on providing shared services, research in public sector is required in view of their specific institutional context. Second research direction relates to the variety element of Big data. There is a need for the development of open data standards and sharing protocols for linking the variety of data sources (e.g. formal report, quantitative data, textual data, social media data, sensors, maps, speech, video, crowdsourced data etc.) applicable to public services in a privacy preserving manner. This would support the cause of Big data integration without compromising the privacy of the citizens.

CONCLUSION

Big data is being widely utilized in the private sector to support the management and strategies for digital enterprise transformation. This chapter notes the potential of Big data for digital transformation of public services. Seven Vs of Big data are discussed in the context of public service, noting that volume and variety are perhaps more crucial for public service than the velocity alone. Big data applications from the area of tax administration, transportation, energy, public health, and disaster management, are discussed with relevant examples from across the globe. However, there are also challenges associated with data quality, infrastructure cost, availability of suitable human resources, privacy and security. These challenges can be mitigated with initiatives such as shared services, cloud computing, open source software, open data framework, and regulatory compliance. For these initiatives to be successful, future research should focus upon Big data management strategies and architectural approaches, along with the development of open data standards and sharing protocols in privacy preserving manner. This would allow the governments to realize the full potential of Big data application in digital transformation of public services.

ACKNOWLEDGMENT

This research received no specific grant from any funding agency in the public, commercial, or not-for-profit sectors.

REFERENCES

Akter, S., & Wamba, S. F. (2019). Big data and disaster management: A systematic review and agenda for future research. *Annals of Operations Research, 283*(1-2), 939–959. doi:10.100710479-017-2584-2

Anbalagan, B., & Valliyammai, C. (2016, December). #ChennaiFloods: Leveraging Human and Machine Learning for Crisis Mapping during Disasters Using Social Media. In *2016 IEEE 23rd International Conference on High Performance Computing Workshops (HiPCW)* (pp. 50-59). IEEE.

Atanasijević, J., Jakovetić, D., Krejić, N., Krklec-Jerinkić, N., & Marković, D. (2019). Using big data analytics to improve efficiency of tax collection in the tax Administration of the Republic of Serbia. *Ekonomika Preduzeća, 67*(1-2), 115–130. doi:10.5937/EkoPre1808115A

Bertot, J. C., Gorham, U., Jaeger, P. T., Sarin, L. C., & Choi, H. (2014). Big data, open government and e-government: Issues, policies and recommendations. *Information Polity, 19*(1, 2), 5-16.

Bourgoin, M. O., & Smith, S. J. (1995). *Big data—Better Returns, Leveraging Your Hidden Data Assets to Improve ROI. In Artificial Intelligence in the Capital Markets.* Probus Publishing Company.

Boyle, R. (2006). *Measuring public sector productivity: lessons from international experience.* CPMR Discussion Paper 35. Institute of Public Administration.

Brown, B., Chui, M., & Manyika, J. (2011). Are you ready for the era of 'big data'? *The McKinsey Quarterly, 4*(1), 24–35.

Campbell, N. (2014). Tax Policy and Administration in an Era of Big data. *Tax Planning International, 12*(12), 2–6.

Carey, G., & Crammond, B. (2015). What works in joined-up government? An evidence synthesis. *International Journal of Public Administration, 38*(13-14), 1020–1029. doi:10.1080/01900692.2014.982292

Chamikara, M. A. P., Bertók, P., Liu, D., Camtepe, S., & Khalil, I. (2020). Efficient privacy preservation of big data for accurate data mining. *Information Sciences, 527*, 420–443. doi:10.1016/j.ins.2019.05.053

Chen, F. M., Feng, M. C., Chen, T. C., Hsieh, M. H., Kuo, S. H., Chang, H. L., Yang, C. J., & Chen, Y. H. (2020). Big data integration and analytics to prevent a potential hospital outbreak of COVID-19 in Taiwan. *Journal of Microbiology, Immunology, and Infection.* Advance online publication. doi:10.1016/j.jmii.2020.04.010 PMID:32327328

Chiauzzi, E., Rodarte, C., & DasMahapatra, P. (2015). Patient-centered activity monitoring in the self-management of chronic health conditions. *BMC Medicine, 13*(1), 77. doi:10.118612916-015-0319-2 PMID:25889598

Davenport, T. H., & Dyché, J. (2013). *Big data in big companies.* International Institute for Analytics.

Dixon, P. (2017). A Failure to "Do No Harm"—India's Aadhaar biometric ID program and its inability to protect privacy in relation to measures in Europe and the US. *Health and Technology, 7*(4), 539–567. doi:10.100712553-017-0202-6 PMID:29308348

Dremel, C., Wulf, J., Herterich, M. M., Waizmann, J. C., & Brenner, W. (2017). How AUDI AG Established Big data Analytics in Its Digital Transformation. *MIS Quarterly Executive*, *16*(2), 81–100.

Dutta, R., Das, A., & Aryal, J. (2016). Big data integration shows Australian bush-fire frequency is increasing significantly. *Royal Society Open Science*, *3*(2), 150241. doi:10.1098/rsos.150241 PMID:26998312

Gaardboe, R., Svarre, T., & Kanstrup, A. M. (2015). Characteristics of business intelligence and big data in e-government: Preliminary findings. *Innovation and the Public Sector*, 109.

Goldstein, P. (2019). *Data Lakes: What They Are and How They Can Benefit Feds.* Retrieved from https://fedtechmagazine.com/article/2019/01/data-lakes-what-they-are-and-how-they-can-benefit-feds-perfcon

Gruschka, N., Mavroeidis, V., Vishi, K., & Jensen, M. (2018, December). Privacy issues and data protection in big data: a case study analysis under GDPR. In *2018 IEEE International Conference on Big data* (pp. 5027-5033). IEEE. 10.1109/BigData.2018.8622621

Hay, S. I., George, D. B., Moyes, C. L., & Brownstein, J. S. (2013). Big data opportunities for global infectious disease surveillance. *PLoS Medicine*, *10*(4), e1001413. doi:10.1371/journal.pmed.1001413 PMID:23565065

Heaphy, L. (2019). Data ratcheting and data-driven organisational change in transport. *Big Data & Society*, *6*(2), 1–12. doi:10.1177/2053951719867359

Heudecker, N. (2015). *Big data Isn't Obsolete. It's Normal.* Retrieved from https://blogs.gartner.com/nick-heudecker/big-data-is-now-normal/

HMRC. (2019). *Tax gap remains low.* Retrieved from https://www.gov.uk/government/news/tax-gap-remains-low

Höchtl, J., Parycek, P., & Schöllhammer, R. (2016). Big data in the policy cycle: Policy decision making in the digital era. *Journal of Organizational Computing and Electronic Commerce*, *26*(1-2), 147–169. doi:10.1080/10919392.2015.1125187

Internal Revenue Service. (2019). *The Tax Gap.* Retrieved from https://www.irs.gov/newsroom/the-tax-gap

Jnr, B. A., Petersen, S. A., Ahlers, D., & Krogstie, J. (2020). Big data driven multi-tier architecture for electric mobility as a service in smart cities. *International Journal of Energy Sector Management.* . doi:10.1108/IJESM-08-2019-0001

Joseph, R. C., & Johnson, N. A. (2013). Big data and transformational government. *IT Professional*, *15*(6), 43–48. doi:10.1109/MITP.2013.61

Kepes, B. (2015). *How big data predicts and helps prevent train delays in Sweden.* Retrieved from https://www.networkworld.com/article/2982447/how-big-data-predicts-and-helps-prevent-train-delays-in-sweden.html

Khan, M. A., Uddin, M. F., & Gupta, N. (2014, April). Seven V's of Big data understanding Big data to extract value. In *Proceedings of the 2014 zone 1 conference of the American Society for Engineering Education* (pp. 1-5). IEEE. 10.1109/ASEEZone1.2014.6820689

Kim, G. H., Trimi, S., & Chung, J. H. (2014). Big-data applications in the government sector. *Communications of the ACM, 57*(3), 78–85. doi:10.1145/2500873

Kitchin, R. (2014). *The data revolution: Big data, open data, data infrastructures and their consequences.* Sage.

Kitchin, R. (2016). Getting smarter about smart cities: Improving data privacy and data security. Data Protection Unit, Department of the Taoiseach, Dublin, Ireland.

Klievink, B., & Janssen, M. (2009). Realizing joined-up government—Dynamic capabilities and stage models for transformation. *Government Information Quarterly, 26*(2), 275–284. doi:10.1016/j.giq.2008.12.007

KPMG. (2019). *Harvey Nash/KPMG CIO Survey – A Changing Perspective.* Retrieved from https://home.kpmg/xx/en/home/insights/2019/06/harvey-nash-kpmg-cio-survey-2019.html

Laney, D. (2001). *Application delivery strategies.* META Group.

Lnenicka, M., & Komarkova, J. (2019). Developing a government enterprise architecture framework to support the requirements of big and open linked data with the use of cloud computing. *International Journal of Information Management, 46*, 124–141. doi:10.1016/j.ijinfomgt.2018.12.003

Luengo, J., García-Gil, D., Ramírez-Gallego, S., García, S., & Herrera, F. (2020). *Big Data Preprocessing: Enabling Smart Data.* Springer Nature. doi:10.1007/978-3-030-39105-8

Mashey, J. R. (1997, October). *Big data... And the next wave of infrastress.* Paper presented in Computer Science Division Seminar, University of California, Berkeley, CA.

McAfee, A., Brynjolfsson, E., Davenport, T. H., Patil, D. J., & Barton, D. (2012). Big data: The management revolution. *Harvard Business Review, 90*(10), 60–68. PMID:23074865

Mergel, I., Rethemeyer, R. K., & Isett, K. (2016). Big data in public affairs. *Public Administration Review, 76*(6), 928–937. doi:10.1111/puar.12625

Mikalef, P., Boura, M., Lekakos, G., & Krogstie, J. (2019). Big data analytics and firm performance: Findings from a mixed-method approach. *Journal of Business Research, 98*, 261–276. doi:10.1016/j.jbusres.2019.01.044

Munné, R. (2016). Big data in the public sector. In New horizons for a data-driven economy: a roadmap for usage and exploitation of big data in Europe (pp. 195-208). London: Springer Open. doi:10.1007/978-3-319-21569-3_11

Norheim-Hagtun, I., & Meier, P. (2010). Crowdsourcing for crisis mapping in Haiti. *Innovations: Technology, Governance, Globalization, 5*(4), 81–89. doi:10.1162/INOV_a_00046

Pastorino, R., De Vito, C., Migliara, G., Glocker, K., Binenbaum, I., Ricciardi, W., & Boccia, S. (2019). Benefits and challenges of Big data in healthcare: An overview of the European initiatives. *European Journal of Public Health, 29*(Supplement_3), 23–27. doi:10.1093/eurpub/ckz168 PMID:31738444

Patel, B., Roy, S., Bhattacharyya, D., & Kim, T. H. (2017). Necessity of big data and analytics for good e-governance. *International Journal of Grid and Distributed Computing*, *10*(8), 11–20. doi:10.14257/ijgdc.2017.10.8.02

Pauwels, K. (2014). *It's Not the Size of the Data—it's how You Use it: Smarter Marketing with Analytics and Dashboards*. Amacom.

Poiani, T. H., dos Santos Rocha, R., Degrossi, L. C., & de Albuquerque, J. P. (2016, January). Potential of collaborative mapping for disaster relief: A case study of OpenStreetMap in the Nepal earthquake 2015. In *2016 49th Hawaii International Conference on System Sciences (HICSS)* (pp. 188-197). IEEE 10.1109/HICSS.2016.31

Pradhan, P., & Shakya, S. (2018). Big data Challenges for e-Government Services in Nepal. *Journal of the Institute of Engineering*, *14*(1), 216–222. doi:10.3126/jie.v14i1.20087

Rajagopalan, M. R., & Vellaipandiyan, S. (2013, November). Big data framework for national e-governance plan. In *2013 Eleventh International Conference on ICT and Knowledge Engineering* (pp. 1-5). IEEE. 10.1109/ICTKE.2013.6756283

Rao, T. R., Mitra, P., Bhatt, R., & Goswami, A. (2019). The big data system, components, tools, and technologies: A survey. *Knowledge and Information Systems*, *60*(3), 1165–1245. doi:10.100710115-018-1248-0

Richter, P. C., & Brühl, R. (2020). Ahead of the game: Antecedents for the success of shared service centers. *European Management Journal*, *38*(3), 477–488. doi:10.1016/j.emj.2019.10.006

Rubin, V., & Lukoianova, T. (2013). Veracity roadmap: Is big data objective, truthful and credible? *Advances in Classification Research Online*, *24*(1), 4.

Sarker, M. N. I., Hossin, M. A., Frimpong, A. N. K., & Xiaohua, Y. (2018, August). Promoting information resource management for e-government through big data approach. In *Proceedings of the 2018 International Conference on Information Management & Management Science* (pp. 99-104). 10.1145/3277139.3277155

Saxena, D., & McDonagh, J. (2019). Evaluating ERP implementations: The case for a lifecycle-based interpretive approach. *Electronic Journal of Information Systems Evaluation*, *22*(1), 29–37.

Shukla, P. S., & Mathur, M. (2020). Conceptualizing the Role of Data Analytics and Technology in E-Governance: An Insight. *International Journal of Business Analytics*, *7*(2), 1–12. doi:10.4018/IJBAN.2020040101

Singh, P., Sawhney, R. S., & Kahlon, K. S. (2018). Sentiment analysis of demonetization of 500 & 1000 rupee banknotes by Indian government. *ICT Express*, *4*(3), 124–129. doi:10.1016/j.icte.2017.03.001

Stagnaro, C., & Leoni, I. B. (2019). Second-generation smart meter roll-out in Italy: A cost-benefit analysis. Paper presented in Eurelectric Power Summit 2019, Florence, Italy.

Tammel, K. (2017). Shared services and cost reduction motive in the public sector. *International Journal of Public Administration*, *40*(9), 792–804. doi:10.1080/01900692.2016.1204617

Ushakova, A., & Mikhaylov, S. J. (2020). Big data to the rescue? Challenges in analysing granular household electricity consumption in the United Kingdom. *Energy Research & Social Science*, *64*, 101428. doi:10.1016/j.erss.2020.101428

Van Oort, N., & Cats, O. (2015, September). Improving public transport decision making, planning and operations by using big data: Cases from Sweden and the Netherlands. In *2015 IEEE 18th international conference on intelligent transportation systems* (pp. 19-24). IEEE. 10.1109/ITSC.2015.11

Van Rijmenam, M. (2013). *Why the 3v's are not sufficient to describe big data.* Retrieved from https:// datafloq.com/read/3vs-sufficient-describe-big-data/166

Walker-Munro, B. (2020). Use of Big Data Analytics by Tax Authorities. In M. Jackson & M. Shelly (Eds.), *Legal Regulations, Implications, and Issues Surrounding Digital Data* (pp. 86–110). IGI Global. doi:10.4018/978-1-7998-3130-3.ch005

Wamba, S. F., Gunasekaran, A., Akter, S., Ren, S. J. F., Dubey, R., & Childe, S. J. (2017). Big data analytics and firm performance: Effects of dynamic capabilities. *Journal of Business Research*, *70*, 356–365. doi:10.1016/j.jbusres.2016.08.009

Woerner, S. L., & Wixom, B. H. (2015). Big data: Extending the business strategy toolbox. *Journal of Information Technology*, *30*(1), 60–62. doi:10.1057/jit.2014.31

Yang, C., Huang, Q., Li, Z., Liu, K., & Hu, F. (2017). Big data and cloud computing: Innovation opportunities and challenges. *International Journal of Digital Earth*, *10*(1), 13–53. doi:10.1080/17538947.2016.1239771

Zavattaro, S. M., French, P. E., & Mohanty, S. D. (2015). A sentiment analysis of US local government tweets: The connection between tone and citizen involvement. *Government Information Quarterly*, *32*(3), 333–341. doi:10.1016/j.giq.2015.03.003

Zhang, Y., Huang, T., & Bompard, E. F. (2018). Big data analytics in smart grids: A review. *Energy Informatics*, *1*(1), 8. doi:10.118642162-018-0007-5

Zhou, K., Fu, C., & Yang, S. (2016). Big data driven smart energy management: From big data to big insights. *Renewable & Sustainable Energy Reviews*, *56*, 215–225. doi:10.1016/j.rser.2015.11.050

Zhu, L., Yu, F. R., Wang, Y., Ning, B., & Tang, T. (2018). Big data analytics in intelligent transportation systems: A survey. *IEEE Transactions on Intelligent Transportation Systems*, *20*(1), 383–398. doi:10.1109/TITS.2018.2815678

ADDITIONAL READING

Baig, A., Cadena, A., Chui, M., & Dua, A. (2014). *Innovation in local government: Open data and information technology*. McKinsey & Company.

Cavanillas, J. M., Curry, E., & Wahlster, W. (Eds.). (2016). *New horizons for a data-driven economy: a roadmap for usage and exploitation of big data in Europe*. Springer. doi:10.1007/978-3-319-21569-3

Dey, N., & Tamane, S. (2019). *Big data Analytics for Smart and Connected Cities*. IGI Global. doi:10.4018/978-1-5225-6207-8

Information Resources Management Association. (2016). *Big data: concepts, methodologies, tools, and applications*. IGI Global.

Radnor, Z. J., Bateman, N., Esain, A., Kumar, M., Williams, S. J., & Upton, D. M. (Eds.). (2015). *Public service operations management: A research handbook*. Routledge. doi:10.4324/9781315747972

Sandhu, K. (Ed.). (2019). *Leadership, Management, and Adoption Techniques for Digital Service Innovation*. IGI Global.

Sun, Z. (Ed.). (2019). *Managerial Perspectives on Intelligent Big data Analytics*. IGI Global. doi:10.4018/978-1-5225-7277-0

KEY TERMS AND DEFINITIONS

Big Data: Datasets characterized by Volume, Velocity, Variety, Variability, Veracity, Visualization, and Value.

Digital Enterprise Transformation: End-to-end value creation for the enterprise via the management and application of digital technology aligned with business strategy.

E-Governance: Application of digital technology for the purpose of efficient, effective, and responsive public governance.

Enterprise: An organizational entity with a definite objectives, scopes, and operational rules. An enterprise focus may be conducting a business or providing public services.

Management: The set of principles and actions geared toward implementing the strategy to attain the objectives of the enterprise.

Public Service: Essential service (e.g., health, electricity, law and order), that are required by the citizens for proper functioning of the society.

Strategy: A long term direction outlining the value proposition and growth of the enterprise to attain its objective.

Value: Intended outcomes, for instance efficiency or reputational gains, made possible by Big data analytics.

Variability: Variation in the meaning when processing natural language data.

Variety: Various forms of data in disparate formats.

Velocity: The speed with which data is generated.

Visualization: Visual interpretation of data and analysis to assist in decision-making.

Volume: Amount of data generated.

Chapter 14
Share or Lose:
A Radical Challenge for the Traditional Economy

Kamil Yagci
https://orcid.org/0000-0001-8130-7060
Tourism Faculty, Pamukkale University, Turkey

Mahmut Efendi
https://orcid.org/0000-0002-7388-5239
Adnan Menderes University, Turkey

Sureyya Akçay
https://orcid.org/0000-0002-5176-4444
Gazi University, Turkey

ABSTRACT

In addition to the development of social technology and the widespread use of the internet, the fact that people are getting used to sharing their goods and services has made the concept of sharing economy a popular issue. Sharing economy is "a potential new way for sustainability," and it is noted that it would disrupt the unsustainable hyper-consumption practices directing capitalist economies. In this regard, the importance of sharing economy becomes prominent. In this study, first of all, basic information was given about sharing economy and then the concepts about how it made progress were introduced. In the next step, the definitions of sharing economy were given, the importance of sharing was mentioned, and then the products used in sharing economy were mentioned. In the following stage, the benefits of sharing economy to nature were addressed, and the weaknesses and dark sides of sharing economy were revealed. Finally, the impact of the sharing economy on the service sector was emphasized, and opinions were presented for future research on this subject.

DOI: 10.4018/978-1-7998-8583-2.ch014

INTRODUCTION

For the enterprises prior to digital transformation, the concept of digital transformation was a holistic form of business transformation accompanied by fundamental economic and technological changes provided by information systems at both organizational and industrial levels (Chanias, Myers & Hess, 2019: 17). In addition to the development of social technology and the widespread use of the Internet, the fact that people are getting used to sharing their goods and services has made the concept of sharing and collaboration a popular issue (Kaplan & Haenlein, 2010). Sharing also continues to be a daily practice in today's world (Wittel, 2011); while families share their fruits with their workers, societies share the access to water resources. For this reason, it is not surprising that sharing forms mediated by the digital world have emerged. Digital planning is a strategy that involves a "fusion view" in which both information systems and business strategy are equalized. In other words, it is now difficult to distinguish between business strategy and information technology strategies (Chanias, Myers & Hess, 2019: 17).

Rather, it is the present framing of these forms of sharing as a radical and disruptive action that can be accepted as unique (Belk, 2014). Nonetheless, such advocates as Botsman and Rogers (2010a) identified sharing economy mediated by the digital in the late 1990s and early 2000s and framed these sharing forms as incredible. In this period, online platforms emerged through which peers could communicate with each other on such a scale never seen before. The attitudes towards consumption has changed in the recent years, which has brought increasing concerns about ecological, social and developmental effects. Increasing concerns about climate change and the desire to be socially embedded in terms of locality and social consumption (Albinsson&Perera, 2012; Belk, 2010; Botsman& Rogers, 2010a) have transformed the concept of "collaborative consumption/sharing economy *"into a peer-to-peer activity coordinated with community-based online services that involve access to obtain, give or share the goods and services.*

The rapid growth of the sharing economy (SE) have increasingly triggered the effects on the different aspects of the socio-economic system (Cheng, 2016: 60). Among classic examples are; open source software platforms (e.g.SourceForge and Github), collaborative online encyclopedias (e.g. Wikipedia), other content sharing websites (e.g. YouTube, Instagram) and peer-to-peer file sharing (e.g. The Pirate Bay). More recent examples include peer-to-peer financing platforms such as micro debt (e.g. Kiva) and crowdfunding services (e.g. Kickstarter). Open source software, online collaboration, file sharing and peer-to-peer financing are the different areas of what is called "sharing economy". The phenomenon of sharing economy emerges as the technological development that simplifies sharing with the availability of different information systems of both physical and non-physical goods and services on the Internet. While introducing new players in many areas, some (e.g. Airbnb, 2014) replaced older players, and others became dominant in their own fields (PwC, 2015a).

In this study, first of all, basic information was given about sharing economy and then, information was presented regarding digital learning, digitalization and digital transformation. In the next step, the definitions of sharing economy were given, the importance of sharing was mentioned, and then the products used in sharing economy were mentioned. In the following stage, the benefits of sharing economy to nature were addressed and the weaknesses and dark sides of sharing economy were revealed. Finally, the impact of the sharing economy on the tourism sector was emphasized and opinions were presented for future research on this subject. As the study was designed as a book chapter and accordingly involved certain criteria, it was designed as a literature review on technology, digitalization and sharing economy.

DIGITAL LEARNING

Digital learning can be considered as a driving force for enhancing skill development in the enterprises. In fact, digital transformation will be achieved the time when the enterprises embrace digital learning. Digital learning is a complex phenomenon associated with many people (Sousa & Rocha, 2019: 328). Hager (1998) and Sousa and Rocha (2019) defined digital learning as an implicit and unplanned process the consequences of which cannot be predicted, whereas Tjepkema (2002) and Van Biesen (1998) described digital learning as a process in which the devices such as smartphones, tablets, computers and others are used, which possesses an obvious character and is involved within everyday learning. Traditional store labels have also been included in this change through multi-channel strategies (Reinartz, Wiegand&Imschloss, 2019: 351). As Oliver Samwer,CEO of Rocket Internet stated; "There were only stores at first, but then Internet was invented. Many physical retailers began to experience a decline in their business as more and more customers opted for the convenience of digital shopping and delivery" (Kapner, 2016, Reinartz et al., 2019: 351),which was actually indicating the footsteps of this development.

DIGITALIZATION AND DIGITAL TRANSFORMATION

Pre-digitization organizations the title attributed to traditional companies such as retail, automotive etc. These enterprises had a certain amount of success before digitization. Retailing was at the heart of all the economies as a function combining the various requirements of the consumers with the special offers of the manufacturers (Reinartz, Wiegand & Imschloss, 2019: 350). In addition to this, since the digital economy plays an existential role, it seems that the traditional enterprises like retail and automotive are under threat (Chanias, Myers & Hess, 2019). Today, it can be argued that there are radical changes in our lives together with digitalization. The emergence of new and powerful digital technologies, digital platforms and digital infrastructures has shaped innovation and entrepreneurship (Nambisan, Wright & Feldman, 2019). Digital change involves the changes in the society and industries using high-level digital technologies (Vial, 2019: 118). It is a true phenomenon that radical changes have emerged in terms of shopping habits, business life and accessibility to products together with the use of mobile phones, tablets and smart devices. Furthermore, digitalization has caused the enterprises to make changes. For example, it has caused the enterprises to seek for new ways to create value by changing their structure, processes and culture (Vial, 2019: 118). According to Nambisan, Write and Feldman (2019), with digital transformation with the emergence of digital technologies, new business models, new kinds of products and services, and new types of customer experience have emerged. The superiority of traditional retailing within the retailer value chain is structurally being questioned with the online transactions of the manufacturers and with different platforms (Reinartz, Wiegand & Imschloss, 2019: 351). This can, in fact, explain the fact that digitalization causes destructive effects on the enterprises. Indeed, it can be considered that the enterprises that cannot keep up with digitalization will be destroyed or downsized. The companies like Alphabet, Tencent or Amazon can be called "digital by nature". The domain of digital technology systems involves the transformation of major structural resources rather than digitizing the resources.

Consumers traditionally make purchasing decisions in front of the shelves of the stores (Reinartz, Viegand & Imschloss, 2019: 350).

According to Lam and Law (2019), digitalization cannot be called a new development for hotels. In fact, hotels have been using airline and global distribution systems since the 1950s to achieve higher productivity and cost efficiency, and expand their accessibility worldwide (Buhalis & Main, 1998; Lam & Law, 2019). In addition to this, hotels are required to keep up with the digital changes in such an increasingly competitive environment so as to be able to take precedence over both traditional competitors and the malfunctions of the industry, and meet the changing demands of their customers (Lam & Law, 2019: 60).

BACKGROUND

Why "Sharing"?

Sharing producers, whose main goal is to create benefits by sharing, can offer services in many different fields depending on their target groups (Kaçar&Yakın, 2018: 725). Sharing does not just belong to the communities before the modern era; such practices are still common in the working class, the poor and minority communities. The discourse of innovation can be an inaccurate universality that excludes people preserving non-digital sharing in their daily lives (Schor, 2016: 13). Uber, which has brought an unpredictable change into the transportation sector (Defossez, 2017: 22), eliminates the driver's requirement to wander around and look for customers, and thus, reduces fuel consumption and provides less traffic density.

It is observed that the sharing economy may be more appropriate compared to the consumption of other goods (Queensland Tourism Industry Council, 2014). It is inevitable that new technological entrepreneurs emergeas the network platforms that are able to sell their own products, produce substitute goods and combine them with the good/service providers who can commercialize them at affordable prices keep being preferred (Sigala, 2015). In the table below, the reasons for preferring sharing economy are given.

A study describing the perceived benefits of Airbnb, which is one of the most advanced platforms of sharing economy in the field of accommodation, with customer responses (Nguyen, 2016), listed these benefits as follow: It frames as a platform that reduces accommodation expenses, provides easy booking and private accommodation areas, makes you feel at home, provides the opportunity to experience the local culture, opens up ways to set up social relations and meet new people, and sheds light on new lifestyles.

Apart from attracting innovation and new technologies, participants are often motivated by economic, environmental and social factors. Sharing economy areas generally have lower prices when compared to market alternatives. The desire to increase social connections is also a common motivation. Many websites recognize these features of their activities, and participants often express their desire to meet new people or neighbors. Even though they have heartwarming expressions about making new friends, many platforms fail to offer intimate social ties. For example, a recent study conducted on vehicle sharing revealed that both sides of the process never met remote access technology (Schor, 2016: 13). Tourists who perform destination choice tend towards the sharing economy platforms that allow to participate in tourism activities at lower costs (Kurt &Ünlüönen, 2017: 10) by taking into account the limited budget, current vacation time and people with whom they go on vacation (family, friends and foreigners) (Alegre &Pou, 2006; Fesenmaier&Jeng, 2000).

"Sharing economy" is thought to create great excitement with the promise of transforming business and consumption through technology and new socio-economic relations. The advocates of this view (Botsman& Rogers, 2010a) suggested that using idle capacity is efficient in terms of social connections and environmental benefits. In addition to this, other academicians argued that the concept of "shar-

Table 1. The Reasons for Preferring Sharing Economy

Factors	ORGANIZED Tourism Enterprises	DISORGANIZED Sharing Companies
Price	Additional obligations such as licenses and permits are included in product prices.	Additional obligations are not included with the consent of the property. It is more convenient.
Authenticity	Hotels, taxis and other tourism products have similar and consistent features everywhere.	You can feel freer and more alive in a local accommodation.
Environment	Businesses make large purchases of products when buying products. The activities of businesses also include the buildings as physical space.	Sharing companies allow to use resources with more capacities.
Communication	There are systems that will find immediate answers for complaints, problems and responses. Problems are aimed to be solved quickly.	An optional and timely communication takes place between the consumer and the supplier. A negative situation experienced is not the responsibility of the supplier.
Reliability	Reservation systems are accurate and developed. Alternatives can be offered to the consumer in case of a reservation mistake to be experienced.	Reservation systems depend on the regular updating of the supplier's profile. It is difficult to compensate for the problems experienced.
Transparency	Businesses often define their addresses, costs and present their products as photographic evidence.	False list submissions are potentially high. The products offered may differ from the products advertised on the sharing website.
Health and Reliability	Enterprises obtain all the permits and licenses that will ensure the health and security of consumers.	There is no guarantee of the products. People can be at risk, so they are responsible for their own health and safety.
Quality	Quality is guaranteed by minimum standard regulations. Expert reviews are the indicator of the quality of the product.	The quality of the product cannot be guaranteed. It can be controlled by peer reviews and comments made to general sharing companies.

Source: Queensland Tourism Industry Council, 2014.

ing economy" does not involve sharing in reality (Belk, 2014; Ravenelle, 2017) and suggested that the framework of sharing initiatives is increasingly focusing on the traditional discourse of economic opportunities (Martin, 2015). It can also be argued that sectors are calling for another neoliberal surplus by using "platform capitalism" (Lobo, 2014) and creating more insecurity on behalf of "sharing". The winners are defined as "micro entrepreneurs" (Ravenelle, 2016).

Digital workforce "works hard and gets insufficient money" (Scholz, 2016). Increasing monetization of private homes and cars, which were once mutual practices, fosters the market logic that harms the culture including the perspective reflected by Hochschdild's "outsourced self" (2012), Neff's "risk workforce" (2012) and Brown's "undoing demos" (2015). Concerns about such market attacks help to explain the resurgence of the interest in Polinayi (see Gemici, 2008), the dominance of the "enemy worlds" perspective identified and criticized by Zelizer (2010), and the popularity of insecurity discourse. However, wider economic effects of sharing economy are still unknown. Despite their incredible commercial success, Airbnb and Uber also received serious resistance and criticism because they opened an unregulated peer-to-peer marketplace with serious social effects (e.g. Schofield, 2014). Sharing economy has also been subjected to criticism itself. For example, Morozov (2013) stated that "it is the type of neo-liberalism that uses steroids, which commercializes other aspects of life beyond the point the market can reach".

The rapid growth of the sharing economy (SE) in the last decade has a strong relationship with socio-economic conditions such as better value distribution in the supply chain (Gansky, 2010), reduction of ecological impacts (Schor& Fitzmaurice, 2015), technological developments and ultimately the change in the attitudes of users towards their need for product ownership and social connectivity (Botsman& Rogers, 2010a). The socio-technical and sustainability transition research area (Markard, Raven &Truffer, 2012; Smith et al., 2010) has evolved over the past two decades to understand how societies and economies can transform. Researchers focused on the transformational change processes in which societies can become sustainable. Multi-Level Perspective (MLP) (Geels, 2005) is a dominant and widely applied theoretical model in transition research (Smith et al., 2010). This model suggests that transformational change processes can be understood in terms of the interactions between the multi-level socio-technical structures forming the society. The three structure levels suggested by MLP are as follows:

The first is a setting formed of slowly changing structures that are deeply embedded in the fabric of society including culture, social values and dominant economic paradigms. The second is the regime formed of common socio-cultural systems serving the needs of the society including consumption, production, digital communication and transportation systems. The third one is the protective area in which innovations emerge and develop (Smith & Raven, 2012). Niche innovations occur in the market economy and civil society: For instance; electric vehicles (Bakker & Farla, 2015), sharing economy (Martin & Upham, 2015), and community currencies (Seyfang & Longhurst, 2013).

Industry practitioners predicted that sharing economy would increase speculatively from 15 billion in 2015 to 335 billion in 2025 (PwC, 2015b). Sharing economy initiatives are also thought to reflect the broader "servicing" trend. Hereby, instead of selling products for free, companies can expand their potential markets by providing access to products (leasing) that people use (Cusumano, 2015: 32). Tourism and accommodation academics predict that sharing economy can change the future dynamics of the accommodation and tourism industry (Guttentag, 2015; Sigala, 2015).

At the same time, serious attention is paid to sharing economy in order to support sustainable consumption practices. While Heinrichs (2013: 228) heralded sharing economy as "a potential new way for sustainability", Botsman and Rogers (2010b) noted that it would disrupt the unsustainable hyperconsumption practices directing capitalist economies. The main argument of the latter one is that sharing economy allows consumers to switch to a culture where their own assets (from cars to excavation vehicles) let them access the assets.

The interest in the effects of nature and sharing economy on entrepreneurs, innovators, enterprises, policy makers, media commentators and academic researchers is growing rapidly. Much of the interest in this field stems from the two sharing economy platforms that are described as success stories in Silicon Valley: Airbnb, an online peer-to-peer platform that allows people to rent houses, including their own homes, for a short term; and Uber, an online peer-to-peer platform that provides taxi and "car sharing" services. Both platforms have been transformed from being start-up companies into multibillion dollar international companies within just five years (Lashinsky, 2015; Konrad & Mac, 2014).

MAIN FOCUS THE CHAPTER

The Definition of Sharing Economy

Sharing economy is considered as a system fostered by the value creation processes of creative enterprises. It is important what kind of values it offers depending on the field of activity. Within the framework of the values it offers, it is discussed how it will remain sustainable as consumer oriented (Kaçar & Yakın, 2018: 736). Since the term is different in the way it is used in practice, it is quite difficult to define the concept of "sharing economy" in such a way to ensure that it is inclusive while maintaining transparency (Schor, 2014). What lies at the heart of these descriptive difficulties is perhaps the controversial meaning of the word "sharing" (Belk, 2014). For instance, the general meaning of sharing excludes swap forms that provide monetary benefits to one or more parties.

Sharing economy is a rising economic-technological phenomenon that is supported by the developments in information and communication technologies (ICT), increased customer awareness, emergence of collaborative internet communities and social trade/sharing (Botsman& Rogers, 2010b; Kaplan & Haenlein, 2010; Wang & Zhang, 2012). Belk (2007: 127), on the other hand, defines the concept as follows: Sharing economy is the process of giving what people have to others and getting what others have for the purpose of using and benefiting. According to Acuner and Acuner (2017: 207), sharing economy is a new and rapidly developing system in which people who do not know each other at all make various shares to provide mutually economic and social benefits. Sharing economy is also defined as a new way to economic, social and environmental sustainability (Heinrichs, 2013). Sharing economy is used to define the applications for the use of products sometimes for free and sometimes not. By defining sharing economy as "access-based consumption", it is also defined as "transactions arising from the shares whose ownership transfer is not a point in question" (Bardhi & Eckhardt, 2012).

The Most Common Sharing Examples of Product Service Systems

- *Car Sharing:* There are examples like Zipcar, Streetcar, and GoGet. In Zipcar service, which is the most popular among them and whose users are called "Zipster", users have a card called "zipcard" that can be reserved for a certain period of time. They can insert their cards into the cars in various parts of the city and use the cars until the limit in the card is fully used. In Turkey, there are such examples as "AtlaGit" and "Mobilizm".
- *Person-to-person Car Sharing:* It is the rental of private cars to one another by the individuals instead of companies. There are websites like "Whipcar", "RelayRides", and"Getaround".
- *Bicycle sharing:* It is the bicycle rental services available in the city ready for common use. There are examples like "Bixi" and "Smartbike".
- *Driving sharing:* It provides the vehicle sharing of people heading to the same place. People not only save money but also consume less. There are examples like "Zimride" and "Nuride" abroad, and there is also an initiativein Turkey called "UcuzaGidelim".
- *Toy Sharing:* Toys are perhaps the items with the shortest period of life. For this reason, they can reach their new owners who can evaluate them rather than throwing away. It is possible to rent toys on websites such as "Rent-a-toy" and"BabyPlays".
- *Renting Clothes:*Products like clothes, jewelry, shoes, etc. can be rented on such websites as "Fashionhire", "Bag", "Borrow & Steal" and"From Bagsto Riches".
- *Renting Movies:*The best known example is "Netflix". It allows unlimited number of watching movies in return for a monthly fee.
- *Person-to-person Rental:* The most famous of the websites where all kinds of goods can be rented is "Zilok" from France. There are also examples such as "Ecomodo" and"Hire Things".
- *Renting from the Neighbor:* The websites like "Sharesomesugar", "Neighborrow" and"Neighborgoods", as their names also suggest, are the websites that bring people living close together and enable them to rent goods from each other(Tosuner, 2011).

The Benefit of Sharing Economy for Nature

While sharing economy websites advertise their green references, many users also consider ecological effects. The ecological effects of sharing are often evident; secondary markets reduce the demand for new products, and therefore, footprints are decreased. Staying in the present homes reduces the demand for new hotels, while car sharing reduces the demand of buying new cars. In a study on car sharing, it was found that although the greenhouse gas emission decreased at a measurable level, this was due to the decrease within the houses (Schor, 2016: 14).

Together with the fact that it is, as an alternative approach, is the subject to change relationship of a wide variety of goods and services along with sharing behavior, this approach also attracts attention due to its sustainable structure (Marangoz, Bayrakdaroğlu& Aydın, 2017: 139). Since the idea of effective use of resources is very positive, this idea, which will benefit all the stakeholders within the system and the society on a larger scale, is increasingly adopted (Teubner, 2014).

Ordinary assumptions regarding ecological effects are generally related to the first and visible change made by the consumer, such as "buying a second-hand product instead of buying a new one or staying in a house instead of a hotel"'. Nonetheless, it is thought that the wave effect should be considered in order to evaluate the total ecological effects. What does the seller or landlord do with the money they earn? They can use the money to buy high-impact products. Does the outlook of the used-product market cause people to buy more new things with the intention of selling them later? Do people travel more if it is cheaper to travel? All these effects are thought to increase ecological and carbon footprints (Schor, 2016: 14).

The Weaknesses of Sharing Economy

Sharing economy initiatives also have weaknesses. For example, the late verification of reservations on Airbnb makes travel plans complicated. Uber offers dynamic pricing like airlines and some hotels. In other words, the prices may increase as the demand will be high during rush hours or when it is raining. Uber drivers may decrease the quality of the service provided since they do not like the destination or because of customer ratings (in Uber, both the customer and driver can grade). The taxis can take advantage of this as Uber has to go to anyone offering standard prices.

In short, sharing economy heralds a new era in which under-used assets are turned into peer-to-peer rental services thanks to the Internet and smartphones. In addition to all these, it can be said that there are still many uncertainties, one of which is that it is easy to start internet initiatives, but they cannot survive when their financing is over. Furthermore, the network effect causes positive feedback loops, increases scaling and involves larger platforms – such as Amazon and Google dominating the internet retail and search industry. It is obvious that Airbnb and Uber have certain potentials and will work hard to preserve these potentials. They can be bigger, better and more diverse in terms of service. In this regard, despite the fact that traditional companies in these markets will not collapse, they are considered to be shaken. As a result, they will demonstrate their advantageous aspects and either gain competitive advantage or be destroyed (Cusumano, 2015: 34).

The Negative Side of Sharing Economy

Some initiatives experienced legal and regulatory problems from city administrations, courts and traditional unions (Cusumano, 2015: 32). In this regard, various studies have documented similar patterns of exploitation and segregation on the platforms related to sharing economy. Sharing economy has been criticized as another neoliberal innovation by ignoring the legal framework that supports security, competition and balanced societies (Interian, 2016). Sharing economy initiatives can engage in practices such as tax avoidance and unfair competition (Lyons &Wearing, 2015). Citizens do not need to purchase a taxi license plate when they offer vehicle sharing services. At the same time, they do not take the license exam or buy commercial insurance. For these reasons and because they do not have to fulfill these requirements, the German court banned Uber's basic services throughout the country. Licensed taxi drivers cannot compete with car sharing because they pay more for these requirements mentioned above. Car sharing uses the existing legal gaps so as to avoid the regulations and taxes. In this case, sharing economy is thought to be transformed into an elusion economy (Malhotra & Van Alstyne, 2014: 23). An Uber driver who did not work last Christmas killed a pedestrian by car while looking for customers. The sharing service did not give any compensation to the victim's family as the driver was "contracted". The contract declares that the service is a matching platform and "the company does not provide any transportation services and does not take responsibility for the services provided by the third parties...". Sharing economy requires providing full information and reliable reputation to all parties (Malhotra & Van Alstyne, 2014: 24).

Although sharing economy is economically efficient, it can be thought to cause different losses in different sectors. For example, it could harm the Netflix demand and filmmakers. Broadcasters have sued the Aereo initiative, where individuals can capture the broadcasts on television signals and display them on other screens. In this case, where sharing can be permitted, complex situations may also be experienced. Besides, it is also revealed that the employees who depend on the income from sharing economy are more unstable (Schoret al., 2017).

Considering from the perspective of market competition, hotel managers and government institutions also perceive sharing economy (e.g. Airbnb) as a threat to traditional tourism and hospitality enterprises, particularly for the hotels with lower prices (Queensland Tourism Industry Council, 2014). Airbnb is regarded as a counter-threat which leads the security and living communities to be reasonably priced, and more importantly, which causes long-term tenants to be evicted and the lack of rental houses (Edelman &Geradin, 2015). It is even documented that participants are motivated by openness and opportunities for social ties (Schor et al., 2016; Ladegaard, 2018).

Malhotra and Van Alstyne (2014) reported that shared rooms disturbed neighbors and increased socio-economic inequality due to the fact that it is a factor which increases income. On the other hand, the biased criticisms that can be made to real professionals and such risks as endangering the professions or fraud are considered as the main problems of sharing economy. It is also thought that the spread of the locals to the economic arena through sharing economy by carrying passengers, opening the doors of private kitchens to travelers, renting rooms and guiding will affect the professional lives of hotel enterprises, taxi drivers, chefs and tour guides, and may even lead to the disappearance of some professions.

The Effect of Sharing Economy on Tourism Industry

In a travel destination, individuals can make many accommodation choices. One of them is to stay in a house. In this respect, buying Real Estate is not realistic for many people (Fang, Ye & Law, 2015). Sharing economy expands the tourism supply options. It also offers alternative tourism movements and responds to high demand better. Tourists seek the better for an authentic tourism experience (Akyol&Ünlüönen, 2020: 630). Multiple prompters exhibit sharing as one of the mainstream practices of many aspects of tourism and accommodation today. The study conducted by Tussyadiah and Pesonen (2015), which focuses on the travelers in the USA and Finland, stated that peer-to-peer accommodation changed the travel patterns significantly by reducing accommodation expenses and providing meaningful social interaction with locals.

Since the emergence of sharing economy, it has been one of the leading sectors in terms of growth in tourism and accommodation due to the fact that tourists and home owners shared their homes, cars, meals and expert local information (locals as tour guides) (OECD, 2016; Sigala, 2015; Lyons & Wearing, 2015). Accordingly, online platforms today are designed to lend people free resources. Individuals can find those renting the asset on these platforms and rent these free resources from their owners. Thanks to this process, a new economic phenomenon called sharing economy emerged. The most common example of sharing economy in the tourism industry is Airbnb, where vacant houses or rooms are rented for short-term by their owners. The tenants can stay at lower prices compared to hotels in many cities thanks to Airbnb (Airbnb vs Hotels: A Price Comparison, 2013). In this regard, the online platform Airbnb provides gains for both the homeowners and tenants. Homeowners earn extra income by renting their unused houses or rooms, while tenants stay at lower prices. Visitors are seeking for better value for their money, sustainable tourism products and authentic tourism experiences (Forno & Garibaldi, 2015; Sigala, 2015; OECD, 2016). In addition to this, the food companies within the tourism sector also use the sharing economy system. The examples to these platforms bringing together people who produce food and would like to share it with others and those who wish to consume this food can be given as;Eatwith, BonAppetour, Casserole Club, Lets Lunch, Landshare, Yeat up, and evpismis.com (Demir, 2020: 56).

Above all, Airbnb has raised different concerns in governments. For example, it is complicated to place Airbnb's operations on a legal basis with the existing laws and policies. The question of the legality of Airbnb has caused controversies in many cities (Bort, 2014; Brustein, 2014). An important question for governments is how sharing economy will change the tourism industry. Zervas, Proserpio and Byers (2017) claim that Airbnb takes the role of low segment hotels. Considering the fact that Airbnb room owners are not required to employ staff, social unemployment levels may increase due to closing down such low-segment hotels. However, the fact that Airbnb enters the market can contribute to the entire tourism industry since people who prefer to stay with Airbnb tend to stay longer when they travel (Airbnb, 2014). Hence, the market share of the tourism industry is growing with the increase in the number of visitors. Together with the arrival of tourists in a destination, more restaurants need to meet the increasing demand for food. In this regard, employment opportunities are provided for the unemployed people through the tourism industry. Based on the points mentioned above, the question of whether Airbnb is beneficial for the hotel industry is still controversial (Fang, Ye & Law, 2015).

Considering from the perspective of the supplier, it can be said that sharing industry has increased the supply of tourism options in general as the initial cost of setting up the tourism enterprise is relatively low (Nadler, 2014). Online platforms allowed the sharing economy initiatives to grow by accessing the consumers' wide range of product and service scales, and offering more affordable opportunities rather than high standards when compared to their traditional counterparts (Shaheen, Mallery& Kingsley, 2012; Juul, 2015). More importantly, the nature of sharing economy has allowed destinations to better respond to the demands in the most popular period by offering alternative tourism services (Juul, 2015).

FUTURE RESEARCH DIRECTIONS

In the future, researchers may conduct studies that will determine the opinions and thoughts of consumers regarding food sharing platforms, and how to make legal arrangements and supervisions in the houses that are registered to this platform (Demir, 2020: 67). In this respect, it can be seen how broad area the concept of sharing economy is spread. The concept of sharing economy spreads from internet sharing to car sharing, room sharing and even bed sharing, as well as clothes sharing. In fact, it can be said that in this regard, it has an enormous area for researchers working in many fields.

The structure of social networks and the dissemination of the content produced in these networks have a determining role in the change of consumer behavior and in the development of sharing economy. In this respect, it is thought that analyzing the websites and performing a content analysis, diversifying the sub-elements, and carrying out studies spread to all nations will contribute to the field.

In addition to all these, the studies to be carried out by using the quantitative and qualitative data collection techniques with the communities and users involved in the common use movement will support to access to reliable data on the functioning and status of the sharing economy system. Besides, together with the quantitative and qualitative studies, the reasons for sharing and common use can be revealed in a single study. Furthermore, conducting studies involving information on how to use those shared will be beneficial for the researchers studying in the field of marketing.

CONCLUSION

Sharing behavior and common consumption movement, which is a revolt approach to the ownership-based economic system, is expanding its scope with the help of internet technologies day by day and spreading throughout the universal society (Kiracı, 2017: 51). Despite the fact that the moral projects of the participants in the sharing economy initiatives are rooted in their moral local order dreams, another dream equally shapes its practices: the perception of economy as abrader. If consumers can purchase a service or product from anywhere and enjoy the moment, their satisfaction level increases and traditional stores become vacant (Reinartz & Imschloss, 2017, Reinartz, Wiegand & Imschloss, 2019). Nonetheless, they choose to bring their economic production and market relations to the "local" area. Instead of seeing these initiatives as intrusive, colonizing or destroying, it is believed that the providers will allow to create a domestic market in which sharing initiatives can create social connections and gain autonomy in their working lives (Fitzmaurice et al., 2020: 99).

Traditional enterprises can offer broader, more reliable, consistent and secure services instead of their competitors in sharing economy. In this new environment where digitalization has emerged, the enterprises which have various traditional structures are aware that they cannot compete with online platforms and retailers in terms of price and product range (Reinartz, Wiegand & Imschloss, 2019). There are no obstacles for traditional companies to be just like their competitors in sharing economy. For example, Marriott sets up partnership with boutique hotels around the world and offers access to "Autography

Collection" features with reservation systems and loyalty programs that customers can access via mobile devices or computers. Due to the fact that digital technologies provide more information, data processing and communication and connectivity function as the actors that provide new cooperation among diversified distributed networks (Vial, 2019: 137). Perhaps this feature of enterprises should grow and develop. In another case, MetroCap Boston launched the smartphone application where potential customers can call a taxi and pay by credit card. Taxi companies can also work with local governments so as to reduce regulations, increase the number of license plates and hire more drivers (Cusumano, 2015: 34). In this respect, it is thought that it can gain a competitive advantage with the steps taken by the local people and sharing economy. Accordingly, it will not only reduce unemployment but also increase the working areas together with this arrangement. In addition to these, it is thought that it will provide equality for the competition by enabling easy access and being informed about the taxi prices in advance thanks to the internet applications prepared by taxi companies.

It is observed that more than half of the world uses the Internet and individuals access the Internet through their smart phones, and in such a structure, online platforms will gradually become more and more active within the scope of sharing economy. Digital technology systems are always under construction, without having a predictable end. These systems are always active targets. Digital technology systems need to be constantly renewed and improved by adding new information and insights (Chanias, Myers & Hess, 2019: 31). Therefore, it is inevitable that sharing economy will affect the tourism sector just as it affects all other sectors. It is necessary for the tourism sector reshape the sector by taking into account the concept of developing sharing economy. Hotels must adapt to digital changes so as to be able to meet the changing demands of customer experiences because today's travelers and those who book individually without traveling are digitally informed (Lam & Law, 2019). More secure measures should be taken on critical issues such as the privacy of personal information and personal security on the platforms of sharing economy (Akyol & Ünlüönen, 2020: 638). In this respect, tourism enterprises can create their own participation in sharing economy by creating a common platform and providing services at one place in mobile applications. In this regard, it is thought that tourism enterprises will establish a system that identifies those who rent their houses and rooms by participating in sharing economy and that they will either be excluded or made to pay taxes by offering it to the relevant authorities. For this reason, it is obvious that the important issue in this respect is not only to protect themselves but also to support the economy of the country.

It turns out that the discourses supporting sharing ignore the dark side of these innovations, so it is thought that the criticism is very harsh. In terms of creating new work areas, sharing economy has the potential to distribute money fairly, have a more democratic structure, reduce the ecological footprint and bring people together in new ways. Accordingly, there is excitement felt about sharing economy. Sharing economy has moved towards exciting new technologies. It is extremely transformative for individuals and even foreigners to easily connect, make a change, share information and collaborate. This is the issue almost everyone agrees on regarding sharing platforms. In addition to this, technologies are only as good as the political and social context they adopt. Software, crowdfunding and information provides powerful tools to build social solidarity, democracy and sustainability (Schor, 2016: 19). It is understood that the concept of sharing economy involves profitable and harmful situations for companies and individuals. In this regard, it becomes necessary for companies to act by taking into consideration their profitability and the harmful aspects. Due to the fact that individuals always consider their benefits and economic aspects, they are thought to be involved in this system.

Furthermore, the things to be done in confronting sharing economy in different situations (epidemics) at different times today are complicated. In case of epidemic diseases, it is thought that people will not find demand for the services and products they open to sharing. The reason for this is that in pandemic cases such as Covid-19, individuals have the desire to fully preserve their personal health. It is believed that individuals will see the service and product opened to sharing appropriate for utilizing in healthy situations and will exhibit their purchasing behavior accordingly. In this regard, it is thought that those who provide goods and services through sharing economy should take certificates and hygienic measures that comply with different marketing strategies standards (ISO) for extraordinary conditions. Of the sectors that will probably be affected by this situation are the accommodation, travel and food and beverage sectors within the tourism sector.

Sharing economy platforms, which are extremely significant in terms of accommodation sector, are not only limited to the accommodation aspect of tourism but they also function in many tourism activities from transportation to travel agency services, and from catering services to recreational activities (Kurt & Ünlüönen, 2017: 14). In other words, a wind of sharing economy is thought to be blowing within the tourism sector. In this regard, it is considered that setting off by the tourism enterprises or the new tourism establishments according to the conditions of sharing economy will be beneficial for the future and profitability of these companies. It should not be ignored that all the goods and services will be included in this trend with successful marketing strategies.

Regarding the sharing economy, it is thought that gathering the authorities together and reviewing the legal regulations, and re-evaluating the issues that are not clear enough within the law and setting up additional arrangements on the country basis will contribute to the sustainability of the system. In addition to all these, it is also thought that introducing the actors of sharing economy accurately and initiating efforts to increase the reliability of the sharing economy platforms will be beneficial for the future of this innovative business model (Kişi, 2018: 65). Its support for the country's economy will be greater in this way and it will lead to those who run their businesses through official means.

REFERENCES

Acuner, S., & Acuner, E. (2017). Turizmde paylaşım ekonomisi ve vergilendirilmesi. *Journal of Tourism and Gastronomy Studies*, *5*(2), 188–212. doi:10.21325/jotags.2017.77

Airbnb vs Hotels: A Price Comparison. (2013, June 17). *Priceonomics*. Retrieved from https://priceonomics.com/hotels/

Akyol, B., & Ünlüönen, K. (2020). Effects of sharing economy on tourism sector: A study on Kırıkkale University students. *Journal of Tourism and Gastronomy Studies*, *8*(1), 623–644. doi:10.21325/jotags.2020.568

Albinsson, P. A., & Perera, B. Y. (2012). Alternative marketplaces in the 21st century: Building community through sharing events. *Journal of Consumer Behaviour*, *11*(4), 303–315. doi:10.1002/cb.1389

Alegre, J., & Pou, L. (2006). The length of stay in the demand for tourism. *Tourism Management*, *27*(6), 1343–1355. doi:10.1016/j.tourman.2005.06.012

Bakker, S., & Farla, J. (2015). Electrification of the car—will the momentum last?: Introduction to The Special Issue. *Environmental Innovation and Societal Transitions, 14*, 1–4. doi:10.1016/j.eist.2014.07.002

Bardhi, F., & Eckhardt, G. M. (2012). Access-based consumption: The case of car sharing. *The Journal of Consumer Research, 39*(4), 881–898. doi:10.1086/666376

Belk, R. (2007). Why not share rather than own? *The Annals of the American Academy of Political and Social Science, 611*(1), 126–140. doi:10.1177/0002716206298483

Belk, R. (2010). Sharing. *The Journal of Consumer Research, 36*(5), 715–734. doi:10.1086/612649

Belk, R. (2014). You are what you can access: Sharing and collaborative consumption online. *Journal of Business Research, 67*(8), 1595–1600. doi:10.1016/j.jbusres.2013.10.001

Bort, J. (2014). San Francisco makes Airbnb legal at last. *Business Insider*. Retrieved from https://www.businessinsider.com/sanfrancisco-makes-airbnb-legal-at-last-2014-10

Botsman, R., & Rogers, R. (2010a). *What's mine is yours: How collaborative consumption is changing the way we live*. Collins.

Botsman, R., & Rogers, R. (2010b). Beyond Zipcar: Collaborative consumption. *Harvard Business Review, 88*(10), 30.

Brown, W. (2015). *Undoing the demos: Neoliberalism's stealth revolution*. Zone Books. doi:10.2307/j.ctt17kk9p8

Brustein, J. (2014). An Airbnb rival challenges San Francisco's Airbnb law. *Bloomberg Businessweek*. Retrieved from https://www.bloomberg.com/bw/articles/2014-11-03/san-francisco-faces-a-lawsuit-over-its-airbnb-law

Buhalis, D., & Main, H. (1998). Information technology in peripheral small and medium hospitality enterprises: Strategic analysis and critical factors. *International Journal of Contemporary Hospitality Management, 10*(5), 198–202. doi:10.1108/09596119810227811

Chanias, S., Myers, D. M., & Hess, T. (2019). Digital transformation strategy making in pre-digital organizations: The case of a financial services provider. *The Journal of Strategic Information Systems, 28*(1), 17–33. doi:10.1016/j.jsis.2018.11.003

Cheng, M. (2016). Sharing economy: A review and agenda for future research. *International Journal of Hospitality Management, 57*, 60–70. doi:10.1016/j.ijhm.2016.06.003

Cusumano, M. A. (2015). How traditional firms must compete in the sharing economy. *Communications of the ACM, 58*(1), 32–34. doi:10.1145/2688487

Defossez, D. A. L. (2017). The regulation of a project of the deregulation: UBER in Brazil and the European Union. *Journal of Law and Regulation, 3*(1), 1–28.

Demir, Y. (2020). Paylaşım ekonomisi kapsamında yemek paylaşma sitelerinin analizi. *Güncel Turizm Araştırmaları Dergisi, 4*(1), 54–69. doi:10.32572/guntad.678419

Edelman, B. G., & Geradin, D. (2015). Efficiencies and regulatory shortcuts: How should we regulate companies like Airbnb and Uber. *Stan. Tech. L. Rev., 19*, 293. doi:10.2139srn.2658603

Fang, B., Ye, Q., & Law, R. (2015). Effect of sharing economy on tourism industry employment. *Population, 1*.

Fesenmaier, D. R., & Jeng, J. M. (2000). Assessing structure in the pleasure trip planning process. *Tourism Analysis, 5*(1), 13–27.

Fitzmaurice, C. J., Ladegaard, I., Attwood-Charles, W., Cansoy, M., Carfagna, L. B., Schor, J. B., & Wengronowitz, R. (2020). Domesticating the market: Moral exchange and the sharing economy. *Socio-economic Review, 18*(1), 81–102. doi:10.1093er/mwy003

Forno, F., & Garibaldi, R. (2015). Sharing economy in travel and tourism: The case of home-swapping in Italy. *Journal of Quality Assurance in Hospitality & Tourism, 16*(2), 202–220. doi:10.1080/1528008X.2015.1013409

Gansky, L. (2010). *The mesh: Why the future of business is sharing?* Portfolio Trade.

Geels, F. W. (2005). The dynamics of transitions in socio-technical systems: A multi-level analysis of the transition pathway from horse-drawn carriages to automobiles (1860–1930). *Technology Analysis and Strategic Management, 17*(4), 445–476. doi:10.1080/09537320500357319

Gemici, K. (2008). Karl Polanyi and the antinomies of embeddedness. *Socio-economic Review, 6*(1), 5–33. doi:10.1093er/mwl034

Guttentag, D. (2015). Airbnb: Disruptive innovation and the rise of an informal tourism accommodation sector. *Current Issues in Tourism, 18*(12), 1192–1217. doi:10.1080/13683500.2013.827159

Hager, P. (1998). Understanding workplace learning: General perspectives. In Current Issues and New Agendas in Workplace Learning (pp. 31–46). Springfield, VA, NCVER.

Heinrichs, H. (2013). Sharing economy: A potential new pathway to sustainability. *GAIA-Ecological Perspectives for Science and Society, 22*(4), 228–231. doi:10.14512/gaia.22.4.5

Hochschild, A. R. (2012). *The outsourced self: Intimate life in market times*. Metropolitan Books.

Interian, J. (2016). Up in the air: Harmonizing the sharing economy through Airbnb regulations. *BC Int'l & Comp. L. Rev., 39*, 129.

Juul, M. (2015). The sharing economy and tourism. *Tourist accommodation. European Parliament Research Service Briefing*. Retrieved from http://www.europarl.europa.eu/RegData/etudes/BRIE/2015/568345/EPRS BRI(2015)568345 EN.pdf

Kaçar, İ. A., & Yakın, V. (2018). Sharing economy and creating value: Business model canvas. *Third Sector Social Economic Review, 53*(3), 724–739. doi:10.15659/3.sektor-sosyal-ekonomi.18.09.962

Kaplan, A. M., & Haenlein, M. (2010). Users of the world, unite! The challenges and opportunities of Social Media. *Business Horizons, 53*(1), 59–68. doi:10.1016/j.bushor.2009.09.003

Kapner, S. (2016). Retail slump shows Amazon effect. *The Wall Street Journal*. Retrieved from https://www.wsj.com/articles/kohls-shows-effects-of-retail-slump-as-someponder-the-amazon-factor-1463084218

Kiracı, H. (2017). Ortak tüketim ekseninde paylaşılan/paylaşılamayan varlıklar ve bireylerin paylaşım davranışlarını etkileyen faktörler üzerine bir araştırma. *Uluslararası İktisadi ve İdari İncelemeler Dergisi*, 51-70.

Kişi, N. (2018). Paylaşım Ekonomisinin Ulaşım Sektörüne Yansımaları: Uber Örneği. *Uluslararası Yönetim ve Sosyal Araştırmalar Dergisi*, *5*(10), 57–68.

Konrad, A., & Mac, R. (2014). Airbnb cofounders to become first sharing economy billionaires as company nears $10 billion valuation. *Forbes, 3*, 20. Retrieved from http://www.forbes. com/sites/alexkonrad/2014/03/20/airbnb-cofounders-are-billionaires/

Kurt, S., & Unluönen, K. (2017). Paylaşım ekonomisi kapsamında turizm sisteminin değerlendirilmesi. *Gazi Üniversitesi Turizm Fakültesi Dergisi*, *1*, 1–21.

Ladegaard, I. (2018). Hosting the comfortably exotic: Cosmopolitan aspirations in the sharing economy. *The Sociological Review*, *66*(2), 381–400. doi:10.1177/0038026118758538

Lam, C., & Law, R. (2019). Readiness of upscale and luxury-branded hotels for digital transformation. *International Journal of Hospitality Management*, *79*, 60–69. doi:10.1016/j.ijhm.2018.12.015

Lashinsky, A. (2015). Uber: An oral history. *Forbes*. Retrieved fromhttps://fortune.com/ 2015/06/03/uber-an-oral-history/

Lobo, S. (2014). SPON-Die Mensch-Maschine: Auf Dem Weg in Die Dumpinghölle. *Spiegel Online, 3*.

Lyons, K., & Wearing, S. (2015). *The sharing economy: Issues, ımpacts and regulatory responses in the context of the NSW visitor economy*. NSW Business Chamber.

Malhotra, A., & Van Alstyne, M. (2014). Thedarkside of thesharingeconomy… and how tolighten it. *Communications of the ACM*, *57*(11), 24–27. doi:10.1145/2668893

Marangoz, M., Bayraktaroğlu, F., & Aydın, A. E. (2017). Tüketimde alternatif bir yaklaşım olarak paylaşım ekonomisi: ortak kullanım ağlarının içerik analizi ile incelenmesi. *Dumlupınar Üniversitesi Sosyal Bilimler Dergisi*, 134-148.

Markard, J., Raven, R., & Truffer, B. (2012). Sustainability transitions: An emerging field of research and its prospects. *Research Policy*, *41*(6), 955–967. doi:10.1016/j.respol.2012.02.013

Martin, C. J., & Upham, P. (2016). Grassroots social innovation and the mobilisation of values in collaborative consumption: A conceptual model. *Journal of Cleaner Production*, *134*, 204–213. doi:10.1016/j.jclepro.2015.04.062

Morozov, E. (2013). The "sharing economy"undermines workers'rights. *Financial Times*. Retrieved from http://evgenymorozov.tumblr.com/post/64038831400/the-sharing-economyundermines workers-rights

Nadler, S. S. N. (2014). *The sharing economy: What is it and where is it going?* (Unpublished doctoral dissertation). Massachusetts Institute of Technology.

Nambisan, S., Write, M., & Feldman, M. (2019). The digital transformation of innovation and entrepreneurship: Progress, challenges and key themes. *Research Policy*, *48*(8), 103773. doi:10.1016/j.respol.2019.03.018

Neff, G. (2012). *Venture labor: Work and the burden of risk in innovative industries*. MIT Press. doi:10.7551/mitpress/9780262017480.001.0001

Nguyen, H. N. (2016). *Customer value in Sharing economy: The case of Airbnb* (Unpublished master's thesis). Tampere University Business competence, Finland.

OECD. (2016). *Policies for the tourism sharing economy OECD tourism trends and policies 2016*. OECD Publishing.

PwC. (2015a). *The sharing economy*. PwC.

PwC. (2015b). *The sharing economy—Sizing the revenue opportunity*. Retrieved from http://www.pwc.co.uk/issues/megatrends/collisions/sharingeconomy/the-sharing-economy sizing-the-revenue-opportunity.html

Queensland Tourism Industry Council. (2014). *The sharing economy: How it will impact the tourism landscape and what businesses can do?* Queensland Tourism Industry Council, Brisbane.

Ravenelle, A. (2016). *Microentrepreneur or Precariat? Exploring the sharing economy through the experiences of workers for Airbnb, Taskrabbit, Uber and Kitchensurfing*. Manuscript in preparation.

Ravenelle, A. J. (2017). Sharing economy workers: Selling, not sharing. *Cambridge Journal of Regions, Economy and Society*, *10*(2), 281–295. doi:10.1093/cjres/rsw043

Reinartz, W., Wiegand, N., & Imscholos, M. (2019). The impact of digital transformation on the retailing value chain. *International Journal of Research in Marketing*, *36*(3), 350–366. doi:10.1016/j.ijresmar.2018.12.002

Schofield, H. (2014). Short-letapartmentsspark Paris row as Airbnbthrives. *BBC News*. Retrieved from https://www.bbc.co.uk/news/world-europe-30580295

Scholz, T. (2016). *Uberworked and underpaid: How workers are disrupting the digital economy*. Polity Press.

Schor, J. (2014). *Debating the sharing economy*. Retrieved fromhttps://greattransition.org/publication/debating-the-sharing-economy

Schor, J. (2016). Debating the sharing economy. *Journal of Self-Governance and Management Economics*, *4*(3), 7–22. doi:10.22381/JSME4320161

Schor, J. B., Attwood-Charles, W., Cansoy, M., Ladegaard, I., & Wengronwitz, R. (2017). *Dependence and precarity in the platform economy*. Unpublished paper, Boston College.

Schor, J. B., & Fitzmaurice, C. J. (2015). Collaborating and connecting: the emergence of the sharing economy. In *Handbook of research on sustainable consumption*. Edward Elgar Publishing. doi:10.4337/9781783471270.00039

Seyfang, G., & Longhurst, N. (2013). Desperately seeking niches: Grassroots innovations and niche development in the community currency field. *Global Environmental Change*, *23*(5), 881–891. doi:10.1016/j.gloenvcha.2013.02.007

Shaheen, S. A., Mallery, M. A., & Kingsley, K. J. (2012). Personal vehicle sharing services in North America. *Research in Transportation Business & Management*, *3*, 71–81. doi:10.1016/j.rtbm.2012.04.005

Sigala, M. (2015). Collaborative commerce in tourism: Implications for research andindustry. *Current Issues in Tourism*, 1–10.

Smith, A., & Raven, R. (2012). What is protective space? Reconsidering niches in transitions to sustainability. *Research Policy*, *41*(6), 1025–1036. doi:10.1016/j.respol.2011.12.012

Smith, A., Voß, J. P., & Grin, J. (2010). Innovation studies and sustainability transitions: The allure of the multi-level perspective and its challenges. *Research Policy*, *39*(4), 435–448. doi:10.1016/j.respol.2010.01.023

Sousa, M. J., & Rocha, A. (2019). Digital learning: Developing skills for digital transformation of organizations. *Future Generation Computer Systems*, *91*, 327–334. doi:10.1016/j.future.2018.08.048

Teubner, T. (2014). Thoughts on the sharing economy. In *Proceedings of the International Conference on e-Commerce* (*Vol. 11*, pp. 322-326). Academic Press.

Tjepkema, S. (2002). *The learning infrastructure of self managing workteams*. Twente University Press.

Tosuner, A. (2011). *Ortak kullanım ağlarındaki içerik üretiminin, tüketim davranışının azaltılmasındaki teşvik edici rolünün web siteleri üzerinden incelenmesi: Zumbara, Freeconomy, Community Exchange Network, Freecycle Network* (Unpublished master's thesis). İstanbul Üniversitesi Sosyal Bilimler Enstitüsü, İstanbul.

Tussyadiah, I. P., & Pesonen, J. (2015). Impacts of peer-to-peer accommodation use on travel patterns. *Journal of Travel Research*, *55*(8), 1022–1040. doi:10.1177/0047287515608505

Van Biesen, F. (1989). Everyday learning in labour organisations. *Ontwerp*, *1*(1), 4–11.

Vial, G. (2019). Understanding digital transformation: A review and a research agenda. *The Journal of Strategic Information Systems*, *28*(2), 118–144. doi:10.1016/j.jsis.2019.01.003

Wang, C., & Zhang, P. (2012). The evolution of social commerce: The people, management, technology, and information dimensions. *Communications of the Association for Information Systems*, *31*(1), 105–127. doi:10.17705/1CAIS.03105

Wittel, A. (2011). Qualities of sharing and their transformations in the digital age. *International Journal of Information Ethics*, *15*(9), 3–8.

Zelizer, V. A. (2010). *Economic lives: How culture shapes the economy?* Princeton University Press.

Zervas, G., Proserpio, D., & Byers, J. W. (2017). The rise of the sharing economy: Estimating the impact of Airbnb on the hotel industry. *JMR, Journal of Marketing Research*, *54*(5), 687–705. doi:10.1509/jmr.15.0204

KEY TERMS AND DEFINITIONS

Customers: Any bodies of demand side of a marketplace wanting goods and services.

Gig Economy: Systems that break up a traditional company 'job' into individual 'gigs' that independent workers are paid to do for a defined time.

Platforms: The network, marketplace or any other digitally enabled mechanism used to facilitate an exchange between peers.

Providers: Supplier side of marketplaces providing goods and services.

Sharing Economy: Systems that facilitate the sharing of underused/unused assets or services, for free or for a fee, directly between individuals or organizations.

Chapter 15
A Usability Audit Model for Destination Websites Management in the Digital Economy

Simón Alba-Muñoz
University of Malaga, Spain

María-Mercedes Rojas-de-Gracia
https://orcid.org/0000-0002-5006-039X
University of Malaga, Spain

Plácido Sierra-Herrezuelo
https://orcid.org/0000-0003-1783-9024
University of Malaga, Spain

ABSTRACT

In a globalized world, tourist destinations must have a website containing accurate information for potential tourists. However, there is currently no model that serves as a guide to evaluate the usability of tourism websites. A web usability audit manual is presented in this work with the application of a case study methodology, which combines theoretical contributions with those of a real audit of a tourism institution. Apart from the description of the manual itself, the results of this work have made it possible to identify a series of actions to be taken into account, as well as others that should be avoided when a usability audit is being carried out in the tourism field.

DOI: 10.4018/978-1-7998-8583-2.ch015

INTRODUCTION

Due to the phenomenon of globalization, the tourism sector today can be considered a single market in which each country, region or city competes with others to attract tourists (Manhas, Manrai, & Manrai, 2016). This gives rise to a concern on the part of the governments of the different destinations to generate an attractive image that allows them to settle in a competitive position within the tourism market. One of the most effective ways to promote this competitive position is the construction of a recognized brand that can represent its identity in an attractive way for potential clients (Gallarza, Saura, & García, 2002).

It is in this competitive and global context that tourist destination websites play a decisive role (Fernández-Cavia et al., 2013; Fernández-Cavia, Rovira, Díaz-Luque, & Cavaller, 2014). This implies that it is not enough for tourist destinations to work on the creation of a competitive image on the Internet. The large amount of information currently available to users on the network complicates the task of capturing the attention of the tourist, increasingly demanding in terms of easy use, speed or design of websites based on a single website. This has resulted in a tendency among different tourist destinations to put greater emphasis on improving the website, in order to meet the demands and expectations of users and thus ensure that they have a satisfactory experience during their interaction with its web portals (Martinis, Papadatou, & Kabassi, 2019; McCartney, Butler, & Bennett, 2008).

This means that tourist destinations want to offer a promotional website that not only provides information about the destination, but is also presented in the appropriate way so that it is useful and simple for the user seeking information or intending to plan a trip. This implies that the presence of information about the destination on a website is not enough, and that it must be presented in the appropriate way. This is where the concept of usability arises, meaning the degree to which a product or system can be used by specified users to achieve specific goals effectively, efficiently and satisfactorily, as defined by ISO standards. However, on many occasions, managers of tourist destination websites have felt lost, since they do not have a model to serve as a guide for evaluating the usability of their website. This is precisely the objective of this work: the elaboration of a manual that explains the steps to follow when auditing the usability of a website in the tourism sector.

BACKGROUND

In a study whose main theme is the web usability audit of tourist destinations, we should start with a brief theoretical compilation based on the doctrines and explanations of some of the most prominent authors in this field. Therefore, before delving into the project, it is necessary to clearly and precisely define the terms that will be used in this manual. This is vital, considering that the usability audit field is still new and unknown to a large part of the population. Specifically, there are three key elements in this study: usability, usability audit and user experience (UX).

It is also necessary to indicate that, although many of the concepts presented here can be used by all brands in a general sense, this manual is focused on tourism destinations, so it presents a series of specific features. It is important to mention that they are websites that are often managed by public authorities focusing on the interests of a series of tourism enterprises that depend on the flow of tourists attracted by the destination at issue.

Usability

As stated by the International Organization for Standardization in its Standard ISO 25000, the term usability is defined as the *degree to which a product or system can be used by specified users to achieve specific goals effectively, efficiently and satisfactorily in a specific context*. This capacity is related to very different aspects, from software design to its navigability. That is why these standards also present a broader outlook and specify that usability is divided into the following sub-characteristics:

- **Appropriateness/recognizability:** Degree to which users can recognize whether a product or system is appropriate for their needs.
- **Learnability:** Degree to which a product or system can be used by specified users to achieve specific learning goals to use the product or system *effectively, efficiently and satisfactorily in a specific context*
- **Operability:** Degree to which a product or system has attributes that make it easy to operate and control.
- **User error protection**: Degree to which a system protects users against committing errors.
- **User interface aesthetics**: Degree to which a user interface enables pleasing and satisfying interaction for the user.
- **Accessibility:** Degree to which a product or system can be used by people with the widest range of characteristics and capabilities to achieve a specified goal in a specific context.

Based on the above, we can affirm that we are not dealing with an absolute characteristic or capacity of the product or system, but something gradual, or rather, that can be considered to a greater or lesser extent. In this respect, the degree of usability of a system or website is an empirical and relative measure. According to Maldonado (2015), it is an empirical measure because it is based on usability tests that are carried out through field work or in laboratories; and it would be a relative measure because the result that can be obtained from these tests will be good or bad depending on the goals previously established in each case.

Usability Audit

According to Rubin and Chisnell (2008), the general objective of a usability audit is to identify and rectify existing usability errors in a system in order to create products that are easy to handle and use satisfactorily, and that provides the utility and functionality sought by the target audience. This evaluation is particularly important, since a website with low usability is unattractive to the user in the commercial field and, in a context as competitive as that of tourist destinations, this can lead potential customers to seek competitors.

According to the classification of Nielsen and Molich (1990), the following audit methods would be used:

- **Formal method:** This method consists in conducting the audit based on technical analyses.
- **Automatic method:** It is based on the use of automated or computerized procedures.
- **Heuristic method:** This method enables us to examine the user interface, based on the auditor's own opinion.

- **Empirical method:** Although it requires more time than other methods, it is currently the most widespread and consists in analyzing the usability of the system through tests with users to obtain full information about the interaction between it and the system.

In this context, the proposals of Nielsen (1994) and Jeffrey and Chisnell (2008) are the most popular. Although both models have small differences and different levels of detail at some points, they propose the application of the empirical method with a very similar structure. Therefore, the two resort to real users, considering that they provide direct information on how people interact with the system and what the exact problems in the interface being evaluated are.

Nielsen Model

Firstly, the Nielsen (1994) model proposes the creation of an audit plan in the form of an initial report that establishes the general aspects of the process, such as the objectives, duration or profiles of the users involved. This audit plan is followed by budgeting, which includes the financial requirements of the audit. After these tasks, Nielsen (1994) recommends the performance of pilot tests before executing the final tests, in order to identify eventual technical or planning errors. Upon completion of these tests, new or expert representative users who will carry them out are selected.

The auditors who will carry out the evaluation must also be selected. This author emphasizes the importance of the fact that the auditor should be a person with previous auditing experience and knowledge of the system to be evaluated. However, he also states that auditor profiles that do not fit in perfectly with those characteristics can also guarantee the effectiveness of the audit. After the selection of users and auditors, this model proposes that the next step be the identification of those tasks to be performed by users. These tasks must fulfill the main requirement of being representative, meaning that they act as typical users in their interaction with the website.

The next step is the performance of the tests. According to this model, it is divided into four phases:

1. **Preparation:** You have to ensure that everything is ready.
2. **Introduction:** Auditors explain to users what they should know before starting to perform tasks.
3. **Test performance:** An official auditor should be appointed to intervene and interact with the user only if strictly necessary.
4. **Interrogation:** Questions are asked so that the user may complement the information extracted during the tests.

Finally, the last step marked by this model is the measurement of results. This stage aims to convert the usability of the audited website into measures and ratios, such as the time required to carry out a task or the number of errors made by the user during the interaction.

Jeffrey and Chisnell Model

On the other hand, the Jeffrey and Chisnell (2008) model follows a structure similar to that of Nielsen (1994), but, while the latter focuses mainly on the phases from the beginning of the audit to the execution of the tests, the former is much more detailed in those phases occurring after performing the tests. That is, the Jeffrey and Chisnell (2008) model shows greater development in the phases during which the results are analyzed. Therefore, the proposal of these authors also begins with the elaboration of an audit plan that fulfills functions similar to those indicated by Nielsen (1994).

The next step is the selection of representative users who will participate in the audit, so it is obvious that it does not refer to budgets or pilot tests. This selection is followed by the preparation phase of the materials needed to carry out the audit. It is followed by the development phase, which differs considerably from the one proposed by Nielsen (1994), since this model does not include an auditor selection phase with guidelines as to the ideal profile. In fact, in the testing phase, Jeffrey and Chisnell (2008) almost limit themselves to indicating how the auditors should act, with indications regarding how to control their tone or gestures to adopt a position as neutral as possible, intervene only when it is very necessary, etc. However, it makes a new contribution, since it refers to the need to use the "thinking aloud" technique, which means that users express their thoughts aloud during their interaction with the website.

After performing the tests, Jeffrey and Chisnell (2008) also recommend the questioning of users as a source of complementary information. The interrogation is followed by a phase of transforming data into findings and recommendations, which includes a preliminary analysis process and a comprehensive one in which statistics help to organize and summarize data to identify patterns. Once this task has been completed, these authors propose to continue with the task of identifying user errors and difficulties and their origins. This phase is supported by data organization carried out previously. In addition, these errors must be organized by severity level. After this analytical phase, the next step is the development of recommendations, which should be carried out by a team with some knowledge of usability and design. Finally, this model ends with the proposal to prepare a final report that includes an executive summary, methodology, results, findings and recommendations and an appendix with the raw information used.

User Experience

User experience or simply UX, is a concept that is closely linked to usability. In fact, we can say that one is a consequence of the other. That is, if the usability of a product or system works well, this will result in an improvement in the UX. Therefore, it is important to know what exactly it is and what consequences it has.

Similar to the concept of usability, we should start with an official definition to understand the user experience concept. Therefore, its ISO definition states that the UX is *the person's perceptions and responses that result from the use or anticipated use of a product, system or service*. According to this definition, this concept includes emotions, beliefs, preferences, perceptions, physical and mental responses, behavior and skills that occur before, during and after use.

Nowadays, improvement of the UX is a fundamental pillar in a successful marketing strategy. In the web field it is a key factor for Search Engine Optimization (SEO) since, in fact, Google gives more and more priority to this factor over others. This is because what is very important to them is that users are as satisfied as possible with the content they find through their searches (Au et al., 2008).

In any case, regardless of the above, trying to improve in UX is of great importance, since its proper use has a significant and desirable impact in the internet world:

- It decreases bounce rate.
- It increases the duration of visits.
- It provides greater feedback from the user.
- It increases conversions.

- Users are loyal, so they return (thus increasing the traffic of recurring users).
- Users recommend the web to others, which results in an increase in new user traffic.

These are powerful reasons to seek improvement of the UX on any website. Therefore, usability is one of the paths to follow to achieve this goal, and a usability audit is the first step to take (Dominguez, Hammill, & Brillat, 2015).

USABILITY AND USER EXPERIENCE OF TOURISM WEBS

Internationalization in the Tourist Field

The unbridled evolution of ICT has changed the way people search for and digest information. Today the vast majority of travelers use the internet as a means to search for information and plan their trips. Its characteristics are also closely linked to each local culture, that is, the tourist's requirements vary greatly depending on the culture from which they come (Degen, Lubin, Pedell, & Ji, 2005). The websites of tourist destinations play an essential role in the traveler's decision before leaving. Then, the attractiveness of these websites has a great impact on travelers' choices. Therefore, the UX has a great influence on tourism during interaction with the website. However, as the depth and scope of these websites have increased, the usability problems have become more apparent.

On the other hand, due to globalization, the usability of tourist destination websites must be considered as being closely linked to an internationalized or cross-cultural context. In fact, tourist demand is influenced by factors such as the design of the user interface, which has different requirements for each culture. Therefore, cross-cultural design should be considered from the beginning of the website creation process and should not consist of its mere translation to different languages once the original version is done (Zhou & DeSantis, 2005). In short, and given its trait of internationalization, when it comes to improving its usability, tourist destination websites should pay special attention and consider the different ways of browsing and searching for information that exist between users of different cultures.

Usability Audit on Tourist Destination Websites

Many studies have attempted to measure the quality of a tourist destination website. However, even today there is no clear consensus as to the proper evaluation of the usability of a website in the tourism sector, due to the great disparity in the tools and factors considered when evaluating it. This makes it very difficult to find general guidelines on how the audit should be carried out. However, according to Fernández-Cavia et al. (2013), the empirical method has the most support in the case of tourist destination websites. It also recommends a review of all methods, so that a combination of tools from all of them is used, but without making a more specific proposal.

Despite the aforementioned lack of consensus as to the type of methodology to be followed in relation to the results of the few publications on audits in the field of tourist destination websites (Carstens & Patterson, 2005; Finn & Johnson, 2013; Hung, Hu, & Lee, 2013; Martínez-Sala, Monserrat-Gauchi, & Alemany-Martínez, 2020; Zhou & DeSantis, 2005), some conclusions and recommendations of interest can be drawn and taken into account when improving a destination website, among which are:

- **Giving users a starting point**. Normally, the homepage, being the web entry or the path most commonly taken from search engines, is the page that receives the most clicks. It is therefore essential that it be a starting point for users who access it, offering content that generates engagement (Nielsen & Tahir, 2011).
- **Seeking simplicity**, given that the web environment is circumscribed within a world full of distractions, users appreciate the absence of noise, that is, unnecessary information (Nielsen, 1999).
- **Providing users with maps and directions**, as they offer crucial information for the potential user of these types of websites (Zhou & DeSantis, 2005).
- **Offering useful functionalities**, since the users need to have content according to their needs. Therefore, as Zhou and DeSantis (2005) argue, it is of no use to offer the user the possibility to search within the website by terms, dates or other criteria if this functionality does not return results consistent with the user's interests.
- **Making navigation intuitive**. This characteristic is reinforced by the law of simplicity defended by Nielsen (1999).
- **Clarifying information on visas and immigration policies**, since, according to Adukaite, Gazizova and Cantoni (2014), this type of information helps to better serve tourists by facilitating the work not only of the traveler, but also of the receiving country with an increase in tourist flow.
- **Using content, terminology and functions in several languages**, given the aforementioned international nature of tourism (Zhou & DeSantis, 2005).
- **Inserting images and multimedia content**. Previous studies conclude that this type of content stimulates the interest of users who will plan a trip and improve their experience during their visit to the website (Lian & Yu, 2019; Shani, Chen, Wang, & Hua, 2010).
- **Offering information on exchange rates**, which helps travelers from countries with different currencies to estimate the different prices of the country they intend to visit (Dwyer, Forsyth, & Rao, 2002).
- **Providing information about the climate and local weather**, due the interest it arouses in tourists who decide to visit a place (Becken, 2013).
- **Including personal stories**. Intelligent use of these personal stories by the managers of these tourist destinations can cause a great increase in engagement on the web. Hence the importance of "peer to peer" and of assessment, comments and recommendations made by other users, since they add a personality to the website that can make it connect emotionally with potential customers, which is especially true for the case of tourism (Cam, Anh, Moslehpour, & Thanh, 2019).
- **Showing the benefits that trips provide to tourists**. That is, showing users explicitly what benefits they can obtain on the website in a pleasant, visible and simple way is always more user friendly than exposing cold data that bothers them (Zhou & DeSantis, 2005).

All these recommendations and the absence of a model that serves as a guide to assess the usability of tourist destination websites show the need for a manual explaining the steps to follow to audit the usability of a website that allows proper management in the digital economy, which is the objective of this work.

The Case Study

The case study methodology was chosen in order to achieve the objective proposed in this work. This technique is appropriate when a holistic, in-depth investigation is required and for cases with a limited amount of prior research or data compiled in studies (Feagin, Orum, & Sjoberg, 1991). Specifically, as Yin (1994) states, the case study is an empirical investigation that studies a contemporary phenomenon in its own context in real life. This allows the researcher to take advantage of previous theoretical proposals that can guide the collection and analysis of data. From this perspective, the relevant use of case studies as a research methodology has been verified in various subjects, including several associated with business management, management and organizational change, and innovation (Brown & Hayes, 2008; De-Laguno-Alarcón, Sierra-Herrezuelo, & Rojas-de-Gracia, 2019; Higgins-Desbiolles, 2018).

As the name indicates, the case study requires a real case. The usability audit recently carried out by the Costa del Sol Tourism and Planning institution (Turismo y Planificación Costa del Sol, in Spanish), the entity that manages the website visitacostadelsol.com, has been chosen to create this manual. This entity emerged in January 2015 to promote the tourist destination of the province of Malaga under the Costa del Sol brand and support the growth of the economy, designing and executing projects at the service of private companies and public entities.

According to George, Bennett, Lynn-Jones and Miller (2005), the following steps must be followed to carry out a case study:

Step 1: Study design
Step 2: Development of the study
Step 3: Analysis and conclusions

The first step is to establish the objective of the study. As already mentioned, in this case, it consists of creating a manual that explains the steps to follow when auditing the usability of a website in the tourism sector. During the second step, data collection is planned and implemented using the different sources considered for the case. Specifically, an exhaustive review of the literature on this topic has been carried out first to obtain the necessary information to create this manual. This theoretical basis has served to extract some general canons, resulting in an initial model proposed for carrying out a usability audit on a tourist destination portal. Second, this initial model has been empirically compared with a real usability audit that, in this case, has been the recent one on the website visitacostadelsol.com carried out during 2017. This has warranted in-depth interviews to be conducted with those responsible for the audit.

The third step, involving analysis and conclusions, has been made possible by the actual audit conducted by the Costa del Sol Tourism and Planning institution where recommendations and implementation improvements were obtained, not only from the web, but from the audit process itself. Consequently, we are urged to fill a gap existing in the literature and develop a detailed manual as a guide for auditors of tourist destination websites through comparing the initial model based on the actual usability audit case.

SOLUTIONS AND RECOMMENDATIONS

At this point and based mainly on recommendations made by Nielsen (1994) and Jeffrey and Chisnell (2008), together with information taken from the Costa del Sol Tourism and Planning case, we will finally describe how to carry out a usability audit on a tourist destination website. The basic objective of this is to identify any eventual errors the website may have, and to propose solutions that make it a useful, easy to learn, easy to use tool that makes it very unlikely for users to commit errors that are not easily remedied.

Contributions of the Costa del Sol Tourism and Planning Audit

The contributions that, in principle, were not specifically considered in the theoretical models and that have been extracted from the audit conducted by the Costa del Sol Tourism and Planning institution are summarized in the following:

1. **Methodology combined with the user test as a core.** Regarding the method to follow, it has been very useful to implement additional methodologies, together with that of the user test, as they enrich the audit by identifying errors and generating recommendations from different perspectives.
2. **Focus on devices.** The audit adopted a model called "Mobile first", since it was based on the fact that users mainly access destination websites from their mobile devices and mobile access figures have increased through the abolition of roaming. The fact that visits to destination websites are eminently mobile has conditioned the usability of the portal. In this context, for example, the size of the device and the fact that it has a touch screen change the way users interact with the web and, therefore, usability requirements. Therefore, the usability analysis was carried out on the mobile phone and then moved to devices with larger screens. This approach organizes all of your information according to the different versions of the web, which is very useful when it comes to understanding and implementing the recommended improvements.
3. **Selection of external auditors with previous experience in the sector.** Selecting auditors with experience in conducting usability audits on websites and who are familiar with or are specialized in the tourism sector was the right thing to do. This is due to the advantage of these auditors being able to better guarantee what mistakes are usually made and what solutions usually work.
4. **Description of the user profile based on their tourist habits.** The audit revealed the relevance of tourist habits as key variables when determining web usability. Therefore, when describing the profiles of users selected to perform the user tests, it is important that they be based on tourist behavior such as their accommodation preferences, their preferred means of transport or activities in which they are interested.
5. **Selection of personalized tasks for user tests.** The tasks that were selected to perform the user test were very specific actions of the destination website to be audited, that is, those actions most repeated by users on the site and, therefore, the most representative. For example, in the case of the Costa del Sol, they were asked to look for an event on the agenda, navigate through this agenda and consult that particular event. The objective of this is to underline the importance of testing the major paths and tools offered by a specific website to know if they are useful or if they work correctly.
6. **Benchmarking as an additional source of recommendations.** This technique was used, based on other tourist destination websites which have worked well in those aspects in which the audited website makes mistakes, in order to serve as a source of inspiration to solve them.

Once the audit carried out on the website visitacostadelsol.com was implemented, Costa del Sol Tourism and Planning compared the key performance indicators (KPI) for the first four months of 2018 (period in which the improvements proposed after the audit had not yet been implemented) and those for the first four months of 2019 (period in which the proposed improvements had already been implemented). In this comparison, several improvements were observed, which are shown in Figure 1. It is clear that, after the audit, an increase in web traffic has been achieved, which comes largely from new users and organic traffic. It should also be noted that indicators such as the increase in page time and conversions reveal that it is very likely that users' experience in their interaction with the website is now more satisfactory compared to the period before the improvements had been made.

Usability Audit Procedure

Before starting with the audit itself, it is essential to carry out a previous web analysis since it will be necessary to know which users visit the web, as well as the actions most executed by them. Specifically, the web analysis will show us which tourist profiles and which actions are more relevant for the case of the destination web in question, which will be necessary for the audit proposed in this model. For this previous phase, the use of tools such as Google Analytics is recommended. It is also recommended that the website creators themselves carry out this analysis since they are familiar with the content and operation of the website.

On the other hand, the empirical methodology has turned out to be the most suitable for use, or rather the user test, complemented with techniques of two methodologies, the heuristic (based on expert criteria) and the automatic (based on the use of automated software). Therefore, the final model proposed will be based on the user test technique as the main tool. The results achieved through this will be combined with those from the professional criteria of specialists in the field, as well as those from automated analysis tools. This combination aims to guarantee the detection of the greatest number of errors, to which the relevant recommended solutions will finally be assigned.

Specifically, the process proposed in this manual is organized in the phases shown in Figure 2, which are: (1) Audit plan; (2) Preparation of pilot tests; (3) User selection; (4) Auditor selection; (5) Task selection; (6) Development of tests; (7) Organization and analysis of results; (8) Generation of recommendations; (9) Preparation of a final report.

Developing tests (user tests –neutral official auditor–minimum intervention–thinking aloud; critical analysis of auditors; automated analysis).

Organization and analysis of results (preliminary analysis, comprehensive analysis).

Developing recommendations (auditors' criteria, benchmarking, assigning priority).

Final report (single document, executive summary, methodology, results, recommendations (breakdown), appendix).

Audit Plan

Before beginning any test it is necessary to be clear about the purpose of the audit, since this will condition the type of method to be implemented. Therefore, it has to start from an audit plan. This audit plan will differ according to the type of tests to be performed and the degree of formality that the company in question requires, but it should include the following matters:

- Purpose of the audit
- Problems to be solved/Objectives of the tests.
- Place and time at which it will take place.
- Estimated duration of each session.
- Equipment needed to carry out the tests.
- Necessary status of the system at the time the tests begin.

Figure 1. Evolution of the KPI of the web visitacostadelsol.com

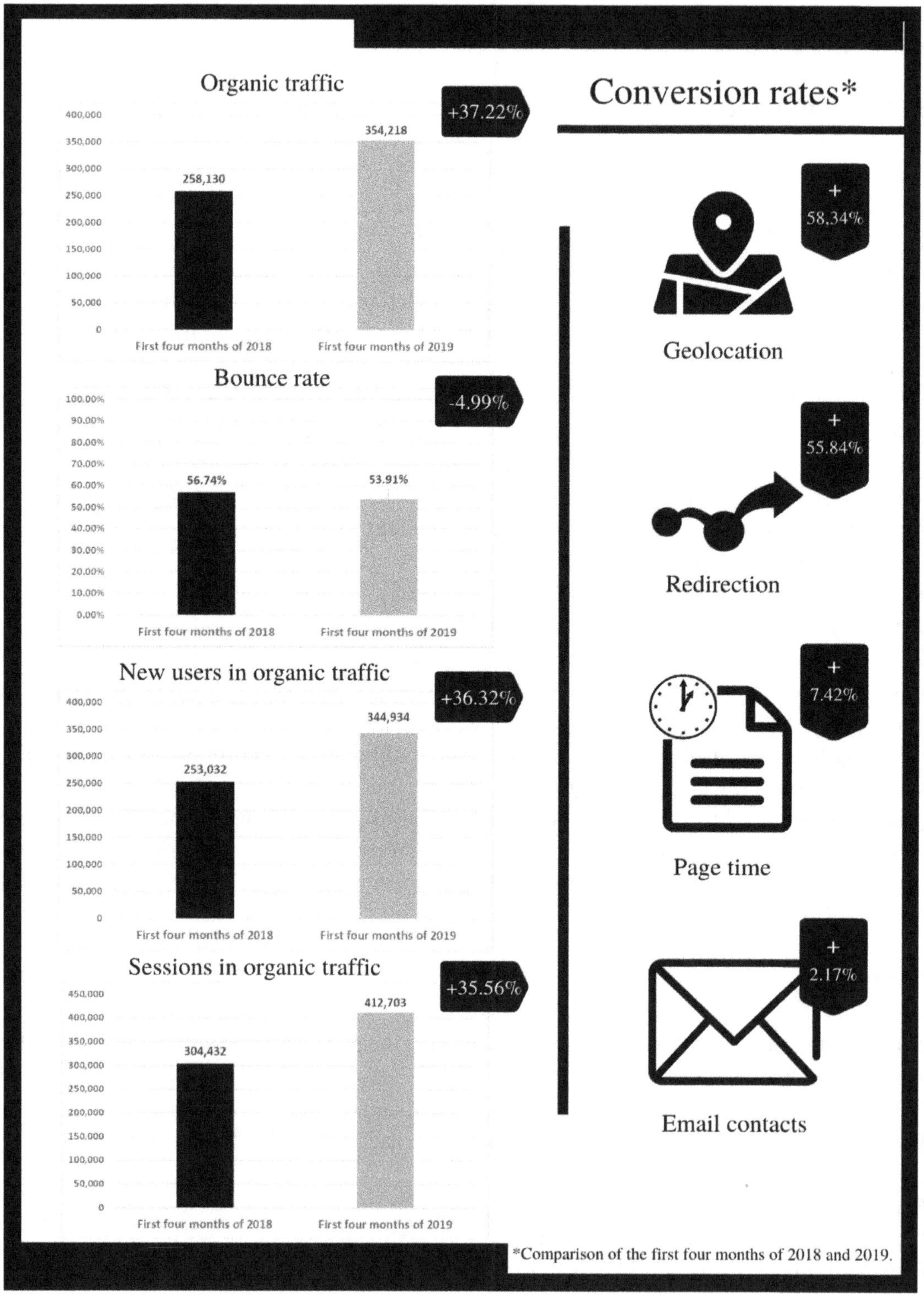

Figure 2. Phases of the usability audit model for tourist destination websites

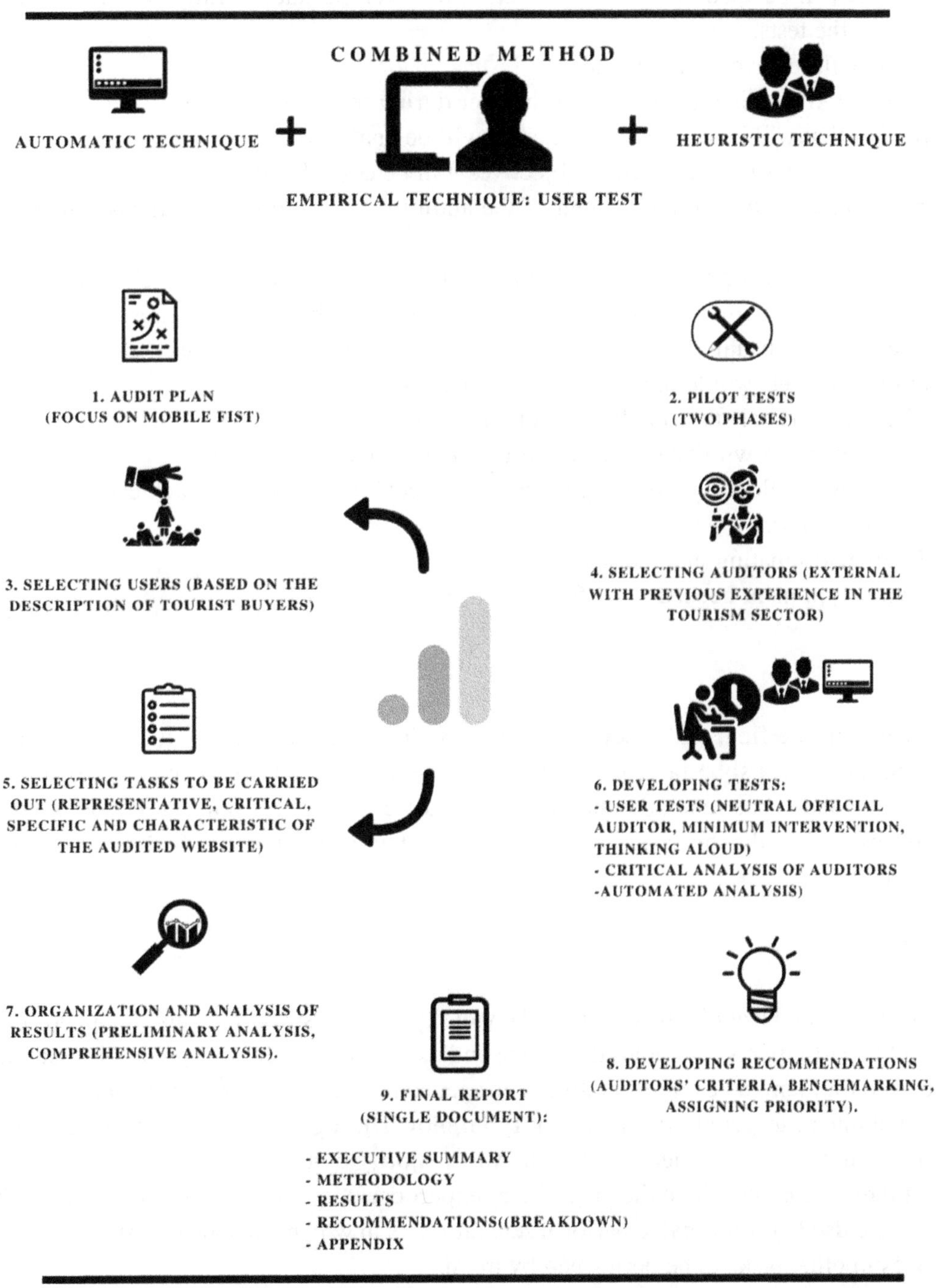

- Desired speed of expected system response, so that the estimate is realistic.
- Identification of the auditors.
- Identification of users who will participate in the tests and how they will be reached.
- Criteria that will be used to determine whether the user has successfully performed the tasks established in the tests.
- Help users will receive during the tests.
- Limit presented by the auditor to assist the user during the tests.
- Information that will be collected and how it will be analyzed.
- Expected level after which usability objectives will be considered satisfied.
- Report and presentation of the content of the audit that will guide auditors and precede the final report.
- Audit budgets. At this point, it is also advisable to separate fixed from variable costs since it will be easier to plan how many users to include in the tests. Although the figures vary widely in each case, the costs are usually around €2,700 of fixed costs and €800 per user test. A general breakdown of the budgets would include the following points:
    - Usability specialists who plan, direct and analyze the tests.
    - Administrators who schedule user tests, enter data, etc.
    - Software developers who change codes to collect information or to achieve the desired modifications to perform the tests.
    - Users participating in the tests.
    - Extra equipment needed to perform the tests.

Pilot Tests

Before carrying out the final audit, several pilot tests should be carried out to identify any possible deficiencies in the previously established audit plan. The number of tests to be performed will depend on the size of the audit, but generally one or two are sufficient. At this point, it is not essential to use representative users. Ideally, this task should be performed with an initial batch of users similar to those used in the final tests.

User Selection

This is a crucial step in the audit process since the validity of the results of the audit depends on whether the profile of the participants resembles that of the end user. Therefore, at this point it is essential to bear in mind the need for them to be representative. The user source can be of a different nature: from current clients who volunteer, to people from temporary employment agencies, students (in case this profile will enter the system's target audience), etc. The vast majority of audits require the use of new users in the field, but there are cases where the presence of expert users is also required. In the case where both types of users are used, it is normal to perform separate tests in which some tasks are common, but there are differences in other tasks to be performed by them.

In the case of tourism, when selecting users, the most representative profiles must be taken as a reference according to the previous web analysis carried out. This representativeness that is taken as a reference must focus mainly on the user's tourist profile, that is, on those factors that are truly relevant for tourist entities, based primarily on their tourist behavior (leisure, culture, accommodation interests, transport, etc.). In addition, because this is a website that is being audited, the device through which they access it is also an important factor to take into account in the selection of users, with the use of mobile devices being particularly important. The internationality of a typical user profile on tourist destination websites must also be taken into account. Therefore, it is convenient to select users that represent the different cultural profiles that normally visit the website.

Auditor Selection

When choosing the auditors, it is obviously preferable to assign the position to people with previous experience in the matter and, specifically, in the execution of the evaluation method to be used. It is evident that the effectiveness of the audit depends largely on the method used and, therefore, it is important that the people who carry it out have prior knowledge. This does not mean that the presence of experienced auditors is essential, since it is also possible to perform an evaluation without them, although the chances of achieving the desired effectiveness are lower.

In addition to experience in the method to be used, another important factor to consider is the knowledge of the system to be evaluated, its applications and its interfaces. This knowledge is necessary to understand what users do when trying to carry out the tasks in the system and to draw reasonable conclusions about their eventual intentions while interacting with the system. This does not mean that the auditor should know how the system is implemented. In fact, the presence of programmers in the system is also recommended in case intervention is necessary to solve any problems that may arise during the audit.

An easy way to find auditors with knowledge of the system to be evaluated is to assign designers themselves for this position. This has its advantages, since the position is attributed to the person entrusted with the task of introducing the possible usability improvements resulting from the audit. In other words, the usability improvement process is shortened since the person who obtains recommendations for improvements and implements them is the same. However, this also has its disadvantage, since the degree of objectivity required of an auditor is at risk in these cases and there is a tendency to provide excessive help to users during the tests.

Based on this, in the tourism sector a good profile would be considered that of professional auditors not belonging to the organization, specialized in usability audits and with experience in the tourism sector. This guarantees great objectivity when it comes to inspecting the website and interesting contributions based on their experience in the sector, that is, it enables the heuristic methodology to be implemented.

Task Selection

A basic rule when selecting the tasks for users to perform during the audit is that these should closely represent the uses to be made of the system. This selection should cover the most prominent parts of the user interface. To carry out this work, users should make use of the information supplied by data analyses, as they do to understand the profile of the representative user. Furthermore, the tasks entrusted must be concise enough to enable them to be carried out within the established time limits, but without falling into the error that they are so simple that they become insignificant. Another important aspect of this point is that the tasks must clearly specify which final result the user is expected to achieve.

Along the same lines, in the case of tourist destination websites, it is necessary to select those that were most representative according to the web analysis, as well as those that, at the discretion of the auditors, turn out to be critical actions on a tourist destination website: check the events agenda, find accommodation or make a reservation, for example. As long as they are better defined and more specific, it is more likely to detect possible errors associated with the corresponding task.

Development of tests

Focusing on the user test, usability tests generally have four phases:

Phase 1: Preparation. In this phase, the auditor must ensure that everything is ready: the materials to be used, instructions for users, questionnaires, that all legal requirements that may exist be met, that the system is in the initial status according to the plan or that everything necessary for data collection is available.

Phase 2: Introduction. At this point, the auditors give users a brief explanation about the purpose of the tests and the configuration of the system in case it is something they are not familiar with. Other aspects such as willingness to participate in the tests, confidentiality, etc. are also discussed.

Phase 3: Test development. At this stage, it is essential for the audit to be carried out on all elements of the audited product which, in the case at hand, are the tourist destinations, not on individual parts thereof. However, the reliability of an audit on a particular item would not be affected as long as the results of this audit were shared with the results of others on the other product items. The following are some key factors to consider when carrying out the audit:

- Previously assigning the position of officer to one of the auditors, who would be the only one who could speak during the tests, but only if necessary.
- Monitoring the session impartially. The auditor's attitude should not differ when faced with different results and he should react in the exact same way to a user error as to correct behavior.
- Being aware of the effects that the voice and body language of the auditor may have on the user during the tests.
- Treating each new participant individually. The auditor should not be influenced by his experience with the previous participant.
- Not "rescuing" participants when they find it difficult to carry out any task, unless it is obvious that the user is frustrated.
- If an error is committed as an auditor, such as releasing information to the participant, the tests must proceed without any interruption.
- Ensuring that the participant completes one task before continuing with the next one.
- Maintaining a relaxed atmosphere and making it clear to the participants that there are no right or wrong answers.
- Using the "thinking aloud" technique, which consists in making the participants express their thoughts aloud while carrying out the tasks entrusted to them. However, although this technique can help users focus and the auditor to obtain clues about the confusion that leads users to make mistakes, it slows down the thinking process and can be disturbing and unnatural for participants.
- Interacting with users appropriately. Interaction must be minimal, and direct questions should not always be used. The auditor must act as a mirror that reflects users' thoughts in order to help them express what impressions they have during the course of the tests.
- Helping users as a last resort.
- Using checklists to guide the test development process.

Phase 4: Interrogation. In this last phase, users are provided with a questionnaire for them to make any comments and suggestions about the system. During the interrogation, questions are also asked about specific moments or events during the user's interaction with the system, all by way of review. The objective of this step is to understand the reason for each error made by users and the difficulty encountered by them. This is the last opportunity to resolve these issues before users end their participation.

However, as already mentioned, apart from the user test, it has also proved very useful to perform two more types of tests. On the one hand, it is advisable to perform an analysis of the external auditors. In this test, it is the auditors themselves, as experts in web usability and connoisseurs of other tourist destination websites, who analyze the website in question to identify errors at their discretion. The auditors will work on the main pages of the website, as well as the different elements of same (forms, search engines, content, etc.). This would provide us with the second source of results. To complement the two previous tests, it is also recommended that participants carry out an automated analysis using different software tools in order to measure different aspects of the website, such as its adaptation to the different devices or loading speed. This analysis would constitute the third source of results.

Organization and Analysis of Results

The task of measuring usability is complex since it requires quantification of an aspect of tremendous ambiguity. The following are some of the most commonly used measures:

- Time required to complete a task.
- Number of different tasks that can be carried out in a given period of time.
- Interaction/error ratio.
- Number of errors committed by users during the interaction.
- Number of commands or other system features implemented by the user.
- Number of commands or other system features not implemented by the user.
- Number of times that users showed obvious frustration or clear satisfaction.

Once the results are in the form of raw data, this information must be organized and polished to facilitate the task of identifying errors and their possible origins. For this purpose, it is important to carry out two different processes. The first is to carry out a preliminary analysis to quickly ascertain the most serious usability problems. This enables developers work on solving them as soon as possible. This should be done immediately upon completion of the audit in the form of small written report or a brief verbal presentation of recommendations. Once this analysis has been completed, a comprehensive analysis follows, which is carried out between the second and fourth week after the audit. Its format is an exhaustive report that includes both the updated recommendations of the preliminary analysis and the new findings.

Data collected during the tests performed in the audit must first be compiled and summarized in order to carry out these analyzes. The key to compiling the data is to organize it into patterns. Inferential statistics (means, medians, time ranges, etc.) help identify these patterns. Subsequently, descriptive summaries should be produced to provide a snapshot of what happened during the tests, such as the points at which users acted correctly and at what point they erred. Once these two steps have been completed, it will not be difficult to identify the errors and problems found by users.

However, the greatest difficulty will be in finding the true source of these errors, that is, in attributing a reason related to the audited product resulting in user problems or errors. This requires many areas to be analyzed: annotations and reports made during the audit by each auditor, recordings made during the tests or the knowledge of auditors and developers on how the system and its user interface work. It will also be necessary to take into account the background of the users who made the mistakes. When the errors and problems are identified, as well as the reason for them, the next step is to assign each of these problems a priority depending on whether the errors are more or less critical; considering criticality as the combination of severity with probability of occurrence. In this way, those problems that are considered more critical should be solved first.

Regardless of whether the error has been identified by the user test, by the auditors' judgment or by automated methods, it is necessary to emphasize the need to search for general errors of the website as well as those in each of its different language or device versions. Since the tourism industry is an international business, webs must be adapted to cultural differences that may exist between potential users coming from the different markets we wish to analyze.

Generation of Recommendations

After the previous analysis, the auditors will work together to propose recommendations for each of the errors identified. This step is the *raison d'être* of a usability audit. Knowledge of the principles of usability and user-centered design are always very beneficial in the process of developing appropriate recommendations. However, this task should not be carried out by a single person, but by a team, since this allows different perspectives to be provided, which is considered essential. Furthermore, those who have to implement the recommendations are consequently convinced of their usefulness since they have participated in their development. There are certain useful key factors to bear in mind when making recommendations:

- It is necessary to focus on solutions with the most general impact on the web.
- When making the first draft, the possibilities of being able to implement the recommendations that are going to be proposed should not be taken into account, even if they have to be discarded later.
- After the initial draft, and after weighing up the errors, it is advisable to propose recommendations that can be implemented in both the short and long term.
- It is necessary to indicate those areas that are found to need a deeper study after the audit.
- It is necessary to address every problem identified in the audit.

In this way, based on their knowledge of web usability and on their experience in audits performed on similar websites, auditors may have a greater knowledge of the problem. Additionally, the benchmarking technique should be used, which will use as a reference other tourist destination websites that have been able to function in those aspects in which the audited website makes mistakes. Depending on the errors for which a solution is provided, the recommendations will have greater or lesser priority when they are implemented, so the auditors should make it clear which ones are priorities.

Preparation of a Final Report

The final report is the document that the external auditors must present to the internal team of the entity whose website has been audited. It is essential that it be perfectly organized, and that it clearly inform the reader and facilitate the task of implementing the improvements. It should thus be organized in the following way:

- **Executive Summary**. This is an initial section that constitutes a brief presentation of the main recommendations and benefits that the website will achieve with their implementation.
- **Methodology**. Everything related to the criteria, tools and methods used to find recommendations for improvement of the website appears in this section.
- **Results**. The results obtained from each test performed are organized in as many graphs as possible, by type of test (user test, evaluation of professional auditors and automated tests) and, in turn, by the different variants thereof, as well as the different sections audited in each variant. This will make it easy for the reader to identify the results each audited section of the website has obtained in each test.
- **Recommendations**. This is the most important part of the report, as it contains the improvements that should be implemented. It is advisable that these recommendations be organized into general recommendations, that is, those whose implementation affects the website in general, and specific recommendations or, which is the same, recommendations directed towards a specific version of the website, by device or by language. Both categories of recommendations should then be organized by section of the website, for example, sections dedicated to accommodation, activities, destinations, etc., as well as by priority. All recommendations should be shown, where possible, using graphics and comparative examples "before/after", making it easier for the internal team to understand them.
- **Appendices**. It is advisable to include an annex that informs the recipient of the final report of the raw data on which the auditors' recommendations are based. In this section, recordings of user tests can be added to demonstrate their opinions while interacting with the website, as well as the data obtained from the different tests to which the website has been submitted through the different automated software packages.

FUTURE RESEARCH DIRECTIONS

Despite the obvious practical application of the model developed in this work, its contributions have certain limitations. Although Costa del Sol Tourism and Planning has verified the improvement experienced in the KPIs used as indicators by the entity after the usability audit, this is a recent experience and a study of its evolution in the longer term is pending. Regardless of this improvement, it would also be risky to attribute it solely and exclusively to the implementation of the usability audit, as this agency carries out other marketing initiatives during the same period.

Due to these limitations, and given that it is a pioneering manual in the sector, it would be advisable that future lines of research be devoted to the empirical comparison of the proposed model in order to verify its effectiveness. It would therefore be useful to make comparative empirical studies, for example, following the steps of the manual in the audit of different tourist destination websites in order to identify the relationship between the implementation of the usability audit and the resulting subsequent improvements.

CONCLUSION

In a globalized world, tourist destinations are forced to offer a promotional website that provides information about them presented in the appropriate way so that it is useful and simple for the user who seeks information or intends to plan a trip. This implies that the presence of information about the destination on a website is not enough, but that it must be presented in the appropriate manner. This is where the concept of usability arises, that is, the degree to which a product or system can be used by specific users to achieve specific objectives with effectiveness, efficiency and satisfaction in a particular context. This work fills an existing gap in the literature since, in many cases, those responsible for tourist destination websites have felt lost by not having a manual to serve as a guide for assessing the usability of their website.

A case study methodology has been chosen to prepare this manual. General theoretical knowledge on web usability audits found in the literature and the empirical contrast thereof have been combined in a real web usability audit in the tourism field. The real audit case was carried out by Costa del Sol Tourism and Planning, which is the entity in charge of promoting the tourist destination of the province of Malaga under the Costa del Sol brand through its website visitacostadelsol.com.

Apart from the description of the manual itself, the results of this work have made it possible to identify a series of actions to be taken into account, as well as others that should be avoided when a usability audit is being carried out in the tourism field. The recommendation to use external auditors and experts in the tourism sector, the application of a combined method that is enriched by the techniques of different methods, beyond the use of the solo user test, or the use of benchmarking as an additional source of recommendations have proved to be key factors in the audit of tourist websites. On the contrary, it has been shown that it is not advisable to segregate the final audit report into several documents by subject matter since it makes it difficult to implement improvements.

REFERENCES

Adukaite, A., Gazizova, E., & Cantoni, L. (2014). When e-gov deals with tourists: The case of visa information. In *ACM International Conference Proceeding Series* (pp. 334–337). Association for Computing Machinery. 10.1145/2691195.2691283

Au, I., Boardman, R., Robin, J., Larvie, P., Pavese, A., Riegelsberger, J., ... Stevens, M. (2008). User experience al Google-Focus on the user and all else will follow. In *CHI'08 Extended Abstracts on Human Factors in Computing Systems* (pp. 3681–3686). ACM.

Becken, S. (2013). Measuring the effect of weather on tourism: A destination- and activity-based analysis. *Journal of Travel Research*, *52*(2), 156–167. doi:10.1177/0047287512461569

Brown, D., & Hayes, N. (2008). *Influencer Marketing. Who really influences your customers?* Taylor & Francis.

Cam, L. N. T., Anh, T. T., Moslehpour, M., & Thanh, X. D. T. (2019). Exploring the impact of traditional and electronic word of mouth on travel intention. In *ACM International Conference Proceeding Series* (pp. 83–87). Association for Computing Machinery. 10.1145/3317614.3317617

Carstens, D. S., & Patterson, P. (2005). Usability study of travel websites. *Journal of Usability Studies*, *1*(1), 47–61.

De-Laguno-Alarcón, C., Sierra-Herrezuelo, P., & Rojas-de-Gracia, M. M. (2019). Results-oriented influencer marketing manual for the tourism industry. In K. Mezghani & W. Aloulou (Eds.), *Business transformation in the era of digitalization* (pp. 249–275). IGI Global. doi:10.4018/978-1-5225-7262-6.ch014

Degen, H., Lubin, K. L., Pedell, S., & Ji, Z. (2005). Travel planning on the web: a cross-cultural case study. In N. Aykin (Ed.), *Usability and internationalization of information technology* (pp. 313–343). Lawrence Erlbaum Associates, Publishers.

Dominguez, G., Hammill, S. J., & Brillat, A. I. (2015). Toward a usable academic library web site: A case study of tried and tested usability practices. *Journal of Web Librarianship*, *9*(2-3), 99–120. doi:10.1080/19322909.2015.1076710

Dwyer, L., Forsyth, P., & Rao, P. (2002). Destination price competitiveness: Exchange rate changes versus domestic inflation. *Journal of Travel Research*, *40*(3), 328–336. doi:10.1177/0047287502040003010

Feagin, J. R., Orum, A. M., & Sjoberg, G. (1991). *A case for the case study*. UNC Press Books.

Fernández-Cavia, J., Díaz-Luque, P., Huertas, A., Rovira, C., Pedraza-Jimenez, R., Sicilia, M., ... Máguez-González, M. I. (2013). Marcas de destino y evaluación de sitios web: Una metodología de investigación. *Revista Latina de Comunicación Social*, (68), 622–638. doi:10.4185/RLCS-2013-993

Fernández-Cavia, J., Rovira, C., Díaz-Luque, P., & Cavaller, V. (2014). Web Quality Index (WQI) for official tourist destination websites. Proposal for an assessment system. *Tourism Management Perspectives*, *9*, 5–13. doi:10.1016/j.tmp.2013.10.003

Finn, K., & Johnson, J. (2013). A usability study of websites for older travelers. In Lecture Notes in Computer Science (including subseries Lecture Notes in Artificial Intelligence and Lecture Notes in Bioinformatics) (vol. 8010 LNCS, pp. 59–67). doi:10.1007/978-3-642-39191-0_7

Gallarza, M. G., Saura, I. G., & García, H. C. (2002). Destination image: Towards a conceptual framework. *Annals of Tourism Research*, *29*(1), 56–78. doi:10.1016/S0160-7383(01)00031-7

George, A. L., Bennett, A., Lynn-Jones, S. M., & Miller, S. E. (2005). *Case studies and theory development in the social sciences*. MIT Press.

Higgins-Desbiolles, F. (2018). Event tourism and event imposition: A critical case study from Kangaroo Island, South Australia. *Tourism Management*, *64*, 73–86. doi:10.1016/j.tourman.2017.08.002

Hung, Y. H., Hu, P. C., & Lee, W. T. (2013, August). *Improving the design and adoption of travel websites: An user experience study on travel information recommender systems*. Paper presented at 5th IASDR International Conference, Tokio, Japan.

Jeffrey, R., & Chisnell, D. (2008). *Handbook of usability testing: How to plan, design, and conduct effective test.* Jonh Wiley & Sons.

Lian, T., & Yu, C. (2019). Impacts of online images of a tourist destination on tourist travel decision. *Tourism Geographies, 21*(4), 635–664. doi:10.1080/14616688.2019.1571094

Maldonado, S. (2015). *Analítica web: Medir para triunfar.* ESIC.

Manhas, P. S., Manrai, L. A., & Manrai, A. K. (2016). Role of tourist destination development in building its brand image: A conceptual model. *Journal of Economics, Finance and Administrative Science, 21*(40), 25–29. doi:10.1016/j.jefas.2016.01.001

Martínez-Sala, A. M., Monserrat-Gauchi, J., & Alemany-Martínez, D. (2020). User usable experience: A three-dimensional approach on usability in tourism websites and a model for its evaluation. *Tourism Management Perspectives, 33*(July), 100579. doi:10.1016/j.tmp.2019.100579

Martinis, A., Papadatou, A., & Kabassi, K. (2019). An analysis of the electronic presence of national parks in Greece. In V. Katsoni & M. Segarra-Oña (Eds.), *Smart Tourism as a Driver for Culture and Sustainability* (pp. 433–449). Springer. doi:10.1007/978-3-030-03910-3_30

McCartney, G., Butler, R., & Bennett, M. (2008). A strategic use of the communication mix in the destination image-formation process. *Journal of Travel Research, 47*(2), 183–196. doi:10.1177/0047287508321201

Nielsen, J. (1994). *Usability engineering.* Elsevier.

Nielsen, J. (1999). *Designing web usability: The practice of simplicity.* New Riders Publishing.

Nielsen, J., & Molich, R. (1990). Heuristic evaluation of user interfaces. In *Proceedings of the SIGCHI conference on Human factors in computing systems* (pp. 249–256). ACM.

Nielsen, J., & Tahir, M. (2011). *Homepage usability: 50 websites deconstructed.* New Riders Publishing.

Nielsen. (2015). Global trust in advertising: Winning strategies for an evolving media landscape. *Nielsen.* Retrieved from http://www.nielsen.com

Rubin, J., & Chisnell, D. (2008). *Handbook of usability testing: How to plan, design and conduct effective tests.* John Wiley & Sons.

Shani, A., Chen, P. J., Wang, Y., & Hua, N. (2010). Testing the impact of a promotional video on destination image change: Application of china as a tourism destination. *International Journal of Tourism Research, 12*(2), 116–133. doi:10.1002/jtr.738

Yin, R. K. (1994). Case study research. Design and methods (2nd ed.). London: SAGE Publications.

Zhou, Q., & DeSantis, R. (2005). Usability issues in city tourism website design: A content analysis. In *IEEE International Professional Communication Conference* (pp. 789–796). IEEE.

Chapter 16
Motives for the New Disruptive Technologies:
Focus on the Blockchain Technology

Nermin Brkovic
University of Gothenburg, Sweden

Shahryar Sorooshian
https://orcid.org/0000-0001-5336-827X
University of Gothenburg, Sweden

ABSTRACT

This literature review presents a number of motives and opportunities for Supply Chain 4.0 transition with underlying pillars in focus that are IoT, AI, big data, and blockchain technology. All technologies and systems are described briefly concerning the existing literature, with an extensive focus on blockchain technology. It becomes apparent that we are standing in front of a massive supply chain transition, where connectivity and digital networks will create competitive advantages. Aspects like efficiency, traceability, visibility, transparency, auditability, and flexibility will play significant roles for organisations and their ability to successfully adapt to future supply chain transformations.

1. INTRODUCTION

Traditional supply chains are stacking up on disadvantages related to more extended supply chains. Supply chains are becoming more complex due to rapidly changing market environments, growing international competition as well as demand and output volatility. These features are happening side by side with increasing global connectivity by advanced new technologies (Rejeb et al. 2019). Customers, on the other side, want more product and service customisation with the higher service level, and lower prices. To embrace the new complicated market environment, firms need to be more agile and have better risk capabilities to respond quickly. But this is costly, and according to Ben-Daya et al. (2019), firms need

DOI: 10.4018/978-1-7998-8583-2.ch016

to gain better visibility throughout the whole supply chain and have better collaboration with all actors, from the suppliers to the customers, in order to balance the costs.

Challenges today can be risks such as more involved intermediaries, increasing amount of corruption, lack of quality control and difficulties of evaluating impacts of disruptions along the chain (Manners-Bell 2017). Challenges regarding information sharing between the entities are also important because that creates trust issues, and poor transparency throughout the supply chain for the customers (Loop 2016). With the lack of information sharing also comes visibility issues. It is challenging to verify the sources of the materials and the information when there are different kinds of inconsistencies throughout the supply chain (Frederico et al. 2019).

According to Chopra & Meindl (2010), supply chain management often includes trade-offs, where it is said that responsiveness cannot improve without increasing capability costs. Still, new technology development could change this. The new disruptive technologies consist of Internet of Things, Artificial Intelligence, Big Data Analysis, Robotics, Wearables, 3D printing, Blockchain Technology etc. and can reshape the supply chain management. Wiedenmann & Größler (2019) argues that the new technologies have opened up a range of potentials and opportunities with networking throughout the whole supply chain. The new disruptive technologies would have implications on all business areas that will lead to considerable changes in the supply chains. It is about connecting the physical world to the digital world, and it will depend on how companies in the future acquire, handle and share data along their supply chains and its stakeholders (Barata et al. 2018).

2. MOTIVATION AND METHODOLOGY

This literature review aims to examine how different entities and actors in the supply chain can adapt and determine their motives behind and for Supply Chain 4.0 deployment to gain competitive advantage. Focus is limited to four disruptive technologies - which are IoT, AI, Big Data and Blockchain Technology.

A collection of articles was collected and analysed systematically to evaluate relevant literature. An up-to-date literature review is presented where pertinent keywords to Supply Chain 4.0 was conducted in the first steps. The keywords were used in databases such as Google Scholar and GU Supersök to find appropriate literature. The search period was from 2016 to 2019. A screening and extraction process was later made based on titles and abstracts to eliminate irrelevant literature. All the sources were reviewed for peer-review and number of citations, to get higher reliability. Few sources are not from academic journals or articles, but they are only used when describing a phenomenon.

3. SUPPLY CHAIN 4.0

3.1. Supply Chain Management

A supply chain is a network of units, products and services tied together with actors that can be suppliers, factories, distributors, wholesalers, retailers and end customers. The role of supply chain management is to integrate different entities in the supply chain and efficiently manage and coordinate order flows, physical flows and financial flows both upstream and downstream, to reach the goal of maximising the added value. The aim is to minimise the costs and still meet customer requirements (Simchi-Levi & Kaminsky 2007).

The new era of supply chain management, also called Supply Chain 4.0, has developed from Industry 4.0. This is a term that marks the beginning of digitisation and digitalisation in the manufacturing processes with the help of new technologies. Industry 4.0 is characterised by products and services that flexibly connects to networks, where digital connectivity enables automated and optimised production and deliveries without human interaction (Hofmann & Rüsch 2017).

3.2. Towards Development

The critical enabler of visibility is connectivity which removes technological barriers amongst entities in the supply chain. Visibility leads to better supply chain integration and better supply chain performance (Somapa et al. 2018). Thereby the motives of enhancing more visibility gives benefits such as better inventory control, shorter lead times, improved forecasting, a better understanding of customer behaviour, greater flexibility and better risk management (Calatayud et al. 2019). Before Industry 4.0 and the new disruptive technologies, supply chain collaboration and monitoring were difficult as identification, and data availability was limited, with a lack of system interoperability (Gnimpieba et al. 2015).

In Supply Chain 4.0, the performance will be monitored by a massive amount of data in collaboration with many disruptive technologies to forecast and identify risks. There will be simulation models that will allow to predict the future with minimal errors and allow taking actions automatically to prevent ongoing and future risks which will lead to greater agility and proactivity (Calatayud et al. 2019). The adoption of Supply Chain 4.0 will in most cases allow organisations to have better visibility and reduce the disruptions by having a flexible and digital integrated ecosystem. This is also a way to leverage new technologies to create smart and efficient processes (Makris et al. 2019).

3.3. Supply Chain 4.0 Characteristics

Supply Chain 4.0 in general will create new ways of creating competitive advantage. Radanliev et al. (2019) claims that when different entities and actors connect and exchange information, they will provide optimised transportation and production, along with better inventory management. The throughput time and labour costs could also be reduced due to smarter inventory management which is enabled by new technology implementation (Rejeb et al. 2019). Another work, Frederico et al. (2019), found out that this will enable self-adjustment and self-optimisation of the performance and result in cost reductions and potential increase of market share. The key is interoperability to ensure that different systems can understand each other. Furthermore, Supply Chain 4.0 can enable opportunities like resource savings and economies of scale with smart manufacturing and more likely to meet personalised customer requirements to give better value. Supply Chain 4.0 is expected to have an impact on customer requirements with faster response. There would also be improvements in collaboration and transparency, which would benefit suppliers and avoid disruptions in the supply chain. Operational improvements would reduce costs and improve flexibility, where profitability would be increased. All this would result in a better competitive advantage for adaptive organisations (Frederico et al. 2019).

With larger supply chain flows, more integrated entities and increasing adoption of automatization, the visibility becomes essential. The new technologies within Supply Chain 4.0 have the capabilities to capture real-world visibility and feedback in precision (Radanliev et al. 2019). With more connection between people, places and information, the more interaction it will satisfyingly be between customers and companies. It will enable and create motives for new business models, integrate every link in the supply chain and allow for new ways to make a profit in business processes and supply chains (Andrews et al. 2016). According to Shanley (2017), the usage of the new technologies will improve coordination and real-time monitoring of location, temperature, waste, recalls etc. and allow modes of transports and shipments to be tracked instantaneously along the route.

3.4. Internet of Things

The undergoing digital development has made much impact on supply chain structures already, both with internal and external integration. One of the disruptive technologies in Supply Chain 4.0 is the Internet of Things. IoT takes communication in the supply chains to another step, especially between humans and things. IoT relates to the extension of the internet into tangible things where entities can interact within a company or its supply chain, where IoT emits data from smart objects and then collects, analyses and turns it into useful information (Ben-Daya et al. 2019). The added value from IoT comes from the integration of sensors and by setting the data available to the users (Calatayud et al. 2019).

If the implementation of IoT is successful in the supply chains of organisations, it could result in a more intelligent and agile supply chain consisting of physical machines and objects that are integrated with sensors, processes and human factors (Vaidya et al. 2018). IoT has the motive of enabling effective decision making when data acquisition is more rapid, which enables quick reactions to changes in real-time, allowing for higher agility. This has also enabled new levels of visibility and adaptability into all aspects of the supply chain. It is, for example, easier to provide forecasts and early signs of potential risks (Ben-Daya et al. 2019).

IoT also has the ability to improve cost savings, improve inventory accuracy and enhance product tracking, which will be helpful for planning and the coordination of vertical and horizontal integration (Pereira & Romero 2017). Some significant fundamental changes that will occur due to IoT is different customer requirements where production can be applicable to last-minute changes. The flexibility can thereby be infused with more dynamic configuration of time, price and quality. Increased flexibility can also be good for the suppliers where they can put better value into products with more knowledge acquired more easily. The motives behind implementing IoT is that it leads to better-optimised decisions, along with better resource efficiency, since there will be pressure to constantly have the highest output possible in the supplier and production entities. IoT will provide more valuable opportunities to Supply Chain 4.0 with its data and algorithm handling by new implementing ways of downstream services and products reaching the markets (Ben-Daya et al. 2019).

Based on the results of the work from Ben-Daya et al. (2019), Industry 4.0 and Supply Chain 4.0 will continue to shift how things are done in the industry sectors. Smart manufacturing will enable faster decisions and smarter operations where visibility, as mentioned earlier, will play a significant role due to the use of real-time information in all aspects of the supply chain. Companies have according to Hofmann (2017) started to give some visibility in their business data to partners. However, it gets complicated when suppliers and customers are spread globally. Bag et al. (2018) report that since IoT enables a more digitalised supply chain, it also allows buyers and sellers to track goods in the supply chain and perform required planning and quality controls. Transparency and communication in the chain are essential for successful adoption of Supply Chain 4.0.

Effective performance measurement has an impact on how fast changes can be identified. Deliveries in the supply chain have some challenges with different measurement standards and lack of compatibility between partners in the supply chain, which results in inefficiency and reduced amount of analysed data that could be used as a competitive advantage (Ben-Daya et al. 2019). Tadejko (2015) named that integration of IoT applications in the deliveries with visibility and real-time monitoring would reduce the costs and delays. It would also allow synchronisation between the transports and the production. (Rejeb 2018) states that multiple IoT devices could transform transportation processes where GPS can be used to position trucks and optimise routing, together with RFID and other connected sensors, to increase the visibility of conditions like temperature and location with analysis of the traffic data.

3.5. CPS and RFID

There are underlying systems that have significant importance concerning Supply Chain 4.0 and IoT. One of them is CPS, cyber-physical systems. CPS consists of machines and facilities that enable management of connected systems that autonomously exchange information and trigger wanted actions. CPS brings the digital and physical attributes together which allows for new types of control, efficiency and transparency implementations to the supply chain. CPS might also reduce overall inventory level and safety inventory (Hofmann & Rüsch 2017). The other important system is radio frequency identification, RFID. RFID is mostly used to gather data and make decisions alongside with a broad IoT framework in Supply Chain 4.0. It also can provide identification for goods. RFID identifies targets using radio signals and reads relevant data without contact between the system and the target (Yan et al. 2017). RFID tags could trigger alerts for specific situations, like empty stations, and lead to improvements in the supply chain planning process and flows (Rejeb et al. 2019). In combination with IoT, it will ensure steady operations with real-time information availability and increased visibility. This will, in most cases, lead to production flexibility and new possibilities and are great motives to deploy in supply chains (Bag et al. 2018).

3.6. Bullwhip Effects

Distortions and variances in demand can occur in the upstream of the supply chains. It is often an effect of increased order variability with goods and information not being transferred throughout the supply chain in right time and quantity. This is called the bullwhip effect. The bullwhip effect results in increased storage, shortage, manufacturing and transportation costs.

Benefits from the disruptive technologies can reduce time delays and processing time which reduces the bullwhip effect. AI can also reduce time delays by spotting patterns in the data, which results in better processing without human irrationality (Wiedenmann & Größler 2019). Closer collaboration due to new technologies in the supply chain leads to better information consistency and higher trust with less forecast uncertainty, and thereby also fewer bullwhip effects (Longo et al. 2019). According to Wiedenmann & Größler (2019) a reduction of the bullwhip effect often reduces the costs, other inefficiencies related to upstream problems and improves the performance of the supply chain.

3.7. Big Data Analytics

Big Data is another disruptive technology in Supply Chain 4.0. This technology has many connections with IoT, but the difference is the amount of data that is managed. Big Data is a model for data and computing resources that will be conducted with minimal effort to increase the value. It is extracted value from a large volume of data, with variety of algorithms that are translated into analytics and stored from different entities, operations and stakeholders in the supply chain (Raman et al. 2018). The motives behind Big Data is that it will provide real-time information and visibility inside the supply chain where demand will be forecasted in a more accurate and safe way. Big Data transmission with networks of smart devices will thereby also support real-time decision making, and give companies increased operating margin. This will result in less manufacturing and assembly costs according to Zhong et al. (2016). Big Data is an essential component and the motives for adoption are that it will bring competitive advantage by solving problems and improving coordination and agility across the supply chains (Wang et al. 2016).

3.8. Artificial Intelligence

A newer disruptive technology that relates to IoT and Big Data is Artificial Intelligence. AI is using algorithms of collected data to make computers understand what data to use and make autonomous decisions from that. It is often related to a computer that thinks and behaves like a human. AI has perception, language processions and can solve problems while simultaneously acting on its environment. AI also has the ability to handle high-speed data transmission and case learning (Ustundag & Cevikcan 2018). Systems based on AI work to optimise both deliveries and inventory management in the supply chains, where growing data availability is expected to make AI as one of the most critical technologies in supply chain management (Merlino & Sponge 2017).

Calatayud et al. (2019) claims that the use of predictive technologies like AI will improve many of the supply chain operations. AI applications in the supply chains will have automated systems that will adjust to real-time information and decide the best options regarding factors such as shortages or disruptions in the supply chain. AI, together with IoT and Big Data, will be able to produce more accurate forecasting and machines will make decisions with reduced lead times as the manual processes are minimized. This will mainly improve supply chain performance in the more increasingly complex world. Guszsca (2018) convicts that reducing human involvement in repetitive tasks will save money and time for the companies, as well as the error rate. The biggest advantage of AI may be that it does not need sleep and food, and thereby can continue to work as much as wanted. This will lead to increased productivity all across the supply chain, and may in the future revolutionise the human dependent transportation industry.

3.9. Just in Time and KANBAN

One of the pull orientation in supply chain management is JIT, Just in Time. The objective by JIT systems is to have a low stock supply system where materials are only produced and supplied if there is demand. It aims for short delivery, short cycle times and agility throughout the supply chain. Supply Chain 4.0 will enable more automated and accurate planning in JIT systems where real-time tracking of flows can improve the planning. Supply Chain 4.0 technologies would also increase the transparency across the supply chain with the JIT systems. Further potential benefits with JIT systems would be reduced bullwhip effects and more integrated supply chains. The second pull orientation is the scheduling system Kanban. It is a system of materials that are supplied with precise quantities at the moment they are needed. By producing when given a demand signal, there is a reduction in inventory levels and costs. Kanban is expected to have improved shortened cycle times due to technology development. The information between buyers and sellers along with the ability to react, will affect the Kanban systems positively, where flexibility will increase due to higher amount of available and processed data (Hofmann & Rüsch 2017).

3.10. Challenges for Supply Chain 4.0

High technology companies are improving at a fast pace due to direct interactions with the different entities in the supply chain. At the same time, the food and retail industry is a bit slower with the adoption. The implementation of Supply Chain 4.0 will have a considerable impact, especially on the digital infrastructure. It will depend on if the organisations have entered the market with a digital business model or adopted one along the way. The investment costs will vary, where the selection and education of employees in all areas will be vital because of integration and transparency. To succeed with the implementation, it will require new skill sets and collaboration across the entities in the supply chain (Makris et al. 2019). Nevertheless, the implementation of the new technologies can have issues like job losses, lack of knowledge, lack of specialised actors in the supply chain, lack of funding and digital security issues which can create uncertainties and risks (Bag et al. 2018). With solved interoperability issues by clear visibility from end-to-end will imply for better competitive advantage. This is not mainly pointed to developed and stable industries indicated by Cataluyud (2017). With increased connectivity, less developed companies and poorer countries can participate more globally since digital barriers are reduced and entering thresholds lowered. It will be easier to use Supply Chain 4.0 capabilities and participate in global trade with fewer investments and assets.

3.11. Transparency Issues

Globalisation is emerging, and supply chains are getting more complex. There are several cases of mismanaged supply chains with corruption, delays, child labour, counterfeits etc. where demand for increased transparency and visibility is required by the entities in the supply chain (Abeyratne & Monfared 2016). The disruptive technologies within Supply Chain 4.0 have reduced the information asymmetry a lot, but many companies are still not inclined to share their data if it is sensible because of trust issues. Many centralised systems also provide with limited access to information from third and second layer actors, which gives limited insight into the supply chain (Petersen et al. 2018). As transparency is one of the crucial standpoints in supply chain management, the disruptive technology called blockchain, which is in early-stage, has the possibility to further transform supply chain flows (Christodoulou et al. 2018).

4. BLOCKCHAIN TECHNOLOGY

4.1. Decentralised Infrastructure

Nakamoto (2008) published ''Bitcoin: A Peer-to-Peer Electronic Cash System'', where he formulated an infrastructure that would allow transactions digitally without third parties involved in a decentralised way. He explained the infrastructure as a chain of connected encrypted blocks that cannot be deleted or changed. Blockchain technology has since been seen as one of the most promising advances in technology in the last decade and promising to help to share information more transparently in the supply chain (Tapscott 2017). The lack of transparency is often associated lack of shared information where the information is stored in silos and hard to come in possession of. As actors do not know each other or have no real interaction, there can be trust issues with lag times, and most of all lack of desired oversight in the supply chain (Norberg 2019).

The information in the blockchain is stored and distributed across all participants, where everyone has a replicated version, in the decentralised network simultaneously, cryptographically and chronologically (Norberg 2019). The decentralised network reduces the single point failure risks with centralised networks, where one failure can shut down or create severe problematic issues. Compared to centralised networks, the decentralised networks also provides better scalability and reduces unnecessary traffic flows (Dorri et al. 2017). The blockchain updates in real-time with built-in immutability, which allows for secure exchange of data and makes the system resilient to attacks and impossible to change stored information (Norberg 2019). So every time new information is added as a new block, it is time-stamped and linked with previous blocks that cannot be deleted. This creates a chain with a single point of truth with only one version, which shows true ownership of a product just by accessing the transaction in the blockchain (Tapscott & Tapscott 2016).

4.2. Distributed and Immutable

The features of distribution and immutability do not only make the transactions secure but are important for preventing fraud and corruption. Collomb & Sok (2016) indicates that blockchain with its transparency, could expose one of the world's biggest corruption problems within international trade. The features with blockchain give the ability to follow products, cargo or keep track of records from their origin with a clear end-to-end traceability (Thurner 2018). In this way, all actors become equally powerful, where no actors control the data everyone (Wang et al. 2019). As companies are looking for ways to share their information more securely where authenticity and integrity are important, blockchain technology is a cost-effective approach. It is a solution where there is one immutable truth that can be viewed by all those who have the right access to it (Longo et al. 2019). Actors can, for example, check if shipments have been inspected, if the temperature was correct during the shipment, audit certificates, and if the negotiated route was taken. Different actors could have different access that only pertains to them in the supply chain, like adding information in some areas but only have the ability to follow the process without interaction in other areas (Gurtu & Johny 2019).

4.3. Motives for Deployment

Calatayud et al. (2019) found in their study that one of the motives of embracing blockchain technology in supply chain management is the increasing actors in the supply chains globally. There are many constraints, and the process between each actor is time-consuming. Blockchain can incorporate all suited actors together and eliminate those who are not needed, like third parties. Blockchain technology is likely to transform the supply chain by removing intermediaries and third parties that was needed for validation. It will also eliminate physical documents for verification. The steps in the supply chain will thereby be reduced, which saves money and time. The data is shared publicly and self-verifiable on the network. Dinh & Thai (2018) explains that the historical trail of information stored in the blockchain is more transparent than centralised solutions, and information sharing is vital for the integration of actors and technologies in the Supply Chain 4.0.

Blockchain technology has the potential for relieving bottlenecks in the supply chains by enabling trust in every step. The information about the companies is in open access, and the stakeholders that are involved can trust the information like they could not do prior blockchain. Shipments can be more reliably controlled about location and conditions, and fraud with third parties will no longer be an issue. Products could be traced during their whole life cycle, from raw materials to waste. There is an ability to evaluate the suppliers or manufacturers before deciding to sign a contract by looking at past transactions (Christodoulou et al. 2018). In relation to this, blockchain technology provides conditions for better operational performance and optimised process flow. This would be done due to the shorter process time and less manual work (Philipp et al. 2019). This would generate more awareness about the supply chain and most likely lead to a reduction of the bullwhip effect in the supply chain (Longo et al. 2019).

Costs of trade and common transactions costs will decrease, which will allow for even greater globalisation (Norberg 2019). Small and medium-sized businesses will have benefits with lower participation costs, because of reduced needs of administration and third-party involvement, which will develop new competitiveness. One important factor is the reduced involvement of intermediaries that will be value-adding (Philipp et al. 2019). Businesses are also dealing with discounts when making procurements. Those are often based on the amount of purchases made, which is hard to trace. Blockchain collects data from all appropriate actors and can audit them without intermediaries which reduces the costs compared to a regular audit process. This is accomplished by having all the actors integrated into one decentralised network that benefits both buyers and sellers (Calatayud et al. 2019).

4.4. Financing Solutions

The supply chain finance could also get improved by blockchain technology. Banks between importers and exporters could guarantee payments much faster, with less need for manual verifications (Norberg 2019). Blockchain could also help to reduce frictions when different parties are signing international deals. If an actor does not approve the letter of credit from the other actor, because they do not trust the bank or worries that the goods or payments will not be delivered securely, blockchain can with a solution like smart contracts solve this (Cong & He 2019). By replacing banks as intermediaries, the processing time for transactions could decrease from one week to just some hours (Guo & Liang 2016). The speed of the transactions is especially important as they can be immediate in seconds in some cases, where decision making in real-time will be crucial. The cost structure is also another motive of adopting blockchain technology as it can almost make the transactions free to any actors all over the world at any time (Maltaverne 2017).

4.5. Synchronisation With IoT and AI

Blockchain technology is also evolving into synchronisation with other disruptive technologies. Blockchain presents solutions for some IoT issues like interoperability, where blockchain supports the network to scale up across the supply chain industries and borders (Rejeb et al. 2019). A combination of IoT and blockchain would bridge the gap of data interoperability but remain secure and reliable. IoT devices would also speed up the automation in the supply chain together with blockchain because of a more secure system with immutable and self-audited transactions (Casino et al. 2017).

With the integration of disruptive technologies and the shift to Supply Chain 4.0, blockchain could, for example, be used to have secure and permanent records of every moment in the supply chain, like a digital footprint (Aryal et al. 2018). This would create better efficiency for the whole global economy with stronger visibility and legitimacy. IoT devices can be used on products that are shipped, with a blockchain system that records data for self-verification and as a proof of action or proof of delivery (Wang et al. 2019). For example, in ports, terminals and docking stations during loading activities, IoT devices could store real-time data in a decentralised way due to blockchain technology. All documents and information about critical processes and product attributes would be immutable and transparent that all involved actors could access. The integration between IoT devices and blockchain will lead development to more automated process flows according to Philipp et al. (2019). These aspects reduce transaction and enforcement costs along supply chains, minimise delays and make reliable to predict production and delivery times (Christodoulou et al. 2018).

4.6. Traceability

To manage the risk of any step will be easier, and every actor in the supply chain will enter their information in the blockchain that others can audit. With the help of QR codes and RFID, product information can be recorded on the blockchain and easier accessible where organisations can obtain greater control of their supply chains (Rejeb et al. 2019). Another motive for blockchain deployment is that consumers also pay more attention to authenticity and want to know where, when and how the products were made and sourced (Wang et al. 2019). Consumers can with new technologies and blockchain see, for example, what ingredients have been used, where they originally came from and transportation of its route (Mao et al. 2019). It can be more into detail, like what has an animal been fed with or what the living conditions were during specific periods etc. that would raise the awareness about food safety. This will help consumers make better-enlightened choices among a variety of products and give capabilities for the producers to compete with other methods than price. Suppliers would have the ability to convince authenticity and have open reports of the transfer of ownership, while retailers and manufacturers could respond quicker to food safety issues and product recalls (Francisco & Swanson 2018).

4.7. Smart Contracts

The most important application for supply chains within blockchain technology is smart contracts. A smart contract is a protocol recorded on the blockchain that does not need any human interaction (Cong & He 2019). The contract is set up with lines of code with conditions that need to be met, to execute pre-specified tasks or actions like payments autonomously. It can trigger real-time actions if certain rules are fulfilled to which all involved actors agreed upon (Liao & Wang 2018). The agreements are stored on the blockchain, which is immutable and makes it accessible for all involved actors if they have permission. The smart contract audits the agreed conditions and can thereby trigger intended actions. If the contract is not following the agreement or violates the agreement, the underlying blockchain technology will stop it from moving along (Gurtu & Johny 2019). Smart contracts are especially applicable to payments and proof of delivery situations. If a shipment is received, an automated payment is sent. This reduces payments that are withheld and improves the transaction flow in the supply chain. There are also many actors in the supply chain, and it can be hard to follow all agreed conditions. Smart contracts could automate the process in combination with IoT and Big Data to make it more efficient (Wang et al. 2019).

A smart contract can verify that a product or service meets specific standards related to sustainability, labour rights, origin etc. Smart contracts enable secure transactions with different actors without any intermediaries. All transactions are traceable and transparent due to blockchain technology (Christodoulou et al. 2018). Motives behind adopting smart contracts are that it will decrease the need for third parties like banks, lawyers, brokers etc. Thereby it will also lower transaction costs and redesign current structures for the supply chains. As negotiations can include counteroffers and disagreements, it becomes a very time-consuming process. Smart contract implementation would achieve great benefit in these areas (Philipp et al. 2019). Smart contracts could be useful regarding food supply chains. When information about a product is received, it could accept or deny the product based on conditions in the smart contract like temperature or humidity. If the conditions have been violated, the product can be sent back, or if accepted, a payment could be triggered (Rejeb et al. 2019). Other benefits smart contracts provide are trackable flows, automated data transfer, and time-saving. There is no unnecessary forwards and backwards sending of documents since everything is stored on the blockchain with constant visibility for everyone with permission (Philipp et al. 2019). This raises trust and decreases costs by shorter lead times and less manual work which is associated with traditional contracts. It will drop the transaction costs and lower entry barriers for small and medium-sized businesses (Wang et al. 2019).

4.8. Challenges

The logistics and transportation industry anticipates for an integrated system of technologies in the future. This would consist of shippers, forwarders, carriers, terminals, ports, customs, banks etc. in a network with blockchain as an underlying technology (Cong & He 2019). However, according to Saberi et al. (2019), behind all the promising solutions and opportunities that blockchain technology can bring into Supply Chain 4.0, there are also challenges. There are many technological barriers in the industry with immaturity that needs to be fixed. There is a need for a common framework of international regulations because different businesses and actors have different policies. Nevertheless, there is also many regulatory uncertainties and profound understanding of the technology among policymakers. Many organisations operate their own blockchains, while the idea from Nakamoto (2008) was that it should interact and integrate different systems. There is much work to solve all the interoperability issues. According to Kshetri (2018) should all actors in the supply chains work together and aim to set principles to deploy the blockchain technology as fast as possible. International standards would need to be developed to suit blockchain development and as a requirement for interoperability between the different systems (Korpela et al. 2017). Currently, there is a committee developing ISO standards covering issues such as interoperability, transactions and smart contracts (Norberg 2019).

5. CONCLUSION

As briefly examined in this literature review, Supply Chain 4.0 will include features from all the disruptive technologies and aid with desired motives from the industry as transparency, visibility, knowing location, conditions of shipments, instant feedback and flexibility to uncertainties. Through blockchain, the information flow will be reorganised in a distributed and decentralised way. The main motives in which blockchain technology will improve the supply chains are transparency, security and trust. Blockchain approaches will make the symmetric information more immutable, retrievable and self-verifiable. This literature review has examined various motives of how different disruptive technologies will shape and influence the Supply Chain 4.0. Identified main motives are highlighted for Supply Chain 4.0 and how different technologies and systems can provide the most value for future supply chains. The previous research studies are optimistic with a variety of solutions that would make the supply chain flows more efficient.

This review can assist with knowledge of potential deployments and opportunities in areas like IoT, AI, Big Data and Blockchain technology related to supply chain management. Further studies could focus on how specific organisations have implemented the Supply Chain 4.0 approach, or create a framework for different functions or industries and their motives for Supply Chain 4.0.

ACKNOWLEDGMENT

This work was part of assignments in Master of Science by the first authors; the second author was tutor of the course and taught the subject.

REFERENCES

Abeyratne, S., & Monfared, R. (2016). Blockchain ready manufacturing supply chain using distributed ledger. *International Journal of Research in Engineering and Technology*, *5*(9), 1–10. doi:10.15623/ijret.2016.0509001

Andrews, H., Berttram, P., Espie, V., Geissbauer, R., Khurana, A., Kinder, M., Malmgren, P., Mueller, R., Phillips, D., Potter, J., Romac, B., Schrauf, S., & Strom, M. (2016). *Industry 4.0 - How digitization makes the supply chain more efficient, agile, and customer-focused*. PWC.

Aryal, A., Liao, Y., Nattuthurai, P., & Li, B. (2018). The emerging big data analytics and IoT in supply chain management: A systematic review. Supply Chain Management, pp. *Supply Chain Management*, *25*(2), 2018. doi:10.1108/SCM-03-2018-0149

Bag, S.H. (2018). Industry 4.0 and supply chain sustainability: framework and future research directions. *Benchmarking*.

Barata, J., Da Cunha, P. R., & Stal, J. (2018). Mobile supply chain management in the Industry 4.0 era An annotated bibliography and guide for future research. *Journal of Enterprise Information Management*, *31*(1), 173–193. doi:10.1108/JEIM-09-2016-0156

Ben-Daya, M., Hassini, E., & Bahroun, Z. (2019). Internet of things and supply chain management: A literature review. *International Journal of Production Research*, *57*(15-16), 4719–4742. doi:10.1080/00207543.2017.1402140

Calatayud, A. (2017). *The connected supply chain: enhancing risk management in a changing world*. Discussion Paper No. 508, Inter-American Development Bank, Washington, DC.

Calatayud, A., Mangan, J., & Christopher, M. (2019). The self-thinking supply chain. *Supply Chain Management*, *24*(1), 22–38. doi:10.1108/SCM-03-2018-0136

Casino, F., Azpilicueta, L., Lopez-Iturri, P., Aguirre, E., Falcone, F., & Solanas, A. (2017). Optimized Wireless Channel Characterization in Large Complex Environments by Hybrid Ray Launching-Collaborative Filtering Approach. *IEEE Antennas and Wireless Propagation Letters*, *16*, 780–783. doi:10.1109/LAWP.2016.2604021

Chopra, S., & Meindl, P. (2010). *Supply Chain Management: Strategy, Planning and Operation* (E. Svendsen, Ed.; 4th ed.). Pearson Education Limited.

Christodoulou, P., Christodoulou, K., & Andreou, A. (2018). A Decentralized Application for Logistics: Using Blockchain in Real-World Applications. *The Cyprus Review*, *30*(2), 181–18.

Collomb, A., & Sok, K. (2016). Blockchain / Distributed Ledger Technology (DLT): What Impact on the Financial Sector? *Communications & Stratégies*, (103), 93–111, 212, 214.

Cong, L. W., & He, Z. (2019). Blockchain Disruption and Smart Contracts. *Review of Financial Studies*, *32*(5), 1754–1797. doi:10.1093/rfs/hhz007

Dinh, T. N., & Thai, M. T. (2018). AI and Blockchain: A Disruptive Integration. *Computer*, *51*(9), 48–53. doi:10.1109/MC.2018.3620971

Dorri, A. (2017). Blockchain for IoT security and privacy: The case study of a smart home. *2017 IEEE International Conference on Pervasive Computing and Communications Workshops (PerCom Workshops),* 618–623.

Francisco, K. & Swanson, D. (2018). The Supply Chain Has No Clothes: Technology Adoption of Blockchain for Supply Chain Transparency. *Logistics, 2*(1).

Frederico, G. F. F. (2019). Supply Chain 4.0: Concepts, maturity and research agenda. Supply Chain Management, pp. *Supply Chain Management.*

Gnimpieba, Z. D. R., Nait-Sidi-Moh, A., Durand, D., & Fortin, J. (2015). Using Internet of Things Technologies for a Collaborative Supply Chain: Application to Tracking of Pallets and Containers. *Procedia Computer Science*, *56*(C), 550–557. doi:10.1016/j.procs.2015.07.251

Guo, Y., & Liang, C. (2016). Blockchain application and outlook in the banking industry. *Financial Innovation*, *2*(1), 1–12. doi:10.118640854-016-0034-9

Gurtu, A., & Johny, J. (2019). Potential of blockchain technology in supply chain management: A literature review. *International Journal of Physical Distribution & Logistics Management*, *49*(9), 881–900. doi:10.1108/IJPDLM-11-2018-0371

Guszcza, J. (2018). *Smarter together: Why artificial intelligence needs human-centered design* (Vol. 22). Deloitte Review.

Hofmann, E. (2017). Big data and supply chain decisions: The impact of volume, variety and velocity properties on the bullwhip effect. *International Journal of Production Research*, *55*(17), 5108–5126. doi:10.1080/00207543.2015.1061222

Hofmann, E., & Rüsch, M. (2017). Industry 4.0 and the current status as well as future prospects on logistics. *Computers in Industry*, *89*, 23–34. doi:10.1016/j.compind.2017.04.002

Korpela, K., Hallikas, J., & Dahlberg, T. (2017). Digital supply chain transformation toward blockchain integration. *Proceedings of the 50th Hawaii international conference on system sciences*. 10.24251/HICSS.2017.506

Kshetri, N. (2018). 1 Blockchain's roles in meeting key supply chain management objectives. *International Journal of Information Management*, *39*, 80–89. doi:10.1016/j.ijinfomgt.2017.12.005

Liao, D.-Y. Y., & Wang, X. (2018, November 27). Applications of blockchain technology to logistics management in integrated casinos and entertainment. Informatics, 5(4), pp. *Informatics (MDPI)*, *5*(4), 44. doi:10.3390/informatics5040044

Longo, F., Nicoletti, L., Padovano, A., d'Atri, G., & Forte, M. (2019). Blockchain-enabled supply chain: An experimental study. *Computers & Industrial Engineering*, *136*, 57–69. doi:10.1016/j.cie.2019.07.026

Loop, P. (2016). Blockchain: the next evolution of supply chains: blockchain technology could help lead to a reinvention of retail supply chains. *Material Handling & Logistics*, *71*(10), 22.

Makris, D., Hansen, Z. N. L., & Khan, O. (2019). Adapting to supply chain 4.0: an explorative study of multinational companies. *Supply Chain Forum: An International Journal, 20*(2), 116–131.

Maltaverne, B. (2017, July 17). Blockchain: what are the opportunities for Procurement? *Medium*.

Manners-Bell, J., (2017). *Supply chain risk management: understanding emerging threats to global supply chains*. Kogan Page Publishers.

Mao, D. (2019). Novel Automatic Food Trading System Using Consortium Blockchain. *The Arabian Journal for Science and Engineering. Section B. Engineering*, *44*(4), 3439–3455.

Merlino, M., & Sproģe, I. (2017). The Augmented Supply Chain. *Procedia Engineering*, *178*, 308–318. doi:10.1016/j.proeng.2017.01.053

Nakamoto, S. (2008). *Bitcoin: A peer-to-peer electronic cash system*. Available at https://bitcoin.org/bitcoin.pdf

Norberg, H. (2019). Unblocking the Bottlenecks and Making the Global Supply Chain Transparent: How Blockchain technology stands to update global trade. *The School of Public Policy Publications*, *12*(9), 1–24.

Pereira, A. C., & Romero, F. (2017). A review of the meanings and the implications of the Industry 4.0 concept. *Procedia Manufacturing*, *13*(C), 1206–1214. doi:10.1016/j.promfg.2017.09.032

Petersen, M., Hackius, N. & von See, B. (2018). Mapping the sea of opportunities: Blockchain in supply chain and logistics. *IT - Information Technology, 60*(5), 263–271.

Philipp, R., Prause, G., & Gerlitz, L. (2019). Blockchain and Smart Contracts for Entrepreneurial Collaboration in Maritime Supply Chains. *Transport and Telecommunication*, *20*(4), 365–378. doi:10.2478/ttj-2019-0030

Radanliev, P. (2019). *The Industrial Internet of Things in the Industry 4.0 supply chains: Literature review and future trends.* arXiv.org, pp.arXiv.org.

Raman, S., Patwa, N., Niranjan, I., Ranjan, U., Moorthy, K., & Mehta, A. (2018). Impact of big data on supply chain management. *International Journal of Logistics Research and Applications, 21*(6), 579–596. doi:10.1080/13675567.2018.1459523

Rejeb, A. (2018). Blockchain Potential in Tilapia Supply Chain in Ghana. *Acta Technica Jaurinensis, 11*(2), 104–118. doi:10.14513/actatechjaur.v11.n2.462

Rejeb, A., Keogh, J. & Treiblmaier, H. (2019). Leveraging the Internet of Things and Blockchain Technology in Supply Chain Management. *Future Internet, 11*(7).

Saberi, S., Kouhizadeh, M., Sarkis, J., & Shen, L. (2019). Blockchain technology and its relationships to sustainable supply chain management. *International Journal of Production Research, 57*(7), 2117–2135. doi:10.1080/00207543.2018.1533261

Shanley, A. (2017). Real-Time Logistics. *Pharmaceutical Technology Europe, 29*(10), 46–48.

Somapa, S., Cools, M., & Dullaert, W. (2018). Characterizing supply chain visibility – a literature review. *International Journal of Logistics Management, 29*(1), 308–339.

Tadejko, P. (2015). Application of Internet of Things in Logistics–Current Challenges. *Economics and Management, 7*(4), 54–64.

Tapscott, D. (2017). *How will blockchain change banking? How won't it?* Available at: www. huffingtonpost.com/don-tapscott/how-will-blockchain-chang_b_9998348.html

Tapscott, D., & Tapscott, A. (2016). *Blockchain revolution: how the technology behind bitcoin is changing money, business and the world.* Portfolio/Penguin.

Thurner, T. (2018). Business innovation through Blockchain: The B3 perspective. *Foresight, 20*(5), 583–584.

Ustundag, A., & Cevikcan, E. (2018). *Industry 4.0: Managing The Digital Transformation.* Springer International Publishing. doi:10.1007/978-3-319-57870-5

Vaidya, S., Ambad, P., & Bhosle, S. (2018). Industry 4.0 – A Glimpse. *Procedia Manufacturing, 20*, 233–238. doi:10.1016/j.promfg.2018.02.034

Wang, G., Gunasekaran, A., Ngai, E. W. T., & Papadopoulos, T. (2016). Big data analytics in logistics and supply chain management: Certain investigations for research and applications. *International Journal of Production Economics, 176*, 98–110. doi:10.1016/j.ijpe.2016.03.014

Wang, Y., Han, J. H., & Beynon-Davies, P. (2019). Understanding blockchain technology for future supply chains: A systematic literature review and research agenda. *Supply Chain Management, 24*(1), 62–84. doi:10.1108/SCM-03-2018-0148

Wiedenmann, M., & Größler, A. (2019). The impact of digital technologies on operational causes of the bullwhip effect – a literature review. *Procedia CIRP, 81*, 552–557. doi:10.1016/j.procir.2019.03.154

Yan, B., Jin, Z., Liu, L., & Liu, S. (2018). Factors influencing the adoption of the internet of things in supply chains. *Journal of Evolutionary Economics*, *28*(3), 523–545. doi:10.100700191-017-0527-3

Zhong, R. Y., Newman, S. T., Huang, G. Q., & Lan, S. (2016). Big Data for supply chain management in the service and manufacturing sectors: Challenges, opportunities, and future perspectives. *Computers & Industrial Engineering*, *101*, 572–591. doi:10.1016/j.cie.2016.07.013

Chapter 17
Emerging Technologies in Financial Services

Deepika Dhingra
https://orcid.org/0000-0001-5967-8834
Bennett University, India

Vasuman Agarwal
Bennett University, India

Shruti Ashok
Bennett University, India

ABSTRACT

Emerging technologies have redesigned the financial services industry through innovative means to cater to evolving customer expectations of personalisation and ease. FinTech has been progressed as one of the most pioneering and cost-effective disruptive technologies. Initial adaptation of FinTech solutions has permitted several start-ups, financial service providers, and other assorted sectors to accomplish an augmented pace of growth. This chapter highlights how emerging technologies are altering the subtleties of doing business for financial services benefactors, possibility of emerging technologies, advantages and disadvantages, technology linked issues/challenges in financial services, and also highlights drivers of this revolution.

INTRODUCTION

We are living in a world where digital transformation is taking place sooner than we are, as humans. The lives of each one of us have been affected by modern technology in several ways. Technological innovation clasps immense opportunities in financial services - with increasing access to market, while also lowering expenses for customers and workload for the service providers. The advancement in management and strategies for digital enterprise transformation has shaped innovative prospects for economic and social growth in the technological sector. The combination of financial service start-ups

DOI: 10.4018/978-1-7998-8583-2.ch017

and the advent of new technologies such as artificial intelligence (AI), machine learning (ML), blockchain, big data, and online transactions are transforming the way business is done and has given rise to a large number of cybercrime threats. Hence, opportunities and threats coupled with the advent of these technologies deserve undeterred attention. Talking about opportunities, low barriers to entry cannot go unnoticed - many new start-ups have sprung up.

Atom and Metro are examples of success stories of the same, in the banking sector. The simultaneous entry of new and large firms into the financial services domain, including Fintech and BigTech firms, have been game-changers for the financial services providers. This has and can impact the grade of clustering and disputes in financial services. These new entrants are posing challenges for the conventional financial services framework. This paper articulates significant trends in the FinTech landscape aligning them with the advancements in technology that have been disrupting the financial service space and provides recommendations for fostering the growth of Fintech.

BACKGROUND

The FinTech market in India has been witnessing a constant growing curve for over past five years. In a span of 5 years (January 2013 - October 2018), India has seen the rise of about 2000 FinTech companies, starting an entrepreneurial movement (Figure 1). With an increase in the availability of Fintech solutions, customers adapted to the digital transformation, like fish takes to water. This further resulted in India (2018), ranking second globally after China (83.5%), in FinTech adoption rate with 57.9% FinTech users. This rate is more than any developed countries. A robust technological network as its backbone and a large market-base with low penetration of financial services (FS) further exhibits a great potential for the Indian FinTech industry.

Figure 1. Entrepreneurial activity on the rise in India Y-o-Y number of Fintech Companies founded (2013-2018), Source: Traxcn 2018

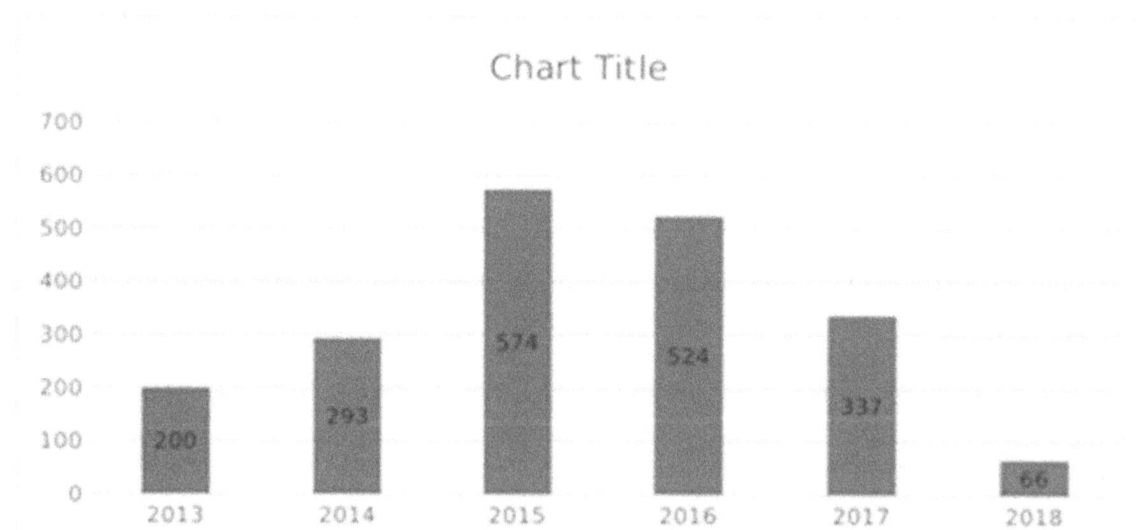

The industry saw a total transaction value of $66.1 billion in 2019, predicted to jump to $137.8 billion by 2023, growing at a CAGR of 20.18% (Figure 2). The total transaction value in the global FinTech space was $5.49 trillion in 2019, being predicted to grow to $9.82 trillion by 2023, with a CAGR of 15.64% (Figure 3).

Figure 2. India Fintech transaction value projections 2019 to 2023 (USD million), Source: Statista 2019

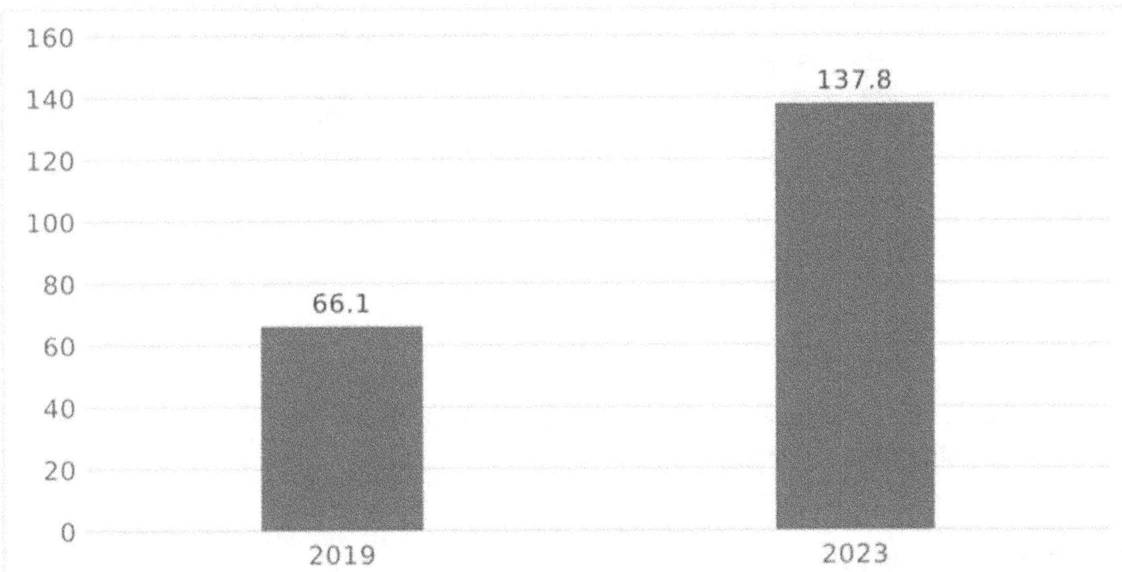

FUNDING PROSPECTS IN INDIA

Constant venture capital (VC) investments in the Indian FinTech market have been seen during the past few years. In 2018, India completed 97 deals with a value of $1.79 billion through VC funding. This created a record high, in terms of the number of deals, however, $2.4 billion was raised in VC funding in 2017 with a total deal count of 48. As per a CB Insights report, FinTech companies being backed by global VC increased to almost $39.57 billion across 1,707 deals, both of which created a new record in the Fintech market.

Digital Payments

The evolution and growth of FinTech is being boosted with the increasing volume of digital transactions touching $24.13 billion in 2018. Due to mobile wallets and Unified Payment Interface (UPI) transactions being used excessively, the case for digital payments became even stronger. There has also been a monumental growth of e-commerce with the support of innovative digital payment technologies such as AI blockchain, IoT, real-time payments, mobile Point of Sale (POS). From a funding perspective, investors have been showing interest in the Indian payments' space. 'Payments' earned the prestigious

Figure 3. Global Fintech transaction value projections, 2019-2023 (USD trillion), Source: Statista, 2019

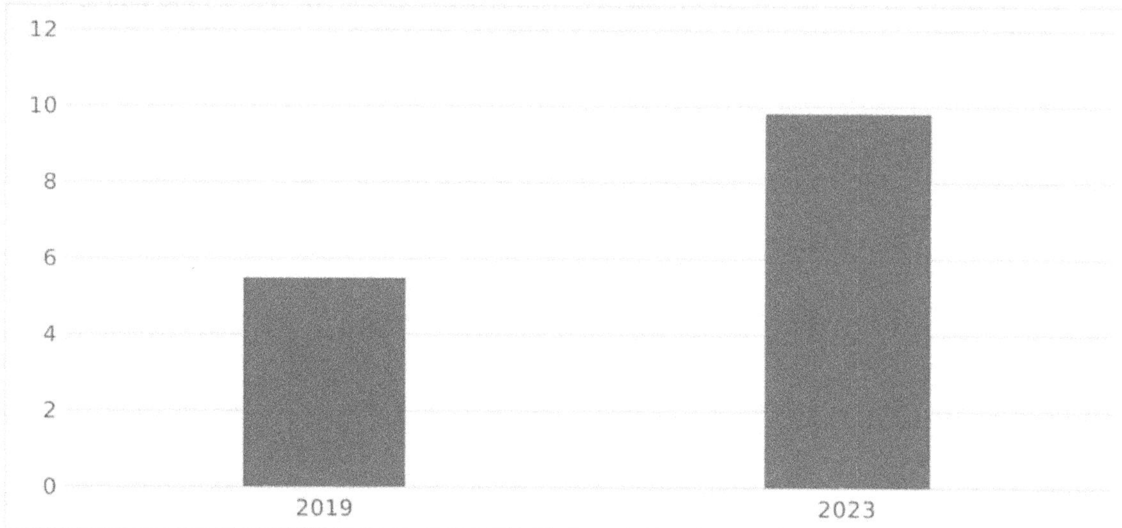

position of being the highest funded segment in the Indian Fintech industry with approximately $709 million worth investments in 21 deals.

LITERATURE REVIEW

The most dramatic change in the post-crisis global financial system has been in global banking. Though this segment has experienced chief alterations over the period owing to fluctuations in geo-political system and regulation, authors (Mareev, 2016; Shim and Shin, 2016) opine that a unique era has emerged for banks with the growth of fintech. This concept still needs to be explored as that signifies an impera-

Figure 4. Global VC-backed FinTech funding and deal count, 2014 - 2018 (USD billion)

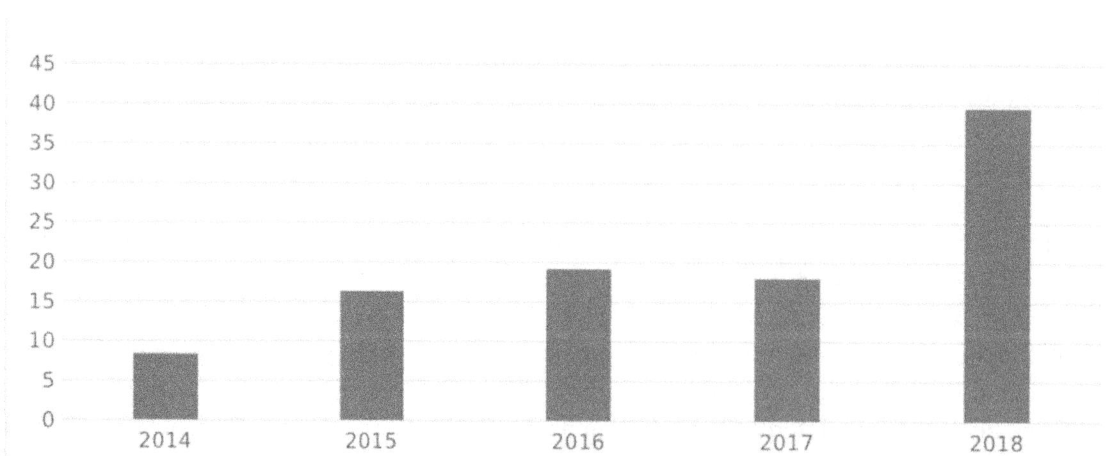

tive trial for academe and executives in the financial industry (DeYoung, 2005; Dapp, 2014; Gábossy, 2016; Iwata, 2017).

Created by an amalgamation of the words finance and technology, the term fintech refers to companies that use technology to function outside conventional frameworks of the financial industry. Looking to alter the approach with which these services are presented (Fortnum et al., 2017), using communication, the internet and the automated processing of information (Arner et al., 2016; Chen, 2016; Gabor and Brooks, 2017; Szpringer, 2016).

According to Christensen's (2003) theory of disruptive innovation, FinTech firms can be categorized into two types: 'Sustainable FinTech's' for well-known financial institutions that work to guard their market locations by using IT through incremental innovations and 'Disruptive FinTech's' that are pioneering companies and start-ups that test recognized benefactors by contributing novel offerings. (Jesse McWaters, 2015; Lacasse et al., 2016). Business models of these enterprises offer better resistance, security, capability and prospects than obsolete financial services (Gomber et al., 2017). Even though the financial industry has been an initial user and a meticulous customer of new IT solutions, the rise of innovative business models and entrants have had a farfetched impact on the prevailing dynamics of the industry. In a swiftly varying financial environment, demanding and expensive regulation requirements, the accepted companies in banking and financial services are fronting considerable change with the upsurge of digital finances (Gomber et al., 2017). Consequently, fintech start-ups and big IT companies enter the sphere of the financial industry, create ground and acquire customers who had been customarily served by deep rooted providers.

Gomber et al. (2017) mentions three reasons for the same. First, offerings by the fintech companies satisfy the requirement of customers which were unmet earlier or had been inadequately offered by conventional contributors of financial services. Subsequently, fintech companies presented innovative openings for sales through applications of novel concepts & technologies. MarketInvoice (www.marketinvoice.com) for example, offers small and medium industries the prospect to fasten up their billing to attain working capital more swiftly in exchange for payment of a commission, and they do not have to rely on receipt of the unique invoice data (an operation known as factoring, marketing or commercial development) (Buckley and Webster, 2016). Third, IT companies have an approach that is fundamentally different from the conventional financial services providers. They are adequately nimble and advanced to put the reputable opponents under burden. Fintech companies focus on technology-oriented business scaffolds, accessible and lucrative, to contest with outdated financial service providers. Experts in the financial extent believe that at some point banks will be used only for deposits, while the remaining will be done using fintech services (Hemmadi, 2015, cited in Gomber et al., 2017).

RESEARCH GAP

A rapid development in Management and Strategies for Digital Enterprise Transformation is giving way to disruptive innovations in financial services. Financial institutions have been altering their business models according to regulatory frameworks and are gradually getting used to it. Emerging technologies in financial services have changed the way firms perform their businesses and day-to-day operations. From peer-to-peer lending to big data to artificial intelligence, fintech innovations have been the focal point of discussion across almost all business spheres. "Innovation in financial services is deliberate and predictable; incumbent players are most likely to be confronted where the greatest sources of customer friction meet the largest profit pools" (World Economic Forum Report by Deloitte, 2015).

By employing a qualitative approach, this paper discusses how emerging technologies are changing the dynamics of management and strategies for financial services providers and hence answer these questions:

1. What are the various emerging technologies in financial services
2. How are the diverse emerging technologies being adopted and changing the rules of the game, their scope, pros & cons
3. What are the emerging technology-related issues in Finance?
4. What are the primary factors driving the growth of emerging technologies in the Financial services ecosystem?

PAYMENT - BUSINESS MODELS & METHODS

With the emergence of a number of payment methods in India - usage of cards has been the most prevalent. UPI, mobile wallets and prepaid cards have further unlocked the doors for more convenient and efficient payment options. Some of the examples include fast tag tolls and transit payments, peer-to-peer lending, smart city payments, and cross-border remittances.

Banks, NBFCs, or other issuing entities give cards or access to mobile wallets to customers who can then avail the service at the respective PoS terminals for making digital payments. Device manufacturers facilitate in making the payment gateway for these payments, including scanners, readers, PoS machines, and ATMs available to the users. Once the transaction is complete, back-end systems like switches, card management, and reconciliation systems are leveraged. Support services are also integral in addressing customer grievances, providing loyalty solutions, and a lot more for a complete and smooth payment experience.

Demystifying the Incumbent Landscape

The widespread acceptance of digital wallets and regulatory efforts led to newer opportunities to emerge in the Indian market. These opportunities were capitalised on by many players by entering the digital payments segment themselves or by fostering partnerships. This further led to a widespread transformation of the competitive digital payments landscape, becoming all-encompassing - telecom players, banks and e-commerce became a part of the same.

Digital Payments Funding

A substantial influx of funds from an eclectic set of stakeholders were a key factor for the rise in digital payments.

1. **Large MNCs**: Global corporations wishing to enter the high potential market of India have been a big source of funds for the largest wallet players, along with other multinationals.
2. **VC firms**: Both international and Indian VC firms have been investing in the Indian wallet and payment space.

3. **E-commerce players**: International e-commerce players have been actively investing in the Indian Fintech market, resulting in an increase of in-app retail on wallet platforms.
4. **Financial Service providers**: With Japanese payment firms leading the charts, FS providers have been making significant contributions in the domestic payments segment.

Alternative Lending

Product and Process have been at the heart of technological innovations, augmenting customer experience, and operational efficiency. Digital transformations deployed by unconventional lenders improve the customer acquisition process, thereby reducing costs. These technologies also deploy alternative information for credit underwriting and adopting robust risk management solutions to improve the flow of lending activities like collection management and loan resolution.

Alternative lenders have witnessed a massive inflow of funds globally, demonstrating the huge potential of the sector to be unlocked. During 2018, alternative lending was most widely leveraged in the Indian Fintech sector, with the value of transactions worth approximately $530 million from 617 deals. As of September 2018, Indian alternative lending space witnessed a cumulative investment of more than $1 billion, making it a watershed period. In totality, the global funding in this segment crossed approximately $21.7 billion mark during September 2018, further adding to its growth.

Alternative Lending Business Models

Alternative lenders use both traditional and alternative data sources, focusing on technology to cater to the customer base which remains outside the purview of services for traditional lenders. This section discusses the various alternative lending models:

Peer-to-Peer Lending

P2P lenders act as an intermediary between the borrowers (individuals as well as organizational) and the lenders. This provides easy access of loans to borrowers at a lower cost, as mutually decided by borrowers and lenders. For availing these services, both parties are required to pay a fee to the intermediary. The borrowers pay an initiation fee, which can either be a flat rate or a pre-determined percentage of the loan amount, depending on the credit rating of the borrower whereas the lenders pay an administrative charge and any additional services such as legal advice.

Invoice Financing

Invoice financing focuses on fulfilling short-term liquidity needs of a borrower. It encompasses the working capital facilities, extended by lenders based on the due invoices of MSMEs, which helps them to accelerate their account receivables.

Crowdfunding

When investees share their business ideas, monetary requirements, anticipated future trajectories, and investors judge them on their communication skills and business acumen, it is referred to as crowdfunding. A considerable number of investors invest a small portion of the required funding, creating a pool for investments being amassed by the investee. Finance may also be acquired in exchange of equity, with the given company offering shares to investors.

Pay Later Loans

Many banks and payment-based start-ups' have been using this model, where the lenders disburse instant loans that borrowers can use to finance their purchases. These loans are generally of small denomination. Customers can repay the debt through payment wallet/apps. No interest needs to be paid till a pre-determined date, after which a late fee is levied. Based on the individual customer's financial capacity, limits on customer spending can also be redefined and/or extended.

Mobile Lending

Based on creditworthiness of borrowers deciphered using mobile calling patterns and other available data such as mobile transactions and mobile e-money usage, small mobile loans are provided to the borrowers.

Digital Mortgage

The lenders modernize the traditional borrowing processes by creating an online space ranging from the application process to the delivery stage. Online channels enable faster completion of the process and hence, a better customer experience.

Direct Lending Models

Entities that directly lend one's capital to borrowers. A primary example of this model is the NBFCs.

Various direct lending models are emerging in India – determining the basis of borrowers' working capital, as well as unsecured and short-tenure loans.

- PoS lending: By collaborating with Financial Service lenders, these players finance the purchases of e-commerce shoppers. For underwriting, they leverage conventional data like bank account statements also AI models to demystify consumer behaviour using past transaction data.
- Supply chain financing: Due to the emergence of e-commerce, lenders need to target merchants selling their products and services apart from having a narrow focus on just retail consumers. These platforms have access to enormous volumes of data on sale cycles of the respective merchants. This acts as an input for advanced analytical models for credit underwriting.

InsurTech

The Indian InsurTech space received total funding of approximately $378 million from 17 deals, gaining momentum for this space only to make it the third largest funded FinTech segment.

Key Business Models

InsurTech refers to the use of technology-based innovations throughout the insurance value chain. It is also leveraged to attain cost efficiencies and product democratization. Ranging from lead management to underwriting, sales, distribution, and renewal, the segment is currently dominated by budding start-ups.

Digital Insurance Advisors

Digital advisors are online service providers who aggregate and sell traditional as well as the new product offerings to digital insurers. Not only does the insured enjoy a seamless digital experience, but they also get access to a platform enabling them to compare various insurance schemes and select the one that best suits them. Whereas, the insurer works based on commissions.

PoS Insurance Providers

Partnering with online service providers, they offer insurance by bundling it along with other products and services purchased by customers, who target the consumer needs like purchasing a car or an electronic appliance or house. Personalized insurance products as per customer specific needs are also offered. Access to a huge spectrum of consumers is gained through collaboration with online service providers as well as e-commerce aggregators. Upselling and cross-selling of traditional insurance products - life and health insurance are also done.

WealthTech

WealthTech players use the power of advanced analyses to offer online solutions with the potential to recreate wealth and investment management services. Apart from the technical acumen of financial advisors, technology has made the role of AI and ML models in evaluating lucrative investment options, optimizing portfolios, and risk management important. An increase in the number of investors and start-ups signify the widespread popularity of this industry. In 2008, WealthTech was prized as the fourth-best funded FinTech segment in India, with investments from 23 deals of approximately $122 million. There has been an impressive growth in the amount of capital raised by WealthTech start-ups globally as well.

Democratizing Investment Advisory

The growth of tech-enabled wealth managers has blurred the line between high net worth individuals (HNWI) and small investors, making focused advisory services possible, for both HNWIs and the general public.

Hybrid Models with a Human Touch

Human capabilities and Robo-advisors along with other technologically influenced wealth and portfolio management tools are complementing one another in providing smooth and efficient financial services like never. This hybrid model has surely been a game-changer.

Sentiment Analysis

The power of data analytics is not unknown. Not just number crunching but an in-depth real-time analysis of the sentiments of people as well. Findings from the social media data are leveraged in this entire process. This coupled with historical data and an analysis of the current can help in predicting the future trajectory, of say, a company's future stock price.

The Exodus of Payment Players into the Systematic Investment plan (SIP) space

E-wallet companies in India are penetrating the wealth management market by introducing low-value SIPs (Systematic Investment Plan) which may be as low as INR 100. The easy access to these investment avenues due to easy link of wallets and low commission charged by these firms help in this market penetration process.

Individual Investment Advisory

The process of selection of an investment product has witnessed the magic of gamification. An investor is provided with certain pre-developed investment choices that act as a bridge towards reaching the individual investment goal. The process of selecting the most suitable investment option becomes more robust and simpler as a result.

Various Emerging Technologies in Financial Services

The most overpowering feature of the modern financial system is a high stride of innovations - both for their number and value. Emerging fads in the financial services industry like chatbots and automation help in the reduction of working hours, improve customer relationships and improve profitability. These benefits to the financial institutions in recent years is what came to be known as the '*fintech revolution*'.

Blockchain

In simple terms, a traditional ledger converted to a Distributed ledger technology (DLT) is commonly known as Blockchain. The DLT system helps to create, securely transfer, and store information all at the same time. The functioning of blockchain is however extremely different from the traditional ledgers. The ledger is not administered and controlled centrally, rather each user of DLT gets the data to administer and verify the transactions. DLT appeared as the technology that inspired the use of cryptocurrencies. One of the most significant has been the Ether cryptocurrency using the Ethereum blockchain. However, abundant possible applications of DLT to financial services outside digital currencies are becoming apparent. Keeping in view, the connect of DLT to the payments system, DLT is becoming more prevalent in comparison to other technologies, as controllers see the necessity to comprehend the fundamental concept, identify its implications and to address probable limitations and apprehensions on the consumer protection front. This technology has the potential to be used in any sort of financial transaction such as trade, post-trade settlement, monitoring money supply, etc. The working of a Blockchain is shown in Figure.5

Figure 5.
Source: "Money is no object: Understanding the evolving cryptocurrency market," PwC, 2015/"A Strategist's Guide to Blockchain," strategy business, January, 2016/"How Blockchain Technology Is Disrupting Everything," TechDay, 2016

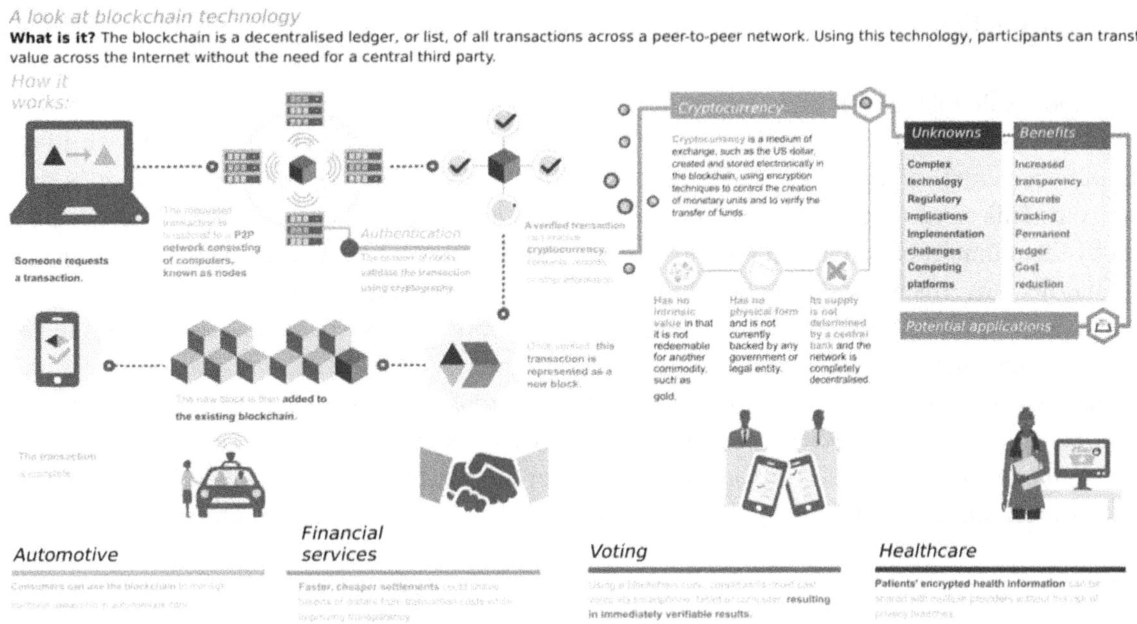

Artificial Intelligence

Artificial intelligence is designed and expected to mimic human intelligence. This technology focuses on recognition, understanding, human interaction, learning, problem-solving, decision making, and reasoning. AI and machine learning (ML) always go hand in hand. Machines are fed with historical data to identify patterns and thereby interpret and categorize new data, which then learns design with new experiences to improve its performance with algorithms.

Machines can also be fed with algorithms to perform various tasks like data entry, customer interaction, risk evaluation, documentation, etc. which saves a lot of employee hours and hence saves a lot of capital for the company. However, this technology might help the bots to learn patterns, but this isn't possible without human input.

The presence of AI in human lives is quite noteworthy nowadays. Chatbots available on almost every website are the most publicly available example of AI. However, what most people are unaware of is that today it has a vital role in functions - back-office, product delivery, shipping, marketing, security, etc.

Automation in Financial Services

Automation is mostly associated with robots, because both automation and robots have one thing in common, i.e. reducing human work. Robotic process automation is one of the most commonly used tools for automation, that simply mechanizes monotonous and repetitive processes. RPAs can take both grouped (charts, graphs) or ungrouped (forms, surveys) information as input to automate various processes like logging data, generating reports, etc. For example, a bot is fed in primary information out of surveys, it will then structure this data and log it into the database, then create a report and publish it in the respective servers.

Big Data Analytics

'World's most valuable resource is no longer oil, but data'.

Digitalization of day to day activities has led people to leave behind their traces on the world wide web, and hence create an extremely large database of the habits of people, their daily activities on the internet, etc. This collection of data is commonly referred to as big data. Traces on the internet are left behind by the minutest of activities undertaken. It is observed that when one searches about something on the internet, advertisements of related things are shown all over the webpage.

The traces that we leave behind is a commodity, much more valuable than oil. This data is then sold in the market and analysed by companies. This process of analysis is known as *big data analytics*. It can potentially be used at each step-from ideation to sale. This tool is being used by companies to improve their market research and target a specific audience. It is also used to improve product design based the client's wants. In the financial service industry, firms can customize financial products based on the risk appetite (which can be determined by the traces left) of the client and hence cater to them individually.

Internet of Things

The largest source of big data presently is the Internet of things (IoT). Every physical device (phone, laptop, smartwatch, etc) that we operate in our day to day lives emits information through the sensors and is then transferred to a common cloud, provided by IoT. This information is the analysed by big data analytics and AI to draw conclusions and processes. The IoT industry is predicted to boom with the increased dependency of human on technology.

Cloud Computing

Collecting data on hard drives seems to be distant past now. Imagine a company trying to store data about the product usage patterns of customers on a hard/pen drive. It's tough to even estimate several devices that would be required to store so much data. This is exactly why cloud computing is used. This technology has increased the capacity of companies to store information on the cloud, enabling further analysis and utilization of the data.

Biometric Technologies

Biometric technologies rely on the recognition of unique characters of individuals to identify authentication. There are various biometric technologies which have already been developed, and there may be many more which may develop to further authenticate identities. Technologies like - fingerprint, voice recognition, iris scanner, face recognition, etc have already been developed to secure the various transactions, hence reducing the risk of fraud or theft.

Further research into this technology would develop an even secure system that would eliminate the risk of frauds, thefts, and cyber-crimes by manifold.

Augmented/ Virtual Reality

Both AR and VR are technologies that aim to create an enhanced view for consumers to perceive and interact with their environment. The only difference between the two is that AR provides an enhanced view of the environment, whereas VR creates a simulated environment. Imagine purchasing furniture but getting a view of how it would look like in your living room even before you purchase it.

Leveraging Digital Technology for Seamless Delivery Of Financial Services

Ubiquitous enough, technological advances and related innovations have transformed the way financial products and services are provided to the final users. Wave of change is on the cards for pre-existing entities and has been embraced by new entities as well. While some technologies have a universal application in the field of financial services others are more niche and context specific. Coupled together, the two have potential to make the industry bigger and better. Payment mechanisms, planning, lending and funding, trading and investment, insurance, cybersecurity, operations, and communication; all have been at the forefront of change. The sections that follow elucidate the repercussions of these developments on financial contracting.

Payments

Payment mechanisms lie at the heart of the application of digital technology for providing financial services. The advent of physical instruments like credit cards marked a watershed period for the digital payments industry. The two categories of innovative payment mechanisms services include online payments and mobile payments. The access to internet over mobile phones has blurred the line between the two. Payments through peer to peer currency exchange platforms for exchanges across borders are also gaining traction. Online payments include online banking, electronic commerce, and payment services like 'Amazon Payments.' Mobile payments are those made using devices connected to a mobile communication network and include mobile money transactions using mobile network operators (e.g. payments by SMS) and pre-paid cards connected to mobile phones. Special attention needs to be paid to developments in cryptocurrencies which can be used like regular currency and are managed with digital wallets stored on a smartphone. All transactions are permanently recorded on blockchain. New currency can be generated by 'miners' by solving the required algorithm. Smart contracts are also being increasingly used, leveraging DLT for payments. These are self-enforcing agreements that automatically execute a transaction on fulfilment of certain criteria and can be used for many purposes such as facilitating swap payments. Smart contracts coupled with Internet of Things related technologies establish an automatic linking between connected devices and related insurance policy. They are being progressively used in the insurance sector for paying insurance claims when the insured event occurs. Market participants are endeavouring to design an apparatus to use DLT to complete post-trade payments and facilitate faster clearing and settlement. The use of DLT makes the process more transparent and efficient. The question of the wide and successful adoption of these technologies is still left to the test of time.

Advice and Planning

Digital platforms have a huge potential for becoming the ultimate financial planning assistance tool for users. Omnipresent websites and online courses can be used to understand essentials of the big, intriguing world of finance. Augmented reality and gamification combined, provide an incredibly interesting and interactive learning experience that can help users with better financial planning. Easy to comprehend data visualization using augmented reality can help to improve understanding of complex data sets. With an increasing number of financial products being provided with competitive features, tools to facilitate comparison and to facilitate selection of the best investment options are in huge demand indeed. Retirement and budget-related planning tools help consumers in better planning and foster healthy saving habits in the long run. There exist chatbots that monitor spending habits of consumers and give suggestions regarding spending, saving, and investing whenever a deviation in the spending pattern occurs. Artificial Intelligence-powered Robo-advisors can also be used to provide valuable investment advice. Countries have also started developing pension dashboards that help beneficiaries to gain an understanding of their sources of pension income; assisting them to plan respective steps like adjusting contribution rates to be undertaken. Thus, digital platform is being used for both financial education and financial planning services.

Investment and Trading

Better ways to access and optimize trading and investment can also be deciphered using the digital platform. As a proof of concept, direct trading and investment platforms are increasing bandwidth of the markets available for institutional investors (implying reduced dependence on market makers for trading) and retail consumers (lower prices through disintermediation and availability of best-designed portfolios). By allowing investors to reiterate trading strategies of traders they desire to follow, social trading platforms are also gaining eminence. High-frequency trading is the result of implementation of algorithms to trading, ensuing greater speed. Algorithmic trading is also being expanded to new applications. Chatbots and Robo-advisors providing investment and portfolio management services to automatically trade and to keep the level of portfolio risk at an equilibrium level are on the rise.

AI can also help in financial decision making by predicting future star performers and best investment options. Hedge funds are incumbent users of this technique. In yet another financial innovation, augmented reality has been deployed and tested to help traders have a better and quicker understanding of financial market data and the trends that follow.

Lending and Funding

Thanks to digital technology, funds and credit can now reach those individuals and businesses that earlier did not have access to them or found them highly expensive to attain. Peer to peer platforms and other channels have promoted the idea of disintermediation and the creation of new channels for lending and funding. There are different forms that peer-to-peer platforms can take:

- **Donation and reward-based platforms** - They help investors to donate funds, say for a social cause, or in exchange for a product/service that would be generated through a funded project.

- **Loan-based platforms** - These are useful in cases where investors desire a return on their investments.
- **Equity-based platforms** - A stake in a company raising funds may be attained using it.

Lending related risks can be gauged using the power of data analytics and Big Data. Lending related risk valuation begins with finding a robust estimate of an individual's credit score. Newer methods that use variables like social networks are becoming indispensable. Another spectacular example of the application of Big Data is the payment processor, Worldpay that helps in giving loans to SMEs in partnership with London-based company Liberis. Crunching past numbers including payment abilities and time required by customers, Worldpay uses past data to yield information for the future. By making a forecast of sales, unsecured cash is advanced to the recipients. This keeps the risk factor well in check.

Insurance

Insurance industry is no exception to the use of digital platforms for enhancing scale and efficiency. Accessibility as well as distribution pattern of insurance policies has been transformed. Peer-to-peer insurance platforms to pool risk along with co-investors, mobile phones for premium payments have been the game-changers. Underwriting and pricing of risk have been the focal point of change in the insurance sector on account of the advent of technology. Data analytics, including Artificial Intelligence and Big Data, provides precise data that can be used to predict risk. Care must be taken to use power of technology the right way, concentrating on the major areas of concern to avoid an absolute shift in the behaviour of the insured who may consider insurance to pool risks rather than considering the most important aspect of the risks considered "bad and detrimental." That said, the application of technology has not just benefitted the pre-existing insurance products but has also given birth to new kinds of products. Insurance ranging from long term to very short-term driven contracts can be issued.

The insurance underwriting process has also been rewritten. Instead of making subjective judgments, facial recognition technology may be used to gauge the health and age of the individual for underwriting life insurance. To arrive at the premium value for auto insurance, sensors, and cameras in cars may be utilized to evaluate the driver's road behaviour.

Cybersecurity

Like a two-sided sword, increased reliance on digital technology has led to cybersecurity issues. Digital technology can answer its problem as well by making the delivery of digital financial services seamless and secure. High powered data encryption can help protect digitally stored data. Biometric technology has the potential to help in seamless identity verification and authentication, thereby mitigating the risk of passwords being stolen or transactions being fraudulently presented. Any deviation in standard behaviour can be used as a red alert signal to identify and prevent fraud using data analytics. DLT also makes transactions more transparent and easier to track.

Operations

Making processes more efficient and effective is what the application of digital technology in operations is all about, thereby reducing overhead costs. Automation helps to save valuable resources for the esoteric issues while making day-to-day repetitive processes fully automatic. Compliance functions can also be performed better by use of technology. RegTech is the short form for regulatory technology that uses the financial technology industry to make regulatory processes better. For example, DLT may be used to facilitate Know Your Customer (KYC) requirements. The technology developers are also in the run-up to design applications that can be used to facilitate risk management functions.

Communications

Instead of requiring the omnipresence of a human interface to communicate with the clients, the application of digital technology has also helped to modify the communication process. Marketing methodology used for financial products has also been changed. Marketing is all about reaching the right consumer at the right time using the right way and through the right channel. Targeted online ads serve this purpose well and are quick enough to reach the intended audience. The online behaviour and browsing patterns of users that are observed using the latest technology are the building blocks for this process. We belong to an era of personalization and customization which is best demonstrated through user-specific online advertising. Text message reminders and intimation for meeting payment commitments for a financial plan or providing customer support functions through chatbots and augmented reality can all facilitate in changing the face of the industry.

Issues Related to Emerging Technologies in Financial Services

Cybercrime

There has been a 480% rise in data breaches involving financial service from 2017 to 2018. Innovative solutions are required if they are to be stopped as each attack costs millions to financial institutions. Blockchain technology is the foundation for any kind of cybercrime solutions emerging to protect financial services. With more institutions implementing distributed ledger technology (DLT), blockchain is becoming the go-to solution to keep financial data protected while not in use. Putting together DLT with the present financial infrastructure is posing severe hindrances, which must be overcome.

Regulatory Compliance

The dynamic regulatory environment has been a persistent challenge for financial institutions of all types. RegTech is an evolving market that is easing the onus of enforcement. RegTech start-ups have started acting as a link to fulfill the gap between regulators and the financial service industry by using the newest FinTech. There are various benefits offered by RegTech applications, a few of them would be - Automated reporting, automated audits, and process streamlining.

Drivers of Emerging Technologies in Financial Services

Unfulfilled Financial Requirements

Due to incomplete information about the features of financial services and a host of other reasons, majority of the Indian population has been omitted from the authorized financial system. These problems have seen some improvement with the inauguration of schemes like Jan Dhan Yojana and Direct Benefit Transfer. The section that had not been supporting the use of these services has now started embracing these. Sadly, incumbents have not been able to meet their banking and financial requirements. This means that there is massive scope for FinTech's to aid this segment in India with its cost-effective digital products.

Altering Consumer Demographics, Varying Needs, and Rising Digital Expectations

The needs of consumers of today keep changing at an unprecedented pace. The young population is internet and technology-friendly, spends an ample amount of time (approximately 130 minutes per day for premium segment users) on smartphones, and has openly welcomed the idea of accessing financial products using digital platforms. Financial services players must make their mark in this market where the customer experience standards have already been set so high by the non-FS technology players. Consequently, financial services players have begun offering innovative digital services that have led to the incumbent redesign and rethink their pre-existing business models. These players have started joining hands with start-ups and have also started marking their digital presence.

Government Policies, Regulations, and Infrastructure

The Indian Government and regulators have been pivotal in facilitating the adoption of FinTech solutions across the country through the launch of several initiatives to this end. Some of these key initiatives have been categorized below:

Driving Financial Inclusion

1. **Goods and Services Tax (GST) regime:** GST regime has been a crucial step in streamlining the Indian economy's unorganized sector, with many FinTech's taking benefit of the digital footmark created from the Goods and Services Tax Network (GSTN). The network has 1.21 crore registered taxpayers to credit score and lend to micro, small and medium enterprises (MSMEs)
2. **Jan Dhan Yojana:** Jan Dhan Yojana is the leading ambition of the Government of India. The scheme intends to augment the level of financial inclusion across the Indian economy, raising the number of people with bank accounts in India (approximately 320 million accounts were opened under the scheme), laying the basis for the distribution of banking services to the unbanked. This has raised the demand for financial services related products, accompanied by a marked behavioural transformation among unbanked consumers. Opportunities for FinTech companies are definitely on the rise

Fabricating the Digital Infrastructure

Unified Payments Interface (UPI)

The National Payments Corporation of India (NPCI) introduced UPI to facilitate the roll-out of interoperable payment services between FinTech's and incumbent institutions. The success of UPI can be judged from the exemplary adoption of digital payments by the business players including merchants and customers. The platform became one of the primary platforms used across the world. It was used by

92 banks and observed 620 million transactions worth INR 1 trillion in December 2018. In 2019, UPI 2.0 was launched with an overdraft facility to aid thin-file customers in getting credit access.

Digital India Program

The use of FinTech based solutions was boosted through the government's active involvement in spreading and improving digital literacy across the Indian economy through initiatives relating to infrastructure, literacy, and the ease of accessing digital services.

Accessibility to the Internet

Over the previous decade, there has been a noteworthy growth in internet speed as well as access (approximately 520 million mobile internet users) across the country. This is a precondition from an infrastructural perspective to access FinTech services. The cost of internet usage has dipped significantly in the last five years, ensuring an increase in the number of internet users, augmenting FinTech adoption.

Supporting Innovation and Competition in the Industry

Start-up India

This is the flagship scheme of the Government to endorse the endeavours of start-ups in the country by ensuring regulatory and financial funding which has directed growth in the number of FinTech start-ups.

License for Payment Banks

Licenses to 11 FinTech companies by RBI for offering e-banking services including, but not limited to remittances, deposits, and savings, have further paved the way for the quintessential branchless banking services offered by FinTech companies.

Cognizance of Peer-To-Peer (P2P) Lenders as Non-Banking Financial Companies (NBFCs)

There has been no turning back for the sector after RBI has provided legitimacy to the P2P lending segment by bringing them under the NBFC category.

Regulatory Sandbox by the RBI for FinTechs

The norms for the regulatory sandbox for FinTech start-ups planned by RBI are expected to be announced by June 2019. The central bank has the objective of attaining a balance between innovation and regulation that can be instrumental in helping the FinTech industry unlock its potential. Before the planned scale-up, this sandbox shall help in the development of innovative solutions and products on a small scale is expected to provide temporarily relaxed regulatory norms for the conceptualization of new solutions or products on a small scale, thereby providing incentives to those planning to enter the industry. Off late, many state governments have also followed to contribute towards the success of the

FinTech agenda, with the Maharashtra and Andhra Pradesh Governments setting up a Mumbai FinTech Hub and FinTech Valley in Vizag, respectively.

SOLUTIONS AND RECOMMENDATIONS

The intricacies of banking risks have been at the helm of change as well on account of the increasing role of fintech in the business landscape. The good part is that these risks also unfold new kinds of opportunities for banks and consumers. Significant risks related to the advent of fintech for existing banks as well as the new entrants comprise strategic, operational, cyber, and compliance risks. The players in the sector have been promoting the adoption of the latest set of technologies to provide the right mix of financial products and services, such as artificial intelligence, machine learning, advanced data analytics, distributed ledger technology, cloud computing, and application programming interfaces as per consumer needs. Talking about risks, banks have become increasingly dependent on arbitrators for providing technology-based services to the end customers. Consequently, the distribution of services offered by these entities has become more commercialized. The main drivers of contracting out are a significant reduction in costs, flexibility in operations, and augmented safety and operational endurance. There is scope for operations to be outsourced, but, in that case, the risks and liabilities related to those operations shall remain with the banks. With the advancements in Fintech, the risks associated with consumer data protection and interests as well as cybersecurity risks are also on the rise. Several fintech firms, especially the lending and investing based ones presently run at a regional or national level scale. Fintech firms like those specializing in making wholesale payments or cross-border remittances have a great potential to go ahead with cross-border operations. Fintech shall revolutionize conventional banking business models and the modus operandi as well as the delivery of financial services. This calls for a rethinking of old business models and their replacement and modification using the latest models. The transition needs to be seamless and all-encompassing. Bank managers and executives need to provide their inputs based on their experiences and learnings. In return, these institutions shall not just experience better financial performance but their managers shall also become more competent and efficient.

Bank regulatory, administrative, and accrediting frameworks herald the emergence of technology-enabled innovation in the present day. Provident authorities do not have a remit for non-bank entities in some regions. Consequently, many services formerly provided by banks are now being provided by other firms that may not be controlled by bank administrators.

FUTURE RESEARCH DIRECTIONS

The advancement of human life and technology go hand in hand. With the demand for mobility increasing, we saw the rise of mobile phones, with the rise in demand for internet on the go, we saw smartphones coming up and today with demand for banking on the go, we have experienced an overwhelming change in the banking experience for an individual through the mobile banking apps. Today, with the progress that fintech has already achieved, we can experience chatbots, ML algorithms for fraud detection, online transactions through blockchain, biometric-enabled security, etc. The conventional banks are being overshadowed and replaced by the technology-enabled banking services in the market, leaving the conventional banks with no choice but to invest in these disruptive technologies. Doing this will enable them to improve their operations, by making it more efficient and at the same time reduce the contact hours for the client, enabling them to save their own time – avoiding standing in long queues in the banks, waiting to get their problems resolved. However, nothing is perfect, and hence the author has identified some future trends for the fintech services offered:

Digital Payments

The problems of low industry margin on account of a cashback-driven culture are further pulled down by increasing competition and inefficient processes including barriers in the KYC process and transactional security-related challenges. To solve this problem of low margins, efforts need to be diverted towards setting up an apparatus wherein FS players can make use of accumulated data through transactions and make use of that data to analyse the credit needs of customers and therefore use it to disburse loans. This co-action between payment and borrowing space can be exploited and taken advantage of.

Alternative Lending

Alternative lending shall continue growing upwards and onwards. The government's goal of financial inclusion shall aim to provide the impetus for its sustained growth. Some issues do need to be addressed. First and foremost is the issue of data privacy. Lenders have access to a wide pool of data including the transactions' history of users, which needs to be handled with the utmost care, respecting the need for privacy of the borrowers and users of funds. Consumer consent must be obtained upfront, and data governance standards must be adhered to. Model biases must also be taken care of while using AI and ML techniques.

Insurtech

Telematics and HealthTech driven insurance is proof of the concept of innovations taking the world by storm in the respective insurance space. India is no exception - with a majority of the Indian population still uninsured, there exists great scope for growth. With better risk-based pricing inputs in the form of real-time, well-connected data available, the segment is a safe bet. Regulatory barriers posing a major challenge for collecting pertinent data need to be taken care. With the insurance industry embracing digital business models, growth in this segment is bound to happen. An increase in awareness and a decrease in costs, with the help of low-cost technology-based distribution models, imply that InsurTech is all set to disrupt the Financial Service space in years to come.

WealthTech

As the wealth of a country increases, so does the need to manage the wealth. The Indian economy saw an increasing CAGR of 18.67% in the number of HNWIs between 2011 and 2017. This growth is predicted to rise over the years and reach a massive total of $3 trillion by 2025, creating a massive opportunity for the WealthTech players.

By increasing financial literacy in the country, wealth management will cross the bounds of HNWIs and reach the masses. The Mutual fund industry aims to grow the AUM by approximately 5 times to

$1.47 trillion and the number of investors by more than 3 times to 130 million, by 2025. Which will hence, increase the demand for WealthTech industry to sustain the increase in demand of retail investors.

Blockchain

The inflexibility of the primary code and ensuing irreversibility of the transactions could present possible hurdles for financial transactions, as eventually the accuracy of the underlying code is still unprotected to human error. Flexible blockchains have been projected as a way forward, even though such a method may put the original purpose of the technology, or at least some significant aspects of it (e.g. finality), in question.

Artificial Intelligence

Even though all the functions of AI seem flawless, but there are various challenges that the company faces while using AI. The biggest challenge being humans' input being required to feed algorithms and how efficiently do they do it. To maintain the quality of customer interaction chatbots is a widely faced challenge by the smaller companies. Many organizations also face compliance issues and fear that AI might fail to do the desired job, which is why manual regulations are set up to avoid machine errors. This is one of the imperative reasons for the delay in the adoption of AI in financial institutions.

However, the only way forward in the coming times of technology are to comply with the changes and automate the processes of human interaction through AI.

Big Data

Big data provides FS industry with opportunities, but at the same time impedes them. Drawing out data through social media, customer databases, a news feed, etc. is helping the FS providers customize customer experience and at the same time safeguard their interests. Even though the availability of data is equal for everyone, how to draw out beneficial conclusions from that available data with the strong tool of data analytics is the necessary skill. This skill is what will be wanted in the coming years, with humans leaving trails of data everywhere.

CONCLUSION

FinTech is now restructuring the nuances of trade as many upcoming firms design new pioneering product lines for customers. FinTech shall usher in transformation and disruptive innovation in the financial services industry through widespread usage of new-age technology and automation that can help make the customer experience seamless. Rather than viewing FinTech as competition, traditional financial service firms are starting to leverage the tools and openings this sector offers. The last five years have been especially phenomenal in terms of funding and customer adoption rates. Firms are expected to set up intellectual incubator platforms, which link FinTech start-ups and recognized financial firms to assist in developing futuristic ideas while delivering real capital for firms to invest and adapt to the transient landscape. Financial firms are also finding and assessing FinTech with the finest value propositions for profitable collaborations. In turn, FinTech firms gather sustenance, access to big client groups, and proficient knowledge. Governments and market regulators across the globe have also played a supportive role during the formative years of the technology. The contribution of the Unified Payments Interface (UPI) based ecosystem, availability of well-performing low-cost internet and rising smartphone penetration cannot be understated in this regard. Access to capital and market, coupled with impeccable regulatory support can take the industry to much greater heights.

Innovative technologies such as AI to DLT are transforming the domain of financial services, creating prospects as well as challenges for consumers, service providers, and regulators. These skills might drive substantial potent gains in the financial sector, also in the zone of payments, financing, investments, asset management, and insurance. Competition along with a variety of service offerings can move the industry towards greater efficiency and effectiveness.

The digital payments space has witnessed maximum innovations. The development of alternative payment channels and payment hubs has been exceptionally good. However, the same benefits including greater competition and financial stability can also squeeze the profits of financial institutions, thereby raising margin pressure for incumbents and questioning their stability due to excessive dependence over third parties. The pace of development has not been the same for all markets and the future trajectory of each market depends on its regulatory ecosystem. This points towards a greater threat to the stability and integrity of the financial system, especially in cases where it functions outside the purview and boundaries of financial regulation.

REFERENCES

Allen, F., McAndrews, J., & Strahan, P. (2002). E-finance: An introduction. *Journal of Financial Services Research*, *22*(1/2), 5–27.

Alt, R., & Puschmann, T. (2012). The rise of customer-oriented banking - electronic markets are paving the way for change in the financial industry. *Electronic Markets*, *22*(4), 203–215. doi:10. 100712525-012-0106-2

Arner, D. W., Barberis, J., & Buckley, R. P. (2016). The evolution of FinTech: A new post-crisis paradigm? *Georgetown Journal of International Law*, *47*(4), 1271–1319.

Arner, D. W., Barberis, J., & Buckley, R. P. (2017). FinTech, RegTech and the reconceptualization of financial regulation. Northwestern. *Journal of International Law and Business*, *37*(3), 371–413.

Bain & Company. (2017). *Evolving the customer experience in banking*. http://www.bain.de/en/Images/BAIN_REPORT_Evolving_the_Customer_Experience_in_Banking.pdf

Beck, H. (2001). Banking is essential, banks are not. The future of financial intermediation in the age of the internet. *NETNOMICS: Economic Research and Electronic Networking*, *3*(1), 7–22. doi:10.1023/A:1009927623530

Berger, A. N. (2003). The economic effects of technological progress: Evidence from the banking industry. *Journal of Money, Credit and Banking*, *35*, 141–176. doi:10.1353/mcb.2003.0009

Bons, R. W. H., Alt, R., Lee, H. G., & Weber, B. (2012). Banking in the internet and mobile era. *Electronic Markets*, *22*(4), 197–202. doi:10.100712525-012-0110-6

CBInsights. (2018). *Global Fintech report Q1 2018*. https://www.cbinsights.com/research/report/fintech-trends-q1-2018/

Chen, L. (2016). From fintech to finlife: The case of fintech development in China. *China Economic Journal, 9*, 225–239. doi:10.1080/17538963.2016.1215057

Chiu, I. H.-Y. (2016). FinTech and disruptive business models in financial products, intermediation and markets- Policy implications for financial regulators. *Journal of Technology Law & Policy, 21*, 55–112. doi:10.3868050-004-015- 0003-8

Christensen, C. M. (2003). The innovator's dilemma: The revolutionary book that will changed the way you do business. *The American Political Science Review*.

Dapp, T. (2014). Fintech–The digital (r) evolution in the financial sector. *Deutsche Bank Res., 39*. https://goo.gl/UcZJFz

Davies, S., Jackett, D., Kashyap, M., Nicolacakis, D., Qureshi, M., & Shipman, J. (2016). *Customers in the spotlight: How FinTech is reshaping banking - Global FinTech Survey 2016*. PricewaterhouseCoopers. https://www.pwc.com/il/he/bankim/ assets/fin-tech-banking.pdf

Deloitte. (2016). *RegTech is the new FinTech: How regulatory technology is helping firms better understand and manage their risks*. Deloitte. https://www2.deloitte.com/content/dam/Deloitte/ie/Documents/FinancialServices/IE_2016_FS_RegTech_is_the_new_FinTech. pdf

DeYoung, R. (2005). The performance of internet-based business models: Evidence from the banking industry. *The Journal of Business, 78*, 893–948. doi:10.1086/ 429648

Dhar, V., & Stein, R. M. (2017). FinTech platforms and strategy - integrating trust and automation in finance. *Communications of the ACM, 60*(10), 32–35. doi:10.1145/3132726

Fortnum, D., Pollari, I., Mead, W., Hughes, B., & Speier, A. (2017). *The pulse of fintech Q1 2017: Global analysis of investment in fintech*. KPMG technical report. Available at: https://assets.kpmg.com/content/dam/kpmg/xx/pdf/2017/04/ pulse-of-fintech-q1.pdf

Gabor, D., & Brooks, S. (2017). The digital revolution in financial inclusion: International development in the fintech era. *New Political Economy, 22*, 423–436. doi:10.1080/13563467.2017.1259298

Gábossy, Á. (2016). New directions in crowdfunding. *Public Finance Quarterly, 61*(4), 533–544.

Garcia, R., & Calantone, R. (2002). A critical look at technological innovation typology and innovativeness terminology: A literature review. *Journal of Product Innovation Management, 19*(2), 110–132.

Gimpel, H., Rau, D., & Röglinger, M. (2018). Understanding FinTech start-ups - a taxonomy of consumer-oriented service offerings. *Electronic Markets, 28*(3). Advance online publication. doi:10.100712525-017- 0275-0

Gomber, P., Kauffman, R. J., Parker, C., & Weber, B. W. (2018). On the FinTech revolution: Interpreting the forces of innovation, disruption, and transformation in financial services. *Journal of Management Information Systems, 35*(1), 220–265. doi:10.1080/ 07421222.2018.1440766

Gomber, P., Koch, J.-A., & Siering, M. (2017). Digital finance and FinTech: Current research and future research directions. *Journal of Business Economics*, *87*(5), 537–580. doi:10.1007/ s11573-017-0852-x

Goodale, J. (2012). *Bank 1.0 and Bank 2.0 success entails learning from each other's best practices.* Whitepaper TSYS. https:// digitalpayments.files.wordpress.com/2013/03/bank-1-0-and-bank2-0.pdf

Hemmadi, M. (2015). FinTech is both friend and FOE. *Canadian Business*, *88*(6), 10–11.

Iwata, D. (2017). *A new relationship between financing and technology in the FinTech era.* NEC Technical Journal.

Jesse McWaters, F. (2015). *The Future of Financial Services – How disruptive innovations are reshaping the way financial services are structured, provisioned and consumed.* Academic Press.

Lacasse, R. M., Lambert, B. A., Osmani, E., Couture, C., Roy, N., Sylvain, J., & Nadeau, F. (2016). A digital tsunami: FinTech and Crowdfunding. *International Scientific Conference on Digital Intelligence*, 1–5.

Lee, I., & Shin, Y. J. (2018). Fintech: Ecosystem, business models, investment decisions, and challenges. *Business Horizons*, *61*(1), 35–46. doi:10.1016/j.bushor.2017.09.003

Mareev, S. N. (2016). Understand global capitalism (Reflections on the Book "Global Capital", by A.V. Buzgalin and A.I Kolganov). *Voprosy Filosofii*, 60–67.

Mishra, V., & Singh, V. (2015). Selection of appropriate electronic banking channel alternative. *International Journal of Bank Marketing*, *33*(3), 223–242.

Nejad, M. G. (2016). Guest editorial: Challenges and opportunities for innovation in financial services. *International Journal of Bank Marketing*, *34*(1), 1–7.

PricewaterhouseCoopers. (n.d.a). https://www.pwc.com/il/he/bankim/assets/fin-tech-banking.pdf

PricewaterhouseCoopers. (n.d.b). https://www.pwc.com/gx/en/industries/financial-services/publications/ financial-services-technology-2020-and-beyond-embracing-disruption.html

Schueffel, P. (2016). Taming the beast: A scientific definition of fintech. SSRN *Electronic Journal, 4*, 32–54. doi:10.2139srn.3097312

Shim, Y., & Shin, D. H. (2016). Analyzing China's fintech industry from the perspective of actor-network theory. *Telecommunications Policy*, *40*, 168–181. doi:10. 1016/j.telpol.2015.11.005

Stöckli, E., Dremel, C., & Uebernickel, F. (2018). Exploring characteristics and transformational capabilities of InsurTech innovations to understand insurance value creation in a digital world. *Electronic Markets*, *28*(3). Advance online publication. doi:10.100712525-018-0304-7

Szpringer, W. (2016). FinTech – New phenomena in the financial services market. *eMentor*, 56–69.

World Economic Forum. (2012). *Rethinking financial innovation.* World Economic Forum.

APPENDIX

List of Abbreviations

AI	Artificial Intelligence
AMFI	Association of Mutual Funds in India
API	Application Programming Interfaces
AR	Augmented Reality
AUM	Asset Under Management
CAGR	Compounded Annual Growth Rate
DLT	Distributed Ledger Technology
ESG	Environmental, Social and Governance
FinTech	Financial Technology
FS	Financial Service
GST	Goods and Service Tax
GSTN	Goods and Services Tax Network
HNWI	High Net Worth Individuals
IMPS	Immediate Payment Service
InsurTech	Insurance Technology
IoT	Internet of Things
KYC	Know Your Customer
ML	Machine Learning
MSME	Micro, Small And Medium Enterprises
NBFC	Non-Banking Financial Company
NEFT	National Electronic Funds Transfer
NPCI	National Payments Corporation of India
P2P	Peer to Peer
POS	Point of Sale
PoS	Point of Service
PPI	Prepaid Payment Instruments
RegTech	Regulatory Technology
RPA	Robotic Process Automation
SIP	Systematic Investment Plan
SME	Small And Medium Enterprises
SMS	Short Message Service
UPI	Unified Payment Interface
VC Firms	Venture Capitalist Firms
VR	Virtual Reality
WealthTech	Wealth Management Technology

Compilation of References

Abdinoor & Mbamba. (2017). Factors influencing consumers' adoption of mobile financial services in Tanzania. *Cogent Business & Management, 4*(1392273).

Abdou, H. A., English, J., & Adewunmi, P. O. (2014). An investigation of risk management practices in electronic banking: The case of the UK banks. *Banks and Bank Systems, 9*(3).

Abeyratne, S., & Monfared, R. (2016). Blockchain ready manufacturing supply chain using distributed ledger. *International Journal of Research in Engineering and Technology*, *5*(9), 1–10. doi:10.15623/ijret.2016.0509001

Abiteboul, S. (1997). Querying semi-structured data. In *International Conference on Database Theory* (pp. 1-18). Berlin: Springer

Abrutyn, S. (2016). *Handbook of contemporary sociological theory*. Springer International Publishing. doi:10.1007/978-3-319-32250-6

Acohido, P., & Swartz, J. (2008). *Zero-day threat: The shocking truth of how banks and credit bureaus help cyber crooks steal your money and identity*. Union Square Press.

Acs, Z., Åstebro, T., Audretsch, D., & Robinson, D. T. (2016). Public policy to promote entrepreneurship: A call to arms. *Small Business Economics*, *47*(1), 35–51. doi:10.100711187-016-9712-2

Acuner, S., & Acuner, E. (2017). Turizmde paylaşım ekonomisi ve vergilendirilmesi. *Journal of Tourism and Gastronomy Studies*, *5*(2), 188–212. doi:10.21325/jotags.2017.77

Adner, R., & Kapoor, R. (2010). Value creation in innovation ecosystems: How the structure of technological interdependence affects firm performance in new technology generations. *Strategic Management Journal*, *31*(3), 306–333. doi:10.1002mj.821

Adukaite, A., Gazizova, E., & Cantoni, L. (2014). When e-gov deals with tourists: The case of visa information. In *ACM International Conference Proceeding Series* (pp. 334–337). Association for Computing Machinery. 10.1145/2691195.2691283

Agwu, E. (2018). The role of e-banking on operational efficiency of banks in Nigeria. *Basic Research Journal of Business Management and Accounts*, *6*(1), 1–10. doi:10.2139srn.3122498

Ahanger, R. G. (2011). An investigation into the determinants of customers' preferences and satisfaction of internet banking. *Journal of Applied Sciences*, *11*(3), 426–437. doi:10.3923/jas.2011.426.437

Airbnb vs Hotels: A Price Comparison. (2013, June 17). *Priceonomics*. Retrieved from https://priceonomics.com/hotels/

Akçura, A. (2019). *Global Practices In the Taxation of The Digital Economy and The Position of Turkey*. Retrieved From https://www.verginet.net/dtt/1/dijital-ekonomi-vergilendirilmesi-dunya-Turkiye-uygulamalari.aspx

Akter, S., & Wamba, S. F. (2019). Big data and disaster management: A systematic review and agenda for future research. *Annals of Operations Research, 283*(1-2), 939–959. doi:10.100710479-017-2584-2

Akyol, B., & Ünlüönen, K. (2020). Effects of sharing economy on tourism sector: A study on Kırıkkale University students. *Journal of Tourism and Gastronomy Studies, 8*(1), 623–644. doi:10.21325/jotags.2020.568

Al-Amoush, A. B., & Sandhu, K. (2019). A new model for acceptance of analytics in learning management systems at Jordanian universities (JLMS). In Modern Technologies for Teaching and Learning in Socio-Humanitarian Disciplines (pp. 138-161). IGI Global.

Albinsson, P. A., & Perera, B. Y. (2012). Alternative marketplaces in the 21stcentury: Building community through sharing events. *Journal of Consumer Behaviour, 11*(4), 303–315. doi:10.1002/cb.1389

Alcaide–Muñoza, L., Rodríguez–Bolívara, M. P., Cobob, M. J., & Herrera–Viedmac, E. (2017). Analysing the scientific evolution of e-Government using a science mapping approach. *Government Information Quarterly, 34*, 545–555. doi:10.1016/j.giq.2017.05.002

Al-Debei, M., & Avison, D. (2010). Developing a unified framework of the business model concept. *European Journal of Information Systems, 19*(3), 359–376. doi:10.1057/ejis.2010.21

Aldrich, E. H., & Waldinger, R. (1990). Ethnicity and Entrepreneurship. Annual Review of Sociology, 16, 25.

Alegre, J., & Pou, L. (2006). The length of stay in the demand for tourism. *Tourism Management, 27*(6), 1343–1355. doi:10.1016/j.tourman.2005.06.012

Ali, S., Peters, L. D., Khan, I. U., Ali, W., & Saif, N. (2020). Organizational Learning and Hotel Performance: The Role of Capabilities' Hierarchy. *International Journal of Hospitality Management, 85*, 102349. doi:10.1016/j.ijhm.2019.102349

Alkhaleefah, A. (2018). What to do to improve the international saudi innovation Rank/Score. *International Journal of Mechanical Engineering and Technology, 9*(3), 435–442.

Allen, F., McAndrews, J., & Strahan, P. (2002). E-finance: An introduction. *Journal of Financial Services Research, 22*(1/2), 5–27.

Allen, J. P. (2019). *Digital Entrepreneurship*. Routledge. doi:10.4324/9780429506567

Almeida, A. M. P., Almeida, H. S., & Figueiredo-Braga, M. (2018). Mobile solutions in depression: Enhancing communication with patients using an SMS-based intervention. *Procedia Computer Science, 138*, 89–96. doi:10.1016/j.procs.2018.10.013

Almeida, R. K., Fernandes, A. M., & Viollaz, M. (2020). Software Adoption, Employment Composition, and the Skill Content of Occupations in Chilean Firms. *The Journal of Development Studies, 56*(1), 169–185. doi:10.1080/00220388.2018.1546847

Al-Sukkar, A. S. (2005). *The application of information systems in the Jordainan banking sector: A study of the acceptance of the Internet*. Doctoral Universty of Wollongong.

Altman, E. (2015). *Platform and Ecosystem Transitions: Strategic and Organizational Implications. Doctoral dissertation.* Boston: Harvard Business School.

Alt, R., & Puschmann, T. (2012). The rise of customer-oriented banking - electronic markets are paving the way for change in the financial industry. *Electronic Markets, 22*(4), 203–215. doi:10. 100712525-012-0106-2

Alvarez, S. A., & Barney, J. B. (2017). Resource-based theory and the entrepreneurial firm. *Strategic entrepreneurship: Creating a new mindset*, 87-105.

Alves, C., Oliveira, J., & Jansen, S. (2017). Software ecosystems governance-a systematic literature review and research agenda. *Proc. 19th Int. Conf. Enterprise Inf. Syst. (ICEIS)*, 1, pp. 215-226. 10.5220/0006269402150226

Amin, H. (2008). Factors affecting the intentions of customers in Malaysia to use mobile phone credit cards. *Management Research News Journal*, *31*(7), 493–503. doi:10.1108/01409170810876062

Amorim, A. C., Mira da Silva, M., Pereira, R., & Gonçalves, M. (2020). Using agile methodologies for adopting COBIT. *Information Systems*, *101496*, 101496. Advance online publication. doi:10.1016/j.is.2020.101496

Amorós, J. E., Ciravegna, L., Mandakovic, V., & Stenholm, P. (2019). Necessity or opportunity? the effects of State fragility and economic development on entrepreneurial efforts. *Entrepreneurship Theory and Practice*, *43*(4), 725–750. doi:10.1177/1042258717736857

Anas, N., Zulkipli, S. N., Noor, M. S. M., Noh, A. M. M., Ariff, M. I. M., Ghazali, Z. M., ... Rosli, H. M. (2019). *Usefulness and Effectiveness of Mind Mapping: An Analysis of CTU101 and CTU151*. Academic Press.

Anbalagan, B., & Valliyammai, C. (2016, December). # ChennaiFloods: Leveraging Human and Machine Learning for Crisis Mapping during Disasters Using Social Media. In *2016 IEEE 23rd International Conference on High Performance Computing Workshops (HiPCW)* (pp. 50-59). IEEE.

Andreo, S., & Bosch, J. (2019). API Management Challenges in Ecosystems. In S. Hyrynsalmi, M. Suoranta, A. Nguyen-Duc, P. Tyrväinen, & P. Abrahamsson (Eds.), *Software Business. ICSOB 2019. Lecture Notes in Business Information Processing* (Vol. 370). Springer. doi:10.1007/978-3-030-33742-1_8

Andrews, H., Berttram, P., Espie, V., Geissbauer, R., Khurana, A., Kinder, M., Malmgren, P., Mueller, R., Phillips, D., Potter, J., Romac, B., Schrauf, S., & Strom, M. (2016). *Industry 4.0 - How digitization makes the supply chain more efficient, agile, and customer-focused.* PWC.

Anen, C. (2007). *Neural correlates of economic and moral decision-making* (Tesis doctoral).

Angeren, J., Kabbedijk, J., Popp, K., & Jansen, S. (2013). Managing software ecosystems through partening. In S. Jansen, S. Brinkkemper, & M. Cusumano (Eds.), Software Ecosystems: analyzing and managing business networks in the software industry (pp. 85-102). Edward Elgar Publishiing.

Annosi, M. C., Martini, A., Brunetta, F., & Marchegiani, L. (2020). Learning in an agile setting: A multilevel research study on the evolution of organizational routines. *Journal of Business Research*, *110*, 554–566. doi:10.1016/j.jbusres.2018.05.011

Antunes, H. de J. G., & Pinheiro, P. G. (2020). Linking knowledge management, organizational learning and memory. *Journal of Innovation & Knowledge*, *5*(2), 140–149. doi:10.1016/j.jik.2019.04.002

Arcos-Medina, G., & Mauricio, D. (2020). The Influence of the Application of Agile Practices in Software Quality Based on ISO/IEC 25010 Standard. *International Journal of Information Technologies and Systems Approach*, *13*(2), 27–53. doi:10.4018/IJITSA.2020070102

Arner, D. W., Barberis, J., & Buckley, R. P. (2016). The evolution of FinTech: A new post-crisis paradigm? *Georgetown Journal of International Law*, *47*(4), 1271–1319.

Arner, D. W., Barberis, J., & Buckley, R. P. (2017). FinTech, RegTech and the reconceptualization of financial regulation. Northwestern. *Journal of International Law and Business*, *37*(3), 371–413.

Aryal, A., Liao, Y., Nattuthurai, P., & Li, B. (2018). The emerging big data analytics and IoT in supply chain management: A systematic review. Supply Chain Management, pp. *Supply Chain Management*, *25*(2), 2018. doi:10.1108/SCM-03-2018-0149

Ashmore, S., & Wedlake, M. (2016). Developing the Product Your Customer Really Wants: The Value of an Agile Partnership. *Information Resources Management Journal*, *29*(3), 1–11. doi:10.4018/IRMJ.2016070101

Atanasijević, J., Jakovetić, D., Krejić, N., Krklec-Jerinkić, N., & Marković, D. (2019). Using big data analytics to improve efficiency of tax collection in the tax Administration of the Republic of Serbia. *Ekonomika Preduzeća*, *67*(1-2), 115–130. doi:10.5937/EkoPre1808115A

Attaran, M. (1999). Internet-based business opportunities: Buyers beware of scams. *Information Management & Computer Security*, *7*(4), 176–178. doi:10.1108/09685229910292682

Au, I., Boardman, R., Robin, J., Larvie, P., Pavese, A., Riegelsberger, J., ... Stevens, M. (2008). User experience al Google-Focus on the user and all else will follow. In *CHI'08 Extended Abstracts on Human Factors in Computing Systems* (pp. 3681–3686). ACM.

Axoft Argentina, S. A. (2019). *Tango Tiendas*. Retrieved November 11, 2019, from https://www.tangonexo.com/tiendas/

Axoft Argentina, S. A. (2019, November 8). *Tango nexo*. Retrieved November 8, 2019, from https://www.tangonexo.com/

Axoft Argentina, S. A. (2019, September 16). *Tango software*. Retrieved from https://www.axoft.com/

Aydin, E., Polat, A., & Ergene, L. T. (2016, November). Vector control of DFIG in wind power applications. In *2016 IEEE International Conference on Renewable Energy Research and Applications (ICRERA)* (pp. 478-483). IEEE. 10.1109/ICRERA.2016.7884383

Bag, S.H. (2018). Industry 4.0 and supply chain sustainability: framework and future research directions. *Benchmarking*.

Bagdadli, S., & Gianecchini, M. (2019). Organizational career management practices and objective career success: A systematic review and framework. *Human Resource Management Review*, *29*(3), 353–370. doi:10.1016/j.hrmr.2018.08.001

Bag, S., Wood, L. C., Xu, L., Dhamija, P., & Kayikci, Y. (2020). Big data analytics as an operational excellence approach to enhance sustainable supply chain performance. *Resources, Conservation and Recycling*, *153*, 104559. doi:10.1016/j.resconrec.2019.104559

Bagwell, S. (2018). From mixed embeddedness to transnational mixed embeddedness An exploration of Vietnamese businesses in London. *International Journal of Entrepreneurial Behaviour & Research*, *24*(1), 104–120. doi:10.1108/IJEBR-01-2017-0035

Bain & Company. (2017). *Evolving the customer experience in banking*. http://www.bain.de/en/Images/BAIN_REPORT_Evolving_the_Customer_Experience_in_Banking.pdf

Baiyere, A., Salmela, H., & Tapanainen, T. (2020). Digital transformation and the new logics of business process management. *European Journal of Information Systems*, *29*(3), 1–22. doi:10.1080/0960085X.2020.1718007

Baker, C. R. (1999). An analysis of fraud on the internet. *Internet Research*, *9*(5), 348–360. doi:10.1108/10662249910297750

Bakker, S., & Farla, J. (2015). Electrification of the car—will the momentum last?: Introduction to The Special Issue. *Environmental Innovation and Societal Transitions*, *14*, 1–4. doi:10.1016/j.eist.2014.07.002

Balaji, S., Babu, M. M., & Aravind, L. (2007). Interplay between network structures, regulatory modes and sensing mechanisms of transcription factors in the transcriptional regulatory network of E. coli. *Journal of Molecular Biology*, *372*(4), 1108–1122. doi:10.1016/j.jmb.2007.06.084 PMID:17706247

Baltagi, B. H., Egger, P. H., & Kesina, M. (2016). Bayesian Spatial Bivariate Panel Probit Estimation', Spatial Econometrics: Qualitative and Limited Dependent Variables (Advances in Econometrics, Volume 37). Emerald Group Publishing Limited.

Baltar, F., & Icart, I. B. (2013). Entrepreneurial gain, cultural similarity and transnational entrepreneurship. *Global Networks-a Journal of Transnational Affairs, 13*(2), 20. doi:10.1111/glob.12020

Bandura, A., & Walters, R. H. (1977). *Social learning theory* (Vol. 1). Prentice-hall.

Banerjee, M. (2009). *Internet banking: An interaction building channel for bank customer relationships. In Self-Service in the Internet Age.* Springer-Verlag.

Baptista, P., Fernández, C., & Hernández, R. (2006). *Metodología de la investigación* (6th ed.). Editorial McGraw Hill.

Baptista, R., & Karaöz, M. (2006). Entrepreneurial human capital and the early survival chances of new start-ups: Opportunity-based vs. necessity-based entrepreneurship. *Small Business Economics, 36*(3), 249–270. doi:10.100711187-009-9226-2

Barata, J., Da Cunha, P. R., & Stal, J. (2018). Mobile supply chain management in the Industry 4.0 era An annotated bibliography and guide for future research. *Journal of Enterprise Information Management, 31*(1), 173–193. doi:10.1108/JEIM-09-2016-0156

Bardhi, F., & Eckhardt, G. M. (2012). Access-based consumption: The case of car sharing. *The Journal of Consumer Research, 39*(4), 881–898. doi:10.1086/666376

Barki, H., Rivard, S., & Talbot, J. (1993). Toward an Assessment of Software Development Risk. *Journal of Management Information Systems, 10*(2), 203–225.

Barney, J. B. (2018). Why resource-based theory's model of profit appropriation must incorporate a stakeholder perspective. *Strategic Management Journal, 39*(13), 3305–3325. doi:10.1002mj.2949

Basole, R. (2016, November/December). Accelerating Digital Transformation. Visual Insights from the API Ecosystem. *IT Pro*, 20-25.

Basole, R., & Park, H. (2019). Interfirm Collaboration and Firm Value in Software Ecosystems: Evidence From Cloud Computing. *IEEE Transactions on Engineering Management, 66*(3), 368–380. doi:10.1109/TEM.2018.2855401

Batı, M. (2019). *The New Tax Draft with All Its Articles.* Retrieved From https://t24.com.tr/haber/doc-dr-murat-bati-yazdi-madde-madde-yeni-vergi-taslagi,845205

Batth, R. S., Nayyar, A., & Nagpal, A. (2018, August). Internet of robotic things: driving intelligent robotics of future-concept, architecture, applications and technologies. In *2018 4th International Conference on Computing Sciences (ICCS)* (pp. 151-160). IEEE. 10.1109/ICCS.2018.00033

Bazhair, A., & Sandhu, K. (2015). Factors for the Acceptance of Enterprise Resource Planning (ERP) Systems and Financial Performance. *Journal of Economics, Business and Management, 14*(7).

Bazhair, A. H., & Sandhu, K. (2015). Factors for the acceptance of enterprise resource planning (ERP) systems and financial performance. *System, 14*(7), 16.

Beck, K., Beedle, M., van Bennekum, A., Cockburn, A., & Cunningham, W. (2001). *Manifesto for Agile Software Development.* Retrieved July 19, 2020, from Manifesto for Agile Software Development website: https://agilemanifesto.org/

Becken, S. (2013). Measuring the effect of weather on tourism: A destination- and activity-based analysis. *Journal of Travel Research, 52*(2), 156–167. doi:10.1177/0047287512461569

Beckers, P., & Blumberg, B. F. (2013). Immigrant entrepreneurship on the move: A longitudinal analysis of first- and second-generation immigrant entrepreneurship in the Netherlands. *Entrepreneurship and Regional Development, 25*(7-8), 654–691. doi:10.1080/08985626.2013.808270

Beck, H. (2001). Banking is essential, banks are not. The future of financial intermediation in the age of the internet. *NETNOMICS: Economic Research and Electronic Networking, 3*(1), 7–22. doi:10.1023/A:1009927623530

Beliaeva, T., Ferasso, M., Kraus, S., & Damke, E. J. (2019). Dynamics of digital entrepreneurship and the innovation ecosystem. *International Journal of Entrepreneurial Behaviour & Research, 26*(2), 266–284. doi:10.1108/IJEBR-06-2019-0397

Belk, R. (2007). Why not share rather than own? *The Annals of the American Academy of Political and Social Science, 611*(1), 126–140. doi:10.1177/0002716206298483

Belk, R. (2010). Sharing. *The Journal of Consumer Research, 36*(5), 715–734. doi:10.1086/612649

Belk, R. (2014). You are what you can access: Sharing and collaborative consumption online. *Journal of Business Research, 67*(8), 1595–1600. doi:10.1016/j.jbusres.2013.10.001

Bělohlávek, R., Dauben, J. W., & Klir, G. J. (2017). *Fuzzy logic and mathematics: a historical perspective.* Oxford University Press.

Ben-Daya, M., Hassini, E., & Bahroun, Z. (2019). Internet of things and supply chain management: A literature review. *International Journal of Production Research, 57*(15-16), 4719–4742. doi:10.1080/00207543.2017.1402140

Benson, V., Morgan, S., & Filippaios, F. (2014). Social career management: Social media and employability skills gap. *Computers in Human Behavior, 30*, 519–525. doi:10.1016/j.chb.2013.06.015

Benzecry, C. E., Krause, M., & Reed, I. A. (Eds.). (2017). *Social theory now.* University of Chicago Press. doi:10.7208/chicago/9780226475318.001.0001

Ber, H. (2018). *An Overview of the Issue of Taxing the Digital Economy.* Retrieved From https://vergialgi.net/dijital-ekonominin-vergilendirilmesi-sorunsalina-genel-bir-bakis

Berger, A. N. (2003). The economic effects of technological progress: Evidence from the banking industry. *Journal of Money, Credit and Banking, 35*, 141–176. doi:10.1353/mcb.2003.0009

Bertot, J. C., Gorham, U., Jaeger, P. T., Sarin, L. C., & Choi, H. (2014). Big data, open government and e-government: Issues, policies and recommendations. *Information Polity, 19*(1, 2), 5-16.

Bingöl, O. (2019). *On Taxation: Digital Services Tax on the Horizon.* Retrieved From https://vergiyedair.com/2019/10/24/dijital-hizmet-vergisi-geliyor/

Birinci, N. (2019). The Effect of Digitalization on Tax Base and Unilateral Measures. *Finance Journal*, (176), 505–527.

Black, N. J., Lockett, A., Winklhofer, H., & Ennew, C. (2001). The adoption of Internet financial services: *A qualitative study. International Journal of Retail & Distribution Management, 29*(8), 390–398. doi:10.1108/09590550110397033

Bloomberg, J. (2018). Digitization, digitalization, and digital transformation: confuse them at your peril. *Forbes.*

Boccia, F. (2016). Introduction: The Digital Economy and Fiscal Policy In The Age of E-Commerce. In Francesco Boccia, Robert Leonardi (Ed.), The Challenge of the Digital Economy, Market, Taxation and Appropriate Economic Models (pp. 1-17). Academic Press.

Bogdanowicz, M. (2015). *Digital Entrepreneurship Barriers and Drivers.* Retrieved from: https://ec.europa.eu/jrc/en/publication/digital-entrepreneurship-barriers-and-drivers-need-specific-measurement-framework

Bons, R. W. H., Alt, R., Lee, H. G., & Weber, B. (2012). Banking in the internet and mobile era. *Electronic Markets, 22*(4), 197–202. doi:10.100712525-012-0110-6

Boonsiritomachaia, W., & Pitchayadejanant, K. (2017). Determinants affecting mobile banking adoption bygeneration Y based on the Unified Theory of Acceptance andUse of Technology Model modified by the TechnologyAcceptance Model concept. *Journal of Social Sciences*, *1*(10).

Bort, J. (2014). San Francisco makes Airbnb legal at last. *Business Insider*. Retrieved from https://www.businessinsider.com/sanfrancisco-makes-airbnb-legal-at-last-2014-10

Bosh-Sijtsema, P., & Bosch, J. (2015). Plays nice with others? Multiple ecosystems, various roles and divergent engagement models. *Technology Analysis and Strategic Management*, *27*(8), 960–974. doi:10.1080/09537325.2015.1038231

Botsman, R., & Rogers, R. (2010a). *What's mine is yours: How collaborative consumption is changing the way we live*. Collins.

Botsman, R., & Rogers, R. (2010b). Beyond Zipcar: Collaborative consumption. *Harvard Business Review*, *88*(10), 30.

Bouaziz, F. (2006). Managing e-government projects failure and risks. *7th International Business Information Management (IBIMA) Conference*.

Bouaziz, F., & Chaabouni, J. (2013). Criteria for assessing the success of e-government projects. In E-Government Success Factors and Measures: Concepts, Theories, Experiences, and Practical Recommendations. Centro de Investigacin y Docencia Econmicas, Mexico.

Bouaziz, F. (2020a). From E-government to Digital Government: the Public Value Quest in the Tunisian Public Administration. In V. Ponnusamy, K. Rafique, & N. Zaman (Eds.), *Employing Recent Technologies for Improved Digital Governance* (pp. 107–127). IGI Global.

Bouaziz, F. (2020b). Digital government competences for digital public administration transformation. In K. Sandhu (Ed.), *Leadership, Management, and Adoption Techniques for Digital Service Innovation* (pp. 244–263). IGI Global.

Bouaziz, F., & Chaabouni, J. (2012). A framework to analyze the alignment of e-government projects. *International Journal of Electronic Government Research*, *8*(2), 75–90. doi:10.4018/jegr.2012040104

Boudreau, K. (2010). Open platform strategies and innovation: Granting access vs. devolving control. *Management Science*, *56*(10), 1761–1777. doi:10.1287/mnsc.1100.1215

Bourgoin, M. O., & Smith, S. J. (1995). *Big data—Better Returns, Leveraging Your Hidden Data Assets to Improve ROI. In Artificial Intelligence in the Capital Markets*. Probus Publishing Company.

Bousquet, J., Bedbrook, A., Czarlewski, W., Onorato, G. L., Arnavielhe, S., Laune, D., ... Morais-Almeida, M. (2019). Guidance to 2018 good practice: ARIA digitally-enabled, integrated, person-centred care for rhinitis and asthma. *Clinical and Translational Allergy*, *9*(1), 1–19.

Boyle, R. (2006). *Measuring public sector productivity: lessons from international experience*. CPMR Discussion Paper 35. Institute of Public Administration.

Bozdoğanoğlu, B., & Haspolat Kaya, I. (2019). Opportunities and Challenges Created by Digitalization for Tax Administrations: The Digitalization Process of Tax Administrations While The Economy Is Digitalized. *MHD*, *15*(176), 1647–1676.

Brenk, S. (2020). Open Business Model Innovation – The Impact of Breadth, Depth, and Freedom of Collaboration. Academy of Management Proceedings, 1, 1-6. doi:10.5465/AMBPP.2020.19

Briley, D. A., Livengood, J., Derringer, J., Tucker-Drob, E. M., Fraley, R. C., & Roberts, B. W. (2019). Interpreting behavior genetic models: Seven developmental processes to understand. *Behavior Genetics*, *49*(2), 196–210. doi:10.100710519-018-9939-6 PMID:30467668

Bromwich, M. (1999). Thoughts on management accounting and strategy. *Pacific Accounting Review*, *11*(1/2), 41–48. doi:10.1108/eb037925

Brown, B., Chui, M., & Manyika, J. (2011). Are you ready for the era of 'big data'? *The McKinsey Quarterly*, *4*(1), 24–35.

Brown, D., & Hayes, N. (2008). *Influencer Marketing. Who really influences your customers?* Taylor & Francis.

Brown, J. S. (2000). Growing up: Digital: How the web changes work, education, and the ways people learn. *Change: The Magazine of Higher Learning*, *32*(2), 11–20. doi:10.1080/00091380009601719

Brown, R., Mawson, S., Lee, N., & Peterson, L. (2019). Start-up factories, transnational entrepreneurs and entrepreneurial ecosystems: Unpacking the lure of start-up accelerator programmes. *European Planning Studies*, *27*(5), 885–904. doi:10.1080/09654313.2019.1588858

Brown, T. E., Davidsson, P., & Wiklund, J. (2001). An operationalization of Stevenson's conceptualization of entrepreneurship as opportunity-based firm behavior. *Strategic Management Journal*, *22*(10), 953–968. doi:10.1002mj.190

Brown, W. (2015). *Undoing the demos: Neoliberalism's stealth revolution*. Zone Books. doi:10.2307/j.ctt17kk9p8

Brustein, J. (2014). An Airbnb rival challenges San Francisco's Airbnb law. *Bloomberg Businessweek*. Retrieved from https://www.bloomberg.com/bw/articles/2014-11-03/san-francisco-faces-a-lawsuit-over-its-airbnb-law

Brynjolfsson, E., Dick, A., & Smith, M. (2010). A nearly perfect market? *Quantitative Marketing and Economics*, *8*(1), 1-33.

Brynjolfsson, E., & McAfee, A. (2011). *Race against the machine: how the digital revolution is accelerating innovation, driving productivity, and irreversibly transforming*. Digital Frontier Press.

Brzozowski, J., Cucculelli, M., & Surdej, A. (2017). The determinants of transnational entrepreneurship and transnational ties' dynamics among immigrant entrepreneurs in ICT sector in Italy. *International Migration (Geneva, Switzerland)*, *55*(3), 105–125. doi:10.1111/imig.12335

Budak, T. (2018). *Taxing the Digital Economy*. On İki Levha Publishing.

Budu, J. (2018). Applying Agile Principles in Teaching Undergraduate Information Technology Project Management. *International Journal of Information and Communication Technology Education*, *14*(3), 29–40. doi:10.4018/IJICTE.2018070103

Buhalis, D., & Main, H. (1998). Information technology in peripheral small and medium hospitality enterprises: Strategic analysis and critical factors. *International Journal of Contemporary Hospitality Management*, *10*(5), 198–202. doi:10.1108/09596119810227811

Bultum, A. G. (2014). Factors Affecting Adoption of Electronic Banking System in Ethiopian Banking Industry. *Journal of Management Information System and E-commerce*, *1*(1).

Calatayud, A. (2017). *The connected supply chain: enhancing risk management in a changing world*. Discussion Paper No. 508, Inter-American Development Bank, Washington, DC.

Calatayud, A., Mangan, J., & Christopher, M. (2019). The self-thinking supply chain. *Supply Chain Management*, *24*(1), 22–38. doi:10.1108/SCM-03-2018-0136

Cam, L. N. T., Anh, T. T., Moslehpour, M., & Thanh, X. D. T. (2019). Exploring the impact of traditional and electronic word of mouth on travel intention. In *ACM International Conference Proceeding Series* (pp. 83–87). Association for Computing Machinery. 10.1145/3317614.3317617

Campbell, N. (2014). Tax Policy and Administration in an Era of Big data. *Tax Planning International*, *12*(12), 2–6.

Canonica, G. W., Antó i Boqué, J. M., Mullol i Miret, J., & Valero Santiago, A.MASK study group. (2019). Guidance to 2018 good practice: ARIA digitally enabled, integrated, person-centred care for rhinitis and asthma. *Clinical and Translational Allergy, 9.*

Cantú-Ortiz, F. J., Sánchez, N. G., Garrido, L., Terashima-Marin, H., & Brena, R. F. (2020). An artificial intelligence educational strategy for the digital transformation. *International Journal on Interactive Design and Manufacturing*, 1-15.

Carey, G., & Crammond, B. (2015). What works in joined-up government? An evidence synthesis. *International Journal of Public Administration, 38*(13-14), 1020–1029. doi:10.1080/01900692.2014.982292

Carstens, D. S., & Patterson, P. (2005). Usability study of travel websites. *Journal of Usability Studies, 1*(1), 47–61.

Casino, F., Azpilicueta, L., Lopez-Iturri, P., Aguirre, E., Falcone, F., & Solanas, A. (2017). Optimized Wireless Channel Characterization in Large Complex Environments by Hybrid Ray Launching-Collaborative Filtering Approach. *IEEE Antennas and Wireless Propagation Letters, 16*, 780–783. doi:10.1109/LAWP.2016.2604021

Castagna, F., Centobelli, P., Cerchione, R., Esposito, E., Oropallo, E., & Passaro, R. (2020). Customer Knowledge Management in SMEs Facing Digital Transformation. *Sustainability, 12*(9), 3899. doi:10.3390u12093899

Cavusoglu, H. (2003). *The economics of information technology investments.* Doctoral Degree University of Texas at Dallas.

CBInsights. (2018). *Global Fintech report Q1 2018.* https://www.cbinsights.com/research/report/fintech-trends-q1-2018/

CEPAL. (2004). Novena conferencia regional sobre la mujer de América Latina y El Caribe. *Consenso de México.*

Chamikara, M. A. P., Bertók, P., Liu, D., Camtepe, S., & Khalil, I. (2020). Efficient privacy preservation of big data for accurate data mining. *Information Sciences, 527*, 420–443. doi:10.1016/j.ins.2019.05.053

Chandler, A. D. (1990). *Strategy and structure: Chapters in the history of the industrial enterprise* (Vol. 120). MIT Press.

Chand, M. T., & Rosalie, L. (2011). Global competitiveness, consumer choice and 'country of origin' effect: An exploratory East-West study. *Asia Pacific Journal of Management, 17*(3), 15.

Chand, M., & Ghorbani, M. (2011). National culture, networks and ethnic entrepreneurship: A comparison of the Indian and Chinese immigrants in the US. *International Business Review, 20*(6), 13. doi:10.1016/j.ibusrev.2011.02.009

Chand, M., & Tung, R. L. (2014). Bicultural identity and economic engagement: An exploratory study of the Indian diaspora in North America. *Asia Pacific Journal of Management, 31*(3), 763–788. doi:10.100710490-014-9375-y

Chanias, S., Myers, D. M., & Hess, T. (2019). Digital transformation strategy making in pre-digital organizations: The case of a financial services provider. *The Journal of Strategic Information Systems, 28*(1), 17–33. doi:10.1016/j.jsis.2018.11.003

Chao, X., Kou, G., Peng, Y., & Alsaadi, F. E. (2019). Behavior monitoring methods for trade-based money laundering integrating macro and micro prudential regulation: A case from China. *Technological and Economic Development of Economy, 25*(6), 1–16. doi:10.3846/tede.2019.9383

Chau, T., & Maurer, F. (2004). Tool Support for Inter-team Learning in Agile Software Organizations. In G. Melnik & H. Holz (Eds.), *Advances in Learning Software Organizations* (pp. 98–109). Springer Berlin Heidelberg., doi:10.1007/978-3-540-25983-1_10

Chen, F. M., Feng, M. C., Chen, T. C., Hsieh, M. H., Kuo, S. H., Chang, H. L., Yang, C. J., & Chen, Y. H. (2020). Big data integration and analytics to prevent a potential hospital outbreak of COVID-19 in Taiwan. *Journal of Microbiology, Immunology, and Infection.* Advance online publication. doi:10.1016/j.jmii.2020.04.010 PMID:32327328

Cheng, M. (2016). Sharing economy: A review and agenda for future research. *International Journal of Hospitality Management, 57*, 60–70. doi:10.1016/j.ijhm.2016.06.003

Chen, L. (2016). From fintech to finlife: The case of fintech development in China. *China Economic Journal, 9*, 225–239. doi:10.1080/17538963.2016.1215057

Chen, T., Drennan, J., & Andrews, L. (2012). Experience sharing. *Journal of Marketing Management, 28*(13-14), 1535–1552. doi:10.1080/0267257X.2012.736876

Cheung, J. (2015). *Exploring Consumers' Experiential Responses and Shopping Intentions toward Visual User-Generated Content in Online Shopping Environments* (PhD Thesis). The University of Manchester, Manchester UK.

Chiauzzi, E., Rodarte, C., & DasMahapatra, P. (2015). Patient-centered activity monitoring in the self-management of chronic health conditions. *BMC Medicine, 13*(1), 77. doi:10.118612916-015-0319-2 PMID:25889598

Chiou, J. (2000). Antecedents and Moderators of Behavioral Intention:Differences between US and Taiwanese Students. *Genetic, Social, and General Psychology Monographs, 126*(1), 105–124. PMID:10713903

Chircu, A. M., & Kauffman, R. J. (2002). Limits to value in electronic commerce- related I. T investments. *Journal of Management Information Systems, 19.*

Chiu, I. H.-Y. (2016). FinTech and disruptive business models in financial products, intermediation and markets- Policy implications for financial regulators. *Journal ofTechnology Law & Policy, 21*, 55–112. doi:10.3868050-004-015- 0003-8

Chopra, S., & Meindl, P. (2010). *Supply Chain Management: Strategy, Planning and Operation* (E. Svendsen, Ed.; 4th ed.). Pearson Education Limited.

Choudhari, R. D., Banwet, D. K., & Gupta, M. P. (2007). Identifying Risk Factors in for E-governance Projects. In A. Agarwal & V. V. Ramana (Eds.), *Foundations of E-government* (pp. 270–277). Computer Society of India.

Christensen, C. M. (2003). The innovator's dilemma: The revolutionary book that will changed the way you do business. *The American Political Science Review.*

Christodoulou, P., Christodoulou, K., & Andreou, A. (2018). A Decentralized Application for Logistics: Using Blockchain in Real-World Applications. *The Cyprus Review, 30*(2), 181–18.

Clear, T. (2019). Software Ecosystems: What Do We Need to Know? *ACM Inroads, 10*(2). Advance online publication. doi:10.1145/3395963

Cleveland, M., & Cleveland, S. (2020). Culturally Agile Leadership: A Relational Leadership Development Approach. *International Journal of Public and Private Perspectives on Healthcare, Culture, and the Environment, 4*(1), 1–9. doi:10.4018/IJPPPHCE.2020010101

Collins, J. (2002). The Chinese diaspora in Australia. *International Journal of Entrepreneurial Behaviour & Research*, 8.

Collins, P. H. (2019). Intersectionality as critical social theory. *Duke University Press Books.*

Collomb, A., & Sok, K. (2016). Blockchain / Distributed Ledger Technology (DLT): What Impact on the Financial Sector? *Communications & Stratégies*, (103), 93–111, 212, 214.

Compeau, D. R., & Higgins, C. A. (1995). Computer Self-Efficacy: Development of a Measure and Initial Test. *Management Information Systems Quarterly, 19*(2), 189–211. doi:10.2307/249688

Cong, L. W., & He, Z. (2019). Blockchain Disruption and Smart Contracts. *Review of Financial Studies, 32*(5), 1754–1797. doi:10.1093/rfs/hhz007

Constantinides, E. (2004) Influencing the online consumer's behavior: the Web experience. *Internet Research, 14*(2), 111-126.

Correani, A., De Massis, A., Frattini, F., Petruzzelli, A. M., & Natalicchio, A. (2020). Implementing a digital strategy: Learning from the experience of three digital transformation projects. *California Management Review, 62*(4), 37–56. doi:10.1177/0008125620934864

Cowart, K. O., & Goldsmith, R. E. (2007). The influence of consumer decision-making styles on online apparel consumption by college students. *International Journal of Consumer Studies, 31*(6), 639–647. doi:10.1111/j.1470-6431.2007.00615.x

Cozby, P. C. (1997). *Methods in behavioral research*. Mayfield Publishing Company.

Crespo, N. F., & Crespo, C. F. (2016). Global innovation index: Moving beyond the absolute value of ranking with a fuzzy-set analysis. *Journal of Business Research, 69*(11), 5265–5271. doi:10.1016/j.jbusres.2016.04.123

Cronista. (2019, May 3). *La crisis no pudo con MercadoLibre: vendió más en Argentina y ganó u$s 94 millones*. Retrieved November 11, 2019, from https://www.cronista.com/apertura-negocio/empresas/La-crisis-no-pudo-con-MercadoLibre-vendio-mas-en-Argentina-y-gano-us-94-millones-20190503-0004.html

Cusumano, M. A. (2015). How traditional firms must compete in the sharing economy. *Communications of the ACM, 58*(1), 32–34. doi:10.1145/2688487

Cusumano, M., Gawer, A., & Yoffie, D. (2019). *The Business of Platforms. Strategy in the Age of Digital Competition, Innovation, and Power*. HarperCollins publishers.

Dannenberg, M., & Kellner, D. (1998). The bank of tomorrow with today's technology. *International Journal of Bank Marketing, 16*(2), 90–97. doi:10.1108/02652329810206743

Dapp, T. (2014). Fintech–The digital (r) evolution in the financial sector. *Deutsche Bank Res., 39*. https://goo.gl/UcZJFz

Davcik, N. S., & Grigoriou, N. (2016). How dynamic marketing capabilities affect market share performance output: An innovative brand oriented approach. In Groza M., Ragland, C. (Eds.), *Marketing challenges in a turbulent business environment. Developments in marketing science: Proceedings of the academy of marketing science*. Springer. 10.1007/978-3-319-19428-8_37

Davenport, T. H., & Dyché, J. (2013). *Big data in big companies*. International Institute for Analytics.

Davey, T., Plewa, C., & Struwig, M. (2011). Entrepreneurship perceptions and career intentions of international students. *Education + Training, 53*(5), 335–352. doi:10.1108/00400911111147677

Davidson, E., & Vaast, E. (2010). Digital entrepreneurship and its sociomaterial enactment. In *2010 43rd Hawaii International Conference on System Sciences* (pp. 1-10). IEEE. 10.1109/HICSS.2010.150

Davidson, R. J., Jackson, D. C., & Kalin, N. H. (2000). Emotion, plasticity, context, and regulation: Perspectives from affective neuroscience. *Psychological Bulletin, Vol, 126*(6), 890–909. doi:10.1037/0033-2909.126.6.890 PMID:11107881

Davies, S., Jackett, D., Kashyap, M., Nicolacakis, D., Qureshi, M., & Shipman, J. (2016). *Customers in the spotlight: How FinTech is reshaping banking - Global FinTech Survey 2016*. PricewaterhouseCoopers. https://www.pwc.com/il/he/bankim/ assets/fin-tech-banking.pdf

Davis, F. (1989). Perceived Usefulness, Perceived Ease of Use, and User Acceptance of Information Technology. *Management Information Systems Quarterly, 13*(3), 319–339. doi:10.2307/249008

Davis, F. D., Bagozzi, R. P., & Warshaw, P. R. (1989). User Acceptance of Computer Technology: A Comparison of Two Theoretical Models. *Management Science, 35*(8), 982–1003. doi:10.1287/mnsc.35.8.982

Day, S. W., & Jean-Denis, H. (2016). Resource Based View of social entrepreneurship: Putting the pieces together. *Journal of Strategic Innovation and Sustainability*, *11*(2).

De Clercq, D., & Belausteguigoitia, I. (2019). Coping and laughing in the face of broken promises: Implications for creative behavior. *Personnel Review*, *49*(4), 993–1014. doi:10.1108/PR-11-2018-0441

de Haan, E. (2019). *Critical Moments in Executive Coaching: Understanding the Coaching Process Through Research and Evidence-based Theory*. Routledge. doi:10.4324/9781351180764

de Reuver, M., Sorensen, C., & Basole, R. (2018). The digital platform: A research agenda. *Journal of Information Technology*, *33*(2), 24–35. doi:10.105741265-016-0033-3

Defossez, D. A. L. (2017). The regulation of a project of the deregulation: UBER in Brazil and the European Union. *Journal of Law and Regulation*, *3*(1), 1–28.

Degadt, J., Lambrecht, J., & Broekaert, W. (2019). Business Modelling of Digital Entrepreneurship and Digital Collaboration Solutions to Increase Global Growth in Businesses Owned by Happy Women Entrepreneurs. In *Conference Proceedings Chapters* (pp. 241-264). Bulgarian Association for Management Development and Entrepreneurship.

Degen, H., Lubin, K. L., Pedell, S., & Ji, Z. (2005). Travel planning on the web: a cross-cultural case study. In N. Aykin (Ed.), *Usability and internationalization of information technology* (pp. 313–343). Lawrence Erlbaum Associates, Publishers.

De-Laguno-Alarcón, C., Sierra-Herrezuelo, P., & Rojas-de-Gracia, M. M. (2019). Results-oriented influencer marketing manual for the tourism industry. In K. Mezghani & W. Aloulou (Eds.), *Business transformation in the era of digitalization* (pp. 249–275). IGI Global. doi:10.4018/978-1-5225-7262-6.ch014

Deloitte. (2016). *RegTech is the new FinTech: How regulatory technology is helping firms better understand and manage their risks*. Deloitte. https://www2.deloitte.com/content/dam/Deloitte/ie/Documents/ FinancialServices/IE_2016_FS_RegTech_is_the_new_FinTech. pdf

Demir, Y. (2020). Paylaşım ekonomisi kapsamında yemek paylaşma sitelerinin analizi. *Güncel Turizm Araştırmaları Dergisi*, *4*(1), 54–69. doi:10.32572/guntad.678419

Dengler, K., & Matthes, B. (2018). The impacts of digital transformation on the labour market: Substitution potentials of occupations in Germany. *Technological Forecasting and Social Change*, *137*, 304–316. doi:10.1016/j.techfore.2018.09.024

Denning, S. (2019). Lessons learned from mapping successful and unsuccessful Agile transformation journeys. *Strategy and Leadership*, *47*(4), 3–11. doi:10.1108/SL-04-2019-0052

Derby, E., & Larsen, D. (2006). *Agile retrospectives: Making good teams great*. Pragmatic Bookshelf.

Deshmukh, A. (2006). *Digital accounting: The effects of the internet and ERP on accounting*. IGI Global. doi:10.4018/978-1-59140-738-6

Deuringer, C. (2000). *Organisation und Change-Management: Ein ganzheitlicher Strukturansatz zur Förderung organistorischer Flexibilität*. Dt. Univ.-Verl. doi:10.1007/978-3-322-81381-7

DeYoung, R. (2005). The performance of internet-based business models: Evidence from the banking industry. *The Journal of Business*, *78*, 893–948. doi:10.1086/ 429648

Dhar, V., & Stein, R. M. (2017). FinTech platforms and strategy - integrating trust and automation in finance. *Communications of the ACM*, *60*(10), 32–35. doi:10.1145/3132726

Digital Marketing Institute. (2020). *6 digital skills that will future-proof a workforce*. Retrieved from https://digitalmarketinginstitute.com/blog/6-digital-skills-that-will-future-proof-a-workforce

Digital Skills Global. (2020). *The top 10 digital skills tech companies are looking for today.* Retrieved from https://digitalskillsglobal.com/blog/the-top-10-digital-skills-tech-companies-are-looking-for-today

Dimitratos, P., Voudouris, I., Plakoyiannaki, E., & Nakos, G. (2012). International entrepreneurial culture—Toward a comprehensive opportunity-based operationalization of international entrepreneurship. *International Business Review, 21*(4), 708–721. doi:10.1016/j.ibusrev.2011.08.001

Dinh, T. N., & Thai, M. T. (2018). AI and Blockchain: A Disruptive Integration. *Computer, 51*(9), 48–53. doi:10.1109/MC.2018.3620971

Dixon, P. (2017). A Failure to "Do No Harm"—India's Aadhaar biometric ID program and its inability to protect privacy in relation to measures in Europe and the US. *Health and Technology, 7*(4), 539–567. doi:10.100712553-017-0202-6 PMID:29308348

Doğan, N. Ö., & Derici, S. (2019). Project Management and Efficiency of the Projects in the Industry 4.0 Era. In Agile Approaches for Successfully Managing and Executing Projects in the Fourth Industrial Revolution (pp. 188-209). IGI Global.

Doll, W. J., Raghunathan, T. S., Lim, J., & Gupta, Y. P. (1995). A confirmatory factor analysis of the user information satisfaction instrument. *Information Systems Research, 6*(2), 177–189. doi:10.1287/isre.6.2.177

Doll, W. J., Xia, W., & Torkzadeh, G. (1994). A confirmatory factor analysis of the end-user computing satisfaction instrument. *Management Information Systems Quarterly, 18*(4), 453–461. doi:10.2307/249524

Dominguez, G., Hammill, S. J., & Brillat, A. I. (2015). Toward a usable academic library web site: A case study of tried and tested usability practices. *Journal of Web Librarianship, 9*(2-3), 99–120. doi:10.1080/19322909.2015.1076710

Donner, J., & Tellez, C. A. (2008). Mobile banking and economic development: Linking adoption. *Asian Journal of Communication, 18*(4), 318–322. doi:10.1080/01292980802344190

Dorri, A. (2017). Blockchain for IoT security and privacy: The case study of a smart home. *2017 IEEE International Conference on Pervasive Computing and Communications Workshops (PerCom Workshops),* 618–623.

Dremel, C., Wulf, J., Herterich, M. M., Waizmann, J. C., & Brenner, W. (2017). How AUDI AG Established Big data Analytics in Its Digital Transformation. *MIS Quarterly Executive, 16*(2), 81–100.

Drori, I., Honig, B., & Wright, M. (2009). Transnational Entrepreneurship: An Emergent Field of Study. *Entrepreneurship Theory and Practice, 33*(5), 1001–1022. doi:10.1111/j.1540-6520.2009.00332.x

Drucker, F. P. (1985). Innovation and Entrepreneurship. *Routledge Classic 2015.*

Duan, C., Kotey, B., & Sandhu, K. (2020b). Transnational immigrant entrepreneurship: effects of home-country entrepreneurial ecosystem factors. International Journal of Entrepreneurial Behavior & Research, (ahead-of-print). doi:10.1108/IJEBR-05-2020-0300

Duan, C., Kotey, B., & Sandhu, K. (2020a). *Digital Entrepreneurship for Immigrants: Motivation, Strategies, Ecosystems, and Performance*. IGI Global. doi:10.4018/978-1-7998-2799-3.ch009

Duan, C., Kotey, B., & Sandhu, K. (2021). *Understanding immigrant entrepreneurship: home-country entrepreneurial ecosystem perspective.* New England Journal of Entrepreneurship., doi:10.1108/NEJE-05-2020-0013

Duarte, M. P., & Carvalho, F. M. (2020). *Portugal in the Global Innovation Index: A panel data analysis* (No. 0144). Gabinete de Estratégia e Estudos, Ministério da Economia.

Dutia, T. (1995). The restructuring of the system of accounting in Romania during the period of transition to the market economy. *European Accounting Review*, *4*(4), 739–748. doi:10.1080/09638189500000047

Dutilh, N. (2018). *Taxation and the Digital Economy: European and International Initiatives to Create a Fair Tax System*. Retrieved From https://www.lexology.com/library/detail.aspx?g=5b609b46-77bb-4061-b091-11333b1f5f9e

Dutta, R., Das, A., & Aryal, J. (2016). Big data integration shows Australian bush-fire frequency is increasing significantly. *Royal Society Open Science*, *3*(2), 150241. doi:10.1098/rsos.150241 PMID:26998312

Du, W. Y., Pan, S. L., Zhou, N., & Ouyang, T. H. (2018). From a marketplace of electronics to a digital entrepreneurial ecosystem (DEE): The emergence of a meta-organisation in Zhongguancun, China. *Information Systems Journal*, *28*(6), 1158–1175. doi:10.1111/isj.12176

Dwyer, L., Forsyth, P., & Rao, P. (2002). Destination price competitiveness: Exchange rate changes versus domestic inflation. *Journal of Travel Research*, *40*(3), 328–336. doi:10.1177/0047287502040003010

E-Banking. (2020). In *Banka Ekonomike*. Retrieved from https://www.bekonomike.com/en/%C3%87ka-eshte-E-Banking-Inidividet

E-Banking. (2020). In *Encyclopedia*. Retrieved from https://www.encyclopedia.com/finance/encyclopedias-almanacs-transcripts-and-maps/electronic-banking

Ecer, F. (2018). An Integrated Fuzzy AHP and ARAS Model to Evaluate Mobile Banking Services. *Technological and Economic Development of Economy*, *24*(2), 670–695. doi:10.3846/20294913.2016.1255275

Edelman, B. G., & Geradin, D. (2015). Efficiencies and regulatory shortcuts: How should we regulate companies like Airbnb and Uber. *Stan. Tech. L. Rev.*, *19*, 293. doi:10.2139srn.2658603

Edo, A. (2019). The Impact Of Immigration On The Labor Market. *Journal of Economic Surveys*, *33*(3), 922–948. doi:10.1111/joes.12300

Eisenhardt, K., & Graebner, M. (2007). Theory building from cases: Opportunities and callenges. *Academy of Management Journal*, *50*(1), 25–32. doi:10.5465/amj.2007.24160888

Eisenmann, T., Parker, G., & Van Alstyne, M. (2007). Platform envelopment. *Strategic Management Journal*, *32*(12), 1270–1285. doi:10.1002mj.935

Ekinci, E., & Pala, O. (2020). Reflections of the Developments In The Digital Economy on Taxation: Evaluating Tax Audits Within Digital Companies Resident Abroad. *Tax World Journal*, *39*(462), 113–130.

Elgahwash, F. O. (2013). *The Role of Information and Communication Technologies in Enhancing Customer Relationships in the Libyan Banking Sector*. UOW.

Elgahwash, F. O. (2016). Factors have affected Mobile Services adoption in Libyan banking system: A qualitative evidence. *Journal of Al-Haqiqah in University of Adrar*, (38), 1–30.

Elgahwash, F. O., & Freeman, M. B. (2013). Self-Service Technology Banking Preferences: Comparing Libyans' Behaviour in Developing and Developed Countries. *International Journal of Intelligent Information Technologies*, *9*(2), 7–20. doi:10.4018/jiit.2013040102

Epstein, S. (1994). Integration of the cognitive and the psychodynamic unconscious. *The American Psychologist*, *49*(8), 709–724. doi:10.1037/0003-066X.49.8.709 PMID:8092614

Etienne-Nugue, J. (2009). *Hablame de las artesanias*. UNESCO.

European Commission, (2016). *Digital Entrepreneurship Scoreboard 2015*. Directorate-General for intermarket, Industry, Entrepreneurship and SMEs.

European Commission. (2018). *Digital Taxation: Commission Proposes New Measures to Ensure That All Companies Pay Fair Tax In the EU*. European Commission Press Release. Retrieved From https://ec.europa.eu/commission/presscorner/detail/en/IP_18_2041

Evangelidis, A. (2004). FRAMES-A Risk Assessment Framework for e-Services. *Electronic. Journal of E-Government, 2*(1), 21–30.

Faghih, N., & Sazegar, M. (2019). A Taxonomy of Country Performance Based on GDP and Innovation Indicators for the Group of Twenty (G20). In *Globalization and Development* (pp. 163–200). Springer. doi:10.1007/978-3-030-14370-1_7

Fairooz & Wickramasinghe. (2019). Innovation and Development of Digital Finance: A Review on Digital Transformation in Banking & Financial Sector of Sri Lanka. *Asian Journal of Economics, Finance and Management, 1*(2), 69-78.

Falco, E., & Kleinhans, R. (2018). Beyond Information-Sharing. A Typology of Government Challenges And Requirements For Two-Way Social Media Communication With Citizens. *The Electronic. Journal of E-Government, 16*(1), 18–31.

Fang, B., Ye, Q., & Law, R. (2015). Effect of sharing economy on tourism industry employment. *Population, 1.*

Feagin, J. R., Orum, A. M., & Sjoberg, G. (1991). *A case for the case study*. UNC Press Books.

Feher, P., Szabo, Z., & Varga, K. (2017). *Analysing Digital Transformation among Hungarian Organizations. In 30th Bled E-Conference: Digital Transformation – From Connecting Things To Transforming Our Lives. Academic Press.*

Fehrer, J., Woratscheck, H., & Brodie, R. (2018). A systemic logic for platform business models. *Journal of Service Management, 29*(4), 546–568. doi:10.1108/JOSM-02-2017-0036

Felipe, L., Beukes, E. W., Fox, B. A., & Manchaiah, V. (2020). Quality and readability of English-language internet information for vestibular disorders. *Journal of Vestibular Research*, (Preprint), 1-10.

Felix, P. (2014). Prospects and challenges of electronic banking in Ghana: The case of Zenith Bank, Sunyani. *International Journal of Advances in Management. Economics and Entrepreneurship, 1*(1), 6–14.

Fernández-Cavia, J., Díaz-Luque, P., Huertas, A., Rovira, C., Pedraza-Jimenez, R., Sicilia, M., ... Máguez-González, M. I. (2013). Marcas de destino y evaluación de sitios web: Una metodología de investigación. *Revista Latina de Comunicación Social*, (68), 622–638. doi:10.4185/RLCS-2013-993

Fernández-Cavia, J., Rovira, C., Díaz-Luque, P., & Cavaller, V. (2014). Web Quality Index (WQI) for official tourist destination websites. Proposal for an assessment system. *Tourism Management Perspectives, 9*, 5–13. doi:10.1016/j.tmp.2013.10.003

Fesenmaier, D. R., & Jeng, J. M. (2000). Assessing structure in the pleasure trip planning process. *Tourism Analysis, 5*(1), 13–27.

Fettry, S., Anindita, T., Wikansari, R., & Sunaryo, K. (2019, July). The future of accountancy profession in the digital era. In *Global Competitiveness: Business Transformation in the Digital Era: Proceedings of the First Economics and Business Competitiveness International Conference (EBCICON 2018), September 21-22, 2018, Bali, Indonesia* (p. 8). Routledge. 10.1201/9780429202629-2

Figueroa-Armijos, M., & da Motta Veiga, S. (2019). Predictors of Early-Career Self-Employment among Millennials in the Digital Economy: The Role of The Great Recession. *Proceedings of the 52nd Hawaii International Conference on System Sciences*. 10.24251/HICSS.2019.546

Finn, K., & Johnson, J. (2013). A usability study of websites for older travelers. In Lecture Notes in Computer Science (including subseries Lecture Notes in Artificial Intelligence and Lecture Notes in Bioinformatics) (vol. 8010 LNCS, pp. 59–67). doi:10.1007/978-3-642-39191-0_7

Fiol, C. M., & Lyles, M. A. (1985). Organizational Learning. *The Academy of Management Review, 10*(4), 803–813. doi:10.2307/258048

Fischer, M., Imgrund, F., Janiesch, C., & Winkelmann, A. (2020). Strategy archetypes for digital transformation: Defining meta objectives using business process management. *Information & Management, 57*(5), 103262. doi:10.1016/j.im.2019.103262

Fitzmaurice, C. J., Ladegaard, I., Attwood-Charles, W., Cansoy, M., Carfagna, L. B., Schor, J. B., & Wengronowitz, R. (2020). Domesticating the market: Moral exchange and the sharing economy. *Socio-economic Review, 18*(1), 81–102. doi:10.1093er/mwy003

Florina, V., Liliana, M., & Viorica, I. (2008). *Risk management of e-banking activities.* Retrieved December 1, 2019, from http://steconomice.uoradea.ro/anale/volume/2008/v3-financesbanksaccountancy/160.pdf

FONART. (2009). *Manual de Diferenciación entre Artesania y Manualidad.* Recovered from https://www.fonart.gob.mx/web/pdf/DO/mdma.pdf

Foote, W. (September 29, 2015). Tapping the potential of the artisan economy. *Forbes.* Recovered from https://www.forbes.com/sites/willyfoote/2015/09/29/tapping-the-potential-of-the-worlds-fourth-largest-economy/#3ea27e3f1aa2

Forbes. (2017). *The Amazing Ways Coca Cola Uses Artificial Intelligence and Big Data To Drive Success.* Retrieved May, 2020, from https://www.forbes.com/sites/bernardmarr/2017/09/18/the-amazing-ways-coca-cola-uses-artificial-intelligence-ai-and-big-data-to-drive-success/#61b4504a78d2

Forbes. (2018). *How Much Data Do We Create Every Day? The Mind-Blowing Stats Everyone Should Read.* Retrieved May 2020, from https://www.forbes.com/sites/bernardmarr/2018/05/21/how-much-data-do-we-create-every-day-the-mind-blowing-stats-everyone-should-read/#514a5ebb60ba

Ford, D. H. (2019). *Humans as self-constructing living systems: A developmental perspective on behavior and personality.* Routledge.

Forgas, J. P. (Ed.). (2001). *Feeling and thinking: The role of affect in social cognition.* Cambridge University Press.

Forno, F., & Garibaldi, R. (2015). Sharing economy in travel and tourism: The case of home-swapping in Italy. *Journal of Quality Assurance in Hospitality & Tourism, 16*(2), 202–220. doi:10.1080/1528008X.2015.1013409

Fortnum, D., Pollari, I., Mead, W., Hughes, B., & Speier, A. (2017). *The pulse of fintech Q1 2017: Global analysis of investment in fintech.* KPMG technical report. Available at: https://assets.kpmg.com/content/dam/kpmg/xx/pdf/2017/04/pulse-of-fintech-q1.pdf

Francisco, K. & Swanson, D. (2018). The Supply Chain Has No Clothes: Technology Adoption of Blockchain for Supply Chain Transparency. *Logistics, 2*(1).

Frederico, G. F. F. (2019). Supply Chain 4.0: Concepts, maturity and research agenda. Supply Chain Management, pp. *Supply Chain Management.*

Frennert, S. (2018). Lost in digitalization? Municipality employment of welfare technologies. *Disability and Rehabilitation. Assistive Technology.* PMID:30264649

Furst, K., Lang, W. W., & Nolle, D. (2000). *Internet banking: Developments and prospects.* Economic and Policy Analysis Working Paper, 1-58. Retrieved June 11, 2016, from http://199.83.40.54/publications/publications-by-type/economics-working-papers/2008-2000/wp2000-9.pdf

Gaardboe, R., Svarre, T., & Kanstrup, A. M. (2015). Characteristics of business intelligence and big data in e-government: Preliminary findings. *Innovation and the Public Sector*, 109.

Gabor, D., & Brooks, S. (2017). The digital revolution in financial inclusion: International development in the fintech era. *New Political Economy*, *22*, 423–436. doi:10.1080/13563467.2017.1259298

Gábossy, Á. (2016). New directions in crowdfunding. *Public Finance Quarterly*, *61*(4), 533–544.

Gachanja, I. M., Nga'nga', S. I., & Kiganane, L. M. (2020). Influence of organization learning on innovation output in manufacturing firms in Kenya. *International Journal of Innovation Studies*, *4*(1), 16–26. doi:10.1016/j.ijis.2020.02.001

Gaikwad, P. K., Jayakumar, C. T., Tilve, E., Bohra, N., Yu, W., & Spichkova, M. (2019). Voice-activated solutions for agile retrospective sessions. *Procedia Computer Science*, *159*, 2414–2423. doi:10.1016/j.procs.2019.09.416

Gallarza, M. G., Saura, I. G., & García, H. C. (2002). Destination image: Towards a conceptual framework. *Annals of Tourism Research*, *29*(1), 56–78. doi:10.1016/S0160-7383(01)00031-7

Gansky, L. (2010). *The mesh: Why the future of business is sharing?* Portfolio Trade.

Gao, J., Huang, C., Su, J., & Xie, Q. (2019). Examining the Factors Behind the Success and Sustainability of China's Creative Research Group: An Extension of the Teamwork Quality Model. *Sustainability*, *11*(4), 1195. doi:10.3390u11041195

Garay-Rondero, C. L., Martinez-Flores, J. L., Smith, N. R., Morales, S. O. C., & Aldrette-Malacara, A. (2019). Digital supply chain model in Industry 4.0. *Journal of Manufacturing Technology Management*, *31*(5), 887–933. doi:10.1108/JMTM-08-2018-0280

Garcia, R., & Calantone, R. (2002). A critical look at technological innovation typology and innovativeness terminology: A literature review. *Journal of Product Innovation Management*, *19*(2), 110–132.

Garrido-Baserba, M., Corominas, L., Cortés, U., Rosso, D., & Poch, M. (2020). The fourth-revolution in the water sector encounters the digital revolution. *Environmental Science & Technology*, *54*(8), 4698–4705. doi:10.1021/acs.est.9b04251 PMID:32154710

Gartner, B. W. (1985). A Conceptual Framework for Describing the Phenomenon of New Venture Creation. *Academy of Management Review, 10*(4), 12.

Garud, R., Kumaraswamy, A., Roberts, A., & Xu, L. (2020). Liminal movement by digital platform-based sharing economy ventures: The case of Uber Technologies. *Strategic Management Journal*, •••, 1–29. doi:10.1002mj.3148

Gassmann, O., Frankenberger, K., & Csik, M. (2014). *The business model navigator: 55 models that will revolutionise your business*. Pearson.

Gawer, A. (2014). Bridging differing perspectives on technological platforms: Toward and integrative framework. *Research Policy*, *43*(7), 1239–1249. doi:10.1016/j.respol.2014.03.006

Gawer, A., & Cusumano, M. (2014). Industry Platforms and Ecosystem Innovation. *Journal of Product Innovation Management*, *31*(3), 417–433. doi:10.1111/jpim.12105

Geels, F. W. (2005). The dynamics of transitions in socio-technical systems: A multi-level analysis of the transition pathway from horse-drawn carriages to automobiles (1860–1930). *Technology Analysis and Strategic Management*, *17*(4), 445–476. doi:10.1080/09537320500357319

Geissinger, A., Laurell, C., Sandström, C., Eriksson, K., & Nykvist, R. (2019). Digital entrepreneurship and field conditions for institutional change–Investigating the enabling role of cities. *Technological Forecasting and Social Change, 146*, 877–886. doi:10.1016/j.techfore.2018.06.019

GEM. (2017/2018). *GEM Global Report 2017/18.* Retrieved from https://www.gemconsortium.org/report/gem-2017-2018-global-report

Gemici, K. (2008). Karl Polanyi and the antinomies of embeddedness. *Socio-economic Review, 6*(1), 5–33. doi:10.1093er/mwl034

George, A. L., Bennett, A., Lynn-Jones, S. M., & Miller, S. E. (2005). *Case studies and theory development in the social sciences.* MIT Press.

Gerrard, P., & Cunningham, B. (2003). The diffusion of internet banking among Singapore consumers. *International Journal of Bank Marketing, 21*(1), 16–28. doi:10.1108/02652320310457776

Ghezzi, A., & Cavallo, A. (2018). Agile business model innovation in digital entrepreneurship: Lean Startup approaches. *Journal of Business Research.*

Ghobakhloo, M. (2020). Determinants of information and digital technology implementation for smart manufacturing. *International Journal of Production Research, 58*(8), 2384–2405. doi:10.1080/00207543.2019.1630775

Gil-Garcia, J. R., Dawes, S. S., & Pardo, T. A. (2018). Digital government and public management research: Finding the crossroads. *Public Management Review, 20*(5), 633–646. doi:10.1080/14719037. 2017.1327181

Gil-Garcia, J. R., Pardo, T. A., & Baker, A. (2007). Understanding context through a comprehensive prototyping experience: A tested research strategy for emerging technologies. In *Proceedings of the 40th. Hawaii International Conference on System Sciences.* Waikoloa, HI: IEEE Computer Society

Gimpel, H., Rau, D., & Röglinger, M. (2018). Understanding FinTech start-ups - a taxonomy of consumer-oriented service offerings. *Electronic Markets, 28*(3). Advance online publication. doi:10.100712525-017- 0275-0

Ginsberg, A., Horwitch, M., Mahapatra, S., & Singh, C. (2010, 18-22 July 2010). *Ecosystem strategies for complex technological innovation: The case of smart grid development.* Paper presented at the Picmet 2010 Technology Management for Global Economic Growth.

Giones, F., & Brem, A. (2017). Digital technology entrepreneurship: A definition and research agenda. *Technology Innovation Management Review, 7*(5), 44–51. doi:10.22215/timreview/1076

GitHub, Inc. (2019). *GitHub.* Retrieved November 11, 2019, from https://github.com/TangoSoftware/ApiTiendas

Gjøystdal, S., & Karunaratne, T. (2020). Effect of Inadequate Self-Organized Teams in Agile Project Management: A Case Study From the Oil and Gas Industry. *International Journal of Information Technology Project Management, 11*(3), 95–106. doi:10.4018/IJITPM.2020070106

Glimcher, P. (2003). *Decisions, Uncertainty and the Brain: The Science ofNeuroeconomics.* The MIT Press. doi:10.7551/mitpress/2302.001.0001

Glimcher, P. W., & Rustichini, A. (2004). Neuroeconomics: The Consilience of Brain and Decision. *Science, 306*(5695), 447–452. doi:10.1126cience.1102566 PMID:15486291

Glyptis, L., Christofi, M., Vrontis, D., Del Giudice, M., Dimitriou, S., & Michael, P. (2020). E-Government implementation challenges in small countries: The project manager's perspective. *Technological Forecasting and Social Change, 152*, 1–11. doi:10.1016/j.techfore.2019.119880

Gnimpieba, Z. D. R., Nait-Sidi-Moh, A., Durand, D., & Fortin, J. (2015). Using Internet of Things Technologies for a Collaborative Supply Chain: Application to Tracking of Pallets and Containers. *Procedia Computer Science, 56*(C), 550–557. doi:10.1016/j.procs.2015.07.251

Goldstein, P. (2019). *Data Lakes: What They Are and How They Can Benefit Feds*. Retrieved from https://fedtechmagazine.com/article/2019/01/data-lakes-what-they-are-and-how-they-can-benefit-feds-perfcon

Gomber, P., Kauffman, R. J., Parker, C., & Weber, B. W. (2018). On the FinTech revolution: Interpreting the forces of innovation, disruption, and transformation in financial services. *Journal of Management Information Systems, 35*(1), 220–265. doi:10.1080/ 07421222.2018.1440766

Gomber, P., Koch, J.-A., & Siering, M. (2017). Digital finance and FinTech: Current research and future research directions. *Journal of Business Economics, 87*(5), 537–580. doi:10.1007/ s11573-017-0852-x

Gomes, D. F., da Eira Dias, A. S. M., da Costa Abreu, A. J. F. P., & Guitiss Navas, H. V. (2020). Organizational and Methodological Influence of Risk Management in Projects. *International Congress on Engineering - Engineering for Evolution*, 209-221. DOI 10.18502/keg.v5i6.7035

Gomez-Uribe, C. A., & Hunt, N. (2015). The Netflix recommender system: Algorithms, business value, and innovation. *ACM Transactions on Management Information Systems, 6*(4), 1–19. doi:10.1145/2843948

Gong, Y., Yang, J., & Shi, X. (2020). Towards a comprehensive understanding of digital transformation in government: Analysis of flexibility and enterprise architecture. *Government Information Quarterly, 37*, 1–13. doi:10.1016/j.giq.2020.101487

González, M. (2016). 31% del PIB nacional es aportado por mujeres empresarias. *Informa BTL*. Recovered from https://www.informabtl.com/31-del-pib-nacional-es-aportado-por-mujeres-empresarias/

Goodale, J. (2012). *Bank 1.0 and Bank 2.0 success entails learning from each other's best practices*. Whitepaper TSYS. https:// digitalpayments.files.wordpress.com/2013/03/bank-1-0-and-bank2-0.pdf

Gottdiener, M. (2019). *The new urban sociology* (6th ed.). Routledge. doi:10.4324/9780429244452

Grant, R. M. (2008). *Contemporary Strategy Analysis*. Wıley.

Greenhaus, J. H., Callanan, G. A., & Godshalk, V. M. (2010). Career management. *Sage (Atlanta, Ga.)*.

Gruschka, N., Mavroeidis, V., Vishi, K., & Jensen, M. (2018, December). Privacy issues and data protection in big data: a case study analysis under GDPR. In *2018 IEEE International Conference on Big data* (pp. 5027-5033). IEEE. 10.1109/BigData.2018.8622621

Guiltinand, J. P., & Donnelly, J. H. (1983). The use of product portfolio analysis in bank marketing planning. In Management Issues for Financial Institutions. Academic Press.

Gulati, R., Puranam, P., & Tushman, M. (2012). Meta-Organization Design: Rethinking Design in Interorganizational and Community Contexts. *Strategic Management Journal, 33*(6), 571–586. doi:10.1002mj.1975

Gullkvist, B. (2011). Drivers of diffusion of digital accounting practice. *Contributions to Accounting, Auditing and Internal Control, 25*.

Gunasekaran, A., Papadopoulos, T., Dubey, R., Wamba, S. F., Childe, S. J., Hazen, B., & Akter, S. (2017). Big data and predictive analytics for supply chain and organizational performance. *Journal of Business Research, 70*, 308–317. doi:10.1016/j.jbusres.2016.08.004

Guo, Y., & Liang, C. (2016). Blockchain application and outlook in the banking industry. *Financial Innovation, 2*(1), 1–12. doi:10.118640854-016-0034-9

Gurau, G. (2011). *Online Self-Services: Investigating the Stages of CustomerSST Systems Interaction.* www.igi-global.com/e-resources/library-recommendation/?id=1

Gurtu, A., & Johny, J. (2019). Potential of blockchain technology in supply chain management: A literature review. *International Journal of Physical Distribution & Logistics Management, 49*(9), 881–900. doi:10.1108/IJPDLM-11-2018-0371

Guszcza, J. (2018). *Smarter together: Why artificial intelligence needs human-centered design* (Vol. 22). Deloitte Review.

Gutnik, L., Forogh, A., Yoskowitz, N., & Patel, V. (2006). The role of emotions in decision making: a cognitive neuroeconomic approach towards understanding sexual risk behavior. *Journal of Biomedical Information.* doi:10.1016/j.jbi.2006.03.002

Guttentag, D. (2015). Airbnb: Disruptive innovation and the rise of an informal tourism accommodation sector. *Current Issues in Tourism, 18*(12), 1192–1217. doi:10.1080/13683500.2013.827159

Gwinner, K. P., Gremler, D. D., & Bitner, M. J. (1998). Relational benefits in services industries: The customer's perspective. *Journal of the Academy of Marketing Science, 26*(2), 101–114. doi:10.1177/0092070398262002

Haapio, H., & Karjaluoto, H. (2019). Antecedents of Market Orientation in The Banking Sector During Its Digital Transformation. In 32nd Bled eConference. Humanizing Technology for a Sustainable Society. University of Maribor.

Hafezieh, N., Akhavan, P., & Eshraghian, F. (2011). Exploration of process and competitive factors of entrepreneurship in digital space: A multiple case study in Iran. *Education, Business and Society, 4*(4), 267–279. doi:10.1108/17537981111190051

Hager, P. (1998). Understanding workplace learning: General perspectives. In Current Issues and New Agendas in Workplace Learning (pp. 31–46). Springfield, VA, NCVER.

Hair, N., Wetsch, L. R., Hull, C. E., Perotti, V., & Hung, Y. T. C. (2012). Market orientation in digital entrepreneurship: Advantages and challenges in a Web 2.0 networked world. *International Journal of Innovation and Technology Management, 9*(06), 1250045. doi:10.1142/S0219877012500459

Hall, S. (2020). *What is digital transformation?* https://enterprisersproject.com/what-is-digital-transformation

Hanafizadeh, P., & Zare-Ravasan, A. (2018). A model for selecting IT outsourcing strategy: The case of e-banking channels. *Journal of Global Information Technology Management, 21*(2), 111–138. doi:10.1080/1097198X.2018.1462070

Hanelt, A., Bohnsack, R., Marz, D., & Antunes, C. (2020). A systematic review of the literature on digital transformation: Insights and implications for strategy and organizational change. *Journal of Management Studies*, joms.12639. doi:10.1111/joms.12639

Hannah, D., & Eisenhardt, K. (2018). How firms navigate cooperation and competition in nascent ecosystems. *Strategic Management, 39*(12), 3163–3192. doi:10.1002mj.2750

Hasibović, A. Ć., & Tanović, A. (2019, May). PRINCE2 vs Scrum in digital business transformation. In *2019 42nd International Convention on Information and Communication Technology, Electronics and Microelectronics (MIPRO)* (pp. 1514-1518). IEEE. 10.23919/MIPRO.2019.8756716

Hausman, A., & Siekpe, J. (2009). The effect of web interface features on consumer online purchase intentions. *Journal of Business Research, 62*(1), 5–13. doi:10.1016/j.jbusres.2008.01.018

Hay, S. I., George, D. B., Moyes, C. L., & Brownstein, J. S. (2013). Big data opportunities for global infectious disease surveillance. *PLoS Medicine, 10*(4), e1001413. doi:10.1371/journal.pmed.1001413 PMID:23565065

Hayvalı, A. (2019). *New Taxes, New Rates.* Retrieved From https://www.habergazetesi.com.tr/yazarlar/19605/yeni-vergiler-yeni-oranlar

Heaphy, L. (2019). Data ratcheting and data-driven organisational change in transport. *Big Data & Society, 6*(2), 1–12. doi:10.1177/2053951719867359

Heeks, R. (2003). Most eGovernment-for-Development Projects Fail: How Can Risks be Reduced? *iGovernment Working Paper Series.* http://idpm.man.ac.uk/publications/wp/igov/index.shtml

Heilig, L., Lalla-Ruiz, E., & Voß, S. (2017). Digital transformation in maritime ports: Analysis and a game theoretic framework. *NETNOMICS: Economic Research and Electronic Networking, 18*(2-3), 227–254.

Heinrichs, H. (2013). Sharing economy: A potential new pathway to sustainability. *GAIA-Ecological Perspectives for Science and Society, 22*(4), 228–231. doi:10.14512/gaia.22.4.5

He, J., Nazari, M., Zhang, Y., & Cai, N. (2020). Opportunity-based entrepreneurship and environmental quality of sustainable development: A resource and institutional perspective. *Journal of Cleaner Production, 256*, 120390. doi:10.1016/j.jclepro.2020.120390

Heller, L. (2010). Mujeres emprendedoras en América Latina y el Caribe: realidades, obstáculos y desafíos. Santiago de Chile: United Nations.

Hemmadi, M. (2015). FinTech is both friend and FOE. *Canadian Business, 88*(6), 10–11.

Henderson, R., & Robertson, M. (2000). Who wants to be an entrepreneur? Young adult attitudes to entrepreneurship as a career. *Career Development International, 5*(6), 279–287.

Hernández-Girón, J., Yexcas, M., & Domínguez-Hernández, M. (2007). Factores de éxito en los negocios de artesanía en México. *Estudios Gerenciales, 23*(104), 77–99. doi:10.1016/S0123-5923(07)70018-9

Heudecker, N. (2015). *Big data Isn't Obsolete. It's Normal.* Retrieved from https://blogs.gartner.com/nick-heudecker/big-data-is-now-normal/

He, X. H. (2019). Digital entrepreneurship solution to rural poverty: Theory, practice and policy implications. *Journal of Developmental Entrepreneurship, 24*(1), 32. doi:10.1142/S1084946719500043

Hidalgo, E. S. (2019). Adapting the scrum framework for agile project management in science: Case study of a distributed research initiative. *Heliyon, 5*(3), e01447. doi:10.1016/j.heliyon.2019.e01447 PMID:30976706

Higgins-Desbiolles, F. (2018). Event tourism and event imposition: A critical case study from Kangaroo Island, South Australia. *Tourism Management, 64*, 73–86. doi:10.1016/j.tourman.2017.08.002

Hirschheim, R., Heinzl, A., & Dibbern, J. (2020). *Information Systems Outsourcing: The Era of Digital Transformation.* Springer Nature. doi:10.1007/978-3-030-45819-5

Hitt, W. D. (1995). The learning organization: Some reflections on organizational renewal. *Leadership and Organization Development Journal, 16*(8), 17–25. doi:10.1108/01437739510097996

HMRC. (2019). *Tax gap remains low.* Retrieved from https://www.gov.uk/government/news/tax-gap-remains-low

Hochschild, A. R. (2012). *The outsourced self: Intimate life in market times.* Metropolitan Books.

Höchtl, J., Parycek, P., & Schöllhammer, R. (2016). Big data in the policy cycle: Policy decision making in the digital era. *Journal of Organizational Computing and Electronic Commerce, 26*(1-2), 147–169. doi:10.1080/10919392.2015.1125187

Hofmann, E. (2017). Big data and supply chain decisions: The impact of volume, variety and velocity properties on the bullwhip effect. *International Journal of Production Research*, *55*(17), 5108–5126. doi:10.1080/00207543.2015.1061222

Hofmann, E., & Rüsch, M. (2017). Industry 4.0 and the current status as well as future prospects on logistics. *Computers in Industry*, *89*, 23–34. doi:10.1016/j.compind.2017.04.002

Hostler, R. E., Yoon, V. Y., Guo, Z., Guimaraes, T., & Forgionne, G. (2011). Assessing the impact of recommender agents on on-line consumer unplanned purchase behavior. *Information & Management*, *48*(8), 336–343. doi:10.1016/j.im.2011.08.002

Howe, J. L., Penrod, J. D., Gottesman, E., Bean, A., & Kramer, B. J. (2019). The rural interdisciplinary team training program: A workforce development workshop to increase geriatrics knowledge and skills for rural providers. *Gerontology & Geriatrics Education*, *40*(1), 3–15. doi:10.1080/02701960.2018.1454917 PMID:29583103

Huang, R., Spector, J. M., & Yang, J. (2019). Learning in the Context of Technologies. In *Educational Technology* (pp. 33–48). Springer. doi:10.1007/978-981-13-6643-7_2

Huber, A. S. (2013). Das Ziel Digital Enterprise: Die professionelle digitale Abbildung von Produktentwicklung und Produktion. In U. Sendler, G. Baum, H. Borcherding, M. Broy, M. Eigner, H. K. Kohler, ... M. Stümpfle (Eds.), *Industrie 4.0: Beherrschung der industriellen Komplexität mit SysLM*. Springer Vieweg. doi:10.1007/978-3-642-36917-9_7

Huda, M., Qodriah, S. L., Rismayadi, B., Hananto, A., Kardiyati, E. N., Ruskam, A., & Nasir, B. M. (2019). Towards Cooperative with Competitive Alliance: Insights into Performance Value in Social Entrepreneurship. In Creating Business Value and Competitive Advantage with Social Entrepreneurship (pp. 294-317). IGI Global.

Hull, C. E., Caisy Hung, Y. T., Hair, N., Perotti, V., & DeMartino, R. (2007). Taking advantage of digital opportunities: A typology of digital entrepreneurship. *International Journal of Networking and Virtual Organisations*, *4*(3), 290–303. doi:10.1504/IJNVO.2007.015166

Hung, Y. H., Hu, P. C., & Lee, W. T. (2013, August). *Improving the design and adoption of travel websites: An user experience study on travel information recommender systems*. Paper presented at 5th IASDR International Conference, Tokio, Japan.

Hurwitz, J. S., Nugent, A., Halper, F., & Kaufman, M. (2013). *Big data for dummies*. John Wiley & Sons.

Hussain, A. (2013). El potencial del comercio electrónico: oportunidades para las PYME de los países en desarrollo. *Revista del centro de comercio internacional*. Recovered from http://www10.iadb.org/intal/intalcdi/PE/2014/14253.pdf

Hutchinson, D., & Warren, M. (2001). *A framework of security authentication for internet banking*. Paper presented at the 3rd International Conference on Information Integration and Web-based Applications & Services, Linz, Austria.

İleri, Y. (2019). *The Danger Posed by Google, Facebook, Twitter, and Instagram for Digital Taxation*. Retrieved From https://odatv.com/dijital-vergide-google-facebook-twitter-ve-instagram-tehlikesi-30101959.html

Indego Africa. (2016). How the artisan sector can change the world. *ONE*. Recovered from https://www.one.org/us/2016/05/13/how-the-artisan-sector-can-change-the-world/

INEGI. (2009). *Censo Económico*. Micro, pequeña, mediana y gran empresa. Recovered from https://www.inegi.org.mx/est/contenidos/espanol/proyectos/censos/ce2009/default.asp?s=est&c=14220

INEGI. (2012). *Conociendo México*. Análisis de la demografía de los establecimientos 2012. Recovered from http://buscador.inegi.org.mx/search?tx=analisis+de+la+demografia+de+los+establecimientos&q=analisis+de+la+demografia+de+los+establecimientos&site=sitioINEGI_collection&client=INEGI_Default&proxystylesheet=INEGI_Default&getfield

Informs. (2016). *UPS On-Road Integrated Optimization and Navigation (ORION) Project*. Retrieved May 2020, from https://www.informs.org/Impact/O.R.-Analytics-Success-Stories/UPS-On-Road-Integrated-Optimization-and-Navigation-ORION-Project

Inglis, D., & Thorpe, C. (2018). *An invitation to social theory* (2nd ed.). Polity.

Interian, J. (2016). Up in the air: Harmonizing the sharing economy through Airbnb regulations. *BC Int'l & Comp. L. Rev., 39*, 129.

Internal Revenue Service. (2019). *The Tax Gap*. Retrieved from https://www.irs.gov/newsroom/the-tax-gap

International Telecommunication Union. (2015). Measuring the Information Society Report. Ginebra: ITU.

Investopedia. (2020). *7 Ways Amazon Uses Big Data to Stalk You*. Retrieved May 2020, from https://www.investopedia.com/articles/insights/090716/7-ways-amazon-uses-big-data-stalk-you-amzn.asp

İpek, İ. (2019). Organizational learning in exporting: A bibliometric analysis and critical review of the empirical research. *International Business Review, 28*(3), 544–559. doi:10.1016/j.ibusrev.2018.11.010

Isenberg, D. (2011). The entrepreneurship ecosystem strategy as new paradigm for economic policy: principles for cultivating entrepreneurship: The Babson entrepreneurship ecosystem project. Babson College.

Islam, N., Mustafi, M. A. A., Rahman, N., Nower, N., Rafi, M. A., Natasha, M. T., Hassan, R., & Afrin, S. (2018). *Factors Affecting Customers' Experience in Mobile Banking of Bangladesh*. 13th Annual International Conference - Convergence, Bengaluru, India. 10.2139srn.3305925

Ivatury, G., & Pickens, M. (2006). *Mobile phone banking and low-income customers -evidence from South Africa: Consultative Group to Assist the Poor, The World Bank and United Nations Foundation. U. N. F.* CGAP.

Iwata, D. (2017). *A new relationship between financing and technology in the FinTech era*. NEC Technical Journal.

Jansen, S., Brinkkemper, S., & Finkelstein, A. (2009). Business Network Management as a Survivial Strategy: A Tale of Two Software Ecosystems. In *Proceedings of the First Workshop on Software Ecosystems* (pp. 34-48). Falls Church: CEUR Workshop Proceedings.

Jansen, S. (2020). A focus area maturity model for software ecosystem governance. *Information and Software Technology, 118*, 106219. doi:10.1016/j.infsof.2019.106219 PMID:32490064

Jansen, S., Finkelstein, S., & Brinkkemper, A. (2009). A sense of community: A research agenda for software ecosystems. In *31st International Conference on Software Engineering, New and Emerging Research Track* (pp. 187-190). Vancouver: IEEE Press. 10.1109/ICSE-COMPANION.2009.5070978

Jeffrey, R., & Chisnell, D. (2008). *Handbook of usability testing: How to plan, design, and conduct effective test*. Jonh Wiley & Sons.

Jesse McWaters, F. (2015). *The Future of Financial Services – How disruptive innovations are reshaping the way financial services are structured, provisioned and consumed*. Academic Press.

Jnr, B. A., Petersen, S. A., Ahlers, D., & Krogstie, J. (2020). Big data driven multi-tier architecture for electric mobility as a service in smart cities. *International Journal of Energy Sector Management*. . doi:10.1108/IJESM-08-2019-0001

Johnsen, A. (2016). Strategic Planning and Management in Local Government in Norway: Status After Three Decades. *Scandinavian Political Studies, 39*(4), 333–365. doi:10.1111/1467-9477.12077

Johnson, C., Mekikian, G., & Barnett, W. (2020). The Rise of Mercado Libre. Case IB-109. Stanford Graduate School of Business.

Jones, P., & Bradbury, L. (2017). *Introducing social theory* (3rd ed.). Polity.

Joseph, R. C., & Johnson, N. A. (2013). Big data and transformational government. *IT Professional, 15*(6), 43–48. doi:10.1109/MITP.2013.61

Journal, T. (2018). Taxation of the Digital Economy: Unilateral Measures. *Insight and Analysis for the Business Tax Community, 1389*, 7–13.

Jun, M., & Cai, S. (2001). The key determinants of Internet banking service quality: A content analysis. *International Journal of Bank Marketing, 19*(7), 276–291. doi:10.1108/02652320110409825

Juul, M. (2015). The sharing economy and tourism. *Tourist accommodation. European Parliament Research Service Briefing*. Retrieved from http://www.europarl.europa.eu/RegData/etudes/BRIE/2015/568345/EPRS BRI(2015)568345 EN.pdf

Kaçar, İ. A., & Yakın, V. (2018). Sharing economy and creating value: Business model canvas. *Third Sector Social Economic Review, 53*(3), 724–739. doi:10.15659/3.sektor-sosyal-ekonomi.18.09.962

Kajuju, N. K. (2016). *The effect of electronic banking on liquidity of commercial banks in Kenya* (Unpublished doctoral thesis). School of Business, University of Nairobi, Kenya.

Kamaludin, I. A. M. M. H., Saad, M. M., & Aziz, N. A. (2012). Sustainability–Driven Entrepreneurship: The Mediating Effect of Opportunity-Based Management Structure on the Relationship between Entrepreneurial Orientation and Environmental Sustainability Management of SMEs: A Conceptual Framework. *European Jounrla of Business and Management, 4*(13), 148–156.

Kane, G. (2017, April 17). Digital Maturity, Not Digital Transformation. *MIT Sloan Management Review*. Retrieved from https://sloanreview.mit.edu/article/digital-maturity-not-digital-transformation/

Kane, G., Palmer, D., Phillips, A., Kiron, D., & Buckley, N. (2015). *Strategy, not technology, drives digital transformation*. MIT Sloan Management Review.

Kaplan, A. M., & Haenlein, M. (2010). Users of the world, unite! The challenges and opportunities of Social Media. *Business Horizons, 53*(1), 59–68. doi:10.1016/j.bushor.2009.09.003

Kapner, S. (2016). Retail slump shows Amazon effect. *The Wall Street Journal*. Retrieved from https://www.wsj.com/articles/kohls-shows-effects-of-retail-slump-as-someponder-the-amazon-factor-1463084218

Karabulut, Ş. (2020). Financial Implications of theDigital Age: Digital Service Tax. *Finance Journal, 178*, 263-288.

Karimi, S. (2013). *A purchase decision-making process model of online consumers and its influential factor a cross sector analysis* (PhD thesis). Manchester Business School.

Kariv, D., Menzies, T. V., Brenner, G. A., & Filion, L. J. (2009). Transnational networking and business performance: Ethnic entrepreneurs in Canada. *Entrepreneurship and Regional Development, 21*(3), 239–264. doi:10.1080/08985620802261641

Kashmari, A., Nejad, A. H. G., & Nayebyazdi, A. (2016). Impact of electronic banking innovations on bank deposit market share. *Journal of Internet Banking and Commerce, 12*(1), 1–12.

Kautonen, T., Kibler, E., & Minniti, M. (2017). Late-career entrepreneurship, income and quality of life. *Journal of Business Venturing, 32*(3), 318–333. doi:10.1016/j.jbusvent.2017.02.005

Kawai, N. (2019). Historical Transition of Psychological Theories of Fear: The View of Fear in Behaviorism. In *The Fear of Snakes* (pp. 1–18). Springer. doi:10.1007/978-981-13-7530-9_1

Kefallinos, D., Lambrou, M. A., & Sykas, E. D. (2009). An Extended Risk Assessment Model for Secure E-Government Projects. *International Journal of Electronic Government Research, 5*(2), 72–92.

Kelestyn, B., & Henfridsson, O. (2014). *Everyday digital entrepreneurship: The inception, shifts, and scaling of future shaping practices*. Academic Press.

Kellermanns, F., Walter, J., Crook, T. R., Kemmerer, B., & Narayanan, V. (2016). The resource-based view in entrepreneurship: A content-analytical comparison of researchers' and entrepreneurs' views. *Journal of Small Business Management, 54*(1), 26–48. doi:10.1111/jsbm.12126

Kendall, K. E., Kong, S., & Kendall, J. E. (2010). The Impact of Agile Methodologies on the Quality of Information Systems: Factors Shaping Strategic Adoption of Agile Practices. *International Journal of Strategic Decision Sciences, 1*(1), 41–56. doi:10.4018/jsds.2010103003

Kepes, B. (2015). *How big data predicts and helps prevent train delays in Sweden*. Retrieved from https://www.networkworld.com/article/2982447/how-big-data-predicts-and-helps-prevent-train-delays-in-sweden.html

Kerr, S. P., & Kerr, W. (2019). *Immigrant entrepreneurship in America: Evidence from the survey of business owners 2007 & 2012*. Retrieved from https://www.nber.org/papers/w22385

Kerr, G., & Armstrong-Stassen, M. (2011). The bridge to retirement: Older workers' engagement in post-career entrepreneurship and wage-and-salary employment. *The Journal of Entrepreneurship, 20*(1), 55–76. doi:10.1177/097135571002000103

Kettunen, J., & Makela, J. P. (2019). Practitioners' conceptions of ethical practice in social networking in career services. *International Journal for Educational and Vocational Guidance, 19*(3), 345–362. doi:10.100710775-018-9383-4

Kettunen, J., & Sampson, J. P. Jr. (2019). Challenges in implementing ICT in career services: Perspectives from career development experts. *International Journal for Educational and Vocational Guidance, 19*(1), 1–18. doi:10.100710775-018-9365-6

Ke, W., & Wei, K. K. (2006). Organizational Learning Process: Its Antecedents and Consequences in Enterprise System Implementation. *Journal of Global Information Management, 14*(1), 1–22. doi:10.4018/jgim.2006010101

Khalid, A., Butt, S. A., Jamal, T., & Gochhait, S. (2020). Agile Scrum Issues at Large-Scale Distributed Projects: Scrum Project Development At Large. *International Journal of Software Innovation, 8*(2), 85–94. doi:10.4018/IJSI.2020040106

Khan, S. (2009). *Adoption issues of internet banking in Pakistani' firms* (Unpublished master thesis). Lulea University of Technology, Lulea.

Khan, S. (2016). *Leadership in the digital age: A study on the effects of digitalisation on top management leadership*. Academic Press.

Khanagha, S., Ansari, S., Paroutis, S., & Oviedo, L. (2020). Mutualism and the dynamics of new platform creation: A study of Cisco and fog computing. *Strategic Management Journal*, (Special issue), 1–31. doi:10.1002mj.3147

Khan, G. F., Swar, B., & Kon Lee, S. (2014). Social Media Risks and Benefits: A Public Sector Perspective. *Social Science Computer Review, 32*(5), 606–627. doi:10.1177/0894439314524701

Khan, H. H., Ahmad, R. B., & Chan, S. G. (2018). Market structure, bank conduct and bank performance: Evidence from ASEAN. *Journal of Policy Modeling, 40*(5), 934–958. doi:10.1016/j.jpolmod.2018.02.001

Khan, M. A., Uddin, M. F., & Gupta, N. (2014, April). Seven V's of Big data understanding Big data to extract value. In *Proceedings of the 2014 zone 1 conference of the American Society for Engineering Education* (pp. 1-5). IEEE. 10.1109/ASEEZone1.2014.6820689

Khatri, A., & Kurnia, K. (2011). *Mobile banking adoption: In Australian rural areas.* The Pacific Asia Conference on Information Systems (PACIS). Brisbane, Australia.

Kim, Jin, & Swinney. (2009). The role of etail quality, e-satisfaction and e-trust in online loyalty development process. *Journal of Retailing and Consumer Services, 16*(4), 239-247.

Kim, G. H., Trimi, S., & Chung, J. H. (2014). Big-data applications in the government sector. *Communications of the ACM, 57*(3), 78–85. doi:10.1145/2500873

Kim, H., Suh, K., & Lee, U. (2013). Effects of collaborative online shopping on shopping experience through social and relational perspectives. *Information & Management, 50*(4), 169–180. doi:10.1016/j.im.2013.02.003

Kim, J., Park, J., Kim, J., & Park, J. (2005). A consumer shopping channel extension model: Attitude shift toward the online store. *Journal of Fashion Marketing and Management, 9*(1), 106–121. doi:10.1108/13612020510586433

Kiracı, H. (2017). Ortak tüketim ekseninde paylaşılan/paylaşılamayan varlıklar ve bireylerin paylaşım davranışlarını etkileyen faktörler üzerine bir araştırma. *Uluslararası İktisadi ve İdari İncelemeler Dergisi*, 51-70.

Kirkpatrick, R. (2009). *1969: The year everything changed.* Skyhorse Publishing Inc.

Kişi, N. (2018). Paylaşım Ekonomisinin Ulaşım Sektörüne Yansımaları: Uber Örneği. *Uluslararası Yönetim ve Sosyal Araştırmalar Dergisi, 5*(10), 57–68.

Kitchin, R. (2016). Getting smarter about smart cities: Improving data privacy and data security. Data Protection Unit, Department of the Taoiseach, Dublin, Ireland.

Kitchin, R. (2014). *The data revolution: Big data, open data, data infrastructures and their consequences.* Sage.

Klievink, B., & Janssen, M. (2009). Realizing joined-up government—Dynamic capabilities and stage models for transformation. *Government Information Quarterly, 26*(2), 275–284. doi:10.1016/j.giq.2008.12.007

Knudsen, D. R. (2020). Elusive boundaries, power relations, and knowledge production: A systematic review of the literature on digitalization in accounting. *International Journal of Accounting Information Systems, 36*, 100441. doi:10.1016/j.accinf.2019.100441

Köhler, E., & Schimanovich, W. (2017, February). Kurt Gödel: A Godfather of Computer Science. In *International Conference on Computer Aided Systems Theory* (pp. 49-65). Springer.

Kohtamäki, M., Parida, V., Oghazi, P., Gebauer, H., & Baines, T. (2019). Digital servitization business models in ecosystems: A theory of the firm. *Journal of Business Research, 104*, 380–392. doi:10.1016/j.jbusres.2019.06.027

Komba, M. M., & Lwoga, E. T. (2020). Systematic Review as a Research Method in Library and Information Science. In *Handbook of Research on Connecting Research Methods for Information Science Research* (pp. 80–94). IGI Global. doi:10.4018/978-1-7998-1471-9.ch005

Konrad, A., & Mac, R. (2014). Airbnb cofounders to become first sharing economy billionaires as company nears $10 billion valuation. *Forbes, 3*, 20. Retrieved from http://www.forbes. com/sites/alexkonrad/2014/03/20/airbnb-cofounders-are-billionaires/

Korachi, Z., & Bounabat, B., (2020). *Towards a Frame of Reference for Smart City Strategy Development and Governance.* Academic Press.

Korobov, S. A., Moseyko, V. O., Novoseltseva, E. G., Epinina, V. S., & Marusinina, E. Y. (2017). Socio-economic Development of Small and Medium Entrepreneurship: Potential of Resource-Based Approach. In *Russia and the European Union* (pp. 453–459). Springer. doi:10.1007/978-3-319-55257-6_58

Korotov, K., Khapova, S., & Arthur, M. (2010). Career entrepreneurship. *Published in Organizational Dynamics*, *40*(2), 127–135. doi:10.1016/j.orgdyn.2011.01.007

Korpela, K., Hallikas, J., & Dahlberg, T. (2017). Digital supply chain transformation toward blockchain integration. *Proceedings of the 50th Hawaii international conference on system sciences.* 10.24251/HICSS.2017.506

Kotey, B. (2006). Entrepreneurship and Regional Development: A Theoretical Frame Work. *Small Enterprise Research*, *14*(2), 25. doi:10.5172er.14.2.20

Kotey, B., & Meredith, G. G. (1997). Relationships among Owner/Manager Personal Values, Business Strategies, and Enterprise Performance. *Journal of Small Business Management*, *1997*(April), 27.

Kotey, B., Sharma, B., & Gao, K. (2013). The Configuration of Entrepreneurial Strategy in Chinese Small Textile Manufacturing Firms. *Journal of New Business Ideas and Trends*, *11*(1).

KPMG. (2019). *Harvey Nash/KPMG CIO Survey – A Changing Perspective*. Retrieved from https://home.kpmg/xx/en/home/insights/2019/06/harvey-nash-kpmg-cio-survey-2019.html

Kruskopf, S., Lobbas, C., Meinander, H., Söderling, K., Martikainen, M., & Lehner, O. M. (2019). Digital accounting: Opportunities, threats and the human factor. *ACRN Oxford Journal of Finance and Risk Perspectives*, *8*, 1–15.

Kshetri, N. (2018). 1 Blockchain's roles in meeting key supply chain management objectives. *International Journal of Information Management*, *39*, 80–89. doi:10.1016/j.ijinfomgt.2017.12.005

Kuak, D., Dolezal, M., Kerous, B., Eichler, Z., Vasek, J., & Liarokapis, F. (2019). An interactive and multimodal virtual mind map for future workplace. *Frontiers in ICT (Lausanne, Switzerland)*, *6*, 12.

Kumar, M., Sareen, M., & Barquissau, E. (2012). Relationship between types of trust and level of adoption of internet banking. *Problems and Perspectives in Management*, *10*(1), 82–92.

Kurt, S., & Unluönen, K. (2017). Paylaşım ekonomisi kapsamında turizm sisteminin değerlendirilmesi. *Gazi Üniversitesi Turizm Fakültesi Dergisi*, *1*, 1–21.

Kushnirovich, N. (2015). Economic Integration of Immigrant Entrepreneurs. *Entrepreneurial Business and Economics Review*, *3*(3), 9–27. doi:10.15678/EBER.2015.030302

Kuťák, D., Doležal, M., Kerouš, B., Eichler, Z., Vašek, J., & Liarokapis, F. (2019). An Interactive and Multimodal Virtual Mind Map for Future Workplace. *Frontiers in ICT (Lausanne, Switzerland)*, *6*, 12. doi:10.3389/fict.2019.00014

Lacasse, R. M., Lambert, B. A., Osmani, E., Couture, C., Roy, N., Sylvain, J., & Nadeau, F. (2016). A digital tsunami: FinTech and Crowdfunding. *International Scientific Conference on Digital Intelligence*, 1–5.

Ladegaard, I. (2018). Hosting the comfortably exotic: Cosmopolitan aspirations in the sharing economy. *The Sociological Review*, *66*(2), 381–400. doi:10.1177/0038026118758538

Laloux, F. (2015). *Reinventing organizations: Ein Leitfaden zur Gestaltung sinnstiftender Formen der Zusammenarbeit* (M. Kauschke, Trans.). Verlag Franz Vahlen. doi:10.15358/9783800649143

Lam, C., & Law, R. (2019). Readiness of upscale and luxury-branded hotels for digital transformation. *International Journal of Hospitality Management*, *79*, 60–69. doi:10.1016/j.ijhm.2018.12.015

Landaeta, R. E., Viscardi, S., & Tolk, A. (2011). Strategic management of scrum projects: An organizational learning perspective. In *First International Technology Management Conference*, (pp. 651–656). San Jose, CA: IEEE. 10.1109/ITMC.2011.5996039

Laney, D. (2001). *Application delivery strategies.* META Group.

Lankshear, C., & Knobel, M. (Eds.). (2008). *Digital literacies: Concepts, policies and practices* (Vol. 30). Peter Lang.

Lan, T., & Zhu, S. J. (2014). Chinese apparel value chains in Europe: Low-end fast fashion, regionalisation, and transnational entrepreneurship in Prato, Italy. *Eurasian Geography and Economics*, *55*(2), 156–174. doi:10.1080/15387216.2014.948471

Larsson, Z. Y., Di Gangi, P. M., & Teigland, R. (2019). Sharing my way to success: A case study on developing entrepreneurial ventures using social capital in an OSS community. *Information and Organization*, *29*(1), 23–40. doi:10.1016/j.infoandorg.2018.12.001

Lashinsky, A. (2015). Uber: An oral history. *Forbes*. Retrieved fromhttps://fortune.com/ 2015/06/03/uber-an-oral-history/

Laudon, K. C., & Laudon, J. P. (2020). *Management information systems: Managing the Digital Firm.* Pearson.

Laudon, K. C., & Traver, C. G. (2001). *E-commerce: Business, technology, society.* Addison-Wesley.

Laukkanen, T., & Pasanen, M. (2008). Mobile banking innovators and early adopters: How they differ from other online users. *Journal of Financial Services Marketing*, *13*(2), 86–94. doi:10.1057/palgrave.fsm.4760077

Laukkanen, T., Sinkkonen, S., & Laukkanen, P. (2009). Communication strategies to overcome functional and psychological resistance to Internet banking. *International Journal of Information Management*, *29*(2), 111–118. doi:10.1016/j.ijinfomgt.2008.05.008

Lee, I., & Shin, Y. J. (2018). Fintech: Ecosystem, business models, investment decisions, and challenges. *Business Horizons*, *61*(1), 35–46. doi:10.1016/j.bushor.2017.09.003

Lee, J.-C., & Chen, C.-Y. (2019). Investigating the environmental antecedents of organizations' intention to adopt agile software development. *Journal of Enterprise Information Management*, *32*(5), 869–886. doi:10.1108/JEIM-06-2018-0119

Leek, S., Turnbull, P. W., & Naude, P. (2003). How is information technology affecting business relationships? Results from a UK survey. *Industrial Marketing Management Journal*, *32*(2), 119–126. doi:10.1016/S0019-8501(02)00226-2

Leelayouthayotin, L. (2004). *Factors influencing online purchase intention: the case of health food consumers in Thailand* (PhD thesis). Universidad Southern Queensland, Australia.

Legislative Proposal on the Digital Service Tax Law and The Amendments to Certain Tax Laws Dated 24. From https://www2.tbmm.gov.tr/d27/2/2-2312.pdf doi:10.2019. Retrieved

Legros, M., Karuranga, E. G., Lebouc, M.-F., & Mohiuddin, M. (2013). Ethnic Entrepreneurship In OECD Countries: A Systematic Review Of Performance Determinants Of Ethnic Ventures. *The International Business & Economics Research Journal (Online)*, *12*(10), 1199. doi:10.19030/iber.v12i10.8131

Lemert, C. (2019). *Social theory: The multicultural, global, and classic readings* (6th ed.). Routledge.

Lemons, C. J., & Toste, J. R. (2019). Professional Development and Coaching: Addressing the "Last Mile" Problem in Educational Research. *Assessment for Effective Intervention*, *44*(4), 300–304. doi:10.1177/1534508419862859

Lethmate, R. (2016). *Auf einen Kaffee mit Ralf Lethmate* (N. Wolf, Interviewer) [Agile Review]. Retrieved from https://www.itagileshop.de/lesen/agile-review/2016-sonderausgabe-kunden-begeistern/#cc-m-product-10651914598

Levitt, B., & March, J. G. (1988). Organizational Learning. *Annual Review of Sociology, 14*, 319–340. Retrieved from https://www.jstor.org/stable/2083321

Li, P., Liu, S. W., Zhang, S. B., & Li, C. H. (2017). A Study on Factors Affecting Students' Entrepreneurial Intentions in HIT. In M. A. Tao (Ed.), *2017 24th Annual International Conference on Management Science & Engineering* (pp. 358-362). New York: IEEE.

Liakhovych, G., Bezruchuk, S., Ivanenko, V., & Laichuk, S. (2019). SWOT-analysis of accounting outsourcing. *European Cooperation, 3*(43), 7–19. doi:10.32070/ec.v3i43.50

Lian, T., & Yu, C. (2019). Impacts of online images of a tourist destination on tourist travel decision. *Tourism Geographies, 21*(4), 635–664. doi:10.1080/14616688.2019.1571094

Liao, D.-Y. Y., & Wang, X. (2018, November 27). Applications of blockchain technology to logistics management in integrated casinos and entertainment. Informatics, 5(4), pp. *Informatics (MDPI), 5*(4), 44. doi:10.3390/informatics5040044

Libert, B., Beck, M., & Wind, J. (2016). *The Network Imperative. How to survive and grow in the age of digital business models*. Harvard Business Review Press.

Li, C. G., Isidor, R., Dau, L. A., & Kabst, R. (2018). The More the Merrier? Immigrant Share and Entrepreneurial Activities. *Entrepreneurship Theory and Practice, 42*(5), 698–733. doi:10.1177/1042258718795344

Limani, Y., Hajrizi, E., Stapleton, L., & Retkoceri, M. (2019). Digital Transformation Readiness in Higher Education Institutions (HEI): The Case of Kosovo. *IFAC-PapersOnLine, 52*(25), 52–57. doi:10.1016/j.ifacol.2019.12.445

Lin, D. M., Zheng, W., Lu, J. Y., Liu, X. H., & Wright, M. (2019). Forgotten or not? Home-country embeddedness and returnee entrepreneurship. *Journal of World Business, 54*(1), 1–13. doi:10.1016/j.jwb.2018.08.003

Lin, X., & Tao, S. (2012). Transnational entrepreneurs: Characteristics, drivers, and success factors. *Journal of International Entrepreneurship, 10*(1), 50–69. doi:10.100710843-011-0082-1

Liu, D., Chen, S., & Chou, T. (2011). Resource fit in digital transformation: Lessons learned from the CBC Bank global e-banking project. *Management Decision, 49*(10), 1728–1742. doi:10.1108/00251741111183852

Liu, J. Y., Nandhakumar, J., & Zachariadis, M. (2018). When guanxi meets structural holes: Exploring the guanxi networks of Chinese entrepreneurs on digital platforms. *The Journal of Strategic Information Systems, 27*(4), 311–334. doi:10.1016/j.jsis.2018.10.003

Liu, J.-W., Ho, C.-Y., Chang, J. Y. T., & Tsai, J. C.-A. (2019). The role of Sprint planning and feedback in game development projects: Implications for game quality. *Journal of Systems and Software, 154*, 79–91. doi:10.1016/j.jss.2019.04.057

Li, Y., Spigt, R., & Swinkels, L. (2017). The impact of FinTech start-ups on incumbent retail banks' share prices. *Financial Innovation, 3*(1), 26. doi:10.118640854-017-0076-7

Lnenicka, M., & Komarkova, J. (2019). Developing a government enterprise architecture framework to support the requirements of big and open linked data with the use of cloud computing. *International Journal of Information Management, 46*, 124–141. doi:10.1016/j.ijinfomgt.2018.12.003

Lobo, S. (2014). SPON-Die Mensch-Maschine: Auf Dem Weg in Die Dumpinghölle. *Spiegel Online, 3.*

Lobschata, Muellerb, Eggersd, Brandimartee, Diefenbachf, Kroschkea, & Wirtzh. (2019). Corporate digital responsibility. *Journal of Business Research.*

Lo, F. Y., Huarng, K. H., & Rey-Martí, A. (2019). Entrepreneur subsidiary of business groups from emerging markets: A multi-level perspective. *The International Entrepreneurship and Management Journal, 15*(2), 471–483. doi:10.100711365-019-00563-y

Longo, F., Nicoletti, L., Padovano, A., d'Atri, G., & Forte, M. (2019). Blockchain-enabled supply chain: An experimental study. *Computers & Industrial Engineering, 136*, 57–69. doi:10.1016/j.cie.2019.07.026

Loop, P. (2016). Blockchain: the next evolution of supply chains: blockchain technology could help lead to a reinvention of retail supply chains. *Material Handling & Logistics, 71*(10), 22.

Loukis, E., & Charalabidis, Y. (2011). Why Do e-Government Projects Fail? Risk Factors of Large Information Systems Projects in the Greek Public Sector: An International Comparison. *International Journal of Electronic Government Research, 7*(2), 59–77. doi:10.4018/jegr.2011040104

Luengo, J., García-Gil, D., Ramírez-Gallego, S., García, S., & Herrera, F. (2020). *Big Data Preprocessing: Enabling Smart Data*. Springer Nature. doi:10.1007/978-3-030-39105-8

Luna-Reyes, L. F., Gil-Garcia, J. R., & Celorio-Mansi, J. A. (2010). *Reporte de Resultados de Talleres con Directores de Informática Municipales.* Universidad de las Américas Puebla-INFOTEC.

Luna-Reyes, L. F., Gil-Garcia, J. R., & Cruz, C. B. (2007). Collaborative digital government in Mexico: Some lessons from federal web-based interorganizational information integration initiatives. *Government Information Quarterly, 24*(4), 808–826.

Lyons, K., & Wearing, S. (2015). *The sharing economy: Issues, ımpacts and regulatory responses in the context of the NSW visitor economy.* NSW Business Chamber.

Lyytinen, K., Mathiassen, L., & Ropponen, J. (1998). Attention shaping and software risk- a categorical analysis of four classical risk management approaches. *Information Systems Research, 9*(3), 233–255.

Ma'ruf, A. H., Syafii, M., & Kusuma, A. P. (2019). Pengaruh Model Pembelajaran Mind Mapping Berbasis HOTS terhadap Motivasi dan Hasil Belajar Siswa. *Mosharafa: Jurnal Pendidikan Matematika, 8*(3), 503–514.

Madariaga, J., Buenadicha, C., Molina, E., & Ernst, C. (2019). *Economía de plataformas y empleo: ¿cómo es trabajar para una app en Argentina?* CIPPEC - BID - OIT.

Madu, A. A., & Madu, A. A. (2002). Dimension of e-quality. *International Journal of Quality & Reliability Management, 19*(3), 246–258. doi:10.1108/02656710210415668

Magsamen-Conrad, K., Dillon, J. M., Hanasono, L. K., & Valdez, P. A. (2020). Developing an intergroup communication intervention curriculum: Enhancing workforce skills across generations. In *Five Generations and Only One Workforce: How Successful Businesses Are Managing a Multigenerational Workforce* (pp. 148–176). IGI Global. doi:10.4018/978-1-7998-0437-6.ch008

Mahmood, Y. N. (2019). The impact of quality service factors on banking service sector case study in Erbil banks. *Tikrit Journal of Administration and Economics Sciences, 2*(42).

Mahmoodi, S., & Naderi, H. (2016). Assessment of modern banking services to achieve and realization of e-commerce and its impact on the profitability of banks listed on the Tehran stock exchange. *Modern Applied Science, 10*(9), 263. doi:10.5539/mas.v10n9p263

Makris, D., Hansen, Z. N. L., & Khan, O. (2019). Adapting to supply chain 4.0: an explorative study of multinational companies. *Supply Chain Forum: An International Journal, 20*(2), 116–131.

Maldonado, S. (2015). *Analítica web: Medir para triunfar*. ESIC.

Malhotra, A., & Van Alstyne, M. (2014). Thedarkside of thesharingeconomy… and how tolighten it. *Communications of the ACM*, *57*(11), 24–27. doi:10.1145/2668893

Maltaverne, B. (2017, July 17). Blockchain: what are the opportunities for Procurement? *Medium*.

Manhas, P. S., Manrai, L. A., & Manrai, A. K. (2016). Role of tourist destination development in building its brand image: A conceptual model. *Journal of Economics, Finance and Administrative Science*, *21*(40), 25–29. doi:10.1016/j.jefas.2016.01.001

Manners-Bell, J., (2017). *Supply chain risk management: understanding emerging threats to global supply chains*. Kogan Page Publishers.

Mao, D. (2019). Novel Automatic Food Trading System Using Consortium Blockchain. *The Arabian Journal for Science and Engineering. Section B. Engineering*, *44*(4), 3439–3455.

Marangoz, M., Bayraktaroğlu, F., & Aydın, A. E. (2017). Tüketimde alternatif bir yaklaşım olarak paylaşım ekonomisi: ortak kullanım ağlarının içerik analizi ile incelenmesi. *Dumlupınar Üniversitesi Sosyal Bilimler Dergisi*, 134-148.

March, J. G., & Shapira, Z. (1987). Managerial perspectives on risk and risk taking. *Management Science*, *33*(11), 1404–1418.

Mareev, S. N. (2016). Understand global capitalism (Reflections on the Book "Global Capital", by A.V. Buzgalin and A.I Kolganov). *Voprosy Filosofii*, 60–67.

Mariotto, F., Zanni, P., & Salati, G. (2014). What is the use of a single-case study in management research? *Revista de Administração de Empresas*, *54*(4), 358–369. doi:10.1590/S0034-759020140402

Markard, J., Raven, R., & Truffer, B. (2012). Sustainability transitions: An emerging field of research and its prospects. *Research Policy*, *41*(6), 955–967. doi:10.1016/j.respol.2012.02.013

Maropoulos, P. G., Zhang, D., Chapman, P., Bramall, D. G., & Rogers, B. C. (2007). Key digital enterprise technology methods for large volume metrology and assembly integration. *International Journal of Production Research*, *45*(7), 1539–1559. doi:10.1080/00207540600942326

Martin, C. J., & Upham, P. (2016). Grassroots social innovation and the mobilisation of values in collaborative consumption: A conceptual model. *Journal of Cleaner Production*, *134*, 204–213. doi:10.1016/j.jclepro.2015.04.062

Martínez-Sala, A. M., Monserrat-Gauchi, J., & Alemany-Martínez, D. (2020). User usable experience: A three-dimensional approach on usability in tourism websites and a model for its evaluation. *Tourism Management Perspectives, 33*(July), 100579. doi:10.1016/j.tmp.2019.100579

Martinis, A., Papadatou, A., & Kabassi, K. (2019). An analysis of the electronic presence of national parks in Greece. In V. Katsoni & M. Segarra-Oña (Eds.), *Smart Tourism as a Driver for Culture and Sustainability* (pp. 433–449). Springer. doi:10.1007/978-3-030-03910-3_30

Mashat, Ritchie, Lovatt, & Pratten. (2005). The Social Role of Accounting: Views and Perceptions of the Accounting Community in Libya towards Corporate Social Responsibility and Accountability. *M. M. U. s. Research*, 1-24.

Mashey, J. R. (1997, October). *Big data... And the next wave of infrastress*. Paper presented in Computer Science Division Seminar, University of California, Berkeley, CA.

Matt, C., Hess, T., & Benlian, A. (2015). Digital Transformation Strategies. *Business & Information Systems Engineering*, *57*(5), 339–343. doi:10.100712599-015-0401-5

Maya, F. F. (2018). Mobile-banking adoption: Empirical evidence from the banking sector in Pakistan. *International Journal of Bank Marketing*, *36*(7), 1386–1413. doi:10.1108/IJBM-10-2017-0215

McAfee, A., & Brynjolfsson, E. (2017). *Machine, Platform, Crowd. Harnessing our digital future*. W. W. Norton & Company Ltd.

McAfee, A., Brynjolfsson, E., Davenport, T. H., Patil, D. J., & Barton, D. (2012). Big data: The management revolution. *Harvard Business Review*, *90*(10), 60–68. PMID:23074865

McCartney, G., Butler, R., & Bennett, M. (2008). A strategic use of the communication mix in the destination image-formation process. *Journal of Travel Research*, *47*(2), 183–196. doi:10.1177/0047287508321201

McCartney, S. (2001). *ENIAC: The triumphs and tragedies of the world's first computer*. Berkley Publishing Group.

McDonald, I. J., Mcphee, A. D., Haldenby, P. A. J., Chan, P. M. W., & Lee, J. J. S. (2018). *U.S. Patent Application No. 15/287,815*. US Patent Office.

McGaughey, R., & Mason, K. (1998). The Internet as a marketing tool. *Journal of Marketing Theory and Practice*, *6*(6), 1–11. doi:10.1080/10696679.1998.11501800

McKinney, V., Yoon, K., & Zahedi, F. M. (2002). The measurement of web-customer satisfaction: An expectation and disconformation approach. *Information Systems Research*, *13*(3), 296–331. doi:10.1287/isre.13.3.296.76

Medium. (2019). *Benefits of Using Big Data in Supply Chain Management*. Retrieved May 2020, from https://medium.com/@erpsolutionsoodles/benefits-of-using-big-data-in-supply-chain-management-1bcc1f6c915f

Meijer, A., Rodríguez Bolívar, M.P., & Gil-Garcia, J.R. (2018). From E-Government to Digital Era Governance and Beyond: Lessons from 15 Years of Research into Information and Communications Technology in the Public Sector. *Journal of Government organizations Research and Theory*, 1-6.

Mergel, I., Edelmann, N., & Haug, N. (2019). Defining digital transformation: Results from expert interviews. *Government Information Quarterly*, *36*(4), 101385. doi:10.1016/j.giq.2019.06.002

Mergel, I., Rethemeyer, R. K., & Isett, K. (2016). Big data in public affairs. *Public Administration Review*, *76*(6), 928–937. doi:10.1111/puar.12625

Merlino, M., & Sproģe, I. (2017). The Augmented Supply Chain. *Procedia Engineering*, *178*, 308–318. doi:10.1016/j.proeng.2017.01.053

Merton, R. K. (1967). *On theoretical sociology*. Free Press.

Mesas-Carrascosa, F. J., de Castro, A. I., Torres-Sánchez, J., Triviño-Tarradas, P., Jiménez-Brenes, F. M., García-Ferrer, A., & López-Granados, F. (2020). Classification of 3D point clouds using color vegetation indices for precision viticulture and digitizing applications. *Remote Sensing*, *12*(2), 317. doi:10.3390/rs12020317

Meske, C., & Junglas, I. (2020). Investigating the elicitation of employees' support towards digital workplace transformation. *Behaviour & Information Technology*, 1–17. doi:10.1080/0144929X.2020.1742382

Mikalef, P., Boura, M., Lekakos, G., & Krogstie, J. (2019). Big data analytics and firm performance: Findings from a mixed-method approach. *Journal of Business Research*, *98*, 261–276. doi:10.1016/j.jbusres.2019.01.044

Milway, K. S., & Saxton, A. (2011). *The Challenge of Organizational Learning*. Retrieved July 19, 2020, from Stanford Social Innovation Review website: https://ssir.org/articles/entry/the_challenge_of_organizational_learning

Min, H., & Galle, W. P. (1999). Electronic commerce usage in business-to-business purchasing. *International Journal of Operations & Production Management, 19*(9), 909–921. doi:10.1108/01443579910280232

Mintzberg, H. (1979). Patterns in strategy formation. *International Studies of Management & Organization, 9*(3), 67–86. doi:10.1080/00208825.1979.11656272

Mishra, V., & Singh, V. (2015). Selection of appropriate electronic banking channel alternative. *International Journal of Bank Marketing, 33*(3), 223–242.

Mnjala, D. M. (2014). The Challenges of Creating Sustainable Competitive Advantage in the Banking Industry in Kenya. *IOSR Journal of Business and Management, 16*(4), 82-87.

Moe, N. B., Dingsøyr, T., & Kvangardsnes, O. (2009). Understanding Shared Leadership in Agile Development: A Case Study. In *2009 42nd Hawaii International Conference on System Sciences*, (pp. 1–10). Waikoloa, HI: IEEE. 10.1109/HICSS.2009.480

Mohamed, A. (2013). Improving the Libyan customers' trust and acceptance for online banking technology (PhD). University of Salford.

Moktadir, M. A., Dwivedi, A., Rahman, A., Chiappetta Jabbour, C. J., Paul, S. K., Sultana, R., & Madaan, J. (2020). An investigation of key performance indicators for operational excellence towards sustainability in the leather products industry. *Business Strategy and the Environment, 29*(8), 3331–3351. doi:10.1002/bse.2575

Möller, K., Schäffer, U., & Verbeeten, F. (2020). *Digitalization in management accounting and control: an editorial*. Academic Press.

Moll, J., & Yigitbasioglu, O. (2019). The role of internet-related technologies in shaping the work of accountants: New directions for accounting research. *The British Accounting Review, 51*(6), 100833. doi:10.1016/j.bar.2019.04.002

Monizza, G. P., Bendetti, C., & Matt, D. T. (2018). Parametric and Generative Design techniques in mass-production environments as effective enablers of Industry 4.0 approaches in the Building Industry. *Automation in Construction, 92*, 270–285. doi:10.1016/j.autcon.2018.02.027

Monostori, L., Erdős, G., Kádár, B., Kis, T., Kovács, A., Pfeiffer, A., & Váncza, J. (2010). Digital enterprise solution for integrated production planning and control. *Computers in Industry, 61*(2), 112–126. doi:10.1016/j.compind.2009.10.008

Moon, B.J. (2004). Consumer adoption of the internet as an information search and product purchase channel: some research hypotheses. *International Journal of Internet Marketing and Advertising, 1*(1), 104-118.

Moore, G. C., & Benbasat, I. (1991). Development of an Instrument to Measure The Perceptions of Adopting an Information Technology Innovation. *Information Systems Research, 2*(3), 192–222. doi:10.1287/isre.2.3.192

Morales, D., & Trinidad, F. (2019). Predictors of acceptability of digital mortgage service of universal banks in the Philippines: An empirical study. *International Journal of Modern Trends in Business Research, 2*(8), 79–92.

Morgan, R. M., & Hunt, S. D. (1994). The commitment-trust theory of relationship marketing. *Journal of Marketing, 58*(3), 20–38. doi:10.1177/002224299405800302

Morinobu, S. (2018). *Strategies for Taxing the Digital Economy*. The Tokyo Foundation for Policy Research. Retrieved From https://www.tkfd.or.jp/en/research/detail.php?id=24

Morozov, E. (2013). The "sharing economy"undermines workers'rights. *Financial Times*. Retrieved from http://evgeny-morozov.tumblr.com/post/64038831400/the-sharing-economyundermineswworkers-rights

Moses, J. (2015). Agile Writing: A Project Management Approach to Learning. *International Journal of Sociotechnology and Knowledge Development, 7*(2), 1–13. doi:10.4018/IJSKD.2015040101

Motiwalla, L., Albashrawi, M., & Kartal, H. (2018). Understanding Mobile Banking Success through User Segmentation *Proceedings of the 51st Hawaii International Conference on System Sciences.* 10.24251/HICSS.2018.110

Motoyama, Y., & Knowlton, K. (2017). Examining the Connections within the Startup Ecosystem: A Case Study of St. Louis. *Entrepreneurship Research Journal, 7*(1). Advance online publication. doi:10.1515/erj-2016-0011

Mowrer, R. R., & Klein, S. B. (2019). A contrast between traditional and contemporary learning theory. *Contemporary Learning Theories: Volume II: Instrumental Conditioning Theory and the Impact of Biological Constraints on Learning*, 1.

Mtima, L. (2009). Copyright Social Utility and Social Justice Interdependence: A Paradigm for Intellectual Property Empowerment and Digital Entrepreneurship. *West Virginia Law Review, 112*, 97.

Müller-Stewens, P. D. G. (n.d.). *Definition: Strategie.* Retrieved July 19, 2020, from Https://wirtschaftslexikon.gabler.de/definition/strategie-43591

Munné, R. (2016). Big data in the public sector. In New horizons for a data-driven economy: a roadmap for usage and exploitation of big data in Europe (pp. 195-208). London: Springer Open. doi:10.1007/978-3-319-21569-3_11

Murphy, E., Dingwall, R., Greatbatch, D., Parker, S., & Watson, P. (1998). Qualitative Research Methods in Health Technology Assessment: A Review of the Literature. *Health Technology Assessment, 2*(16). Advance online publication. doi:10.3310/hta2160 PMID:9919458

Mutahar, A. M., Daud, N. M., Ramayah, T., Isaac, O., & Aldholay, A. H. (2018). The effect of awareness and perceived risk on the technology acceptance model (TAM): Mobile banking in Yemen. *Int. J. Services and Standards, 12*(2), 27. doi:10.1504/IJSS.2018.091840

Mutanov, G., Mamykova, Z., Kopnova, O., & Bolatkhan, M. (2020). Applied research of data management in the education system for decision-making on the example of Al-Farabi Kazakh National University. In *E3S Web of Conferences* (Vol. 159, p. 09003). EDP Sciences. doi:10.1051/e3sconf/202015909003

Nadler, S. S. N. (2014). *The sharing economy: What is it and where is it going?* (Unpublished doctoral dissertation). Massachusetts Institute of Technology.

Nair, H., Staat, H. J., Tran, T., van Houselt, A., Prosperetti, A., Lohse, D., & Sun, C. (2014). The Leidenfrost temperature increase for impacting droplets on carbon-nanofiber surfaces. *Soft Matter, 10*(13), 2102–2109. doi:10.1039/C3SM52326H PMID:24651906

Nakamoto, S. (2008). *Bitcoin: A peer-to-peer electronic cash system.* Available at https://bitcoin.org/bitcoin.pdf

Nambisan, S. (2017). Digital Entrepreneurship: Toward a Digital Technology Perspective of Entrepreneurship. *Entrepreneurship Theory and Practice, 41*(6), 1029–1055. doi:10.1111/etap.12254

Nambisan, S., Siegel, D., & Kenney, M. (2018). On Open Innovation, Platforms, and Entrepreneurship. *Strategic Entrepreneurship Journal, 12*(3), 354–368. doi:10.1002ej.1300

Nambisan, S., Write, M., & Feldman, M. (2019). The digital transformation of innovation and entrepreneurship: Progress, challenges and key themes. *Research Policy, 48*(8), 103773. doi:10.1016/j.respol.2019.03.018

Naranjo-Gil, D. (2004). The role of sophisticated accounting system in strategy management. *International Journal of Digital Accounting Research, 4*(8), 125–144.

Nasermoadeli, A., Ling, K. C., & Severi, E. (2013). Exploring the Relationship between Social Environment and Customer Experience. *Asian Social Science*, *9*(1), 130–141.

Nason, R. S., & Wiklund, J. (2018). An assessment of resource-based theorizing on firm growth and suggestions for the future. *Journal of Management*, *44*(1), 32–60. doi:10.1177/0149206315610635

Nazaritehrani, A., & Mashali, B. (2020). Development of e-banking channels and market share in developing countries. *Financial Innovation*, *6*(12), 12. Advance online publication. doi:10.118640854-020-0171-z

Neff, G. (2012). *Venture labor: Work and the burden of risk in innovative industries*. MIT Press. doi:10.7551/mitpress/9780262017480.001.0001

Nejad, M. G. (2016). Guest editorial: Challenges and opportunities for innovation in financial services. *International Journal of Bank Marketing*, *34*(1), 1–7.

Ngoasong, M. Z. (2018). Digital entrepreneurship in a resource-scarce context: A focus on entrepreneurial digital competencies. *Journal of Small Business and Enterprise Development*, *25*(3), 483–500. doi:10.1108/JSBED-01-2017-0014

Ng, T. W., & Wang, M. (2019). An actor–partner interdependence model of employees' and coworkers' innovative behavior, psychological detachment, and strain reactions. *Personnel Psychology*, *72*(3), 445–476. doi:10.1111/peps.12317

Nguyen, H. N. (2016). *Customer value in Sharing economy: The case of Airbnb* (Unpublished master's thesis). Tampere University Business competence, Finland.

Nicotra, M., Romano, M., Giudice, D. M., & Schillaci, E. C. (2018). The causal relation between entrepreneurial ecosystem and productive entrepreneurship: A measurement framework. *The Journal of Technology Transfer*, *43*(3), 33. doi:10.100710961-017-9628-2

Nielsen. (2015). Global trust in advertising: Winning strategies for an evolving media landscape. *Nielsen*. Retrieved from http://www.nielsen.com

Nielsen, J. (1994). *Usability engineering*. Elsevier.

Nielsen, J. (1999). *Designing web usability: The practice of simplicity*. New Riders Publishing.

Nielsen, J., & Molich, R. (1990). Heuristic evaluation of user interfaces. In *Proceedings of the SIGCHI conference on Human factors in computing systems* (pp. 249–256). ACM.

Nielsen, J., & Tahir, M. (2011). *Homepage usability: 50 websites deconstructed*. New Riders Publishing.

Nkongolo-Bakenda, J.-M., & Chrysostome, V. (2019). Dual environments of home and host countries of diasporic transnational entrepreneurs: an empirical study in the Canadian context. *International Journal of Entrepreneurship and Small Business*.

Noguera, I., Guerrero-Roldán, A.-E., & Masó, R. (2018). Collaborative agile learning in online environments: Strategies for improving team regulation and project management. *Computers & Education*, *116*, 110–129. doi:10.1016/j.compedu.2017.09.008

Norberg, H. (2019). Unblocking the Bottlenecks and Making the Global Supply Chain Transparent: How Blockchain technology stands to update global trade. *The School of Public Policy Publications*, *12*(9), 1–24.

Norheim-Hagtun, I., & Meier, P. (2010). Crowdsourcing for crisis mapping in Haiti. *Innovations: Technology, Governance, Globalization*, *5*(4), 81–89. doi:10.1162/INOV_a_00046

Nowlis, S., & McCabe, D. (2000). The effect of the inability to touch merchandise on the likelihood of choosing products online. In *American Marketing Association. Conference Proceedings.* (Vol. 11, p. 308). American Marketing Association.

Nuri, M. (2019). An empirical study on measurement of efficiency of digital transformation by using data envelopment analysis. *Management Science Letters*, *9*, 549–556.

Obukhova, Merzlyakova, Ershova, & Karakulina. (2020). Introduction of digital technologies in the enterprise. In *E3S Web of Conferences*. EDP Sciences.

OECD. (2013). *Action Plan on Base Erosion and Profit Shifting*. OECD Publishing. Retrieved From https://www.oecd.org/ctp/BEPSActionPlan.pdf

OECD. (2014). *Recommendation of the Council on Digital Government Strategies*. Retrieved from http:// www.oecd.org/gov/digital-government/Recommendation-digital-government-strategies.pdf

OECD. (2015). Addressing the Tax Challenges of the Digital Economy, Action 1-2015 Final Report. In *Series: OECD/G20 Base Erosion and Profit Shifting Project, French*. OECD Publishing.

OECD. (2015). *OECD/G20 Base Erosion and Profit Shifting Project: Executive Summaries 2015 Final Reports*. OECD Publishing. Retrieved From https://www.oecd.org/ctp/beps-reports-2015-executive-summaries.pdf

OECD. (2016). *Energy and Air Pollution: World Energy Outlook Special Report 2016*. OECD.

OECD. (2016). *Policies for the tourism sharing economy OECD tourism trends and policies 2016*. OECD Publishing.

OECD. (2018). *Tax Challenges Arising From Digitalization- Interim Report 2018: Inclusive Framework on BEPS*. OECD/G20 Base Erosion and Profit Shifting Project, OECD Publishing. Retrieved From https://www.oecd.org/tax/beps/brief-on-the-tax-challenges-arising-from-digitalisation-interim-report-2018.pdf

Olbert, M., & Spengel, C. (2017). International Taxation In The Digital Economy: Challange Accepted? *World Tax Journal*, (February), 3–46.

Oliveira, R. C. (2010). The determinants of immigrant entrepreneurship and employment creation in Portugal: Chapter 4 of Migrant Entrepreneurship in OECD Countries. Academic Press.

Oliver, K. M., & Williams-Duncan, S. (2019). Faith Leaders Developing Digital Literacies: Demands and Resources across Career Stages According to Theological Educators. *The Journal of Media Literacy Education*, *11*(2), 122–145. doi:10.23860/JMLE-2019-11-2-7

Omar, S., & Tajudeen, F. P. (2020). The Influence of Career Adaptability and Career Commitment to Minimize Intention to Leave Among ICT Professionals. *International Journal of Human Capital and Information Technology Professionals*, *11*(2), 23–38. doi:10.4018/IJHCITP.2020040102

Omigie, N. O., Zo, H., Rho, J. J., & Ciganek, A. P. (2017). Customer pre-adoption choice behavior for M-PESA mobile financial services Extending the theory of consumption values. *Industrial Management & Data Systems*, *117*(5), 910–926. doi:10.1108/IMDS-06-2016-0228

Osmundsen, K., Lden, J., & Bygstad, B. (2018). *Digital Transformation: Drivers, Success Factors and Implications*. The 12th Mediterranean Conference on Information Systems MCIS, Corfu, Greece.

Osterwalder, A., & Pigneur, Y. (2010). *Business Model Generation: A Handbook for Visionaries, Game Changers, and Challengers*. John Wiley & Sons, Inc.

Osterwalder, A., Pigneur, Y., & Tucci, C. (2005, July). Clarifying business models: Origins, present, and future of the concept. *Communications of the Association for Information Systems*, *15*, 1–25. doi:10.17705/1CAIS.01601

Outhwaite, W. (2016). *Social theory: Ideas in profile*. Profile Books.

Overby, S. (2020). *What is digital transformation?* https://enterprisersproject.com/what-is-digital-transformation

Owusu, P. A., & Duah, H. (2018). Evaluating total quality management as a competitive advantage tool in mobile telecommunication services in Ghana. *European Journal of Research and Reflection in Management Sciences*, *6*(1).

Oyson, M., & Whittaker, D. H. (2010). *An opportunity-based approach to international entrepreneurship: Pursuing opportunities internationally through prospection*. Academic Press.

Öz, E., & Kara, M. C. (2016). A Global Look at Digital Taxation. *Tax World Journal*, *36*(424), 30–37.

Padirayon, L. M., Pagudpud, M. V., & Cruz, J. S. D. (2019). Exploring constructivism learning theory using mobile game. *IOP Conference Series. Materials Science and Engineering*, *482*(1), 012004. doi:10.1088/1757-899X/482/1/012004

Pan, G., & Seow, P. S. (2016). Preparing accounting graduates for digital revolution: A critical review of information technology competencies and skills development. *Journal of Education for Business*, *91*(3), 166–175. doi:10.1080/08832323.2016.1145622

Parker, G., Van Alstyne, M., & Choudary, S. (2016). *Platform Revolution. How networked markets are transforming the economy and how to make them work for you*. W. W. Norton & Company.

Parker, S. K., Wang, Y., & Liao, J. (2019). When is proactivity wise? A review of factors that influence the individual outcomes of proactive behavior. *Annual Review of Organizational Psychology and Organizational Behavior*, *6*(1), 221–248. doi:10.1146/annurev-orgpsych-012218-015302

Passerini, K., El Tarabishy, A., & Patten, K. (2012). *Information technology for small business: managing the digital enterprise*. Springer Science & Business Media. doi:10.1007/978-1-4614-3040-7

Pasteur, L. (2013). *Características y diferencias de la investigación documental, de campo y experimental*. Formación de competencias para la investigación.

Pastorino, R., De Vito, C., Migliara, G., Glocker, K., Binenbaum, I., Ricciardi, W., & Boccia, S. (2019). Benefits and challenges of Big data in healthcare: An overview of the European initiatives. *European Journal of Public Health*, *29*(Supplement_3), 23–27. doi:10.1093/eurpub/ckz168 PMID:31738444

Patel, B., Roy, S., Bhattacharyya, D., & Kim, T. H. (2017). Necessity of big data and analytics for good e-governance. *International Journal of Grid and Distributed Computing*, *10*(8), 11–20. doi:10.14257/ijgdc.2017.10.8.02

Pauwels, K. (2014). *It's Not the Size of the Data—it's how You Use it: Smarter Marketing with Analytics and Dashboards*. Amacom.

Pawson, R., Greenhalgh, T., Harvey, G., & Walshe, K. (2005). Realist review-a new method of systematic review designed for complex policy interventions. *Journal of Health Services Research & Policy*, *10*(1, suppl), 21–34. doi:10.1258/1355819054308530 PMID:16053581

Pedro, C. P., Ramalho, J. J. S., & Silva, J. V. (2018). The main determinants of banking crises in OECD countries. *Review of World Economics*, *154*(1), 203–227. doi:10.100710290-017-0294-0

Peharda, P., Munđar, D., & Vrček, N. (2011). Methodology for risk assessment and corresponding costs in e-government projects. *Proceedings of the 22nd Central European Conference on Information and Intelligent Systems*, 335-342.

Pellizzoni, E., Trabucchi, D., & Buganza, T. (2019). Platform strategies: How the position in the network drives succes. *Technology Analysis and Strategic Management*, *31*(5), 579–592. doi:10.1080/09537325.2018.1524865

Peng, G., & Gala, C. (2014). Cloud ERP: A New Dilemma to Modern Organisations? *Journal of Computer Information Systems, 54*(4), 22–30. doi:10.1080/08874417.2014.11645719

Penz, E., & Hogg, M. (2011). The role of mixed emotions in consumer behaviour: Investigating ambivalence in consumers' experiences of approach-avoidance conflicts in online and offline settings. *European Journal of Marketing, 45*(1/2), 104–132. doi:10.1108/03090561111095612

Pereira, A. C., & Romero, F. (2017). A review of the meanings and the implications of the Industry 4.0 concept. *Procedia Manufacturing, 13*(C), 1206–1214. doi:10.1016/j.promfg.2017.09.032

Peter, M. K., Kraft, C., & Lindeque, J. (2020). Strategic action fields of digital transformation: An exploration of the strategic action fields of Swiss SMEs and large enterprises. *Journal of Strategy and Management, 13*(1), 160–180. doi:10.1108/JSMA-05-2019-0070

Petersen, M., Hackius, N. & von See, B. (2018). Mapping the sea of opportunities: Blockchain in supply chain and logistics. *IT - Information Technology, 60*(5), 263–271.

Petrova, P. (2018). Industry 4.0 and Accounting: Challenges and Opportunities. *Nauchni trudove*, (3), 135-144.

Petticrew, M., & Roberts, H. (2008). *Systematic reviews in the social sciences: A practical guide.* John Wiley & Sons.

Phau, I., & Poon, S. (2000). Factors influencing the types of products and services purchased over the Internet. *Internet Research, 10*(2), 102–113. doi:10.1108/10662240010322894

Philipp, R., Prause, G., & Gerlitz, L. (2019). Blockchain and Smart Contracts for Entrepreneurial Collaboration in Maritime Supply Chains. *Transport and Telecommunication, 20*(4), 365–378. doi:10.2478/ttj-2019-0030

Picazo-Vela, S., Gutiérrez-Martínez, I., & Luna-Reyes, L. F. (2012). Understanding risks, benefits, and strategic alternatives of social media applications in the public sector. *Government Information Quarterly, 29*, 504–511. doi:10.1016/j.giq.2012.07.002

Pichelr, P., Summer, M., Weber, B., & Goodhart, C. (2019). *Does digitalization require Central Bank Digital Currencies for the general publ.* Monetary Policy & The Economy – First View.

Poiani, T. H., dos Santos Rocha, R., Degrossi, L. C., & de Albuquerque, J. P. (2016, January). Potential of collaborative mapping for disaster relief: A case study of OpenStreetMap in the Nepal earthquake 2015. In *2016 49th Hawaii International Conference on System Sciences (HICSS)* (pp. 188-197). IEEE 10.1109/HICSS.2016.31

Porter, M. (1991). Towards a Dynamic Theory of Strategy. *Strategic Management Journal, 12*(S2), 95–117. doi:10.1002mj.4250121008

Porter, M., & Heppelmann, J. (2015). How Smart, Connected Products are Transforming Companies. *Harvard Business Review*, 1–19.

Portes, A., Guarnizo, L. E., & Haller, W. J. (2002). Transnational entrepreneurs: An alternative form of immigrant economic adaptation. *American Sociological Review, 67*(2), 278–298.

Portes, A., Guarnizo, L. E., & Landolt, P. (1999). The study of transnationalism: Pitfalls and promise of an emergent research field. *Ethnic and Racial Studies, 22*(2), 237. doi:10.1080/014198799329468

Portes, A., & Yiu, J. (2013). Entrepreneurship, transnationalism, and development. *Migration Studies, 1*(1), 20. doi:10.1093/migration/mns036

Portes, A., & Zhou, M. (1996). Self-employment and the earnings of immigrants. *American Sociological Review, 61*(2), 219. doi:10.2307/2096332

Pousttchi, K., & Schurig, M. (2004). *Assessment of today's mobile banking applications from the view of customer requirements. 37th Hawaii International Conference on System Sciences (HICSS)*, Big Island, HI. 10.1109/HICSS.2004.1265440

Powers, J., & Magnoni, B. (2010). *Dueña de tu propia empresa: identificación, análisis y superación de las limitaciones a las pequeñas empresas de las mujeres en América Latina y el Caribe.* Fondo Multilateral de Inversiones, BID.

Pradhan, P., & Shakya, S. (2018). Big data Challenges for e-Government Services in Nepal. *Journal of the Institute of Engineering*, *14*(1), 216–222. doi:10.3126/jie.v14i1.20087

Prensario TI Latin America. (2016, October). Software ERP en América Latina. Nuevo perfil de negocio cambia el mercado. *Prensario TILA*, *14*(184), 4–12.

PricewaterhouseCoopers. (n.d.a). https://www.pwc.com/il/he/bankim/assets/fin-tech-banking.pdf

PricewaterhouseCoopers. (n.d.b). https://www.pwc.com/gx/en/industries/financial-services/publications/financial-services-technology-2020-and-beyond-embracing-disruption.html

PwC. (2015a). *The sharing economy.* PwC.

PwC. (2015b). *The sharing economy—Sizing the revenue opportunity.* Retrieved from http://www.pwc.co.uk/issues/megatrends/collisions/sharingeconomy/the-sharing-economy sizing-the-revenue-opportunity.html

Queensland Tourism Industry Council. (2014). *The sharing economy: How it will impact the tourism landscape and what businesses can do?* Queensland Tourism Industry Council, Brisbane.

Qureshi, M. R. J., & Kashif, M. (2009). Seamless long term learning in agile teams for sustainable leadership. In *2009 International Conference on Emerging Technologies*, (pp. 389–394). Islamabad, Pakistan: IEEE. 10.1109/ICET.2009.5353140

Rabiu, I. D., Ladan, S., Usman, H. A., & Garba, M. (2019). Impact of e-banking on the operational efficiency of banks in Nigeria. *International Journal of Academic Research in Business & Social Sciences*, *9*(2). Advance online publication. doi:10.6007/IJARBSS/v9-i2/5527

Radanliev, P. (2019). *The Industrial Internet of Things in the Industry 4.0 supply chains: Literature review and future trends.* arXiv.org, pp.arXiv.org.

Rahi, S. (2017). Research design and methods: A systematic review of research paradigms, sampling issues and instruments development. *International Journal of Economics & Management Sciences*, *6*(2), 1–5. doi:10.4172/2162-6359.1000403

Rajagopalan, M. R., & Vellaipandiyan, S. (2013, November). Big data framework for national e-governance plan. In *2013 Eleventh International Conference on ICT and Knowledge Engineering* (pp. 1-5). IEEE. 10.1109/ICTKE.2013.6756283

Rajenderan, M., & Zawawi, D. (2019). Leaky Pipeline Syndrome in Information and Communication Technology (ICT) Industry of Malaysia: A Conceptual Study on Female Career Barriers and Retention Management. *International Journal of Academic Research in Business & Social Sciences*, *9*(2). Advance online publication. doi:10.6007/IJARBSS/v9-i2/5672

Raman, S., Patwa, N., Niranjan, I., Ranjan, U., Moorthy, K., & Mehta, A. (2018). Impact of big data on supply chain management. *International Journal of Logistics Research and Applications*, *21*(6), 579–596. doi:10.1080/13675567.2018.1459523

Rao, T. R., Mitra, P., Bhatt, R., & Goswami, A. (2019). The big data system, components, tools, and technologies: A survey. *Knowledge and Information Systems*, *60*(3), 1165–1245. doi:10.100710115-018-1248-0

Rathmell, W. K., Brown, N. J., & Kilburg, R. R. (2019). Transformation to academic leadership: The role of mentorship and executive coaching. *Consulting Psychology Journal*, *71*(3), 141–160. doi:10.1037/cpb0000124 PMID:31787830

Rauch, E., Linder, C., & Dallasega, P. (2020). Anthropocentric perspective of production before and within Industry 4.0. *Computers & Industrial Engineering*, *139*, 105644. doi:10.1016/j.cie.2019.01.018

Ravenelle, A. (2016). *Microentrepreneur or Precariat? Exploring the sharing economy through the experiences of workers for Airbnb, Taskrabbit, Uber and Kitchensurfing*. Manuscript in preparation.

Ravenelle, A. J. (2017). Sharing economy workers: Selling, not sharing. *Cambridge Journal of Regions, Economy and Society*, *10*(2), 281–295. doi:10.1093/cjres/rsw043

Reidl, L., Cuevas, C., & López, R. (2010). *Métodos de Investigación en Psicología*. Universidad Nacional Autónoma de México. Recovered from https://www.rua.unam.mx/objeto/7987/metodos-de-investigacion-en-psicologia

Reinartz, W., Wiegand, N., & Imscholos, M. (2019). The impact of digital transformation on the retailing value chain. *International Journal of Research in Marketing*, *36*(3), 350–366. doi:10.1016/j.ijresmar.2018.12.002

Reis, D. A., de Moura, F. R., & de Aragao Gomes, I. M. (2019, May). The Linkage between Intellectual Property and Innovation in the Global Innovation Ecosystem. In *European Conference on Intangibles and Intellectual Capital* (pp. 218-XIII). Academic Conferences International Limited.

Rejeb, A., Keogh, J. & Treiblmaier, H. (2019). Leveraging the Internet of Things and Blockchain Technology in Supply Chain Management. *Future Internet, 11*(7).

Rejeb, A. (2018). Blockchain Potential in Tilapia Supply Chain in Ghana. *Acta Technica Jaurinensis*, *11*(2), 104–118. doi:10.14513/actatechjaur.v11.n2.462

Ren, N., & Liu, H. (2015). Traversing between transnationalism and integration: Dual embeddedness of new Chinese immigrant entrepreneurs in Singapore. *Asian and Pacific Migration Journal*, *24*(3), 298–326. doi:10.1177/0117196815594719

Resego Morakanyane, R., Reilly, P. O., & McAvoy, J. (2020). Determining Digital Transformation Success Factors. *Proceedings of the 53rd Hawaii International Conference on System Sciences*. 10.24251/HICSS.2020.532

Reynolds, D. P., Bygrave, D. W., Autio, E., Cox, W. L., & Hay, M. (2002). *Global Entrepreneurship Monitor: 2002 Executive Report*. Academic Press.

Reynolds, J. H., Chelazzi, L., & Desimone, R. (1999). Competitive mechanisms subserve attention in macaque areas V2 and V4. *The Journal of Neuroscience: The Official Journal of the Society for Neuroscience*, *19*(5), 1736–1753. doi:10.1523/JNEUROSCI.19-05-01736.1999 PMID:10024360

Richard & Mandari. (2018). *Factors influencing usage of mobile banking services: The case of ilala district in Tanzania*. Academic Press.

Richter, C., Kraus, S., Brem, A., Durst, S., & Giselbrecht, C. (2017). Digital entrepreneurship: Innovative business models for the sharing economy. *Creativity and Innovation Management*, *26*(3), 300–310. doi:10.1111/caim.12227

Richter, C., Kraus, S., & Syrjä, P. (2015). The shareconomy as a precursor for digital entrepreneurship business models. *International Journal of Entrepreneurship and Small Business*, *25*(1), 18–35. doi:10.1504/IJESB.2015.068773

Richter, P. C., & Brühl, R. (2020). Ahead of the game: Antecedents for the success of shared service centers. *European Management Journal*, *38*(3), 477–488. doi:10.1016/j.emj.2019.10.006

Rickwood, C., & White, L. (2009). Pre-purchase decision-making for a complex service: retirement planning. *Journal of Services Marketing*, *23*(3), 145-153.

Rider, C. I., Thompson, P., Kacperczyk, A., & Tåg, J. (2019). Experience and entrepreneurship: A career transition perspective. *Industrial & Labor Relations Review*, *72*(5), 1149–1181. doi:10.1177/0019793919852919

Rieger, K. L., Chernomas, W. M., McMillan, D. E., & Morin, F. L. (2019). The arts as a catalyst for learning with undergraduate nursing students: Findings from a constructivist grounded theory study. *Arts & Health*, 1–20. doi:10.1080/17533015.2019.1608569 PMID:31038419

Robbins, S. P., Chatterjee, P., Canda, E. R., & Leibowitz, G. S. (2018). *Contemporary human behavior theory: A critical perspective for social work practice (What's new in social work)* (4th ed.). Pearson.

Rogers, E. M. (2003). *Diffusion of innovations* (5th ed.). Simon and Schuster.

Rogers, E. M., & Shoemaker, F. (1974). Communication of innovations: A cross-cultural approach. *Man*, *9*(2).

Rogers, E. M., & Shoemaker, F. F. (1971). *Communication of Innovations: A Cross- Cultural Approach*. The Free Press.

Rohan, D. (2013). *Neuroeconomic Studies on Personality and Decision-Making* (Tesis doctoral). The University of Minessota, Minessota EUA.

Rong, K., Lin, Y., Li, B., Burström, T., Butel, L., & Yu, J. (2018). Business ecosystem research agenda: More dynamic, more embedded, and more internationalized. *Asian Business & Management*, *17*(3), 167–182. doi:10.105741291-018-0038-6

Roock, S., & Wolf, H. (2016). Scrum—Verstehen und erfolgreich einsetzen (1. Auflage). Heidelberg: dpunkt.verlag.

Rosa, P. (2019). Entrepreneurial Growth Through Portfolio Entrepreneurship: The Entrepreneurial Career Ladder. In The Family Business Group Phenomenon (pp. 111-144). Palgrave Macmillan.

Rose, S., Clark, M., Samouel, P., & Hair, N. (2012). Online Customer Experience in e-Retailing: An empirical model of Antecedents and Outcomes. *Journal of Retailing*, *88*(2), 308–322. doi:10.1016/j.jretai.2012.03.001

Ross, J., Sebastian, I., & Beath, C. (2016). How to Develop a Great Digital Strategy. *MIT Sloan Management Review*.

Rotchanakitumnuai, S., & Speece, M. (2003). Barriers to internet banking adoption: A qualitative study among corporate customers in Thailand. *International Journal of Bank Marketing*, *21*(6/7), 312–323. doi:10.1108/02652320310498465

Rouse, M. (2019). *ICT (Information and Communications technologies)*. https://searchcio.techtarget.com/definition/ICT-information-and-communications-technology-or-technologies

Rubin, J., & Chisnell, D. (2008). *Handbook of usability testing: How to plan, design and conduct effective tests*. John Wiley & Sons.

Rubin, V., & Lukoianova, T. (2013). Veracity roadmap: Is big data objective, truthful and credible? *Advances in Classification Research Online*, *24*(1), 4.

Rydehell, H., Isaksson, A., & Löfsten, H. (2019). Effects of internal and external resource dimensions on the business performance of new technology-based firms. *International Journal of Innovation Management*, *23*(01), 1950001. doi:10.1142/S1363919619500014

Saberi, S., Kouhizadeh, M., Sarkis, J., & Shen, L. (2019). Blockchain technology and its relationships to sustainable supply chain management. *International Journal of Production Research*, *57*(7), 2117–2135. doi:10.1080/00207543.2018.1533261

Sacristan, J. (2013). La pyme tiene problema para lanzar su e-commerce. *El economista*. Recovered from https://www.eleconomista.es/catalunya/noticias/4766122/04/13/La-pyme-tiene-problemas-para-lanzar-su-ecommerce.html

Sadek, D., Zainal, N., Taher, M., & Yahya, A. (2010). Service quality perceptions between Cooperative and Islamic Banks of Britain. *American Journal of Economics and Business Administration*, *2*(1), 1–5. doi:10.3844/ajebasp.2010.1.5

Sahut, J.-M., Luca, I., & Frédéric, T. (2019). The age of digital entrepreneurship. *Small Business Economics*, •••, 1–11.

Säisä, M. E. K., Tiura, K., & Matikainen, R. (2019). Agile Project Management in University-Industry Collaboration Projects. *International Journal of Information Technology Project Management, 10*(2), 8–15. doi:10.4018/IJITPM.2019040102

Sakhdari, K., & Burgers, J. H. (2018). The moderating role of entrepreneurial management in the relationship between absorptive capacity and corporate entrepreneurship: An attention-based view. *The International Entrepreneurship and Management Journal, 14*(4), 927–950. doi:10.100711365-017-0477-0

Sandhu, K. (2008). E-Services Acceptance Model (E-SAM). In SAdvances in Computer and Information Sciences and Engineering. Springer.

Sandhu, K. (2008). E-services acceptance model (e-sam). In *Advances in Computer and Information Sciences and Engineering* (pp. 224–229). Springer. doi:10.1007/978-1-4020-8741-7_40

Sandhu, K. (2009). Measuring the performance of the electronic service acceptance model (E-SAM). *International Journal of Business Information Systems, 4*(5), 13. doi:10.1504/IJBIS.2009.025205

Sandhu, K., & Corbitt, B. J. (2002). *Assessing web-based electronic services adoption model (E-SAM)*. Deakin University School of Information Systems.

Sandoval, E., & Guerra, E. (2010). *Migrantes e indígenas: acceso a la información en comunidades virtuales interculturales*. Recuperado de www.eumed.net/libros/2010b/684/

Santos, V., Goldman, A., Shinoda, A. C. M., & Fisher, A. L. (2011). A view towards Organizational Learning: An empirical study on Scrum implementation. In *Proceedings of the 23rd International Conference on Software Engineering & Knowledge Engineering*, (pp. 583–589). https://www.researchgate.net/publication/221391284_A_view_towards_Organizational_Learning_An_empirical_study_on_Scrum_implementation

Santos, V., & Goldman, A. (2011). An Approach on Applying Organizational Learning in Agile Software Organizations. In A. Sillitti, O. Hazzan, E. Bache, & X. Albaladejo (Eds.), *Agile Processes in Software Engineering and Extreme Programming* (pp. 324–325). Springer Berlin Heidelberg. doi:10.1007/978-3-642-20677-1_27

Sarantakos, S. (2013). *Social research*. Palgrave Macmillan. doi:10.1007/978-1-137-29247-6

Sarker, M. N. I., Hossin, M. A., Frimpong, A. N. K., & Xiaohua, Y. (2018, August). Promoting information resource management for e-government through big data approach. In *Proceedings of the 2018 International Conference on Information Management & Management Science* (pp. 99-104). 10.1145/3277139.3277155

Saxena, D., & McDonagh, J. (2019). Evaluating ERP implementations: The case for a lifecycle-based interpretive approach. *Electronic Journal of Information Systems Evaluation, 22*(1), 29–37.

Saxenian, A. (2005). From Brain Drain to Brain Circulation: Transnational Communities and Regional Upgrading in India and China. *Studies in Comparative International Development, 40*(2), 26. doi:10.1007/BF02686293

Sayın, A. (2019). *What Provisions Does the New Tax Proposal Include?* Retrieved From https://www.habergazetesi.com.tr/yazarlar/19605/yeni-vergiler-yeni-oranlar

Schatz, D., Bashroush, R., & Wall, J. (2017). Towards a more representative definition of cyber security. *Journal of Digital Forensics, Security and Law, 12*(2).

Schenkel, M. T., Farmer, S., & Maslyn, J. M. (2019). Process improvement in SMEs: The impact of harmonious passion for entrepreneurship, employee creative self-efficacy, and time spent innovating. *Journal of Small Business Strategy, 29*(1), 64–77.

Schenkel, M. T., Farmer, S., & Maslyn, J. M. (2019). Process improvement in SMEs: The impact of harmonious passion for entrepreneurship, employee creative self-efficacy, and time spent innovating. *Journal of Small Business Strategy, 29*(1), 64–77.

Scherer, N. W., & Wangenheim, V. (2015). The Value of Self-Service: Long-Term Effects of Technology based Self-Services usage on Customer Retention. *Journal of MIS Quarterly, 39*(1), 177–200. doi:10.25300/MISQ/2015/39.1.08

Schiller, N. G., Basch, L., & Blanc, C. S. (1995). From immigrant to transmigrant - Theorising transnational migration. *Anthropological Quarterly, 68*(1), 48–63. doi:10.2307/3317464

Schofield, H. (2014). Short-letapartmentsspark Paris row as Airbnbthrives. *BBC News*. Retrieved from https://www.bbc.co.uk/news/world-europe-30580295

Scholarios, D., Van der Heijden, B. I., Van der Schoot, E., Bozionelos, N., Epitropaki, O., Jedrzejowicz, P., Knauth, P., Marzec, I., Mikkelsen, A., & Van der Heijde, C. M. (2008). Employability and the psychological contract in European ICT sector SMEs. *International Journal of Human Resource Management, 19*(6), 1035–1055. doi:10.1080/09585190802051337

Scholz, T. (2016). *Uberworked and underpaid: How workers are disrupting the digital economy*. Polity Press.

Schor, J. (2014). *Debating the sharing economy*. Retrieved fromhttps://greattransition.org/publication/debating-the-sharing-economy

Schor, J. B., Attwood-Charles, W., Cansoy, M., Ladegaard, I., & Wengronwitz, R. (2017). *Dependence and precarity in the platform economy*. Unpublished paper, Boston College.

Schor, J. (2016). Debating the sharing economy. *Journal of Self-Governance and Management Economics, 4*(3), 7–22. doi:10.22381/JSME4320161

Schor, J. B., & Fitzmaurice, C. J. (2015). Collaborating and connecting: the emergence of the sharing economy. In *Handbook of research on sustainable consumption*. Edward Elgar Publishing. doi:10.4337/9781783471270.00039

Schroeder, R. (2018). Social theory after the internet: Media, technology, and globalization. *UCL Press*. doi:10.2307/j.ctt20krxdr

Schueffel, P. (2016). Taming the beast: A scientific definition of fintech. SSRN *Electronic Journal, 4*, 32–54. doi:10.2139srn.3097312

Schultis, K., Elsner, C., & Lohmann, D. (2014). *Architecture challenges for internal software ecosystems: A large-scale industry case study. In Proceedings of the 22nd ACM SIGSOFT International Symposium on Foundations of Software Engineering*. ACM. https://doi.acm.org/10.1145/2635868.2635876

Schumpeter, A. J. (1943). Capitalism, Socialism and Democracy (3rd ed.). Harperperennial Modernthought.

Schwertner, K. (2017). Digital transformation of business. *Trakia Journal of Sciences in Trakia University, 15*(1), 388–393. doi:10.15547/tjs.2017.s.01.065

Scott, J., & Marshall, G. (2009). *A dictionary of sociology* (3rd ed.). Oxford University Press. doi:10.1093/acref/9780199533008.001.0001

Scott, M. G., & Twomey, D. F. (1988). The long-term supply of entrepreneurs: Students' career aspirations in relation to entrepreneurship. *Journal of Small Business Management, 26*(4), 5.

Selamat, Z., & Jaffar, N. (2011). Information technology acceptance: From the perspective of Malaysian bankers. *International Journal of Business and Management, 6*(1), 207–217.

Sequeira, J. M., Carr, J. C., & Rasheed, A. A. (2009). Transnational Entrepreneurship: Determinants of Firm Type and Owner Attributions of Success. *Entrepreneurship Theory and Practice*, *33*(5), 1023–1044. doi:10.1111/j.1540-6520.2009.00333.x

Sestino, A., Prete, M. I., Piper, L., & Guido, G. (2020). Internet of Things and Big Data as enablers for business digitalization strategies. *Technovation*, *98*, 102173. doi:10.1016/j.technovation.2020.102173

Seyfang, G., & Longhurst, N. (2013). Desperately seeking niches: Grassroots innovations and niche development in the community currency field. *Global Environmental Change*, *23*(5), 881–891. doi:10.1016/j.gloenvcha.2013.02.007

Shaheen, S. A., Mallery, M. A., & Kingsley, K. J. (2012). Personal vehicle sharing services in North America. *Research in Transportation Business & Management*, *3*, 71–81. doi:10.1016/j.rtbm.2012.04.005

Shah, M., Maitlo, A., Jones, P., & Yusuf, Y. (2019). An investigation into agile learning processes and knowledge sharing practices to prevent identity theft in the online retail organisations. *Journal of Knowledge Management*, *23*(9), 1857–1884. doi:10.1108/JKM-06-2018-0370

Shani, A., Chen, P. J., Wang, Y., & Hua, N. (2010). Testing the impact of a promotional video on destination image change: Application of china as a tourism destination. *International Journal of Tourism Research*, *12*(2), 116–133. doi:10.1002/jtr.738

Shanley, A. (2017). Real-Time Logistics. *Pharmaceutical Technology Europe*, *29*(10), 46–48.

Shareefa, M. A., Baabdullahb, A., Duttac, S., Kumard, V., & Dwivedie, Y. K. (2018). Consumer adoption of mobile banking services: An empirical examination of factors according to adoption stages. *Journal of Retailing and Consumer Services*, *43*, 54–67. doi:10.1016/j.jretconser.2018.03.003

SharmaM.SharmaC.KhanA. (2019). *Smart ATM: Technology acceptance modeling and analysis*. doi:10.2139srn.3356363

Shen, L., & Cheung, S. O. (2018). How forming joint ventures may affect market concentration in construction industry? *International Journal of Construction Management*, *18*(2), 151–162. doi:10.1080/15623599.2017.1301026

Shewhart, W. A., & Deming, W. E. (1986). *Statistical method from the viewpoint of quality control*. Dover.

Shim, Y., & Shin, D. H. (2016). Analyzing China's fintech industry from the perspective of actor-network theory. *Telecommunications Policy*, *40*, 168–181. doi:10. 1016/j.telpol.2015.11.005

Shinnar, S., & Nayir, Z. (2019). Immigrant Entrepreneurship in an Emerging Economy: The Case of Turkey. *Journal of Small Business Management*, *57*(2), 559–575. doi:10.1111/jsbm.12408

Shukla, M. (2011). *Entrepreneurship and small business management*. Kitab Mahal.

Shukla, P. S., & Mathur, M. (2020). Conceptualizing the Role of Data Analytics and Technology in E-Governance: An Insight. *International Journal of Business Analytics*, *7*(2), 1–12. doi:10.4018/IJBAN.2020040101

Sievi-Korte, O., Richardson, I., & Beecham, S. (2019). Software architecture design in global software development: An empirical study. *Journal of Systems and Software*, *158*, 110400. doi:10.1016/j.jss.2019.110400

Sigala, M. (2015). Collaborative commerce in tourism: Implications for research andindustry. *Current Issues in Tourism*, 1–10.

Singanamalla, S., Potluri, V., Scott, C., & Medhi-Thies, I. (2019). PocketATM: Understanding and improving ATM accessibility in India. In *Proceedings of the Tenth International Conference on Information and Communication Technologies and Development*. ACM. 10.1145/3287098.3287106

Singh, A., & Hess, T. (2017). How Chief Digital Officers Promote the Digital Transformation of their Companies. *MIS Quarterly Executive*, *16*(1), 1–17.

Singh, J. S. K. (2020). Social Competencies, Job Performance and Cultural Adjustment Among Expatriate Assignees In Malaysia. *Malaysian Management Journal*, *21*, 17–32.

Singh, P., Sawhney, R. S., & Kahlon, K. S. (2018). Sentiment analysis of demonetization of 500 & 1000 rupee banknotes by Indian government. *ICT Express*, *4*(3), 124–129. doi:10.1016/j.icte.2017.03.001

Sivarajah, U., & Irani, Z. (2013). A theoretical model for the application of web 2.0 in e-government. *European, Mediterranean & Middle Eastern Conference on Information Systems (EMCIS2013)*, 1-18.

Skilton, M. (2015). *Building the digital enterprise: A guide to constructing monetization models using digital technologies*. Palgrave Macmillan. doi:10.1057/9781137477729

Slovic, P., Finucane, M. L., Peters, E., & MacGregor, D. G. (2004). Risk as analysis and risk as feelings: Some thoughts about affect, reason, risk, and rationality. *Risk Analysis*, *24*(2), 311–322. doi:10.1111/j.0272-4332.2004.00433.x PMID:15078302

Smith, A., & Raven, R. (2012). What is protective space? Reconsidering niches in transitions to sustainability. *Research Policy*, *41*(6), 1025–1036. doi:10.1016/j.respol.2011.12.012

Smith, A., Voß, J. P., & Grin, J. (2010). Innovation studies and sustainability transitions: The allure of the multi-level perspective and its challenges. *Research Policy*, *39*(4), 435–448. doi:10.1016/j.respol.2010.01.023

Smith, S. S. (2018). Digitization and financial reporting–how technology innovation may drive the shift toward continuous accounting. *Accounting and Finance Research*, *7*(3), 240–250. doi:10.5430/afr.v7n3p240

Sohn, S. Y., Kim, D. H., & Yoon, J. H. (2016). Technology credit scoring model with fuzzy logistic regression. *Applied Soft Computing*, *43*, 150–158. doi:10.1016/j.asoc.2016.02.025

Solli-Sæther, H., & Karlsen, J. T. (2014). Enablers and Barriers of Knowledge Sharing for Offshore Outsource ISD Project: A Case Study. *International Journal of Information Technology Project Management*, *5*(2), 44–59. doi:10.4018/ijitpm.2014040104

Somapa, S., Cools, M., & Dullaert, W. (2018). Characterizing supply chain visibility – a literature review. *International Journal of Logistics Management*, *29*(1), 308–339.

Song, A. K. (2019). The Digital Entrepreneurial Ecosystem-a critique and reconfiguration. *Small Business Economics*, *53*(3), 569–590. doi:10.100711187-019-00232-y

Sousa, M. J., & Rocha, A. (2019). Digital learning: Developing skills for digital transformation of organizations. *Future Generation Computer Systems*, *91*, 327–334. doi:10.1016/j.future.2018.08.048

Spathis, C., & Georgakopoulou, E. (2007). The adoption of IFRS in South Eastern Europe: The case of Greece. *International Journal of Financial Services Management*, *2*(1), 50–63. doi:10.1504/IJFSM.2007.011671

Stagnaro, C., & Leoni, I. B. (2019). Second-generation smart meter roll-out in Italy: A cost-benefit analysis. Paper presented in Eurelectric Power Summit 2019, Florence, Italy.

Stake, R. (2000). The case study method in social inquiry. In N. Denzin & Y. Lincoln (Eds.), *The American tradition in qualitative research* (Vol. 2). Sage Publications.

Stam, E. (2015). Entrepreneurial Ecosystems and Regional Policy: A Sympathetic Critique. *European Planning Studies*, *23*(9), 10. doi:10.1080/09654313.2015.1061484

Statista. (2018a). *E-commerce share of total global retail sales in 2016, by region.* The Statistics Portal. Recovered from https://www.statista.com/statistics/239300/number-of-online-buyers-in-selected-countries/

Statista. (2018b). *Number of digital buyers worldwide from 2014 to 2021 (in billions).* The Statistics Portal. Recovered from https://www.statista.com/statistics/251666/number-of-digital-buyers-worldwide/

Statista. (2018c). *Retail e-commerce sales worldwide from 2014 to 2021 (in billions US dollars).* The Statistics Portal. Recovered from https://www.statista.com/statistics/379046/worldwide-retail-e-commerce-sales/

Statista. (2020a). *Big Data Market Size Revenue Forecast Worldwide From 2011 to 2027.* Retrieved May 2020, from https://www.statista.com/statistics/254266/global-big-data-market-forecast/

Statista. (2020b). *Internet Usage Statistics: The Internet Big Picture.* Retrieved May 2020, from https://www.internetworldstats.com/stats.htm

Staunton, T. (2019). Icarus, Grannies, Black Holes and the death of privacy: Exploring the use of digital networks for career enactment. *British Journal of Guidance & Counselling*, 1–12. doi:10.1080/03069885.2019.1698007

Steininger, D. M. (2019). Linking information systems and entrepreneurship: A review and agenda for IT-associated and digital entrepreneurship research. *Information Systems Journal*, *29*(2), 363–407. doi:10.1111/isj.12206

Stevens, T. (2018). Global cybersecurity: New directions in theory and methods. *Politics and Governance*, *6*(2), 1–4. doi:10.17645/pag.v6i2.1569

Stewart, K. (1999). Transference as means of building trust in World Wide Web sites. *Proceedings of the 20th ICIS.*

Stöckli, E., Dremel, C., & Uebernickel, F. (2018). Exploring characteristics and transformational capabilities of InsurTech innovations to understand insurance value creation in a digital world. *Electronic Markets*, *28*(3). Advance online publication. doi:10.100712525-018-0304-7

Stormi, K. T., Laine, T., & Korhonen, T. (2019). Agile performance measurement system development: An answer to the need for adaptability? *Journal of Accounting & Organizational Change*, *15*(2), 231–256. doi:10.1108/JAOC-09-2017-0076

Strandhagen, J. W., Alfnes, E., Strandhagen, J. O., & Vallandingham, L. R. (2017). The fit of Industry 4.0 applications in manufacturing logistics: A multiple case study. *Advances in Manufacturing*, *5*(4), 344–358. doi:10.100740436-017-0200-y

Suh, H., & Han, I. (2002). Effect of trust on customer acceptance of internet banking. *Electronic Commerce Research and Applications*, *1*(4), 7–63. doi:10.1016/S1567-4223(02)00017-0

Sun, M., Wang, M., & Wegerif, R. (2019). Using computer-based cognitive mapping to improve students' divergent thinking for creativity development. *British Journal of Educational Technology*, *50*(5), 2217–2233. doi:10.1111/bjet.12825

Sussan, F., & Acs, Z. J. (2017). The digital entrepreneurial ecosystem. *Small Business Economics*, *49*(1), 55–73. doi:10.100711187-017-9867-5

Szakolczai, A., & Thomassen, B. (2019). *From anthropology to social theory: Rethinking the social sciences.* Cambridge University Press.

Szpringer, W. (2016). FinTech – New phenomena in the financial services market. *eMentor*, 56–69.

T.C. Ministry of Treasury and Finance. (2019). *Ministry of Treasury and Finance of the Republic of Turkey, New Economic Programme: Steps for Structural Transformation.* Retrieved From https://ms.hmb.gov.tr/uploads/2019/04/Yeni-Ekonomi-Program%C4%B1-2019-v5.pdf

Taber, B. J. (2019). Career Counselling Interventions to Enhance Career Adaptabilities for Sustainable Employment. In *Handbook of Innovative Career Counselling* (pp. 103–115). Springer. doi:10.1007/978-3-030-22799-9_7

Tadejko, P. (2015). Application of Internet of Things in Logistics–Current Challenges. *Economics and Management, 7*(4), 54–64.

Tammel, K. (2017). Shared services and cost reduction motive in the public sector. *International Journal of Public Administration, 40*(9), 792–804. doi:10.1080/01900692.2016.1204617

Tapscott, D. (2017). *How will blockchain change banking? How won't it?* Available at: www. huffingtonpost.com/don-tapscott/how-will-blockchain-chang_b_9998348.html

Tapscott, D., & Tapscott, A. (2016). *Blockchain revolution: how the technology behind bitcoin is changing money, business and the world.* Portfolio/Penguin.

Tarassov, V. B. (2018, September). Enterprise total agentification as a way to industry 4.0: Forming artificial societies via goal-resource networks. In *International Conference on Intelligent Information Technologies for Industry* (pp. 26-40). Springer.

Taylor, S., & Todd, P. A. (1995). Understanding Information Technology Usage: A Test of Competing Models. *Information Systems Research, 6*(2), 144–176. doi:10.1287/isre.6.2.144

Tekic, Z., & Koroteev, D. (2019). From disruptively digital to proudly analog: A holistic typology of digital transformation strategies. *Business Horizons, 62*(6), 683–693. doi:10.1016/j.bushor.2019.07.002

Temenos. (2017). Top 5 regulatory burdens faced by banks. Retrieved from https://www.temenos.com/en/blog/2015/august/regulation-headaches/#

Teubner, T. (2014). Thoughts on the sharing economy. In *Proceedings of the International Conference on e-Commerce* (*Vol. 11*, pp. 322-326). Academic Press.

The Enterprisers Project. (2020). What is digital transformation? https://enterprisersproject.com/what-is-digital-transformation

The Financial Brand. (2018). *The four pillars of digital transformation in banking.* https://thefinancialbrand.com/71733/four-pillars-of-digital-transformation-banking-strategy/

Thurner, T. (2018). Business innovation through Blockchain: The B3 perspective. *Foresight, 20*(5), 583–584.

Timmers, P. (1999). *Electronic commerce: Strategies and models for business-to-business trading.* Wiley and Sons Ltd.

Tjepkema, S. (2002). *The learning infrastructure of self managing workteams.* Twente University Press.

Tomac, N., Radonja, R., & Bonato, J. (2019). Analysis of Henry Ford's contribution to production and management. *Pomorstvo, 33*(1), 33–45. doi:10.31217/p.33.1.4

Tortorella, G. L., Cawley Vergara, A. M., Garza-Reyes, J. A., & Sawhney, R. (2020). Organizational learning paths based upon industry 4.0 adoption: An empirical study with Brazilian manufacturers. *International Journal of Production Economics, 219*, 284–294. doi:10.1016/j.ijpe.2019.06.023

Tosuner, A. (2011). *Ortak kullanım ağlarındaki içerik üretiminin, tüketim davranışının azaltılmasındaki teşvik edici rolünün web siteleri üzerinden incelenmesi: Zumbara, Freeconomy, Community Exchange Network, Freecycle Network* (Unpublished master's thesis). İstanbul Üniversitesi Sosyal Bilimler Enstitüsü, İstanbul.

Tsai, C. F. (2007). On Classifying Digital Accounting Documents. *International Journal of Digital Accounting Research, 7*(13).

Tsiatsis, V., Karnouskos, S., Holler, J., Boyle, D., & Mulligan, C. (2018). *Internet of Things: technologies and applications for a new age of intelligence*. Academic Press.

Tura, N., Kutvonen, A., & Ritala, P. (2017). Platform design framework: Conceptualisation and application. *Technology Analysis and Strategic Management, 30*(8), 881–894. doi:10.1080/09537325.2017.1390220

Turban, E., Pollard, C., & Wood, G. (2018). *Information Technology for Management: On-demand Strategies for Performance, Growth and Sustainability*. John Wiley & Sons.

Turi, J. A., & Sorooshian, S. (2019). The impact of organisational structure on organisational learning. *Middle East J. of Management, 6*(2), 204. doi:10.1504/MEJM.2019.097817

TÜSİAD. (2019). *The Legislative Proposal on New Tax Provisions Include Items that Need to be Reconsidered for All Segments of Society*. Retrieved From https://tusiad.org/tr/basin-bultenleri/item/10459-yeni-vergi-duzenlemesine-i-liskin-kanun-teklifi-tum-toplum-kesimleri-i-cin-yeniden-degerlendirilmeye-muhtac-duzenlemelere-sahiptir

Tussyadiah, I. P., & Pesonen, J. (2015). Impacts of peer-to-peer accommodation use on travel patterns. *Journal of Travel Research, 55*(8), 1022–1040. doi:10.1177/0047287515608505

Twati. (2008). The influence of societal culture on the adoption of information systems: The case of Libya. *Communications of the IIMA Journal, 8*(1), 1-12.

Ulusoy, A. (2019). *Digital Services Tax On The Horizon*. Retrieved From https://www.yenisafak.com/yazarlar/ahmetulusoy/dijital-hizmet-vergisi-geliyor-2053220

UNESCO. (2001). *Artesanías creadoras*. París: Unesco, Sección de Artesanías y Diseño.

United Nations Industrial Development Organisation (UNIDO). (2001). *Women Entrepreneurship Development in Selected African Countries*. Working Paper No. 7, United Nations Industrial Development Organisation.

Ünker, P. (2019). *How Will the New Taxes Affect the Consumer?* Retrieved From https://www.dw.com/tr/yeni-vergiler-t%C3%BCketiciyi-nas%C4%B1l-etkileyecek/a-51090228

UPS. (2016). *ORION: The algorithm proving that left isn't right*. Retrieved May 2020, from https://www.ups.com/us/en/services/knowledge-center/article.page?kid=aa3710c2

Uricchio, A. (2016). A Few Ideas for Reforming Internet Taxation. In F. Boccia & R. Leonardi (Eds.), *The Challenge of the Digital Economy, Market, Taxation and Appropriate Economic Models* (pp. 83–96). Academic Press. doi:10.1007/978-3-319-43690-6_6

Ushakova, A., & Mikhaylov, S. J. (2020). Big data to the rescue? Challenges in analysing granular household electricity consumption in the United Kingdom. *Energy Research & Social Science, 64*, 101428. doi:10.1016/j.erss.2020.101428

Ustundag, A., & Cevikcan, E. (2018). *Industry 4.0: Managing The Digital Transformation*. Springer International Publishing. doi:10.1007/978-3-319-57870-5

Vaidya, S., Ambad, P., & Bhosle, S. (2018). Industry 4.0 – A Glimpse. *Procedia Manufacturing, 20*, 233–238. doi:10.1016/j.promfg.2018.02.034

Van Alstyne, M., Parker, G., & Choudary, P. (2016, April). Pipelines, Platforms, and the New Rules of Strategy. *Harvard Business Review*, 54–60, 62.

Van Biesen, F. (1989). Everyday learning in labour organisations. *Ontwerp, 1*(1), 4–11.

van der Zwan, P., Thurik, R., Verheul, I., & Hessels, J. (2016). Factors influencing the entrepreneurial engagement of opportunity and necessity entrepreneurs. *Eurasian Bus Rev, 6.*

Van Oort, N., & Cats, O. (2015, September). Improving public transport decision making, planning and operations by using big data: Cases from Sweden and the Netherlands. In *2015 IEEE 18th international conference on intelligent transportation systems* (pp. 19-24). IEEE. 10.1109/ITSC.2015.11

Van Rijmenam, M. (2013). *Why the 3v's are not sufficient to describe big data.* Retrieved from https://datafloq.com/read/3vs-sufficient-describe-big-data/166

Van Ruler, B. (2019). Agile communication evaluation and measurement. *Journal of Communication Management (London), 23*(3), 265–280. doi:10.1108/JCOM-12-2018-0136

Van Tubergen, F. (2005). Self-Employment of Immigrants: A Cross-National Study Study of 17 Western Societies. *Social Forces, 84*(2), 23. doi:10.1353of.2006.0039

Vance, C. M., & Bergin, R. (2019). The Social Expat-Preneur: Examining a Growing International Career Model Supporting Global Social Entrepreneurship. In Creating Business Value and Competitive Advantage With Social Entrepreneurship (pp. 186-204). IGI Global.

VanderMeer, D., Dutta, K., & Datta, A. (2012). A Cost-Based Database Request Distribution Technique for Online e-Commerce Applications. *Management Information Systems Quarterly, 36*(2), 479–507. doi:10.2307/41703464

Varela, J. A., Bande, B., Del Rio, M., & Jaramillo, F. (2019). Servant Leadership, Proactive Work Behavior, and Performance Overall Rating: Testing a Multilevel Model of Moderated Mediation. *Journal of Business-To-Business Marketing, 26*(2), 177–195. doi:10.1080/1051712X.2019.1603417

Venkataraman, S. (2019). The distinctive domain of entrepreneurship research. In *Seminal Ideas for the Next Twenty-Five Years of Advances* (pp. 5–20). Emerald Publishing Limited. doi:10.1108/S1074-754020190000021009

Venkatesh, V., & Davis, F. D. (2000). A theoretical extension of the Technology Acceptance Model: Four Longitudinal Field Studies. *Management Science, 46*(2), 186–204. doi:10.1287/mnsc.46.2.186.11926

Venkatesh, V., Morris, M. G., Davis, G. B., & Davis, F. D. (2003). User Acceptance of Information Technology: Toward a Unified View. *Management Information Systems Quarterly, 27*(3), 425–478. doi:10.2307/30036540

Venkatesh, V., Thong, J. Y. L., & Xu, X. (2012). Consumer Acceptance and Use of Information Technology: Extending The Unified Theory of Acceptance and Use of Technology. *Management Information Systems Quarterly, 36*(1), 157–178. doi:10.2307/41410412

Venkatraman, V. (2017). *The Digital Matrix. New Rules for Business Transformation Through Technology.* LifeTree Media Ltd.

Vertovec, S. (2003). Migration and other modes of transnationalism: Towards conceptual cross-fertilisation. *The International Migration Review, 37*(3), 641–665. doi:10.1111/j.1747-7379.2003.tb00153.x

Vézina, S., & Bélanger, A. (2019). Impacts of education and immigration on the size and skills of the future workforce. *Demographic Research, 41*, 331–366. doi:10.4054/DemRes.2019.41.12

Vial, G. (2019). Understanding digital transformation: A review and a research agenda. *The Journal of Strategic Information Systems, 28*(2), 118–144. doi:10.1016/j.jsis.2019.01.003

Victor, L. (2008). Systematic reviewing. *Social Research Update, 54*(1), 1–4.

Viet, N. Q., Behdani, B., & Bloemhof, J. (2020). Data-driven process redesign: Anticipatory shipping in agro-food supply chains. *International Journal of Production Research, 58*(5), 1302–1318. doi:10.1080/00207543.2019.1629673

Vogel, M. A. (2005). *Leveraging information technology competencies and capabilities for a competitive advantage. Doctoral Degree*. University of Maryland.

Von Bloh, J., Mandakovic, V., Apablaza, M., Amoros, J. E., & Sternberg, R. (2019). Transnational entrepreneurs: Opportunity or necessity driven? Empirical evidence from two dynamic economies from Latin America and Europe. *Journal of Ethnic and Migration Studies*. Advance online publication. doi:10.1080/1369183X.2018.1559996

Vondracek, F. W., Lerner, R. M., & Schulenberg, J. E. (2019). *Career development: A life-span developmental approach*. Routledge. doi:10.4324/9781315792705

Vrooman, J. C. (2009). *Rules of relief: institutions of social security, and their impact*. Academic Press.

Walker-Munro, B. (2020). Use of Big Data Analytics by Tax Authorities. In M. Jackson & M. Shelly (Eds.), *Legal Regulations, Implications, and Issues Surrounding Digital Data* (pp. 86–110). IGI Global. doi:10.4018/978-1-7998-3130-3.ch005

Walker, R. H., Craig-Lees, M., Hecker, R., & Francis, H. (2002). Technology- enabled service delivery: An investigation of reasons affecting customer adoption and rejection. *International Journal of Service Industry Management, 13*(7), 91–106. doi:10.1108/09564230210421173

Wamba, S. F., Gunasekaran, A., Akter, S., Ren, S. J. F., Dubey, R., & Childe, S. J. (2017). Big data analytics and firm performance: Effects of dynamic capabilities. *Journal of Business Research, 70*, 356–365. doi:10.1016/j.jbusres.2016.08.009

Wang, C., & Zhang, P. (2012). The evolution of social commerce: The people, management, technology, and information dimensions. *Communications of the Association for Information Systems, 31*(1), 105–127. doi:10.17705/1CAIS.03105

Wang, G., Gunasekaran, A., Ngai, E. W. T., & Papadopoulos, T. (2016). Big data analytics in logistics and supply chain management: Certain investigations for research and applications. *International Journal of Production Economics, 176*, 98–110. doi:10.1016/j.ijpe.2016.03.014

Wang, H., Feng, J., Zhang, H., & Li, X. (2020). The effect of digital transformation strategy on performance. *International Journal of Conflict Management, 31*(3), 441–462. doi:10.1108/IJCMA-09-2019-0166

Wang, Q., & Liu, C. Y. (2015). Transnational activities of immigrant-owned firms and their performances in the USA. *Small Business Economics, 44*(2), 345–359. doi:10.100711187-014-9595-z

Wang, Y. R., & Warn, J. (2019). Break-out strategies of Chinese immigrant entrepreneurs in Australia. *International Journal of Entrepreneurial Behaviour & Research, 25*(2), 217–242. doi:10.1108/IJEBR-03-2017-0108

Wang, Y., Han, J. H., & Beynon-Davies, P. (2019). Understanding blockchain technology for future supply chains: A systematic literature review and research agenda. *Supply Chain Management, 24*(1), 62–84. doi:10.1108/SCM-03-2018-0148

Wang, Y., Minor, M., & Wei, J. (2011). Aesthetics and the online shopping environment: Understanding consumer responses. *Journal of Retailing, 87*(1), 46–58. doi:10.1016/j.jretai.2010.09.002

Wannes, A., & Ghannouchi, S. A. (2019). KPI-Based Approach for Business Process Improvement. *Procedia Computer Science, 164*, 265–270. doi:10.1016/j.procs.2019.12.182

Warner, K. S. R., & Wäger, M. (2018). Building dynamic capabilities for digital transformation: An ongoing process of strategic renewal. *Long Range Planning, 52*(3), 326–349. doi:10.1016/j.lrp.2018.12.001

WeConnect International. (n.d.). *Prospere como mujer empresaria*. Recovered from https://weconnectinternational.org

Weerakkody, V., Irani, Z., Lee, H., Osman, I., & Hindi, N. (2015). E-government implementation: A bird's eye view of issues relating to costs, opportunities, benefits and risks. *Information Systems Frontiers*, *17*, 889–915. doi:10.100710796-013-9472-3

WEF. (2013). *Entrepreneurial Ecosystems Around the Globe and Company Growth Dynamics*. Retrieved from: https://www.weforum.org/reports/entrepreneurial-ecosystems-around-globe-and-company-growth-dynamics

Wei, K. (2009). Service quality index: A study on Malasian banks. *Journal of Contemporary Management Research*, *5*(2), 109–124. doi:10.7903/cmr.1179

Weill, P., & Woerner, S. (2015). Thriving in an increasingly digital ecosystem. *MIT Sloan Management Review*, *56*(4), 27–34.

Wen, W., & Zhu, F. (2019). Threat of Platform-Owner Entry and Complementor Responses: Evidence from the Mobile App Market. *Strategic Management Journal*, *40*(9), 1336–1367. doi:10.1002mj.3031

Westland, C. (2002). Transaction risk in e-commerce. *Decision Support Systems*, *33*(1), 187–103. doi:10.1016/S0167-9236(02)00010-6

Wiedenmann, M., & Größler, A. (2019). The impact of digital technologies on operational causes of the bullwhip effect – a literature review. *Procedia CIRP*, *81*, 552–557. doi:10.1016/j.procir.2019.03.154

Wiewiora, A., Chang, A., & Smidt, M. (2020). Individual, project and organizational learning flows within a global project-based organization: Exploring what, how and who. *International Journal of Project Management*, *38*(4), 201–214. doi:10.1016/j.ijproman.2020.03.005

Willcocks, L., & Margetts, H. (1994). Risk assessment and information systems. *European Journal of Information Systems*, *3*(2), 127–137.

Williamson, A. J., Battisti, M., Leatherbee, M., & Gish, J. J. (2019). Rest, zest, and my innovative best: Sleep and mood as drivers of entrepreneurs' innovative behavior. *Entrepreneurship Theory and Practice*, *43*(3), 582–610. doi:10.1177/1042258718798630

Williams, W., & Elmore, R. F. (Eds.). (2014). *Social Program Implementation: Quantitative Studies in Social Relations*. Academic Press.

Wilson, F., Kickul, J., & Marlino, D. (2007). Gender, entrepreneurial self–efficacy, and entrepreneurial career intentions: Implications for entrepreneurship education. *Entrepreneurship Theory and Practice*, *31*(3), 387–406. doi:10.1111/j.1540-6520.2007.00179.x

Wittel, A. (2011). Qualities of sharing and their transformations in the digital age. *International Journal of Information Ethics*, *15*(9), 3–8.

Woerner, S. L., & Wixom, B. H. (2015). Big data: Extending the business strategy toolbox. *Journal of Information Technology*, *30*(1), 60–62. doi:10.1057/jit.2014.31

Wolf, H., van Solingen, R., & Rustenburg, E. (2011). *Die Kraft von Scrum: Eine inspirierende Geschichte über einen revolutionären Projektmanagementansatz*. Addison-Wesley.

Won Jeong, S., Fiore, A., Niehm, L., & Lorenz, F. (2009). The role of experiential value in online shopping: The impacts of product presentation on consumer responses towards an apparel web site. *Internet Research*, *19*(1), 105–124. doi:10.1108/10662240910927858

Woodford, C. (2017). *A brief history of computers*. Academic Press.

Wooldridge, J. M. (2016). *Introductory econometrics: A modern approach.* Nelson Education.

World Economic Forum. (2012). *Rethinking financial innovation.* World Economic Forum.

Wu, X., Lyu, Y., Kwan, H. K., & Zhai, H. (2019). The impact of mentoring quality on protégés' organization-based self-esteem and proactive behavior: The moderating role of traditionality. *Human Resource Management, 58*(4), 417–430. doi:10.1002/hrm.21968

Wu, Y.-L., & Li, E. Y. (2018). Marketing mix, customer value, and customer loyalty in social commerce. *Internet Research, 28*(1), 74–104. doi:10.1108/IntR-08-2016-0250

Xu, J. (2014). *Managing digital enterprise.* Springer. doi:10.2991/978-94-6239-094-2

Xu, Q., Zhang, G., & Chan, A. (2019). Abusive supervision and subordinate proactive behavior: Joint moderating roles of organizational identification and positive affectivity. *Journal of Business Ethics, 157*(3), 829–843. doi:10.100710551-017-3691-3

Xu, X. (2020). Application Research of Accounting Archives Informatization Based on Big Data. In *Data Processing Techniques and Applications for Cyber-Physical Systems (DPTA 2019)* (pp. 55–62). Springer. doi:10.1007/978-981-15-1468-5_9

Yablonsky, S. (2016). *Intermediaries in E-Commerce. Encyclopedia of E-Commerce Development.* Implementation, and Management., doi:10.4018/978-1-4666-9787-4.ch005

Yan, B., Jin, Z., Liu, L., & Liu, S. (2018). Factors influencing the adoption of the internet of things in supply chains. *Journal of Evolutionary Economics, 28*(3), 523–545. doi:10.100700191-017-0527-3

Yang, R. (2020). *Analysing the impact of digital transformation on corporate travel management* (Master Thesis). University of Vaasa.

Yang, C., Huang, Q., Li, Z., Liu, K., & Hu, F. (2017). Big data and cloud computing: Innovation opportunities and challenges. *International Journal of Digital Earth, 10*(1), 13–53. doi:10.1080/17538947.2016.1239771

Yang, J., Whitefield, M., & Boehme, K. (2007). New issues and challenges facing e-banking in rural areas: An empirical study. *International Journal of Electronic Finance, 1*(3), 336. doi:10.1504/IJEF.2007.011503

Yeboah, J., & Ewur, G. D. (2014). Quality Customer Service as a Competitive Advantage in the Telecommunication Industry in the Western Region of Ghana. *Journal of Education and Practice, 5*(5), 11.

Yeung, H. W. C. (2002). Entrepreneurship in International Business: An Institutional Perspective. *Asia Pacific Journal of Management,* 19.

Yin, R. K. (1994). Case study research. Design and methods (2nd ed.). London: SAGE Publications.

Ying, Z., Caixia, C., Wen, G., & Xiaogang, L. (2018). Impact of recommender systems on unplanned purchase behaviours in e-commerce. In *2018 5th International Conference on Industrial Engineering and Applications (ICIEA)* (pp. 21-30). IEEE. 10.1109/IEA.2018.8387066

Yin, R. K. (2002). *Case study research: Design and methods.* SAGE Publications.

Yin, Y., Stecke, K. E., & Li, D. (2018). The evolution of production systems from Industry 2.0 through Industry 4.0. *International Journal of Production Research, 56*(1-2), 848–861. doi:10.1080/00207543.2017.1403664

You, T., & Zhou, M. (2019). Simultaneous Embeddedness in Immigrant Entrepreneurship: Global Forces Behind Chinese-Owned Nail Salons in New York City: PROD. *The American Behavioral Scientist*, *63*(2), 166–185. doi:10.1177/0002764218793684

Yüce, M., & Akbulut, N. (2018). Measures Adopted Concerning the Taxation of the Digital Economy within the Scope of the BEPS Action Plan. *Academic View Journal*, *68*, 105-123.

YuSheng, K., & Ibrahim, M. (2019). Service innovation, service delivery and customer satisfaction and loyalty in the banking sector of Ghana. *International Journal of Bank Marketing*, *37*(5), 1215–1233. doi:10.1108/IJBM-06-2018-0142

Zaheer, H., Breyer, Y., & Dumay, J. (2019). Digital entrepreneurship: An interdisciplinary structured literature review and research agenda. *Technological Forecasting and Social Change*, *148*, 148. doi:10.1016/j.techfore.2019.119735

Zavattaro, S. M., French, P. E., & Mohanty, S. D. (2015). A sentiment analysis of US local government tweets: The connection between tone and citizen involvement. *Government Information Quarterly*, *32*(3), 333–341. doi:10.1016/j.giq.2015.03.003

Zeithaml, V. A., Parasuraman, A., & Malhotra, A. (2000). *A conceptual framework for understanding e-service quality: Implications for future research and managerial practice.* Marketing Science Institute, Working paper report no. 00-115.

Zeithaml, V. A., & Gilly, M. C. (1987). Characteristics affecting the acceptance of retailing technologies: A comparison of elderly and non-elderly consumers. *Journal of Retailing*, *63*(1), 49–68.

Zeithaml, V. A., Parasuraman, A., & Malhotra, A. (2002). Service 1uality delivery through websites: A critical review of extant knowledge. *Academy of Marketing Science Journal*, *30*(4), 3620–3675. doi:10.1177/009207002236911

Zelizer, V. A. (2010). *Economic lives: How culture shapes the economy?* Princeton University Press.

Zeng, M. (2018). *Smart Business. What Alibaba's Success Reveals about the Future of Strategy*. Harvard Business Review Press.

Zervas, G., Proserpio, D., & Byers, J. W. (2017). The rise of the sharing economy: Estimating the impact of Airbnb on the hotel industry. *JMR, Journal of Marketing Research*, *54*(5), 687–705. doi:10.1509/jmr.15.0204

Zhang, Lu, & Kizildag. (2018). Banking "on-the-go": examining consumers' adoption of mobile banking services. *International Journal of Quality and Service Sciences*, 1-19.

Zhang, T., Agarwal, R., & Lucas, H. (2011). The value of IT-enabled retailer learning: personalized product recommendations and customer store loyalty in electronic markets. *MIS Quarterly-Management Information Systems*, *35*(4), 859.

Zhang, J. H., & Lee, J. H. (2019). Beyond the Hawthorne research: Relationship between IT company employees' perceived physical work environment and creative behavior. In *International Conference on Software Engineering Research, Management and Applications* (pp. 147-159). Springer.

Zhang, J. H., & Lee, J. H. (2019). Beyond the Hawthorne Research: Relationship Between IT Company Employees' Perceived Physical Work Environment and Creative Behavior. In *International Conference on Software Engineering Research, Management and Applications* (pp. 147-159). Springer.

Zhang, Y., Huang, T., & Bompard, E. F. (2018). Big data analytics in smart grids: A review. *Energy Informatics*, *1*(1), 8. doi:10.118642162-018-0007-5

Zhao, Tsai, & Wang. (2019). *Improving Financial Service Innovation Strategies for Enhancing China's Banking Industry Competitive Advantage during the Fintech Revolution: A Hybrid MCDM Model*. Academic Press.

Zheng, L. (2013). Social media in Chinese government: Drivers, challenges and capabilities. *Government Information Quarterly*, *30*, 369–376. doi:10.1016/j.giq.2013.05.017

Zheng, M. (2015). Economic and Business Dimensions. Three Paradoxes of Building Platforms. *Communications of the ACM*, *58*(2), 27–29. doi:10.1145/2700343

Zhong, R. Y., Newman, S. T., Huang, G. Q., & Lan, S. (2016). Big Data for supply chain management in the service and manufacturing sectors: Challenges, opportunities, and future perspectives. *Computers & Industrial Engineering*, *101*, 572–591. doi:10.1016/j.cie.2016.07.013

Zhou, K., Fu, C., & Yang, S. (2016). Big data driven smart energy management: From big data to big insights. *Renewable & Sustainable Energy Reviews*, *56*, 215–225. doi:10.1016/j.rser.2015.11.050

Zhou, Q., & DeSantis, R. (2005). Usability issues in city tourism website design: A content analysis. In *IEEE International Professional Communication Conference* (pp. 789–796). IEEE.

Zhu, F., & Liu, Q. (2018). Competing with complementors: An empirical look at Amazon.com. *Strategic Management Journal*, *39*(10), 2618–2642. doi:10.1002mj.2932

Zhu, L., Yu, F. R., Wang, Y., Ning, B., & Tang, T. (2018). Big data analytics in intelligent transportation systems: A survey. *IEEE Transactions on Intelligent Transportation Systems*, *20*(1), 383–398. doi:10.1109/TITS.2018.2815678

Ziyadin, Suieubayeva, & Utegenova. (2020). *Digital Transformation in Business*. Springer Nature Switzerland AG.

Ziyae, B., Sajadi, S. M., & Mobaraki, M. H. (2014). The deployment and internationalization speed of e-business in the digital entrepreneurship era. *Journal of Global Entrepreneurship Research*, *4*(1), 15. doi:10.118640497-014-0015-2

Zugelder, M. T., Flaherty, T. B., & Johnson, J. P. (2000). Legal issues associated with international Internet marketing. *International Marketing Review*, *17*(3), 253–271. doi:10.1108/02651330010331651

Zwass, V. (2006). The web-internet compound as the infrastructure of digital government. *Business Process Management Journal*, *12*(1), 7–12. doi:10.1108/14637150610643715

About the Contributors

Kamaljeet Sandhu is an active, experienced researcher, who is passionate about research in Digital Innovation and Strategy, Business Analytics, Digital Health, AI, IoT, Cryptocurrency, Blockchain, Cloud Computing, IT Startup, FinTech, Cybersecurity, Accounting, Corporate Governance and CSR, Supply Chain, ERP, SMEs, and Entrepreneurship. The editor held multiple leadership positions including Senior Research Fellow at the University of South Australia, and Senior Academic position in Canada at the University of Northern British Columbia, and in Australia that include University of Wollongong, Charles Darwin University, Deakin University, and in Fiji at the University of South Pacific. As a PhD Principal Supervisor, the editor has supervised and mentored several PhD research students to successful completion, and students have successfully gained academic and research appointments at international universities and other organizations. Dr. Sandhu's PhD students' research is funded by international government and industry scholarships. The editor has multidisciplinary experience working across different faculties such as business, accounting, finance, management, economics, IT and IS, software, and computer science.

* * *

Süreyya Akçay is a graduate of Giresun University, Department of Tourism and Hotel Management. She completed her master's degree at Gazi University, Department of Tourism Management. Her work focuses on sharing economy in tourism, tourist guidance education, gastronomy tourism and organizational behavior in tourism businesses.

Simón Alba-Muñoz completed a Master in Digital Marketing Management and Management at the University of Malaga. He has worked in several companies doing tasks within the scope of Digital Marketing.

Shruti Ashok specializes in the area of Finance. She earned her Ph. D degree from Faculty of Management Studies, Delhi University. She has expertise in financial planning, risk management, financial aspect of mergers and acquisitions. During her doctoral research, she investigated the opportunities and challenges of reverse mortgage in the Indian context. One notable contribution of her doctoral research is the exploration of reverse mortgage as a financial planning tool for the elderly in India. Dr. Shruti Ashok is currently working in the capacity of Assistant Professor with Bennett University, Greater Noida. Her current teaching responsibilities include facilitating students in Security Analysis, Risk Management and Behavioral Finance at both UG and PG level. Dr. Shruti has contributed to various internationally acclaimed peer reviewed journals, conferences and publications. Her research papers are published in ABDC category and Scopus indexed journals. She has presented her scholarly work at conferences organised by IIT and Pan IIM. Shruti's scholarly interests are financial aspect of mergers and acquisitions, integration of AI into financial planning, reverse mortgage - a golden stick for the Indian elderly. Dr. Shruti also chairs the Entrepreneur society at her department where she spearheads students into developing entrepreneurial skills. In the past, Dr. Shruti has also worked with Bombay Stock Exchange as a guest faculty for Technical Analysis. She also has rich banking experience of 3 years, working with banks such as HSBC Dubai, Citibank, HDFC Bank and State Bank of India.

Fatma Bouaziz is assistant professor in Management at the Faculty of Economics and Management of Sfax - Tunisia. She got her Ph.D. in management in 2011 from the same faculty. Her doctoral thesis deals with the risk management of e-government projects in the case of the Tunisian government. Her research interests include the use of ICTs by government, their organizational impacts and abilities to improve public services delivery, human resource management and organizational resilience in the context of transition.

Nermin Brkovic is a MSc student within the Department of Business Administration, University of Gothenburg. His research area is Blockchain Technology in relation to Supply Chain Management and Accounting.

Jovanna Nathalie Cervantes Guzmán, holds a PhD in management science at the University of Guadalajara. She is a professor for the bachelor's degree in marketing from at U de G. She directs a special project in the university which is focused on incentivizing entrepreneurship for young students of the university. She was selected in a program of entrepreneurial professors by Santander X and the University of Oxford. As an entrepreneur she was selected in the program "Young Leaders of the Americas (YLAI)" 2020-2021, by the U.S. Department and IREX, where they select entrepreneurs with the greatest potential in LATAM, Canada and the Caribbean.

Joana Costa is a researcher in the area of Economics, Management, Industrial Engineering and Tourism. Teacher of Bachelor's, Master's and Doctorate courses at the University of Aveiro and Minho

Fatmanur Deniz has been working as a research assistant at Nevşehir Hacı Bektaş Veli University, Faculty of Economics and Administrative Sciences, Department of Banking and Finance since 2020. Deniz received her bachelor's degree in Gazi University Elementary Mathematics Teaching Department in 2014 and at the same time received her bachelor's degree in Anadolu University, Department of Economics in 2015. She received her master's degree in Ankara Hacı Bayram Veli University at finance in 2019. She is currently continuing her doctoral studies in the field of Accounting and Finance at Sakarya University.

Deepika Dhingra is an academician, Finance professional, trainer and consultant. She has over 12 years of experience & is currently working as an Assistant Professor (Finance) with Bennett University, India. She holds a Ph.D. in Finance from Faculty of Management Studies, Delhi University and a M.B.A from Indraprastha University, Delhi. Dr. Deepika has moderated panel discussions, chaired sessions and delivered invited talks at seminars. She has undertaken trainings for several PSU's such as Engineers

India Limited, NBCC GAIL etc. She has also presented her research at various conferences held at IIM Bangalore, IIM Raipur, IIM Calcutta, NMIMS Bangalore, Goa Institute of Management, BITS Pilani, IIT Roorkee, Delhi University. She teaches finance courses to postgraduate as well as undergraduate students.

Carson Duan is a PhD candidate at the University of New England, Australia. His doctoral research project is about immigrant entrepreneurship process in relation to immigrants' host and home country entrepreneurial ecosystem. He has years of experiences as a digital entrepreneur engaged in document digitalisation.

Mahmut Efendi was born in 24.021980 in Söke/Aydın/Türkiye. He is an independent researcher. He graduated from Faculty of Tourism Management, Aydın Adnan Menderes University, Turkey in 2005. He completed his MSc in field of Business Administration in 2009 at Yaşar University, İzmir/Turkey. His Ph.D. in the field of Tourism Management in 2018 at Aydın Adnan Menderes University. His main research interests lie in the area of Tourist Ethics, Quality Management, Sharing Economy and Tour Guidance in tourism industry. He is a professional tour guide. He has also taken part in several workshops and conferences related to his research fields.

Farid Huseynov received his PhD in Information Systems in 2016 from the Middle East Technical University (METU), Turkey. He received his BS in Management and MS in Information Systems from the METU in 2009 and 2013, respectively. His research interests include digital business models, behavioural issues in B2C electronic commerce, online recommender agents, mobile consumer behavior, and information technology (IT) acceptance and use.

Bernice Kotey is a Professor of Entrepreneurship at the University of New England in Armidale, Australia. Her publications cover a range of management issues affecting Small and Medium firms (SMEs) and the impact of the macro-environment on their operations. Her current focus is on Human Resource Management practices in SMEs. In relation to context, her research examines SMEs in local, regional, developing and developed economies. Bernice is a Certified Practicing Accountant (Australia) and completed the Education Management Program in Harvard in 2010.

Fahri Özsungur is an Associate Professor. He was graduated from Ataturk University Faculty of Law, Hacettepe University Department of Family and Consumer Sciences PhD. and Aksaray University Department of Business Ph.D. He serves as a Higher Degrees by Research (HDR) Examiner /Ph.D. Examiner for the University of New England. He is a Eurostars Technical Expert (EUREKA Secretariat). He is affiliated with Mersin University Vocational School of Social Sciences Department of Social Work and Counseling, Adana Science and Technology University, Rotary International, Osmaniye Korkut Ata University, Çağ University, WEGATE- European Gateway for Women's Entrepreneurship, and Canadian Institute for International Law Expertise (CIFILE). He has 4 books, 9 book chapters, and more than 78 (4 SSCI/SCI/SCI-Expanded,10 ESCI) published articles and 18 international conference papers. He is the editor of 14 Journals (1 SSCI/SCI/SCI-Expanded), and the reviewer of 109 Journals (9 SSCI/SCI/SCI-Expanded,26 ESCI).

Tansif ur Rehman has a PhD in European Studies. He has also completed 56 Certification/Credit Courses, 11 Miscellaneous Diplomas, 08 Government of Pakistan Trainings, 04 Certification Courses and Diploma (Languages) - Deutsch, English, Italian, and Russian. He has several publications and has over 20 years teaching as well as 14 years research experience.

María-Mercedes Rojas-de-Gracia earned her PhD degree from University of Málaga. She is a Professor of the Department of Economics and Business Administration, University of Málaga (Spain). Her lines of research consist on the study of destination image and family vacation decision making. Currently, she is working on the study of Destination Image through the use of social media.

Marisa Analía Sánchez received a Doctorate degree in Computer Science from Universidad Nacional del Sur in Bahía Blanca, Argentina. She is currently Full Professor of graduate and post-graduate courses at Department of Management Sciences at Universidad Nacional del Sur. Her research interests include the role, value and governance of digitization in organizations.

Deepak Saxena is an Assistant Professor of Management Information Systems at Birla Institute of Technology & Science Pilani (India). Prior to this, he has worked as a Research Fellow with the Trinity College Dublin, and as an Assistant Lecturer with Dublin Institute of Technology. His research interest includes the application of technology in the public service context. He has published in journals such as Australasian Journal of Information Systems, Journal of Information Science, Electronic Journal of Information Systems Evaluation, and Electronic Journal of e-Government.

Plácido Sierra-Herrezuelo is an Executive Consultant at Malaga - Costa del Sol Tourism Board an Associate Professor of Marketing and Market Resesrch at University of Malaga. Interested in tourism marketing and digital marketing.

E. Suganya is currently pursuing a Ph.D. in Computer Science at Bharathiar University, Coimbatore, India. She has completed a Master of Science in Computer Science and a Master of Philosophy in Computer Science. Her research areas include data mining, web mining, and big data. She has published research papers in international journals. She also presented research papers at national and international conferences. Her research areas include data mining and web mining.

S. Vijayarani is an Assistant Professor at the Department of Computer Science of Bharathiar University, Coimbatore, India. She has obtained M.C.A., M.Phil., and Ph.D., in Computer Science. She has 10 years of teaching/research and 10 years of technical experience. Her research interests include data mining, privacy issues in data mining, text mining, web mining, data streams, and information retrieval. She has published more than 80 research articles in national/international journals. She also presented research papers at international/national conferences. She has authored a book and guided more than 25 research scholars. She is a lifetime member of professional bodies such as CSI, ISCA, IAENG, IRED, and UACEE.

Atilla Wohllebe has already worked in several agile teams and organizations in various roles. He is a certified Scrum Product Owner and PhD student at the Doctoral School in Management and Organizational Sciences, MATE Hungarian University of Agriculture and Life Sciences - Kaposvár Campus, Kaposvár, Hungary. In his research and work he combines the theoretical and practical view. Atilla Wohllebe currently lives and works in Hamburg, Germany. He holds a B. A. in Business Administration from the Hamburg School of Business Administration and a M. Sc. in E-Commerce from the University of Applied Sciences Wedel.

Kamil Yagci is an Associate Professor in the Department of Tourist Guidance at the University of Pamukkale (Turkey) where he has been a member since 2014. He graduated from Faculty of Business, Department of Tourism Management, Dokuz Eylul University, Turkey in 1999. He completed his MSc in the field of Total Quality Management in 2003 at Dokuz Eylul University and his Ph.D. in the field of Tourism Management in 2010 at Dokuz Eylul University (Izmir,Turkey). His main research interests lie in the area of Quality Management, ICT in tourism, E-tourism, Supply chain management practices in tourism, Organization theories and their application in tourism industry. He is also certified as lead auditor for ISO 9001:2000 and ISO 14001:2004 Quality Management Systems. He has also taken part in several workshops and conferences related to his research fields.

Juana I. Zuntini received a Master degree in Business Administration from Universidad Nacional del Sur, Argentina. Owner of Zuntini Soluciones Integrales (technology company). She is currently an Adjunct Professor at Department of Management Sciences at Universidad Nacional del Sur. Her research interests include Information Technology Management.

Index

E

F

G

I

K

M

N

O

P

R

S

www.ingramcontent.com/pod-product-compliance
Lightning Source LLC
LaVergne TN
LVHW062112300926
849161LV00010B/2439
* 9 7 8 1 7 9 9 8 8 5 8 3 2 *